T0003094

ALL THE POWERS OF EARTH

The
Political Life
of
Abraham Lincoln,
1856–1860

SIDNEY BLUMENTHAL

Simon & Schuster Paperbacks

New York   London   Toronto   Sydney   New Delhi

Simon & Schuster Paperbacks
An Imprint of Simon & Schuster, Inc.
1230 Avenue of the Americas
New York, NY 10020

First Simon & Schuster trade paperback edition September 2020

SIMON & SCHUSTER PAPERBACKS and colophon are registered
trademarks of Simon & Schuster, Inc.

For information about special discounts for bulk purchases, please contact
Simon & Schuster Special Sales at 1-866-506-1949 or
business@simonandschuster.com.

The Simon & Schuster Speakers Bureau can bring authors to your live event.
For more information or to book an event contact the Simon & Schuster Speakers
Bureau at 1-866-248-3049 or visit our website at www.simonspeakers.com.

Interior design by Joy O'Meara

Manufactured in the United States of America

10 9 8 7 6 5 4 3 2 1

Library of Congress Cataloging-in-Publication Data is available.

ISBN 978-1-4767-7728-3
ISBN 978-1-4767-7730-6 (pbk)
ISBN 978-1-4767-7731-3 (ebook)

For John Ritch and Christina Ritch

CONTENTS

TIMELINE OF MAJOR EVENTS

March 4, 1853: Inauguration of Franklin Pierce as president

May 30, 1854: Kansas-Nebraska Act passes the Congress

October 4, 1854: Lincoln speaks against the Kansas-Nebraska Act at the Illinois House of Representatives

February 8, 1855: Lincoln, the Whig candidate for the U.S. Senate, recognizes he lacks the votes in the state legislature to win, and throws his support to the antislavery Democrat Lyman Trumbull to defeat the pro-Douglas candidate

August 16, 1855: Andrew Reeder, the first territorial governor of Kansas, removed by President Pierce for his objections to fraudulent elections

September 28, 1855: New York Republican Party created out of fusion of Whigs, Democrats, and Free Soilers

October 7, 1855: John Brown arrives in Kansas

October 23, 1855: Free state settlers meet at Topeka to adopt a constitution banning slavery in the territory, elect a governor, and designate Andrew Reeder its congressional delegate

November 1855: Wakarusa War in Kansas between free state and proslavery forces

December 25, 1855: Christmas dinner at Maryland home of Francis P. Blair to found the national Republican Party

February 22, 1856: The Know Nothing Party, or American Party, nominates former president Millard Fillmore as its presidential candidate

February 22, 1856: First national convention of the Republican Party takes place at Pittsburgh

February 22, 1856: Lincoln writes the platform at a meeting of antislavery editors at Decatur as the founding document of the Illinois Republican Party and calls for its first convention

March 12, 1856: Stephen A. Douglas submits his report on Kansas to the Senate

May 19–20 1856: Charles Sumner delivers his speech to the Senate, "The Crime Against Kansas"

May 21, 1856:   Missouri Ruffians led by former senator David Rice Atchison sack the Kansas free state capital of Lawrence

May 22, 1856:   Congressman Preston S. Brooks of South Carolina canes Charles Sumner in the Senate

May 24–25, 1856:   John Brown and his men murder five proslavery settlers at Pottawatomie, Kansas

May 29, 1856:   Lincoln delivers his "Lost Speech" as the keynote of the founding convention of the Illinois Republican Party

June 6, 1856:   James Buchanan defeats Stephen A. Douglas at the Democratic Party national convention to win nomination as the presidential candidate

June 19, 1856:   John C. Frémont nominated as the first Republican Party presidential candidate; Lincoln's name put into nomination for vice president but loses to William Dayton, a former U.S. senator from New Jersey

November 4, 1856:   James Buchanan elected president

March 4, 1857:   Inauguration of James Buchanan as president

March 6, 1857:   Chief Justice Roger B. Taney issues decision in the Dred Scott case

June 12, 1857:   Douglas defends the Dred Scott decision in a speech at Springfield

June 15, 1857:   Fraudulent election in Kansas elects proslavery delegates to a constitutional convention

June 26, 1857:   Lincoln assails the Dred Scott decision in a speech at Springfield, declaring of the captive slave, "All the powers of earth seem rapidly combining against him."

August 24, 1857:   The Ohio Life Insurance and Trust Company collapses, triggering an economic panic

October 19, 1857:   Proslavery delegates meeting at Lecompton to ratify a Kansas constitution legalizing slavery

November 26, 1857:   Kansas territorial governor Robert J. Walker confronts President Buchanan at the White House on the Lecompton Constitution and is rebuffed

December 3, 1857:   Douglas visits Buchanan at the White House, demands he reject the Lecompton Constitution as a violation of "popular sovereignty," and is threatened by the president that he will be "crushed"

December 8, 1857:   Buchanan endorses the Lecompton Constitution in his first annual message to the Congress

December 9, 1857:   Douglas denounces Buchanan in a speech before the Senate

December 11, 1857:   Frederick P. Stanton, acting territorial governor serving in Walker's absence, dismissed by Buchanan

December 15, 1857:   Walker resigns as territorial governor

December 21, 1857:   Fraudulent referendum in Kansas approves the Lecompton Constitution

January 4, 1858:   Free state Kansas legislature conducts a referendum that overwhelmingly rejects the Lecompton Constitution

February 2, 1858:   Buchanan submits Lecompton Constitution to the Congress to approve for admission of Kansas as a slave state

March 4, 1858:   Senator James Henry Hammond of South Carolina declares in a speech, "Cotton is king"

April 1, 1858:   The House of Representatives rejects the admission of Kansas as a state under the Lecompton Constitution

April 30, 1858:   The Congress passes the English bill stipulating a new referendum on the Lecompton Constitution

June 17, 1858:   Lincoln delivers his "house divided" speech in accepting the Republican nomination for the Senate

August 2, 1858:   Kansas voters by a large margin reject the Lecompton Constitution

August 21, 1858:   Lincoln-Douglas debate, Ottawa, Illinois

August 27, 1858:   Lincoln-Douglas debate, Freeport

September 15, 1858:   Lincoln-Douglas debate, Jonesboro

September 18, 1858:   Lincoln-Douglas debate, Charleston

October 7, 1858:   Lincoln-Douglas debate, Galesburg

October 13, 1858:   Lincoln-Douglas debate, Quincy

October 15, 1858:   Lincoln-Douglas debate, Alton

November 2, 1858:   Douglas reelected, Lincoln defeated

November 4, 1858:   The *Illinois Gazette* of Lacon publishes an editorial: "Abraham Lincoln for President in 1860"

January 5, 1859:   Inner circle of Lincoln men meet at the Illinois State Capitol and propose running Lincoln for president or vice president

April 7, 1859:   Illinois Republican State Committee meets at Bloomington, decides to support Lincoln as a presidential candidate and to keep him in the background for the moment

April 1859:   Lincoln secretly buys a German language newspaper, the *Illinois Staats-Anzeiger*

September 1859:   Douglas publishes an article in *Harper's Monthly,* "Popular Sovereignty in the Territories"

September 13, 1859: Senator David C. Broderick, Democrat of California, a Douglas ally, killed in a duel with California Supreme Court chief justice David Terry, ally of Senator William Gwin, Democrat of California, an enemy of Douglas

September 1859:   Lincoln speaks in Ohio cities, following Douglas, in off-year election campaign; Republicans sweep statewide offices

October 12, 1859:   Lincoln receives a telegram inviting him to speak to a group of Republicans in New York

October 16–18, 1859: John Brown's raid on Harpers Ferry

December 2, 1859:   John Brown hanged

February 27, 1860:   Lincoln poses for a photograph at the studio of Mathew Brady in New York City

February 27, 1860:   Lincoln delivers speech at the Cooper Union: "Right makes might"

April 30, 1860:   Seven Southern state delegations walk out of the Democratic Party national convention at Charleston to stop Douglas's nomination and protest the failure to endorse the Alabama Platform in favor of the extension of slavery to the territories

May 3, 1860:   The Democratic Party national convention at Charleston adjourns without nominating a candidate

May 9, 1860:   Illinois Republican convention nominates Lincoln for president; he is dubbed "The Railsplitter"

May 10, 1860:   Constitutional Union Party convention nominates John Bell of Tennessee for president and Edward Everett of Massachusetts for vice president

May 18, 1860:   Republican Party national convention at Chicago nominates Lincoln for president

June 18–23, 1860:   Democratic Party national convention reconvenes at Baltimore, refusing to seat Southern delegations that had bolted at Charleston; nominates Douglas for president

June 23, 1860:   National Democratic Party convention at Baltimore, comprised of Southern bolters, nominates Vice President John C. Breckinridge of Kentucky for president and Senator Joseph Lane of Oregon for vice president

November 6, 1860:   Lincoln elected president

December 20, 1860: South Carolina secedes from the Union

CAST OF MAJOR CHARACTERS

PRESIDENTS

Zachary Taylor, 12th President

Millard Fillmore, 13th President

Franklin Pierce, 14th President

James Buchanan, 15th President

THE SENATE

David Rice Atchison, Missouri, Democrat, president pro tempore, F Street Mess

Edward D. Baker, Oregon, Republican, former Illinois congressman and friend of Lincoln

James A. Bayard, Delaware, Democrat

Judah P. Benjamin, Louisiana, Democrat

Jesse Bright, Indiana, Democrat, president pro tempore

David C. Broderick, California, Democrat

Andrew Butler, South Carolina, Democrat, F Street Mess

Simon Cameron, Pennsylvania, Democrat/Know Nothing/Republican

Salmon P. Chase, Ohio, Republican

Clement Clay, Alabama, Democrat

John J. Crittenden, Kentucky, Whig/Know Nothing

Jefferson Davis, Mississippi, Democrat

Stephen A. Douglas, Illinois, Democrat

William Pitt Fessenden, Maine, Republican

Henry S. Foote, Mississippi, Democrat

John C. Frémont, California, Republican candidate for president 1856

William M. Gwin, California, Democrat

John P. Hale, New Hampshire, Republican

James Henry Hammond, South Carolina, Democrat, former governor

Robert M.T. Hunter, Virginia, Democrat, F Street Mess

Preston King, New York, Republican

Joseph Lane, Oregon, Democrat, National Democratic candidate for vice president 1860

James M. Mason, Virginia, Democrat, F Street Mess

William Seward, New York, Republican

John Slidell, Louisiana, Democrat

Charles Sumner, Massachusetts, Republican

Lyman Trumbull, Illinois, antislavery Democrat, Republican
Benjamin Wade, Ohio, Republican
Henry Wilson, Massachusetts, Republican

THE HOUSE OF REPRESENTATIVES

William Barksdale, Mississippi, Democrat
Thomas Hart Benton, Missouri, Democrat
Francis P. Blair, Jr., Missouri, Republican
Preston S. Brooks, South Carolina, Democrat
Anson Burlingame, Massachusetts, Republican
Schuyler Colfax, Ohio, Republican
Henry A. Edmundson, Virginia, Democrat
Galusha Grow, Pennsylvania, Republican
Thomas Harris, Illinois, Democrat, friend of Douglas
Philemon Herbert, California, Democrat
Laurence M. Keitt, South Carolina, Democrat
Edwin Morgan, New York, Republican
James L. Orr, South Carolina, Democrat, Speaker of the House
Roger Pryor, Virginia, Democrat
William Richardson, Illinois, Democrat, friend of Douglas
John Sherman, Ohio, Republican
Alexander H. Stephens, Georgia, Whig/Democrat
Thaddeus Stevens, Pennsylvania, Whig/Republican
Eli Thayer, Massachusetts, Republican, founder of New England Emigrant Aid
Society
Robert Toombs, Georgia, Whig/Democrat
Clement Vallandigham, Ohio, Democrat
Elihu Washburne, Illinois, Republican, friend of Lincoln
David Wilmot, Pennsylvania, Democrat/Republican
Robert C. Winthrop, Massachusetts, Whig, Speaker of the House

ALABAMA

John Forsyth, editor of the *Mobile Register*
William Lowndes Yancey, fire-eater, author of the Alabama Platform

ILLINOIS

William B. Archer, former state legislator, Whig/Know Nothing/Republican
Edward L. Baker, editor of the *Illinois State Journal*

William H. Bissell, former Democrat, first Republican governor

Orville Hickman Browning, lawyer, former state legislator, Whig/Republican

Jacob Bunn, merchant, funder of Lincoln's campaigns

John Whitfield Bunn, merchant, funder of Lincoln's campaigns

Theodore Canisius, editor of the *Illinois Staats-Anzeiger* secretly owned by Lincoln

J.O. Cunningham, editor of the *Urbana Union,* Republican

David Davis, judge of the Eighth Circuit, Lincoln's convention manager

T. Lyle Dickey, judge, Whig

Adele Cutts Douglas, wife of Stephen A. Douglas, grand-niece of Dolley Madison

Jesse K. DuBois, former state legislator, Whig/Republican, state auditor

Zebina Eastman, abolitionist editor of the *Free West*

Jesse W. Fell, lawyer, publisher of the *Bloomington Pantagraph,* educator, abolitionist, Whig/Republican

Joseph Gillespie, former state legislator, Whig/Know Nothing/Republican

Jackson Grimshaw, lawyer, Republican

Ozias Hatch, former state legislator, state secretary of state, Republican

Friedrich Hecker, German revolutionary, Republican presidential elector

William Henry Herndon, Lincoln's law partner

Abraham Jonas, former state legislator, Lincoln law associate

Norman Judd, state senator from Chicago, chairman Republican State Central Committee

Gustave Koerner, German American leader, former judge on the state Supreme Court, lieutenant governor, Democrat/Republican

Ward Hill Lamon, Lincoln law associate

Stephen Trigg Logan, Lincoln's former law partner, Whig/Republican

Owen Lovejoy, abolitionist, Republican and congressman

James H. Matheny, Springfield lawyer, Lincoln's best man at his wedding, Whig/Know Nothing

Joseph Medill, editor of the *Chicago Tribune*

Richard J. Oglesby, lawyer, planner of the Illinois Republican convention 1860

John M. Palmer, former state legislator, Democrat/Republican

Ebenezer Peck, state legislator, Republican

Henry B. Rankin, Lincoln-Herndon law clerk

Charles H. Ray, editor and publisher of the *Chicago Tribune*

George Schneider, editor of the *Illinois Staats-Zeitung*

John Locke Scripps, reporter for the *Chicago Democratic Press,* records Lincoln's autobiography

James W. Sheahan, editor of the *Chicago Times*

John Todd Stuart, Lincoln's former law partner, Whig
Leonard Swett, Lincoln law associate
Leonard Volk, sculptor
John "Long John" Wentworth, mayor of Chicago, Democrat/Republican
Henry Clay Whitney, Lincoln law associate
Richard Yates, congressman, governor, Whig/Republican

KANSAS

George W. Brown, editor of the *Herald of Freedom*
John Calhoun, proslavery surveyor general
Mark Delahay, free state newspaper editor, Lincoln's distant cousin
John W. Geary, third territorial governor
Samuel Jones, proslavery sheriff
Samuel Lecompte, proslavery judge
Andrew Reeder, first territorial governor
Charles Robinson, free state governor
Sara Robinson, wife of Charles Robinson
Wilson Shannon, second territorial governor
Frederick P. Stanton, deputy to Governor Walker
Robert J. Walker, fourth territorial governor, former U.S. senator from Mississippi, former secretary of the treasury

MASSACHUSETTS

Charles Francis Adams, Conscience Whig, son of President John Quincy Adams
John A. Andrew, lawyer, Republican, governor
Frank W. Bird, businessman, Republican power broker
Caleb Cushing, Pierce's attorney general, chairman of the Democratic national convention 1860
Ralph Waldo Emerson, philosopher, abolitionist
Edward Everett, former governor, senator, and president of Harvard
Thomas Wentworth Higginson, Unitarian minister, member of the Secret Six
Samuel Gridley Howe, social reformer, member of the Secret Six
Abbott Lawrence, industrialist, influential Whig
Amos A. Lawrence, industrialist, funder of the New England Emigrant Aid Society
Theodore Parker, Unitarian minister, member of the Secret Six
Benjamin Roberts, African American lawyer
George Luther Stearns, industrialist, abolitionist donor, member of the Secret Six

Henry David Thoreau, writer, abolitionist

George Ticknor, Harvard professor, social arbiter of Boston

NEW YORK

August Belmont, U.S. head of Rothschild bank, uncle of John Slidell's wife, Buchanan's campaign manager 1856

John Bigelow, editor of the *New York Evening Post*

William Cullen Bryant, editor of the *New York Evening Post*

Horace Greeley, editor of the *New York Tribune*

James S. Pike, reporter for the *New York Tribune*

Henry J. Raymond, editor of the *New York Times,* lieutenant governor of New York

Dean Richmond, cochairman of the New York Central Railroad, Democratic power broker

Henry Villard, reporter for the *New Yorker Staats-Zeitung, New York Tribune,* and *New York Herald*

Thurlow Weed, editor of the *Albany Evening Journal,* Seward intimate, Whig, and Republican political boss

Walt Whitman, former editor of the *Brooklyn Eagle,* author *Leaves of Grass*

Fernando Wood, mayor of New York City, grand sachem of Tammany Hall

SOUTH CAROLINA

Christopher G. Memminger, commissioner for secession

Robert Barnwell Rhett, editor of the *Charleston Mercury*

VIRGINIA

John Minor Botts, former congressman, Whig/Know Nothing, Unionist

George Fitzhugh, editor of the *Richmond Enquirer,* author of *Sociology for the South, or The Failure of Free Society*

Edmund Ruffin, fire-eater, author, agronomist

Henry A. Wise, governor

SLAVES AND FREE BLACKS

Mary Mildred Botts, child emancipated by Charles Sumner

Anthony Burns, fugitive slave captured in Boston

Frederick Douglass, fugitive slave, author, abolitionist, confidant of John Brown

Margaret Garner, fugitive slave who killed her child rather than submit her family to slavery

Polly Mack, free black in Springfield who sought out Lincoln to free her son about to be sold as a slave in New Orleans

John Shelby, free black from Springfield, held captive in New Orleans to be sold as a slave, his liberty purchased by Lincoln; son of Polly Mack

ABOLITIONISTS

Gamaliel Bailey, editor of *The National Era* newspaper in Washington, D.C.

Henry Ward Beecher, pastor of the Plymouth Church of Brooklyn

Lydia Maria Child, Boston abolitionist, poet, author, journalist

Margaret Douglass, Virginia schoolteacher jailed for educating blacks

William Lloyd Garrison, editor of *The Liberator*

Julia Ward Howe, abolitionist, wife of Samuel Gridley Howe

Wendell Phillips, Boston abolitionist

Harriet Beecher Stowe, author of *Uncle Tom's Cabin*

Theodore Weld, assistant to Congressman John Quincy Adams, author, organizer

JOHN BROWN'S RAID

Jeremiah G. Anderson, white member of Brown's band, killed

Osborne Perry Anderson, free black member of band, escaped

Fontaine Beckham, mayor of Harpers Ferry and B&O agent, killed by Brown's men

Thomas Boerley, grocer, killed by Brown's men

John Brown, revolutionist, executed

Oliver Brown, son of John Brown, member of band, killed

Owen Brown, son of John Brown, member of band, escaped

Watson Brown, son of John Brown, member of band, killed

John Edwin Cook, white member of the band, executed

John Anthony Copeland, Jr., free black, student at Oberlin College, executed

Barclay Coppoc, white member of the band, escaped

Edwin Coppoc, white member of the band, killed Mayor Beckham, executed

Hugh Forbes, English soldier of fortune

Shields Green, fugitive slave member of the band, executed

Albert Hazlett, white member of band

George H. Hoyt, Brown's defense attorney

Thomas Jackson, major and professor, Virginia Military Institute

John Henry Kagi, white member of the band, killed

Lewis Leary, free black member of the band, killed

Robert E. Lee, colonel of U.S. Marines

Willie H. Leeman, white member of the band, killed

Francis Jackson Meriam, white member of Brown's band, conduit to the Secret Six, escaped

Dangerfield Newby, black member of the band, killed

James Redpath, reporter for the *New York Tribune*

Franklin Sanborn, secretary of the Massachusetts Kansas Aid Committee, member of the Secret Six

Hayward Shepherd, black railway porter killed by Brown's men

Gerrit Smith, funder of abolitionist causes and John Brown, member of the Secret Six

Aaron Stevens, white member of Brown's band, executed

J.E.B. Stuart, lieutenant of U.S. Marines

Stewart Taylor, white member of band, killed

Dauphin Thompson, white member of band, killed

Will Thompson, white member of band, killed

Charles Plummer Tidd, white member of band, escaped

Lewis W. Washington, great-grandnephew of George Washington, held as hostage

REPUBLICANS

Edward Bates, St. Louis lawyer, Whig/Know Nothing, candidate for Republican presidential nomination 1860

Francis Preston Blair, member of President Andrew Jackson's Kitchen Cabinet, founder of the national Republican Party

Lewis Clephane, business editor of *The National Era,* organizer of the Republican Club of Washington, D.C.

Andrew G. Curtin, Republican candidate for governor of Pennsylvania, Lincoln supporter

William Dayton, former U.S. senator from New Jersey, Republican candidate for vice president 1856

Jessie Benton Frémont, daughter of Thomas Hart Benton, wife of John C. Frémont, campaign manager

Hinton Rowan Helper, author, *The Impending Crisis: How to Meet It*

Henry S. Lane, Republican candidate for governor of Indiana 1860, Lincoln supporter

Alexander K. McClure, Pennsylvania newspaper editor and Curtin's campaign manager

Carl Schurz, German language newspaper editor, friend of Lincoln

Caleb Smith, former congressman from Indiana, Lincoln supporter

Gideon Welles, editor of the *Hartford Press,* Democrat/Republican, Lincoln supporter

DRED SCOTT CASE

Montgomery Blair, son of Francis P. Blair, Dred Scott's attorney

Taylor Blow, son of Dred Scott's original owner, who emancipated him after the decision

John Catron, associate justice of the Supreme Court, friend of James Buchanan

Benjamin R. Curtis, associate justice of the Supreme Court, dissenter in the Dred Scott case

Robert C. Grier, associate justice of the Supreme Court, friend of James Buchanan

Reverdy Johnson, defense attorney in the case before the Supreme Court, former attorney general

John McLean, associate justice of the Supreme Court, Republican candidate for president in 1856, dissenter in the Dred Scott case

John Sanford, owner of Dred Scott

Dred Scott, slave who sued for his freedom

Harriet Scott, slave, Dred Scott's wife

Roger Taney, chief justice of the Supreme Court, author of the Dred Scott decision

THE BUCHANAN ADMINISTRATION AND ENTOURAGE

Samuel L.M. Barlow, Wall Street financier and political funder

Jeremiah Black, attorney general, former judge on the Pennsylvania Supreme Court

John C. Breckinridge, vice president, former member of Congress, presidential candidate of the National Democratic Party 1860

Lewis Cass, secretary of state, former senator from Michigan

Howell Cobb, secretary of the treasury, former governor of Georgia, former Speaker of the House

John B. Floyd, secretary of war, former governor of Virginia

John W. Forney, Pennsylvania newspaper editor and political operative

Harriet Lane, niece of Buchanan and acting first lady

Jacob Thompson, secretary of the interior, former congressman from Mississippi

Isaac Toucey, secretary of the navy, former congressman from Connecticut

LINCOLN'S FAMILY

Ninian Edwards, Jr., brother-in-law, married to Mary's sister, Whig/Democrat

John Hanks, cousin

Mary Lincoln, wife

Robert Todd Lincoln, son

Thomas "Tad" Lincoln, son

William Wallace "Willie" Lincoln, son

"When in the Course of human events it becomes necessary for one people to dissolve the political bands which have connected them with another and to assume among the powers of the earth, the separate and equal station to which the Laws of Nature and of Nature's God entitle them, a decent respect to the opinions of mankind requires that they should declare the causes which impel them to the separation.

We hold these truths to be self-evident, that all men are created equal, that they are endowed by their Creator with certain unalienable Rights, that among these are Life, Liberty and the pursuit of Happiness.—That to secure these rights, Governments are instituted among Men, deriving their just powers from the consent of the governed,—That whenever any Form of Government becomes destructive of these ends, it is the Right of the People to alter or to abolish it, and to institute new Government, laying its foundation on such principles and organizing its powers in such form, as to them shall seem most likely to effect their Safety and Happiness."

THE DECLARATION OF INDEPENDENCE,
JULY 4, 1776

"In those days, our Declaration of Independence was held sacred by all, and thought to include all; but now, to aid in making the bondage of the negro universal and eternal, it is assailed, and sneered at, and construed, and hawked at, and torn, till, if its framers could rise from their graves, they could not at all recognize it. All the powers of earth seem rapidly combining against him. Mammon is after him; ambition follows, and philosophy follows, and the Theology of the day is fast joining the cry. They have him in his prison house; they have searched his person, and left no prying instrument with him. One after another they have closed the heavy iron doors upon him, and now they have him, as it were, bolted in with a lock of a hundred keys, which can never be unlocked without the concurrence of every key; the keys in the hands of a hundred different men, and they scattered to a hundred different and distant places; and they stand musing as to what invention, in all the dominions of mind and matter, can be produced to make the impossibility of his escape more complete than it is."

ABRAHAM LINCOLN, JUNE 26, 1857

"At any time, the South can raise, equip, and maintain in the field, a larger army than any Power of the earth can send against her, and an army of soldiers—men brought up on horseback, with guns in their hands. . . . No, you dare not make war on cotton. No power on earth dares to make war upon it. Cotton is king. . . . The Senator from New York said yesterday that the whole world had abolished slavery. Aye, the name, but not the thing; all the powers of the earth cannot abolish that."

SENATOR JAMES HENRY HAMMOND,
OF SOUTH CAROLINA, MARCH 4, 1858

"Our best people do not understand the danger. They are besotted. They have compromised so long that they think principles of right and wrong have no more any power on this earth."

JOHN BROWN, 1859

PART ONE

THE PRESENT CRISIS

———————◦•◦———————

"We see dimly in the Present what is small and what is great . . ."

JAMES RUSSELL LOWELL,
"THE PRESENT CRISIS"

CHAPTER ONE

THINGS FALL APART

In 1850, the Union was proclaimed to have been saved again in a great compromise that removed slavery as a controversy from national politics. President Millard Fillmore declared it nothing less than "the final settlement." The issue tearing the country apart, whether the vast territory conquered in the Mexican War would be slave or free, was no longer to be a matter of debate. "We have been carried in safety through a perilous crisis," Franklin Pierce announced at his inauguration on March 4, 1853.

The Compromise of 1850 settled the borders of Texas and admitted California as a free state, and avoided determining the status of New Mexico until far into the future. Only a few agitators trying to shield fugitive slaves from being returned to their masters under the new federal law continued to be nuisances. Slavery as a question that would divide the country was now safely consigned to the past as it had once before.

Most importantly, this new compromise left sacrosanct the Compromise of 1820, the Missouri Compromise, the

Franklin Pierce

original "final settlement." The Missouri crisis had aroused all the issues and arguments revived in the crisis in the aftermath of the Mexican War. The admission of Missouri as a slave state would upset the balance of eleven free and eleven slave states. Its admittance would also establish a precedent for admitting further Western states as slave states. The Northern objection was mirrored in Southern fears that the entire West would be denied to slavery and the balance of power inevitably shifted. Secretary of State John Quincy Adams wrote in his diary that the Missouri problem was "a flaming sword . . . a mere preamble—a title page to a great tragic volume." He believed it was based in the Constitution's "dishonorable compromise with slavery," a "bargain between freedom and slavery" that was "morally vicious, inconsistent with the principles upon which alone our revolution can be justified." He prophesied that "the seeds of the Declaration are yet maturing" and that its promise of equality would become "the precipice into which the slave-holding planters of his country sooner or later much fall." In the Senate, the Southerners' anxiety that slavery might be prohibited in the territories assumed a hostility congealed into ideology against the egalitarian premise of the Declaration of Independence. Senator Nathaniel Macon of North Carolina, the former Speaker of the House, posed the question, "A clause in the Declaration of Independence has been read declaring that 'all men are created equal'; follow that sentiment and does it not lead to universal emancipation?" The Declaration, Macon stated, "is not part of the Constitution or of any other book" and there was "no place for the free blacks in the United States." Senator Henry Clay of Kentucky managed to hammer together a narrow majority for a compromise that brought in Maine as a free state to balance the slave state of Missouri and established a line restricting slavery north of 36°31' latitude excepting Missouri. The debate inspired a sense of panic in Thomas Jefferson retired at Monticello. "This momentous question, like a fire bell in the night, awakened and filled me with terror. I considered it at once as the knell of the Union."

Jefferson's nightmare hung over the Senate debate of the Compromise of 1850, filled with frightful images of death, premonitions of catastrophe, and curses of doom if slavery were allowed to persist as a vital issue. The Great Triumvirate of Henry Clay, Daniel Webster, and John C. Calhoun, the representative political men of their age, hurled lightning bolts from their Olympian heights. Henry Clay, young Abraham Lincoln's "beau ideal of a statesman," who invented the power of the Speaker of the House, who as a senator crafted the Compromise of 1820, who served as secretary of state, and who was nearly elected president, warned that the nation stood "at the edge of the precipice before the fearful and disastrous leap is taken in the yawning abyss below, which will inevitably lead to certain and irretrievable destruction." Daniel Webster of Massachusetts, the Godlike Daniel, the voice of "liberty and Union, one and inseparable, now and forever," whose framed picture hung in Lincoln's law office, cautioned, "Secession! Peaceable secession! Sir, your eyes and mine are never destined to see that miracle. The dismemberment of this vast country without convulsion! . . . Sir, he who sees these States, now revolving in harmony around a common center, can expect to see them quit their places and fly off without convulsion, may look the next hour to see the heavenly bodies rush from their spheres and jostle against each other in the realms of space without producing a crash of the universe." John C. Calhoun of South Carolina, whose stunning career included every office—congressman, senator, secretary of war, vice president, secretary of state—but the one he coveted most—president of the United States—sat wrapped wraithlike in a black cape on the Senate floor. The great nullifier, who insisted the states had preeminent authority over the federal government, objected to any compromise that would thwart the extension of slavery anywhere in the country, an "injustice" which he called the "oppression" of the South. "No, sir," he prophesied, "the Union can be broken." Calhoun's acolyte, Jefferson Davis of Mississippi, in opposing the admission of California as a free state, threatened, "If sir, this spirit of sectional aggrandizement, or if gentlemen prefer, this love they bear for the African race, shall cause the disruption of these states, the last chapter of our history will be a sad commentary upon the justice and the wisdom of our people." Calhoun died less than a month after his final appearance in the Senate. Clay and Webster were dead within two years. The old order passed. By then Secretary of War Jefferson Davis was the power behind the president.

Two years earlier, in 1848, a different sort of warning was delivered in the House of Representatives from a backbench congressman, Abraham Lincoln of Illinois, in a bloodcurdling speech that attempted to get to the root of the crisis created by the Mexican War. Lincoln called himself "a Proviso man," after the Wilmot Proviso, an act that would prohibit slavery in all the seized territory, which he voted for numerous times but that never passed the Congress. Opening the West to slavery had roiled politics for a decade. In 1844, Lincoln had supported Henry Clay's presidential campaign against the annexation of Texas, which Clay called "wicked." Clay lost to James K. Polk of Tennessee, who launched the Mexican War that gained territory that would become the states of California, Nevada, Utah, and parts of Arizona, New Mexico, Colorado, and Wyoming. The balance of political power between North and South, slave states and free, hung on whether slavery would be extended into what was called the Mexican Cession or halted in its tracks.

Lincoln the "Proviso Man" rose to challenge the narrative of the war in order to undermine the legitimacy of slavery extension. He insisted that the origin of the war was fraudulent and demanded the evidence for the "spot" where it began. Lincoln the devotee of Shakespeare described President Polk as a Macbeth-like despot, "deeply conscious" of his guilt and stained by blood he could not wipe away—"he feels the blood of this war, like the blood of Abel, is crying to Heaven against him . . . and trusting to escape scrutiny, by fixing the public gaze upon the exceeding brightness of military glory—that attractive rainbow, that rises in showers of blood—that serpent's eye, that charms to destroy." Polk's message on the war that had opening the issue of the extension of slavery, said Lincoln, was "the half insane mumbling of a fever-dream."

For Lincoln's criticism of the war the newspaper owned by his longtime rival, Senator Stephen A. Douglas, dubbed him "Ranchero Spotty"—"ranchero" being the word for Mexican guerrilla fighters—tainting his patriotism. Lincoln served only one term. He had run for office continually since the age of twenty-three, risen to become the Whig Party floor leader in the state legislature, the leading Whig of his state, but he was thrust out of politics. Isolated in his two-man law office in Springfield, he gloomily stared for hours as he contemplated a life he considered would be insignificant. "How hard, oh! How hard it is to die and leave one's country no better than if one had never lived for it!" he despaired to his law partner, William Henry Herndon. Lincoln could not anticipate that after he sank from public view to the county courthouses of central Illinois he would be "thunderstruck and stunned" by Douglas's Kansas-Nebraska Act of 1854 that unhinged the basic structure of politics and "striking in the direction of the sound" would launch on a journey that would miraculously carry him to the presidency.

Lincoln's reinvention required that he invent a whole new politics. He would temper his melancholy and disappointment into the base metal of his determination. He had to break free from past political bonds, focus his concentrated intellectual powers entirely self-taught to reframe political argument, forge a completely new party from the wreckage, draw together in a common enterprise men who hated and distrusted each other, from abolitionists to Old Whigs, from Democrats to Know Nothings, overcome after suffering defeat after defeat and one famous and powerful opponent after another, and through his mastery in the whirlwind create new "powers of earth" to struggle against the greatest power in the country, the Slave Power, "all the powers of earth."

Lincoln would have to begin by rising from the ashes of the Whigs. The Compromise of 1850 split the Whigs between its Northern and Southern wings, and by 1852 it was no longer a viable national party. Its candidate, General Winfield Scott, nominated in the Whig tradition of forwarding military heroes to compensate for its incoherence, stumbled to the worst showing in presidential elections. The Whig Party never recovered from its defeat in the 1852 election. It cracked beneath Lincoln's feet. But the realignment of politics was not yet apparent.

On March 1, 1853, during the week that Washington put on its finery for the inauguration of a new president, Lincoln deposited $310 in fees gained from his law practice into an account at the Springfield Marine and Fire Insurance Company. The day before the inauguration he bought a wheelbarrow for work around his house on the corner of Eighth and Jackson Streets. On March 8, his mind was on "a little Ejectment case" coming up in the Edgar County Circuit Court. He could not attend and asked a colleague whether he could handle the matter. "I have been paid a little fee. Now I dislike to keep their money without doing the service; and I also hate to disgorge."

In a time of peace and prosperity, after more than a decade of war and panic, Franklin Pierce swept into the presidency in the greatest landslide in the country's history—greater than Thomas Jefferson's, greater than Andrew Jackson's. Handsome and charming, well-educated and well-spoken, Pierce at forty-eight years old was the youngest man ever to attain the highest office. He had a "fascination of manner that has since proved so magical in winning him an unbounded personal popularity," wrote the novelist Nathaniel Hawthorne, his classmate at Bowdoin College and biographer. "Few men possess anything like it; so irresistible as it is, so sure to draw forth an undoubting confidence, and so true to the promise which it gives."

Pierce recited his inaugural address from memory to universal admiration. Few of those warmed by the sun in the crisp air at the dawn of the new era on March 4, 1853, felt the barest shiver of convulsions to come. The fortunate president did not have the slightest hint that the members of the Congress cheering him on that cloudless day would unravel the peace and bring about his downfall, or that he would fecklessly cooperate in his own undoing to precipitate the crisis before the war. Four years after assuming office, on his way out, Pierce simply remarked to his private secretary, Sidney Webster, "There's nothing left to do but to get drunk."

"So amiable, so friendly in his manner, so affectionate," a friend observed about the new president. It was a warm description of a nice boy. He had no log cabin. Pierce was the product of a privileged upbringing with a powerful, alcoholic father and provocative, unstable mother. Good things happened for him effortlessly. The hidden hand of his early success was Benjamin Pierce, a gruff Revolutionary War hero, "the General," and governor of New Hampshire, who stage-managed his son's anointment as Speaker of the New Hampshire House of Representatives at the age of twenty-seven and glided him into seats in the Congress and the Senate.

Southern senators welcomed Franklin Pierce into their club in 1837 as a pluperfect and pliable Northern man of Southern sympathy. He could have retained his place forever as an unmemorable fixture like a flickering sconce in the Senate chamber. Then, abruptly, he quit. His stern wife was determined to rescue him from a life of depravity.

Jane Appleton Pierce, the daughter of the president of Bowdoin College and the niece of Amos Lawrence, the wealthy Massachusetts mill owner, had a visceral distaste for politicians, whom she regarded as common and grimy, and blamed her husband's chronic drunkenness on his association with the riffraff. Once, attending a Washington theater, the pleasant Pierce recklessly threw himself into a brawl. He sometimes discovered himself waking up in a daze of blinding hangovers, inevitably followed by bouts of self-reproach and apologies until he would repeat the cycle. Mrs. Pierce demanded that he leave the Senate, believing she was saving his soul and protecting her family reputation.

Death opened another door. On the eve of the 1852 presidential contest, one of Pierce's mentors and the favorite son of the New Hampshire Democrats, Supreme Court justice Levi Woodbury, who had run unsuccessfully for the presidential nomination in 1848, suddenly expired. The Concord Cabal, the political directorate of New Hampshire's Democratic Party, acting almost in loco parentis, brought Pierce forward to the starting gate as a dark horse candidate. He easily raced past a stable of stumbling "old fogies" without giving the slightest offense to those left in the dust. None resented the upstart because he fulfilled each one's desire to deprive the prize to the others, especially to the most dangerous rival of all—that dynamo of raw ambition, Senator Stephen A. Douglas of Illinois, thirty-nine years old, nine years younger than the youthful Pierce.

Pierce's levitation was a marvel of political preferment that allowed him to transcend his vagueness without the slightest mental focus. His wife, above all, understood him. When a breathless messenger reached the Pierces with news of his nomination as they were placidly touring the landscaped tombs of the Mount Auburn Cemetery in Cambridge, Massachusetts, she fainted.

Even before Pierce arrived in Washington, his natural optimism was knocked off-kilter. During the transition the tragic death of his only surviving son, slipping just out of his grasp in a bizarre railroad accident in New Hampshire, sent his emotionally fragile wife into reclusive mourning and him back to the brandy bottle. She wore black to the inauguration and the ball was canceled.

Pierce's effortless ascent lifted him into the presidency, but poorly prepared him for its rigors. While he promised almost everyone whatever they asked of him and wished to satisfy all sides, he often failed to deliver the goods and seemed genuinely hurt when people expressed disappointment. There was little political rhyme or reason to his frequently broken personal pledges. "He was so absurdly false to his promises, that, where it did not cut too hard, it was positively ludicrous," wrote one influential Democrat. Pierce's boyish impulse for ingratiation heightened his wishful thinking, his predominant mode of thought. Upsetting anyone or anything was the last thing he ever sought, and so he upset nearly everyone and everything. Whenever there was not a happy ending, he was baffled. Paradox and complication perplexed him. He was confounded not only when he failed to deliver but also when he did.

While the others clawed at each other during the struggle for the nomination, Pierce's passivity had allowed him to escape unscathed. But once he became president his well-intentioned gestures to smooth over his party's fissures perversely pried them open. With the bounty of patronage spread before the Democrats their hatreds reemerged with a vengeance.

The crack-up appeared first within the New York party, whose endless fractious hostilities went back at least to the beginning of the Republic, to Aaron Burr's founding of Tammany Hall, which he had used to undermine Alexander Hamilton. In 1848, antislavery Democrats joined with political abolitionists to create the Free Soil Party, which was organized to oppose the extension of slavery in the Mexican Cession. The New York Democratic faction, known as the Barnburners or the Softs, was instrumental in nominating former president Martin Van Buren of New York, who had been denied the Democratic nomination, as the Free Soil candidate. He was an unlikely standard-bearer of the cause. As president, Van Buren had been resolutely pro-Southern and proslavery in sympathy. After the election Van Buren returned to his usual position and the Free Soil Party disintegrated. Pierce's patronage to the Softs was his effort to let bygones be bygones. He wished to reunite the party around him and the new consensus. But his goodwill enraged the proslavery Hards.

Nothing was forgotten and nothing forgiven. The Hards retaliated by torpedoing Pierce's nomination of former senator John A. Dix, a leading Soft, as secretary of state. Then the Hards launched into pitched battle against the Softs for control of the patronage-rich New York Custom House, assailing Pierce as a betrayer for failing to hand them every job. The Hards, meanwhile, attempted to wreck Pierce's next appointment to be secretary of state—William L. Marcy, the New York party warhorse, former governor, senator, and secretary of war—the old Jacksonian who had coined the phrase: "To the victor belong the spoils." Marcy's crime had been to call for party unity. To the spoils belonged the victor.

From the beginning, Pierce was dependent for emotional support and political guidance on his Mexican War comrade, who, completing the sympathetic bond, would also lose a beloved son. "How I shall be able to summon my manhood and gather up my energies for all the duties before me, it is hard for me to see," Pierce confided to Jefferson Davis on the eve of his inauguration. The former senator from Mississippi, scion of plantation wealth, was an imperious aristocrat with the streak of a martinet, who instinctively reacted to differences of opinion as though they were mortal attacks on his sacred honor and occasionally threatened duels. Suffering from an incurable venereal disease, herpes simplex 2, which rendered him periodically blind for weeks at a time, his rigidity redoubled. Davis, however, was a man of vision—of a vast slave empire encompassing Cuba, the Caribbean, and Latin America, and a transcontinental railroad linking the South to the West, which would be drawn into slavery. For all intents and purposes, Secretary of War Jefferson Davis was the acting president of the United States.

Within a year of Pierce's overwhelming election his popularity unraveled in a downward spiral of factional fighting over the patronage that he mishandled through political ineptitude to alienate all sides. His advent had been hailed by "cheering events" and "unparalleled unanimity," when "not a voice was heard to disparage the President-elect," according to the proslavery *New York Herald*. "Twelve months have elapsed, and now not a voice, save those of hirelings, utters a syllable in his praise. He has forfeited the esteem of a whole people, broken every pledge he gave, violated each separate promise of his inaugural, trampled on the sentiment which elected him, plunged the country into disorders whose issue appalls the most stout-hearted, and for all this has earned the indignant reproaches of an injured Nation. His government has fallen lower after ten months of office than any of its predecessors ever fell in four years."

Pierce was discredited even though his party controlled every branch of government and the opposition was smashed into pieces. It was not the opposition party that ripped apart Pierce's presidency; it was broken from within.

Yet only minor tremors were enough to cause his fall from grace. The volcanic eruption was yet to come. Soon the fissures of the political earth would crack open. The molten elements of politics—ambition, influence, and reputation—would pour onto the landscape. Those raw elements were personified in the single most disruptive character in American politics, the perpetual rival to one and all—the once and future rival of Abraham Lincoln.

Pierce pointedly excluded one man from the patronage—Stephen A. Douglas of Illinois, the wild child banished to the dark forest. But Douglas would not be denied. The attempt to isolate him only made him free-ranging and menacing. He took every sign of Pierce's weakness as an incentive, every deprivation of patronage as an insult. Douglas had no motive to play for anyone but himself, which was his natural instinct. With almost every speech and gesture, he battered down the limits and conventions of politics. Douglas had been the chief floor manager of the Compromise of 1850, but he could not help himself from undoing it, reopening the issue of slavery and unhinging his party.

CHAPTER TWO

VAULTING AMBITION

"Vaulting ambition, which o'erleaps itself . . ."

SHAKESPEARE, *MACBETH*

S tephen A. Douglas had not yet turned forty years old when he observed the fortunate, popular, and incapable Franklin Pierce swear to the oath of office of president. Douglas's whole being was consumed with envy that Pierce should be the one standing on the Capitol Portico with his right hand raised and his left one on the Bible. His frustration stoked the furnace of his ambition, beyond resentment, anger, and vengeance—it was a rage for power rooted in wounded pride.

The Little Giant projected himself as "the spirit of the age," an irresistible force of nature and fate, carried forward on the whirlwind of industrialization and the gale of Manifest Destiny. After Henry Clay faltered both politically and physically handling the Compromise of 1850, which crumbled in his frail hands, the younger Douglas assumed its management as Senate floor leader, masterfully passing it. Never was the transfer of power from one generational leader to another within the Congress more sud-

Stephen A. Douglas

den and dramatic. The curtain came down on one and rose for the other. For Clay, the abruptness was a poignant moment of decline; for Douglas, it was a ruthless ascent. Immediately after passage of the Compromise, he maneuvered through passage of the Illinois Central Railroad Tax Act, establishing the first federally chartered railroad corporation, stretching from the lakeshore of Chicago (whose real estate he sold at a windfall profit for the right-of-way) to the Gulf of Mexico, an alternate Mississippi River on wheels.

In his assault to capture the Democratic presidential nomination in 1852 he inflicted damage on himself that never healed. His campaign systematically insulted almost every major figure within the party. The name-calling was vicious, childish, and, worst of all, often deadly accurate. Douglas's offense against the party's elders, the "old fogies," as he called them, remained vivid as a forewarning of the ever-present threat of his still radiant political promise, his vibrant youth, boundless energy, legislative skill, stunning accumulation of power through his linkage to far-flung financial and industrial interests, and astounding feats of oratorical bombast, bellowed in floor performances of name-calling, illogic, flying spit and sweat, accompanied by shouting in a drumbeat, and flinging about the word "nigger." Imposing and intimidating, the Little Giant's heights of demagogy highlighted his underlying anxiety.

Even before Pierce's inauguration Douglas began planning his campaign to seize the 1856 Democratic presidential nomination. His scramble was already frantic. Douglas's previously unmarred confidence was tinged with desperation. Seeking to recover his untarnished glimmer he burned with an ever more intense nervous energy. The death of his wife, Martha, in January 1853, shortly after Pierce's election, brought home to Douglas his mortality. He was always driven and uncontrollable, but now he was compelled and haunted. His drinking got worse and appearance shabby as it would during his cycles of stress.

Then Douglas conceived an even more stupendous feat to transport his ambition to the White House, the construction of a transcontinental Pacific railroad. He had strategically invested in real estate to profit from both potential central and northern routes, dealing in his fellow legislators North and South, and was the beneficiary of his close relationships with bankers from Washington to Wall Street to Chicago. But there was an obstacle. The railroad must cross land that stretched a thousand miles from the western border of Missouri to the continental divide of the Rocky Mountains. In order to lay track across the Great Plains, which was federal territory, an act of Congress was required. Lining the pockets of Douglas's fellow politicians was only one part in lining up the politics.

The Kansas and Nebraska territories, commonly referred to solely as Nebraska, were north of the line established in the Compromise of 1820—the Missouri Compromise—that had permitted admission of Missouri as a slave state but no other above that demarcation. The territory north of the line was a vast land containing what would ultimately become not only the states of Kansas and Nebraska, but also South Dakota, North Dakota, Colorado, Wyoming, and Montana. If admitted as states under the terms of the Missouri Compromise their representatives and senators would decisively tilt the balance of power against the South, and almost inevitably a large Northern majority in the Congress would pass legislation against the expansion of slavery.

When Douglas as chairman of the Senate Committee on Territories originally filed his bill to organize the Nebraska territories he triggered a bidding war. Singlehandedly he broke the dam of the Compromise of 1850 that had been constructed to quarantine slavery from national politics. From the moment Douglas introduced his bill, he lost control to Southerners who seized the opening to repeal the Missouri Compromise. While the notion that the federal government could not interfere with slavery as a "local" institution in the Southern states was a nearly universal consensus except among a tiny fringe of abolitionists, the Southern Rightists insisted that their "liberty" could not be restricted anywhere. They used Douglas's bill to erase the line prohibiting slavery in the North as only a preliminary step to nationalizing it.

Douglas hailed his Nebraska Act (as it was often called) as a glorious new dawn of democracy, which he marketed under the phrase "popular sovereignty," a watery concept he raised to a high principle and waved as his banner. Whether or not a new territory would be slave or free, he argued, would be determined by the vote of its citizens. But just who those hypothetical people might be and what legal conditions might govern their decisions he could and would not say. Indeed, that lack of definition on the most important matters was at the heart of his doctrine. His ill-defined means were contrived to achieve his political ends. Both Southern Rightists and antislavery Northerners considered "popular sovereignty" to be little more than Douglas's expedient gambit to advance his ambition. But a number of the most influential Southerners, even if they privately acknowledged his cynicism, grabbed Douglas's Nebraska Act as a convenient mechanism for the conquest of Kansas, which would be secured when Missourians swooped across the state line to claim it for slavery. His concept was regarded as vacant as the territory of Kansas itself (the tribe of Wyandotte Native Americans who inhabited it conveniently overlooked). "Border Ruffians" rushed in to fill Douglas's theoretical vacuum.

The first territorial governor, Andrew Horatio Reeder, a Democratic railroad lawyer from Pennsylvania, had no objection to slavery and even jocularly suggested he might bring his own slave to the territory, though he didn't happen to own one. A dignified, portly figure with well-tended side-whiskers, upon his arrival in Kansas delivered a windy oration worthy of Polonius, hailing "our glorious Union" and the "*vox populi*" of popular sovereignty. He saw the New England Emigrant Aid Society, which funded antislavery settlers to travel to Kansas, as the only potential source of friction and that could be easily handled.

The first election in the territory, for a Kansas delegate to the Congress, on November 29, 1854, was the signal for an invasion of hundreds of heavily armed proslavery men from the western border counties of Missouri. They organized into groups called Blue Lodges and Sons of the South, equipped with weapons provided from state armories, and pledged to make Kansas a slave state. Threatening poll judges and intimidating free state men from voting, the Ruffians installed their favored candidate. Governor Reeder scheduled an election for the legislature for March 30, 1855. On that day more than five thousand men lubricated with whiskey, flying flags and banners, overran the polls to stuff ballots for what the free staters called the "bogus legislature."

Reeder's refusal to certify rigged elections came as a shock to the proslavery forces. His actual belief in the orotund phrases he had uttered about the popular will surprised all sides and infuriated the Missourians. Pierce summoned him to Washington to fire him.

Reeder's replacement as territorial governor, Wilson Shannon, a former Democratic governor and congressman from Ohio, who had voted for the Kansas-Nebraska Act, appeared at a rally at Westport, Missouri, the headquarters town for the Ruffians, where he blessed the proslavery "bogus legislature" as legal and announced, "He was for slavery in Kansas."

Abraham Lincoln feared the worst-case scenario, driven by those exploiting "the spirit of violence." "That Kansas will form a Slave constitution, and, with it, will ask to be admitted into the Union, I take to be an already settled question," he had written his friend Joshua Speed on August 24, 1855. "By every principle of law, ever held by any court, North or South, every negro taken to Kansas is free; yet in utter disregard of this—in the spirit of violence merely—that beautiful [Bogus] Legislature gravely passes a law to hang men who shall venture to inform a negro of his legal rights."

Despite two invasions, the Border Ruffians failed to drive off the antislavery settlers, most of whom had been recruited to the territory by the New England Emigrant Aid Society in a deliberate effort to use the popular sovereignty concept to keep Kansas free. In September 1855, in Kansas, a gathering of Free Soilers, Whigs, and some Democrats formed a new political party, the Free State Party, under the banner: "A Free State; Opposition To Tyranny By Peaceable Measures First; When They Fail, By Force." The newly formed party resolved, "That we owe no allegiance or obedience to the tyrannous enactment of this spurious Legislature. . . . the monstrous consummation of an act of violence, usurpation, and fraud." Then the free state men reconvened at Topeka on October 23 to ratify a constitution emblazoned, "Slavery shall not exist in the state." To accommodate the Democrats in the Free State coalition, however, the constitution banned free blacks. Governor Shannon, meanwhile, attended the founding of the proslavery Law and Order Party as a delegate, representing Lawrence, where he did not reside, and was elected the convention's chairman. He informed the cheering crowd that the Topeka Constitution was "treasonable," adding, "The president is behind you."

In late November 1855, a series of startlingly tragic and absurd events precipitated yet another Ruffian invasion. In a dispute over a land claim, a proslavery man brutally murdered a free state man. The killer fled for safety to the sanctuary of Missouri. His protector was Samuel J. Jones, postmaster of Westport, the hotbed of the Ruffians, who had participated in the first invasion of Kansas to threaten election judges and destroy a ballot box, and was appointed sheriff of Douglas County (named after Stephen A. Douglas) by the "bogus legislature." A contemporary Kansan historian described him as "the most consummate rogue" of "contemptible meanness." Jones arrested the only eyewitness to the murder, a free state leader named Jacob Branson. But an armed band of free state men confronted Jones, rescuing the prisoner. The humiliated Jones informed Governor Shannon he faced "an open rebellion." Then the governor summoned the militia to suppress it, though less than a hundred men answered his call, followed by an official order, a bugle call, to bring in about 1,500 heavily armed Missourians to exterminate the foe. They anticipated a turkey shoot. "We expect bloodshed," read the editorial in the proslavery *Squatter Sovereign* newspaper, "and we . . . expect to wade in the blood of the abolitionists."

The Ruffians descended on Lawrence bristling with muskets and bowie knives, toting whiskey jugs to stoke their bravado, and expected to stage a swift massacre to settle the question of Kansas for good. They were stunned to encounter a well-drilled militia entrenched in breastworks and five forts, and wielding hundreds of Sharps rifles, the most modern, rapid-firing, and accurate long-range weapon in the world, of which the Ruffians had not one, aimed in their direction. They "will give us the victory without firing a shot," the leader of the free staters Charles Robinson wrote Lawrence. The shaken Ruffians pleaded for intervention from the governor, who instead chose to negotiate. They felt Shannon, like Reeder, betrayed them. The Missourians sullenly retreated for the winter, losers of what was called the Wakarusa War, to prepare for a bloody spring offensive.

On January 15, 1856, the free staters named their own governor and legislature. Kansas was now divided by dual and dueling powers. There were two legislatures, two constitutions, and two armed camps. The proslavery party's government had come into existence under federal legal authority, yet in defiance of the presidentially appointed governor and every rule of fair elections. The antislavery party's government had no legal status but claimed the mantle of justice. Both claimed the other was illegitimate.

In February, Lincoln attended a meeting in Springfield, Illinois, to hear firsthand accounts from free state Kansans on the front lines. Lincoln spoke up, advising a political strategy against creating a separate government, unaware that the free staters had already done so in their effort to resist making Kansas a slave state. "You can better succeed with the ballot," Herndon recounted him saying. "Let there be peace. Revolutionize through the ballot box. . . . Your attempt, if there be such, to resist the laws of Kansas by force is criminal and wicked; and all your feeble attempts will be follies and end in bringing sorrow on your heads and ruin the cause you would freely die to preserve!" When a subscription was taken up, Lincoln chipped in, "showing his sincerity," and it was sent "to our friends in Kansas."

Under Douglas's exalted "popular sovereignty" free elections were being trampled. The congressional committee investigating the "troubles" in Kansas would conclude, "each election in the Territory . . . has been carried by organized invasion from the State of Missouri, by which the people of the Territory have been prevented from exercising the rights secured to them."

The conflict on the distant plains of Kansas exposed the contradiction between Douglas's doctrine and the squalid reality. His problem was not theoretical. Douglas had attached his fate to that of Kansas. He saw the opening of the 34th Congress as a new opportunity to recast the crisis and resolve his danger.

CHAPTER THREE

THE SPIRIT OF VIOLENCE

W ho names Douglas for the next President now?" mocked an editorial in the *New York Times* after the passage of his Nebraska bill provoked an outcry in 1854. Under the headline "The Prophet on the Nebraska Question," the newspaper approvingly quoted the sermon of the famous Hartford theologian Horace Bushnell: "But tidings out of the East and out of the West shall trouble him; therefore shall he go forth with great fury to destroy and utterly to make waste, yet he shall come to his end and none shall help him."

"I could then travel from Boston to Chicago by the light of my own effigies," Douglas would later observe during his 1858 campaign for the Senate against Lincoln, when he also boasted that he had envisioned his resurrection and his enemies' demise. "I predicted that in less than five years you would have to get out a search warrant to find an anti-Nebraska man."

Not quite two years after the New England evangelist had cast a malediction on him, Douglas announced he was seeking "perfect and complete vindication," as he wrote to Howell Cobb, trying to ingratiate himself with the former

Lyman Trumbull

Georgia governor. Cobb was one of the wealthiest slaveholders, just returned to the Congress where he had been Speaker of the House under Polk, and as establishment a Southern Democrat as there was. Despite the devastation of the Northern Democrats in the midterm elections of 1854, Douglas took heart from the comeback of Democrats in state contests the following year and the rapid dissolution of the Whig Party. Even as the anti-Nebraska forces claimed control of the U.S. House of Representatives, Douglas plotted his next presidential campaign. His prospective rivals seemed damaged and weak. Pierce was ruined, mainly for signing Douglas's Nebraska bill, and Douglas believed he could rise on Pierce's ashes.

"Douglas first!" was his new slogan, proclaiming his self-confidence. "Ohio is as sure for us as Illinois," he wrote James W. Sheahan, whom he had installed as editor of the *Chicago Times*. Douglas intended to play the inside game rather than repeat the failed strategy of storming the citadel. For his campaign managers Douglas enlisted two seasoned politicos, David T. Disney, a former congressman from Ohio, and James W. Singleton, an Illinois state legislator and railroad builder by way of Virginia and Kentucky who had been an Old Whig. Singleton slyly filled Southern newspapers with letters touting Douglas, while Disney set up shop at New York's Astor House, where he tried to forge peace between the proslavery Hards and antislavery Softs, hostile factions of the New York Democratic Party, to promote Douglas's candidacy. But Disney could no more achieve an armistice between the scorpions in the bottle than had Pierce.

Still, Douglas believed the leadership of the Democratic Party was a vacuum that he alone could fill. The exhausted ambition of Secretary of State William L. Marcy had left his New York backers searching for an alternative. For two generations Marcy had been the towering Democratic figure in the state and a recurrent presidential hopeful. His disdain for Pierce, who treated him shabbily, and Buchanan, an old rival, exceeded his distaste for Douglas. Dean Richmond, Marcy's key man and the vice president of the New York Central Railroad, traveled to Washington to confer secretly with Douglas. Richmond promised a winning scenario: if his delegation of Softs would be seated at the convention and the Hards were excluded, he guaranteed New York would vote as a unit for Douglas and deliver to him the nomination.

When the 34th Congress reconvened on March 4, 1856, Douglas stepped on to the stage for the first scene of the drama that he hoped would end with his inauguration as president. He had returned to Washington recovered

from one of his periodic physical collapses brought on by his chronic alcoholism. ("It is well known in Chicago that he is a drunken little blackguard,"
jibed the *Cleveland Leader,* a Republican Party newspaper tied to antislavery senator Benjamin Wade.) The Democratic majority anxiously awaited
Douglas's move. He planned to use his chairmanship of the Committee on
Territories to deliver a report on Kansas to tout his "great principle" of popular sovereignty, and expected it would prove "a crusher, and would cut down
Pierce completely," according to his close ally, Congressman Thomas L. Harris of Illinois. Douglas's presentation was carefully produced as the launch of
his presidential campaign.

On March 12, Senator Andrew Butler of South Carolina formally requested that Douglas read aloud his entire report before the Senate. For two
hours, Douglas held forth to make his whole constitutional, historical, and
political case. It was a transparent bid for Southern support. He offered the
Calhoun explanation of the Union as a compact of states with the "reserve
right" of slavery.

Butler's introduction and Douglas's tribute to Calhoun suggested the tactical alliance that Douglas believed was essential for his next run for the presidency. He could not rise without the blessing of the Southern Democrats.
They had blocked him from the Democratic nomination in 1852, but he had
accomplished the Kansas-Nebraska Act with their cooperation.

Butler was an elder member of the F Street Mess, the epicenter of power
in Washington, where the most powerful Southern senators, all chairmen
of the most influential committees, resided together in a boardinghouse in
the shadow of the Capitol. Butler was chairman of the Committee on the
Judiciary. Secretary of War Jefferson Davis was an ex officio member of the
F Street Mess. Individually each of these great beasts claimed the mantle of
John C. Calhoun, the "cast-iron man" from South Carolina, who had died
in 1850 but still cast his spell. Collectively the F Street Mess amounted to a
Senate Select Committee on the Legacy of John C. Calhoun. After their
deaths Clay's and Webster's influence waned along with their party. Only
Calhoun's shadow remained. His tragic odyssey and bleak vision foretold the
radicalization of the South.

Calhoun's definition of the highest form of civilization was a chain of
hierarchy from master to slave. The crusader for states' rights, nullifier of
federal authority, and prophet of secession had proclaimed slavery nothing
less than "a positive good" and condemned any compromise to restrain its
reach. Sensing a darkening horizon lowering over the country as approach-

ing mortality clouded over him, Calhoun furiously composed dense tracts filled with tortuous formulas to perpetuate minority rule over the majority.

Despite his manifestos Calhoun was no mere ideologue. His driven and dry logic was the distilled product of an embittered lifetime at the pinnacle of American politics. He was the antithesis of a rabble-rousing, tobacco-stained, populist provincial. Nor did he ever make any demagogic appeals to the poor white forgotten man. There was nothing homespun, naive, or commonplace about Calhoun. He was Yale educated, married into Charleston wealth, and a consummate politician operating in Washington for decades.

In the deepest recesses of his brain and to the marrow of his bones Calhoun understood one thing above all: that slavery was power—economic power, political power, social power. Confining slavery to its regional cage would inevitably lead to a dwindling Southern political minority and force a crisis of its whole system. He knew that the future of the Slave Power depended on adroit mastery of the federal government's inner levers, which as secretary of state he had manipulated in precipitating the Mexican War. He believed that slavery must become an imperial project claiming Cuba and other Latin American lands that would become slave states to tip the balance for the South. If Southern domination over the federal government was ever broken, there could be—should be—no Union. Peering into the abyss, he darkly predicted that the future loss of the executive branch to an antislavery president would trigger secession. Calhoun's fatal damage outlived him. His overreaching failure provided a pessimistic and cautionary tale for Southern Rightists that they must eternally rule the Democratic Party and the citadel of the federal government to sustain their increasingly precarious power.

Anyone seeking to be the candidate for president of the Democratic Party had to span simultaneously the party's Northern base and accommodate the Southern powers-that-be that constituted Calhoun's living legacy. Pierce's attempt to satisfy the

Statue of John C. Calhoun in Statuary
Hall in the U.S. Congress

Soft faction of the New York party through the patronage was sufficient for the F Street Mess to wreak retribution that early on hobbled his administration. And Douglas's relationship with the Southerners was far more fraught than Pierce's.

Despite his first wife's ownership of a Mississippi plantation, which Douglas retained after she died through paperwork trying to disguise it, Southern aristocrats viewed his transparently concealed status as a large slaveholder as another aspect of his uncouth social climbing. No matter how brutal Douglas's thrusts against antislavery senators, Southern legislators would never truly accept him as a member of their inner club. Douglas tried every device to court them, confiding in them, drinking with them, throwing his arms around them, and lining their pockets with lucrative real estate deals. They shared his company and shots of whiskey, but his gestures of intimacy only confirmed for Jefferson Davis and others like him Douglas's unreliable and low character. To the Southerners, he was always undependable. His shifting positions, even when it momentarily appeased them, confirmed the suspicion. His "great principle" of popular sovereignty still remained anathema because he left open the possibility of the territories becoming free states. It did not take extraordinary insight to see through Douglas to his neediness. In private the Southerners spoke of him as a vulgar confidence man, "our little grog drinking, electioneering demagogue," as Davis described him in a letter to Pierce in 1860. They would use him as far as he could be used, but they would never trust him. For all Douglas's canniness he lacked the disinterested ability to see himself as others did.

The poor boy from Vermont who set off for Illinois to make his fortune could not escape being perceived as unrefined. Douglas's meteoric rise from lowly Northern origins always made him seem suspect in Southern eyes. Douglas was the most brilliant, dynamic, and skillful Northern Democrat, but fatally flawed as his own man, an exemplar of Yankee individualism making himself on the frontier, unwilling to fall into line, and eternally erratic. It would not really have mattered to them if he were polished, distinguished, and cultured. Nor would his alcoholism have bothered them. But Douglas flamboyantly and unapologetically pursued his own interests, political and financial, and his supreme ambition defined him as a party unto himself. He owed no political debt for his rise to the Southerners. Yet Douglas needed the powers-that-be to attain his ultimate goal of the presidency. His schemes to put a host of Southern politicians into his financial debt did nothing to allay suspicion of him even as he enriched them. They happily pocketed the cash, while still regarding him as dubious. Douglas conceived himself as the true heir of Andrew Jackson, the still reigning spirit of Western democracy and his party. President Jackson had crushed Vice President Calhoun's movement for states' rights nullification of federal law and ambition to be president. He saw Calhoun's maneuver as an attempted coup d'état. Calhoun hastily retreated in the face of Jackson's threat of military force. To his dying day, Jackson regretted not hanging him.

Douglas wished to be the new Jackson, but was compelled to gain the tacit approval of Calhoun's heirs. He had to hold the North while finessing the South. To realize his dream, he had to square the circle. The necessity of Douglas's ambition within his party dictated his deliberate ambiguity. He spun out his doctrine of popular sovereignty as the simultaneous solution for the future of the Union and himself.

Douglas wrote his report on Kansas as a brief to appeal for Southern support even as he defended his doctrine. If popular sovereignty was the crux of democracy, for Douglas its core was the "right" of a new Northern state to choose slavery or not. He claimed that the Constitution granted each new state "the right . . . to decide the question of slavery for itself." He insisted that popular sovereignty as applied to territories was rooted in the Constitution; that the Missouri Compromise had violated the Constitution because it "assumed to deny to the people forever the right to settle the question of slavery for themselves"; and that the Kansas-Nebraska Act restored "the cardinal principles of State equality and self-government, in obedience to the constitution." His short history of the United States was bowdlerized to deny the basis on which Illinois itself was created a free state. He deliberately omitted mention of the Jefferson-inspired Ordinance of 1787 prohibiting slavery in the Northwest Territory, agreed upon in the Constitutional Convention and incorporated as one of the nation's first laws. He knowingly ignored the legislative history behind the Missouri Compromise restricting slavery in the North. He purposely elided Jackson's Proclamation Against Nullification condemning Calhoun's states' rights definition of the nation. He consciously failed to recall President Zachary Taylor's resolve to close to slavery the territory gained through the Mexican War. Instead, he posited popular sovereignty as the Constitution's original intent, carefully forgetting its recent origin, that the Democratic candidate in the 1848 presidential contest, Lewis Cass, had contrived it as a campaign gambit, which Douglas repackaged as an enduring principle. But he was unpersuasive in lifting it above controversy. Nearly everyone, whether antislavery or proslavery, considered his doctrine transparently self-serving. Douglas's pastiche of Calhounism, fallacious history, and hackneyed legalisms were the talking points of his strategy to win Southern support and thereby the Democratic nomination. His tower of babble was a monument to his ambition.

Douglas built his intricate but rickety intellectual scaffolding to support his prosecutorial case against the antislavery forces in Kansas and defense of the Border Ruffians. He traced the source of violence threatening "the rights and liberties of the people" to a malevolent distant power engaged in an "act of aggression" in violation of "constitutional law," and "in perversion of the plain provisions of an act of Congress passed in pursuance of the constitution" and "the laws of nations." The native Vermonter finally identified the locus of subversion, the dangerous "foreign" menace to be the entire "State of Massachusetts," which had authorized the Emigrant Aid Society. It was Massachusetts that was the "foreign State" seeking to impose "their own peculiar institutions," twisting John C. Calhoun's branding of slavery as the South's "peculiar institution." It was Massachusetts that was the tyranny trampling democracy. It was Massachusetts that would inspire foreign attack on the United States. "The same principle of action, when sanctioned by our example," said Douglas, "would authorize all the kingdoms, and empires, and despotisms in the world to engage in a common crusade against republicanism in America, as an institution quite as obnoxious to them, as domestic slavery is to any portion of the people of the United States."

Douglas's accusation condensed into that single sentence a perfect illustration of his inimitable demagogic style: daring innuendo, false equivalence, bullying, absurd hypotheticals, and inverted meanings. He made it seem that those defending democracy in Kansas were its enemies and those suppressing it its defenders. Anyone attempting to engage Douglas on his own terms risked getting lost in the bramble of his mischief and made the object of his malice.

Douglas's description of Massachusetts as an evil "foreign" power was central to his indictment. The "determined hostility" of the Emigrant Aid Society had aroused the reluctant opposition of the innocent citizens of Missouri, he said, having "created apprehensions that the object of the company was to abolitionize Kansas as a means of prosecuting a relentless warfare upon the institutions of slavery within the limits of Missouri." The innocent Missourians were "excited by a sense of common danger to the necessity of

protecting their own firesides from the apprehended horrors of servile insurrection and intestine war." They were defending hearth and home from
invading hordes of New England barbarians.

At the conclusion of Douglas's tour de force, Senator Jacob Collamer of
Vermont calmly stood to read the minority report into the record, refute his
points, and propose the admission of Kansas as a free state under the antislavery Topeka Constitution. Then Senator Charles Sumner of Massachusetts took the floor.

"In the report of the majority," Sumner said, "the true issue is smothered; in that of the minority, the true issue stands forth as a pillar of fire to
guide the country." He defended the Emigrant Aid Society from Douglas's
"assault," declaring the society had "done nothing for which it can be condemned under the laws and Constitution of the land." It was in fact Douglas, said Sumner, who had misrepresented the facts: "Very well, sir; a bad
cause is naturally staked on untenable ground. You cannot show the misconduct. Any such allegation will fail. And you now begin your game with
loaded dice."

Douglas seized upon the gambling metaphor and upped the ante. "The
Senator says that we begin our game with 'loaded dice.' I understand that to
be a gambler's phrase. He may be able to explain it; certainly it will require
explanation before the majority of the Senate will be able to understand it.
If he means that he is prepared to go to the country to justify treason and
rebellion, let him go; and I trust he will meet the fate the law assigns to such
conduct." Douglas, who had been a judge on the Illinois Supreme Court,
ruled Sumner guilty of "treason" and deserving a death sentence.

The *New York Tribune* reported that Douglas had threatened Sumner
along with the "Free-State men of Kansas," saying, "We mean to subdue you,
sir." The article, reprinted in the *Chicago Tribune,* agitated Douglas, and at
his insistence the official record of the *Congressional Globe* may have been altered so that Douglas was recorded to have called for "submission to the laws
and to the constituted authorities . . . and to punish rebellion and treason."
But the phrase—"We mean to subdue you"—assumed a life of its own, and
it would never cease to haunt Douglas.

Two days later, Lyman Trumbull stood to make his maiden speech in
the Senate. When Trumbull presented his credentials to the Senate, members of Douglas's faction of the Illinois state legislature presented a petition
asserting that he had been illegally elected because his term as a judge extended to 1861. It was a spurious nuisance claim swiftly dismissed by the

Judiciary Committee as lacking merit, but it revealed Douglas's fury at Trumbull's presence.

Now Trumbull stood in the Senate to protest the government printing of Douglas's report on Kansas without the minority report attached. Trumbull also emphasized that his election in Illinois was a repudiation of the repeal of the Missouri Compromise—by logical extension a repudiation of Douglas. Like Lincoln, Trumbull was intimately familiar with Douglas's methods of invective and illogic. Both Trumbull and Douglas had been state judges; now Judge Trumbull judged Judge Douglas. For the first time in the Senate, an equal from his own state rose to challenge him.

Trumbull was a formidable figure in his own right, well-educated, talented, and skillful, a former judge on the state Supreme Court who had been swept into the U.S. House of Representatives in 1854 on the wave of opposition to the Kansas-Nebraska Act, but he owed his presence in the Senate entirely to the gesture of one man—Abraham Lincoln. He was there because Lincoln wished to thwart his lifelong rival, Stephen A. Douglas.

Yet another of the Kansas-Nebraska Act's consequences was to destroy the Democratic majority in the Illinois state legislature, which elected U.S. senators. The new alignment drew challengers to Douglas's suddenly vulnerable longtime ally, James Shields, who held the other Senate seat. "They don't care two pence about Nebraska," Shields confided to other Douglas men, "but Douglas they have sworn to destroy." Trumbull emerged the leader of the anti-Douglas Democrats in Illinois, and in 1855 he threw his hat into the ring against Shields, but his support from anti-Douglas Democrats in the legislature only amounted to a handful, not close to win.

The Whig candidate, Abraham Lincoln, the last of the Whigs, like the last of the Mohicans, was the strong front-runner. When Shields faltered in the early balloting and Lincoln raced ahead, just short of a majority, the Douglas Democrats threw their backing behind the pliable and corrupt governor, Joel Matteson, who began bribing legislators. On the tenth ballot, as Lincoln's numbers fell, he calculated he could not win, so in order to avoid a Matteson victory he instructed his followers to cast their ballots for Trumbull. Lincoln gracefully accepted his loss, gratified at the vicarious defeat of Douglas. "On the whole, it is perhaps as well for our general cause that Trumbull is elected," he wrote his friend Congressman Elihu Washburne of Illinois. "The Neb. men confess that they hate it worse than anything that could have happened. It is a great consolation to see them worse whipped than I am." Lincoln's self-sacrifice to make Trumbull the senator became the foundation stone in the forging of the coalition that would become the Illinois Republican Party. Soon Lincoln would leave the husk of the Whig Party behind.

Standing on the floor of the Senate to confront Douglas, Trumbull declared he was not "frightened from a statement of what I believe to be the true condition of things in Kansas by the cry of insurrection and treason where none exist." He called out Douglas for using the epithets "abolitionize" and "Black Republicans" in his report. "The veriest simpleton in your streets may cry out 'Black Republican' or 'Abolitionist,'" Trumbull said. The former judge dismissed Douglas's attempt to wrap his Nebraska Act in constitutional legitimacy as "not very material" and filled with "inconsistencies." He ruled Douglas in contempt of logic, law, and history. "The men who framed our Constitution understood the English language," he said.

Then Trumbull cited the antislavery Ordinance of 1787 that Douglas had conspicuously left unmentioned. Quoting at length a particularly dense passage of Douglas's that justified the Missouri Compromise repeal, "maintaining the fundamental principle of equality among all the States," Trumbull ridiculed it as an absurdity: "I would like to know from the committee what under heaven the organization of a territorial government in Kansas has to do with equality among all the States?"

Reading further portions from Douglas's report, he systematically demolished his sophistry, especially Douglas's doctrine of popular sovereignty: "that boasted principle of the Kansas-Nebraska Act, which is claimed to be of such vital moment, has no sort of importance except for evil in consequence of its vagueness and uncertainty." Never before had Douglas been treated so roughly within the Senate. But Trumbull was not done. He debunked Douglas's skewed account of the Kansas conflict, citing chapter and verse of Border Ruffian violence, reading accounts from incendiary proslavery newspapers. "Had the Emigrant Aid Society been guilty of half the outrages which are here published to the world with impunity by the Missourians, do you believe the facts would have been smothered up by this report?"

When Trumbull concluded and as the Senate prepared to adjourn, Douglas went on the warpath. He played both the victim and the prosecutor in turning on Charles Sumner, who had not spoken that day. "Last year," he said, "when the Nebraska bill was under consideration, the Senator from Massachusetts asked of me the courtesy to have it postponed for a week, until he could examine the question. I afterwards discovered that, previous to that time, he had written an exposition of the bill—a libel upon me—and sent it off under his own frank." Douglas referred to the manifesto written by Senators Salmon P. Chase of Ohio and Sumner, "Appeal of the Independent Democrats," that rallied antislavery opinion against Douglas's bill as "a criminal betrayal of precious rights."

Douglas wheeled on Trumbull to accuse him of appearing in the Senate under fraudulent pretenses. "I desire now to say a word upon another point. I understand that my colleague has told the Senate, as being a matter very material to this issue, that he comes here as a Democrat, having always been a Democrat. Sir, that fact will be news to the Democracy of Illinois. I undertake to assert there is not a Democrat in Illinois who will not say that such a statement is a libel upon the Democracy of that state. I undertake to say that there is not a man here . . ."

But before Douglas could continue his tirade, Senator John J. Crittenden of Kentucky interrupted him mid-sentence calling him to order. Crittenden claimed the mantle of Henry Clay, the legacy of the border state statesman. He had been Fillmore's attorney general and drifted from stalwart conservative Old Whig to the nativist Know Nothing Party, which was popular in Kentucky. "I really think this debate is transcending all the rules of decorum which have been usually observed in the Senate," Crittenden chided Douglas. He requested that Douglas stop accusing other senators of "libel" and instead show "respect." Douglas replied that he would "keep myself within the rules; but I should have been better satisfied if the Senator from Kentucky, when the Black Republicans were denouncing us in coarse terms the other day, had arrested them for a want of courtesy towards the friends of the Constitution." Having suggested Sumner hang for treason, Douglas demanded the imprisonment of "Black Republicans" for failing to show "respect" to him.

"I do not know to what the gentleman alludes," Crittenden replied. Douglas pointed an accusing finger at Trumbull, guilty of "the most vulgar and coarse of all partisan assaults ever made on the Democratic side of the house by a senator on the other side." Crittenden again tried to dampen Douglas's rancor, explaining that he had called Douglas to order "with reluctance, exceeding reluctance," warning him of his "personal language," "whatever his passion may have prompted," and appealing to him as a "distinguished senator," with the "eyes of the public" upon "this body." Crittenden admonished him, "We are not here for the purpose of personal encounter or personal vituperation. Questions of a personal character may be settled elsewhere. The floor of the Senate is not the place to settle them. . . . This is a matter on which I cannot be misunderstood."

But Crittenden's appeal to courtesy only incited Douglas to lash out at Trumbull's "political character," which "would be deemed by the Illinois Democracy a libel on them." Then he struck out at Crittenden. "I am better capable of judging than the Senator from Kentucky. I do not regard him as good authority on the character of the Illinois Democracy," he said. To prove his point, Douglas made another assault on Trumbull. "How can a man who was elected as an Abolition-Know-Nothing, come here and claim to be a Democrat, in good standing with the Democracy of Illinois?" That, he said, "means a Black Republican. My colleague is the head and front of Black Republicanism in Illinois in opposition to Democracy."

An affronted Crittenden replied, "I cannot fail to think there was some purpose of a personal application in those reproaches and denunciations which it has pleased him, in the heroism of his eloquence.... I repel every denunciation of that sort, so far as it was aimed at, or was intended to embrace me, or those with whom I am associated. I repel it with scorn—utter scorn." Douglas replied that he "distinctly said" he was discussing Illinois, where "every Know Nothing lodge adopted the abolition creed, and those were the 'miserable' factions by which my colleague was brought into power here."

Trumbull leaped to his feet to refute Douglas's "totally untrue" charges. "I am not to be driven into the defense of either Abolitionism or Know Nothingism. I have nothing to do with them."

"I said he received every Abolition and every Know Nothing vote in the legislature," Douglas shot back. "Does he deny the statement? He dare not." On he went, "I say, it will be news to the people of Illinois to hear that he is a Democratic Senator in the Senate of the United States." Then, charging Trumbull with attempting "to mislead the country as to the state of parties in Illinois," he said, "I will not occupy the attention of the Senate further," and would save "what strength I may have" to reply "to the champions of Black Republicanism, of whom, it seems, my colleague has become the chief." He would "avoid as far as possible personal controversy."

Trumbull was incredulous. It was "extraordinary to me," he said, that after Douglas had insulted him he "should sit down with a declaration that he intends to avoid all personal matters.... Why did he provoke the controversy?" Again, Douglas accused him of being the candidate of "the Know Nothing and Abolition parties." Again, Trumbull repelled his accusation. "I shall never permit him, here or elsewhere to make an assault on me personally, without meeting it with the best power that God has given me, feeble though it be."

Now Douglas wheeled on Sumner for committing "a gross libel." But Sumner insisted that the facts upheld his version of the incident. "The Senator has alluded to facts," said Sumner. "I answer on facts." Then the former Harvard professor made a classical reference. "Now, as to the character of the address—the senator has chosen to revive that ancient matter. He had better go, perhaps to the siege of Troy and revive that again."

"Why do you not reprove your agitators on that side of the chamber," Douglas replied, "who have been going back to the siege of Troy ever since the Nebraska bill was passed?" Finally, Douglas declared himself the victim in the fracas. "I am not the one who has disturbed the repose of the Senate."

The rattled Senate adjourned.

The following week, on March 17, Douglas filed his statehood bill for Kansas. The election there, he insisted, was completely legitimate, the so-called "bogus legislature" was indeed the true government, and it should conduct its election of delegates to a convention to write a state constitution. In fact, the "bogus legislature" had already adopted the Missouri constitution, which protected slavery.

On March 20, Douglas took to the Senate floor to resume his diatribes. Trumbull, he charged, was guilty of "innuendo of unfairness," and had invented "personal issues with myself for the purpose of diverting public attention from the great questions involved in this contest between the Democracy and allied forces of northern Know Nothingism and Abolitionism."

Douglas flung his newly coined and racially charged phrases to tar the Republicans—the "Black Republican Party," "Black Republicanism," and the "Black Republican camp." The free state men in Kansas, he added, were "an invading army from a foreign State"—"that things should be called by their right names—that revolution should be checked—that rebellion should be suppressed."

The fundamental issue, Douglas said, was between his position, which "affirms the principles of non-intervention from without, and self-government within . . . while the other insists that the domestic affairs and internal concerns of the Territories may be controlled by associations and corporations from abroad. . . . They have succeeded by this system of foreign interference in producing violence, and bloodshed, and rebellion in Kansas." He accused the "agents" of "mischievous schemes of foreign interference" to be operating with secret "political designs," until "all disguise was thrown aside, and the purpose of the company openly avowed, to abolitionize Kansas, with the view of erecting a cordon of free States as a perpetual barrier against the formation and admission of any more slave States." Douglas warned, "My opinion is that, from the signs of the times, and in view of all that is passing around us, as well as at a distance, there will be very little difficulty in arresting the traitors—and that, too, without going all the way to Kansas to find them!" Those "traitors" were in the chamber of the Senate. The *Congressional Globe* recorded: ("Laughter.") But it was not laughter of derision but agreement.

Douglas built to a crescendo. "This Government has shown itself the most powerful of any on earth in all respects except one. It has shown itself equal to foreign war or to domestic defense—equal to any emergency that may arise in the exercise of its high functions in all things except the power to hang a traitor!" He appealed to a higher authority: "I trust in God that the time is not near at hand, and that it may never come, when it will be the imperative duty of those charged with the faithful execution of the law to execute that power." But he proclaimed his resolve that "if treason against the United States shall be consummated, far be it from my purpose to express the wish that the penalty of the law may not fall upon the traitor's head!" Off with Trumbull's head! Off with Sumner's!

Calmly and deliberately, Senator William Henry Seward of New York rose to oppose the admission of Kansas on the basis of the proslavery "bogus legislature" and to introduce a substitute based instead on the antislavery To-peka Constitution. Douglas's histrionics hardly ruffled him. At his residence in Washington, Seward hosted dinner parties with an eclectic group of guests, occasionally including Douglas, featuring fine wine, good cigars, and indiscreet gossip. At his home in Auburn, New York, he and his wife, Fran-ces, a highly educated woman and abolitionist, ran a station of the Under-ground Railroad for fugitive slaves. They also helped secretly fund Frederick Douglass's newspaper, the *The North Star.* Above all, Seward was central within his party, its consummate politician. He had launched his career in the conspiracy-minded Anti-Masonic Party of upstate New York, a region that was also the seedbed of abolitionism, the evangelical Great Awakening, and Mormonism. Protégé and biographer of John Quincy Adams during the former president's last phase as an antislavery crusader in the House of Rep-resentatives, Seward possessed the adroit political skills his hero lacked. Along with his alter ego with whom he bonded in the Anti-Masonic cam-paign, Thurlow Weed, editor and publisher of the *Albany Evening Journal,* Seward was the maker of New York's Whig Party. Weed often operated from luxurious rooms at the Astor House on Broadway, padding like a large feline through politics with an acute sixth sense, listening, purring, and sniffing. "I once heard Seward declare," recalled Gideon Welles, Lincoln's secretary of the navy, "that 'Seward is Weed and Weed is Seward. What I do, Weed approves. What he says, I endorse. We are one.'" Together they were "the firm," as Horace Greeley, one of their early creations, called them. Greeley, however, fell out with "the firm" when they failed to slate him for lieutenant governor in favor of Henry J. Raymond, editor of the *New York Times,* that newspaper and its editor also among their inventions—both the *Times* and Raymond. Raymond was a reliable partner, unlike the mercurial Greeley, given to unpredictable bouts of grandiosity, hysteria, and sudden enthusiasms, and who would never forgive Seward for being passed over.

The history of "the firm" charted the rise and fall of the Whig Party. After Weed was instrumental in electing Seward governor of New York in 1838, the two men acted as prime movers behind every Whig presidential candidate. William Henry Harrison's nomination and election in 1840 signaled their mastery of New York politics and emergence as national power brokers. Henry Clay's candidacy in 1844, however, fell just short from defections in New York to the radical antislavery Liberty Party and local nativists who despised Seward.

Seward wore the badges and scars of his vast and varied experience, was both respected and despised, sometimes considered too radical and sometimes too crafty, clear in his purposes and ruthless in his tactics, appealing to a "higher law" than the Constitution against slavery even as he bid for control of the patronage at the New York Custom House. He was charged at the same time with holding dangerous principles and having none. Henry Clay said of him, after Seward abandoned the marked Clay for the unblemished military hero Zachary Taylor in 1848, "Mr. Seward is man of no convictions." Like Clay, Seward had his beliefs, but was also adroit, sometimes too adroit. He was ironically coming to resemble Clay, who never reached the presidency, burdened with his past. An army of followers mobilized in Seward's wake, but a phalanx of enemies, some former acolytes like the irascible Greeley, tracked

William Henry Seward,
painting by Henry Inman

after him. After the 1852 debacle, the Whig Party no longer functioned as a working organism. Seward and Weed tried to breathe life into the corpse, but the body had expired. "How strange the mutations of politics," Seward wrote his wife.

At Syracuse, on September 28, 1855, Weed choreographed a convention for the merger of a breakaway faction of Softs and the remnant of the Whigs into a new Republican Party. Greeley gave it a name; Raymond sat as a delegate. Seward consecrated the party in a speech delivered on October 12 at the State House at Albany. He excoriated "the privileged class" of slaveholders in control of the government. "The President of the United States is reduced to the position of a deputy of the privileged class," he declared. Slavery would end, he prophesied, but the method was uncertain. "Slavery is not, and never can be, perpetual. It will be overthrown either peacefully or lawfully under this Constitution, or it will work the subversion of the Constitution, together with its own overthrow. Then the slaveholders would perish in the struggle." Now Seward bade farewell to the Whig Party that had been his life's work, reduced to a ruin.

> Shall we report ourselves the Whig party? Where is it? "Gentle shepherd, tell me where?" Four years ago, it was a strong and vigorous party, honorable for energy, noble achievements, and still more for noble enterprises. In 1852, it was united and consolidated, and moved by panics and fears to emulate the Democratic Party in its practiced subserviency to the privileged class, and it yielded in spite of your remonstrances and mine. The privileged class, who had debauched it, abandoned it, because they knew that it could not vie with its rival in the humiliating service it proffered them; and now there is neither Whig party nor Whig south of the Potomac. . . . We have maintained it here, and in its purity, until the aiders and abettors of the privileged class, in retaliation, have wounded it on all sides, and it is now manifestly no longer able to maintain and carry forward, alone and unaided, the great revolution that it inaugurated. . . . Any party, when reduced so low, must ultimately dwindle and dwarf into a mere faction. Let, then, the Whig party pass. It committed a grievous fault, and grievously hath it answered it. Let it march out of the field, therefore, with all the honors.

Neither "true Democrats" nor "true Whigs" should raise "a stained banner, upon the other." It was time for a new organization. "Its banner is untorn in former battles, and unsullied by past errors. That is the party for us."

Back in Washington Seward was dismayed at the disarray. After attending an anti-Nebraska congressional caucus on March 12, 1856, he wrote Weed, "I came away with feelings of my own, sad and unhopeful. . . . It is manifest that here, the tone of anti-slavery feeling is becoming daily more and more modified, under the pressure of the 'Know-Nothing' influences. . . . I feel as if I was already half demoralized." But, he observed, Kansas "may present an issue on which we can rally the party," though he had no strategy.

Seward's downcast letter to Weed was written the day after Douglas introduced his report on Kansas. The anti-Nebraska men had dissolved into squabbling, divided among antislavery Whigs, dissident Democrats, Free Soilers, and Know Nothings, and if left to their own devices might have endlessly emphasized their sectarian differences. But Douglas could not leave them alone. His ambition was impatient. He was intent on justifying what he had done in Kansas in order to advance his presidential campaign. His will to power forced upon his scattered adversaries new political realities they lacked the ability to create themselves. While the inchoate and nascent Republican movement had no acknowledged national leader, Douglas filled the vacuum, hectoring his opponents into common cause. The more he tarred them as "Black Republicans," the more he galvanized them into becoming Republicans; the more he insisted on popular sovereignty as the means to take slavery off the agenda, the more he made slavery the unavoidable issue; the more he insisted on his unassailable correctness on Kansas, the more his position became contestable.

On April 9, Seward proposed admitting Kansas as a state based on the antislavery Topeka Constitution. His speech before the Senate was a carefully prepared brief, placing responsibility for the violence on the Border Ruffians, citing incident after incident, quotation after quotation, to prove his case. He compared Pierce to George III for imposing a tyranny and described his offenses in the style of the Declaration of Independence. He proclaimed the Topeka Constitution a "revolution" against "usurpation and tyranny," "a remedy peaceful and simple." And he dismissed Douglas's doctrine: "Shall we confess that the proclamation of popular sovereignty was not merely a failure, but was a pretense and a fraud?" He finished with a dark vision of civil war. "Do you look through this incipient war quite to the end, and see there peace, quiet, and harmony, on the subject of slavery? . . . But if disunion could ever come, it would come in the form of a secession of the slaveholding States." Then "the slaveholding power" would "have fastened his grappling irons upon the fountains of the Missouri and the slopes of the Rocky

Mountains. Then that power would either be intolerably supreme in this Republic, or it would strike for independence or exclusive domination." Then the "free States and slave States" would be "divided and warring with each other." Then, when "we have forgotten moral right . . . we shall have become reckless of the obligations of Eternal Justice, and faithless to the interests of universal freedom."

Douglas soon found a way to retaliate. When James Lane was named the free state U.S. senator and appeared with a petition for admission of Kansas under the Topeka Constitution, Douglas accused him of presenting an altered document without a provision that would prohibit free blacks. "You withheld the part you would not defend!" Douglas crowed at Seward. "I drove the Senator from New York to the wall on this point the other day. Let there be an end to this system of fraud."

To Douglas's intense displeasure three senators decided to tangle with him. His display of ferocity had not intimidated them. They were practiced politicians with the scars to prove it. Benjamin Wade of Ohio spoke up first. "Supposed the fact to be one way or the other, what differences does it make now?" he said. Douglas hardly frightened "Bluff" Ben. Wade, who embraced the forbidden label of "abolitionist" flung at him, was the former law partner of Congressman Joshua Giddings of the notorious boardinghouse known as "Abolition House," had been an Ohio state senator, where he had opposed a state fugitive slave act in 1839, a stand for which he lost his seat, and had been a district court judge. An old Whig turned Free Soiler, Wade despised Fillmore and was friendly with Seward. He was renowned for his scorn and sarcasm. During the debate over the Compromise of 1850, Senators Andrew Butler of South Carolina and Archibald Dixon of Kentucky had ganged up on him, jibing whether, if he believed that "all men are created equal," according to the Declaration of Independence, blacks and whites should work side by side. "By the law of God Almighty," replied Wade, "your slave is your equal, and so you will find out at the day of judgment, though probably not before, at your rate of progress." Now, acting like the judge he once was, he rejected Douglas's objection to the Kansas free state petition as "immaterial," adding, "Is it because you were driven from the real merits of the controversy?"

Senator John P. Hale, Pierce's nemesis in New Hampshire, who had been prominent in the earliest antislavery party, the Liberty Party, next took on Douglas, dismissing his demagogy: "It does not seem to me to be possible that there can be any sophistry which can mislead anybody upon so simple a proposition."

Then Senator Henry Wilson of Massachusetts confronted Douglas, who he charged, "has endeavored today to put some of us in a false position in regard to this question." Of impoverished working-class origin and self-schooled, learning his trade as a shoemaker and campaigning as the "Natick cobbler," Wilson was fervently antislavery. He built his own political organization on the loyalty of the Middlesex Regiment of the Massachusetts militia of which he was a colonel, published the Free Soil newspaper in Boston, and had been president of the State Senate. "I am proud of the name of 'abolitionist.' I glory in it," he declared in 1846. Two years later, he defected from the Whigs to the Free Soil Party. Wilson was an adroit dealmaker and coalition builder, and the hidden hand behind the rise of Sumner to the Senate. Striking an alliance with the Know Nothings in the legislature in 1855, he installed himself in the Senate as the successor to the distinguished Old Whig Edward Everett, the cobbler replacing the president of Harvard.

"The Senator often talks to us about 'abolition agitators,' and 'abolitionism,'" said Wilson to Douglas. But he "knows as well as I know" that he was distorting the position of senators "opposed to the extension of slavery and to the connection of slavery with the Federal Government." Yet Douglas had persisted in his distortions. "Sir, this is not the first time, during the present session that the Senator from Illinois has indulged in the profuse use of mere partisan catch-words. These partisan phrases, I tell the honorable Senator frankly, are unworthy of him and of the Senate. He talks again today about 'Black Republicans.' This is a favorite phrase of the honorable Senator from Illinois. . . . He should leave such petty warfare to little men. . . . You may sneer at us as Abolition agitators. . . . We have passed beyond that. The people of this country are being educated up to a standard above all these little sneering phrases. We will accept your issue, but you will not, cannot subdue us. . . . You may vote us down, but we shall live to fight another day."

Douglas jumped in on that line to depict his opponents as cowards. "He who fights and runs away, may live to fight another day," he derided. "If we fall," replied Wilson, "we shall fall to rise again." Again, he urged Douglas "had better discuss this grave question without the application of taunts and epithets." But Douglas fired back that it was Wilson who had "forgotten what was due to the proprieties of the Senate." And he offered a new definition of the pejorative term "Black Republicans." "The new creed," he said, "adjures and ignores every question which has for its object the welfare and happiness of the white man—every question which does not propose to put the negro on an equality with the white man, politically and socially. . . .

Every plank in their platform rests on a black basis—every clause relates to the negro. . . . I wish to call things by their right names. . . . For these reasons the whole country seem, by common consent, to recognize the propriety of calling this new party, the 'Black Republican Party.'"

"We claim our principles are national," Wilson replied. And Wade interjected that in the Republican-controlled House of Representatives a bill was being introduced to restore the Missouri Compromise—"the Jefferson proviso," Wade called it, after the Ordinance of 1787—raising the icon of the Democratic Party against Douglas.

Douglas challenged these "Black Republicans." "I wish to bring these gentlemen to the test," he said. In the coming election, "the standard-bearer on our side" (whom Douglas hoped would be himself) would "take issue with you on every one of the points which you tender—'no more slave State,' 'the repeal of the fugitive slave law,' 'the abolition of the slave trade between the States,' and 'the abolition of slavery in the District of Columbia.' Upon each and all of them you need have no fear that our candidate will not stand firmly, immovably and unequivocally, upon the Democratic platform."

Douglas now threw the epithet of "abolitionist" at Seward. "If the Senator is aiming at the reputation of being a martyr to his cause, I think he is adopting the proper course. . . . I sense that the Senator from New York did not object to be called an Abolitionist. He was looking to the honors of martyrdom." After threatening Trumbull with hanging for treason, he suggested Seward was looking to be strung up.

Then Douglas accused Wilson of the blackest of black accusations against a "Black Republican"—sexual race mixing. Wilson's offense had been to support the petition of Kansas to be admitted as a free state while dissenting from the Topeka Constitution's provision barring free blacks. Douglas mocked that Wilson opposed it as "barbarous." He proudly proclaimed that Illinois had "a similar clause in her constitution; she had a right to put it there; it was our business, and not yours; and if Massachusetts does not like it let her do as she pleases within her own limits, so that she does not violate the Constitution of the United States. We do not believe in the equality of the negro, socially or politically, with the white man. You may practice it, but do not try to force the negro on an equality with us in our State. Our people are a white people; our State is a white State; and we mean to preserve the race pure, without any mixture with the negro. If you wish your blood and that of the African mingled in the same channel, we trust that you will keep at a respectful distance from us, and not try to force that on us as one of your domestic institutions." The *Congressional Globe* recorded: "[Laughter, and applause in the galleries.]" (Unquestionably, the word "negro" was substituted for Douglas's usual use of the word "nigger.")

Douglas's crowd-pleasing riff slid from invidious comparison of state black codes to interracial lust, which prompted Wilson to chide him for his coarseness: "Let me tell the honorable Senator from Illinois, that these taunts so often flung out about the equality of races, about amalgamation, and the mingling of blood, are the emanations of low and vulgar minds." Wilson declared that he was "proud to live in a commonwealth where every man, black or white . . . is recognized as a man, standing upon the terms of perfect and absolute equality before the laws . . . in a commonwealth that recognizes the sublime creed embodied in the Declaration of Independence." He acknowledged that "the people of Massachusetts may not believe that the African race—'Outcast to insolence and scorn'—is the equal of this Anglo-Saxon race of ours in intellectual power; but they know no reason why a man, made in the image of God, should be degraded by unjust laws." He invoked the antislavery spirit of John Quincy Adams, of George Washington who wished for "some plan adopted by which slavery could be abolished by law," of Jefferson who also hoped for an end to it, and of Benjamin Franklin, John Jay, and Alexander Hamilton—all "abolitionists."

"Do I understand," demanded an astonished Douglas, "the gentleman to say that Washington and Jefferson were Abolitionists?" "I certainly say it," replied Wilson. "Then I hope the gentleman will not complain when I call him one," said a triumphant Douglas.

But if Wilson was not an "abolitionist" he was unlike radical abolitionists. He was a political man who understood other political men. Now he called attention to Douglas's political weakness, his "gigantic task" in winning the support of the Southerners of his party for the Democratic nomination. "We all know," explained Wilson, "that he has 'a hard road to travel.' . . . The men for whom he fights cannot afford to be generous. An eminent politician once said that 'political gratitude is a lively sense of favors to come.' He may yet discover that the men for whom he has toiled are governed only by 'a lively sense of favors to come.'" Wilson saw to the heart of Douglas's political conundrum to expose his vulnerability and predict he would not be rewarded with his party's nomination. It was the deepest cut of all.

Among those observing the fevered debate in the galleries was Harriet Beecher Stowe, author of *Uncle Tom's Cabin,* the passion play novel of slavery and fugitives, who recorded her impressions for an abolitionist newspaper.

"This Douglas," she wrote, "is the very ideal of vitality. Short, broad, and thick-set, every inch of him has its own alertness and motion. He has a good head and face, thick black hair, heavy black brows and a keen eye. His figure would be an unfortunate one were it not for the animation which constantly pervades it; as it is, it rather gives poignancy to his peculiar appearance; he has a small, handsome hand, moreover, and a graceful as well as forcible mode of using it—a point speakers do not always understand. . . . He has two requisites of a debater—a melodious voice and a clear, sharply defined enunciation."

She described how he used his peculiar but captivating physical appearance to spin his demagogy. "His forte in debating is his power of mystifying the point," she wrote.

> With the most off-hand assured airs in the world, and a certain appearance of honest superiority, like one who has a regard for you and wishes to set you right on one or two little matters, he proceeds to set up some point which is *not* that in question, but only a family connection of it, and this point he attacks with the very best of logic and language; he charges upon it horse and foot, runs it down, tramples it in the dust, and then turns upon you with—"Sir, there is your argument! Did not I tell you so? You see it is all stuff"; and if you have allowed yourself to be so dazzled by his quickness as to forget that the routed point is not, after all, the one in question, you suppose all is over with it. Moreover, he contrives to mingle up so many stinging allusions to so many piquant personalities that by the time he has done his mystification a dozen others are ready and burning to spring on their feet to repel some direct or indirect attack, all equally wide of the point. His speeches, instead of being like an arrow sent at a mark, resemble rather a bomb which hits nothing in particular, but bursts and sends red-hot nails in every direction.

But Stowe also noticed a telltale flaw in his bravado, a missing element from his repertoire. "It is a merciful providence that with all his alertness and adroitness, all his quick-sighted keenness, Douglas is not witty—that might have made him too irresistible a demagogue for the liberties of our laughter loving people, to whose weaknesses he is altogether too well adapted now." There was another flaw she did not chronicle that was related to his lack of humor. For an experienced politician, Douglas was remarkably sensitive and thin-skinned. He took nearly every criticism as a personal slight. Still, she wrote, the new Republicans "have pitted against them a leader infinite in resources, artful, adroit, and wholly unscrupulous." Two years later Douglas would deploy his panoply of mystification, principally his exploitation of race, in his debates with Lincoln.

Through the spring of 1856, during the Senate debates of March and April, Douglas filled the chamber with personal vilification, racial invective, and death threats. He raised the spirit of violence to achieve several practical results at once: to turn his critics into political foils for his own advantage in his quest for the Democratic presidential nomination; to make himself acceptable to the Southern wing of the party; and to overshadow potential rivals as exhausted men of the past. He could see himself ascendant, the convention bestowing its prize, the telegraph with the news in his hand, his resounding victory over the "Black Republicans," the chief justice administering the oath of office—Stephen Arnold Douglas, the fifteenth president of the United States. But his heated theatrics exposed his fear that his dream was slipping out of his grasp again. His tactics were backfiring.

CHAPTER FOUR

WAR TO THE KNIFE

What hath Douglas wrought? On March 3, 1856, days before Douglas presented his Kansas report, the House of Representatives authorized a Special Committee to Investigate the Troubles in Kansas. The creation of the committee was among the first acts of the new House now controlled by an anti-Nebraska coalition—a repudiation of Douglas.

When the 34th Congress arrived in Washington in the first week of December of 1855 no party held a majority in the House. Douglas's lieutenant there, William A. Richardson of Illinois, declared himself the Democratic candidate for Speaker, and made the Nebraska Act the dividing line. Joshua Giddings of Ohio, the longtime antislavery champion, held together the disparate anti-Nebraska caucus. He still resided across from the Capitol in "Abolition House," where Lincoln had lived during his one term in the House and Giddings had assisted him in writing his stillborn proposal for emancipation in the District of Columbia. The

Andrew Reeder, first territorial governor of Kansas, disguised to escape arrest

anti-Nebraska caucus eventually coalesced around Nathaniel Banks, a former millworker who had risen to become the Free Soil Speaker of the Massachusetts House in alliance with the Know Nothings and helped engineer the election of the antislavery Charles Sumner to the Senate. After seemingly endless balloting, Banks prevailed on February 2, 1856. The House divided exposed both parties divided. In the House vote, Banks received not one ballot from a Southerner. The "lines of demarcation" between North and South, proslavery and antislavery, "are becoming more and distinctly marked," remarked Giddings, who administered the oath of office to the first Republican Speaker.

The majority members of the Committee to Investigate the Troubles in Kansas consisted of William A. Howard of Michigan, John Sherman of Ohio (brother of one William Tecumseh Sherman), and for the minority, Mordecai Oliver of Missouri, who had been a delegate at the proslavery convention of the "bogus legislature" and described the Ruffians as "men of wealth, intelligence and high moral worth" standing for "the high state of civilization and refinement."

"The second month of spring was quickly passing away, and quiet reigned—a quiet which seemed almost fearful from the very stillness," wrote Sara Robinson, wife of the free state "governor," Charles Robinson. The congressmen arrived in Lawrence on April 17 after conducting a first round of inquiries in the rough proslavery town of Lecompton. The free staters "anticipated that quiet would continue while the investigation was entered into; that, from motives of policy alone, the enemy would hide in their lair, and attempt to gain the favor of the committee by a present show of fairness."

Two days after the investigators came to Kansas, Sheriff Samuel Jones, the Ruffian enforcer, reappeared in Lawrence. He grabbed S.N. Wood, who had attended the founding convention in Pittsburgh of the Republican Party, where he had lectured the delegates on the Kansas outrages. A crowd gathered around Jones, diverted him, stole his pistol, and Wood simply walked away. Jones's bafflement quickly turned to anger. The next day he came back with a posse, searched for Wood, and unable to find him seized another free state man, striking him. The man knocked Jones down and escaped, yet another humiliation. Jones rode back to Lecompton, demanding that Governor Shannon send federal troops to "assist me in the execution of the laws." Shannon ordered a squad of ten dragoons to accompany Jones in enforcing his arrest warrants, which he had expanded to encompass forty men, including "Governor" Robinson. The investigating committee, meanwhile, shuttled back and forth between Lecompton and Lawrence. "This first effort of theirs, showing clearly that the work of investigation would be carried on systematically, struck terror into the heart of the wrong-doers," recalled Sara Robinson. "That all their labors hitherto might not be foiled at one blow, they felt that a desperate effort must be made to break up the sittings of the committee, and the plan unfolded itself."

Jones arrested six free state men and imprisoned them in a tent for the supposed felony of failing to help him arrest Wood. "These men were thus kept in Lawrence," wrote William A. Phillips, a free state man who was also a correspondent for the *New York Tribune,* "the design being, beyond all question, to provoke the people of the town to a rescue, when there would be another excuse for attacking the place, and, in the disturbance, destroying the testimony taken, if not killing the commissioners." The free state leaders decided on a policy of "non-resistance" to avoid a provocation. But on the evening of April 23 an unknown shooter wounded Jones. Robinson formally condemned the "criminal" attack. Jones, who had quickly recovered, was now celebrated as a martyr. "His death must be avenged," declared the *Squatter Sovereign,* the newspaper of the proslavery forces. "His murder shall be avenged if at the sacrifice of every abolitionist in the Territory. . . . We are now in favor of leveling Lawrence and chastising the traitors there congregated, should it result in the total destruction of the Union." The paper urged a "war to the knife, and knife to the hilt; neither asking quarters nor granting them."

Jones's deputies raided homes in Lawrence in a dragnet to round up those named in his warrants. The proslavery delegate to the Congress installed through the fraudulent November 1854 election, John W. Whitfield, who had been observing the investigating committee's hearings, claimed it was "unsafe for himself and witnesses to remain there, and requested the Committee to adjourn to some other place," according to a contemporary historian. Congressman Oliver, the pro-Ruffian voice on the committee, made a motion to suspend its work, but the other two members voted to continue. The chairman, Congressman Howard, wrote Speaker Banks that the evidence they had collected so far "deeply implicated" the Ruffians in election fraud. "Some of the most important facts have been proven by leaders of the invasion & even by candidates elected." "We were frequently threatened through anonymous letters," wrote John Sherman. "On one occasion, upon going in the morning to the committee room, I found tacked on the door a notice to the 'Black Republican Committee' to leave Kansas upon penalty of death."

On May 5, the territorial chief justice appointed by Pierce, Judge Samuel Lecompte, convened a grand jury to charge the free state leaders with "high treason" for resisting the "bogus legislature," and in case there was "no resistance" declared that their "intention" was enough to indict them for "constructive treason." These crimes that would seem to carry capital punishment had no legal basis and were wholly fictitious. It was simply impossible for treason to be committed against a territory. Attached to the indictments, Lecompte's grand jury also issued a bill to suppress the two newspapers published in Lawrence, the *Herald of Freedom* and *Kansas A Free State,* which were charged with sedition, "advising assassination," and "demoralizing the public mind," and another bill to destroy the Free State Hotel as "a stronghold of resistance to law." One of the grand jurors, a covert free state man, alerted the people of Lawrence to the indictments before they were disclosed. "What a sweet scented jury it was!" he said. "There were at least fifteen bottles of whiskey in the room all the time."

Judge Lecompte, the founder of the proslavery town of Lecompton, which he developed as a real estate speculation and got the legislature to designate the capital, also invested in railroad companies with his partner, John Calhoun, the federal land agent. "To the charge of a pro-slavery bias," Lecompte declared, "I am proud, too, of this. I am the steady friend of Southern rights under the constitution of the United States. I have been reared where slavery was recognized by the constitution of my state. I love the institution as entwining itself around all my early and late associations."

John Calhoun, surveyor general of the Nebraska and Kansas territories (no relation to John C. Calhoun), was more powerful than the territorial governor. He had the authority to draw the fine lines of the map, chart new towns and apportion land, deciding which interests would be granted real estate, railroads, and schools, and controlled several hundred federal patronage jobs, the greatest number in Kansas, his own political machine. Calhoun had been the most prominent Democrat in Sangamon County, Illinois, elected to the state legislature and three times mayor of Springfield. He was a longtime close ally of Douglas. After the Nebraska Act was enacted, Douglas pressed Pierce to name Calhoun to the post in Kansas, the biggest plum Douglas was able to extract from the president, the most strategic favor he could receive, placing his trusted man where he could help secure his enormous gamble. Through Calhoun a piece of the politics of Illinois was exported and implanted in Kansas. Abraham Lincoln had as complicated a relationship with Calhoun as did Douglas. In his first decent-paying job in the river town of

New Salem, Illinois, Lincoln had apprenticed with him as a surveyor. Calhoun had also been a schoolteacher whose students included William Henry Herndon, later to become Lincoln's law partner. Lincoln had most recently debated Calhoun on September 9, 1854, on the Nebraska Act, in which he had put Lincoln on the defensive, falsely assailing him for "affiliation with abolitionism" and the secretive nativist Know Nothing Party. Calhoun declared the free state men were "vile abolitionists . . . so vile they would lick the slime off the meanest penitentiary in the land," and "would bow down and worship the devil if he would only help them to steal a nigger."

Former governor Reeder, elected the free state delegate to the Congress, was assisting the investigative committee in gathering and questioning witnesses when he was informed of the "high treason" indictments. He believed it was a plan to "paralyze the Free-State party . . . to pick up all our leaders, including all the State officers, members of the Legislature, etc., or an offense not bailable, and keep them shut up for six months, and until after the next election." The committee concluded in its official report that "the obstruction which created the most serious embarrassment to your committee was the attempted arrest of Gov. Reeder. . . . Subsequent events have only strengthened the conviction of your committee, that this was a wanton and unlawful interference by the judge who issued the writ, tending greatly to obstruct a full and fair investigation." The intent, the report stated, was to remove Reeder from providing "local information which would enable us to elicit the whole truth, and it was obvious to every one that . . . would necessarily hinder, delay, and embarrass" the committee.

On May 7, a deputy served Reeder with a subpoena to appear before the Lecompton grand jury. Reeder told him it was "irregular" and he would not obey it. The deputy returned the next day with a posse to present Reeder with an arrest warrant for contempt while he was examining witnesses before the committee. Reeder claimed privilege as an elected delegate to the Congress. He conferred with Howard and Sherman, who agreed; but Oliver, the Missourian, insisted he had no privilege. Reeder said that he had received information that "my life was not safe from private assassination in Lecompton." That evening he, Howard, Sherman, and Robinson decided that he and Robinson should escape to inform sympathetic officials in Washington of the true state of affairs in Kansas. They also vouchsafed with Robinson "the testimony already taken by the Congressional Committee as there was great danger that it might be seized and destroyed."

Reeder fled disguised in a borrowed overcoat and cap, traveling by night to a series of safe houses as though a fugitive slave in an underground railroad until he was ferried across the Mississippi into Illinois. In Chicago a crowd called for him to appear on the balcony of the hotel where he was staying, and he "was received with cheers upon cheers." That evening he took the train to Bloomington, where he found himself on May 29 among the throng assembling for the founding convention of the Illinois Republican Party and to hear Lincoln speak.

Robinson escaped from Lawrence along with his wife, but was captured in Lexington, Missouri, and shipped as a prisoner to Lecompton, where he was held captive for four months. John Sherman believed that those who caught Robinson knew he was carrying the committee's documents. "We believe that a knowledge of that fact caused the arrest," he recalled. But Sara Robinson, who hid copies of those documents in her clothes, continued traveling to St. Louis where she arranged for the delivery of the testimony personally to Speaker of the House Nathaniel Banks in Washington. Then she went on to Bloomington, arriving at the opening of the Illinois Republican convention, where she encountered Reeder, "to my surprise," he observed— the two escapees from Kansas fortuitously coming in time to hear the keynote speaker, Abraham Lincoln.

When Reeder eluded arrest, the chagrined deputy consulted with the U.S. Marshal, J.B. Donaldson, who issued a proclamation on May 11 that "there is every reason to believe that any attempt to execute these writs will be resisted by a large body of armed men," and summoned a posse to assemble at Lecompton. Bands of Ruffians and several hundred of the newly arrived Southerners were instantly deputized and put on the federal payroll as members of the marshal's *posse comitatus*. This provisional army surrounded Lawrence, whose leaderless residents appealed to Governor Shannon for protection. He declared that he would in "no way interfere" and "not interpose to save" those who "resist" from "the legitimate consequences of their illegal acts." A Committee of Public Safety in Lawrence issued a statement that the assertions of the U.S. marshal were false, and that the claim of Senator Douglas and others that they were "rebels and traitors" was a "slanderous charge." The free state men retreated from the town while the Ruffians mustered for their attack.

The fog of impending violence also lowered over Washington. "The border-ruffian policy, which was filling Kansas with alarm and bloodshed, had its representatives in Washington, walking its streets, hanging around its hotels, and stalking through the capitol," recalled Senator Henry Wilson. Menace lurked in the debates.

When Horace Greeley, editor of the *New York Tribune*, antislavery crusader and former Whig congressman, traveled to Washington to cover the spectacle, on the evening of January 29, as he walked down the street with his hands in his coat pockets, he heard a loud voice behind him. "Is your name Greeley?" "It is," he replied. Congressman Albert C. Rust, a proslavery Democrat from Arkansas, suddenly smashed Greeley to the ground with the metal head of his cane. It was a gesture of Southern honor enforcing punishment of an insolence abolitionist who needed to be beaten to a proper station of subservience. "Greeley defended himself as well as he could, but suffered severely, although he is not disabled," reported the *New York Times*. There was no punishment for Rust.

Greeley's caning in January had aroused little outcry. On May 8, Congressman Philemon T. Herbert, a Democrat from California, but originally from Alabama, and ardently proslavery, provoked a squabble with a waiter at the Willard Hotel when he arrived too late to be served breakfast, cursed him as a "damned Irish son of a bitch," pulled out a pistol, and shot him dead. The Southern press defended Herbert for upholding the prerogative of "white men" dealing with "menials," as the *Charleston Standard* put it. In the House, the Democrats thwarted an attempt on the part of some anti-Nebraska members to launch an inquiry. At his trial a sympathetic jury acquitted Herbert of manslaughter. (During the war he served as a Confederate colonel.) "Members of Congress went armed in the streets," wrote Henry Wilson, "and sat with loaded revolvers in their desks."

"The tyranny of the slave oligarchy becomes more revolting day by day," Charles Sumner wrote his friend William Jay, a founder of the American Anti-Slavery Society and son of the nation's first chief justice, on May 6. "For some time I have tried for the floor. . . . I shall expose this whole crime at great length, and without sparing language." Sumner was receiving a stream of correspondence from abolitionists in Kansas on the "warlike" confrontation. On May 17, he wrote Theodore Parker, the preeminent Unitarian minister of Boston, abolitionist leader, and idol of William Herndon. "Alas! The tyranny over us is complete. Will the people submit? When you read this, I shall be saying to the Senate, 'They will not!' . . . I shall pronounce the most thorough philippic ever uttered in a legislative body."

CHAPTER FIVE

THE PURITAN AS PROPHET

Since Charles Sumner was elected to the Senate in 1851, he had been denied and scorned, refused committee assignments, banished as an outcast, deemed unworthy, unclean, and untouchable. He was the constant object of slander yet accused of being the defamer. It was not an irony that the tribune against slavery was the worthiest man from Massachusetts, the most learned in the Senate, his height at six feet two inches the measure of his rectitude, his gaze an image of engaged intellect— Sumner "with his fine presence and lofty carriage, his careful, well-arranged dress, and his deep, rich voice," as his friend Charles Francis Adams described him.

Charles Sumner, 1855

From his admirers, Sumner's virtues inspired deep respect and loyalty. His friend, the antislavery poet John Greenleaf Whittier, dedicated a poem to him in 1855: "In the white light of heaven, / the type of one / Who, momently by Error's host assailed, / Stands strong as Truth." But Sumner repelled others as cold, forbidding, and arrogant. His integrity was "unsullied and unassailable," but his "self-esteem was limitless," recalled Hugh

McCulloch, Lincoln's secretary of the treasury, who ran afoul of his censorious judgment. Sumner could be brittle, prickly, and unforgiving. Those unfortunate to be at the receiving end of his criticism regarded him as conceited, condescending, and harsh. His magnificent bearing, intellectual gifts, and ivory principles aroused resentment from the common run of politicians, even some on his own side. They interpreted his ornate public style as highhanded. They recoiled from his imperious sterling example and his disdain for the ordinary gestures of political life, making them feel as though they were inferior, vulgar, and squalid, which they didn't like to be reminded.

Neither Seward nor Lincoln, however, was among those who permitted themselves to feel aggrieved by Sumner's manner. Seward, who was welleducated, amiable, and foxy, maintained his relationship through thick and thin, though he was sometimes irritated by Sumner's impolitic ineptitude, once telling him, "Sumner, you're a damned fool." Lincoln, unlike nearly all the others, with his acute sense of human nature, had sympathy for Sumner's morbid sensitivity. He knew Sumner far better than Sumner knew himself. Lincoln as president never allowed Sumner's perceived slights, real or not, to create an impenetrable wall of alienation. Lincoln strategically reached out to Sumner with just the right little touch to pull him out of his high dudgeon, like the night of the second inaugural in 1865, when Lincoln directed his carriage to pick up a sulking Sumner at his home and gave him the place of honor of escorting Mary on his arm into the ball. Lincoln had a natural empathy for the inner hurt that Sumner masked by withdrawing behind his condescension. "Mr. Lincoln," recalled Shelby M. Cullom, a Republican congressman from Illinois, "was the only man living who ever managed Charles Sumner, or could use him for his purpose."

Sumner took painstaking care to be comprehensive in his criticisms, to display the astounding scope of his knowledge, and leave no part of his righteous indignation unexpressed. He was determined to smash to dust his opponents' claims through the accumulation of his dazzling erudition. He had emerged by challenging the political powers and social conventions of Boston, splitting and overthrowing the establishment of the Whig Party, an experience that was not only formative but also his template for action once he was elected to the Senate. Considered an inflexible figure in Washington, he agonized over criticism from his abolitionist friends in Boston that he was ever hesitant or craven. Upon his election to the Senate, Theodore Parker, who presided as pastor of the leading Unitarian congregation of Boston as an antislavery beacon, the church of the Transcendentalists, and who was the keeper of the flame of his grandfather, Captain John Parker, who fired the first shot, "the shot heard 'round the world," on Lexington Green, reminded Sumner of his calling in a letter on April 26, 1851: "You told me once that you were in morals, not in politics. Now I hope you will show that you are still in morals although in politics. I hope you will be the senator *with a conscience.* . . . I expect you to make mistakes, blunders; I hope they will be intellectual and not moral; that you will never miss the Right, however you may miss the Expedient. . . . I consider that Massachusetts has put you where you have no right to consult for the ease or the reputation of yourself, but for the eternal Right." But no one was more demanding on Sumner than he was himself, measuring his public actions by an unbending moral yardstick to speak unvarnished truth to the Slave Power.

Sumner was absorbed by politics, played the game by his own lights, yet disdained the idea of a political vocation as belittling. Standing for Massachusetts was his greatest calling. Sumner felt in his soul that he had been confided the greatest trust in representing the higher law of Pilgrims' pride. Speaking at Plymouth Rock on August 1, 1853, he declared, "Better the despised Pilgrim, a fugitive for freedom, than the halting politician, forgetful of principle, 'with a Senate at his heels.' Such, Sir, is the voice from Plymouth Rock, as it salutes my ears. Others may not hear it; but to me it comes in tones which I cannot mistake." Few listening to him echo his words off the famous Rock could mistake that he aligned the Pilgrims with the movement to protect fugitive slaves and that the "politician, forgetful of principle" he rebuked was the recently deceased Daniel Webster, fallen archangel of Massachusetts for his soiled embrace of the Fugitive Slave Act. If Sumner was "despised" for following his inner voice, he was compensated in the knowledge that he was true to the eternal verities of the Puritan compact.

Sumner's exalted oratory served exalted ends. He considered criticism of his flouting of political regularity and its niceties as high praise. "He possessed none of the instinct or experience of the politician, nor that sagacity of mind which appreciates and measures the importance of changing circumstances, or the possibilities and opportunities of the day," wrote his political friend Carl Schurz. "He lacked entirely the genius of organization. He never understood, nor did he value, the art of strengthening his following by timely concession, or prudent reticence, or advantageous combination and alliance. He knew nothing of management and party maneuver. Indeed, not infrequently he alarmed many devoted friends of his cause by bold declarations, for which they thought the public mind was not prepared, and by the unreserved avowal, and straightforward advocacy, of ultimate objects, which they thought might safely be left to the natural development of events. He was not seldom accused of doing things calculated to frighten the people, and to disorganize the antislavery forces."

Schurz was mostly though not completely correct about Sumner's political blindness. Sumner was keenly aware of the world in which he operated, but rather than usually engaged in the subtleties of regular politics he sought to influence its direction mainly through his oratory, the classical subject at which he was best in teaching at Harvard. The alpha of his tactics and omega of his strategies was his language. Sumner was hardly an organization man, but nobody would do more to infuse the Republican Party with a sense of moral purpose through personal self-sacrifice. He was also one of a handful of men who exercised his influence through six presidencies from prewar crisis to Civil War to Reconstruction—and his ideas would live on to inspire the civil rights movement nearly a century later.

Sumner was one of the most cosmopolitan Americans of his generation, as a young man moving easily among lords and literary giants in London, dubbed an honorary member of the theatrical Garrick Club, accepted as an equal by the latter-day philosophes of Paris, learning French and studying law at the Sorbonne, and befriending artists in Rome. He made himself at home abroad. Despite his wide travels and cultural horizons, however, he remained a Puritan at heart and never ceased to be shocked by European mores.

In the Washington of the 1850s, a thoroughly Southern city, dominated by Southerners in the anterooms of Congress and the drawing rooms of the grand houses, Sumner was more than a bit awkward in a society where Southern women exercised their wiles. Handsome and genteel, Sumner strangely lacked the basic elements of attraction. His manner with the fair sex was like his orations, rehearsed and pedagogical. Varina Davis, Jefferson Davis's wife, recalled, "His conversation was studied but brilliant, his manner deferential only as a matter of social policy, consequently, he never inspired the women to whom he was attentive with the pleasant consciousness of possessing his regard or esteem. He was . . . fond of talking to Southern women, and prepared himself with great care for these conversational pyrotechnics, in which, as well as I remember, there was much Greek fire, and the 'set piece' were numerous; he never intruded his peculiar views upon us in any degree, but read up on the Indian mutiny, lace, Demosthenes, jewels, Seneca's morals, intaglios, the Platonian theory, and once gave me quite an interesting resume of the history of dancing." (In 1866, Sumner, at the age of fifty-four, would marry the twenty-seven-year-old Alice Mason Hooper, a beautiful, vivacious, and decidedly nonintellectual widow of Brahmin Boston background, daughter of a wealthy congressman, who preferred dancing and parties, and, when Sumner ignored her, she drifted into the company of a young attaché at the British embassy. The marriage was nasty, brutish, and short. Alice felt neglected and treated cruelly, while Sumner, who "supposed there was an attraction about him superior to balls," felt his "self-esteem was wounded," according to a gossipy account of the ill-suited couple in a Boston newspaper.)

Sumner's ostracism in the Washington of the 1850s hardly came as a surprise; it mirrored the pattern of his experience in Boston. He had been branded by exclusion from the beginning of his political life. His amiability in the capital was accepted only to the degree it was reserved to conversation of the classics about which Southern senators flattered themselves they were learned and did not cross the boundary into slavery. Sumner embraced his status as a political pariah as an affirmation that he was doing right. He proudly wore his dissonance as an adornment of a more profound election. After he had been cast out of the drawing rooms of upper-class Whig Boston, he prefaced an address in 1847 on "Fame and Glory" to the Amherst College literary society with apt quotations, one from Milton's *Paradise Regained* on glory attained "without ambition, war or violence," and another from Shakespeare's *Titus Andronicus*: "He lives in fame that died in virtue's cause." After campaigning for the Free Soil Party in 1848, he wrote his brother, "As a necessary consequence I have been a mark for abuse. I have been attacked bitterly; but I have consoled myself with what John Quincy Adams said to me during the last year of his life: 'No man is abused whose influence is not felt.'"

In an age when oratory was among the most prized political skills, his opponents were awed and repelled by his intellectual firepower, logic, and severity. He was the opposite of the frenzied, shirt-ripping, and snorting Douglas, who sought to crush his enemies with ferocity. One of Sumner's admirers, comparing him to Cicero, described his "magic," which "sways our feelings and thrills our very souls . . . his appropriate and graceful gestures—his rich and mellifluous voice—his grand and elegant diction—his fervid and brilliant eloquence—his deep and stirring pathos—his sound and irresistible logic—his masterly and overpowering argumentation."

Despite his immersion in English literary life, Sumner never relied on wit, irony, or cleverness. He never picked it up or tried it out; it ran against his earnest grain. His speeches were structured according to the classical pattern and he preferred to use words with Latinate roots. "Did you ever see a joke in one of my speeches?" he reproached a friend. "Of course you never did. You might as well look for a joke in the book of Revelations." This might have provoked a laugh, but he wasn't trying to be funny. He was deadly serious.

Sumner's abrupt limits as a politician, his self-conscious violation of acceptable political speech on slavery and its adherents as moral hazards to be avoided, his social maladroitness outside his charmed circle, his guarded dignity, absence of humor, and inability to deflect or absorb anger through self-deprecation or indifference, combined with his brilliant speech and majestic manner, his true profundity and unflinching courage, incited the feverish pitch of responses to him.

Part of Sumner's problem in provoking his enemies was not just his superior air. His fundamental problem was that it was more than any conceit. He was loathed for more than his hauteur, intransigence, and impeccable dress. There were others at least as guilty of those offenses. He was hated even more for his exultant exposure of the shabby claims of the proslavery aristocrats manqué. Nor could he ever be accused of posturing out of mere political ambition. He was the object of unrestrained hostility because of the purity of his convictions, especially his open contempt for the slave owners' social pretenses. He was resented for every perfectly crafted line and classical allusion, the product of his Boston Latin and Harvard education. He was no sloganeer who repeated rote words. His phrases were memorable, his logic persuasive, and his appeal inspiring. Sumner had no power within the institution of the Senate, but those who did feared his broader influence. The more they sought to diminish him, the more they elevated his stature. From the moment he entered the Senate, he was treated as a voice to be silenced.

The sight and sound of Sumner inflamed not simply the fire-eaters of the South, but also the prudent conservative men of more reserved Southern opinion. His very presence was seen as nothing less than a felony. He was declared to be criminal for his condemnation of the Fugitive Slave Act and support for fugitives. Sumner symbolized all they detested about worthy New England, a civilization standing in judgment on their own. He stood for utopian professors, "philanthropists," and Moral Philosophers of wild-eyed antislavery agitation, true believers in the "glittering generality" that "all men are created equal," and other misguided miscreants clamoring for lunatic causes such as votes for women. His political and personal chasteness mocked Southern hypocrisy, especially sexual—the most volatile aspect of slavery, the ultimate dominance of master over slave, the violent sexual control of white men over black women. Sumner's unsparing critique inflamed the slaveholders of the Senate to bait him with lurid fantasies about sex with black women; his response would drive them to the boiling point. Unable to vanquish him in debate or silence him by innuendo, they became determined to force the Puritan to kneel like a slave before them.

Sumner was one of Ralph Waldo Emerson's "representative men," exemplars of their time and place. He was the representative man of more than the antislavery movement or a political party, but of a culture and history. He stood for a certain conception of Massachusetts rooted in the Puritan commonwealth that inspired him to declare of the antislavery cause at the Massachusetts convention of the Free Soil Party in 1848: "It is a continuance of the American Revolution."

The Puritan as prophet, who first decried the fall from grace of the cracked monuments of puritanism, Sumner was moral Boston at war with Brahmin Boston. He exposed the base interests and false idols of the best men. He sought to break the financial and political linkage of Massachusetts and the South forged in the chains of slavery—the Northern money power allied with the Southern Slave Power. His orations were jeremiads by way of Unitarianism in which moral reform usurped Calvinism and sin was ever present in the guise of the evils of slavery, ignorance, and violence. For his relentless truth telling about slavery in the alien Southern capital of Washington he was treated like a fugitive, an identity he embraced. As the representative of the Transcendentalists, this was his personal brand of transcendence. He carried at his core an inner sense of being from the hub of the universe, a Bostonian radiating the magnetism of his moral compass pointing true north. Like all magnetic personalities in politics, he was polarizing.

Sumner's background and rise were a chronicle of the New England enlightenment. He was among other things the Boston Latin and Harvard classmate of the aristocratic abolitionist Wendell Phillips; protégé of Supreme Court justice Joseph Story, William Ellery Channing, and John Quincy Adams; closest friend of Henry Wadsworth Longfellow; sympathetic member within the Transcendentalist circle of Margaret Fuller, Bronson Alcott, Henry David Thoreau, and Ralph Waldo Emerson; a like-minded soul among the uplifting reformers Samuel Gridley Howe and Horace Mann; compatriot of Conscience Whigs Charles Francis Adams and Richard Henry Dana Jr.; cofounder of the Boston Vigilance Committee to protect fugitive slaves with Theodore Parker; and co-sponsor of the Emigrant Aid

Society sending free state settlers to Kansas with Eli Thayer. Before he was elected to the Senate at the age of forty, he "participated actively in the cultural flowering known as the American Renaissance," was "acknowledged as one of America's most important men of letters," and "achieved wide renown and provoked heated controversy as an outspoken champion of legal reform, international peace, education reform, and the reform of prison discipline," according to his biographer Anne-Marie Taylor. But even that summary is cursory.

Sumner's roots ran to the beginnings of the Bay Colony. The original Pilgrim of his family, William Sumner, from Oxfordshire, settled in Massachusetts in 1633, became a freeholder and local selectman, and established a flourishing family whose branches eventually included Increase Sumner, the governor after Samuel Adams. The family of Charles Sumner's mother, Relief Jacob, traced its lineage to William Bradford, who arrived on the *Mayflower,* and was the founder and first governor of the Plymouth Colony. Job Sumner, Charles's grandfather, attended Harvard, fought in the Revolutionary army at Bunker Hill, but died at thirty-five in Georgia, where the pre-constitutional Confederation had sent him trying to resolve its accounts with the state. His son Charles Pinckney Sumner graduated from the Phillips Academy at Andover and Harvard College, where he developed a close friendship with his classmate Joseph Story. At college Charles Pinckney Sumner was inspired by the freethinking writings of Thomas Paine and awarded honors for his poetry. One of his poems imagined a world without slavery: "No sanctioned slavery Afric's sons degrade, / But equal rights shall equal earth pervade." After Harvard, in 1798, he sailed through the West Indies, landing in Haiti in the midst of the slave rebellion against French rule. At a dinner attended by the black revolutionary leaders, he delivered a toast: "Liberty, Equality, and Happiness, to all men!" Upon returning to Boston, he clerked in the law office of Josiah Quincy, who became president of Harvard, a congressman, and mayor of Boston.

The Federalist Party—the party of Josiah Quincy, John Adams, and Increase Sumner—dominated Massachusetts. Charles Pinckney Sumner was a dissenting follower of Thomas Jefferson, who was despised by the Boston elite. During Jefferson's reelection campaign in 1804, C.P. Sumner made public speeches on his behalf, and when the Democratic-Republicans gained a majority in the state legislature, he was rewarded with an appointment as clerk of the Massachusetts House of Representatives, holding his position through 1811 under its Speaker, his old friend Joseph Story. Despite his political connections, his law practice faltered through his inattention. He moved to a house on the poorer side of Beacon Hill, the North Slope down from the State House, one block from the center of the neighboring free black community that was the largest of its kind in the country. In 1819, he was named deputy sheriff of Suffolk County and six years later was appointed sheriff, a plum job, by Governor Levi Lincoln, Jr., a Jeffersonian who became a founder of the Massachusetts Whig Party, and was incidentally a distant cousin of Abraham Lincoln, who would meet him on his campaign swing through the state in 1848.

Charles Sumner always considered his antislavery feelings as his patrimony. From an early age his father regaled him with stories of the Haitian revolution and the heroic Edward Coles, the protégé of Jefferson and private secretary to President James Madison, who freed his own slaves and as the second governor of Illinois defeated the powerful political forces attempting to legalize slavery there. Sumner recalled his father treating black Bostonians as equal citizens, giving them his respectful "customary bow" upon passing them on the street. Sheriff Sumner was unusually outspoken against slavery, denounced the city of Washington as "a slave market," openly opposed segregation of public schools and the legal ban on intermarriage, and insisted on fair trials for blacks as adherence to "that love of equality on which our Commonwealth is based." In 1820, during the contentious debate over the Missouri Compromise, he predicted a civil war over slavery. "Our children's heads will some day be broken on a cannon-ball on this question," he said. He could not know that his prescient remark would apply to his own son.

One of the beneficiaries of C.P. Sumner's enlightened views was William Lloyd Garrison, who began publishing his abolitionist newspaper *The Liberator* in 1831, "within sight of Bunker Hill and in the cradle of liberty," as he proudly announced in its first issue. Almost immediately its appearance provoked denunciations from Boston's leading citizens, merchants and industrialists tied by a thousand golden threads to the Southern economy. Southern state legislatures passed laws declaring possession of the newspaper a felony. In Washington, any free black caught reading *The Liberator* was subject to a large fine and imprisonment, and if unable to pay would be sold into slavery. Two years later, the emergence of the American Anti-Slavery Society, whose Declaration of Sentiments Garrison wrote, incited mobs North and South to riot. When the AASS embarked on an evangelical crusade in 1835 to send antislavery tracts to Southern clergy, their literature was banned from the federal mail and its activists accused of stirring up slave insurrections. After

Boston authorities refused the petition of an antislavery group to use Faneuil Hall for a meeting, on August 21 "the social, political, religious and intellectual elite" filled it to condemn the abolitionists. Harrison Gray Otis, perhaps the most distinguished and wealthiest Bostonian, the former U.S. senator and mayor, ominously warned the crowd that abolishing slavery would be the equivalent of abolishing the Union. With that proclamation a political demarcation line was drawn.

A month later, on September 17, a double gallows was constructed on the street in front of Garrison's Beacon Hill home. One rope was strung for hanging him and another for George Thompson, the leader of the British Anti-Slavery Society, then on a speaking tour of the United States, and the object of assassination threats. When it was rumored that Thompson would appear at a meeting of the Boston Female Anti-Slavery Society on October 21, a mob burst in and seized Garrison, tearing off his clothes and dragging him by a rope through the street. Mayor Theodore Lyman intervened to rescue him, escorting him to safety for the night in the jail. Among those Garrison thanked for saving him was Sheriff Sumner.

Charles Sumner was one of the poorer boys to attend the Boston Latin School alongside the sons of the Beacon Hill elite. He wore rough shoes, cheap clothes, and was taunted as "gawky Sumner." His fellow student, later the radical abolitionist Wendell Phillips, among the most privileged, whose father would soon become mayor, shunned him in an act of childish snobbery. After graduating from Harvard, Sumner went to the law school, where he became the protégé and amanuensis of Joseph Story, his father's old friend, who Jefferson had appointed as associate justice of the Supreme Court and at the same time taught at Harvard. Story "treated him almost as if he were a son; and we were all delighted to welcome in to our family circle," recalled Story's son William. Story escorted Sumner around Washington on his first visit, introducing him to among other notable figures Chief Justice John Marshall with whom they shared most dinners. Sumner edited Story's decisions to be published in three volumes and became an editor of the *American Jurist* journal as well as contributing articles to other publications, including the leading literary magazine, the *North American Review*. While Story was away from Cambridge during the court's session, Sumner filled in for him teaching at the law school. He met weekly with Henry Longfellow, his best friend, Cornelius Felton, the future president of Harvard, and other literary men in a group they called "The Five of Clubs." Bearing a letter of introduction from Story, he traveled to Europe to see the great and the good. Upon his return from his Grand Tour, he joined a law firm, but found day-to-day legal work to be drudgery and was not particularly interested in pursuing clients. He felt trapped as a scrivener of trivial briefs. "My mind, soul, heart are not improved or invigorated by the practice of my profession," he wrote. "The sigh will come, for a canto of Dante, a Rhapsody of Homer, a play of Schiller."

Sumner fell under the sway of William Ellery Channing, the leading theologian of Unitarianism's Moral Philosophy, pastor at Boston's Federal Street Church, and the preacher of conscience in the cause of humanitarian reforms. It was through Channing that Sumner first publicly engaged with the question of slavery. In November 1841, one hundred and twenty-eight American slaves being transported along the Atlantic coast in a ship called the *Creole* staged a revolt and sailed to British territory at Nassau. There they were declared free under British law that had outlawed slavery in 1834. Secretary of State Daniel Webster, the towering figure among Massachusetts Whigs, demanded that they be returned to bondage. The British refused. Channing wrote a pamphlet, edited by Sumner, entitled "The Duty of the Free States," arguing for the position of the British, and warning "the slave-power has been allowed to stamp itself on the national policy, and to fortify itself with the national arm."

Sumner steeped himself in antislavery literature. He read the first book advocating immediate emancipation when it was published in 1833, *An Appeal in Favor of that Class of Americans Called Africans,* written by Lydia Maria Child, a member of the Transcendentalist circle, a friend of Garrison, a novelist, poet, and author of the best-selling *The American Frugal House-wife.* "If a history is ever written entitled, 'The Decay and Dissolution of the North American Republic,'" she wrote, "its author will distinctly trace our downfall to the existence of slavery among us." Child's book heralded the organization of the American Anti-Slavery Society. Since its inception Sumner had subscribed to Garrison's *The Liberator,* but he did not subscribe to Garrison's version of abolitionism that condemned the Constitution as a proslavery charter and the Union as a league with slaveholders; nor did he embrace Garrisonian immediatism and its perfectionism. "I have never been satisfied with its tone," Sumner wrote. "I have been openly opposed to the doctrines on the Union and the Constitution which it has advocated for several years. It has seemed to me often vindictive, bitter, and unchristian." Sumner believed that the Constitution must be the foundation for an antislavery politics, ideas that Salmon P. Chase and the Liberty Party had developed. "Thank God!

the Constitution of the United States does not recognize man as property," he wrote his English friend Lord Morpeth in the aftermath of the *Creole* case. Sumner considered slavery "a local institution" that could be bound within the South and eventually strangled. "You will see how rapidly this question of slavery moves in the country," he wrote Morpeth. "The South seems to have the madness which precedes great reverses."

In 1845, as one of the most prominent young men of Boston, a patron of the arts, admired for his prodigious intellect, and an exemplar of unblemished character, Sumner was invited by the mayor and City Council to deliver the annual Fourth of July oration before a distinguished audience that would include uniformed members of the Massachusetts militia and U.S. military. He informed the city fathers his theme would be international peace, and it was accepted. He was on the executive committee of the Peace Society of which Channing was a founder. War fever was in the air. James K. Polk had been elected president in 1844 on a platform of annexation of Texas as a slave state and threatening war with Mexico. On July 4, 1845, in an act well-advertised in advance, the Texas legislature approved annexation, setting the stage for the coming clash. That day, dressed for his appearance, Sumner "wore a dress-coat with gilt buttons,—a fancy of lawyers at that period,—and white waistcoat and trousers." The Washington Light Guards led the procession of notables across Boston Common to the Tremont Temple to hear the address he entitled "The True Grandeur of Nations." "A war with Mexico would be mean and cowardly," Sumner declared. His speech, filled with classical allusions and lengthy Latin quotations, denounced war in general. "In our age there can be no peace that is not honorable: there can be no war that is not dishonorable," he said. All the glorious battles of English history faded "by the side of that great act of Justice," the emancipation of its slaves. "And when the day shall come" in the United States of "peaceful emancipation . . . then shall there be a victory, in comparison with which that of Bunker Hill [where his grandfather had fought] shall be as a farthing-candle held up to the sun."

At the traditional post-oration dinner at Faneuil Hall, one speaker after another angrily denounced Sumner's effrontery, culminating in a censure from Robert C. Winthrop, the leader of the Whig Party and member of Congress, the direct descendant of the founder of the Massachusetts Bay Colony John Winthrop, protégé of Daniel Webster, and Sumner's Latin and Harvard classmate. Sumner, he said, "seemed to contemplate non-resistance and dissolution of the Union." Winthrop delivered his own toast: "Our Country, whether bounded by Sabine or Del Norte—still our Country—to be cherished in all our hearts—to be defended by all our hands." His tribute to war with Mexico not yet declared before the assembled notables of the Whig establishment was a declaration of war against Sumner and those like him who dared to oppose the coming clash. Earlier, that January, the Massachusetts legislature had passed a resolution opposing Texas annexation. Winthrop's toast was a signal from the Whig leadership that dissent would not be tolerated. Winthrop, after all, had the important matter of the tariff to navigate through the Congress and the waters needed to be calmed.

The censure of Sumner's July 4th speech launched his public life. As his mentors passed from the scene, Channing dying in 1842 and Story in 1845, he found "a Christian statesman" who was proving "the important truth, that *politics & morals* are one & inseparable"—John Quincy Adams. The former president sitting in the House of Representatives had led a relentless crusade against the Gag Rule, which prohibited the Congress from hearing antislavery petitions. Adams finally succeeded in ending the ban in 1845. He and Sumner shared common beliefs in Channing's uplifting Moral Philosophy and in breaking the sordid political grasp of the Slave Power. Like Moses anointing Joshua, Adams wrote the youthful Sumner "beyond my own allotted time, I see you have a mission to perform—I look from Pisgah to the Promised Land. You must enter upon it."

Sumner began meeting at his Court Street law office with a small group of friends, the Young Whigs faction of the party, whose leader was Charles Francis Adams, son of J.Q. Adams. Through the practical political skills of Henry Wilson, a rising working-class state legislator, they forged a tenuous alliance with the volatile Garrisonians and Liberty Party activists to form the Massachusetts State Anti-Texas Committee. Their opponents derisively called them "Conscience Whigs," and they responded by labeling them "Cotton Whigs." Sumner edited the anti-Texas newspaper, wrote the group's resolutions, and delivered his first political speech at a meeting of the group at Faneuil Hall on November 4, 1845, with Charles Adams presiding. "By welcoming Texas as a Slave State we make slavery our own original sin," Sumner said. "Let us wash our hands of this great guilt." Garrison's *Liberator* reported, "The weather was extremely unpropitious,—the rain pouring down violently, the thunder roaring, and the lightning blazing vividly at intervals,—emblematic of the present moral and political aspects of the country."

Winthrop voted for the war, but then spoke against it. Sumner engaged his old classmate in a private correspondence on the "slave-driving war," and urged him to vote against military appropriations. The month the war was launched Sumner, Adams, and their group of Conscience Whigs purchased a newspaper, *The Whig,* to serve as their voice. Writing under the pen name of "Boston," Sumner accused Winthrop of supporting "an unjust war, and national falsehood, in the cause of slavery." Winthrop felt wronged, and wrote Sumner that he sought "to rob him, personally of that 'spotless reputation.'" Sumner followed with another article: "Blood! Blood! is on the hands of the representative from Boston." Winthrop replied that Sumner's articles contained "the coarsest personalities" and "the grossest perversions." He severed their relationship. Sumner ridiculed Winthrop's toast at the July 4th dinner a year earlier: "Our country, right or wrong, or howsoever bounded, is a sentiment of heathen vulgarity and impiety." Behind the polemics over the war lay a subtle conflict over class, the sheriff's boy pulling down the Brahmin. In Massachusetts, the political was the moral, and whoever could claim the high ground could properly speak for Massachusetts and its traditions. Sumner, under his nom de plume "Boston," seized it against the heir of John Winthrop, who had fallen short in "ye duty of ye representative of Boston, a place of conscience, & morality," as Sumner charged.

The Conscience Whigs organized to take over the state convention at Faneuil Hall on September 23. Creating a clamor, they demanded that Sumner be permitted to speak. He dismissed the issues of the tariff and internal improvements as "transient" and "obsolete ideas." "The Whigs," he declared, "ought to be the party of freedom," and called for "REPEAL OF SLAVERY UNDER THE CONSTITUTION." He appealed to the revolutionary tradition of Massachusetts. "Massachusetts can stand alone, if need be." And he attacked Winthrop again, turning his signature word "bounded" against him. "Our party, bounded always by the Right," he declared. Winthrop followed him with a tepid answer about tariffs. Sumner and his faction introduced an antislavery plank, which appeared would carry the hall until Daniel Webster himself mounted the platform calling for unity and muffled it. Sumner urged that the Conscience Whigs run a candidate for the Congress against Winthrop. They thought he was the logical man to run, but he refused the nomination, anxious that he would be perceived as having attacked Winthrop solely "for his own personal promotion." Instead his friend Samuel Gridley Howe received the nomination, and lost decisively.

Sumner's battle with Winthrop coincided with a crusade against yet another Brahmin. The Boston Prison Discipline Society was an institutional pillar of the community, headed by the upright Reverend Louis Dwight, an advocate of harsh discipline and isolation that would presumably lead to religious salvation. Inspired by a report for reform written by Samuel Gridley Howe, Sumner openly challenged Dwight at the group's annual meeting on May 25, 1846. For eight nights he and Howe drew large crowds debating Dwight, whom Sumner called "selfish, Jesuitical and lazy," and the society's treasurer, Samuel A. Eliot, the former mayor, whom he scored for his "vanity or self-esteem." Sumner condemned their "system" of enforced "perpetual solitude" as "an engine of cruelty and tyranny." Dwight and Eliot stood at the pinnacle of Boston society, related by kinship and marriage to the dense network of families that controlled the banks of State Street, the factories, philanthropies, and board of Harvard. Eliot had criticized Sumner for his July 4th address and was closely allied with Winthrop. Dwight suffered a nervous breakdown from the shock of public confrontation, the Prison Society never again held a public meeting, and it dissolved in 1855. The *Boston Post,* a newspaper of the Whig establishment, denounced Sumner as a "malignant defamer" and "having a disordered intellect."

As these controversies simmered to their heated climaxes, a new professor was to be chosen to fill the chair at the Harvard law school left vacant by the death of Joseph Story. He had designated Sumner to be his successor. But Harvard president Edward Everett, the former governor, a close friend of Winthrop who had also treated Sumner with benevolent interest in the past, presided over the board's unanimous rejection of him. The lines in Boston were drawn for and against Sumner.

The largest mansion on Beacon Hill, designed by the famed architect Charles Bulfinch in the Federal style, commanding the strategic corner of Beacon and Park Streets, in the shadow of the golden dome of the State House, and with a sweeping view of the Common, was the temple of Brahmin society. Here resided the arbiter of proper Boston, George Ticknor, wealthy heir to the cofounder of the Provident Bank, married to the daughter of Samuel Eliot, board member of civic institutions, eminent professor at Harvard, where he redesigned its curriculum, acquainted with the most influential people throughout the country and Europe, and author of the monumental *History of Spanish Literature.* Those receiving Ticknor's favor were welcomed into his parlor under a portrait of Sir Walter Scott amid his library of fourteen thousand books and invited to dine at a table graced with such guests as Webster and Hawthorne. He was, according to his biographer, "of the true 'Brahmin caste,'" "refined," and of the "Tory temperament." One of his frequent guests, Edwin Percy Whipple, the literary critic, wrote that "his ample means, his cultivated manners, and his possession of the best house, both as regards situation and elegance, which then existed in the city, made him a leader in the society of the place." "He had his own set of people," observed William Cullen Bryant, the poet and editor of the *New York Post,* "and seems to have looked down upon everybody else." His friends referred to their intimate world as "Ticknorville."

Ticknor had been Sumner's literature professor at Harvard, invited him often into the warmth of his salon, and warned him against making rash public statements against slavery. From this Brahmin Eden, Sumner was banished. "In a society where public opinion governs, unsound opinions must be rebuked," Ticknor wrote a friend referring to Sumner, and denounced in one breath "social democracy" and "demagogues" as a threat to "public morals." It was more than a snub. Coming from an authority on Spanish culture, it was the judgment of an inquisitor. "There was a time when I was welcome at almost every house within two miles of us," Sumner remarked ruefully to Richard Henry Dana, Jr. as they passed along Beacon Street, "but now hardly any are open to me." Dana, too, would be proscribed, and so would Sumner's friend Henry Wadsworth Longfellow, who wrote antislavery poems. Charles Francis Adams described the efforts at "social ostracism; attempts ludicrous now to look back upon, but at the time exasperating to those against whom they were insolently directed. An abolitionist was looked upon as a sort of common enemy of mankind; a Free Soiler was only a weak and illogical abolitionist." Their views were "resented as outrages on decency" and they were "made to feel in many ways the contempt there felt for the cause they had espoused." When Sumner "ceased to be seen" at Ticknor's, it was a signal event in the inner life of Boston. "Slowly but surely the country was working itself up to the war point; and the conservative and reactionary interests, instinctively realizing the fact, demeaned themselves according to their wont." Sumner should not have been surprised. Ticknor had once been the financial and literary benefactor of Lydia Maria Child, but ostracized her for her antislavery views, even cutting her off from library privileges at the Boston Athenaeum. Theodore Parker, blackballed by Ticknor from membership in the Massachusetts Historical Society, took to calling him the "arch devil of the aristocracy."

But the social insulation of the castes of Boston could not prevent unwanted events from intruding. Victory in the Mexican War thrust the question of the extension of slavery in the newly conquered lands to the center of politics. Sumner wrote a resolution adopted by the Massachusetts legislature in February 1847 that protested "the acquisition of any additional territory" unless the Congress prohibited slavery within it—"that there shall be neither slavery nor involuntary servitude in such territory otherwise than for the punishment of crime"—the language of the Northwest Ordinance of 1787 inspired by Jefferson.

Then Sumner led a contingent of Conscience Whigs to the state convention at Springfield on September 29 to battle for the soul of the party. Daniel Webster, intending the convention to be the springboard for his presidential nomination, found himself caught in the crosscurrents. John G. Palfrey, the first Conscience Whig elected to the Congress, introduced a resolution "to support no men for the offices of President and Vice-President of the United States but such as are known by their acts or declared opinions to be opposed to the extension of slavery." Samuel Eliot warned Palfrey, a Unitarian minister, former dean of the Harvard Divinity School, and editor of the *North American Review,* to "be silent . . . or prepared for very rough usage." Palfrey and Charles Adams were heckled and hissed before Sumner rose to speak for the resolution. "Loyalty to principle is higher than loyalty to party," he declared. Winthrop took the lead in arguing against the resolution. Webster, who had been endorsed as a candidate for president, said he was against slavery's extension, but opposed to the resolution. As light faded in the hall and some delegates had already drifted out for the evening, the measure was defeated on a show of hands that the Conscience Whigs felt left their true numbers uncounted.

In 1847 the fratricidal conflict resumed in Washington over Winthrop's designation as the Whig candidate for Speaker of the House. Palfrey assailed him, along with Congressman Joshua Giddings of Ohio, "master of us all in antislavery matters," as Sumner called him. They floated a rumor emanating from Giddings's flawed memory that Winthrop had spoken in favor of the Mexican War in the Whig caucus just before the vote. The *Boston Atlas,* a regular Whig newspaper, attacked Sumner as the ringleader for his "inordinate vanity and self-conceit" and "personal malignity." Finally, Winthrop was elected Speaker through the intervention of J.Q. Adams, who acted out of ancient affection for the Winthrop family above all else. Winthrop promptly denounced C.F. Adams and his comrades Sumner and Palfrey as "a little nest of vipers." Sumner decried "private assassination and assault, which is our lot here—suspected, slandered, traduced by those who profess and call themselves Whigs," and he called for "a new crystallization of parties, in which there shall be, one grand Northern party of Freedom."

"Be not Atticus," J.Q. Adams admonished Sumner, referring to Cicero's friend, Titus Pomponius Atticus, who sequestered himself from the tumult of politics in his library. Both men revered Cicero as their ideal public man and orator. Adams apparently made this remark to Sumner after he had suffered a stroke in the winter of 1847 while preoccupied with the legacy of his political principles. When Adams collapsed at his desk in the House of Representatives and died on February 23, 1848, Sumner stood at his crossroads between Cicero and Atticus.

Sumner was already involved in intense meetings with Charles Francis Adams and the other Conscience Whigs to anticipate "an organized revolt" during the presidential campaign of 1848. Longfellow described those surrounding Sumner as "his captains." In May the Democratic convention nominated Senator Lewis Cass of Michigan. "No Northern politician was ever more abject in his submission to Southern dictation," wrote Edward L. Pierce, Sumner's authorized biographer. Cass's selection was the signal for the walkout of the Barnburners, or the Soft faction from New York. Many were closely linked by a skein of past relationships to former president Martin Van Buren, who had been denied the nomination in 1844 through the imposition of the two-thirds rule that institutionalized Southern control. The Softs' break was partly an act of revenge. Sumner was the Boston group's key contact with the Barnburners, including "Prince" John Van Buren, the former president's son. The "Little Magician" now miraculously transformed himself from a president who had been a Southern instrument into a staunch opponent of slavery's extension partly through guidance in letters from Sumner.

When the Whigs nominated Zachary Taylor, the military hero of the Mexican War, as their presidential candidate to stand on no platform whatsoever, Sumner and his friends staged a well-prepared bolt. On June 28, they held a state convention to create the new Free Soil Party. Sumner delivered a stirring keynote address in which he laid out how the plot to nominate Taylor had brought about the capture of the Whig Party as an arm of the "Slave Power . . . to serve its interests, to secure its supremacy, and especially to promote the extension of Slavery." With thrilling rhetoric, he pointed the finger of blame and shame at the Boston Whigs. "I speak only what is now too notorious, when I say that it was the secret influence which went forth from among ourselves that contributed powerfully to this consummation. Yes! it was brought about by an unhallowed union—conspiracy let it be called—between two remote sections: between the politicians of the Southwest and the politicians of the Northeast,—between the cotton-planters and fleshmongers of Louisiana and Mississippi and the cottonspinners and traffickers of New England,—between the lords of the lash and the lords of the loom."

In August, Sumner attended the national Free Soil convention at Buffalo, where Van Buren was nominated and Charles Francis Adams named his running mate. About the tattered Van Buren's ironic emergence as an antislavery tribune, Webster remarked, "I think the scene would border upon the ludicrous, if not upon the contemptible." He recalled initially encountering Van Buren more than twenty years earlier when he was conniving to overthrow President John Quincy Adams. "If nobody were present," said Webster, "we should both laugh at the strange occurrences and stranger jumbles of political life. . . . That the leader of the Free Spoil party should so suddenly have become the leader of the Free Soil party would be a joke to shake his sides and mine." At a Boston rally, Sumner answered Webster's jibe. "It is not for the Van Buren of 1838 that we are to vote, but for the Van Buren of today."

The *Boston Atlas,* the stalwart Whig newspaper, rained poisonous arrows on the defectors. Adams was "a political huckster," Palfrey a "Judas," and Sumner "a transcendental lawyer." The paper was particularly inventive in its venom toward Sumner, deriding his "cant," "inordinate vanity and self-conceit," "puerile self-consequence," and "vagrant theories." William Schouler, the *Atlas*'s editor, encouraged a promising young congressman from Illinois to campaign in Massachusetts for the Whigs to give the party a fresh look. On his tour, Lincoln appeared on a Boston stage with the party's most prominent figure, William Seward, for their first meeting. None of the Free Soilers bothered to observe the obscure Lincoln's passing presence.

Sumner was drafted to run for the Boston congressional seat against Winthrop, and after wavering plunged in. Longfellow's diary recorded his friend's anxious state of mind. On September 3: "Sumner, full of zeal for the 'Barnburners.' But he shrinks a little from the career just opening before him." On September 17: "He looks somewhat worn. Nothing but politics now. Oh, where are those genial days when literature was the theme of our conversation?" On October 22: "Sumner stands now, as he himself feels, at just the most critical point of his life. Shall he plunge irrevocably into politics, or not?—that is the question; and it is already answered. He inevitably will do so, and after many defeats will be very distinguished as a leader. Let me cast his horoscope: Member of Congress, perhaps; Minister to England, certainly. From politics as a career he still shrinks back. When he has once burned his ships there will be no retreat. He already holds in his hand the lighted torch." Sumner was soundly defeated, but now fully committed to a political life. Leaving Atticus's retreat for good, he entered Cicero's arena.

Sumner's advocacy on behalf of the Free Soil Party was not accepted in Boston as a simple difference of opinion; nor was it understood as just a matter of politics. His words tore apart his personal relationships, alienated him from patrons and friends, and severed his ties to respectable society. His stinging accusation of the conspiracy of "the lords of the lash and the lords of the loom" to nominate Taylor was the final straw. Influential Whigs of Massachusetts, after all, were instrumental in Taylor's nomination. Abbott Lawrence, founder of the mill town of Lawrence with his brothers and the congressman from Boston preceding Winthrop, had supported Taylor in a tentative arrangement that was to conclude with his being named as the vice presidential candidate, but it was foiled when Henry Wilson staged an embarrassing walkout at the Whig convention. Beforehand, Sumner had confronted Lawrence, urging, "Get out of it. . . . It is never too late to begin to do right." To which Lawrence candidly replied, "What can I do about it, I am in up to the eyes." (Taylor would appoint Lawrence the minister to the United Kingdom.)

Samuel Lawrence, Abbott's brother and business partner, had taken an avuncular interest in the brilliant Sumner, even subsidizing his Grand Tour of Europe. But now he was outraged that the scholarly young man had bitten the hand that fed him. "No man regrets the part you are acting more than I do," he wrote Sumner. "You have taken hold of this one idea of slavery, and are in a fair way of becoming severed from a very large circle of friends who give dignity and honor to our common country. I could name scores and scores of men whom you have honored your whole life who regret and condemn the course you have taken." When Sumner tried to explain, Lawrence wrote in another letter:

"How an intelligent Massachusetts man could have given utterance to these words is beyond my comprehension. . . . Your principles tend directly to the breaking up of this glorious republic. You and I never can meet on neutral ground. I can contemplate you only in the character of a defamer of those you profess to love, and an enemy to the permanency of this Union." About Sumner's affiliation with the Free Soil Party, "a Faction," Lawrence wrote: ". . . and Mr. Martin Van Buren!!!!"

Nathan Appleton was equally appalled. "I have regretted to see talents so brilliant as yours, and from which I had hoped so much for our country, take a course in which I consider them worse than thrown away," he wrote Sumner. Appleton was the cofounder of the city of Lowell, where he had introduced the power loom into the manufacture of textiles, was a partner in many enterprises with the Lawrence brothers, and a former congressman representing Boston. Of more intimate interest, his daughter Fanny was married to Longfellow, and Longfellow informed his friend it would be best if he didn't visit his home when his father-in-law was present.

Sumner always believed that Massachusetts must occupy a unique place as the beacon of liberty, true to the principles of the American Revolution. Transforming the nation turned on transforming the commonwealth. In the year after his defeat running for the Congress, he made the first legal argument against school segregation. Benjamin Roberts was a free black and printer who published antislavery pamphlets and several short-lived newspapers for the black community, the *Anti-Slavery Herald* and the *Self Elevator*. He lived on the back slope of Beacon Hill. His five-year-old daughter, Sarah, walked past several schools in order to attend her inferior all-black one. Roberts secured the services of Boston's first black lawyer, Robert Morris, to file a suit to allow Sarah to enter an all-white school. Ellis Gray Loring, scion of an old Boston family and attorney for the Anti-Slavery Society, had trained Morris in the law. Morris was also a leader of the Boston Vigilance Committee to aid fugitive slaves. Morris asked Sumner to act as his co-counsel to write and present the brief before the Massachusetts Supreme Court. Sumner did so without charging a fee.

On December 4, 1849, arguing in the case of *Roberts v. the City of Boston,* Sumner introduced a term that had never before been uttered in an American judicial court—"equality before the law." "In the statement of this proposition I use language which, though new in our country, has the advantage of precision." He traced his definition to France, to the philosopher Diderot's *Encylopédie*, first published in 1751. The principle of equality was rooted in the Declaration of Independence and "embodied" in the Massachusetts constitution: "All men are born free and equal." Denying equality would establish a "system of caste as odious as that of the Hindoos." He observed that John C. Calhoun had assailed the claim of equality in the Declaration as "the most false and dangerous of all political errors." But Sumner declared he would show "the fallacy of the pretension that any exclusion or discrimination founded on race or color can be consistent with Equal Rights." Establishing his basic point, "Separate schools inconsistent with equality," he argued: "It is easy to see that the exclusion of colored children from the

Public Schools is a constant inconvenience to them and their parents, which white children and white parents are not obliged to bear. Here the facts are plain and unanswerable, showing a palpable violation of Equality. The black and white are not equal before the law." Because a segregated school was not a "Common School," it was, he said, "illegal." "It is a mockery to call it an equivalent." He compared this inequality to the anti-Semitism of Europe, where Jews had been "confined to a particular district called the Ghetto," or "the Jewish Quarter." "Compulsory segregation," Sumner declared, was "a vestige of ancient intolerance directed against a despised people. It is of the same character with the separate schools in Boston. Thus much for the doctrine of Equivalents as a substitute for Equality."

In 1850, Lemuel Shaw, chief justice of the Massachusetts Supreme Judicial Court, issued a ruling upholding segregation: "It is urged, that this maintenance of separate schools tends to deepen and perpetuate the odious distinction of caste, founded in a deep-rooted prejudice in public opinion. This prejudice, if it exists, is not created by law, and probably cannot be changed by law." Five years later, in 1855, influenced by Sumner, the Massachusetts legislature prohibited school segregation. But in 1896 Shaw's decision was cited as the basis for the Supreme Court's ruling in the case of *Plessy v. Ferguson* enshrining the segregationist doctrine of "separate but equal." More than a half century later, in its landmark 1954 *Brown v. Board of Education* decision, the Supreme Court overturned *Plessy* on the grounds that Sumner had argued, citing the Roberts case.

While Shaw adjudicated the Roberts case, Massachusetts entered into its own prologue to the Civil War. Within a matter of months both political parties irrevocably split; great men toppled from the heights of reputation; slaves were hunted through Boston streets; and Sumner ascended to the Senate.

The demarcation line between political eras was a date Sumner would refer to as *"Dies Irae"*—the Day of Wrath—March 7 of 1850. It was the day that Daniel Webster stood to address the Senate. "The Godlike Daniel" had once eloquently reviled slavery and famously demolished the states' rights doctrine of slaveholders. He was "the one eminent American of our time," according to Ralph Waldo Emerson. New England looked to him for clarity and guidance. Only Henry Clay to whom he had confided knew what Webster would say, whether he would support the compromise bill that would leave open the question of extending slavery to the new territories gained from Mexico or support President Taylor in opposing it. Then, in what Emerson would call "a fatal hour," Webster not only argued for the compromise but also for the Fugitive Slave Act, declaring that the South had been "injured." He discarded the Wilmot Proviso, which would have prohibited the extension of slavery and which he had previously favored. (Congressman Lincoln had voted for it numerous times, calling himself "a Proviso man.") Webster rebuked the Massachusetts legislature for sending him instructions to vote for it, a resolution written by Sumner, and singled out for praise Sumner's former law partner George Hillard, who as a member of the legislature had voted against it. When Webster finished, Senator Chase overheard him whisper to Douglas, "You don't want anything more than that, do you?"

The Whig Party of Massachusetts was forever ripped apart. "All the drops of his blood have eyes that look downward," said Emerson of Webster. Sumner called Webster's speech "a heartless apostasy," compared him to "Judas Iscariot or Benedict Arnold," and "the rebuke of his former self." Charles Francis Adams observed, "So long as Mr. Webster adhered to the anti-slavery utterances of his earlier days,—so long as he saw fit to claim the Wilmot Proviso as his thunder, and to keep terms with the Liberty party,— the reactionary under-current was scarcely perceptible; but when he changed front openly,—putting in his bid for Southern support,—there was no longer any concealment. Under the guise of loyalty to the Union and the Constitution, social and business Boston by degrees became in its heart, and almost avowedly, a pro-slavery community; and it so remained until 1861."

President Taylor suddenly died on July 9. His successor, Millard Fillmore, reversed his policy. Douglas engineered the compromise bill with the Fugitive Slave Act attached through the Congress on September 18. Within weeks, in October, slave hunters appeared in Boston to track down the escaped slaves William and Ellen Craft living as free blacks on Beacon Hill; they fled to sanctuary in England. President Fillmore appointed Webster his secretary of state. Winthrop replaced him in the Senate. Webster was disgusted at his protégé when Winthrop expressed dismay at the Fugitive Slave Act. To fill Winthrop's open congressional seat the pro-Webster Whigs selected Samuel Eliot and the Free Soilers chose Sumner to oppose him.

On the eve of the election, November 6, Sumner delivered a speech at Faneuil Hall that was the making of his political career. Of the Fugitive Slave Act, he said, "the soul sickens." Speaking of Millard Fillmore, he aroused the crowd to what was described as "Sensation." "Into the immortal catalogue of national crimes it has now passed, drawing, by inexorable necessity, its authors also, and chiefly him, who, as President of the United States, set his name to the Bill, and breathed into it that final breath without which it would bear no life. Other Presidents may be forgotten; but the name signed to the Fugitive Slave Bill can never be forgotten. There are depths of infamy, as there are heights of fame. I regret to say what I must, but truth compels me. Better for him, had he never been born!" By contrast, he proclaimed, "Fugitive Slaves are the heroes of our age." The compromise had not, he said, settled "the Slavery Question." "Nothing, sir, can be settled which is not right." He called for "the overthrow of the Slave Power," which "humbles both great political parties to its will" and must be "openly encountered in the field of politics." New men were needed in Washington to banish it from the "National Government." "Three things at least they must require: the first is *backbone*; the second is *backbone*; and the third is *backbone*."

Sumner's electrifying speech contributed to the crushing defeat of the Whigs, who lost control of the state legislature. Sumner lost his race for the Congress, which was foreordained in the conservative Boston district, but the game all along was being played for higher stakes—Webster's once eternal seat in the Senate. Sumner was the natural candidate of the newly empowered coalition of antislavery Democrats and Free Soilers. Again, he faced off against Winthrop. The splintering of the parties in the legislature, however, kept Sumner just below a majority. And the moneyed interests behind Webster created a slush fund for anti-Sumner legislators. "Everything is being done to prevent Sumner's election . . . that can be," Amos A. Lawrence, the industrialist, informed Samuel Eliot. Former congressman Caleb Cushing, who denounced Sumner as a "one ideaed abolitionist agitator," led a rump group of Democrats dubbing themselves the "Indomitables" to block him. (Pierce would appoint Cushing his attorney general.)

The balloting that began in January dragged on inconclusively for months. After three months of deadlock a seventeen-year-old runaway slave, Thomas Sims, was captured in Boston under the new Fugitive Slave Act. The Boston Vigilance Committee led by Theodore Parker tried to enter the courthouse to free him. Thick iron chains were wrapped across the courthouse doors. Sumner served as Sims's co-counsel, urging his freedom. On April 19, the anniversary of the Battle of Lexington and Concord that began the American Revolution, under the guard of amassed police, local militia, and 250 federal troops the shackled Sims was marched to a ship in the harbor to be returned to slavery. Henry David Thoreau referred to the event as a "moral earthquake." A week later, on April 26, 1851, on the twenty-sixth ballot, Sumner edged to a one-vote victory. Henry Adams, the thirteen-year-old son of Charles Francis Adams, raced with the news from the State House back to the Adams home, where Sumner was dining. "It was," he recalled, "probably the proudest moment in the life of either."

In mourning Whigs wore black armbands on the streets of Boston. A prominent Cotton Whig lawyer and state senator, Benjamin R. Curtis, closely attached to Webster, wrote a letter signed by every Whig member of the legislature charging Sumner of "an indictable offense" and "guilty" of a "criminal" and "factious conspiracy" for making the coalition with Democrats that elected him. A few months later Fillmore would appoint Curtis to the Supreme Court.

"He was sent to work out his own course absolutely," wrote Sumner's friend Thomas Wentworth Higginson, the Unitarian minister and abolitionist. "He had no party; he was to create a party. He had no firm following. The abolitionists watched him with hope, but not without distrust; they had seen so many fail. His opponents were prepared to denounce him as a man of one idea, if he devoted himself to the slavery question alone; or as a demagogue, if he took up any other."

Sumner soon encountered the overriding reality that his Massachusetts colleague Senator John Davis explained to him, "At Washington slavery rules everything." The freshman senator spent his first months clearing his throat. He spoke on several subjects of minor note, but not on slavery. "Surely," editorialized Garrison, "this is 'the play of Hamlet, with the part of Hamlet omitted by particular request.'" Sumner was carefully waiting for the right opportunity, but none arose. On July 27, 1852, he decided to introduce a bill to repeal the Fugitive Slave Act. The next day the Senate refused consent to allow him to speak on his motion. Andrew Butler of South Carolina said Sumner was "pledged to agitate." So Sumner was silenced. "You may speak next term," James M. Mason of Virginia ordered him. "I must speak this term," Sumner insisted. "By God, you shan't," said Mason. "I will and you can't prevent me," Sumner replied. But they could and did. Seward wrote his wife: "When will there be a North? The shutting of the doors against Sumner was wicked and base. . . . Indignation pervaded me to the finger ends."

Sumner's silencing was his rude introduction to the implacable power of the F Street Mess. He had railed against the Slave Power from the distance of Boston, but now he encountered it within the chamber of the Senate. In his first direct conflict, after readying himself for years, he found his voice throttled. He understood that behind his adversaries loomed the shade of John C. Calhoun.

Sumner would envision the future as a clash between the legacies of Calhoun and John Quincy Adams. In a speech campaigning in 1860 for Lincoln, he said, "Never was great conflict destined to involve a great country more distinctly foreshadowed. All that the Republican party now opposes may be found in John C. Calhoun; all that the Republican party now maintains may be found in John Quincy Adams. Choose ye, fellow-citizens, between the two."

Sumner, meanwhile, wrote a lengthy appeal to President Fillmore to pardon the two pilots, Daniel Drayton and Edward Sayres, who had been imprisoned for attempting to help seventy-six fugitive slaves escape from Washington aboard a schooner named the *Pearl* in 1848. The pardon was granted on August 4. Fearful that the men would be arrested on warrants from Virginia, Sumner personally met them at the jail with his carriage and arranged for them to travel that night immediately north. "Here was a point on which Sumner was able to assist us much more effectively than by making speeches in the Senate," wrote Drayton.

Sumner awaited his opening. When the chairman of the Senate Finance Committee, Robert M.T. Hunter, of Virginia and the F Street Mess, routinely introduced the appropriations bill Sumner leaped at his chance. On August 26, 1852, he proposed an amendment that would deny funding for the Fugitive Slave Act. "I am to be heard—not as a privilege, but as a right," he declared. For three and half hours he spoke on his theme of "Freedom National, Slavery Sectional," making a forensic and florid case that slavery was not established in the Constitution as a national institution, that it was forbidden in the territories by the Ordinance of 1787, and that slavery's legitimacy was "constantly misunderstood." "As Slavery assumes to be national, so, by an equally strange perversion, Freedom is degraded to be sectional, and all who uphold it, under the National Constitution, are made to share this same epithet. . . . These terms, now belonging to the commonplaces of political speech, are adopted and misapplied by most persons without reflection. But here is the power of Slavery. . . . It changes word for word. It teaches men to say *national* instead of *sectional,* and *sectional* instead of *national.*"

Sumner argued that the slave was "a person" and therefore entitled to the right under the Constitution of trial by jury. If that were the case, the Fugitive Slave Act was unconstitutional and a dead letter. With ironic approval, he quoted Senator Butler's remark that "a law which can be enforced only by the bayonet is no law." At the heart of his speech, Sumner laid out an incremental strategy for confining slavery to the South that would eventually cause it to "disappear." By denying that the Congress had power to extend slavery and by thwarting the admission of new slave states, the political power behind slavery would inexorably atrophy. Sumner was hardly making an original argument, but rephrasing the old ones going back to the beginnings of antislavery politics in the Liberty Party. His approach contrasted with the radical abolitionists who condemned the Constitution as a pact with the devil and demanded immediate emancipation. Sumner's scenario of slowly strangling slavery, his invocation of Washington and Jefferson as true "abolitionists," and incorporation of the Declaration of Independence's proclamation that "all men are created equal" as the fount of national policy provided the basic arguments that other antislavery speakers, especially Lincoln, would adopt.

When Sumner took his seat after finishing this exhaustive review of history, law, and morality, Southern senators and their allies compared him to a dog, accused him of inciting sexual perversion and murder, and declared him unfit. "The ravings of a maniac may sometimes be dangerous, but the barking of a puppy never did any harm," said Senator Jeremiah Clemens of Alabama. Senator George Badger of North Carolina described Sumner as a slave of free blacks in the abolitionist movement. "This agitation," he said, "was got up and maintained for mischievous purposes. . . . They and their societies are oppressed now by the comparatively few people of color they have among them." Senator Henry Dodge of Iowa claimed that Sumner's real agenda was race mixing. "The idea of equality and amalgamation of those races in the United States of America is utopian in the extreme, and I think wicked and disgraceful. . . . If their doctrines can be brought into practical operation (and they are prepared and are panting for the experiment), they would introduce black-skinned, flat-nosed, and woolly-headed Senators and Representatives, in this Chamber and in the House of Representatives." Douglas argued that Sumner's opposition to the Fugitive Slave Act was itself a violation of his oath of office to defend the Constitution and therefore "has no right to hold office under this Government." Senator John B. Weller of California charged that Sumner's rejection of the Fugitive Slave Act instigated "forcible resistance" and would "bring upon the head of the learned Senator from Massachusetts the blood of murdered men. He who counsels murder is himself a murderer!"

Sumner's amendment was overwhelmingly voted down. The Congress adjourned. His first attempt to make an impression ended. It was an election year, and he went home to campaign.

At the Massachusetts Free Soil Party convention Sumner mounted the platform as the keynote speaker to the applause of the delegates and guests, who included Captain Drayton of the *Pearl,* whose pardon for the crime of attempting to transport fugitive slaves he had arranged. "The rising public opinion against Slavery cannot flow in the old political channels," Sumner said. "It is impeded, choked, and dammed back. But if not *through* the old parties, then *over* the old parties, this irresistible current *shall* find its way. It cannot be permanently stopped. If the old parties will not become its organs, they must become its victims. The party of Freedom will certainly prevail." But Sumner's exciting rhetoric fell flat in the torpid atmosphere. The Free Soil Party suffered defections from Democrats and Whigs, who returned to their natural political homes, and it lost half the vote it had four years earlier. Even more perilous for Sumner, his enemies, the Cotton Whigs, regained control of the legislature, ousting the fragile coalition that had put him into the Senate. If the results of 1852 were a sign of things to come it was that Charles Sumner would be a one-term wonder and his political career would be finished.

CHAPTER SIX

CYCLOPS

——————◆◆◆◆——————

"This Congress is the worst—or rather promises to be the worse—since the Constitution was adopted; it is the 'Devil's Own,'" Sumner wrote his friend Samuel Gridley Howe on December 8, 1853, at the convening of the 33rd Congress. The Mephistophelian drama began at once. With that the laws of political gravity were removed, the planets teetered out of their orbits, and the tidal waves flooded in.

The outsiders at the fringe, the two Free Soil senators, Chase and Sumner, were suddenly thrust to the center. They requested that Douglas postpone introduction of his revision to repeal the Missouri Compromise as part of the Nebraska Act for a week, giving them the opening on January 24 to issue an "Appeal of the Independent Democrats in Congress," denouncing the move as "a criminal betrayal of precious rights." On the Senate floor four days later, Douglas assailed the "abolition confederates" for "an atrocious plot against the cause of free government," and as "the pure, unadulterated representatives of

Senator Andrew Pickens Butler

Abolitionism, Free Soilism, Niggerism in the Congress of the United States." He accused "the freesoilers and Abolitionists" as "the guilty parties" for violating the Missouri Compromise he would now repeal. "Why, then, should we gratify the abolition party in their effort to get up another political tornado of fanaticism, and put the country again in peril, merely for the purpose of electing a few agitators to the Congress of the United States?" Sumner replied that the "Appeal" described "the act, and not its author," and called it "a soulless, eyeless monster—horrid, unshapely, and vast . . . and this monster is now let loose upon the country"—a line paraphrased from Virgil in *The Aeneid* to describe the Cyclops.

Sumner resumed his opposition with a full-blown oration, which he entitled "The Landmark of Freedom," on February 22. As a matter of "Public Faith," he argued against overthrowing the Missouri Compromise, urging that senators "not wantonly and flagitiously discard any obligation, pledge, or covenant, because they chance to possess the power,—that they will not substitute *might* for *right*." In 1860, six years after Sumner introduced these ideas and words into the national debate, Lincoln would memorably restate them in his Cooper Union address: "Let us have faith that right makes might."

After his disquisition on the legislative history of the Missouri Compromise and constitutional history of slavery, Sumner tore into Douglas. Sumner quickly shredded the perverse illogic of popular sovereignty. "By no rule of justice, and by no subtlety of political metaphysics, can the right to hold a fellow-man in bondage be regarded as essential to self-government. The inconsistency is too flagrant. It is apparent on the bare statement. It is like saying *two* and *two* make *three*. In the name of Liberty you open the door to Slavery." Then he called Douglas a "human anomaly, *a Northern man with Southern principles. Sir, no such man can speak for the North.*"

When Sumner had entered the Senate, Andrew Butler enjoyed a little light banter with him about Roman history and Latin. Butler flattered himself with these exchanges with the Harvard professor, whom he otherwise consigned to irrelevance. Sumner's mockery of Douglas was taken as a presumptuous and rude break with senatorial protocol. Southerners were granted full sway to deride "abolitionists," but now the New Englander was stepping out of place.

Two days after Sumner's oration, Butler rose to correct, rebuke, and humiliate him. He intended to give the professor a lesson on the subject of equality. Quoting Sumner's phrase, "Oh, Liberty! What crimes have been committed in thy name!," Butler instructed that "fanatical organization" would result in "breaking down the distinction between the black and the white man, and elevating one, or degrading the other to an equality, the horrors of the French Revolution, in all their frantic ferocity and cruelty, will be nothing compared to the consequences which must flow from such a state of things." Butler chided Sumner for "another remark," which "struck me as inappropriate. It was that in which he chose to draw a contrast between the civilization of the South, and that which must necessarily exist in the northern States, where they have not the institution of slavery." After referring to "General Washington, a slaveholder," Butler appealed to the authority of the Almighty. "Inequality seems to characterize the administration of the Providence of God. . . . Abolitionists cannot make those equal whom God has made unequal, in human estimation." Butler offered his evidence. "All history refutes it. Who ever heard of the African astronomer, statesman, general, poet?"

Having made his points historical and theological, Butler raised the sexual. He had prepared a graphic and pornographic coup de grâce to disgrace the Puritan. "Let us suppose," he began, "the case of a young man who never saw one of this race, and who might therefore be regarded as having no prejudice whatever. Take the case of a young gentleman of a romantic disposition, of high imagination, with all the gifts that could be bestowed upon him by nature." In other words, suppose it was Sumner. "Suppose it were proposed to him, that, if he would consent, he could marry an empress or a princess whose dowry was islands and provinces, who was possessed of the Archipelago of the South. Now, sir, just imagine that young gentleman to have such a proposition brought to him." Here the *Congressional Globe* recorded: "[Laughter.]" "The negotiation commences. The lady is to be introduced to him in a palace highly decorated and prepared for such an occasion. Remember, this young man never saw a black woman before, and therefore he has no prejudice at all. She may have observed all the rules of Marie Antoinette when she passed the confines of France. She may adopt her dress. She may have her ankles covered with pearls, and her fingers with rings of rubies and diamonds." Then Butler undressed her. "The young gentleman is standing near the altar of Hymen, of course with a palpitating heart. His betrothed is led out to him. He sees her white teeth; but lo! She has a black skin and kinky hair. [Laughter.] Now, what do you suppose that youth would say?"

Butler turned to Sumner to deliver his punch line. "Will the gentleman from Massachusetts allow me to borrow one of his quotations, and say, that if he could speak Latin, he would instantly exclaim: "*Monstrum, horren-*

dum, informe, cui lumen ademptum!" "[Laughter.]" Here Butler threw back at Sumner his reference to Virgil's Cyclops: "A monster, horrid, unformed, and blind." Sumner had used Virgil to describe the horror of slavery, but Butler turned the quote against Sumner to depict the sexual licentiousness of a black woman. "He would certainly insist that she was *lumen ademptum*, that the light of the sun had never shown upon her; and I have no doubt he would regard her as the daughter of *Nox*." Butler's reference to Nox was to the Greek goddess of darkness. "But sir, I rather think he would not have stopped to talk Latin at all; and he would not have required an engineer to show him the straightest way out of that palace." "[Laughter.]"

Butler came to the moral of his lascivious story. "Equality! Equality! I should like to see a play written on this subject. I have no doubt that the honorable senator from Massachusetts, with his taste and talent, could draw up one describing the scene which I have mentioned. He could depict the negro princess in search of a husband, and could take this scene as a practical illustration of its results!"

But it was not strictly a play that was on Butler's mind. "Here allow me to notice one remark which was made by the Senator from Massachusetts, which I think even common prudence or common delicacy would have suggested to him that he ought not to have made. He said that, wherever slavery existed, it was followed by sterility, ignorance, and the want of civilization, and that where it was it banished civilization. In what are the South inferior to the North." Sumner's remarks "may furnish materials for the theater," said Butler. "They may furnish materials for what I understand is a very popular novel—'Uncle Tom's Cabin.'"

Butler may have been more familiar with *Uncle Tom's Cabin* than he hinted. It was the greatest best-seller in the country's history, inspired a host of proslavery tracts and novels in reaction, and had been adapted into a play that was a sensational attraction staged in theaters across the country as well as in London and Paris. Harriet Beecher Stowe, the author, was known to be a friend and political ally of Sumner. Butler's *mis en scène* of the young black woman as the seductress of the naive New Englander was a mockery, "of some little ridicule," as he explained, and also one of the plot lines of *Uncle Tom's Cabin*.

The exact Latin line that Butler cited, "*lumen ademptum,*" was the very one that Stowe used to open her chapter on "The Slave Warehouse," describing a New Orleans auction where Uncle Tom and a beautiful mulatto slave girl named Emmeline are sold to the cruel Simon Legree. Before he purchases Emmeline, separating her from her mother, to be held as a sex slave, with his heavy, dirty hand he "drew the girl towards him, passed it over her neck and bust, felt her arms, looked at her teeth . . ." When Emmeline escapes from Legree's plantation as a fugitive, fleeing north to freedom, Uncle Tom, who refuses to divulge where she has gone, is whipped to death, achieving Christian martyrdom.

Butler offered his own counter-Tom morality play of unnatural attraction and natural repulsion in which the black woman was the seductress and the white man the innocent victim. That the man was a Northerner was part of the humor; that he was supposed to be Sumner made it hilarious. Southern men supposedly would have known to flee from the presence of the black temptress. The reality, however, was that black female slaves were exploited sexually by their masters, sold as concubines or "fancy girls," raped without legal consequence, and bore a slave population in the South before the Civil War of 10.4 percent mixed race, according to the historian John Hope Franklin. After the Fugitive Slave Act of 1850 was enacted, 46.5 percent of runaway slaves were identified as mulatto. Butler's perverse sex fantasy was intended to knock down the Puritan as a means of upholding Southern honor. His quotation from Latin was intended to strike down Sumner's erudition. His colorful description of a naked woman with "black skin and kinky hair" was his triumphant conclusion bashing the idea of equality. It was a verbal caning.

The next day, February 25, Butler resumed his attack along a broad front on Sumner, the Commonwealth of Massachusetts, and the North. "The pauperism, the lunacy, and the drunkenness of those States may be attributable to a very different cause, from the fact that they are a non-slaveholding population," Butler said. He ascribed to Sumner "an ideal standard of morality, emblazoned by imagination and sustained in ignorance, or, perhaps, more often planted by a criminal ambition and heartless hypocrisy." Once again, he referred to *Uncle Tom's Cabin*. "I appeal to those who hear me, if gentlemen who have gone to the South, who have lived amidst slaveholders, who have partaken of their hospitality, and have seen the administration of justice and all the graver forms of civilization there, are not better reconciled to the institution of slavery than that class and school of persons who read and take in their notions from 'Uncle Tom's Cabin'?" Abolitionism, he explained, was only one of "the *isms* which now pervade some portions of the North," and were "the cankers of theoretical conceit." "The most extraordinary development of that class of persons and that temper of society that gives rise to such *isms,*" he said, "is to be found in conventions of women, who step from the sphere prescribed to them by God, to enter into the political arena, and claim the rights of men."

Butler derided Sumner with a new scenario. If the South were "disposed to emancipate" the slaves and ship them to, say, Massachusetts, to "hand them over to the gentlemen's philanthropy," it would "resist them with the bayonet." Emancipation, Butler declared, "would be the most cruel act that had ever been done under the authority, or the guise, or the forms of law." The slaves would "inevitably perish," given their "habits, their inclinations, everything connected with them." "It would be a mercy to cut their throats sooner than condemn them to your philanthropy."

Butler concluded his two-day marathon with a flourish to prove that Sumner was little more than a preening hypocrite without moral or scholarly authority. Butler quoted one "Rev. Doctor Belknap," from a document of the Massachusetts Historical Society dated 1795: "Negro children were reckoned an encumbrance in a family; and, when weaned, were given away like puppies." Triumphantly, Butler proclaimed "the extract goes to show that the mind of Massachusetts was not always such as the gentleman would represent it now. It goes to show that she has been an anti-nigger State; and that when she had to deal with this class of persons practically her philanthropy became very much attenuated." Thus, he displayed the fruits of his research, or someone who aided him, to expose that neither Sumner nor Massachusetts had reason for its assumption of moral superiority.

But the surprise obscure quotation Butler used to clinch his argument was not proof of anything but his bogus scholarship and falsification of history. The "Rev. Doctor Belknap" he referenced was Jeremy Belknap, an important early abolitionist, pastor of Boston's Arlington Street Church, and founder of the Massachusetts Historical Society. In 1795, St. George Tucker, a law professor at William and Mary and federal judge, wrote Belknap requesting information on the process of how Massachusetts had abolished slavery by 1788 so that Virginia could follow its example. Belknap consulted more than forty knowledgeable men, from John Adams to Prince Hall, leader of Boston's free black community, in order to inform his history, "Queries Respecting the Slavery and Emancipation of Negroes in Massachusetts." Belknap wrote that only a "few only of our merchants" were engaged in the slave trade. "It was never supported by popular opinion. A degree of infamy was attached to the characters of those who were employed in it." That "Negro children" were "given away like puppies" was a practice Belknap attributed to cruel slave traders and against whom he himself had crusaded as one of the prominent petitioners responsible for passage of the act of the Massachusetts legislature that prohibited the slave trade and protected blacks from being "kidnapped or decoyed away from this commonwealth." Drawing on Belknap's work, Tucker wrote "A Dissertation on Slavery: With a Proposal for the Gradual Abolition of It, In the State of Virginia," which was rejected by the Virginia legislature, though he was sent a polite note.

At midnight on May 24, Sumner rose to speak against final passage of the Douglas bill. He presented a scroll two hundred feet long signed by clergymen from across New England as a petition against the "great moral wrong" of Douglas's Nebraska Act. Harriet Beecher Stowe financed the protest out of her royalties from *Uncle Tom's Cabin*. Douglas had excoriated the "political preachers" for "desecrating the pulpit, and prostituting the sacred desk to the miserable and corrupting influence of party politics." Sumner, however, held up the clergy as moral examples to his adversaries within the Senate, Butler, Mason, and Douglas. "Perhaps the Senator from South Carolina, who is not insensible to scholarship, might learn from them something of its graces. Perhaps the Senator from Virginia, who finds no sanction under the Constitution for any remonstrance from clergymen, might learn from them something of the privileges of an American citizen. And perhaps the Senator from Illinois, who precipitated this odious measure upon the country, might learn from them something of political wisdom.

"Sir, the bill you are about to pass is at once the worst and the best on which Congress ever acted," Sumner said. "Yes, Sir, Worst and Best at the same time. It is the worst bill, inasmuch as it is a present victory of Slavery. . . . Sir, it is the best bill on which Congress ever acted; for it annuls all past compromises with Slavery, and makes any future compromises impossible. Thus it puts Freedom and Slavery face to face, and bids them grapple. Who can doubt the result? It opens wide the door of the Future, when, at last, there will really be a North, and the Slave Power will be broken,—when this wretched Despotism will cease to dominate over our Government, no longer impressing itself upon everything at home and abroad."

Two nights later, on May 26, in Boston, free blacks and members of the Vigilance Committee attempted to enter the courthouse to free a fugitive slave, Anthony Burns, who was being held there. In the scuffle, a guard was killed. Boston was put under martial law as armed police and soldiers escorted the chained Burns to a ship in the harbor to return him to slavery.

The pro-Pierce newspapers in Washington pointed the finger of blame at

Sumner. "Boston in arms against the Constitution," decried the *Union,* "and an Abolition fanatic, the distant leader, safe from the fire and the fagot, he invokes from his seat in the Senate of the United States, *giving the command.* Men shot down in the faithful discharge of duty to a law based upon a Constitutional guaranty, and *the word which encourages the assassin* given by a man who has sworn on the Holy Evangelist and the presence of his Maker to support the Constitution of the country. But our Charles Sumner tell us a new era has been inaugurated." The *Star* threatened, "*Let Sumner and his infamous gang* feel that he cannot outrage the fame of his country, counsel treason to its laws, incite the ignorant to bloodshed and murder, and still receive the support and countenance of the society of this city, which he has done so much to vilify. While the person of a Virginia citizen is only safe from rudeness and outrage behind the serried ranks of armed men, Charles Sumner is permitted to walk among the 'slave-catchers' and fire-eaters' of the South in peace and security."

"Southern Men Threatening Personal Danger to Senator Sumner" ran the headline on the front page of the *New York Times* of May 31. "A strenuous and systematized effort is making here and in Alexandria, to raise a mob against Senator Sumner, in retaliation for the Boston difficulty. The Union newspaper's article on Sunday last is said to have been written by Senator Douglas. It looked directly that way. The Star of this evening has two articles, the incendiary purpose of which cannot be mistaken. Senator Sumner himself has been several times warned today of personal danger, and assured that persons bearing close relation to the Administration are inciting the people to violence against him."

The article in the *Washington Union* "said to have been written" by Douglas excoriated Sumner for his speech against Douglas's bill and issued a thinly veiled threat. "So infamous was this speech of the abolition agitator and incendiary that Judge Douglas rose in his place, and in substance declared it to be an invocation to civil war; predicting that if blood was shed in consequence of the harangue, the dark deed would be laid at the door of Sumner; and declaring his opinion that in the event of a rising against the guarantees of the constitution in Boston, he hoped that the punishment would not fall upon the misguided instruments of fanaticism, but upon the reckless and inhuman instigator to riot and to murder. This rebuke, terrible and sudden, and overwhelming as it was, was felt to be fully deserved by nearly every American citizen on the floor of the Senate."

"If you really think there is any danger worth mentioning, I wish you would telegraph me instantly," Joseph R. Hawley, chairman of the Free Soil Party of Connecticut, wrote Sumner. "I will come to Washington by the next train, and quietly *stay by*. I have revolvers, and can use them—and while there should not be a word of unnecessary provocation, still, if anybody in Alexandria or Washington *really* means to trouble you, or any other free Democrat there, you know several can play at that game." Sumner did not summon bodyguards, and he continued to walk around Washington un-armed. (Hawley would become a Union general, governor of Connecticut, and U.S. senator.)

"Slavery," Sumner pledged to Theodore Parker, "will be discussed with us as never before." And then he wrote defiantly: "The threats to put a bullet through my head, and hang me, and mob me, have been frequent. I have always said, 'Let them come; they will find me at my post.'"

After Southern senators objected to receiving the petition of New En-gland clergy against the Fugitive Slave Act, Sumner spoke again on June 26. Butler sharply attacked him, "whose whole style, tone, and character does not become a Senator." And he demanded, "I would like to ask the Senator, if Congress repealed the Fugitive Slave Law, would Massachusetts execute the constitutional requirements, and send back to the South the absconding slaves?" "Do you ask if I would send back a slave?" "Why, yes," said Butler. "Is thy servant a dog, that he should do this thing?" Sumner replied. Butler mocked his scholarship as effeminate, "the prettiest speeches I ever heard . . . too delicate for my taste." Then he chastised Sumner for saying it was "a dog's office to execute the Constitution of the United States."

Two days later, Sumner again spoke. "I choose to call things by their right name," he said. "And where a person degrades himself to the work of chasing a fellow-man, who, under the inspiration of freedom and the guid-ance of the north star, has sought a freeman's home far away from the coffle and the chain, that person, whomsoever he may be, I call a Slave-Hunter." Sumner called out Butler. "In fitful phrases, which seemed to come from the unconscious excitement so common with the senator, he shot forth var-ious cries about 'dogs,'" Sumner said, observing that Butler "has helped to nurture there a whole kennel of Carolina bloodhounds, trained, with savage jaws and insatiable scent, for the hunt of flying bondsmen. No, sir, I do not believe that there is any 'kennel of bloodhounds,' or even any 'dog,' in the Constitution of the United States." Then Sumner swiveled to address Mason, Butler's "associate leader in the wanton personal assault to which I have been exposed. . . . With imperious look, and in the style of Sir Forcible Feeble, that

Senator has undertaken to call in question my statement that the fugitive slave bill denied the writ of habeas corpus, and, in doing this, he has assumed a superiority for himself which, permit me to tell him now in his presence, nothing in him can sanction." Two days later, on June 28, Senator Clement Clay of Alabama took the floor to describe Sumner as "a sneaking, sinuous, snake-like poltroon," "a leper," "a filthy reptile," and compared him to the Charles Dickens character Uriah Heep of "mean, yet affected honor." Clay proposed to ostracize and expel him, "if we cannot silence him; of disabling, if we cannot disarm him. . . . If we cannot restrain or prevent this eternal warfare upon the feelings and rights of Southern gentlemen, we may rob the serpent of his fangs. We can paralyze his influence by placing him in that nadir of social degradation which he merits."

But the effort to remove Sumner from the Senate was abortive; "his triumph was complete," according to the *New York Times*. "Indeed," its correspondent noted, "it was only a few months ago, at a dinner party in this city, composed chiefly of Southern gentlemen, that one of the guests was covered with confusion in consequence of the open contempt he drew upon himself, by the avowal that he arrested the first 'nigger' under the Fugitive Slave act. Every Southern gentleman present freely expressed his abhorrence of such a 'duty'; and yet it is because of Senator Sumner's declaration that he will not be made a slave catcher, that the vials of personal abuse have been poured out on him."

In late 1854, he engaged in an unusual act to demonstrate the injustice of slavery. He purchased a seven-year-old slave girl whose skin complexion was that of a white child in order to emancipate her. Her name was Mary Mildred Botts. After the Anthony Burns affair, an escaped fugitive slave living as a free black in Boston, John Botts, was fearful that slave hunters would capture him. Working with the attorney for the Boston Vigilance Committee, John A. Andrew, abolitionists raised the money to buy his freedom and that of his wife and three children still held on a plantation in Virginia. Andrew, who was an activist in the Free Soil movement and would become governor of Massachusetts during the Civil War, contacted Sumner, who served as the agent for the transaction. In a letter to the *New York Times,* Sumner described "a child about seven years old, who only a few months ago was a slave in Virginia, but who is now happily free by means sent on from Boston, which I had the happiness of being entrusted with for this purpose. She is bright and intelligent—another Ida May. I think her presence among us will be more effective than any speech I can make."

Sumner's reference to "Ida May" was well understood. *Ida May: A Story of Things Actual and Possible* was a best-selling antislavery novel published in 1854. Inspired by *Uncle Tom's Cabin,* it told the melodramatic story of a beautiful white girl from a wealthy family living in Pennsylvania snatched by slave hunters who blacken her face and sell her into slavery. After many frightening episodes Ida May's long-lost father suddenly appears to rescue her. The notion of the girl's true whiteness made slavery seem even more barbarous. (The author, Mary Hayden Green Pike, was married to Frederick Augustus Pike, Speaker of the House in the Maine legislature, cofounder of the state Republican Party, and elected to the Congress during the Civil War. Her brother-in-law James S. Pike was the crusading antislavery Washington correspondent for the *New York Tribune*.)

Sumner had "created quite a sensation in Washington," the *New York Times* reported under the shocking headline: "A WHITE SLAVE FROM VIRGINIA." Purchasing the slave girl and the other members of her family, "he had thus become a slaveholder," the proslavery *Washington Star* jibed. "This, by the way, gave rise to some scurrilous rumors in reference to Mr. Sumner, which, in justice to him, we contradict." The newspaper referred to malicious gossip that the chaste Sumner was a pedophile. In fact, Sumner had the girl safely escorted by a guardian he designated to the offices of the *Times* in New York for the journalists to see her for themselves. She was, the *Times* reported, "a young female slave, so white as to defy the acutest judge to detect in her features, complexion, hair, or gen-eral appearance the slightest trace of negro blood." She was then taken to Boston where she was reunited with her father, the happy ending of *Ida May* but with a twist.

In the curious and poignant case of Mary Mildred Botts, Sumner advanced the political use of a startling new me-dium to establish indisputable facts—photography. Before she arrived in Boston, Sumner send a daguerreotype of her to his allies in the state legislature, who dis-played the astonishing picture at the State House. No one could doubt her existence. She was not a character from a novel, but a real-live girl.

Mary Mildred Botts

Fact collection was one of the most effective techniques of the antislavery movement. Theodore Weld, John Quincy Adams's assistant, who resided at Abolition House, the boardinghouse where Lincoln would take a room when he was a congressman, was the pioneer of the fact-based method. With the help of his wife, Angelina Grimké and her sister Sarah Grimké, abolitionists from a prominent South Carolina slaveholding family, he produced *American Slavery as It Is: Testimony of a Thousand Witnesses,* published in 1839. Harriet Beecher Stowe had buttressed her startling novel with *A Key to Uncle Tom's Cabin; Presenting the Original Facts and Documents Upon Which the Story Is Founded* in 1853. Sumner now provided through the incontrovertible evidence of photography a new level of fact-based argument, the visual proof of the ambiguity of race, showing a slave as the picture of a lovely white girl, not only possible but actual. But the question of skin color was also a question of sexual domination. Mulatto children were the offspring of masters and slaves. Pointing to the nearly white skin of slaves, he revealed the lurid reality of sexual control. Establishing the malleability of racial identity, Sumner further undermined the rationale for slavery.

Two months after Mary Mildred Botts had appeared as a freed girl in Boston, throughout a week in May 1855, Sumner delivered a lecture he entitled "The Antislavery Enterprise" to packed halls in New York City, reported day after day in the *New York Tribune* and in newspapers across the country. He denounced "the house of bondage" for its "deadly injury to morals, substituting concubinage for marriage, and changing the whole land of Slavery into a by-word of shame, only fitly pictured by the language of Dante, when he called his own degraded country a House of Ill Fame." The Slave Power was sexual power: slavery was rape; slaveholders were rapists. Shaming Southerners, Sumner excited hatred of himself to a fever pitch.

CHAPTER SEVEN

A VOICE FROM THE GRAVE

On Christmas Day 1855 Charles Sumner drove north from Washington to the Silver Spring house in Maryland of Francis P. Blair. It was for more than a holiday dinner. The gathering marked the true founding of the Republican Party.

From the moment that Douglas had introduced the Kansas-Nebraska Act a host of disparate protest groups had proliferated. One of the first consisted of thirty opponents, mostly Whigs, congregating on March 20, 1854, in a schoolhouse in Ripon, Wisconsin, who called themselves the Republican Party. Several thousand met at Jackson, Michigan, on July 6, 1854, under the banner of the Republican Party. All sorts of Free Soilers, Democrats, Whigs, and even some Know Nothings who called themselves Know Somethings rallied in anti-Nebraska groups adopting the Republican identification. In Springfield, Illinois, after Abraham Lincoln delivered a galvanizing speech against the Nebraska bill on October 4, a small group of local abolitionists asked him to

Francis Preston Blair

lead their new Republican Party, but Lincoln demurred, still thinking of himself as a Whig. In Ohio, in 1855, Salmon P. Chase was elected the first Republican governor. New state parties emerged from New York to Indiana, but there was no national party; nor was there a common platform or even general agreement on how to handle the Know Nothings.

Even before his election as governor, Chase was planning a campaign for president as the head of a party that did not yet exist. Imbued with a high sense of morality ingrained from being raised by his uncle who was the Episcopal bishop of Ohio, he had faced down proslavery mobs, earned the reputation of "attorney general of fugitive slaves," and laced his noble rhetoric with theological fervor. An image of dignity and assuredness, Chase's brilliant mind had charted constitutional arguments for a practical antislavery politics to set it apart from Garrison's radical abolitionism that cast the wrath of God on the framers as the source of evil and anything less than immediate emancipation as a pact with the devil. Chase's political odyssey was a map of antislavery politics. Beginning as a proper Whig lawyer in Cincinnati, he became a Democrat, left it for the tiny abolitionist Liberty Party, but felt confined by its rigid sectarianism, and founded the broader Free Soil Party, which he somehow saw as a vehicle for capturing and transforming the Democratic Party. Chase's profound and original insights into the law that framed the most important issues redefined the antislavery movement. But he carried a fatal flaw. He could not clearly read human nature and grasp the motives of others. His formidable intellect was connected to a nervous system that sometimes made his maneuvers seem clumsy and obvious. He had difficulty adjusting his public persona, burdened by a self-conscious vanity that made him avoid wearing glasses onstage, which made him seem condescending as he squinted at his audiences and spoke profundities. He was both visionary and myopic. His resolve to right the ultimate wrong was now matched by his monumental determination to become president. Chase tied his firm convictions and sharp tactics together with his certain belief that he was the best man—not simply the best man for the job, but also the best man of all men. His transparent self-esteem had the effect of putting his limitless ambition on constant parade. He began running for president in 1855 and would never stop plotting how to achieve it until his death in 1873.

"Good! Good! Good!" Sumner wrote Chase upon his narrow victory in winning the governorship of Ohio. In the fall elections of 1855 the old political lines were dissolving, but the new ones were still unformed. Old Whigs clung to the hulk of their sinking party, Democrats suddenly showed unexpected strength in Pennsylvania, anti-immigrant Know Nothings divided into warring factions, an antislavery one calling itself Know Somethings, and faded in some places but surged elsewhere. Chase was not a Know Nothing, but he trafficked with Know Nothings. He had beaten an Old Whig turned Know Nothing, Jacob Brinkerhoff, to gain the Republican nomination, and in private letters he disdained the nativist movement. But he was only able to cobble together the new Ohio Republican Party by giving the Know Nothings half the slots on the ballot. Before his election he worried that he would lose "on both sides, on American because not a member of the [nativist] order and on the naturalized because of the Know-Nothings on the ticket." Now, proposing himself as a presidential candidate he offered that unstable mixture as the foundation for a new party, dubbing it "the Ohio Plan."

Chase and his political agents circulated letters to Republican state chairmen and a few other influential men to seek interest in a preliminary gathering. By initiating the call, Chase hoped to preempt potential rivals such as Seward and Senator John P. Hale In his letter to Hale, Chase wrote that other Republicans were already suggesting him for the party nomination. He also sent a letter to Francis P. Blair, who masked his own plans. Chase had already offered himself "if necessary" as co-counsel in the Dred Scott case to his son Montgomery Blair, who was serving as the lawyer for the slave testing whether living in a free state gave him the right to sue for his freedom. Chase had consistently argued that point in cases on behalf of fugitive slaves since 1837, one of which Harriet Beecher Stowe transformed into a subplot of *Uncle Tom's Cabin*.

Chase was not the sole person who had approached Blair about joining the Republican movement. On June 19, 1855, Lewis Clephane, the business manager of *The National Era,* the antislavery newspaper in Washington, formed "a small club" called the Republican Association of Washington, and issued a platform signed by four others. *The National Era* had published *Uncle Tom's Cabin,* partly on Chase's initial suggestion that Stowe might write something for the paper. Its editor, Gamaliel Bailey, had been Chase's close friend and fellow antislavery crusader from Cincinnati, editor of a newspaper whose printing press was destroyed three times by proslavery mobs, even before Bailey and Chase had campaigned for the Liberty Party. Both were religiously motivated, but believed in political action, not just moral suasion. Bailey had moved to the capital to edit *The National Era* with Chase's encouragement. "In those days," recalled Clephane, "it was a crime to be called a Republican, and every man who was then known as a Republican was denounced as an Abolitionist." Stigmatized and minuscule, the Republican

Association of Washington decided to offer its presidency to the most formidable man they knew.

Francis Preston Blair, sixty-five years old, diminutive, bald, and skeletal, his jutting front teeth lending him a cadaverous look, presented himself as a country gentleman retired from the tumult of politics and devoted to riding his carriage between his mansion on Lafayette Park facing the White House and Silver Spring estate. None of his political acuity, however, had left him.

Blair had been recruited as a young man from Kentucky to edit the *Washington Globe* as President Andrew Jackson's political voice and became a trusted member of his Kitchen Cabinet, fighting Jackson's battles with his sharp pen against nullification and "the money power," against states' rights and privilege. Purged from the *Globe* under Polk at the instigation of Calhoun, Blair supported the presidential candidacy of Martin Van Buren in 1848 when he ran on the Free Soil ticket. Four years later, Van Buren backed Pierce, but Blair did not. His sons Montgomery and Francis Jr., protégés of Thomas Hart Benton, as though in an extended family, were deeply engaged in Missouri politics of which Montgomery's advocacy of the Dred Scott case was their latest project. Blair Sr. was hardly a relic, but as razor sharp as ever, still in possession of the thunder and lightning he let loose for Jackson, and enraged at the old enemies whose nefarious influence he detected in the current crisis. Jackson was dead; Blair was very much alive.

Since the passage of the Nebraska Act, Blair had been pulling wires for an independent presidential candidate. He quietly floated the idea of a Benton candidacy in late 1854, but Benton "kicked over the pail of milk," according to Blair, when he decided to battle his mortal enemy Senator David Rice Atchison for the Senate seat and conceded to the repeal of the Missouri Compromise. Blair turned his attention to Senator Sam Houston of Texas, who Blair wrote to Van Buren was "unstained." But Houston could not be corralled, flirted with the Know Nothings, and responded to Blair's go-betweens with noncommittal ambiguity. By late 1855, Blair began secretly plotting for the candidacy of Senator John C. Frémont of California, a military hero and Western explorer who happened to be Benton's son-in-law.

Blair arranged with the Republican Association that he would be elected its president but decline the honor in a letter explaining his reasons for supporting the organization that was published in newspapers across the country and circulated as a pamphlet. "This letter had a powerful effect upon the Democratic Party and caused many of them to desert their old party ties and unite with the Republican Party," Clephane recalled. Blair carried with him more than the musty mantle of Jackson as an ancient artifact, but acted as translator of the Jacksonian creed into the present. He personified its inner history, the keeper of the flame. Its battles were not over; nor had he mellowed with wealth, comfort, and age.

Blair's letter of December 1, 1855, redefined the Democratic tradition for the new movement. The repeal of the Missouri Compromise, he argued, was nothing less than a new version of nullification. "Yet nothing is clearer in the history of our Government than that this phrase, giving power to Congress 'to make regulations respecting the Territories,' was meant to give it the power to exclude slavery from them." Blair wrested Thomas Jefferson for the Republicans, reviewing the history of his authorship of the Northwest Ordinance prohibiting slavery in Western territories, and read out Stephen A. Douglas for abandoning the true Democratic legacy to "embrace Mr. Calhoun's doctrine." Despite John C. Calhoun's death five years ago, his concept that a state had the power to nullify federal law remained gospel among Southerners. Blair had not ceased railing against it. Now Blair denounced Douglas's unholy alliance and betrayal

> This repeal was the adoption of Mr. Calhoun's nullifying doctrine *in extenso.* The power of Congress to make laws excluding slavery forever from its Territories, *as such,* was denied, and all the Territories were opened to slavery, on the ground of the *"inalienable right"* of every citizen "to move into *any of the Territories with his property, of whatever kind or description"*; and the law of *squatter sovereignty* was superadded, and substituted for the sovereignty of the United States over the public domain. Thus fell, supported by the coalition effected between the Whigs and Democrats of the South, under the pressure and through the intrigues of the Nullifiers, Mr. Jefferson's noble principle, endeared to the country both for its moral grandeur and political wisdom. It is the first thought uttered in the Declaration of Independence; and to the denunciation of the king of Great Britain for the crime of bringing slavery to our shores, the original draft adds, as the deepest aggravation, that *"he has prostituted his negative for suppressing every legislative attempt to prohibit or to restrain this execrable commerce."*

Blair placed Douglas in league against both Jefferson and Jackson. "The Administration has staked itself on the support of the party of privilege—of class interest—which makes it a unit. It confides in the success which has crowned the oligarchy everywhere in the Old World, and secured its triumphs on the maxim, *'Divide and conquer.'* The Whigs and Democrats of the South are a combination, to carry into the next Presidency some candidate absolute in maintaining the repealing clause of the Kansas bill, which nullifies the principles of the Ordinance, the provisions of the Constitution made to give them effect, and all the Compromises which have been made in pursuance of them, with the sanction of all sections of the Union." Blair confidently summoned a future Jackson to the presidency. "Mr. Atchison's attempt by an armed force to carry out the nullification plotted of the caucus which gave birth to the Kansas bill will, like the attempt of his prototype, Mr. Calhoun, to give effect to South Carolina nullification, be paralyzed by the frown of an indignant nation, made potent by as honest and firm Executive. And there will end the career of those gentlemen who arrogate to themselves the exclusive tutelage of the Democracy of the country, as ended that of Mr. Calhoun and his proselytes, who took the peculiar charge of the *'State Rights'* party."

"FRANCIS P. BLAIR TURNED BLACK REPUBLICAN" read the headline in the *Washington Union.* "We have been reluctant to credit the rumor that for several days has represented Francis P. Blair, esq., as a convert to black republicanism . . . the blackest treason to a party on which he reposed for years with all the upholding power of its great champion, Andrew Jackson." "Mr. Blair was prepared for this, as a matter of course," the *New York Times* reported, "and he knew perfectly well what kind of epithets would be heaped upon his head by many of his former political associates; and he will not be dismayed by the Union's attempt to annihilate him."

Blair's fierce argument was finely honed to stigmatize Douglas among Northern Democrats, invoke the household gods of Jefferson and Jackson for the Republicans, avoid the more radical abolitionist demands, and establish the broadest platform for the broadest possible coalition.

His letter set the stage for Christmas at Silver Spring. Only Blair had the authority to convene the select company, and he possessed decades more political experience at the center of power than any of those he invited. He wanted to see the array of men reveal themselves around his table. Sumner and Chase came, as well as Gamaliel Bailey, Nathaniel Banks, and Congressman Preston King of New York. Seward was invited, but he demurred because, as he explained to Thurlow Weed, he was wary of Chase's alliance with the Know Nothings.

The dinner party to create the political party not only brought certain key people together but also laid bare their tensions. While King agreed with Chase that a new Republican Party should adopt Chase's Ohio Plan regarding the Know Nothings, Bailey, who was Chase's oldest and closest friend, called the Know Nothings "detestable" and said, "I cannot go with you into any organization with Republicans and Know Nothings." Sumner was also openly against the Know Nothings. "Ourselves children of the Pilgrims of a former generation, let us not turn from the Pilgrims of the present," he told a crowd in Boston on November 2. Those at the dinner agreed that the first matter at hand was to elect Banks as Speaker of the House, which was accomplished in February 1856. Among the guests, only Chase held presidential aspirations for himself. But Blair raised the possibility of Frémont, whom he had secretly met with in August 1855 as a first step and to whom Banks was confidentially committed. Chase didn't appear to grasp that Blair's suggestion would doom his ambition; nor was he informed of the background of Blair's intrigue. A week later, at Blair's urging, Preston King called on Seward, who had been conspicuously absent. Delegations from all the Northern states were prepared to participate in a convention based on the Ohio Plan, except New York, King told him, and without New York there could be no true national party. Seward replied that he "disavowed all connection or sympathy with such a combination" with Know Nothings, and that he would only support a candidate for president "distinctly on grounds other than, and different from 'Know Nothingism.'" Momentum for the new party gathered without consensus.

The year 1856 opened in Boston with the "lords of the loom" choreographing a public lashing of Sumner. William Appleton and Nathan Appleton, the quintessential Cotton Whigs, cousins living on Beacon Hill, were at the center of a complex web of economic and social networks consisting of dozens of directorships of industries, banks, and cultural institutions. Both had served as Whig congressmen. Now they invited Senator Robert Toombs of Georgia, who owned or controlled more than one thousand slaves, to speak on January 26 at the Tremont Temple. Toombs had been a Whig, but with the dissolution of the party was drifting toward the Democrats and supporting Douglas for the nomination. His speech was a pointed rebuttal of everything Sumner represented. The framers were not antislavery, the Constitution not antislavery, nor could the Congress prohibit slavery in the territories. Slavery was moral, just, and noble, reflecting "a higher civilization." "No stronger evidence of what progress society may make with domestic slavery can be desired, than that which the present condition of the slaveholding States presents." The Appletons led the crowd in giving Toombs three cheers. But a voice shouted out from the back of the hall, "When will Charles Sumner be allowed to speak in the South?"

The palpable sense of disquiet permeating politics, apparent in forums for slavery even at Faneuil Hall, was the consequence of rising uncertainty over the emergence of the Republican Party, the discrediting of the Pierce administration, and fear that control over events was slipping away. Yet events unexpectedly began to fall into place for the Republicans.

After Blair's Christmas summit, Clephane circulated a call for a Republican National Convention. Five governors promptly signed it. The organizing convention took place at Pittsburgh on February 22, 1856. Blair presided as its president. He was depicted as reluctantly drawn back into politics, yet somehow he managed to be at its center and to have his goals achieved. Henry J. Raymond, the editor of the *New York Times* and a Seward protégé, wrote the single plank of the platform urging that "constitutional means" be implemented against the extension of slavery. Horace Greeley supported the cautious but unifying approach, which carefully avoided mention of the Fugitive Slave Act. While some radical abolitionists like Owen Lovejoy of Illinois enthusiastically participated in the new party, others denounced it as impure. "There is not a single warm and living position, taken by the Republican party," Frederick Douglass wrote, "except freedom for Kansas." Meanwhile, the Know Nothing (or American Party) convention held on the same day at Philadelphia splintered with the antislavery faction walking out. Its internal contradictions began to resolve the question for Republicans of an open alliance. On April 29, Blair sent a letter to a meeting in New York of antislavery Democrats to urge them to join the Republicans. It was published as a pamphlet entitled *A Voice from the Grave of Jackson!* "To use a homely phrase," he said, "*the Democracy has sold out*' to Mr. Calhoun's nullifying party."

When Jackson died he bequeathed his papers to Blair as the executor of his literary estate. But Blair served as more than the curator; he felt entitled to judge who was entitled to a claim of the Jacksonian political legacy. In his New York speech, Blair presented a history of Jackson's disillusion with a number of the pretenders to his creed. Blair put Douglas in the list of "the elements of that spurious Democracy which General Jackson's intuitive sagacity foresaw would be the offspring of the political embraces of Calhoun, Tyler, and Polk." Douglas had worshipped Jackson as his hero since he was a boy. It was his formative political experience. He had traveled in a pilgrimage of a group of Democrats in 1844 to pay his respects to the failing Jackson at the Hermitage at Nashville. Upon "convulsively shaking the aged veteran's hand," he was described as "speechless." In January 1853, Douglas delivered the speech to dedicate the statue of Jackson in Lafayette Park, his hat lifted in a permanent salute to the nearby White House that Douglas wished to inhabit. But now Blair relegated him to the category of "traitor."

The walls were closing in on Douglas, the swinging scythe lowering. The inexorable fateful date of the Democratic National Convention, June 2, 1856, could not be avoided. His presidential campaign, well plotted on paper, had flopped in reality. His effort to unite the hostile factions of New York behind him failed. His support in the Northwest states, his home base, crumbled. His backing in the South never materialized. Residual sentiment for Pierce shut him out in New England. Douglas was always a gambler, and he threw the dice on the final breakdown of Pierce and the collapse of the inert but artificially rejuvenated candidacy of James Buchanan. Safely exiled as minister to England and therefore untouched by the administration's downfall, Buchanan had been preserved through a kind of diplomatic mummification.

Pierce's vacuum set nearly everybody within the party scrambling, finger-pointing at would-be culprits and seeking "Anybody But Pierce." Alexander Stephens, of Georgia, who had switched from the Whig to the Democratic Party, blamed the Kansas crisis on Pierce's "fickleness, weakness, folly and vacillations." Douglas's original sin in the eyes of "the most influential men from the North," Stephens wrote, was that his candidacy "defeated Buchanan and caused Pierce an outsider to be taken up," which had created "the almost death struggle before us." Douglas could not be forgiven for the political warfare he had set in motion out of his own ambition; nor could he remove the blot of his disastrous campaign of 1852.

Douglas's room for maneuver for the nomination was rapidly contracting. The party whose nomination he sought was disintegrating in great part from his efforts to gain that prize. The Democrats had lost control of the House of Representatives to the anti-Nebraska coalition drawn from the defection of antislavery Democrats. Douglas was already a rump Northern Democrat. Enemies North and South were determined to deprive him of the nomination. His borrowed principle of popular sovereignty was exposed as a transparent veil for the Ruffians in Kansas. He sought to ascend as a new Jackson, but Blair stripped him of Old Hickory's aura. Between debilitating bouts of the alcoholism that would eventually kill him, Douglas lashed out in the Senate against "the black Republicans," trying to play to the gallery of his party. But he was even gasping for breath in Illinois.

The only way for Douglas to maintain control of the Illinois Democratic Party was to purge it. At the Democratic state convention on May 1, the first order of business was a resolution declaring Senator Lyman Trumbull "a recreant traitor, the representative of fusion, who held his seat in opposition to the Democracy of Illinois, which passed unanimously, amid much enthusiasm and excitement," reported the *Quincy Daily Whig*. "Next a resolution declaring Douglas the true representative of the Democratic party, &c, was passed by acclamation." But one of Douglas's closest allies on the scene, Congressman Thomas L. Harris, wrote him that Douglas's men at the state convention "came near botching the whole business." Until this moment Trumbull had been uncertain about joining the Republicans and hesitant about participating in its upcoming convention on May 29. He was wary of the Whigs on the one hand and of abolitionists on the other. But being purged resolved his dilemma. The cleansing of Trumbull was the decisive sign to antislavery Democrats that they should follow him out of the party. Douglas's purification movement was a reduction. He had to weaken the party in order to save himself. Those eliminated had nowhere to turn but to a new party, even if some still insisted on calling themselves Democrats.

"Doing Him Honor," read the headline on the *Illinois State Journal,* the newspaper closely associated with Lincoln, who, with Herndon, often wrote editorials. "The Douglas Democracy in the late Convention, passed a resolution denouncing Senator Trumbull, in the most savage terms. The people of the State, who believe that the Constitution was formed for some other and higher object than only to extend negro slavery, will be glad of this. Trumbull, by his manly and high-toned course in the U.S. Senate, never stood higher in the public estimation than he does at the present time. His failure to receive the endorsement of the slavery propagandists and Douglas fuglemen, will entitle him still more to the confidence of all conservative and freedom loving people of the State and of the United States. Denunciations from such a source are in an eminent degree honorable, and Senator Trumbull will be gratified, to have received them."

"An Evil Genius" headlined the editorial on Douglas's presidential candidacy in the *New York Times* of May 3.

Before Mr. Douglas began his manipulations upon the party, two years and more ago, it had just emerged from one of its most brilliant campaigns. . . . Opposition was paralyzed, and even discredited. . . . Then began the services of Mr. Douglas to the party, upon which his claims are rested. . . . By what conjuration, what mighty magic, the little enchanter has contributed thus to cover his triumphant friends with shame and disaster, some may be bold enough to inquire. . . . The canvass of 1852 had taught his party how to triumph; he has taught it how to secure defeat, and demands as reward the symbols reserved for victorious leaders. . . . Should his resumption meet no repulse, the fact will class with the curiosities of history. Mr. Douglas is the evil genius of his party . . . he has made a certain busy cunning (with which he happens to be unsparingly gifted) a successful tributary to his ambition. A truculent audacity of language and manner have disguised this low grade of intellectual elevation, and even passed him off upon the unobservant as a man of the most candid purposes, and the most courageous mode of advancing them. . . . In the indulgence of this conscienceless thirst for public attention and discussion, economy of principle and prosperity of party seem to be equally immaterial.

The high-pitched hostility toward Douglas emanating from the *Times,* along with other Republican newspapers, came partly from their concern that he might well emerge as the Democratic nominee.

By mid-May, Douglas established his headquarters in the convention city of Cincinnati at the best hotel, Burnet House, where a New York financier, Edward C. West, picked up the tab for Douglas's contingent and provided a freely flowing bar. The pro-Douglas newspapers in town were hard at work. The *Cincinnati Enquirer* advanced the Douglas-inspired notion of a Pierce-Douglas convention alliance of convenience to thwart Buchanan while the *Cincinnati Gazette* sought to discredit Buchanan's supporters as "weak-backed and weak-kneed syllabub politicians." Meanwhile, the pro-Republican *Cincinnati Commercial* anticipated Douglas's candidacy with coruscating pieces flowing from the acidic pen of Murat Halstead, the newspaper's part-owner, chief editorialist, and political correspondent. On "The Honorable Mister Douglas," he wrote: "An exposed political empyric; a dishonest truckler for unsound popularity; a false pretender to notions of honor, and a foul-mouthed bully self-convicted of cowardice, though a coat of whitewash a foot in thickness would not cause him to pass for a gentleman, it cannot be denied that he will make a most admirable candidate. We hold up multitudinous hands for his nomination. The party should take him—certify him—swear he is what he professes to be. It will not be the first time that an ill-conditioned ape has been exalted to a deity—probably not the last."

In Washington, on May 18, Toombs staged a large dinner party at his house to help promote Douglas's candidacy. He invited former congressman John C. Breckinridge, of Kentucky, who leaned to Douglas, his real estate partner. Senator Lewis Cass, of Michigan, who had been the Democratic nominee in 1848, and now supported Buchanan, was there. So was Howell Cobb, along with the entire Georgia delegation, which had stopped in the capital on the way to the convention. But Cobb also backed Buchanan. Douglas was not making much progress in prying people away, though he hoped that by combining forces with Pierce at the convention to create a stalemate he might produce a political miracle. Douglas's nerves were more on edge than usual; for more than the nomination struggle was coming to a climax.

Newspapers across the country were emblazoned with screaming headlines of the impending final clash in Kansas. Indictments in hand, the U.S. marshal had begun wholesale arrests of free state leaders. On May 15, the proslavery *Lecompton Union* newspaper reported: "Large companies from all sections of the Territory are gathering to Douglas County, in obedience to the proclamation of the United States Marshal. . . . Rebels should be treated as rebels. The people of Lawrence have a great deal to answer for before they can receive quarter." Ruffians were joined by hundreds of newly arrived Southerners under the command of "Major" Jefferson Buford, an Alabama slaveholder, who generously footed their expenses. The militias, calling themselves the "Red Shirts" and "Kickapoo Rangers," swelled around the presence of Senator Atchison near Lecompton, armed with guns and four cannon dispensed from federal arsenals. Deputized on the spot by the U.S. marshal as his posse, the ragtag army of about eight hundred men rallied under two flags. One was red, inscribed "Southern Rights," with a verse underneath, "Let Yankees tremble, abolitionists fall, Our motto is, Give Southern rights to all." Another, a black flag, was inscribed with the inscription, "South Carolina Minute Men," above a coiled snake, the symbol of the revolutionary Gadsden flag. "Blood for Blood! Let us purge ourselves of all abolition emissaries," exclaimed the proslavery newspaper, the *Squatter Sovereign,* published in the town of Atchison.

On May 19, the *New York Tribune* published dispatches from the front lines of Kansas that "show the operation of 'We shall subdue you' in full blast," an intimidating threat attributed to Douglas. "We must respond through the ballot box," the paper editorialized. The approaching national election loomed as a reckoning.

As Charles Sumner carefully prepared his speech on Kansas to be delivered before the Senate in Washington on May 19, he had a sense of foreboding. "The session will not pass without the Senate chamber's becoming the scene of some unparalleled outrage," he wrote a friend in Boston earlier in the year.

CHAPTER EIGHT

THE HARLOT SLAVERY

I n this dark midnight hour," as Stephen A. Douglas steamrolled the Nebraska Act through the Senate in 1854, Sumner pledged, "I struggle against it as against death." He was being informed of the events on the ground in Kansas by a constant stream of letters and reports from free state settlers and the chief organizers of the New England Emigrant Aid Society, including its founder, Eli Thayer, who wrote Sumner he would be in the Senate gallery to hear him deliver his speech, "to do us justice."

The authors of the Kansas debacle had in fact sought to subdue Sumner—Douglas and the members of the F Street Mess, including Andrew P. Butler and James M. Mason, the sponsor of the Fugitive Slave Act, among others. Douglas charged that he had "stolen" his Senate seat through "larceny" and tarred him as one of the soiled "black Republicans." Butler humiliated him for sexual naïveté and luridly suggested he lusted after young black women. Mason insulted him for his "vapid, vulgar declamation," the speech

Margaret Garner and her children, sketch by Thomas Satterwhite Noble

"of a fanatic, one whose reason is dethroned." They denigrated his manner of speaking, his education, and his scholarship. They derided his state of Massachusetts as a bastion of racism no different from any Southern state except for its hypocrisy. They assaulted Sumner's character, his dignity, and his patriotism. They called him "a serpent," "a filthy reptile," "a leper," and "a maniac." Sumner prepared to vindicate himself, his ideals and heritage. He would expose their pretention, duplicity, and shabbiness. He would unmask their gentility as a disguise for a society rooted in violence, sexual predation, and speculation in human property. He would reveal their presumption to claim the American tradition and the values of Western civilization as little more than a deceitful and thinly transparent cover for slavery.

Sumner scorned the Southern aristocratic manner as the pretentious affectation of well-heeled barbarians. His disdain for them was exceeded only by his contempt for Douglas and his "vulgar swagger." "Douglas," he said, "in private life is a brutal vulgar man without delicacy or scholarship; he is filthy in his person; he always looks as if he needed clean linen and should be put under a shower bath."

But any speculative search for Sumner's motives in the deliverance of his speech should look no farther than the first governor of the Massachusetts Bay Colony, John Winthrop, whom he had cited in his 1850 speech against the Fugitive Slave Act as the original authority on resisting unjust laws against liberty. Winthrop's sermon in 1630 had been engraved on Sumner's soul: "We shall find that the God of Israel is among us, when ten of us shall be able to resist a thousand of our enemies; when He shall make us a praise and glory that men shall say of succeeding plantations, 'may the Lord make it like that of New England.' *For we must consider that we shall be as a city upon a hill. The eyes of all people are upon us. So that if we shall deal falsely with our God in this work we have undertaken, and so cause Him to withdraw His present help from us, we shall be made a story and a by-word through the world.*"

No less than George Washington had paraphrased these words after winning the Revolution in his farewell letter to the army in 1783 to challenge Americans with their responsibility to make a new nation: "*This is the time of their political probation, this is the moment when the eyes of the whole World are turned upon them, this is the moment to establish or ruin their national Character forever.*"

Stepping to the well of the Senate on May 19, 1856, to deliver his speech on "The Crime Against Kansas" and surveying the array of notables among the packed galleries, Sumner felt "the eyes of the whole world" upon him as he decried the "hundred eyes" of the Slave Power.

"Notwithstanding the heat, with the thermometer at ninety, nearly all the senators were in their seats, and galleries and lobbies and doorways were crowded with a compact mass of spectators, even the anteroom being opened to ladies after their own gallery had been filled," wrote Charles Sumner's biographer, Edward L. Pierce. "Every journalist's desk was occupied. The members of the House were present in large numbers,—[Joshua] Giddings conspicuous among the Republicans, and [Alexander] Stephens among the Southern leaders. Delegates from the South, on their way to the Democratic national convention soon to meet at Cincinnati, went that morning to the Capitol to witness the novelty of an abolition spectacle. Veteran politicians not in public life—as Francis P. Blair, Sr., Thurlow Weed, and Robert J. Walker, the former senator from Mississippi and Polk's Secretary of the Treasury—were observed in the throng. While the scene was well fitted to inspire the speaker, there was a pervading sense in the audience that violence and bloodshed were imminent in Kansas." Surveying the packed chamber, Douglas remarked, "There are too many people here."

Sumner would speak all day but did not finish that night and so spoke through the next day as well. He began with an appeal to American citizenship as a natural right, undefined in the Constitution until the Fourteenth Amendment. Just as in the case of *Roberts v. the City of Boston* challenging school segregation, in which he had introduced the idea of "equality before the law," and in his speech on "Freedom National, Slavery Sectional," arguing that slavery had no justification as a federally created institution, he invoked the inherent rights of citizenship, which would not be defined in the Constitution until passage of the Fifteenth Amendment in 1870. Summoning from ancient history the cry against tyranny, "I am a Roman citizen," Sumner raised the cry, "I am an American citizen," against "Tyrannical Usurpation" in Kansas.

Sumner explained at length constitutional, historical, and political issues, but his most recurrent metaphor used to describe the Slave Power was sexual. "The wickedness which I now begin to expose is immeasurably aggravated by the motive which prompted it. Not in any common lust for power did this uncommon tragedy have its origin. It is the rape of a virgin Territory, compelling it to the hateful embrace of Slavery, and it may be clearly traced to a depraved desire for a new Slave State, hideous offspring of such a crime, in the hope of adding to the power of Slavery in the National Government." His choice of sexual metaphor—of rape—was not chosen lightly but to shock into recognition of the actual conditions of slavery's submission and oppression—lust, rape, illegitimacy, and prostitution. Now the Slave Power was the rapist, Kansas the virginal victim.

Slavery as a system of political power was nothing less than an all-encompassing criminal enterprise, from the highest office to the lowest.

> Such is the Crime which you are to judge. The criminal also must be dragged into day, that you may see and measure the power by which all this wrong is sustained. From no common source could it proceed. In its perpetration was needed a spirit of vaulting ambition which would hesitate at nothing; a hardihood of purpose insensible to the judgment of mankind; a madness for Slavery, in spite of Constitution, laws, and all the great examples of our history; also a consciousness of power such as comes from the habit of power; a combination of energies found only in a hundred arms directed by a hundred eyes; a control of Public Opinion through venal pens and a prostituted press; an ability to subsidize crowds in every vocation of life,—the politician with his local importance, the lawyer with his subtle tongue, and even the authority of the judge on the bench,—with a familiar use of men in places high and low, so that none, from the President to the lowest border postmaster, should decline to be its tool: all these things, and more, were needed, and they were found in the Slave Power of our Republic.

Here Sumner was reversing the terms of those senators who called him a criminal for opposing the Fugitive Slave Act and instead implicating them in a vast crime. His quotation from *Macbeth*—"vaulting ambition"—alluded to the driven Douglas, the indispensable enabler.

In describing the crime, Sumner argued that Winthrop's Puritan commonwealth and Washington's American nation had been turned inside out and upside down. Rather than being governed by the spirit of Washington, "vaulting ambition" held sway. Reason was overthrown by folly, the Constitution trampled by force and corruption, the people themselves manipulated through a "prostituted press" (another sexual metaphor), and officials betrayed their oaths for the slightest nod from power. Winthrop's "eyes of all the people" and Washington's "eyes of the World" were transformed into "a hundred eyes" of oppressive control, which Sumner further described as a "Great Terrestrial Serpent," slithering to "coil about the whole land."

Sumner explained that his speech would expose the full extent of the

"Crime Against Kansas," the "Apologies for the Crime," and the "True Remedy." It was a report from the front lines, citing letters and newspaper articles; a master class in classical allusion, quoting Roman historians and poets; and a Puritan jeremiad condemning the fall from grace. In style Sumner adopted the formalities of Demosthenes, paragon of ancient reason, to render judgment with the wrath of John Milton.

The first part of his speech tore the mask off Southern honor. The second part demolished the defenses of the "tyrannical" (the Ruffians), the "imbecile" (Pierce), the "absurd" (Douglas's popular sovereignty), and the "infamous" (Douglas's slander), which he compared to the witches of *Macbeth*. "Tyranny, imbecility, absurdity, and infamy all unite to dance, like the weird sisters, about this crime." In the final part, he posed "the Remedy of Injustice and Civil War"—"fratricidal, parricidal war with an accumulated wickedness beyond that of any war in human annals"—against that of "Justice and Peace."

The crime he described was against more than a territory; it was a crime against the whole country. The offense he himself was committing in their eyes—the crime of delivering his speech—was to speak without hesitation or hedging against the Slave Power. "The severity of Sumner's attacks is not altogether shown in their printed form," wrote Anna Laurens Dawes, a biographer and daughter of a U.S. senator from Massachusetts who was a political contemporary of Sumner. "In manner as well as words, this Northern miscreant, this Yankee, showed an absolute and overwhelming scorn and contempt for the Southern chivalry; this was the insult that made injury a crime." Sumner had already given offense, but he had barely begun to offend.

He decided to single out his chief tormentors "who had singled him out for special attack," according to Senator Wilson. It was Sumner's "occasion to repay them for their assaults." But Sumner's reprisal was intended to be far more than any personal rebuke, but to demolish each and every aspect of the Southerners' social identity, political legitimacy, and rhetorical intimidation. He did not stop at the usual harsh condemnations. He defied the unspoken convention not to speak of the sexual hypocrisy at the core of slavery.

His particular targets were Butler and Douglas. "Before entering upon the argument, I must say something of a general character, particularly in response to what has fallen from Senators who have raised themselves to eminence on this floor in championship of human wrong: I mean the Senator from South Carolina and the Senator from Illinois who, though unlike as Don Quixote and Sancho Panza, yet, like this couple, sally forth together in the same adventure."

Using Cervantes's *Don Quixote* as his text, Sumner depicted Butler as addled with delusions of his misplaced medieval code.

> I regret much to miss the elder Senator from his seat; but the cause against which he has run a tilt, with such ebullition of animosity, demands that the opportunity of exposing him should not be lost. . . . The Senator from South Carolina has read many books of chivalry, and believes himself a chivalrous knight, with sentiments of honor and courage. Of course he has chosen a mistress to whom he has made his vows, and who, though ugly to others, is always lovely to him,—though polluted in the sight of the world, is chaste in his sight: I mean the harlot Slavery. For her his tongue is always profuse in words. Let her be impeached in character, or any proposition be made to shut her out from the extension of her wantonness, and no extravagance of manner or hardihood of assertion is then too great for this Senator. The frenzy of Don Quixote in behalf of his wench Dulcinea del Toboso is all surpassed.

Sumner's description of Butler in thrall to "the harlot Slavery" was his riposte to Butler's lascivious portrait of Sumner panting after an African princess. Sumner ridiculed Butler and implicitly his pornography in order to expose the cruelty behind the courtly lord. "The asserted rights of Slavery, which shock equality of all kinds, are cloaked by a fantastic claim of equality. If the Slave States cannot enjoy what, in mockery of the great fathers of the Republic, he misnames Equality under the Constitution,—in other words, the full power in the National Territories to compel fellow-men to unpaid toil, to separate husband and wife, and to sell little children at the auction-block,—then, Sir, the chivalric Senator will conduct the State of South Carolina out of the Union! Heroic knight! Exalted Senator! A second Moses come for a second exodus!"

Sumner threw back at Butler his pejorative words "sectional" and "fanatical," intended to discredit Republicans as hostile to the accepted basis of the Union, which was slavery. "To be sure," said Sumner, "these charges lack all grace of originality and all sentiment of truth; but the adventurous Senator does not hesitate. He is the uncompromising, unblushing representative on this floor of a flagrant sectionalism, now domineering over the Republic,—and yet with a ludicrous ignorance of his own position, unable to see himself as others see him, or with an effrontery which even his white head ought not to protect from rebuke, he applies to those here who resist his sectionalism the very epithet which designates himself."

Sumner turned to Douglas, portraying him as the dutiful assistant to his befuddled lord. "As the Senator from South Carolina is the Don Quixote, so the Senator from Illinois is the squire of Slavery, its very Sancho Panza, ready to do its humiliating offices. This Senator, in his labored address vindicating his labored report,—piling one mass of elaborate error upon another mass,—constrained himself, as you will remember, to unfamiliar decencies of speech."

But Douglas was more than the dutiful subordinate encouraging his superior's delusions. It was Douglas, according to Sumner, who was the originator of the infected debate. "I will not stop to repel imputations which he cast upon myself; but I mention them to remind you of the 'sweltered venom sleeping got,' which, with other poisoned ingredients, he cast into the caldron of this debate." Here Sumner shifted his metaphoric description of Douglas from Cervantes to Shakespeare, quoting the witches' incantation over their boiling pot from *Macbeth*.

"Of other things I speak," said Sumner. "Standing on this floor, the Senator issued his rescript requiring submission to the Usurped Power of Kansas; and this was accompanied by a manner—all his own—befitting the tyrannical threat. Very well. Let the Senator try. I tell him now that he cannot enforce any such submission. The Senator, with the Slave Power at his back, is strong; but he is not strong enough for this purpose."

Sumner was warming to his subject. Butler and Douglas were accessories "to the final Crime"—the crime against democracy. Here Sumner described the crime as sexual and the sexual as treasonous.

If that be the best government where injury to a single citizen is resented as injury to the whole State, what must be the character of a government which leaves a whole community of citizens thus exposed? In the outrage upon the ballot-box, even without the illicit fruits which I shall soon exhibit, there is a peculiar crime, of the deepest dye, though subordinate to the final Crime, which should be promptly avenged. In other lands, where royalty is upheld, it is a special offence to rob the crown jewels, which are emblems of that sovereignty before which the loyal subject bows, and it is treason to be found in adultery with the queen, for in this way may a false heir be imposed upon the State; but in our Republic the ballot-box is the single priceless jewel of that sovereignty which we respect, and the electoral franchise, where are born the rulers of a free people, is the royal bed we are to guard against pollution. In this plain presentment, whether as regards security or as regards elections, there is enough, without proceeding further, to justify the intervention of Congress, promptly and completely, to throw over this oppressed people the impenetrable shield of the Constitution and laws. But the half is not yet told.

Sumner told the story of the crushing of democracy in Kansas as fully as he could piece it together from his sources, but he also referred to other stories about other places. He invoked two notorious incidents whose mere mention would have alarmed his Southern listeners. Both of these stories lifted the flimsy cover of Southern honor to reveal the rape of black female slaves and the reality of mulatto children. This was "the half" that was not yet told.

In pointing to slavery's "dread of which mothers have taken the lives of their offspring," Sumner highlighted the horrific case of Margaret Garner that had recently been the subject of sensational reports filling newspapers across the country. Garner was a twenty-three-year-old mulatto slave who was likely the daughter of her Kentucky plantation owner, John P. Gaines, a former congressman. He sold his estate and slaves to his brother Archibald, who would have been her uncle, and likely and repeatedly impregnated Garner, who gave birth to four children. She fled in January 1856 with other slaves in a dash for freedom to Ohio, but was cornered in a farmhouse by slave catchers and federal marshals. She killed her two-year-old with a knife and attempted to kill the other children and herself before she was captured. Her sensational trial, just three months before Sumner spoke, featured the testimony of Lucy Stone, the abolitionist and feminist, who had become Garner's confidante as she awaited judgment. "The faded faces of the Negro children tell too plainly to what degradation the female slaves submit," Stone told the court. "Rather than give her daughter to that life, she killed it." "The murdered child was almost white, a rare child of beauty," recalled Levi Coffin, the conductor of the Underground Railroad, who had arranged the slaves' escape, in his memoirs. (Garner was returned to slavery and died of typhoid. Her story was the inspiration for Toni Morrison's novel *Beloved,* published in 1987, which was awarded the Pulitzer Prize.)

In Sumner's aside characterizing one of his "hostile" tormentors, Senator James M. Mason of Virginia, "who, as author of the Fugitive Slave Bill, has associated himself with a special act of inhumanity and tyranny," he raised yet another sensational case. "Of him I shall say little," said Sumner, "for he has said little in this debate, though within that little was compressed the bitterness of a life absorbed in support of Slavery. He holds the commission of Virginia; but he does not represent that early Virginia, so dear to our hearts, which gave to us the pen of Jefferson, by which the equality of men was declared, and the sword of Washington, by which Independence was secured: he represents that other Virginia, from which Washington and Jefferson avert their faces, where human beings are bred as cattle for the shambles, and a dungeon rewards the pious matron who teaches little children to relieve their bondage by reading the Book of Life. It is proper that such a Senator, representing such a State, should rail against Free Kansas."

The "pious matron" was Margaret Douglass, a Southern widow and Bible teacher who established a school for black children in Norfolk, Virginia, and in 1854 was sentenced to prison for one month to serve "as an example," according to the judge. In her speech to the court, she spoke plainly about the sexual reality of her mixed race pupils. "Ask how that white blood got beneath those tawny skins. . . . Blame the authors of this devilish mischief, but not the innocent victims of it." After she was released from jail, Douglass wrote a book in which she stated that sexual predation was at the root of the degradation of the South.

> In this truth is to be found the grand secret of the opposition to the instruction of the colored race. . . . It is the one great evil hanging over the Southern slave States, destroying domestic happiness and the peace of thousands. It is summed up in the single word—amalgamation. . . . The white mothers and daughters of the South have suffered under it for years—have seen their dearest affections trampled upon—their hopes of domestic happiness destroyed, and their future lives embittered even to agony. . . . Southern wives know that their husbands come to them reeking with pollution from the arms of their tawny mistresses. . . . Is there any wonder then that people addicted to these habits are rapidly returning to a state of semi-barbarism? The female slave, however fair she may have become, by the various comminglings of her progenitors, or whatever her mental and moral acquirements, knows that she is a slave, and as such, powerless beneath the whims or fancies of her master. . . . How important, then, for these Southern sultans, that the objects of their criminal passions should be kept in utter ignorance and degradation.

Abolitionists widely circulated Douglass's book, and Southern authorities widely resented it. The infamous case of the Virginia schoolteacher and her startlingly frank opinions would have been very familiar to Senator Mason of Virginia.

Images of rape permeated Sumner's speech. He quoted from the Roman poet Ovid's *Metamorphoses* to compare Kansas being raped by the Slave Power to a damsel being raped: "Oh, help, she cried, in this extremist need . . ."

Sumner's exposé of the sexual underside of slavery was his most profound offense. No senator had ever openly discussed the salacious side of slavery from so many different angles. Abolitionist pamphlets and books like Douglass's were routinely banned from the U.S. mail in Southern states or forbidden by local authorities from circulating. But nobody could stop a senator from rightfully holding the floor. Once Sumner spoke, his words were in the *Congressional Globe* and reported far and wide. Breaking the existing gag rules, unofficial and official, he was breaking precedent and protocol. He was opening a new rhetorical front against slavery. The slave South was hardly the highest stage of civilization, but a vast brothel.

Sumner's picture of the domestic life of slavery resonated for years throughout the South. "Sumner said not one word of this hated institution which is not true," wrote Mary Chesnut, the wife of James Chesnut of South Carolina, a U.S. senator and leader of the secession movement, in her diary a month before the war began in March 1860. She was especially fixated on Sumner's remark about "the harlot Slavery."

> Men and women are punished when their masters and mistresses are brutes and not when they do wrong—and then we live surrounded by prostitutes. An abandoned woman is sent out of any decent house elsewhere. Who thinks any worse of a Negro or Mulatto woman for being a thing we can't name. God forgive *us*, but ours is a *monstrous* system and wrong and iniquity. Perhaps the rest of the world is as bad. This is *only* what I see: like the patriarchs of old, our men live all in one house with their wives and their concubines, and the Mulattos one sees in every family exactly resemble the white children—and every lady tells you who is the father of all the Mulatto children in everybody's household, but those in her own, she seems to think drop from the clouds or pretends so to think—.

When Butler drew a picture of an imaginary naked and beckoning black woman on the floor of the Senate in order to humiliate Sumner he was acting as a Southern gentleman, but when the Puritan depicted the sexual degradation of slavery he was cast as a belligerent. Sumner sought to strip Butler of the pretensions that composed his distinguished and refined personage. On a subtle level, Sumner cited in passing St. George Tucker, the antislavery Virginian, a scholarly dismissal of Butler's counterfeit learning. On a less subtle level, he said, "With regret I come again upon the Senator from South Carolina, who, omnipresent in this debate, overflows with rage at the simple suggestion that Kansas has applied for admission as a State, and, with incoherent phrase, discharges the loose expectoration of his speech, now upon her representative, and then upon her people."

Butler had intervened in the debates on Kansas thirty-five times in addition to his formal speeches. He did let loose some expectoration when he spoke as a result of a slight paralysis of his face from a stroke. Yet Sumner's phrase—"the loose expectoration of his speech"—was one he had used in private to refer to the depravity of proslavery justifications. He had written his brother George Sumner in 1852 about the Southern domination of Washington, "In truth, slavery is the source of all our baseness, from gigantic national issues down to the vile manners and profuse expectorations of this place."

Sumner made immediately clear in his speech he was referring to Butler's false, "incoherent," and "foul-mouthed" proslavery positions. "There was no extravagance of the ancient Parliamentary debate which he did not repeat; nor was there any possible deviation from truth which he did not make,— with so much of passion, I gladly add, as to save him from the suspicion of intentional aberration. But the Senator touches nothing which he does not disfigure—with error, sometimes of principle, sometimes of fact. He shows an incapacity of accuracy, whether in stating the Constitution or in stating the law, whether in details of statistics or diversions of scholarship. He cannot ope his mouth, but out there flies a blunder."

Sumner cited a diplomatic episode involving Benjamin Franklin to portray Butler as "a foul-mouthed speaker."

> Surely he ought to be familiar with the life of Franklin; and yet he referred to this household character, while acting as agent of our fathers in England, as above suspicion: and this was done that he might give point to a false contrast with the agent of Kansas,—not knowing, that, however the two may differ in genius and fame, they are absolutely alike in this experience: that Franklin, when entrusted with the petition of Massachusetts Bay, was assaulted by a foul-mouthed speaker where he could not be heard in de-

fense, and denounced as "thief," even as the agent of Kansas is assaulted on this floor, and denounced as "forger." And let not the vanity of the Senator be inspired by parallel with the British statesmen of that day; for it is only in hostility to Freedom that any parallel can be found.

Sumner's disparaging slights were exactly targeted. They homed in on Butler's speech—precisely his incapacity of speech. Belittling Butler's "vanity," Sumner destroyed each element of his argument as well as deriding the manner of his speech. Butler's slavering style represented his substance; his physical deficiency was a manifestation of his intellectual deficiency. Unlike the threats that Douglas made against Sumner, Sumner did not menace with harm but with mockery.

Sumner defended the Bay State's pride denigrating the Palmetto State's disgrace. Butler had accused the Commonwealth of Massachusetts of being the source of disunion and violence. "Pray, Sir," said Sumner, "by what title does he indulge in this egotism? Has he read the history of the 'State' which he represents? He cannot, surely, forget its shameful imbecility from Slavery, confessed throughout the Revolution, followed by its more shameful assumptions for Slavery since. He cannot forget its wretched persistence in the slave trade, as the very apple of its eye, and the condition of its participation in the Union. He cannot forget its Constitution, which is republican only in name, confirming power in the hands of the few, and founding the qualifications of its legislators on 'a settled freehold estate of five hundred acres of land and ten negroes.'" South Carolina, declared Sumner, was "in the very ecstasy of madness." He questioned whether "the whole history of South Carolina blotted out of existence, from its very beginning down to the day of the last election of the Senator to his present seat on this floor, civilization might lose—I do not say how little."

Even more than Butler, Douglas was Sumner's target. Butler carried more social prestige as an elder of the F Street Mess, but Douglas was more formidable and dangerous as an adversary in debate. Sumner unleashed his full repertoire of erudition against him. Douglas was more than Sancho Panza. Sumner quoted at length in Latin from Cicero's denunciation of Catiline, the conspirator against the Roman republic. "As I listened to the Senator from Illinois," said Sumner, "while he painfully strove to show that there is no Usurpation, I was reminded of the effort by a distinguished logician to prove that Napoleon Bonaparte never existed." Sumner called forth the unholy trinity from John Milton's *Paradise Lost*—Satan, Sin, and Death. Again, Sumner raised an image of rape through poetic citation, for Satan raped his daughter Sin, who gave birth to Death. The imposition of slavery on Kansas was "a Dance of Death." "Popular Sovereignty, in whose deceitful name plighted faith was broken and an ancient Landmark of Freedom overturned, now lifts itself before us like Sin in the terrible picture of Milton." Douglas, the author of "popular sovereignty," assumed the role in this allegory of Satan, progenitor of Sin, who is the mother of Death.

> The Senator from Illinois naturally joins the Senator from South Carolina, and gives to this warfare the superior intensity of his nature. He thinks that the National Government has not completely proved its power, as it has never hanged a traitor,—but, if occasion requires, he hopes there will be no hesitation; and this threat is directed at Kansas, and even at the friends of Kansas throughout the country. Again occurs a parallel with the struggles of our fathers; and I borrow the language of Patrick Henry, when, to the cry from the Senator of "Treason! treason!" I reply, "If this be treason, make the most of it." Sir, it is easy to call names; but I beg to tell the Senator, that, if the word "traitor" is in any way applicable to those who reject a tyrannical Usurpation, whether in Kansas or elsewhere, then must some new word, of deeper color, be invented to designate those mad spirits who would endanger and degrade the Republic, while they betray all the cherished sentiments of the Fathers and the spirit of the Constitution, that Slavery may have new spread.

Accused of "treason" Sumner launched in return a quiver of arrows at Butler and Douglas. The word "treason" took several forms in Sumner's speech. One was the sexual "treason" of rape at the root of slavery. There was also the "treason" against the American Revolution and the Constitution. The "treason" that Douglas had accused Sumner of committing for which the punishment would be hanging Sumner transformed into a holy crucifixion and Douglas into the ultimate betrayer. "Let the Senator proceed. Not the first time in history will a scaffold become the pedestal of honor. Out of death comes life, and the 'traitor' whom he blindly executes will live immortal in the cause. 'For Humanity sweeps onward: where to-day the martyr stands, On the morrow crouches Judas, with the silver in his hands.'" The lines casting Douglas as Judas were quoted from the antislavery poem "The Present Crisis" composed by James Russell Lowell, who belonged to Sumner's circle in Boston and would the following year become the founding editor of *The*

Atlantic Monthly. (Lowell's poem would inspire the name of the National Association for the Advancement of Colored People's journal, *The Crisis*, edited by W.E.B. DuBois, and Dr. Martin Luther King would freely quote the poem in his speeches.)

For his peroration, Sumner summoned Dante, who had consigned his enemies to the sufferings of the Inferno for their cowardice—the "Great Refusal." Sumner warned the Congress to abandon its cowardly avoidance of slavery or be condemned to the fires of eternal damnation. "Let it now take stand between the living and dead, and cause this plague to be stayed. All this it can do; and if the interests of Slavery were not hostile, all this it would do at once, in reverent regard for justice, law, and order, driving far away all alarms of war; nor would it dare to brave the shame and punishment of this 'Great Refusal.'"

Rising from the rings of the Inferno, Sumner ascended to the heights of patriotism—to Washington's words to "the good people of Boston" bravely resisting the British in the Revolution. "Above all towers the majestic form of Washington, once more, as on the bloody field, bidding them remember those rights of Human Nature for which the War of Independence was waged. Such a cause, thus sustained, is invincible."

Surrounding himself with the emblems of the American Revolution, Sumner concluded his epic oration. At once the wounded senators leaped up to excoriate him. Senator Lewis Cass, of Michigan, who had been the dreary and defeated Democratic presidential nominee in 1848, pronounced the speech "the most un-American and unpatriotic that ever grated on the ears of the members of this high body."

Douglas took the floor to add his disparagement with more than a hint of threat. "Is it his object to provoke some of us to kick him as we would a dog in the street, that he may get sympathy upon the just chastisement?" He assumed a pose of indignation at Sumner's scholarship as the ravings of a pornographer. Douglas was appealing to the resentment of the Southerners at Sumner's sexual critique of slavery. "We have had another dish of the classics served up—classic allusions, each one only distinguished for its lasciviousness and obscenity—each one drawn from those portions of the classics which all decent professors in respectable colleges cause to be suppressed, as unfit for decent young men to read. Sir, I cannot repeat the words. I should be condemned as unworthy of entering decent society, if I repeated those obscene, vulgar terms which have been used at least a hundred times in that speech."

Then Douglas belittled Sumner by drawing a scene in which he was preening for a black boy with its barely concealed slander of homosexual pedophilia. "The Senator from Massachusetts had his speech written, printed, committed to memory, practiced every night before the glass, with a negro boy to hold the candle and watch the gestures, and annoying the boarders in the adjoining rooms until they were forced to quit the house."

Senator Mason took his turn to condescend to the unworthy member from Massachusetts, the genteel aristocrat acknowledging the unmanly Sumner only to describe him as belonging to a caste beneath contempt—"associations here whose presence elsewhere is dishonor, and the touch of whose hand would be a disgrace. . . . I have said that the necessity of political position alone brings me into relations with men upon this floor who elsewhere I cannot acknowledge as possessing manhood in any form. I am constrained to hear here depravity, vice in its most odious form uncoiled in this presence, exhibiting its loathsome deformities in accusation and vilification against the quarter of the country from which I come; and I must listen to it because it is a necessity of my position, under a common government, to recognize as an equal politically one whom to see elsewhere is to shun and despise."

Sumner would not reply to Cass. "Nothing I say can have anything but kindness for him," he said. He swiveled to Douglas. "To the Senator from Illinois I should willingly yield the privilege of the common scold—the last word; but I will not yield to him, in any discussion with me, the last argument, or the last semblance of it. He has crowned the outrage of this debate by venturing to rise here and calumniate me." After reviewing his previous debate with Butler on the Fugitive Slave Act, Sumner chided Douglas for his personal attacks.

> Perhaps I had better leave that Senator without a word more; but this is not the first, or the second, or the third, or the fourth time that he has launched against me his personalities. Sir, this is the Senate of the United States, an important body under the Constitution, with great powers. Its members are justly supposed, from years, to be above the intemperance of youth, and from character to be above the gusts of vulgarity. . . . Let the Senator bear these things in mind, and remember hereafter that the bowie knife and bludgeon are not proper emblems of senatorial debate. Let him remember that the swagger of Bob Acres and the ferocity of the Malay cannot add dignity to this body. The Senator infused into his speech the venom sweltering for months—ay, for years; and he has alleged matters entirely without foundation, in order to heap upon me some personal obloquy. I will not descend

to things which dropped so naturally from his tongue. I only brand them to his face as false. I say also to that Senator, and I wish him to bear it in mind, that no person with the upright form of man can be allowed . . .

"Say it," demanded Douglas.

"I will say it," replied Sumner. "No person with the upright form of man can be allowed, without violation of all decency, to switch out from his tongue the perpetual stench of offensive personality. Sir, that is not a proper weapon of debate, at least on this floor. The noisome, squat, and nameless animal to which I now refer is not the proper model for an American Senator. Will the Senator from Illinois take notice?"

"I will—and therefore will not imitate you, Sir." "I did not hear the Senator."

"I said, if that be the case, I would certainly never imitate you in that capacity—recognizing the force of the illustration."

"Mr. President," said Sumner, "again the Senator switches his tongue, and again he fills the Senate with its offensive odor. But I drop the Senator."

Douglas took offense, but may not have understood the erudition of the insult. The reference to the "noisome, squat, and nameless animal" was to a creature only disguised as an animal. On November 2, 1855, in a speech at Boston's Faneuil Hall, Sumner had rehearsed some of the themes and language he would use in his "Crime Against Kansas" oration. He declared that the "authors [of popular sovereignty] follow well the example of the earliest Squatter Sovereign—none other than Satan—who, stealing into Eden, was there discovered, by the celestial angels, just beginning his work; as Milton tells us, '—him there they found / Squat like a toad, close to the ear of Eve.'"

Sumner now faced Mason. "There was still another, the Senator from Virginia, who is now also in my eye. That Senator said nothing of argument, and therefore there is nothing of that to be answered. I simply say to him that hard words are not argument, frowns are not reasons, nor do scowls belong to the proper arsenal of parliamentary debate. The Senator has not forgotten that on a former occasion I did something to exhibit the plantation manners which he displays. I will not do any more now."

Thirteen years later, the journalist Donn Piatt recalled that Douglas muttered to him as Sumner spoke: "That damn fool will get himself killed by some other damn fool." Double, double, toil and trouble.

The Senate adjourned.

"You had better go down with Mr. Sumner. I think there will be an assault upon him," Congressman John A. Bingham, Republican from Ohio, warned Senator Wilson of Massachusetts. "Do you think so?" asked Wilson. "I have heard remarks made, from which I think an assault will be made," said Bingham. Bingham would later say that he thought Douglas's remark to "kick" Sumner "was designed to produce or encourage an assault." Wilson recruited two Republican congressmen, Anson Burlingame of Massachusetts and Schuyler Colfax of Ohio, to serve as bodyguards. "I am going home with you today—several of us are going home with you," Wilson told Sumner. But Sumner waved them off. "None of that, Wilson." He walked out alone, caught up with Seward on the street, with whom he had planned to have dinner, but Seward suggested that he go directly to the printing office to oversee the proofs of his speech.

The next day, on the floor of the House, Congressman Thomas Rivers of Tennessee was heard loudly holding forth in conversation that Sumner "ought to be knocked down, and his face jumped into," and that he "hoped" someone "would whip him, and put his foot upon his face."

CHAPTER NINE

THE ASSASSINATION OF CHARLES SUMNER

Early the next morning, on May 21, nearly one thousand Border Ruffians deputized as a posse to enforce writs of treason and sedition appeared on the bluffs overlooking the free state town of Lawrence. Anticipating the attack, the Committee of Safety had decided that able-bodied men should evacuate and residents were urged to offer no resistance.

David Rice Atchison, "Bourbon Dave," the former president pro tempore of the Senate, and acting vice president of the United States, rode as the commander of the Ruffian army. Blustery and belligerent, Atchison had loomed as a monumental figure at the F Street Mess. Born in Frogtown, Kentucky, he had been a rough-hewn classmate at Transylvania University of the polished Jefferson Davis, made his career on the Missouri frontier as a stalwart proslavery Democrat. After Atchison ousted the seemingly

Southern Chivalry, lithograph by John L. Magee

eternal old Jacksonian Thomas Hart Benton in 1851 from his Senate seat, which he had held for thirty years, Benton waged a crusade to regain his rightful place. Benton always fought to the death, sometimes literally, once killing a man in a duel. "Bourbon Dave" equated his endangered career to a mortally threatened South. He swooned from the vertigo of his vulnerability. He had quit his Senate seat to lead the Ruffians on the Kansas battlefield in the belief that a final victory there would enable him to vanquish Benton once and for all in the 1856 Senate race.

Atchison sent a scouting party that discovered "most of the arms-bearing population whisked away like sea-birds blown landward by a tempest," according to an account. The deputy U.S. marshal, however, found three men to arrest for treason. Atchison, Sheriff Samuel J. Jones, the U.S. marshal and his deputy, and the militia officers rode into the town, where the proprietor of the Free State Hotel invited them to have lunch without charge. After finishing the meal, the militias were marched down from the hills under their flags, one proclaiming "Supremacy of the White Race."

The Ruffians broke into the offices of the two newspapers, the *Free State* and the *Herald of Freedom,* and smashed the printing presses. Some men marched around with books stuck on their bayonets. Books and papers were strewn across the streets. The men invaded the Free State Hotel where they raided the wine and liquor cabinets. Five cannon opened fire on the building. Four barrels of gunpowder were ignited to blow up what remained. Observing the flames, Jones said, "This is the happiest moment of my life." The houses and stores were looted. Charles Robinson's house was torched. One Ruffian was killed from a fallen brick at the Free State Hotel. Another accidentally shot himself; yet another fell off his horse. Atchison was observed walking off with a box of cigars stolen from the hotel, a modest prize of war. (In early 1857, the Atchison-Benton contest for the Senate seat ended after forty-one deadlocked ballots in the Missouri legislature with a third candidate walking over their bodies. Their match was a political murder-suicide with both men attempting to murder the other and both committing suicide.)

"LAWRENCE TAKEN! GLORIOUS TRIUMPH OF THE LAW AND ORDER PARTY OVER FANATICISM IN KANSAS!" exulted the *Lecompton Union* on May 21. "Thus fell the Abolition fortress; and we hope this will teach the Aid Society a good lesson for the future. . . . If every man of them had been killed, every house burned, and total and entire extermination had been the motto of the 'Law-and-Order Party,' who would be to blame?"

"Important from Kansas: A General Reign of Terror" ran the *New York*

Times headline on May 22, reporting the march of the Border Ruffians on Lawrence just before its sacking. The *Washington Union* published a lengthy article, "General Jackson Vindicated Against Mr. Blair's Imputation of Black Republicanism," which the paper called "wicked" and a "crime," and another piece attacked the *New York Times* for its "black-Republican" coverage of Kansas, and charged it was "controlled by its abolitionist associations and sympathies." The *Illinois State Journal* of that day featured a call "To the Citizens of Sangamon County," from those "opposed to the repeal of the Missouri Compromise, and who are opposed to the present Administration," to a meeting on the 24th in Springfield to select delegates to the state convention of the new Republican Party to be held the following week. The first name on the list was "A. Lincoln."

As Sumner's crime against Kansas speech was playing out in all its prescient ugliness, it was about to spark another crime, but in Washington. After Sumner had refused Senator Wilson's offer to escort him safely home, Wilson stayed behind to write a letter at his desk. His eye caught that of a congressman who had wandered onto the Senate floor and stationed himself in a nearby seat, and they silently bowed to each other. He was Preston S. Brooks, of South Carolina. At the time, Wilson didn't know his name and watched as Brooks limped away on his cane.

The next evening, with news of the sacking of Lawrence spreading, Brooks and his two congressional companions, Laurence M. Keitt and Henry A. Edmundson, stalked into Gautier's on Pennsylvania Avenue, the best restaurant in Washington, where Sumner often dined, "and, after carefully scanning the faces of the people at the table, walked out without having seated themselves," failing to find their prey, according to an account by a confidant of Sumner.

Preston Smith Brooks was born in 1819 at the pinnacle of the South Carolina plantation elite, the eldest son of one of the oldest and wealthiest families of upcountry Edgefield, the most productive district in the land of cotton. The plantation elite was intricately intermarried and interlinked politically, socially and

Preston Brooks

economically, a class ruling over a small middle class, a larger poor white class, and a majority slave population. The wealthiest, the core of this ruling class, comprised merely 136 people, according to the historian Orville Vernon Burton. Entrance into this class was almost uniformly based on inheritance. Intelligence, ability, and work had little to do with it. This elite fashioned itself an aristocracy, though it was only two or three generations rooted as a ruling class. Its noble tradition was recently invented.

As the natural crucible of John C. Calhoun and the nullification movement, the dynamic in Edgefield drove its political figures relentlessly toward ever more extreme positions, violence, and ultimately secession. The leading men of Edgefield envisioned themselves as the vanguard of South Carolina and South Carolina as the vanguard of the South. Within Edgefield politics was factionalized into shifting warfare among personalities, families, and competing interests. Violence was the fierce and frequent reflex of the slaveholder aristocrats against each other in a primal struggle of ambition (according to the Code Duello), against individual upstart whites that refused to know their place, against slaves repressed through a police state, and against errant Northern outsiders who might have the least criticism of slavery. Physical shows of force, brutality, and intimidation were not only the routine instruments of the system but also customs of the country. Violence was exalted as the bright red banner of true manhood, the test of vigor and courage, the heart of a romantic ideal of dashing conquerors over the conquered. Generations of political violence and extremism would prevail in Edgefield in an unbroken line beyond the Civil War from the Red Shirt militia of Ben "Pitchfork" Tillman that overthrew Reconstruction government and disenfranchised blacks to the career of Tillman's closest adviser's son, J. Strom Thurmond, the U.S. senator, Dixiecrat presidential candidate, and father of the Southern strategy that transformed the modern Republican Party as well as an unacknowledged mulatto daughter.

Preston Smith Brooks, scion of Roseland, a large Edgefield plantation, was bred with the concept of honor. But he spent virtually his entire life in embarrassing episodes failing to fulfill its ideal. He grew up in the shadow of legendary heroes, from Revolutionary War forebears to his cousin James Butler Bonham, who died at the Alamo. Yet Brooks was a constant source of disappointment to his father, Whitfield Brooks, Sr., a veteran of the War of 1812 called the Colonel. At South Carolina College, "a favorite with the ladies," Brooks was disciplined for drinking and suspended for threatening another student with a gun. On the eve of his graduation, he tried to bust his younger brother out of jail, where he was imprisoned for obstreperous behavior, threatened the sheriff, and was expelled. At once, Brooks challenged another wild young man from Edgefield to a duel. Louis T. Wigfall, yet another son of a rich merchant and plantation family, notorious for his violence, drinking, and gambling, had killed Brooks's cousin in a duel. Brooks sought revenge against his father's wishes. "I'll kill Wigfall!" he shouted. On an island in the Savannah River they fired at ten paces, wounding each other. Brooks was left with a limp and a cane. (Wigfall would become a fire-eating secessionist U.S. senator from Texas.) Hoping his wastrel son would improve with responsibility upon his marriage, Brooks's father bestowed upon him a large plantation called Leaside and eighty slaves over whom he could preside as the master. But Brooks proved himself to be indolent and dissolute. "He is deficient in moral energy and decision in mental activity and is too indulgent in mere physical gratifications," sadly wrote Whitfield Sr.

Then an exceptional opportunity appeared. Governor James Henry Hammond, whose political career the Brooks family had long promoted, appointed young Brooks as his aide-de-camp. Brooks soon found himself thrust into the middle of a clash of civilizations. In 1844, the Commonwealth of Massachusetts officially designated Samuel Hoar, the eminent lawyer and former congressman, as commissioner to gather the facts for lawsuits against South Carolina for the imprisonment and selling into slavery of free black seamen from Massachusetts who landed in South Carolina. At Hammond's direction, the legislature passed a resolution calling for the expulsion of the "northern emissary." After a mob threatened the Charleston hotel where Hoar stayed, a delegation led by the sheriff and mayor physically escorted him into a carriage to leave immediately or else face removal by force. Upon his return home, Hoar recounted to his friend Ralph Waldo Emerson that his initial answer was "that he could not and would not go, and that he had rather his broken skull should be carried to Massachusetts by somebody else, than to carry it home safe himself whilst his duty required him to remain." But he finally felt he had no choice. The incident, "contributed largely to the bitter feeling between the two sections of the country, which brought on the Civil War," wrote George F. Hoar, the commissioner's son and later U.S. senator from Massachusetts. Henry David Thoreau, one of Hoar's neighbors, cited the event as part of his justification for protesting slavery and the Mexican War in his essay of 1849, "On the Duty of Civil Disobedience." Sumner gave a case history of "this shameless, lawless act," in a speech in 1854 to the Senate calling for repeal of the Fugitive Slave Act.

Hammond had ordered his new aide-de-camp to go to Charleston and take the Northern agitator to a waiting boat, but Brooks arrived after Hoar had already left. Brooks managed to miss being at the center of the action. Hammond described him as "a mal-apropos young man of little talent, fidgety to be doing [and] always moving in the wrong time and place."

The declaration of war with Mexico provided yet another chance for Brooks to prove himself worthy. His cousin Colonel Pierce Mason Butler offered him a captainship in the Palmetto Regiment of South Carolina Volunteers. Shortly after his arrival in Mexico, however, Brooks collapsed with typhoid fever and returned home an invalid. "[I must regain] before the people of my district the confidence and respect of which I value more than life itself," he wrote a friend, "[and I must overcome] the extreme regret and mortification . . . that I feel on account of being denied the privilege of playing my part in the great battles." Suffering from ridicule he hobbled back to the front without orders only to discover the war had ended. His young brother Whitfield Jr. and two of his cousins, including Colonel Butler, meanwhile, had fallen heroically in battle. His commander reported that the younger Brooks asked as his dying words, "Have I discharged my duty?" Whitfield Sr. eulogized his namesake son as "the noblest son that father ever raised"—a slight to Preston—and died of heartbreak within a year. At the Edgefield Fourth of July celebration of Mexican War veterans in 1849, Brooks was pointedly excluded from participation. Humiliated, he attacked the "courage" of a cousin, Milledge Luke Bonham, who was also kept from the ceremony because he had accidentally been wounded in the foot and missed the war. Bonham, the younger brother of the Alamo martyr, challenged Brooks to a duel. Brooks sought a way out. Through the intervention of Hammond, the two men decided the better part of valor was to avoid murdering each other. (Bonham would serve as a Confederate general and governor during the Civil War.)

Seeking the distinction that had serially eluded him, Brooks ran in 1853 for the congressional seat once held by John C. Calhoun. "My experience in life," he explained to a friend, "has taught me that the best way to keep from being *run over* is to *run over* some body myself, politically." He faced a field of three opponents, the most formidable of whom was Francis W. Pickens, Calhoun's cousin and Andrew Butler's nephew. Pickens was an ardent nullifier, who had criticized Calhoun later in his life for being too moderate. (Pickens would serve as the governor who introduced the South Carolina Ordinance of Secession in 1860.) Brooks won with only 32 percent of the vote. His initial victory with such a narrow plurality was a precarious one, especially in volatile

Edgefield. He identified himself with a faction called the National Democrats that sought to exercise influence for the cause of Southern states' rights within the party. His credibility as a National Democrat rested on the party nominating a reliable proslavery candidate for president. For the first time, South Carolina Democrats held a state convention to select delegates to the national convention. They were exposed to withering charges of betrayal from the pro-secessionist nullifiers such as U.S. senator Robert Barnwell Rhett and his son Robert Barnwell Rhett, Jr., editor of the *Charleston Mercury.* Senator Butler at first reinforced the fire-eaters, but then reluctantly declared he would yield to "the tide of events and the current of public opinion" so long as it did not "let us de-Carolinaize ourselves." Brooks leaned toward the unpopular President Pierce, whose fraying hope dangled on his alliance of convenience with Douglas. But disdain for Pierce ran high among most Southerners and many Northern Democrats, still angry about his early efforts to bring Free Soilers back into the party fold through patronage and his appointment of Reeder as territorial governor to Kansas, which Alexander Stephens wrote "was to make Kansas a free State." Sumner's inflammatory speech was delivered just as tension was building within the Democratic Party to a crescendo over its undecided nominee and unsure future. The more provocative Sumner's language, the more he excited the fire-eating Southern Ultras, in turn menacing the party regular National Democrats who required proof of militancy to hold their ground. With every phrase, Sumner tightened the vise.

Within the House, Brooks was a virtual nonentity. He sponsored no bills, held no responsibility, and wielded no influence. His speeches were conventional Southern apologetics and little noticed. In explaining his support for the Kansas-Nebraska Act, he offered a rote encomium for slavery. "The history of the African contains proof upon every proof of his utter incapacity for self-government. . . . The institution of slavery, which it is so fashionable now to decry, has been the greatest of blessings to this entire country." On December 24, 1855, the day before adjournment for Christmas, in support of a motion upholding the repeal of the Missouri Compromise, which was already an accomplished fact, he postured for the benefit of the Ultras back home: "But, sir, when they [Free Soilers] make a distinct, tangible issue upon the constitutional rights of the South, then I know where to find them. . . . Here is the place to make it, and the place to meet it. I never could understand the magnanimity or chivalry of southern gentlemen, who are content to wear the honors of the country in times of peace, but who propose to leave this Hall and fly to their constituents when dangers threaten. Sir, we are their appointed leaders, and when resistance becomes virtuous we are the very men who should first display it. We are standing upon slave territory, surrounded by slave States, and pride, honor, patriotism, all command us, if a battle is to be fought, to fight it here upon this floor." If the irony of Brooks's statement was lost on him it was revealing nonetheless. He was the one, after all, who wore "the honors of the country," but in time of war left the battlefield and missed the "dangers." And he made clear that the nation's capital, the federal city, was the Southern capital, "slave territory," and its defense against Northern interlopers, "a battle," was a matter of "honor, patriotism," to be fought within the Congress itself.

As Brooks was being squeezed politically on all sides at an uneasy political moment, his main relationships in Washington were with Southern hotspurs in the House, "a set of young enthusiasts inspired with notions of personal honor to be defended and individual glory, fame and military glory to be acquired," as Benjamin F. Perry, the South Carolina Unionist newspaper editor, described them. The antislavery *New York Evening Post* correspondent in Washington observed that outwardly Brooks "generally appeared very pacific in his manner and temperament." But the anonymous backbencher was attracted to the fire-eaters' bombast, quick tempers, and propensity to violence. They acted out his contained emotions.

Laurence M. Keitt was Brooks's closest friend in the Congress. Yet another heir to a slaveholding fortune, from a neighboring district, and a graduate of South Carolina College, he was elected in the same class as Brooks. Five years younger than Brooks, Keitt's fire-eating intensity glowed magnitudes hotter. He felt himself to be on the verge of a "Promethean moment" of "mighty events" leading to "an immortal future" in which he would engrave his name like "an heroic poem." He called for secession if the North did not open all territories to slavery, annex Cuba as a slave state, and transform the United States into a confederation in which the federal government was limited only to foreign policy and defense. Speaking against a bill that would have admitted free blacks to the Kansas-

Laurence M. Keitt

Nebraska territory on May 4, 1854, Keitt raised the specter of interracial sex and suggested that white abolitionists panted after black women. "I want to know, also, whether in the State of Ohio blacks and whites intermarry?" he demanded. Congressman Joshua Giddings of Ohio, the leading abolitionist in the House (and Lincoln's former boardinghouse mate, who had assisted him in writing a bill for emancipation in the District of Columbia), tartly replied: "I move to amend the amendment by inserting after the word 'white' the words 'or more than half white.' . . . The gentleman is more than two thirds colored himself, if you take the color of the people of his district as the criterion of his complexion. [Laughter.]" Congressman Lewis D. Campbell of Ohio jibed, "If the whites do not intermarry with the blacks in his district, in what way can he explain the fact consistently, with a correct state of morals, that there are so many mulatto people there? [Laughter.]" "If they are there," replied Keitt, "I might say that Free-Soil schoolmasters and clock venders had much to do with the condition of things of which the member speaks."

"Between the South and these men there must be war," Keitt declared on April 7, 1856, about the antislavery coalition that was emerging as the Republican Party. "In emergencies bold men triumph. Any one can sow peas for the market; 'tis only the hero who can sow dragon's teeth where they spring up armed men! . . . Let the North refuse admission to a State because of slavery in her constitution, and the history of this Union is closed . . . if it becomes, in our very midst, to us a foreign Government, the South will tear it down from turret to foundation stone."

A few days later, Brooks and Keitt joined a congressional delegation to inspect the Washington Aqueduct being constructed by the U.S. Army Corps of Engineers. Montgomery Meigs, the supervisor of the project and later quartermaster general during the Civil War, wrote in his journal of the two men: "April 12, 1856: They had plenty of drink—whiskey and brandy and champagne and sherry—so that we had an abundance of whatever man might want upon such an occasion. The quiet, temperate men from the North had the beauty of the scenery and looked with interest upon the works of the aqueduct. The rollicking, roistering sons of the South had the good entertainment of the wines and whiskey. . . . I think the party generally found themselves well entertained. Some of the honorable Members used much more wine than I would have liked to take. Several of them had been out on some frolic last night; and drinking now in the day, they slept a good deal upon the boat. There was much loud talking, laughing, and some un-steadiness of gait."

On May 8, 1856, eleven days before Sumner's speech, Congressman Phile-mon T. Herbert, a proslavery member from California, whipped out a pistol to shoot dead an Irish waiter at Willard's Hotel for having the presumption to inform him the dining room hours were over. Keitt openly approved of Herbert for murdering an "inferior," only worried that he might have had the waiter's blood splattered on him.

Brooks's intimate circle was completed by a third musketeer, an Ultra from Virginia, Henry A. Edmundson, heir to a large plantation called Fo-theringay on the Roanoke River and, like Brooks, quick to take offense and use violence. During a long night's debate over the Kansas-Nebraska Act on May 12, 1854, an inebriated Edmundson waved his cane as he rushed to beat Congressman John Wentworth, a Democrat from Chicago, who opposed the bill and evaded his wrath, and then tried to draw a knife on Congressman Lewis Campbell, who grabbed him, after which the sergeant-at-arms had Edmundson arrested at least for the rest of the night. On January 18 1856, after Joshua Giddings taunted Edmundson, quoting Brutus from Shake-speare's *Julius Caesar*: "Go, show your slaves how choleric you are, / And make your bondmen tremble," Edmundson bounded to attack him but was prevented from doing so.

Edmundson became the unreliable narrator of the events as they un-folded, protecting himself as he focused attention on Brooks. He claimed "the first intimation that Mr. Brooks had taken any offense at what Mr. Sumner said" was from a conversation with Senator Robert M.T. Hunter of Virginia, who told him on the morning of the second day of Sumner's speech that Brooks already "had taken exceptions." Hunter was a charter member of the F Street Mess, a mate of Butler, who was absent at his plantation. The encounter between Hunter and Brooks might have occurred naturally in the Capitol, the street, or a social setting. But it also showed the pointed inter-est of the F Street Mess in the matter. Voicing his "exceptions" to Hunter, Brooks was speaking to a figure at the center of power, and whatever Hunter told Brooks he might rightly interpret as the collective F Street view. What Hunter told Brooks, Edmundson did not say. Butler would later describe Brooks enveloped wherever he went in a din of "reproach" for inaction. The focus on Brooks placed the burden on him.

Edmundson recalled that the day after Sumner's speech, on the morn-ing of May 21, as he entered the Capitol with "some other gentlemen," he encountered Brooks on the Capitol steps. Brooks had waited an hour and a half the night before "when he [Sumner] escaped me by taking a carriage."

He was waiting again. "I accosted him," recalled Edmundson, "saying, 'You are going the wrong way for the discharge of your duties.'" His use of the word "accosted" suggested that he was chiding him. Was Brooks going the wrong way because Edmundson thought he was going toward the Senate instead of to the House, or because he was going to the House rather than to the Senate? If it were the former, Brooks would have been confused, but if it were the latter he would have been evasive in "discharging" very different "duties." Brooks complained to Edmundson about Sumner's "insults" and his determination "to punish him" if he failed to make "an ample apology." "I wish you merely to be present, and if a difficulty should occur, to take no part in it. Sumner may have friends with him, and I want a friend of mine to be with me to do me justice." It was a strange invitation for Edmundson to be his second in what was not to be a duel, somehow to "take no part" but also somehow to protect Brooks. Edmundson told him "it had been rumored by Senator Sumner's by friends that he had armed himself in anticipation of an attack, and asked Mr. Brooks what preparation he had made; for I had nothing but a little brier stick. He replied: 'I have nothing but my cane.'" Sumner, of course, was generally known to travel unarmed and to be an advocate of pacifism. But Edmundson stoked Brooks's fear of being physically overwhelmed, hurt, and humiliated.

While Edmundson and Brooks talked, Keitt and Senator Robert Ward Johnson joined them. Johnson, a Calhoun acolyte, was the one of the wealthiest and most powerful men in Arkansas, owner of a plantation with 193 slaves, and chief of the dynasty known as "The Family" that politically controlled the state. "Neither of them was informed of my purpose during that day," Brooks later claimed about the events that followed, though his statement seems dubious. His "exceptions" to Sumner were being widely discussed among the Southerners all around town.

Early on the morning of the 22nd, an exhausted and likely hungover Brooks, who had spent another sleepless night wracked with lubricated visions of vengeance and worry about executing them, seated himself half hidden within the gatehouse of the Capitol waiting to pounce on Sumner. Edmundson spotted him "alone." "I supposed what his object was and stopped in." "You are looking out," Edmundson dryly observed. Brooks explained that he "had scarcely slept any the night before, thinking of it," and laid out his half-baked plan that he was scouting for Sumner to arrive and would confront him before he entered the Senate. Edmundson advised him "that would be an imprudent course." He told Brooks that Sumner was "physically a stronger man than himself." This was the second time in two days that Edmundson had reminded Brooks of his physical inferiority and need to fear Sumner. For all his bravado, Brooks still carried a lead bullet lodged in him from his near fatal and absurd duel with Wigfall, tottered with a limp, and was a smaller man. He moved slowly, quickly tired from his weakness, and lacked endurance. In a fair fight without his cane he would be easily knocked down. His cane was more than a weapon; it represented his physical equality. Undoubtedly, Brooks's frailty intensified his dread. He knew he was not up to the task. "Sumner is a very powerful man and weighs 30 pounds more than myself," Brooks wrote his brother. Edmundson told him "the exertion and fatigue of passing up so many flights of steps would render him unable to contend with Mr. Sumner, should a personal conflict take place." Dragging his crippled leg, Brooks could not walk up the steps without needing to rest. Together he and Edmundson made the climb and entered the Capitol Rotunda. Brooks went one way, to the Senate, and Edmundson another way, to the House. There Edmundson listened to eulogies for a recently deceased member, John Gaines Miller of Missouri, until the House adjourned, and he wandered over to the Senate, where Miller's death was also announced before it too adjourned.

Edmundson noticed that Brooks was hovering at the main aisle near Sumner before he darted to take an empty seat. Edmundson casually walked by him. "I asked him if he was a senator?" Edmundson's goading provoked Brooks's anxiety. "He then said to me he would stand this thing no longer; he would send to Mr. Sumner to retire from the chamber." Brooks raced out of the Senate to stand in the vestibule with a view of Sumner, who was quietly franking copies of his speech for mailing. Edmundson advised Brooks "that if he sent such a message, Mr. Sumner would probably send for him to come into the Senate chamber." In that case, Sumner would have advance notice that Brooks would approach him. Brooks knew that would be an uneven match. He became more nervous, telling Edmundson he "did not desire to have an interview with Mr. Sumner while ladies were present, and I knew there still remained a lady occupying a seat in the lobby not far from where Mr. Sumner was sitting." Edmundson and Brooks walked back into the Senate. Keitt had now positioned himself near the podium. Edmundson suggested to him that they should not be present. "I proposed to Mr. Keitt that we should go down [the] street." "No," replied Keitt. "I cannot leave till Brooks does." Edmundson turned to Senator Johnson to get his opinion on the scenario he had just laid out to Brooks. He asked Johnson "if there would be any impropriety, should an altercation occur between Mr. Brooks and Mr. Sumner, of its taking place in the Senate chamber, the Senate having adjourned at the time? . . . I suggested, in the said conversation, there seemed to me no impropriety in calling on Mr. Sumner in the Senate, it having adjourned some time before, and there being few persons present." But their conversation was interrupted by cries "with exclamations of 'Oh! Oh!'"

Sumner was bent over his desk, his chair pulled close in, writing. "I was addressed by a person who had approached from the front of my desk," he recalled, "so entirely unobserved that I was not aware of his presence until I heard my name pronounced. As I looked up, with pen in hand, I saw a tall man, whose countenance was not familiar, standing directly over me, and at the same moment, caught these words: 'I have read your speech twice over carefully. It is libel on South Carolina, and Mr. Butler, who is a relative of mine—' While these words were still passing from his lips, he commenced a succession of blows with a heavy cane on my bare head, by the first of which I was stunned so as to lose sight." He later had "an indistinct recollection of the words, 'old man.'"

"At the concluding words I struck him with my cane and gave him about 30 first rate stripes with a gutta percha cane," Brooks wrote his brother. "Every lick went where I intended. For about the first five or six licks he offered to make fight but I plied him so rapidly that he did not touch me. Towards the last he bellowed like a calf."

But Sumner made no effort to fight back; nor did Brooks fend him off in self-defense. Sumner was stunned from the first hit, threw his arms up involuntarily, tried instinctively to escape, fell back into his chair, rose again, ripping his desk, fastened to a steel plate, from the floor, staggered blindly, and lost consciousness. Brooks pounded him on the head in an ecstatic frenzy. His cane splintered, but he kept striking. As Sumner reeled, Brooks grabbed him by the lapel of his coat and kept hitting him. Shouts of encouragement rang out. "Don't interfere!" "Go it, Brooks!" "Give the damned Abolitionists hell!" "It is all fair!"

While Brooks beat Sumner, Keitt suddenly "rushed in, running around Mr. Sumner and Mr. Brooks with his cane raised, crying 'Let them alone! let them alone!' threatening myself and others who rushed in to interfere," recalled James Simonton, the *New York Times* correspondent. Senator Crittenden, of Kentucky, in conversation with another senator at the back of the chamber, startled by the commotion, marched down the aisle demanding that Brooks stop. "You had better not interfere, we will lick one at a time," Keitt warned, according to the reporter from the *New York Evening Post*. "Don't strike!" shouted Senator Robert Toombs, of Georgia, to Keitt, who lowered his cane. "Don't kill him!" Crittenden shouted at Brooks. "I had no wish to injure him seriously, but only to flog him," Brooks later claimed he replied. Congressman Ambrose Murray, of New York, seized Brooks by his right arm, trying to stop him from striking, but Brooks freed himself, hitting Sumner again and again, until finally Murray yanked him backward.

Congressman Edwin Morgan, of New York, forced himself between Brooks and Sumner. "I caught Mr. Sumner and saved him from falling violently on the floor. There he laid senseless as a corpse for several minutes, his head bleeding copiously from the frightful wounds, and the blood saturating his clothes." Morgan held his bleeding head on his knee until he slowly regained a dazed consciousness. "While standing there, several Senators and many bystanders were complacently looking on, without the least intention of assisting. . . . Toombs was one. Douglas was another." Morgan lifted Sumner to walk to the anteroom of the Senate, where he lay on a sofa. "As I entered the lobby," Sumner recalled, "I recognized Mr. [John] Slidell, of Louisiana, who retreated."

The three men whose presence were mentioned—Toombs, Douglas, and Slidell—felt compelled to give explanations in speeches to the Senate on May 27. "As for rendering Mr. Sumner any assistance, I did not do it," said Toombs. But as for the caning, "I approved it. That is my opinion." Douglas explained that he was in the reception room chatting with others when a messenger "rushed through, and remarked, as he passed, that somebody was beating Mr. Sumner." Douglas claimed that he stifled his impulse to enter the chamber to "help to put an end to the affray, if I could; but it occurred to my mind, in an instant, that my relations to Mr. Sumner were such that if I came into the Hall, my motives would be misconstrued, perhaps, and I sat down again." He insisted he was innocent of any involvement. "I had not the slightest suspicion that anything was to happen." Nobody had accused Douglas of foreknowledge, but he felt he should deny it. One eyewitness in the public gallery observed, "Senator Douglas stood within five feet of Mr. Sumner, in a free and easy position, with both hands in his pockets, and making no movement toward the assailant."

Senator John Slidell unapologetically stated that he and Douglas reacted at the moment to the messenger's excited report without any feeling whatsoever. "We heard this remark without any particular emotion; for my own part, I confess I felt none. I am not disposed to participate in broils of any kind. I remained very quietly in my seat; the other gentlemen did the same; we did not move." Slidell did not say whether they spoke to each other about the extraordinary act of violence occurring just a few yards away. Instead, he expressed his contempt for Sumner, "I did not think it necessary to express my sympathy, or make any advances towards him." Then he accused Sumner of lying that Slidell was somehow involved with Brooks's attack, "calculated to deceive the public and make a false impression on popular opinion." Nobody, however, had charged Slidell with complicity. "I had not the slightest idea that Mr. Brooks, or anybody else," Slidell insisted, "had any intention of attacking Mr. Sumner."

Standing over Sumner, his unconscious body stretched on the floor with his overturned chair on top of his legs, Brooks still "had a piece of the stick in his hand," said Crittenden. "I took hold of it, and he very gently yielded and allowed me to take it out of his hand." The cane had shattered from the impact of smashing Sumner's skull, with one fragment flying at Brooks's face, cutting near an eye. After washing it, Brooks left the Capitol with Keitt at his side and together they walked down Pennsylvania Avenue.

"I wore my cane out completely but saved the head which is gold," Brooks wrote his brother. Someone, it turned out, retrieved the valuable souvenir for him. When the cane splintered, the section with the head flew off. The Senate messenger, W.H.H. St. John, who had excitedly told Douglas, Toombs, Slidell, and others about the attack, later that day cleaning up strewn papers in the chamber found the head of the cane. Douglas noticed his discovery. "Mr. Douglas then being in the Senate asked him for it," wrote Isaac Bassett, the assistant doorkeeper, in an unpublished memoir. "What Mr. Douglas done with it I never knew." Bassett also observed that during the assault on Sumner "Mr. Douglas, and others stood by but did not interfere." By returning the gold head of the cane to its owner Douglas was not completely passive, after all.

Bassett the doorkeeper pocketed one of the broken pieces of Brooks's cane. "I have a piece now in my possession," he wrote decades later. He also helped carry the limp Sumner to the anteroom and "bathed his head which bled profusely."

The nearest physician summoned, Dr. Cornelius Boyle, saw two wounds "cut to the bone" of Sumner's skull, "very ragged," which he stitched up. Neglecting to clean Sumner's wounds, his hands, or sterilize his instruments, he was undoubtedly a contributing cause of Sumner's subsequent high fever, infection, and prolonged weakness. The science about concussions and trau-matic brain injuries was virtually unknown. Boyle's testimony that Sumner suffered "flesh wounds" would provide the grist for Butler to accuse him of "shamming" in order to playact the martyr.

The doorkeeper of the House, Nathan Darling, who assisted the doctor, offered the most detailed description of Sumner's condition. He had been a captain during the Mexican War. "I have dressed wounds, and could ampu-tate a leg if necessary," he said. "When I arrived there, I found Mr. Sumner all covered with blood. The bystanders did not seem to understand much about it, or seemed frightened, and I went to work. . . . I examined his head, and found two large wounds upon it, and one smaller one under his ear. His hands, his shoulders, and his back, were very much bruised. . . . I be-lieve, if the licks had been struck with half the force on another part of the head, they would have killed him instantly. If they had been inflicted lower down on the side of the head, I believe death would have been the result. I think there is no doubt of it. I have seen a soldier killed with the end of a rawhide struck on the side of his head. He never breathed." Darling said that Sumner's head wounds "were cut right to the bone. The left hand had a black lump on it as large as a butternut. The right hand was hurt, though not so badly. Both his arms and shoulders were black. There was a black streak across his left arms and shoulders, and across both his thighs. The latter, I presume, was made in rising up from his table. The doctor told me that, if no man had seen the cut made on the right side of his head, he would have sworn it was not made with a stick at all. It was what we call a thrust cut, and was as ragged as if it had been made with a brick. . . . There was also a cut on the nose." Sumner's wounds were similar to those inflicted on slaves whipped as punishment, except that they were lashed on their backs, too valuable as property to be beaten on the head, which might kill them.

Even before Sumner delivered his speech, talk of violence had wafted through the Capitol, the boardinghouses, the hotels, the restaurants, and on the streets. "I remember to have heard Mr. Brooks say," according to Ed-mundson, "it was time for southern men to stop this coarse abuse used by the Abolitionists against the southern people and States, and that he should not feel that he was representing his State properly if he permitted such things to be said; that he learned Mr. Sumner intended to do this thing days before he made his speech; that he did it deliberately; and he thought he ought to punish him for it."

Senator Andrew Butler, who had been in South Carolina when the caning occurred, seemed particularly well tuned into the acrid atmosphere that had led to it. Upon his return, on June 11, he explained how Brooks's emotions were played upon, revealing more than he might have imagined. "I said that my friend and relative was not in the Senate when the speech was being delivered, but he was summoned here, as I have learned from others. He was excited and stung by the street rumors and street commentaries, where even ladies pronounced a judgment; and, sir, woman never fails to pronounce a judgment where honor is concerned, and it is always in favor of the redress of a wrong. I would trust to the instinct of woman upon subjects of this kind. He could not go into a parlor, or drawing room, or to a dinner party, where he did not find an implied reproach there as an unmanly submission to an insult to his State and his countrymen. Sir, it was hard for any man, much less for a man of his temperament, to bear this."

Butler did not say who those "others" were who told him about Brooks's feverish state of mind. The "rumors" and "commentaries," coming even from unidentified "ladies," were pointed at Brooks, who would be guilty of "unmanly submission." If he did not act he would betray his family, his state, his people, and Southern womanhood.

Butler dismissed Brooks's legal options and even the Code Duello. "What was my friend to do? Sue him? Indict him? If that was the mode in which he intended to take redress, he had better never go to South Carolina again. Was he to challenge him? That would have been an exhibition of chivalry having no meaning. . . . He would have made himself contemptible, and perhaps might have been committed to the penitentiary for sending a challenge." If Brooks had taken these courses, according to Butler, he would have been shunned or imprisoned.

Butler described Brooks's "temperament" as something with which he was closely familiar. "I have known him from childhood," he said. "I used to have some control over him. . . . Sir, I will tell you who Mr. Brooks is, and why he felt so deeply in reference to these abominable libels." Butler assumed onto himself the patriarchal role of the late Whitfield Brooks, but the would-be father justified the son's rashness that the real father had frowned upon. Butler described Brooks as a decorated soldier whose reputation as a warrior would be tarnished if he were not true to his manly code. He "marched under the Palmetto banner, and his countrymen have awarded to him a sword for his good conduct in the war with Mexico. That sword was in some measure committed to him, that he might use it, when occasion required, to maintain the honor and the dignity of his State. When he heard of this speech first, and read it afterwards, this young man, in passing down the street, heard but one sentiment, and it was, that his State and his blood had been insulted. He could not go into the drawing room, or parlor, or into a reading room, without the street commentary reproaching him. Wherever he went, the question was asked, 'Has the chivalry of South Carolina escaped, and is this to be a tame submission?' "

But Butler would surely have known that Brooks's experience in the Mexican War was a humiliating embarrassment to him, that Brooks had notably been prevented from being honored with its veterans, and that he had staged a ridiculous public feud with his cousin that required the intervention of the governor to stop. There was no award for valor. There was no sword. There was only a man susceptible to taunts.

Since he had been expelled from South Carolina College, Brooks's temperament had been consistent. He was constantly anxious to prove his manhood, sensitive to his shortcomings in asserting them, given to impulsive actions based on poor judgment, plagued by a lack of self-discipline and self-doubt about it, and possessed by wishful thinking distorted into a romantic ideal that he could gain glory, fame, and redemption in a single decisive stroke—a duel or a battle. Time after time, he had proved himself less the chivalrous knight and more the knave. His disgraces only deepened his urge to achieve honor.

Brooks later told a friend in private conversation that he would "quickly put Douglas's suggestion to practice" about Sumner. ("Is it his object to provoke some of us to kick him as one would a dog in the street?") "Gentlemen would understand the significance of a caning."

For all the reasons Brooks and others would eventually offer to justify striking Sumner they would skirt Sumner's recurrent theme of the debased morality of slavery exemplified by masters' rape of their female slaves. Yet sex was on Brooks's brain. He was obsessed with slights to manliness, even when they were not made. Edmundson, in his testimony to the congressional inquiry, stated that Brooks bitterly complained to him on the second day of Sumner's speech about a specific remark he supposedly made the day before about South Carolina: "Disgracefully impotent during the Revolution, and rendered still more so since on account of slavery." Congressman Howell Cobb of Georgia immediately corrected Edmundson. "The language used in his reported speech is, 'shamefully imbecile.'" Brooks, in fact, had not been present during the speech; nor had it yet been printed in the *Congressional*

Globe. But he must have heard an account, interpreted it as a sexual affront, and angrily blurted it out.

While there are no firsthand narratives from masters or slaves on the Brooks family's plantations of what was euphemistically called "amalgamation," the 1850 federal census recorded the presence of a number of mulattos. On Whitfield Brooks, Sr.'s, plantation resided three mulatto males, thirty, sixteen, and one year old, and two females, three and one. Preston Brooks's plantation listed one female aged three. They were not immaculately conceived. The identity of these individuals' white fathers remains unknown, but it is likely they were nearby.

Brooks was tapped to enforce the submission of the "degenerate son," as Butler called Sumner, according to the Washington correspondent for the *New York Times,* who reported on May 24: "A well known personal friend of Mr. Brooks publicly stated, tonight, before a dozen gentlemen, that the assault was premeditated and arranged for at a private conclave, held last evening, at which the individual who made the statement was present. Mr. Brooks then agreed to do this ruffian work which today he has consummated."

Brooks had done his work thoroughly. Sumner's gaping head wounds sewn together, his coat and shirt drenched with blood, Sumner's colleagues brought him in a carriage to his lodging about a half mile from the Capitol. He had rooms in the house of Reverend George W. Samson, pastor of the First Baptist Church. Lying on his bed, one of Sumner's friends recalled that "he presented a ghastly spectacle." But the orator was able to speak a few words. Sumner looked up at those gathered around him and addressed them. "I could not believe that a thing like this was possible," he said.

CHAPTER TEN

ARGUMENTS OF THE CHIVALRY

After leaving Sumner in his bed, the Republican senators gathered that night at Seward's house to agree upon a strategy. Some felt themselves physically endangered by "incensed and inexorable leaders of the Slave Power," according to Henry Wilson. "What new victims would be required, who they should be, and whom their appetite for vengeance, whetted by this taste of blood, would select, they knew not."

The next morning, Wilson rose to speak. "The seat of my colleague is vacant today," he said, and described the basic facts of the assault. "Sir, to assail a member of the Senate out of this Chamber, 'for words spoken in debate,' is a grave offense, not only against the rights of the Senator, but the constitutional privileges of this House, and assault a member in his seat until he falls exhausted and senseless on this floor, is an offense requiring prompt and decisive action of the Senate." He called upon "older Senators" to come up

Arguments of the Chivalry, lithograph by Winslow Homer, 1856. Right to left: Charles Sumner (seated), Preston Brooks, Laurence Keitt, John J. Crittenden (being restrained), Stephen A. Douglas (hands in pockets), Robert Toombs. "The symbol of the North is the pen; the symbol of the South is the bludgeon"—Henry Ward Beecher.

with the proper means "to redress the wrongs of a member of this body and to vindicate the honor and dignity of the Senate."

His appeal was greeted with a prolonged silence until the president pro tempore, Senator Jesse Bright of Indiana, who was himself the slave owner of a plantation in Kentucky, began moving on to other business: "The Chair will lay before the Senate a communication . . ." "Mr. President," interjected Seward, leaping to his feet, "I beg leave to offer the following resolution"—a committee of inquiry. Mason immediately offered an amendment that the Senate should elect its members. At once, a vote was taken. Wilson and Seward were excluded; five Democrats were chosen to fill the five positions.

Five days later, on May 28, the committee chairman, Senator James Pearce, of Maryland, a slaveholder who had recently switched from the Whig to the Democratic Party, read a report blaming Sumner for the incident into the record. "The cause of this assault was certain language used by Mr. Sumner in debate," it stated, and concluded that the Senate had no authority "for a breach of its privileges" because it could not "arrest a member of the House of Representatives," or "try and punish him." That authority rested "solely upon the House of which he is a member." Thus the Senate condemned Sumner and washed its hands of the matter.

On the same day that the Senate committee was formed, the House, in a vote over the objection of nearly all the Democratic members, approved creation of a Select Committee on the Alleged Assault upon Senator Sumner. Its first witness, Charles Sumner, was interviewed in his bedroom on May 26, and gave his account, although his head had a "pulpy feeling," according to a doctor, and was draining pus. Interviewing witness after witness, the Select Committee sought to uncover who had encouraged and assisted Brooks.

"The feeling is pretty much sectional," Keitt wrote his fiancée a week after the assault. "If the northern men had stood up, the city would now float with blood. The fact is the feeling is wild and fierce. . . . Everyone here feels as if we are upon a volcano." ·

"This is not an assault, sir, it is a conspiracy; yes, sir, a conspiracy," Thomas Hart Benton told James S. Pike, the *New York Tribune* correspondent. "These men hunt in couples, sir. It is a conspiracy, and the North should know it." Pike wrote: "To what extent the allegation is true may be partially discovered by the investigations of the House Committee, though, of course, all secrets that should not be disclosed it will be impossible to come at, except inferentially and by indirection. The tone of the Southern press, which is really the best exponent of Southern opinions, and the bold avowal of Mr. Toombs on the floor of the Senate, are alike indicative of unity of feeling and purpose on the part of the slavery men, and imply very conclusively that the attempt to abridge the freedom of speech in Congress is no merely individual affair. The work, it is fair to presume, is done with concert and knowledge."

Brooks was acclaimed as a hero across the South. He boasted, "fragments of the stick are begged for as sacred relics." He was overwhelmed with gifts of canes. Prominent citizens of Charleston gave him one inscribed, "Hit him again." Describing it as "a suitable present," the Columbia *South Carolinian* editorialized, "Well done!" Students at the University of Virginia bought Brooks a cane topped with a gold head in the shape of a cracked human skull.

"The whole South sustains Brooks, and a large part of the North also," the *Charleston Mercury* stated. "All feel that it is time for freedom of speech and freedom of the cudgel to go together." "Sumner and Sumner's friends must be punished and silenced," the *Richmond Enquirer* declared—"with their runaway negroes and masculine women." Elaborating on the theme in another editorial, the newspaper stated:

In the main, the press of the South applaud the conduct of Mr. Brooks, without condition or limitation. Our approbation, at least, is entire and un-reserved. We consider the act good in conception, better in execution, and best of all in consequence. The vulgar Abolitionists in the Senate are getting above themselves. They have been humored until they forget their position. They have grown saucy, and dare to be impudent to gentlemen! Now, they are a low, mean, scurvy set, with some little book-learning, but as utterly devoid of spirit or honor as a pack of curs. Intrenched behind "privilege," they fancy they can slander the South and insult its representatives with impunity. The truth is, they have been suffered to run too long without collars. They must be lashed into submission. Sumner, in particular, ought to have nine-and-thirty early every morning. He is a great strapping fel-low, and could stand the cowhide beautifully. Brooks frightened him, and at the first blow of the cane he bellowed like a bull-calf. There is the black-guard [Henry] Wilson, an ignorant Natick cobbler, swaggering in excess of muscle, and absolutely dying for a beating. Will not somebody take him in hand? [Senator John P.] Hale is another huge, red-faced, sweating scoun-drel, whom some gentleman should kick and cuff until he abates something of his impudent talk. These men are perpetually abusing the people and representatives of the South, for tyrants, robbers, ruffians, adulterers, and what not. Shall we stand it? Mr. Brooks has initiated this salutary discipline, and he deserves applause for the bold, judicious manner in which he chastised the scamp Sumner. It was a proper act, done at the proper time, and in the proper place.

Southern newspapers boldly made the threats that antislavery Northern newspapers warned against. In its first report on Sumner's assault, the *New York Tribune* wrote that "as the South has taken the oligarchic ground that Slavery ought to exist, irrespective of color—that there must be a governing class and a class governed—that Democracy is a delusion and a lie—we must expect that Northern men in Washington, whether members or not, will be assaulted, wounded or killed, as the case may be, so long as the North will bear it. . . . If, indeed, we go on quietly to submit to such outrages, we deserve to have our noses flattened, our skins blacks, and to be placed at work under task-masters; for we have lost the noblest attributes of freemen, and are virtually slaves."

Douglas's purported threat against Sumner on the Senate floor in March—"We will subdue you"—was revived as the subject for an editorial on May 26 in the *Illinois State Journal,* an article possibly written by Lincoln and undoubtedly receiving his approval. Days after the attack on Sumner, under the headline, "We Mean to Subdue You," the *Journal* wrote, "That seems to have been no idle threat which Senator Douglas made to Senator Sumner some time since, in the Senate Chamber—'We mean to subdue you, sir.' On Saturday, we published an account of a cowardly assault made by Preston S. Brooks,—a ruffian from South Carolina, and a member of the Douglas faction,—on the person of Senator Sumner, while occupying his seat within the sacred precincts of the Senate chamber. This outrage is of a piece with those in Kansas, with the additional merit of being bolder and having a more distinguished person for its victim."

Across the North, in city after city, town after town, within several weeks after the assault, packed meetings were held to express "Public Indignation." At New York's Tabernacle, a "jammed up" gathering on May 30 heard Edwin Morgan describe the "undeniable facts" of the beating. "Shame! Shame!" cried the crowd. Henry Ward Beecher, of the Plymouth Church, declared, "Ah, there we have it. "The symbol of the North is the pen; the symbol of the South is the bludgeon. . . . Brooks is not the hero of the cane, but he is Cain himself." The governor of New York, Myron Clark, wrote Sumner to condemn "the sneaking, slave-driving scoundrel Brooks." The Massachusetts legislature passed a resolution to the Congress against the "ruthless attack . . . an outrage of the decencies of civilized life, and an indignity to the Commonwealth of Massachusetts," and "demands for her representatives in the National Legislature entire Freedom of Speech."

On the Sunday after the attack on Sumner, Theodore Parker, paragon of Moral Philosophy, pastor of Transcendentalists, and cochairman with Sumner of the Boston Vigilance Committee, mounted the pulpit. "America is now in a state of incipient civil war," he pronounced.

> We also have a Despotic Power in the United States. There is a Russia in America, a privileged class of three hundred and fifty thousand slaveholders, who own three million five hundred thousand slaves, and control four million poor whites in the South. This despotism is more barbarous than Russia; more insolent, more unscrupulous, more invasive. It has long controlled all the great offices in America. The President is only its tool. . . . At Washington, on a small scale, this despotic power wages war against freedom. There it uses an arm of a different form,—the arm of an Honorable Ruffian, a member of Congress, a (Southern) "gentleman," a "man of property and standing," born of one of the "first families of South Carolina." . . . He skulks about the purlieus of the Capitol, and twice seeks to waylay his victim, honorable, and suspecting no dishonor. But, failing of that meanness, the assassin, a bludgeon in his hand . . . watches in the Senate Chamber till his enemy is alone, then steals up behind him as he sits writing, when his arms are pinioned in his heavy chair and his other limbs are under the desk, and on his naked head strikes him with a club loaded with lead, until he falls, stunned and bleeding, to the floor, and then continues his coward blows. South Carolina is very chivalrous!

"It is the best whom they desire to kill," said Ralph Waldo Emerson, another of Sumner's friends, at a meeting at the Concord, Massachusetts, Town Hall on May 26. "It is only when they cannot answer your reasons that they wish to knock you down. If, therefore, Massachusetts could send to the Senate a better man than Mr. Sumner, his death would be only so much the more quick and certain." But Sumner was merely the object and the victim. "I do not see how a barbarous community and a civilized community can constitute one State," said Emerson. "I think we must get rid of slavery, or we must get rid of freedom."

"You can have little idea of the depth and intensity of the feeling which has been excited in New England," Robert C. Winthrop, Sumner's old rival, wrote John J. Crittenden, who had helped restrain Brooks. For many New

Englanders, the assault on Sumner was Lexington and Concord. But the feeling encompassed the whole North. The train of events that began with the passage of the Kansas-Nebraska Act seemed to have reached a climax. "The Northern blood is boiling at the outrage upon you," George E. Baker, Seward's protégé and close aide, wrote Sumner. "It really sinks Kansas out of sight." The "Public Indignation" meetings were an uprising of the Republican Party before its first convention, its first national demonstration, the first appearance of its breadth and depth.

The Nebraska Act had broken the political consensus; escalating conflict in Kansas accelerated the chaos. But the news reports published day by day in partisan papers from a distant territory were patchy and confusing. Part of Sumner's motive in delivering his speech on "The Crime Against Kansas" was to put these fragmentary pieces into an overarching narrative and to explain their political meaning. Brooks's minute-long fury did more than lend credibility to Sumner's case. The debate over the extension of slavery bursting into violence within the chamber of the Senate obliterated the normal political boundaries. This was no longer a skirmish on the frontier between roughnecks.

The timing fell at a moment of building suspense. President Pierce had been discredited. On the eve of their convention the Democrats were uncertain and uneasy. The Republican Party taking shape out of the shards of broken parties was mysterious. Many politically drifting Old Whigs, discontent Democrats, and nativist but antislavery Know Nothings had kept apart from the new organization. With the cracking of Sumner's skull, the old political order finally and irretrievably shattered. His near killing was the galvanizing event of singular clarity and coherence. "Brooks has knocked the scales from the eyes of the blind, and they now see!" declared E.P. Walton, a newspaper editor in Vermont, who would win a congressional seat as a Republican that year.

"By great odds the most effective deliverance made by any man to advance the Republican Party was made by the bludgeon of Preston S. Brooks," observed Alexander K. McClure, a Pennsylvania Republican who would be instrumental in the rise of Abraham Lincoln. "I well remember the effect of the assault upon Sumner throughout the North in the campaign of 1856. It caused many scores of thousands of Democrats of natural anti-slavery proclivities to sever their connection with the Democratic Party."

Sumner's friend Richard Henry Dana, Jr., wrote him, "When Brooks brought his cane in contact with your head, he completed the circuit of electricity to 30 millions!"

Edward Everett, the most distinguished man of Massachusetts—the former president of Harvard (who had denied Sumner an appointment), governor, and U.S. senator—denounced the attack, but also bemoaned its political benefit to the Republicans. Personification of the old conservative Whiggism, and though not a Know Nothing, he was nonetheless supporting the Know Nothing candidate for president, Millard Fillmore, whom he had served as secretary of state. Everett sadly observed that Brooks's blows "will do more to strengthen the abolition party than any thing that has yet occurred." In a reference to his possible opponent, Fillmore privately wrote, "Brooks' attack on Sumner has done more for Fremont than any 20 of his warmest friends . . . have been able to accomplish."

The Massachusetts legislature's resolution had pronounced the assault on Sumner "brutal and cowardly." On May 27, Wilson echoed those words on the floor of the Senate. "Mr. Sumner was stricken down on this floor by a brutal, murderous, and cowardly assault," he said. Butler jumped up yelling, "You are a liar!" His language was tantamount to a challenge to a duel. The *Congressional Globe* reported that the "impulsively uttered words which Senators advised him were not parliamentary, and he subsequently, at the insistence of Senators, requested that the words might be withdrawn." Brooks stepped into the breach. Two days later he challenged Wilson to a duel. Wilson declined, taking the opportunity to repeat his condemnation. "I characterized, on the floor of the Senate, the assault upon my colleague as 'brutal, murderous, and cowardly.' I thought so then. I think so now. . . . I have always regarded dueling as the lingering relic of a barbarous civilization, which the law of the country has branded as crime." At the National Hotel on Pennsylvania Avenue "a few Southern members" considered "the question of making an assault upon him," which was thwarted only at the insistence of Congressman James L. Orr of South Carolina, a cooler head. Wilson began carrying a pistol for self-protection.

On June 2 the House Select Committee filed its report after only ten days since its formation. The majority laid out the facts of how the assault was premeditated based on the testimony of witnesses, some of whom may not have been completely transparent or were covering up, though the role of Keitt and Edmundson as accessories to Brooks was established. Brooks was found "guilty" of a "breach of privileges" and his expulsion recommended. The majority further urged the House to "declare its disapprobation of the said act of Henry A. Edmundson and Laurence M. Keitt in regard to the said assault," the equivalent of a censure. The majority concluded that the attack on Sumner was "an aggravated assault upon the inestimable right of freedom of speech guaranteed by the Constitution. It asserts for physical force a prerogative over governments, constitutions, and laws; and, if carried to its ultimate consequences, must result in anarchy and bring in its train all the evils of a 'reign of terror.' "

The minority report dissented. It declared the House had "no jurisdiction," and Brooks in any case had not violated any of its privileges. Just as the Senate insisted it had no authority over an act committed by a member of the House, the House Democrats in effect argued that the House had no authority over an act committed in the Senate.

On June 12, Butler took the Senate floor for a two-day-long excoriation of Sumner, "unfit for the art of debate," "a pander to the prejudices of Massachusetts," "a flexible conformist invoking the spirit of Theodore Parker as his muse," and a plagiarist of Demosthenes. Mostly, he emphasized Sumner's "obscenity." Twice Butler quoted Sumner's phrase about "the harlot slavery." "The language used was licentious," Butler said. "I dislike to repeat the obscenity of his illustration." Then Butler repeated it and again apologized: "I beg pardon for repeating it. What in the name of justice and decency could have ever led that man to use such language?" Sumner's phrase should have barred him from polite company, not least for offending female sensibilities. "How any man, who has not been excluded from society, could use such an illustration on this floor, I know not. I do not see how any man could obtain the consent of his own conscience to rise in the presence of a gallery of ladies and give to slavery the personification of a 'mistress,' and say that I loved her because she was a 'harlot.' "

The next day Henry Wilson punctured Butler's pomposity and presumptuousness. "This is not the first time during this session we have heard this kind of talk about 'social influence,' and the necessity of association with gentlemen from the South, in order to have intercourse with the refined and cultivated society of Washington. . . . It is a piney-wood doctrine, a plantation idea." Wilson reviewed the history of how Butler had demeaned Sumner even "before he ever uttered a word" in the Senate, quoting from Butler's copious insults, "every expression calculated to wound the sensibilities of an honorable man, and to draw down upon him sneers, obloquy, and hatred, in and out of the Senate."

Senator Clement Clay, of Alabama, immediately rose to threaten Wilson to a duel unless he withdrew a "personal indignity." Wilson had previously criticized Clay's remark that antislavery senators were hypocrites who "assailed them at home," but in Washington "fawned" on Southern senators "with abject servility." Wilson declared he meant no "personal insult." "That is altogether satisfactory," replied Clay. "If that explanation were not made, I should attempt to vindicate myself from the seeming reproach of the Senator from Massachusetts." Clay explained that he considered antislavery senators such as Sumner to "have denied to me, and to every Senator sitting upon this floor who owns a slave, all the characteristics of gentlemen. They have imputed to us a crime in exercising that right which belongs to us. . . . They have assailed the integrity of every individual who stands in the relation of master to a slave. Still, these Senators thus denying to us all the moral attributes of gentlemen come here, and, as I said before, seek and court our society. . . . I do maintain that this is duplicity unworthy of gentlemen."

Congressman Anson Burlingame of Massachusetts took up Sumner's defense on June 21. "He is the pride of Massachusetts." Burlingame praised Sumner's speech for "the classic purity of its language . . . the nobility of its sentiments . . . severe, because it was launched against tyranny." By contrast, Brooks "had taken an oath to sustain the Constitution, stole into the Senate, that place which had hitherto been held sacred against violence, and smote him as Cain smote his brother." "That is false," shouted Keitt. "I will not bandy epithets with the gentleman," Burlingame replied. "I am responsible for my own language. Doubtless he is responsible for his." "I am," Keitt answered. "I shall stand by mine," said Burlingame, and continued his denunciation of Brooks. "Call you that chivalry? In what code of honor did you get your authority for that?"

Brooks promptly sent word to Burlingame that he wished to face him in a duel. Seeking to avoid it, Burlingame publicly explained he made a distinction between Brooks personally and his act, which he deprecated. The *Boston Courier* criticized him for backing down. Burlingame backtracked that he had not retracted anything. Brooks sent another challenge. Congressman Campbell, acting as Burlingame's second, cutely proposed that they conduct their duel on the Canadian side of Niagara Falls with rifles. Campbell, who was a crack shot, might step in as the second to face Brooks himself. Brooks objected that he could not reach that location "without running the gauntlet of mobs, assassins, prisons and penitentiaries, bailiffs and constables." So Brooks fought no duel. That fall Burlingame emerged as one of the most popular stump speakers for the Republican campaign around the country.

Brooks faced criminal charges before the District of Columbia court on July 7, accompanied by Butler, Mason, and an entourage of Southern legislators. In his defense he argued that he had not intended to harm Sumner,

Sumner hadn't been hurt anyway, and Brooks was the one who should be commended for his self-sacrificing idealism. "I would like to have inquired of him, in person, as to the degree of his personal injuries," Brooks said. "It would have gratified me had he been compelled to answer under oath as to the violence of the first blow, which I aver was but a tap, and intended to put him on his guard." Brooks explained that his true motive was to protect the image of Southern womanhood, his "sister" and "mother," from a defiler. ". . . where a sister's dishonor is blotted out with the blood of her destroyer, an intelligent and wholesome public opinion embodied in an intelligence and virtuous jury, always has, and always will, control the law, and popular sentiment will applaud what the books may condemn. . . . And can it be expected—will it be required—that I, with a heart to feel and an arm to strike, shall patiently hear and ignobly submit while my political mother is covered with insult and obloquy, and dishonor?" According to Brooks's fable, he was shielding imaginary innocent women who might be his sister or mother from the rapacious Sumner. A sympathetic judge fined him $300 and sent him on his way.

Two days later the House debate began consideration of Brooks's expulsion. Congressman Thomas Clingman, of North Carolina, who had switched from the Whig to the Democratic Party, extolled "the liberty of the cudgel." John Savage, of Tennessee, declared that Sumner "did not get a lick more than he deserved," other antislavery House members merited a "good whipping as he deserved," and in honor of Brooks there should be built "a statue in memory of the gallant deed."

The House on July 14 voted 121 to 95 for the expulsion of Brooks and censure of Keitt though not Edmundson—short of the two-thirds majority necessary. Brooks asked to address the body. He declared that he knew Sumner would refuse a duel, giving him no choice but to whip him. His choice of weapon proved he hadn't intended to hurt him, but in explaining his reasoning he exposed how his fear of physical inferiority led him to plan his attack.

If I desired to kill the Senator, why did not I do it? You all admit that I had him in my power. Let me tell the member from New Jersey that it was expressly to avoid taking life that I used an ordinary cane, presented to me by a friend in Baltimore, nearly three months before its application to the "bare head" of the Massachusetts Senator. I went to work very deliberately, as I am charged—and this is admitted,—and speculated somewhat as to whether I should employ a horsewhip or a cowhide; but knowing that the Senator was my superior in strength, it occurred to me that he might wrest it from my hand, and then—for I never attempt any thing I do not perform—I might have been compelled to do that which I would have regretted the balance of my natural life.

Brooks called Congressman Morgan, who had intervened to stop the assault, a "feminine gentleman," for referring to him as a "villain," and issued a threat. "He need not be much alarmed; and, if he will 'hold still' when I get hold of him, I'll not hurt him much; and this is all that I can say about that matter here." Then he resigned his seat with a final flourish assailing "the whole Black Republican crew." "Mr. Brooks retired amid the applause of the South Gallery, which was filled with ladies and gentlemen," reported the *New York Tribune,* "and upon reaching the lobby was embraced and showered with kisses by the ladies. Senators Butler and Mason sat near Brooks during the delivery of his speech and were quite merry over it."

Since the assault, Keitt's temper had raged. The *New York Times* reported that he "beat his washerwoman." He had bizarrely accused Congressman John Hickman, of Pennsylvania, of casting a vote to print the majority report on the assault on Sumner "for Republican Party purposes" and "sprang suddenly from his seat as if to attack Hickman, but was caught by the coat-tail by [Sampson] Harris, of Alabama. As the coat was strong, Keitt was restrained, and immediately resumed his seat," according to the *Times.* "Nobody seems to know why he jumped up, nor why he sat down again. The whole thing is a mystery."

"Today I speak for South Carolina," Keitt declared to denounce his censure. He lamented that "the magic circle of sanctity" within the Congress "has been rudely broken, and licentious utterances have echoed along its walls. Within its very 'holy of holies' we have seen American legislators, dressed up in the cast-off garments of Fred Douglass . . . lepers of history." He defied the House gesture against him. "For what? Because I did not turn public informer. Informer against whom? Against my then colleague—against my friend, my bosom friend, and, as the Black Republican journals have charge complicity on my part and a conspiracy . . . And turn informer in favor of whom?" But he confessed, "I knew that my colleague intended to punish the Senator from Massachusetts." Claiming he had no idea how the attack would unfold, though he had positioned himself strategically in the Senate chamber, he said, "Had I anticipated that act of justice there, I should have been still nearer the scene of action than I was." And he, too, resigned, from Congress.

Three weeks later, on August 1, after special elections in their districts, running without opposition, Brooks and Keitt were returned to the House by the voters where they took the oath of office, and claimed complete vindication. "For inflicting merited punishment, the entire South has applauded and commended me, and placed me in the position of representative," Brooks said.

On his thirty-seventh birthday, August 5, Brooks received a hero's welcome back in Washington at an intimate dinner, "a pleasant party of his friends": Senator Andrew Butler; Secretary of War Jefferson Davis; General Joseph Lane (one of Brooks's seconds in his abortive duel with Burlingame), the delegate from the Oregon Territory; Congressmen John Quitman of Mississippi, Thomas Bocock of Virginia (another of Brooks's seconds), Thomas Clingman of North Carolina—and Senator Stephen A. Douglas of Illinois. At the dinner's close, Quitman presented Brooks with "a beautiful cane," from the citizens of Holmes County, Mississippi, inscribed: "For caning that vile abolitionist and foul-mouthed slanderer, Sumner, of Massachusetts, in the Senate Chamber, on the 22d of May last."

Brooks went on a tour of testimonial dinners in South Carolina, which inspired him to mimic fire-eating rhetoric, though he had been a Unionist. "I have been a disunionist since the time I could think," he said. "The Constitution of the United States should be torn to fragments and a Southern Constitution formed in which every State should be a slave state." At a rally at Columbia, on August 29, he declared that in the event the Republicans should win the presidency "the people of the South should rise in their might, march to Washington, and seize the archives and the treasury of the government. We should anticipate them, and force them to attack us."

Brooks had overnight become an iconic figure of Southern Rights, celebrated as its warrior and martyr. Jefferson Davis spoke for the power center in Washington in writing him on the occasion of one of the dinners honoring him in South Carolina. "I have only to express to you my sympathy with the feeling which prompts the sons of Carolina to welcome the return of a brother who has been the subject of vilification, misrepresentation, and persecution, because he resented a libelous assault upon the reputation of their mother."

Throughout his life, Brooks had sought the laurels of honor. Achieving the status he wished for beyond his dreams, he wilted. Within months after the Sumner incident he could not restrain himself from issuing repeated challenges to duels. Under the glare of attention, he was gripped with depression and drank. He felt that his projected image was fraudulent. He had become a slave to his myth. "I have lost my individuality [and] am regarded to a great extent as the exponent of the South against which Black republicanism is warring in my person," he wrote a friend. He confided to James Orr "he was tired of the new role he had chosen, and heartsick of being the recognized representative of bullies, the recipient of their ostentatious gifts and officious testimonials of admiration and regard."

Brooks caught a cold that suddenly developed into something more serious. Keitt and Orr stood helplessly at his bedside on January 2, 1857, watching him gasp for breath. "Air! Orr, air!" he cried. In a "violent heaving of the chest and lung . . . [his] head dropped back in death from suffocation." He received a state funeral. Crowds viewed his open coffin lying in the Capitol. Effusive eulogies were delivered to an assemblage of members of the Congress, the cabinet, the Supreme Court, President Franklin Pierce, and President-elect James Buchanan.

Privately, James Henry Hammond reflected on the untimely death of his former aide-de-camp to his friend, William Gilmore Simms, a leading Southern literary figure, editor of the *Southern Quarterly Review,* and a poet, historian, and novelist, the author recently of an anti-*Tom* piece of fiction featuring a benign slaveholder to counter *Uncle Tom's Cabin.* The *Southern Quarterly Review* had published a glorifying piece eulogizing Brooks as "a brave soldier, patriot and statesman." "He dies just at his culminating point," Hammond wrote Simms. "The decadence to you and I was clear, but not to the world while his family and many friends have every reason to believe that higher and perhaps the highest honors were in store for him. For him, for them, in every way he is removed at [a] happy moment. . . . This happens to few. He must have found favour with the Deity for it to happen at all. Moreover, it is a proof that his achievement was a true mission which I never thought before. What then? God is with us to use . . . brute force!"

Later that year, just before Christmas, on December 21 and 22, in an auction, Brooks's eighty slaves were all sold to the highest bidders: "Israel" for $1,130; "Calvin," $885; "Henry," $615; "Martha," $1,200; "Amelia," "Hannah," and "Sophie," $750; and children, "Little Harriett," $900; "Green," $400; and "Fox," $170. The dissolution of the Brooks estate was a posthumous confirmation of Sumner's critique. Families were broken up, women likely sold as sexual slaves, and children wrenched from their mothers.

In Edgefield's Willowbrook Cemetery a fourteen-foot-tall marble obelisk was erected to mark Brooks's grave, decorated with a Palmetto tree, symbol of South Carolina, and a laurel wreath of honor beneath which was carved his epitaph: "Ever Able, Manly, Just and Heroic."

CHAPTER ELEVEN

EXTERMINATING ANGEL

"(Weird John Brown), / The meteor of the war."

HERMAN MELVILLE, *THE PORTENT*

Two days after the sack of Lawrence, on May 23, James Blood, treasurer of the New England Emigrant Aid Society in Kansas, was traveling back to the beleaguered town when he encountered a group of eight men headed toward Pottawatomie Creek. "As we approached each other, I could see the gleam of the sun's rays reflected from the moving gun-barrels of the party, in a wagon," he recalled. "Halt!" shouted a man he recognized, and Blood called out his name: "John Brown!" Blood noticed that the wagon was loaded with rifles, revolvers, knives, and broadswords. Brown had given Blood one of those swords during the fall of 1855. Brown was the only one of the group to speak. The rest remained deferentially silent. "I noticed that while we were in conversation the boys watched every look and gesture of the old man—keeping their guns in their hands ready for instant action." Brown's "manner was wild and frenzied, and the whole party watched with excited eagerness every word and motion of the

John Brown, 1857

old man." He gave a sketchy account of what had happened in Lawrence in which his rage was directed at the free state leadership. "He seemed very indignant that there had been no resistance; that Lawrence was not defended, and denounced the member of the committee and leading Free State men as cowards, or worse." As Blood was about to continue his trek to Lawrence, Brown "requested me not to mention the fact that I had met them, as they were on a *secret expedition,* and did not want any one to know that they were in that neighborhood."

Earlier that day, Brown had assembled three of his sons and four followers to a "council" to reveal his plan. "The general purport of our intentions—some radical retaliatory measure—some killing—was well understood by the whole camp," recalled Salmon Brown, one of his sons. "You never heard such cheering as they gave us when we started out." John Brown held in his hand a list of names of proslavery men "who were to be killed." "This was on the crest of the wave of enthusiasm." One member of the group, however, urged "caution." "Caution, caution, sir," replied John Brown. "I am eternally tired of hearing that word caution. It is nothing but the word of cowardice." As they started out, they met a rider, who pulled a news story from his boot about the assault on Sumner. "At that blow the men went crazy—*crazy.* It seemed to be the finishing, decisive touch."

John Brown had followed five of his sons to Kansas, but unlike them he did not go as a settler. He went, according to James Redpath, the correspondent for the *New York Tribune,* who became Brown's promoter and biographer, "to oppose by the sword the armed propagandists of slavery; for a believer in the Bible to emulate the examples of Moses, Joshua, and Gideon, and obey the solemn utterances of the Most High God."

Brown heard the voice of God, the Lord spoke through him, to serve God's will, and God guided his hand. God had preordained his plans. He burned with the unforgiving evangelical fire of New Light Calvinism inspired by the Great Awakening and bent himself in devotion to an angry God, whose divine retribution for sin he would mete out himself. "John Brown is almost the only radical abolitionist I have ever known who was not more or less radical in religious matters also," wrote Thomas Wentworth Higginson, the Boston abolitionist who would become one of his most ardent supporters. "His theology was Puritan, like his practice; and accustomed as we now are to see Puritan doctrines and Puritan virtues separately exhibited, it seems quite strange to behold them combined in one person again."

Brown was an abolitionist who despised other abolitionists, especially

William Lloyd Garrison and his followers, who were pacifists, believers in moral suasion, and modeled their nonviolent actions on the Prince of Peace, Christ the Lamb of God. Brown meant to fight to the death in a holy war against sin. He would not attempt to convince any sinner to abandon their sin, but to punish them. They must bear the full weight of God's wrathful judgment for which he was the agent on earth. He would beat it out, shoot it, or stab it. Just as surely that they must pay the wages of sin, he must be their executioner. Thy will be done.

Brown viewed antislavery politics with at least as much contempt as he did Garrisonian abolitionism. Indeed, he rejected politics in all its forms. To him, they reflected nothing but deadly sins: weakness, faintheartedness, and cravenness. He scorned the building of coalitions of diverse forces for a common objective as not only appeasement with evil but also an evil in itself. Politics was a place of sin and all who practiced it sinful. "He despised the class with all the energy of his earnest and determined nature," wrote John Edwin Cook, one of his followers, who was hanged at Harpers Ferry. "It is asserted that he was a member of the Republican Party; but he despised the Republican Party. . . . He was an abolitionist of the ultra school. He had as little sympathy with Garrison as Seward. . . . That the people would be deceived, that the Republicans would become as conservative of slavery as the Democrats themselves, he sincerely believed. . . . He could 'see no use in this talking,' he said. 'Talk is a national institution; but it does no good for the slave.' He thought it an excuse very well adapted for weak men with tender consciences. . . . He believed in human brotherhood and in the God of Battles."

Just as Brown had no use for political parties or politicians, he disparaged discussion and debate. He was disgusted with compromises, treaties, and the rule of law, which set limits on his visions. He embraced violence as both a means and an end, the only way for the country to atone for slavery, break its bonds, and restore "manhood" to the slave. Frederick Douglass, in their first meeting in 1847, was struck by Brown's fierce insistence on the necessity of violence. "He denounced slavery in look and language fierce and bitter, thought that slaveholders had forfeited their right to live, that the slaves had the right to gain their liberty in any way they could, did not believe that moral suasion would ever liberate the slave, or that political action would abolish the system. . . . He was not averse to the shedding of blood, and thought the practice of carrying arms would be a good one for the colored people to adopt, as it would give them a sense of their manhood." Brown was already at war, he told Douglass. "Slavery was a state of war, and the slave had a right to anything necessary to his freedom." Brown studied the leaders of slave revolts—Spartacus of ancient Rome and Nat Turner of Virginia, Cinqué of the slave ship *Amistad* and Toussaint L'Ouverture of Haiti, and the biographies of Cromwell and Napoleon. He prepared himself for years to assume his godly destiny as the military commander of a black army.

As much as Brown pored over the lives of insurrectionists and generals for lessons, he drew his inspiration from the Book of Hebrews, which he frequently quoted, in particular Hebrews 9:22: "Indeed, under the law almost everything is purified with blood, and without the shedding of blood there is no forgiveness of sins." Violence was not a tactic, but divine anointment like holy oil. This sanguinary book of the New Testament also seemed to offer a scriptural understanding for the American Revolution in 9:18: "Therefore not even the first covenant was inaugurated without blood." It describes Moses sprinkling the law and the people with blood as an act of sanctification in 9:20: "This is the blood of the covenant that God commanded for you." Christ's purification of the world demands his earthly death, according to Hebrews 9:26: "But as it is, he has appeared once for all at the end of the ages to put away sin by the sacrifice of himself."

Brown's self-flagellation, self-sacrifice, and self-disciplined denial of ordinary pleasure, which repelled him as a lure into depravity, steeled him for his task. "He stooped somewhat as he walked; was rather narrow-shouldered," John Edwin Cook described him. "Went looking on the ground almost all the time, with his head bent forward apparently in study or thought. Walked rather rapidly, and very energetically. His features were very sharp, nose prominent, eyes were black or very dark grey. His hair was quite light, and he wore it rather long about the time of the skirmish at Lawrence. He wore a coarse, homespun kind of clothing, and was usually very unpresuming in his appearance and dress. He seemed to be rather taciturn in his habits, and was a sort of meteoric character, appearing very unexpectedly now at one place, and then at another, so that it could never be known where he was to be found. His appearances and disappearances were always sudden, and in a decided manner. He seemed to be ever on the alert."

John Brown presented himself in a direct line of descent from one of the Pilgrims on the *Mayflower,* although the Peter Brown of the *Mayflower* was probably not his ancestor and he likely was descended from another Peter Brown to whom his family tree can be traced. While it was never in dispute that he was a Puritan of Puritans, he claimed a myth from the very creation.

The original Captain John Brown, his grandfather, a soldier of the Revolution, of the Connecticut 18th Regiment, of the Continental Army, died of cholera when his son Owen was five years old. Raised in abject poverty, carted off to various relatives, Owen was swept up in a religious revival that stamped him an orthodox Calvinist. Taken in by the Reverend Jeremiah Hallock, he was daily instructed about sin and salvation, and introduced to the antislavery writings of Jonathan Edwards the Younger, a Congregationalist minister, president of Union College, and one of the early abolitionists. Edwards, son of the most influential Calvinist Puritan theologian, who was a slaveholder, prefaced his 1791 sermon, "The Injustice and Impolicy of the Slave Trade," with a citation from the Gospel of Matthew of the Golden Rule, which John Brown would cite to justify all his actions: "Therefore all things whatsoever you would, that men should do to you, do ye even so to them; for this is the law and the prophets." Owen paid close attention to the trial of a fugitive slave that a Connecticut jury refused to return to his Southern master. After his marriage, he moved to Hudson, Ohio, in the Western Reserve settled by New Englanders, became a tanner, a conductor for the Underground Railroad, and a trustee of the biracial Oberlin College, founded in Hudson.

John Brown, born in 1800 in Torrington, Connecticut, was imbued with his father's Calvinism and abolitionism, one and the same. His mother died when he was eight years old, and his father remarried. On a cattle drive with his father he observed with horror a slave boy his own age beaten with a shovel. John Brown hoped to train as a minister at Amherst College, but the family's money ran out. He became a surveyor, married, and was soon the father of seven children, two of whom died, hid fugitive slaves, and moved to New Richmond, Pennsylvania, where he set up a tannery. His wife died, he married a seventeen-year-old, who cared for his children and bore him thirteen more. Sixteen of them would die, from illness, malnutrition, or bullets, before his death. He whipped them for their sinfulness as his father had whipped him. He beat them with a wooden stick for a host of infractions, from daydreaming (three lashes) to disobeying their mother (eight lashes). In the middle of administering one such punishment, Brown reversed roles, demanding that his son instead beat him until his back bled. "Harder; harder, harder!" He took on his children's sins as his own, refusing to distinguish between them and himself in tribute to God's harsh will.

In 1839, he staged a secret ceremony of oath taking, conducted by a traveling black preacher named Fayette and witnessed by his three sons and wife, in which he "vowed that only by blood atonement could slavery be ended," according to one of his later stalwarts, Richard J. Hinton, to whom he confided the story. "It was then that he declared his purpose to live and to be with those in bonds, as if bound with them, even unto the bitter and bloody end."

Brown had by now begun his Pilgrim's progress through his slough of despond. He failed at twenty businesses, moved seven times, and was usually not at his home, but constantly traveling. He failed with his tannery, failed as a real estate speculator, failed as a farmer, shepherd, cattle dealer, and wool merchant. He borrowed money from a bank cash box without informing the bankers and kited loans. He took out three mortgages on a single piece of property without informing the various lenders of his scheme. He failed in his efforts to repay his debts, declared bankruptcy, and his land, household goods, and tools were sold at auction. He squatted on land that was not his, threatened the rightful owner, was evicted, and briefly jailed. He was hounded by a trail of creditors. Four children died in 1843, on a rented subsistence farm, "a calamity from which father never fully recovered," according to Salmon Brown. His partner in the wool business, Simon Perkins, said of him that he had "little judgment, always followed his own will, and lost much money." When Brown traveled to Britain and Europe in 1849 to market wool his inferior product failed to sell or was sold off at low price and he lost the huge sum of $40,000. He entertained the notion of starting a winery, but spent much of 1851 and 1852 trying to fend off creditors. He rented two farms and lost the crops in a drought. He had no business sense, no entrepreneurial ability, and never grasped the most obvious elements of market economy. His inflexible, arbitrary, and impulsive temperament armored him from learning from experience. He took every setback as the fault of others and a trial imposed by God.

The greater his adversity, the more he identified with the oppression of slaves. He sheltered runaway slaves, talked about adopting "at least one negro boy" as a member of his family and founding a school for blacks, which never materialized. He asked his daughter "if I would be willing to divide my food and clothes" with "some poor little black children." Brown hoped to buy a slave in order to raise him, but he never made the attempt and had no funds in any case.

He moved to Springfield, Massachusetts, in 1846, into a spare house in a working-class neighborhood, to be near the wool warehouse of Perkins & Brown. Springfield had an active antislavery society, which held its meetings in the First Congregational Church and involved a number of the town's prominent citizens as well as its black community of several hundred people. The Hampden County Antislavery Society did more than give lectures denouncing slavery; it ran the Connecticut Valley Line of the Underground Railroad. Brown did not join the society or participate in the Underground Railroad, though he helped fugitives on his own. He befriended free blacks in the town, especially one man named Thomas Thomas, whom he employed as a porter. Thomas, according to one account, posed with Brown in a lost daguerreotype in which Brown has one hand on Thomas's shoulder and the other clutching a banner reading "S.P.W.," letters for the Subterranean Pass Way, Brown's early idea of an Underground Railroad run by a military force. A surviving photograph, the first of Brown, depicts him with one hand solemnly raised as if giving an oath and the other clutching a banner, likely inscribed "S.P.W." Brown did not join the abolitionist First Congregational Church, but instead the Zion Methodist Church, or Free Church, the black church to which Thomas belonged, as its sole white parishioner and was invited to preach from its pulpit. (Thomas left Springfield, Massachusetts, in 1853 for Springfield, Illinois, where he frequently encountered Lincoln as a waiter in the hotel across from Lincoln's law office.)

Through his relationships in the black community, Brown sought out militant black leaders, mostly clergymen, and gained their confidence as a brother in spirit. On a business trip to upstate New York, he met two of the most important figures in the black abolitionist movement. The Reverend Jermain Wesley Loguen was a fugitive slave who became a pastor, educator, and activist in the Liberty Party in Syracuse, New York, where his house was a station in the Underground Railroad. (His daughter would marry Frederick Douglass's son.) The Reverend Henry Highland Garnet, another escaped slave who had become a minister and member of the Liberty Party, presided at a church in Troy, New York. He broke with the pacifism of the Anti-Slavery Society in a speech in 1843 to the National Negro Convention at Buffalo, extolling Nat Turner and embracing armed struggle. "Let your motto be resistance! resistance! resistance!" Brown was familiar with the speech and attempted to publish it as a pamphlet. Both Loguen and Garnet discussed Brown with Frederick Douglass. "In speaking of him their voices would drop to a whisper, and what they said of him made me very eager to see and know him," wrote Douglass.

On a speaking tour through New England in 1847, Douglass went out of his way to come to dinner at Brown's plain house. Brown confided that "he had long had a plan to accomplish" the end of slavery. He unfurled a map of the United States and drew his finger down the length of the Allegheny Mountains stretching from Virginia to Pennsylvania, his Subterranean Pass Way, and declared that God had created the Alleghenies for his plan: "They were placed here for the emancipation of the negro race."

He explained that he would train twenty-five armed men, post them in teams of five stationed twenty-five miles apart, to conduct raids on plantations to "induce the slaves to join them." The value of the slaves would fall and slavery itself would naturally collapse. Brown dismissed Douglass's question about surviving being hunted down by asserting that he would "whip them," and added "but even if the worst came he could but be killed." A few months later, in the February 11, 1848, issue of Douglass's newspaper, *The North Star,* he wrote the first account of Brown, who, "though a white gentleman, is in sympathy a black man, and as deeply interested in our cause, as though his own soul have been pierced with the iron of slavery."

Douglass claimed from that moment his faith in the old nonviolent abolitionism began to ebb.

From this night spent with John Brown in Springfield, Mass., 1847, while I continued to write and speak against slavery, I became all the same less hopeful of its peaceful abolition. My utterances became more and more tinged by the color of this man's strong impressions. Speaking at an anti-slavery convention in Salem, Ohio, I expressed this apprehension that slavery could only be destroyed by bloodshed, when I was suddenly and sharply interrupted by my good old friend Sojourner Truth [the fugitive slave, abolitionist, and feminist] with the question, "Frederick, is God dead?" "No," I answered, "and because God is not dead slavery can only end in blood." My quaint old sister was of the Garrison school of non-resistants, and was shocked at my sanguinary doctrine, but she too became an advocate of the sword, when the war for the maintenance of the Union was declared.

But that was later, and it was the Union army that wielded the sword. Brown was advocating guerrilla warfare even against federal troops sent against him.

Through Douglass, Brown met Willis Hodges and Thomas Van Rensselaer, who edited a small black journal in New York City named *The Ram's Horn.* (Douglass was listed on the masthead as an assistant editor.) In 1848, Brown wrote an article that appeared in the journal but with no byline and in the guise of a confession from a rueful black man, "like others of my colored brethren." "Sambo's Mistakes" was a sermonizing censure of the low and superficial habits of free blacks. "Sambo" had "spent my whole life devouring silly novels and other miserable trash . . . acquiring a taste for nonsense and low wit . . . bought expensive gay clothing . . . Finger rings . . . Nuts, Candy," rather than practicing "self-denial" and "resisting" the "brutal aggressions" of "Southern Slavocrats."

Nearly broke and scrambling to salvage his foundering wool business, Brown wandered in April 1848 to Peterboro in upstate New York to the doorstep of one of the wealthiest men in the country. Gerrit Smith was the heir to the fortune of the partner of John Jacob Astor and had greatly expanded it to project himself as a philanthropist, devoted to temperance, feminism, pacifism, prison reform, the American Bible Society—and chief funder of the abolitionist cause. Smith decided to give 120,000 acres of land in remote North Elba, New York, high in the Adirondacks, for a utopian colony of free blacks and fugitive slaves. Hypochondriac, impulsive and neurotic, he was at once a perfectionist Garrisonian who disdained politics in principle and the main donor to the Liberty Party—a contradiction that did not bother him—and drifted into ever more radical breakaway factions that repeatedly nominated him as their presidential candidate. Brown pledged to Smith that he would teach the "mostly inexperienced" black settlers of North Elba how to operate as farmers and "be a kind of father to them." Smith gave him a grant of land, and Brown ventured to the place in the Adirondacks, "where every thing you see reminds one of Omnipotence," he wrote.

Brown called the North Elba colony of about 150 black families "Timbuctoo," as though it were an African Shangri-La. But the reality of "Timbuctoo" did not match the dream. The ground was rocky and poor for farming. Suffering under primitive conditions, the settlement failed to thrive and began to dissolve by 1855. He moved there in 1849, but kept traveling back and forth to Springfield—and to other points. The burden of his family's survival largely rested on his wife and children. While he encouraged Willis Hodges of *The Ram's Horn* to migrate, he was a mostly absentee patriarch of his black paradise. His assertion of leadership, based on absolute certitude, rectitude, and high enthusiasm, was in the service of an ill-conceived and badly executed plan. Brown's involvement in "Timbuctoo" was of a piece with virtually all of his past and future enterprises.

Back in Springfield in 1851, he found the black community in an anxious state after the passage of federal Fugitive Slave Act. With forty-four black men, he organized a League of Gileadites for armed resistance against any slave catchers who might descend on the town. Brown wrote its manifesto, taking his inspiration from the biblical story of Gideon and his loyal band who slew the Midianites, as recounted in the Book of Judges: "Whosoever if fearful or afraid, let him return and part early from Mount Gilead." According to Brown's "Words of Advice," "all traitors must die," and if any black were arrested the Gileadites should attack at once. "Let the first blow be the signal for all to engage; and when engaged do not do your work by halves, but make clean work with your enemies." He added, ". . . and be hanged, if you must, but tell no tales out of school."

When Senator Charles Sumner spoke in Springfield sometime in the early 1850s, he met with John Brown and the assembled Gildeadites in the back of the shoe store owned by one of its members, Rufus Elmer. "Mr. Brown," said Sumner, "slavery is doomed; but not in your day or in mine." Brown raised his hand high and lowered it as though in judgment, declaring, "I hope to God to die in the cause."

By May 7, 1855, five of John Brown's sons settled in Kansas near Osawatomie in a place they called Brown's Station. Brown did not intend to join them, but instead had his own plans. "If you or any of my family are disposed to go to Kansas or Nebraska, with a view to help defeat Satan and his legions in that direction, I have not a word to say," he wrote John Jr., "but I feel committed to operate in another part of the field." He had already decided to strike at Harpers Ferry to establish the base for his Subterranean Pass Way. Several weeks later, on May 24, John Jr. replied that they needed weapons. "Now we want you to get for us these arms. We need them more than we do bread. Would not Gerrit Smith or some, furnish the money." Drawn to combat Brown decided to go to Kansas.

As the nascent Republican Party was organizing to oppose the extension of slavery, Douglass, Gerrit Smith, and others gathered at a convention in late June 1855 at Syracuse, near Smith's estate, to form a small party called the Radical Political Abolitionists to prepare to run its own presidential ticket. It opposed the Republican position as compromised, instead demanding immediate and complete abolition by direct action if necessary. John Brown spoke from the platform to appeal for funds for weapons to take to Kansas. "Without the shedding of blood there is no remission," he declared. A debate broke out. Lewis Tappan objected. A prominent abolitionist from a family of prominent abolitionists and donor to the movement, Tappan was the founder of the Mercantile Agency, a Wall Street credit rating firm that became Dun

& Bradstreet, and refused to encourage violence. Douglass, however, upheld Brown. Influenced by Brown's fervor, Smith, the onetime pacifist, had also come around to his militant view. He would publish an article in 1856 proclaiming: "Hitherto, I have opposed the bloody abolition of slavery. But now, when it begins to march its conquering bands into the Free states, I and ten thousand other peace men are not only ready to have it repulsed with violence, but pursued even unto death, with violence." Smith gave Brown $60, and he went westward.

By the time Brown arrived at Osawatomie on October 6, 1855, the battle lines were already drawn. He had contempt for the free state government established at Topeka, which in order to bring a significant group of Democrats into the coalition had adopted a position forbidding free blacks in the territory, and he had loathing for its leaders. When the Border Ruffians besieged Lawrence in December Brown and four of his sons made their appearance in a wagon before the Free State Hotel to present themselves as warriors. "To each of their persons was strapped a short, heavy broadsword," said an eyewitness. "Each was supplied with a goodly number of fire-arms and navy revolvers, and poles were standing endwise around the wagon box, with fixed bayonets pointing upwards. They looked really formidable, and were received with great eclat." Free state governor Charles Robinson immediately gave Brown a title: captain of the Liberty Guards of the First Brigade of Kansas Volunteers. John Brown was now Captain John Brown. But several times the Committee on Public Safety stopped him from launching attacks "to draw a little blood," and he refused to attend meetings to which he was invited. "Tell the General," he replied, "that when he wants me to fight, to say so: but that is the only order I will ever obey." On December 10, Robinson assembled the men before the hotel to announce he had negotiated a truce. Brown jumped on a piece of wood and "began to harangue the crowd," and proclaimed, "Without the shedding of blood there is no remission," according to George W. Brown, editor of the *Herald of Freedom* newspaper. John Brown "asked for volunteers to go under his command" to attack at once. None joined him. The committee at first wished to have him placed under arrest but instead sent an officer to calm him. "Leading the Captain away, the storm that he was inciting was soon at an end." Brown was sulfurous in his rage against Robinson, "a perfect old woman," "more talk than cider," and at the free state leaders as "broken-down politicians." "Peace was established, and Old Brown retired in disgust."

But after the free state leaders were charged with "treason," Robinson was held captive and Lawrence was ransacked, there was no one with authority to order Captain John Brown to stand down. "Something is going to be done now," he announced to his "council" of sons and four others, his own band of Gileadites to slay the Midianites. As his inspirational Book of Judges 6:27 said: "Then Gideon took ten men of his servants, and did as the Lord had said unto him; and so it was that he did it by night."

At ten at night on May 24, near Pottawatomie, Brown loudly knocked on the cabin door of James Doyle, a poor white settler. While he sided with the proslavery side he held no slaves. Brown identified himself and his several men as "the Northern Army." At gunpoint he marched Doyle and two of his sons, William and Drury, into the woods. Mrs. Doyle heard two gunshots, moaning, and "wild whoops." John Doyle, the sixteen-year-old surviving son, testified before a congressional committee: "I saw my other brother lying dead on the ground, about one hundred and fifty yards from the house, in the grass, near a ravine. His fingers were cut off; his head was cut open; there was a hole in his breast. William's head was cut open, and a hole was in his jaw, as though it was made by a knife, and a hole was also in his side. My father was shot in the forehead and stabbed in the breast."

At midnight, Brown and his company came to the cabin of Allen Wilkinson, an elected member of the proslavery legislature who did not himself own slaves. Again, Brown presented the group as "the Northern Army," and over the objections of Wilkinson's ill wife dragged him away without allowing him to put on his boots. He was found with gashes on his head and the side of his body and his throat slit.

At two in the morning, Brown went to the cabin of James Harris, likely mistaking it for the house of "Dutch" Henry Sherman, a German immigrant and well-known partisan of the proslavery cause but not a slave owner. Dutch Henry was not there, but his brother "Dutch" Bill happened to be present. They led him out of the house into the woods near a creek. Harris found his body in the morning. "Sherman's skull was split open in two places," he testified, "and some of his brains were washed out by the water; a large hole was cut in his breast, and his left hand was cut off, except a little piece of skin on one side."

Brown and his men washed their knives and swords of blood at daylight in Pottawatomie Creek, and returned to the camp of John Jr. and Jason Brown, two sons who had stayed behind. It was only a day later, but the news had traveled fast. "Hearing this, I was afraid it was true, and it was the most terrible shock that ever happened to my feelings in *my* life," said Jason

Brown. The next day he confronted his father. "Did you have any hand in the killing?" he asked. "I did not, but I stood by and saw it," John Brown replied. "I did not ask further, for fear I should hear something I did not wish to hear." Frederick Brown, another son who had been part of the group, piped up, "I could not feel as if it was right." Another man who had been involved said "it was justifiable as a means of self-defense and the defense of others." "What I said against it seemed to hurt father very much," recalled Jason Brown, "but all he said was, 'God is my judge—we were justified under the circumstances.'" Jason demanded of Frederick whether he knew who had committed the murders. "Yes I do, but I can't tell you." "Did you kill any of them with your own hands?" "No," he said, crying as he spoke. "When I came to see what manner of work it was, I could not do it." John Jr. was sleepless. "I feel that I am going insane," he said.

After the Pottawatomie massacre John Brown and those involved offered many evasive and shifting stories about what happened. Those murdered were foul-mouthed bullies, part of a court intending to arrest him and his family, rape the women, or kill them. He was trying to prevent an even greater outrage. He was ending the conflict in the only way it could be ended. He claimed that he did not personally engage in the butchery. Another time, he told a story that Charles Robinson and James Lane had ordered him to commit the murders. "Captain Brown, did you kill those five men on the Pottawatomie, or did you not?" E.A. Coleman, a Kansan settler friendly with Brown, asked him. "I did not," he replied, "but I do not pretend to say they were not killed by my order; and in doing so I believe I was doing God's service." Coleman's wife said, "Then, Captain, you think that God uses you as an instrument in his hands to kill men." Brown answered, "I think he has used me as an instrument to kill men; and if I live, I think he will use me as an instrument to kill a good many more."

John Brown was now an outlaw, indicted for murder and pursued by posses. Having failed as a revolutionary in a spasm of killing he now set out on a successful path as a self-dramatizing zealot following the higher law of God to justify his purifying violence. To the end he would respond to objections with a quotation from Romans 8:31: "If God is for us, who can be against us?"

"War! War!" shrieked the headline of the Westport, Missouri, *Border Times*. Over the following months more than two hundred men died in a cycle of violence triggered by the Pottawatomie massacre. The proslavery settlers were not scared out of Kansas while the free state men were put on the defensive as the aggressors. Falsely identified as murderers, Jason Brown and John Brown, Jr., were taken as prisoners. Jason was threatened with lynching and John Jr. marched mercilessly in chains for sixty-five miles until they were finally released to federal troops. Jason returned to his house to discover it had been burned and his cattle stolen.

John Brown went into hiding in woods and ravines. "Brown was a presence in Kansas and an active presence all through '56," recalled R.G. Elliott, editor of the *Free State* newspaper in Lawrence. "Yet it was his presence more than his activities, that made his power,—the idea of his being. He was a ghostly influence. . . . Yet after Pottawatomie he moved much in secret." He emerged like a phantom to fight in a series of guerrilla warfare skirmishes. In some of these encounters, he joined free state companies in the field. Brown claimed a great victory in the Battle of Black Jack when he and other free state companies captured a proslavery force that was trying to arrest him, despite being ordered to release it by a federal officer.

The romantic legend of Captain John Brown was already launched. John Redpath of the *New York Tribune* stumbled upon his camp in the woods where he discovered "Old Brown" and his "little band." "He respectfully but firmly forbade conversation on the Pottawattomie affair," Redpath wrote. "Never before had I met such a band of men. They were not earnest, but earnestness incarnate." Brown impressed him as the personification of righteousness. "Often, I was told, the old man would retire to the densest solitudes, to wrestle with his God in secret prayer." Redpath concluded he was at "a sacred spot," and believed "that I had seen the predestined leader of the second and the holier American Revolution." He enthusiastically enlisted as Brown's chronicler and publicist. In his 1860 biography of the martyr, Redpath wrote of the Pottawatomie massacre, "John Brown did not know that these men were killed until the following day," and that "he was twenty-five miles distant at the time."

The proslavery forces meanwhile elevated Brown into the commander of the free state men. "CIVIL WAR IS BEGUN!!!" ran the headline of the *Squatter Sovereign*. Brown, "the notorious assassin and robber," was reported to be leading a murderous army. "The Abolitionists proclaim that 'no quarter will be given. Every Pro-Slavery man must be exterminated.' What will be your reply?" David Atchison and B.F. Stringfellow signed a call to arms to defend against Brown.

The *New York Times* reported from the front lines that Brown had led the free state men and been slain at the Battle of Osawatomie on August

30 in which about four hundred proslavery men razed the settlement and killed Brown's son Frederick. When John Brown appeared alive his reputation grew as death defying. He was now hailed as "Osawatomie Brown," "Old Brown," and Captain John Brown.

"God sees it," Brown said to his son Jason as they stood on a hill above the burning town of Osawatomie. "I have only a short time to live—only one death to die, and I will die fighting for this cause. There will be no more peace in this land until slavery is done for. I will give them something else to do than to extend slave territory. I will carry the war into Africa."

On July 20, his daughter Ruth wrote him from North Elba, "Gerrit Smith has had his name put down for ten thousand dollars towards starting a company of one thousand men to Kansas." Under a warrant of arrest and a cloud of myth John Brown fled eastward.

CHAPTER TWELVE

DEMOCRACY IN AMERICA

Once Charles Sumner felt capable of being moved from his bed he was taken in June 1856 to the home of Francis P. Blair at Silver Spring for convalescence. He spent almost every day lying down, interrupted only by a slow walk around the garden, "hoping daily for strength which comes slowly." William Seward paid him a visit on July 4th, alarmed at his condition. "His elasticity and vigor are gone. He walks, and in every way moves, like a man who has not altogether recovered from a paralysis, or like a man whose sight is dimmed, and his limbs stiffened with age."

Sumner consulted four physicians and traveled to Philadelphia to be evaluated by another, who described him in "a condition of extreme nervous exhaustion, his circulation feeble, and in fact every vital power alarmingly sunken." He sought rest at the seaside resort of Cape May, New Jersey, and a mountain hotel in Pennsylvania, but still felt immense pressure within his head. Doctors could do little for him. The medical science for

Alexis de Tocqueville, painting by
Théodore Chassériau (1855)

diagnosing brain trauma injury and the technology to scan it simply did not exist. No physician could ever determine the lasting neurological damage that may have affected his personality.

Though he was an invalid, the *New York Tribune* urged his nomination as the Republican candidate for vice president as a gesture of tribute. "And would not the entire People applaud his elevation to the office of President of that Senate which has witnessed with disgraceful indifference the recent attempt to suppress Free Speech by the assassin's bludgeon?" He received thirty-five votes. Sumner had no ambition to become vice president, but he did want to campaign. Blair counseled him to continue his recovery. "You have . . . done more to gain the victory than any other," he said.

Sumner's beating was a leitmotif of the Republican campaign, the "free speech" part of its slogan: "Free Soil, Free Labor, Free Speech, Free Men, Fremont!" The Illinois Republican State Committee, under the direction of Abraham Lincoln, published a circular, "Republican Bulletin No. 7," entitled: *Tyranny of the Slave Power "We Will Subdue You." The Outrage Upon Senator Sumner,* which contained a lengthy quote from

> That pure and venerable patriot, Hon. Josiah Quincy, of Mass. . . . upon Preston S. Brooks' crimes as follows: "The blow struck upon the head of Charles Sumner did not fall upon him alone. It was a blow purposely aimed at the North. It was a blow struck at the very tree of liberty. . . . J.Q. Adams once said to me, 'The characteristics of Southern Representatives are boldness, fearlessness, and desperation; while the characteristics of the Northern Representatives have always been dog timidity and fear.' And well the South know this. If we do not act now, the chances may never again return; and all that will be left the North will be to tackle in with the slaves, and drag the carts of slaveholders, only beseeching them to spare the whip, and make the load as light as possible." Heed the advice of the Old Roman, and vote for Fremont and Freedom.

On November 3, 1856, Charles Sumner made a triumphant entrance on his return to Boston in order to vote in the national election to be held the next day. He began his procession from the house of his friend Henry Wadsworth Longfellow on Brattle Street in Cambridge to the Brookline home of Amos A. Lawrence, whose criticism of Sumner was now forgotten. From there a cavalcade of virtually every notable was assembled to accompany him— elected officials, officers of the Massachusetts militia, Harvard professors, and business leaders. When his cortege crossed the city line into Boston a band broke out into "Hail Columbia," and Josiah Quincy, at eighty-four years old the most distinguished citizen of the commonwealth, and Mayor Alexander H. Rice greeted him. Quincy delivered a welcoming address: "He comes, a cheerful and victorious sufferer, out of great conflicts of humanity with oppression, of ideas with ignorance, of scholarship and refinement with barbarian vulgarity, of intellectual power with desperate and brutal violence, of conscience with selfish expediency, of right with wrong." Sumner joined Quincy and the mayor in their carriage drawn by six magnificent gray horses and surrounded by a bodyguard of marshals and police. A contingent of young women threw bouquets of flowers in his path attached with mottoes: "No bludgeon can dim the lustre of our champion of Freedom." "Massachusetts' most honored son. If the ladies could vote, he would be the next President." Then through downtown, around the Common, up to Beacon Hill and the State House, crowds were packed and buildings festooned with flags and banners. One, wreathed in black, read: "May 22, 1856." Another: "Resistance to tyrants is obedience to God." And: "Welcome, Freedom's Defender." At the State House there were more speeches, and Sumner responded in a "feeble" voice: "I shall persevere against all temptations, against all odds, against all perils, against all threats,—knowing well, that, whatever may be my fate, the Right will surely prevail." He was escorted to his house on Hancock Street, where his mother waited at the door. He went to his bedroom, where he stayed for months.

The Massachusetts General Assembly elected Sumner to another term in the Senate by acclamation. His prestige was unassailable, but behind his icon was a guiding political hand called the Bird Club. Francis W. Bird, a paper manufacturer and adherent of the Free Soil Party, began holding weekly lunches at Parker House Hotel after the 1848 loss. Starting with a handful of antislavery friends, the number grew to several dozen men, and the Bird Club over time became the heart and soul of the Massachusetts Republican Party. Ward bosses, journalists, and abolitionists alike belonged. Its first victory was backing Sumner for the Senate, and its second was his reelection. Bird was particularly close to John A. Andrew, a lawyer and antislavery politician, who became governor in 1860 and would appoint Bird to the Governor's Council. At the lunches, Bird sat at the head of the table, with Andrew on his right and Sumner, when he was in town, on his left. The rising influence of the Bird Club was a sign of the insurgent Republicans becoming a regular political organization and governing party.

In early January 1857, John Brown marched into the office of the Massachusetts State Kansas Committee, the local chapter of the Emigrant Aid Society, on School Street in Boston, wearing a gray military-style overcoat with a cape and a fur hat. He presented a letter of introduction to the secretary of the committee, Franklin Benjamin Sanborn, from Sanborn's brother-in-law, George Walker, who was acquainted with Brown in Springfield, Massachusetts. Sanborn, twenty-six years old, was a precocious and radical abolitionist Harvard graduate who had recently founded a college preparatory school at Concord for the children of the leading Transcendentalists. Brown seemed to him to have stepped out of a storybook as an ideal figure from the epic past. "He was, in fact, a Puritan soldier, such as were common enough in Cromwell's day, but have not often been seen since. Yet his heart was averse to bloodshed, gentle, tender and devout." Brown regaled Sanborn with tales of his heroism and famous victories, his plans to "resist aggression," and immediate need for two hundred Sharps rifles and $30,000 in cash.

The enraptured Sanborn brought the "Puritan soldier" to meet the great and the good. At Theodore Parker's house the man of war was introduced to the apostle of peace, William Lloyd Garrison. "They discussed peace and non-resistance together," according to Garrison's grandson and biographer, "Brown quoting the Old Testament against Garrison's citations from the New, and Parker from time to time injecting a bit of Lexington into the controversy, which attracted a small group of interested listeners." Wendell Phillips, who was present, distanced himself, at least then, writing Garrison afterward that Brown's massacre at Pottawatomie "cannot be successfully palliated or excused." His objection underscored that Brown's role in the murders or suspicion of it was not unknown.

George Luther Stearns, a wealthy manufacturer and abolitionist donor, chairman of the Massachusetts State Kansas Committee, after meeting Brown at Theodore Parker's house, invited him to his estate at Medford. "He rose to greet me," wrote Mary Stearns, his wife, "stepping forward with such an erect, military bearing, such fine courtesy of demeanor and grave earnestness, that he seemed to my instant thought some old Cromwellian hero suddenly dropped down before me." "Gentlemen," said Brown, "I consider the Golden Rule and the Declaration of Independence one and inseparable; and it is better that a whole generation of men, women, and children should be swept away than that this crime of slavery should exist one day longer." "These words were uttered like rifle balls," recalled Mary Stearns.

On January 8, Stearns designated Brown the agent of the Massachusetts

State Kansas Committee, assigning him two hundred rifles, $1,000 in military supplies, and $5,000 in cash. Brown raced to see Gerrit Smith, who, in a downward phase of one of his manic-depressive cycles, refused to give him more funds and complained that Brown had not paid him for his land in North Elba. Sanborn traveled with Brown to Chicago to plead with the National Kansas Committee, the governing board of the Emigrant Aid Society, for guns and money, but he was rebuffed.

Brown returned to Boston where Sanborn arranged for him to address a committee of the state legislature on February 18, 1857, to petition for $100,000. He recounted thrilling stories of his adventures, the hardships of settlers, and his sons' victimization. The next day, Amos A. Lawrence, acting for the committee, sent him a meager check for $70.

Sanborn took Brown to Concord for dinner with Ralph Waldo Emerson and Henry David Thoreau. "He spoke of the murder of one of his seven sons, the imprisonment and insanity of another," Sanborn recalled, "and as he shook before his audience the chain which his free-born son had worn, for no crime but for resisting slavery, his words rose to thrilling eloquence, and made a wonderful impression on his audience. From that time the Concord people were on his side, as they afterwards testified on several occasions." He was invited to speak at the Town House in Concord, again telling his tales of Kansas and declaring again, "better that a whole generation of men, women, and children should be swept away than that this crime of slavery should exist one day longer." Emerson gave him a small contribution and Thoreau "subscribed a trifle" because he had "so much confidence in the man—that he would do right."

Charles Sumner had secured his second term in the Senate but was physically incapable of serving. His friends and allies no longer could turn to him as their beacon. He was more symbol than presence. In his absence the practical men who had been instrumental in making his political career went on to build the Republican Party, and they were preoccupied with the machinery of winning elections and governing. Their abolitionism was dedicated to gaining effective political power. A few of the high-minded idealists and radical abolitionists participated in the Bird Club, but they were mostly adrift in the vacuum left by Sumner's withdrawal from public life. John Brown stepped into their drawing rooms to sweep them up with his authentic appearance and urgent stories just as they were enraged at the beating of their infirm champion.

After the legislature rejected his request for funds, Brown had an important call to make. He paid a visit to Charles Sumner at his Beacon Hill home, accompanied by James Redpath, the *Tribune* correspondent, who had come to Boston.

> We spoke of the assault of Brooks, under which Sumner then was suffering. After describing it, as he was stretched in pain on the bed, Captain Brown suddenly asked if he had still the coat. "Yes," said Sumner, "it is in that closet: would you like to see it?" Captain Brown said he would like to see it much indeed. Senator Sumner rose slowly and painfully from the bed, crossed the room, opened a closet and handed the coat to the old hero. . . . I recall the scene as vividly as if I had just seen it: Sumner standing slightly bent and supporting himself by keeping his hand on the bed, Brown, erect as a pillar, holding up the blood besmeared coat in his right hand and intently examining it. The old man said nothing I believe—I could never recall a word; but I remember that his lips compressed & his eyes shone like polished steel.

A week later, Sumner returned to Washington. "Mr. Sumner looks very well as he sits in his chair. He was never, perhaps, looking better," reported the *Boston Traveller.* "But the idea of health is quickly dissipated when he attempts to rise, or more particularly when he commences to walk after rising, when his step appears feeble and uncertain, as though he were walking on a slippery surface and was sensible of its insecurity. He complains of a nervous sensation of his spine, and laughing describes his debility as arising from a want of 'backbone.'" Seated in his chair in the Senate for the first time since the assault, his Republican colleagues thronged around him. "Douglas, Toombs, Slidell, Benjamin, Cass and others, passed and repassed Mr. Sumner's seat and neither gave nor received a look of recognition." Sumner voted on a tariff bill and "returned to his rooms perfectly exhausted." He wrote Theodore Parker, "a cloud began to gather over my brain. I tottered out and took to my bed."

On March 7, 1857, he sailed to Europe on an extensive tour of his familiar sights in search of a cure. Leaving the whirlwind of London society, he sought peace, quiet, and scintillating conversation at the Normandy château of his friend Alexis de Tocqueville. Descended from a millennium-long aristocratic line, Tocqueville was a resolute liberal, appalled by the Old Regime, the Reign of Terror of the French Revolution in which his parents were imprisoned and narrowly escaped the guillotine, and the Bourbon restoration.

He crossed the Atlantic in 1831 as a magistrate to investigate the prison system in the United States, but he wound up writing about every aspect of the American experiment, producing his *Democracy in America*. From his experience with despotism and revolution and with a sociologist's insight he described the New World of social equality, voluntary associations, and civil liberties, as well as the propensity to prejudice and the threat of "the tyranny of the majority," his phrase. Toward the conclusion of his tour d'horizon, he addressed the conundrum of slavery. Tocqueville was an abolitionist who believed that slavery "contrasted with democratic liberty and the intelligence of our age, cannot survive." But he did not know how emancipation might happen in America without setting off "the most horrible of civil wars and perhaps in the extirpation of one or the other of the two races."

The ancient Château de Tocqueville near the English Channel housed a library of six thousand volumes. "Within that large room was a small cabinet, or study, in which he generally sat," recalled Sumner. "What particularly struck me on entering this room was four portraits on the four walls, one of which was of Washington, and another of Hamilton. Of course I could not help exclaiming. When De Tocqueville found that I had recognized them, he seemed much pleased. I, of course, expressed my great pleasure at so high a compliment to our country. We soon were engaged in discussing the character of General Hamilton."

Sumner expressed his certitude that slavery would be overthrown. "There can be no doubt about the result," he said. "Slavery will soon succumb and disappear." "Disappear! In what way, and how soon?" inquired an incredulous Tocqueville. "In what manner, I cannot say," replied Sumner. "How soon I cannot say, but it will be soon. I feel it. I know it. It cannot be otherwise."

"Mr. Sumner is a remarkable man," remarked Tocqueville after he left. "He says that slavery will soon entirely disappear in the United States. He does not know how, he does not know when; but he feels it, he is perfectly sure of it. The man speaks like a prophet."

PART TWO

THE RISE OF ABRAHAM LINCOLN

CHAPTER THIRTEEN

CREATION

"For it is the solecism of power, to think to command the end, and yet not to endure the mean. . . . The rising unto place is laborious; and by pains men come to greater pains; and it is sometimes base; and by indignities men come to dignities. The standing is slippery, and the regress is either a downfall, or at least an eclipse, which is a melancholy thing. . . . All rising to great place is by a winding stair."

FRANCIS BACON, *ESSAYS,*
AMONG LINCOLN'S "FAVORITE BOOKS"

On May 26, 1856, Abraham Lincoln finished up three cases of debt collection in Danville. He had practiced law in the county courthouses of central Illinois for years, familiar stations on the Eighth Judicial Circuit. He was in Danville so often that he maintained a subsidiary law office there with his friend Ward Hill Lamon, whom he called "Hill." None of Lincoln's friends or colleagues called him "Abe." Those who did marked themselves as falsely intimate. He preferred to be called "Lincoln." He did not like being deferentially addressed as "Mr. Lincoln." "I don't recollect of his applying the prefix 'Mr.' to any

Abraham Lincoln, 1858

one," recalled Henry Clay Whitney, a young attorney who traveled from town to town with Lincoln. Lincoln called those in his coterie by their last names, except for Judge David Davis, the chief of the circuit and master of ceremonies, whom Lincoln called "Judge."

Before he rode the railroads Lincoln traveled around by horse—Old Bob and Old Tom—and buggy. "His horse was as rawboned and weird-looking as himself," recalled Whitney, "and his buggy, an open one, as rude as either; his attire was that of an ordinary farmer or stock-raiser, while the sum total of his baggage consisted of a very attenuated carpetbag, an old weather-beaten umbrella, and a short blue cloak reaching to his hips—a style which was prevalent during the Mexican War. This he had procured at Washington while a Congressman, and carried about with him as a winter covering for the years thereafter." The umbrella, originally olive green, was so old it had turned brown and the knob fallen off. No one would mistake it as belonging to anyone but Lincoln, but he had nonetheless sewn the letters of his name in it. In the spring, Lincoln switched his half cloak for a long white linen duster that was wrinkled and covered with dirt. He wore a beaver stovepipe hat that had three indentations on its thin brim from his courteous doffing of it. He often kept papers in it. Despite his wife's best efforts to make him appear a prosperous and thoroughly respectable professional man, he was "oblivious" to style, had "no talent to dress well," and gave a first impression to those from metropolitan centers as a hopeless provincial, "not susceptible to conventionality or to polish."

A few months earlier, in September 1855, Lincoln had suffered a terrible humiliation when he had come to Cincinnati to serve as cocounsel in the landmark Manny-McCormick reaper patent case. He had been hired because it was thought the case might be tried in Illinois. Arguing the case would have been a large step up for him. The imperious corporate attorney in charge, Edwin McMasters Stanton, took one look at him and remarked to another lawyer on the team, "Why did you bring that damned long-armed ape here?" Barred from a chair at the table, Lincoln learned a harsh lesson. If he were to rise beyond his circuit, it would not be by the law. But others who studied him, including eventually Stanton, would learn his "antithetical character," as Whitney described it, "the wide contrast between his exterior and formal guilelessness and simplicity of nature, and the depth of finesse, sagacity, and diplomacy which that exterior simplicity masked and concealed."

Lincoln was always approachable, utterly without affectation or pretense. He told homespun stories to juries, coarse jokes to men in the back of country stores, and played the jester among Judge Davis's traveling troupe of lawyers. His awkward and ungainly physical movements, tousled hair, repertoire of entertaining tales he liked to spin out in his Kentucky accent, and unwavering attention to others' rambling talk made him appear open, direct, and sympathetic. His plainness was authentic, his concern genuine, and his humility natural, but he was conscious that his face and manner were also screens. He could be as remote and distracted as he seemed close and warm. While he had no interest in finer things for himself or an elegant cut of his clothes, though he was happy to buy gifts for Mary and willing to wear better suits to satisfy her, he was acutely aware of the effects of his seeming lack of sophistication on others even as he seemed to be outwardly indifferent to it. He came to rely on misjudgment of his complexity by virtue of easy assumptions drawn from his appearance. Since as a young stranger he had first turned up in overalls at the after-hours debating society of his elders in New Salem and stunned the crowd with his ability to speak and reason, he had drawn together his contradictory pieces into a coherent whole. His experience in New Salem was the first time Lincoln recognized the effect his appearance had on an audience, shocking them out of their low expectations by his performance, a phenomenon that was replicated at every stage of his life from Springfield to Washington and in every new place he entered from Cooper Union to the White House. He both suffered and profited from misplaced perceptions that by his looks he was artless, innocent, or ordinary. Even his regularity as a party politician masked his unconventionality. The basic elements that he worked with were his own mind and matter. He would command an army and navy, but he began as an apprentice of self-command. It had taken Lincoln decades to achieve a self-mastery that he gradually extended over a country and its circumstances.

"His awkwardness of manner, heartiness of welcome, promises, and direct statements were genuine; his dissimulation was never express or affirmative, but always negative, implied, and utilitarian," observed Whitney. ". . . He would frequently launch out or lapse into inappropriate and fatuous themes in order to evade or neutralize those which were *mal apropos* or mischievous. . . . These by-plays of diplomacy served a needed purpose, and met a current emergency, but did not add to the fame or dignity of its possessor. Superficial men who met him on these terms, judged him by the ostensible act, and not by its occult force or ultimate results, and either ascribed to him the tame attributes of the commonplace and prosaic, or disparaged his great qualities and exploitations by ascribing to them no higher qualities than a cheap attribute of vapid and insipid goodness."

After spending the night in Danville, Lincoln boarded a train on May 27, accompanied by a small entourage of young lawyers and journalists following him on the journey to Bloomington, where the convention of a new political party would be held. Since railroad track was laid across the state he took the train using a free pass for regional lines. The group reached Decatur in the late afternoon. There was no train to Bloomington until the morning. "A considerable portion of the day remained before us and the company kept well together, strolling around the town," recalled J.O. Cunningham, the editor of the *Urbana Union*. Standing in front of the courthouse, Lincoln declared that it was "the exact spot where I stood when we moved from Indiana twenty-six years ago." He had come in an oxen-drawn wagon to Illinois in 1830, in a migrating family of thirteen, of which only his father, Thomas, was an immediate relative. The rest were his stepmother, her children and relatives, and his cousins of the Hanks branch of his mother's family. Leaving Decatur behind, they settled in Cole County, where Lincoln departed to set off on his own until he landed in New Salem. His father had rented him out as a laborer in Indiana, collecting his wages. "I used to be a slave," Lincoln would say in 1856. But he turned twenty-one in Illinois, freed from his semiliterate father's control. "No, I didn't know I had sense enough to be a lawyer then," he joked to Whitney.

"Most men forget, or at best have but a hazy abiding consciousness of their experiences, after passing through and beyond them," wrote Henry B. Rankin later, a clerk in the Lincoln-Herndon law office. "With very few are they available immediately when needed. Not so with Lincoln. His whole varied past life was with him an active, vivid, present asset upon which he could depend and draw on effectively at any moment when he needed to use those experiences as resources for any present emergency. Present day psychologists divide life into the conscious and subconscious. If they be correct, Mr. Lincoln's subconsciousness must have been located in the tips of his fingers and tongue, and not hidden away in the silences of the grey matter of any subconscious existence. He was certainly most alertly conscious in every present moment of all that, in the past, had ever existed in his mental or emotional being."

With daylight remaining Lincoln led his traveling group with him into the woods by the Sangamon River. He was no longer thinking about his origins but his future. "Here, seated upon a fallen tree," wrote Cunningham, "Mr. Lincoln talked freely as he had during the afternoon, of his hopes and fears for the coming convention, and of his earnest wish that the Whig element of the southern counties might be well represented there. He was among political friends, there being several lawyers and editors who sympathized politically with him, and he did not attempt to conceal fears and misgivings entertained by him as to the outcome of the gathering. He was well assured that the radical element of the northern counties would be there in force, and feared the effect upon the conservative element of the central and southern parts of the State. It was for the latter he seemed most concerned."

The convention would begin in two days, but Lincoln was staring into a glass darkly. He did not know who would arrive there, whether the disparate delegates would come together and depart prepared to do battle as a unified political party that had no prior existence, no agreed upon antecedents or icons, and no previously acknowledged leader to lead them out of the wilderness. Lincoln's anxieties were small and large, tactical and strategic, personal and political.

Lincoln was a man of the party, a thorough partisan, but now without a party. "I am a Whig," he wrote his old friend Joshua Speed in 1855, "but others say there are no Whigs, and that I am an abolitionist." He had been trained since he was a young man in New Salem in the strictures of party loyalty. His mentor and surrogate father, Bowling Green, the justice of the peace, taught him the basics, encouraged him to read the law, nursed him through his depressions, and boosted him to run for the state legislature. But when Green broke with the party on an issue, Lincoln joined in declining to slate him for office. After Green suddenly died from a stroke, Lincoln was too grief stricken to deliver more than a tearful mumbled eulogy. Lincoln, who had tried being a surveyor and owning a store, studied the law to advance himself in politics. He was the protégé of John Todd Stuart, a leading lawyer of Springfield and state legislator, and learned the mechanics of favors in what was called "log rolling" to pass legislation. By the age of twenty-seven, Lincoln became the floor leader of the Whigs, chief of "the Junto," and instrumental in moving the capital from Vandalia to Springfield. In the first national campaign of the party for "Tippecanoe and Tyler, Too" in 1840 he had achieved pride of place as a presidential elector. He knew the intricacies of vote counting and party allegiance in every town and county. By arranging the convention system to control nominations for elective office he arranged for himself to become a congressman. But he had only one term, made little impression, failed to win a federal patronage position from the incoming Whig administration despite his extensive lobbying, and retreated into his law practice. His political prospects vanished partly for having spoken against the Mexican War. And then the party to which he had pledged his devotion broke into drifting pieces after being swamped in the election of 1852.

Lincoln had just run in early 1855 to become the U.S. senator as the Whig candidate. He had more of the votes in the state legislature than the other two candidates—the incumbent Democratic governor Joel Matteson, an ally of Douglas, and Illinois Supreme Court Judge Lyman Trumbull, an antislavery Democrat—but not enough for a majority. When Matteson began bribing legislators, Lincoln threw his votes to Trumbull. (Mary Lincoln never spoke again to Trumbull's wife, Julia, her longtime friend.) Lincoln's self-sacrifice was the last rite of the Whig Party. It also ingratiated him to the splintered-off antislavery Democrats. Trumbull especially owed him an enormous debt.

There was at the beginning of 1856 only one political party in Illinois, the Democratic Party of Stephen A. Douglas. The rest was flotsam and jetsam, fragments of wreckage. The old Whig Party had no cause, no principle, no chance of winning offices, nothing to hold it together, in short, no further reason for existence. Yet some Old Whigs preferred the lost party that had never quite cohered and could not be restored. They wanted the party as it was, though it was rarely a winning party. They held on to the identity even tighter as it faded, some because it was familiar in a world of unknowns, some out of repulsion of Democrats of any kind, some out of hatred of abolitionists, and some out of accumulated wounds, slights, and resentments. Some clung to the disappearing party's central organizing idea that held together its Northern and Southern wings, the avoidance of principle on slavery. Some joined the American Party, or the Know Nothings, who would bar any but native-born Protestants from holding public office, a more potent nationalist nostalgia defined against the wave of immigrants. Some antislavery Democrats for their part detested Douglas yet remained wary of their old opponents. Abolitionists frightened Old Whigs and Democrats alike. Lincoln had contempt for the bigotry of the Know Nothings, but would say nothing in public to offend them, many of them Whigs he knew well, hoping they would become exhausted. He felt he needed them in the long run. His plan was not to concede to their nativism, but wait for their movement to collapse or be destroyed. Without leaving fingerprints, Lincoln used his political surrogates to undermine them wherever he could. Many of the Old

Whigs, he feared, might either go with the Know Nothings or the Democrats. For all he knew the Republican Party could be a failed experiment.

Illinois was the last large state in which the Republican Party was organized, lagging behind, more fractionalized than the others. With the influx of German immigration and the explosive growth of the city of Chicago the state's social composition was rapidly changing. Until the early 1850s, northern Illinois had been sparsely populated and of little political weight. The Whigs had been rooted in southern and central Illinois in a population originally drawn from poor whites of Kentucky like Lincoln himself. And the balance of power still favored the Democrats, as it always had. Illinois had never voted in a presidential election for the Whig candidate.

Before the Kansas-Nebraska Act, the political antislavery movement in Illinois was negligible. "Up to that date," wrote J.O. Cunningham, an antislavery newspaper editor, "no ballot had ever been cast in perhaps a majority of the counties of the State for the candidates of the 'Liberty' or 'Free Soil' party, and such as had been cast, not exceeding 6 per cent of the entire vote of the State, were in the northern counties; so that slavery agitation before the latter date, had prevailed only within a few of the counties."

After Lincoln delivered his speech in the Hall of Representatives in the State Capitol on October 4, 1854, against the Nebraska Act, a small gaggle of abolitionists approached him to ask if he would join their meeting that night of a group they called the Republican Party. He explained he had legal business in another county. The group put his name on its State Central Committee anyway, but Lincoln declined to attend a November meeting. He explained to one of its members, Ichabod Codding, a minister and abolitionist, "I suppose my opposition to the principle of slavery is as strong as that of any member of the Republican party; but I had also supposed that the *extent* to which I feel authorized to carry that opposition, practically, was not at all satisfactory to that party."

"Finding himself drifting about with the disorganized elements that floated together after the angry political waters had subsided," wrote Herndon, "it became apparent to Lincoln that if he expected to figure as a leader he must take a stand himself. Mere hatred of slavery and opposition to the injustice of the Kansas-Nebraska legislation were not all that were required on him. He must be a Democrat, Know-Nothing, Abolitionist, or Republican, or forever float about in the great political sea without compass, rudder, or sail. At length he declared himself."

But after his failed run for the Senate, through 1855, Lincoln's seeming indecision was mainly the result of his close reading of the fugue state of politics, a period characterized by dissociation and disorder. Old identities had melted but newer ones were not solid. During this confused interregnum, Lincoln was in touch with leaders of all factions who were considering the possibility of "fusionism." Among them was one who had asked him to join the Republicans. Owen Lovejoy, the evangelical abolitionist, whose brother Elijah P. Lovejoy, the antislavery editor, was the first martyr of the antislavery cause in 1837 in Alton, Illinois, when he was murdered defending his printing press. "I shall never forsake the cause that has been sprinkled with my brother's blood," Owen pledged over Elijah's body. Lincoln wrote him on August 11, 1855, to argue why it was premature to proclaim a new party. His objection was purely strategic.

> Not even *you* are more anxious to prevent the extension of slavery than I; and yet the political atmosphere is such, just now, that I fear to do anything, lest I do wrong. Know-nothingism has not yet entirely tumbled to pieces—nay, it is even a little encouraged by the late elections in Tennessee, Kentucky & Alabama. Until we can get the elements of this organization, there is not sufficient materials to successfully combat the Nebraska democracy with. We can not get them so long as they cling to a hope of success under their own organization; and I fear an open push by us now, may offend them, and tend to prevent our ever getting them. About us here, they are mostly my old political and personal friends; and I have hoped their organization would die out without the painful necessity of my taking an open stand against them. Of their principles I think little better than I do of those of the slavery extensionists. Indeed I do not perceive how any one professing to be sensitive to the wrongs of the negroes, can join in a league to degrade a class of white men. I have no objection to "fuse" with any body provided I can fuse on ground which I think is right; and I believe the opponents of slavery extension could now do this, if it were not for this K. N. ism.

Lincoln's letter showed his political state of mind even before he had committed himself to a new course. His willingness to treat Owen Lovejoy as a reasonable partner rather than a radical figure of scorn, like many of Lincoln's Old Whig friends, such as David Davis, for whom the mention of Lovejoy aroused hate "with a burning intensity," already set him apart.

Since 1854, Herndon had assured abolitionists in Illinois who were unfamiliar and wary of Lincoln about his true feelings. He told Zebina Eastman, editor of the abolitionist newspaper *Free West,* published in Chicago, who distrusted "professions of mere politicians," that Lincoln was "a natural-born antislavery man" and "all right."

By the end of the year, over the protests of some of his closest Old Whig colleagues, particularly John Todd Stuart, Lincoln accepted an invitation from a number of antislavery editors to plan the convention for a new party. On February 22, 1856, he presided at the meeting, steering it safely through a conflict over nativism that threatened to tear the gathering apart, ruling in favor of an anti-nativist resolution proposed by the editor George Schneider of the German language *Illinois Staats-Zeitung.*

Herndon served as Lincoln's useful agent in working on the new party. Lincoln's younger law partner was both a devoted Whig and an abolitionist, a Southerner who was inspired by New Englanders beginning with his formative experience as a student at Illinois College, presided over by its president Edward Beecher of the famous theological and antislavery family. Herndon struck up a correspondence with Theodore Parker, "my Ideal," whose writings he passed on to Lincoln. Named along with Lincoln as an executive committee member of the new party from Springfield, Herndon wrote Parker on April 28, 1856, "I hope to live to see the day when I can make slavery feel my influence. That shall be the one object of my life." When the news of the assault on Sumner reached Springfield, Herndon decided to send Sumner a letter. "The people are assaulted through you," he wrote. "A feeling, wild and deep is aroused here."

Despite the apparent consensus among the convention planners, the name "Republican" was discarded as too controversial. "Up to that date," wrote Cunningham, "the term 'Republican,' as the name of a political party had been made use of in other states and in a few localities in this State, as a party designation; but with the use made of it by Senator Douglas in connection with the prefix 'Black,' and the hated epithet 'Abolitionist,' it carried with it much that was obnoxious to the people of a considerable part of the State. So the convention planners made no use of this name, but on the contrary called for a 'State Convention of the Anti-Nebraska Party of Illinois.'"

While on the one hand Lincoln deployed Herndon on the other he also relied upon conservative Old Whig friends. Orville Hickman Browning led a parallel life to Lincoln's: a native Kentuckian, veteran of the Black Hawk War, member of the state legislature, and lawyer on the circuit. He arrived in Bloomington on May 28, a day before Lincoln. He expressed his fears that the convention could go off the rails to Trumbull on May 19: "We wish if possible to keep the party in this state under the control of moderate men, and conservative influences, and if we do so the future destiny of the state is in our own hands and victory will inevitably crown our exertions. On the other hand if rash and ultra counsels prevail all is lost." While Browning and Lincoln were colleagues and ostensible allies, Browning harbored a jealousy rooted in his sense that Lincoln was the inferior man, that "the handsome, stately, suave college man and finished orator regarded himself as superior to the homely, self-educated, rough and ready stump-speaker," according to historian Theodore Calvin Pease, who edited Browning's diaries.

If the convention were to spin apart, dissolve into enmity and recrimination, and fail to give birth to a viable organization, the fiasco would belong to Lincoln. Lincoln's own political career would be finished before it was revived. If the new party emerged in a weakened condition in Illinois, the potential for the national Republican Party would be severely damaged. Without a unified Illinois party, the Republicans might stand little chance of ever winning the presidency. Without Illinois, the Electoral College calculus would be forbidding and the cause of limiting the extension of slavery would be eternally frustrated.

Lincoln was acutely aware of the stakes, not least concerning himself. Since he had run for the Senate, he was determined to run again, the next time in 1858 against his constant rival. Lincoln always envied Douglas's seemingly unstoppable rise far beyond him and felt belittled, even helpless. In his first formal speech, his Springfield Lyceum Address in 1838, Lincoln had warned against Douglas's overreaching ambition, which "thirsts and burns" for "celebrity," "fame," and power. "Distinction will be his paramount object; and although he would as willingly, perhaps more so, acquire it by doing good as harm; yet, that opportunity being past, and nothing left to be done in the way of building up, he would set boldly to the task of pulling down."

The Little Giant had grown into a colossus while Lincoln disappeared into the prairie. During the 1852 campaign, Lincoln observed, "Douglas has got to be a great man, and [be]strode the earth. Time was when I was in his way some; but he has outgrown me and [be]strides the world; and such small men as I am, can hardly be considered worthy of his notice; and I may have to dodge and get between his legs." "Twenty-two years ago," Lincoln recalled later in 1856, "Judge Douglas and I first became acquainted. We were both young then; he a trifle younger than I. Even then, we were both ambitious; I, perhaps, quite as much so he. With *me,* the race of ambition has been a failure—a flat failure; with *him* it has been one of splendid success.

His name fills the nation; and is not unknown, even, in foreign lands. I affect no contempt for the high eminence he has reached. So reached, that the oppressed of my species, might have shared with me in the elevation, I would rather stand on that eminence, than wear the richest crown that ever pressed a monarch's brow."

Douglas had done the work for Lincoln he could not do for himself. Lincoln's chance was Douglas's unintended consequence. Douglas's fierce need to smash everything and everybody in his way cleared a path for Lincoln. Douglas's bedlam invited Lincoln's entrance. The moment Douglas proposed the Kansas-Nebraska Act, Lincoln responded as if it were a cue. "In 1854, his profession had almost superseded the thought of politics in his mind, when the repeal of the Missouri compromise aroused him as he had never been before," Lincoln wrote later in a brief autobiography for the 1860 campaign. But while politics was closed to him after his congressional term and he was immersed in his legal practice, he still prepared himself for some greater political destiny that he could not anticipate.

Lincoln's stark naturalness, his extremes of silliness and melancholy, masked his romantic and fatalistic sense of himself. "Closely allied and interwoven with these traits was an inherent belief in his *destiny,*" wrote Whitney. "I am not aware that a specific destiny was clearly outlined to him; if so, he did not reveal it; but on several occasions he avowed that he was doomed to a violent and bloody end." Whitney recalled Lincoln coming into his law office in October 1854 and pulling Byron's *Childe Harold* from the shelf to read aloud:

> *There is a very life in our despair. . . .*
> *He who ascends to mountain-tops shall find*
> *The loftiest peaks most wrapt in clouds and snow;*
> *He who surpasses or subdues mankind,*
> *Must look down on the hate of those below.*
> *Though high above the sun of glory glow,*
> *And far beneath the earth and ocean spread,*
> *Round him are icy rocks, and loudly blow,*
> *Contending tempests on his naked head,*
> *And thus reward the toils which to those summits led.*

Traveling around central Illinois riding Old Tom or Old Bob was a vocation but not a destiny. Lincoln's ambition, that "little engine that knew no rest," according to Herndon, was stalled but not dampened. Lincoln had not lost such interest in politics that he failed to follow them in the newspapers and study them in books. During the years when he was not running for office or thinking of running for office, he read eclectically the volumes Herndon collected in the best private library in Springfield. He read the *New York Tribune,* the *Richmond Enquirer,* British journals, proslavery and antislavery tracts, works on science, volumes of humor, poetry, Shakespeare, and the geometry of Euclid in order to master the underlying principles of logic. But the telltale book that revealed his inner sense as a man of political destiny was Francis Bacon's *Essays.*

Francis Bacon was the preeminent English Renaissance man of science and politics. His *Novum Organum,* published in 1620, established the principles of the scientific method of experimentation and evidence. After serving as a member of Parliament, attorney general, and Lord Chancellor, he wrote his *Essays,* a series of fifty-eight pieces providing insight into the character and conduct of statecraft. These epigrammatic essays ranged from "Of Truth" to "Of Faction" to "Of Vain Glory," in which he observed, "Glorious men are the scorn of wise men; the admiration of fools; the idols of parasites; and the slaves of their own vaunts." In "Of Honor and Reputation," he categorized ignoble and noble rulers, the virtuous beginning with those who were founders of states, followed by the "second founders" who were the lawgivers, then liberators from the "long miseries of civil wars, or deliver their countries from servitude of strangers or tyrants," and finally the honor that is "the greatest, which happens rarely; that is of such as sacrifice themselves to death or danger of the good of their country."

A politician intent on the discipline of power would seek instruction in Bacon. In "Of Great Place," Bacon wrote, "Men in great place are thrice servants; servants of the sovereign or state; servants of fame; and servants of freedom; so as they have no freedom, neither in their persons, nor in their actions, nor in their times. . . . When he sits in place he is another man." Lincoln, according to Whitney, was also acquainted with Bacon's biography. "He once spoke to me in highly eulogistic terms of Bacon, at which I expressed surprise, and ventured to object that he had been accused of receiving bribes. Lincoln admitted this to be true, but in extenuation said that it had never made any difference in his decisions; in short, he admired him for his strength in spite of his flagitiousness." But Lincoln may also have understood that a man in power subject to envy (the subject of another Bacon essay) could be accused of wrongdoing for reasons of power.

Lincoln applied the empirical and inductive Baconian scientific method by idiosyncratic means. "In his exterior affairs he had no method, system, or order," wrote Whitney.

> He had no library of any sort, law or other, at any time. He had no clerk, stenographer, or typewriter; no letter-copying book, no scrap or common-place book, no diary, no *index rerum,* no cash or account book, no daybook, journal, or ledger. When he received money for law practice, he gave his partner his share at the time, or wrapped it in a bit of paper, awaiting an opportunity to divide. Even when he was President, when he wanted to preserve an unofficial memorandum of any kind, he noted it on a card, and put it in a drawer or, mayhap, in his vest pocket. But in his mental processes and operations he had a most complete method, system, and order; while outside of his mind all was anarchy and confusion, inside all was symmetry and precision. His mind was his workshop; he had little need of an office or pen, ink, and paper; he could perform his chief labor by self-introspection and reflection.

In drawing up his cases, Lincoln sought all the evidence from every source he could muster. He organized his facts in logic that point after point refuted his adversary's. His plain language and fetching stories allowed his arguments to be easily grasped by the juries he knew well and who were indistinguishable from the voters. For his major political addresses, he sometimes spent weeks working on their construction, and they became the template for dozens of stump speeches. His efforts were always a silent internal struggle. When he arrived at his conclusions they were locked into his mind and he would not reverse them. His oratorical method was also his political method. "The great secret of his power as an orator, in my judgment, lay in the clearness and perspicuity of his statements," recalled Leonard Swett, a younger lawyer from Bloomington who was part of his circle.

> When Lincoln had stated a case, it was always more than half argued and the point more than half won. The first impression he generally conveyed was, that he had stated the case of his adversary better and more forcibly, than his opponent could state it himself. He then answered that state of facts fairly and fully, never passing by, or skipping over a bad point. When this was done, he presented his own case. There was a feeling when he argued a case, in the mind of any man who listened to him, that nothing had been

passed over; yet if he could not answer the objections he argued in his own mind and himself arrived at the conclusion to which he was leading others; he had very little power of argumentation. The force of his logic was in conveying to the minds of others the same clear and thorough analysis he had in his own, and if his own mind failed to be satisfied, he had no power to satisfy any body else. His mode and force of argument was in stating how he had reasoned upon the subject and how he had come to his conclusion. . . . From the commencement of his life to its close, I have sometimes doubted whether he ever asked anybody's advice about anything. He would listen to everybody; he would hear everybody, but he never asked for opinions. I never knew him in trying a lawsuit to ask the advice of any lawyer he was associated with.

Boarding an early morning train from Decatur to Bloomington on May 28, Lincoln anxiously walked through every car. "I really would like to know if any of those men are from down south, going to the convention. I don't see any harm in asking them," he announced to those traveling with him. He returned after twenty minutes, "his face radiant with happiness," according to Whitney, having identified a grand total of two delegates, one of them a former legislative colleague, Jesse K. Dubois, a conservative Old Whig. Lincoln was glad to see two, but especially delighted to see Dubois.

The town swarmed with delegates, virtually all from the northern and central counties, the Pike House hotel "full to overflowing and the streets alive with partisans of the 'anti-Nebraska' type," recalled Cunningham. The night before they had excitedly gathered in the square to hear from the hotel's veranda Andrew Reeder, the former governor of Kansas, his hair still tinted from the silver nitrate he had applied for his disguise as a tramp in order to escape. "Poor Reeder is the only public man who has been silly enough to believe that any thing like fairness was ever intended; and he has been bravely undeceived," Lincoln had written Speed on August 24, 1855. Sara Robinson, the wife of the free state leader Charles Robinson, also on the run, mingled in the crowd, along with politicians of all stripes, abolitionists, and German editors (including

Jesse K. Dubois

twenty-three-year-old John G. Nicolay, who would become Lincoln's private secretary in the White House).

Upon his arrival Lincoln walked the short distance from the Illinois Central depot to the mansion of Judge Davis, where he usually stayed when he was in Bloomington. Two old friends joined him there, Judge T. Lyle Dickey and former legislator Archibald Williams, both Old Whigs and regulars on the circuit. Orville Hickman Browning appeared that afternoon and was dispatched to organize the order of business for the next day. "No resolutions had been prepared for the Convention tomorrow, and no program of Proceedings settled; and many discordant elements to be harmonized," he wrote in his diary. He assembled a group of about twenty men "of all shades of opinion" to work on the resolutions, which were based on the template Lincoln had hammered out at the preliminary meeting in February. Once again, the sticking point was a conflict between Know Nothings and Germans that had nearly torn apart the organization, but resolved as Lincoln had resolved it before. "Mr. Lincoln, who was a delegate, counseled every step that was taken, in his quiet, persuasive way," wrote Joseph Medill of the *Chicago Tribune,* who was also a delegate.

As the alpha and omega of unity the resolutions went no further than opposing the extension of slavery. If the platform had embraced other issues, such as opposition to the Fugitive Slave Act, the convention would have spun apart before it had come together. Lincoln "advised the committee to endorse" the Declaration of Independence to underpin its resolution that Congress "possessed full constitutional power to prohibit slavery in all territories." Another resolution that would receive universal acclaim denounced Douglas: "*Resolved,* That Stephen A. Douglas, having laid his 'ruthless hand' upon a sacred compact, which had 'an origin akin to that of the constitution,' and which had 'become canonized in the hearts of the American people,' has given the lie to his past history, proved himself recreant to the free principles of this government, violated the confidence of the people of Illinois, and now holds his seat in the Senate while he misrepresents them." Just as Douglas was damned yet another resolution equally praised Trumbull as "able and consistent." That evening Lincoln wandered back to the depot to spot people he might know coming to the convention on the Chicago train. On the way he stopped at a shop to buy a pair of reading glasses for 37½ cents, explaining to Whitney he "kinder" needed them. When he saw Norman B. Judd, a Chicago attorney and Democratic state senator, he remarked, "That's the best sign yet; Judd is there; and he's a trimmer." "One conspicuous matter

is this," wrote Whitney, "that while Lincoln did not, as a rule, betray enthusiasm under any stress of circumstances, he was in a state of enthusiasm
and suppressed excitement throughout this convention; yet he kept his mental balance, and was not swerved a hair's breadth from perfect equipoise in
speech or action."

At Bloomington he went out of his way to introduce people from disparate political backgrounds to each other. When he brought "the polite and
courtly Browning to the unpolished and irreverent Wentworth"—"Long
John" Wentworth, the Democratic congressman and boss of Chicago—
Browning courteously said, "I have never had the pleasure of meeting you,
but I have heard much of you," to which Wentworth replied, "Damned much
against me." "It struck Lincoln as being very comical," recalled Whitney. "I
heard him repeat it a dozen times that day."

Lincoln had been quietly operating behind the scenes for months, trying
to bring together the patchwork coalition of hostile factions and edgy personalities. He expended much of his energy convincing William H. Bissell,
a Democratic congressman, to head the ticket as its candidate for governor.
Without Bissell at the top of the slate, the party might easily fracture. From
Lincoln's point of view, he was the ideal man, the perfectly crafted Democrat
for the purpose—the law partner of James Shields, the former Democratic
U.S. senator; a Mexican War hero; and member of Congress elected in 1849
as a follower of Douglas.

But, unlike Douglas, Bissell bristled at Southern arrogance. "The Southerners are insolent, overbearing and bullying beyond all belief," he wrote.
When Congressman James Seddon of Virginia delivered a speech in 1850
falsely depicting Northern troops routed and replaced by courageous ones
from Mississippi at the Battle of Buena Vista, Bissell the war veteran was
enraged. "Why, but for the purpose of furnishing materials for that ceaseless,
never-ending eternal theme of 'Southern chivalry'?" The former colonel of
the Mississippi regiment in question, Jefferson Davis, challenged Bissell to
a duel, which, to his surprise, Bissell promptly accepted. President Zachary
Taylor directly intervened to halt it. (Davis, after all, was his former son-
in-law.) "There certainly would have been a fight, and one or both of them
killed had it not been for General Taylor," said Douglas.

At the editors' organizing meeting at Decatur, on February 22, 1856,
Lincoln turned aside an effort to nominate him for governor and instead
advanced the name of Bissell. "If I should be chosen the Democrats would
say, 'it was nothing more than an attempt to resurrect the dead body of the

old Whig party.' I would secure the vote of that party and no more and our defeat would follow as a matter of course. But, I can suggest a name that will secure not only the old Whig vote, but enough Anti-Nebraska Democrats to give us the victory. That name is Col. William H. Bissell."

At first Bissell was receptive to Lincoln's flattery, but on the convention's eve he suddenly cooled. He felt that the Whigs had too much influence and "the anti Nebraska Democrats ought to have rallied, and taken the control and direction of this Bloomington Convention—made it, and its candidates, their own," he wrote Trumbull, and therefore decided "my present inclination is to decline a nomination, should one be tendered me." But the reluctant candidate was finally persuaded, which brightened Lincoln's mood in anticipation of Bloomington. "Lincoln and myself had a long talk in reference to affairs," Herndon wrote Trumbull, "and I have never seen him so sanguine of success, as in this Election—*he is warm*. I gathered this from him,—recollect he has been round our Judicial Circuit—,that the people are warm and full of feeling on this question—this great and mighty issue . . . never saw so much '*dogged determination*' to fight it out;—that the Democrats are coming to us daily."

Early on the morning of the 29th, Isaac N. Arnold, a Chicago lawyer and a former Democratic legislator turned Free Soiler, stood at the top of the main staircase of Pike House to read Chicago newspaper accounts of the Ruffians' assault on Lawrence, Kansas, "with almost tragic emphasis," which served "to inflame the sentiment of listening delegates and others in attendance upon the convention to the highest degree, even the old Whigs."

The convention opened in Major's Hall, the third floor above a hardware store, 270 delegates packed on benches, with Archibald Williams presiding as chairman and a roll call of the counties. From nearly all the southern counties not a single delegate answered. When Lawrence County was called, no one responded. "Mr. Chairman," shouted Lincoln, "let Lawrence be called again; there is a delegate in town from there, and a very good man is it, too." So it was called again, and again it was met with silence. Its delegate, Jesse K. Dubois, "seeing Lovejoy and other Abolitionists there as cherished delegates, he, through indignation or timidity, stayed away for the time being," recalled Whitney.

Before the chairman proceeded with the announcement of convention committees to present reports one Leander Munsell, an Old Whig former legislator, jumped the gun, declaring the nomination of Bissell for governor. "The lapse from conventionalities was little noticed, for the nomination met with a tornado of second from all parts of the hall," recalled Cunningham. Bissell's nomination was "made by acclamation, amid a whirlwind of cheers and huzzas." Then other candidates for state offices were named, including Jesse K. Dubois for state auditor, undoubtedly the doing of Lincoln. Dubois was still not present, though somehow after he was slated he managed to turn up.

Browning was summoned to deliver the opening speech. "His remarks were addressed mainly to the old Clay-Whigs," reported John Locke Scripps of the *Chicago Democratic Press*. "He read extracts from the speeches of Henry Clay from his first entrance upon public life down to the close of his career, all of which proved him to have been steadfastly and uniformly opposed to the spread of slavery into free territory, and that had he still been upon the stage of action when his great measures of pacification—the Missouri Compromise—was ruthlessly violated, his voice and vote would have been the same in 1854, that they were in 1820." But Browning went on "to ever remember that slavery itself was one of the compromises of the Constitution, and was sacredly protected by the supreme law." This was not the view of Lincoln, who cited the founders in his speeches for being antislavery and believing that it would be somehow abolished.

As Browning was the safest and stodgiest speaker, the next one was the least predictable and most exciting. Owen Lovejoy delivered "a terrific declamation against slavery and all its works," according to Medill—"the blazing meteor upon the platform," wrote Cunningham. Then came the surprise. "Many had only known him by what his enemies had said of him and only expected to see the veritable 'Raw Head and Bloody-Bones' of the Abolition Ogre, who surely must be of kin to 'Auld Clootie.'" But Lovejoy proved himself a strategic politician, not just a preacher. He explained that he was opposed to slavery's extension—"that was all." He embraced the platform. He did not make radical demands. He did not use his moral prestige with his followers as a lever for disillusionment. "He broke down much of the unreasonable prejudice against himself and secured for himself a hearing before an audience in Illinois without danger of insult, a treatment he could not, before then, expect." He was, the *Democratic Press* reported, "determined that the cause with which he was identified should not be injured."

Unexpectedly, James S. Emery, a participant at the convention from Lawrence, along with Sara Robinson and Andrew Reeder, was summoned to the platform to speak. Emery was a justice of the peace and an editor whose printing press had been destroyed in the Ruffians' rampage. Medill of the

Tribune had tapped him on the shoulder and sent him up to the podium while the resolutions committee was meeting out of the room, "adding that I must stop when I saw the committee come in, as it had been arranged to have 'a fellow up here from Springfield, Abe Lincoln, make a speech. He is the best stump-speaker in Sangamon county.'" Emery delivered compelling eyewitness stories of "Bleeding Kansas," "with language severe and almost intemperate appeals for armed interference," according to Cunningham. During his vehement talk, Emery felt himself distracted, scanning the audience "trying to pick out Mr. Lincoln." Abruptly, the resolutions committee appeared and Emery's blast ended.

"As I stepped aside, Mr. Lincoln was called for from all sides," Emery recalled. "I then for the first time, and the last, fixed my eyes on the great president. I thought he was not dressed very neatly, and that his gait in walking up to the platform was sort of swinging. His hair was sort of rather rough and the stoop of his shoulders was noticeable; but what took me most was his intense serious look."

Major's Hall was filled with journalists, lawyers, and politicians used to making documentary records. Everyone present felt they were taking part in a momentous historical event that was a watershed in their own lives. Yet there was not one detailed account produced of Lincoln's talk, which became known as his "Lost Speech." "While Mr. Lincoln did not write out even a memorandum of his Bloomington speech beforehand, neither was it extemporary," Medill wrote. "He intended days before to make it, and conned it over in his mind in outline, and gathered his facts, and arranged his arguments in regular order, and trusted to the inspiration of the occasion to furnish him the diction with which to clothe the skeleton of his great oration."

"At first," wrote Medill, "his voice was shrill and hesitating. There was a curious introspective look in his eyes, which lasted for a few moments. Then his voice began to move steadily and smoothly forward, and the modulations were under perfect control from thenceforward to the finish. He warmed up as he went on, and spoke more rapidly; he looked a foot taller as he straightened himself to his full height, and his eyes flashed fire; his countenance became wrapped in intense emotion; he rushed along like a thunderstorm. He prophesied war as the outcome of these aggressions, and poured forth hot denunciations upon the slave power. The convention was kept in an uproar, applauding and cheering and stamping; and this reacted on the speaker, and gave him a tongue of fire."

Several patchy descriptions of the speech were published immediately afterward. The editor of the *Alton Courier,* George T. Brown, reported that Lincoln "enumerated the pressing reasons for the present movement" and "was here ready to fuse with anyone who would unite with him to oppose [the] slave power." The editor of the *Belleville Advocate,* Nathaniel Niles, described how "his wonderful eloquence electrified the audience of two thousand men." The *Bloomington Pantagraph* reported that "without being invidious, we must say that Mr. Lincoln . . . surpassed all others—even himself. His points were unanswerable, and the force and power of his appeals, irresistible."

But Lincoln's speech was never contemporaneously published and recollections of it differed. Whitney claimed decades later to have reconstructed it, but his version was not accepted. When the McLean County Historical Society based in Bloomington held a conference in 1900 on the 1856 convention at which surviving participants gave their reminiscences, the society concluded: "This has been called the 'Lost Speech' of Mr. Lincoln. Since then portions of this speech have lingered in men's minds like some half-forgotten music which one thinks he can recall, but regretfully finds it an elusive dream."

It seems likely though that two remembered passages were accurate. Cunningham recalled: "Seeming to know that there had been wild talk about people going to Kansas armed with Sharpe's rifles, with which to settle the contentions there in issue, he began most gently with a rebuke for such appeals to violence. In words he deprecated the use of force as a means of settling the issue, and concluded this part of his speech with these words as nearly as I remember them: *'No, my friends, I'll tell you what we will do, we will wait until November, and then we will shoot paper ballots at them,'* referring, of course, to the coming presidential election and to the ballots to be then cast." A number of others who were there also recalled Lincoln speaking as though to Southerners and saying, *"We won't go out of the Union, and you shan't!"*

About his closing remark about the Union, Cunningham wrote, "This was said with great deliberation, when he had raised his figure to its greatest height, his eyes, usually so mild and playful, now flashing wild determination, and with vehement gestures with his head and arms. The effect upon his audience was shown by the applause with which it was greeted, amid which the orator withdrew from the stand, and the work of the convention was over. There were then no Whigs, Democrats, nor Free-Soilers, but men of every shade had been fused into a conquering phalanx."

Herndon's reaction captured not only his enthusiasm of the moment but also his sense that Lincoln had entered into a new phase, growing in stature before his eyes. "I give it as my opinion that the Bloomington speech was the grand effort of this life," he insisted. "Heretofore he had simply argued the slavery question on grounds of policy,—the statesman's grounds,—never reaching the question of the radical and the eternal right. . . . I attempted for about fifteen minutes as was usual with me then to take notes, but at the end of that time I threw pen and paper away and lived only in the inspiration of the hour. If Mr. Lincoln was six feet, four inches high usually, at Bloomington that day he was seven feet."

A number of observers believed that the radical tenor of Lincoln's effort was the reason it was not fully documented. "My belief is that," wrote Medill, "after Mr. Lincoln cooled down, he was rather pleased that his speech had not been reported, as it was too radical in expression on the slavery question for the digestion of central and southern Illinois at that time, and that he preferred to let it stand as a remembrance in the minds of his audience. But, be that as it may, the effect of it was such on his hearers that he bounded to the leadership of the new Republican party of Illinois, and no man afterwards ever thought of disputing that position with him."

Another delegate, Eugene F. Baldwin, later the founder of the *Peoria Journal* and *Peoria Star* newspapers, recalled that "the great mass of the leaders felt that Lincoln made too radical a speech and they did not want it produced for fear it would damage the party. Lincoln himself said he had put his foot into it and asked the reporters to simply report the meeting and not attempt to record his words and they agreed to it."

The controversy flared for years about Lincoln's language at the convention, especially his use of the phrase "a house divided, half slave, half free." According to Leonard Swett, one of Lincoln's coterie, the conservative T. Lyle Dickey insisted that Lincoln first publicly spoke of a "house divided" in the Bloomington speech, not as generally believed in 1858. "I was inclined at the time to believe these words were hastily and inconsiderately uttered, but subsequent facts have convinced me they were deliberate and had been matured," Swett told Herndon. "Judge T.L. Dickey says that at Bloomington at the first Republican Convention, in 1856, he uttered the same sentences in a Speech delivered there, and that after the meeting was over, he (Dickey) called his attention to these remarks. Lincoln justified himself in making them, by stating they were true; but finally at Dickey's urgent request, he pronounced that for his sake, or upon his advice, he would not repeat them."

Lincoln at Bloomington put himself at the head of the party that more than anyone else he had created. From the moment he decided to throw himself into the task his abilities were tested. The party had to draw the allegiance of German revolutionaries and abolitionist clergymen as well as suspicious Old Whigs and dissident Democrats, all the while chipping away at Know Nothings. He was able to hold together the odd collection of forces through skills acquired in a lifetime in politics. But the convention was more than a triumph of mechanics. Lincoln had to harmonize the themes to the varied constituencies. He had to frame a platform broad enough to encompass the spectrum of factions and yet narrow enough not to lose viability. Ultimately, he had to accomplish the feat himself. His performance as a speaker aroused the delegates to a novel state of unity. Still, the hazards were hardly removed, and old partisan identities were not easily overcome.

Lincoln was almost completely preoccupied with coaxing recalcitrant Old Whigs. "Your party is so mad at Douglas for wrecking his party that it will gulp down anything," he told former Democrats Norman Judd and Ebenezer Peck, "but our party [Whig] is fresh from Kentucky and must not be forced to radical measures; the Abolitionists will go with us anyway, and your wing of the Democratic party the same, but the Whigs hold the balance of power and will be hard to manage, anyway. Why, I had a hard time to hold Dubois when he found Lovejoy and Codding here; he insisted on going home at once." The difficulties Lincoln encountered in the making of the Illinois Republican Party were a rehearsal for constantly rising political complexity and adversity in which his more conservative friends would threaten his fragile creation.

But Dubois was finally won over by Lincoln's speech. As he walked out of the hall he turned to Whitney and said in a "burst of enthusiasm," "Whitney, that is the greatest speech ever made in Illinois and it puts Lincoln on the track for the Presidency." Whitney claimed to have related the remark to Lincoln, the first suggestion he might be president, and "he walked along without straightening himself up for some thirty seconds, perhaps without saying a word; but with a thoughtful, abstracted look:—then he straightened up and immediately made a remark about some commonplace subject, having no reference to the subject we had been considering."

CHAPTER FOURTEEN

MISS FANCY

The Democratic Party convention opened on June 2 in Cincinnati, within days of the Bloomington event. It was a three-way contest. Franklin Pierce believed he had earned a second term. He certainly wanted another one. His remaining pockets of loyalty within the party were dependent on his distribution of fishes and loaves. "The strength of Pierce consisted in 'possession,' in the enormous amount of patronage at his disposal, in the fact that he presided in the grand central office of the wire-workers of the best drilled party in the country, and was commander-in-chief of office holders," wrote the journalist Murat Halstead. But the toxicity of Pierce's administration was lethal. The events of late May—from the sacking of Lawrence to the caning of Sumner—were hammer blows to his hopes. "The Kansas outrages are all imputable to him, and if he [is] not called to answer for them here, 'In Hell they'll roast him like a herring,'" wrote Benjamin B. French, Pierce's commissioner of public buildings, who became disillusioned and joined the Republicans. John W. For-

James Buchanan, Portrait by George Peter Alexander Healy

ney, editor of the pro-administration *Washington Union,* attributed Pierce's demise to the assault on Sumner. "I have always believed that that outrage secured the nomination for Buchanan," he wrote. Forney had been forced off the newspaper and become one of Buchanan's chief campaign managers.

Alexander H. Stephens, the former Whig congressman from Georgia, who labored for the old party with his colleague Lincoln in 1848 but had abandoned the Whigs, claimed that Pierce's favoritism toward the Softs of New York was the source of his unpopularity. "It was not because he 'shot down' the abolition traitors in Kansas," he wrote, "but rather because he 'shot down' all the true friends of the Kansas Bill in the Northern States two years ago—not with gunpowder it is true but with executive patronage by putting their enemies in power over their necks and heads." But Stephens also blamed the troubles in Kansas on Pierce. "I believe most of the difficulties we now have in Kansas have arisen from the fickleness, weakness, folly and vacillations of his policy in regard to that territory."

Stephen A. Douglas's strategy was to combine with Pierce until Buchanan was broken, shunt Pierce aside, and seize the prize. Douglas's announcement of his candidacy was an embittering shock to Pierce, who thought he had heard Douglas say he would support him against Buchanan. Douglas strutted around Washington as though he were the inevitable nominee, a self-conscious performance. Walking into the National Hotel in May he happened to encounter James Buchanan, who in his inimitably condescending manner spoke of his own coming election. "I expect to choose my Constitutional advisers soon," tartly replied Douglas, "and am most happy thus to receive your acceptance in advance." He and Pierce were, according to Francis P. Blair, "in Cahoot—each calculating that the defeat of Buck in the Convention was essential to give the least Chance for either of them."

Douglas fielded a formidable organization of fixers, financiers, and delegate wranglers. "Much depends on Virginia," he declared on May 14. He also counted on Indiana. And he staked all on New York through a deal with Dean Richmond, the New York Central Railroad vice president and power within the Empire State Democratic Party. In Virginia, however, Governor Henry A. Wise despised Pierce, mistrusted Douglas's tactical alliance with him, and believed Douglas would not be a strong candidate in the South because of his doctrine of popular sovereignty, which theoretically at least provided the basis to deny as well as to open the spread of slavery. There was no available Southerner. The Northern-Southern "doughface," "Old Buck," was an easy choice for Wise. "I have no idea that any slave-holding Democrat can get the next or any nomination for the presidency," wrote Wise. "Our policy is to go in for Buchanan with all our might." (Virginia was lost to Douglas.)

Douglas convinced himself he could rely on support from Senator Jesse Bright of Indiana, the Hoosier political boss, who belligerently represented the state in the interests of slavery. A classmate of Jefferson Davis at Transylvania College, a political ally of the F Street Mess, he owned a plantation and slaves in Kentucky, where he spent much of his time. For all intents and purposes, he behaved as a Southern slaveholder, which he was. He was fiercely jealous of Douglas as a rival for dominance of the Northwest within the Democratic Party and stabbed him in the back in the 1852 nomination battle, throwing Indiana's delegates to Senator Lewis Cass, who could not win, in order to destroy Douglas. Since then Douglas had courted him, even bringing him into a lucrative investment syndicate he created to buy real estate at Superior City in Wisconsin for a terminus of a northern route of a transcontinental railroad. Despite showering Bright with attention and riches, Senator David Yulee of Florida warned Douglas in 1853, "He is your enemy. . . . He does not mean that you shall rise if he can prevent it." Yet Douglas thought he had won him over. "Bright is acting in good faith to you," one of Douglas's operatives assured him. Meanwhile, Buchanan's handlers promised Bright control of federal patronage for the Northwest.

Few men had more distinguished résumés in public life than James Buchanan. He had served at every level of government from the Pennsylvania House of Representatives to the U.S. House and Senate. He had turned down an offer of sitting on the Supreme Court from President John Tyler. He had been a statesman: minister to Russia, secretary of state, and minister to England. He had nearly been the Democratic nominee in 1852 and was a contender in 1848 and 1844. His manner was courtly, his image dignified. He was genteel, proud, and stubborn. He had survived over decades in political controversy since the administration of James Madison. The greatest of his irreducible assets was that he was from Pennsylvania, the Keystone State, the swing state of the North. The Democrats always needed Pennsylvania, and Buchanan stood for Pennsylvania. His survival in its factional bramble was his chief recommendation. Pennsylvania was his ultimate platform.

Buchanan's plodding ambition had previously been a dead weight. He had accumulated a lifetime of political baggage. But magically none of that mattered. It was not Franklin Pierce's or Stephen A. Douglas's baggage. Buchanan's great good fortune was to have been exiled to his ambassadorship in London, where he was preserved unscathed from the political wars. Buchanan had not changed at all, but resurrected from his entombment.

Through a strange political alchemy his dross turned into gold. He was everything the charismatic, exciting, and impulsive Douglas was not. On his fourth attempt for the nomination, his extensive résumé, thorough mediocrity, seeming predictability, and Pennsylvania background made him alluring. Buchanan's enduring quality was his availability. The party did not want the vigorous young man; it sought someone old, tired, and dull. Buchanan's chief recommendation was his absence of certain qualities: originality, independence, and daring. "He was the personification of evasion, the embodiment of an inducement to dodge," wrote the journalist Halstead. Buchanan's recommendation as the most experienced and qualified man for the presidency was enhanced by his negative capability. Buchanan's leadenness made him seem steady, stable, and secure. He was the right man at the right time because this time he wasn't the wrong man. Four years earlier Douglas had derided the older candidates for the nomination as "old fogies." Now the age of the old fogy dawned.

"Mr. Buchanan," President James K. Polk wrote in his diary, "is an able man, but in small matters without judgment and sometimes acts like an old maid." When former president Andrew Jackson objected to Polk naming Buchanan secretary of state, Polk pointed out to Jackson that he had appointed him minister to Russia. "It was as far as I could send him out of my sight and where he could do the least harm. I would have sent him to the North Pole if we had kept a minister there," Jackson replied.

Henry Clay intensely disliked him, once sarcastically dismissing him by remarking "he had made no allusion to the Senator from Pennsylvania. He was referring to the leaders, not to the subordinates of the Democracy." Jackson referred to Buchanan and his intimate friend, Senator William Rufus King, with whom he shared quarters, as "Miss Fancy" and "Miss Nancy." When President Franklin Pierce offered Buchanan the post of minister to England he first accepted but then wished he had rejected it, dithered, and finally went. Pierce's secretary of state, William L. Marcy, observed that "the truth is old bachelors as well as young maids do not always know their own minds. But if he ever meant to go he can assign no sufficient cause for changing his mind."

Buchanan was briefly engaged to the daughter of a wealthy iron manufacturer, but she accused him of holding "affection" only for her "riches." When she died shortly after breaking off the engagement her family barred

Buchanan from the funeral. They were always opposed to the match. There were no more engagements. His close and long friendship with his boardinghouse mate Senator King, a wealthy Alabama plantation owner, had the benefit of having a Southerner promoting his prospects to other Southerners. Governor Aaron V. Brown of Tennessee, President Polk's former law partner, whom Buchanan would name his postmaster general, referred to the two men as "Buchanan and his wife." "Mr. Buchanan looks gloomy and dissatisfied," Brown wrote Polk's wife, Sarah, "and so did his better half until a little private flattery and a certain newspaper puff which you doubtless noticed, excited hopes that by getting a divorce she might set up again the world to some tolerable advantage." In 1840, Buchanan had promoted King as Martin Van Buren's running mate. According to his plan, to which King happily acceded, King would serve four years, announce he would not run for the presidential nomination, and endorse Buchanan. Four years later, Buchanan advanced King's name for vice president. After Polk appointed King as minister to France, King wrote Buchanan, "I am selfish enough to hope you will not be able to procure an associate who will cause you to feel no regret at our separation." When Buchanan lost his bid for the Democratic presidential nomination in 1852, he declined the offer of the vice presidency and offered King in his place, the gambit of the original scheme. Finally, King was nominated. But Vice President King died forty-five days into the Pierce presidency, leaving Buchanan disconsolate. He described his relationship with King as a "communion," and wrote one of his confidants, "I am now 'solitary and alone,' having no companion in the house with me. I have gone a wooing to several gentlemen, but have not succeeded with any one of them." Buchanan's emotional attachment to the South and preserving slavery were entangled with his emotional attachment to King.

The highest accolade that Senator Henry S. Foote of Mississippi could bestow on Buchanan was his talent for "cronyship." Buchanan, he wrote,

> was not known to deliver a single speech remarkable either for eloquence, for potential reasoning, or for valuable practical illustration. He was notably deficient both in ingenuity and in rhetorical brilliancy. I do not think he ever uttered a genuine witticism in his life. . . . Nobody, though, ever heard him talk stupidly or ignorantly; and whenever a subject chanced to be introduced with which he felt himself to be unacquainted he had the good sense to be obdurately and unmovedly silent. . . . He was, as a general thing, exceedingly truthful and confiding, and delighted more than any public man

I have known in what is sometimes called "cronyship," but, unfortunately, selected often as the special partners of his counsels men of very small mental caliber and who had recommended themselves to his regard mainly by their adroitness in the arts of adulation, to the influence of which arts he was indeed most lamentably open.

Buchanan had always been a boilerplate partisan, a stalwart Federalist congressman for four terms before he became a stalwart Democrat. He had periodically announced his retirement from politics since 1830 with an air of exhaustion. He held his utterly conventional views stubbornly until he instantly changed them to fit the circumstances, but he gradually lagged farther and farther behind events, and he had to be prodded to adjust them to stay politically viable. The more detached he became, the more tightly he clung to his anachronistic ideas. He conflated political change with personal offense. Change made him irritated. If he had one lasting position it was his genuine hostility to antislavery advocates, and if he advocated one paramount issue it was the Fugitive Slave Act. Pennsylvania had a long, porous border with the slave state of Maryland, making it a staging ground for the Underground Railroad and a flash point for skirmishes over runaway slaves. The notorious Christiana Riot—a gun battle between abolitionists harboring fugitives and a slave owner seeking the lawful return of his property, ending in his being killed—took place only fifteen miles from Buchanan's residence. The Fugitive Slave Act was close to home.

Buchanan had become a world-weary old gentleman long ago. He lived as a wealthy country squire on his expansive estate in a mansion of twenty-two rooms with a carriage house and other buildings in the village of Wheatland, outside Lancaster, Pennsylvania. He adopted the nickname bestowed on him in the Democratic newspapers—"the Old Public Functionary," even self-referentially calling himself "OPF." The "OPF" also touted himself as "the Sage of Wheatland."

His head tilted to the left side from an eye defect; one of his drooping eyelids twitched. He was myopic, would not wear glasses and tried to focus by squinting. One of his eyes was blue, the other hazel. His angled gaze sometimes gave an impression that he was listening attentively. "Difficulties often arose when those who thought they were close to him realized that they had been reading his looks rather than his mind, and such persons would break off with a sense of personal injury," wrote a biographer, Philip S. Klein.

Buchanan was pedantic, recording his valet's expenditures down to the penny, and worried about others' appearances, once to his detriment chiding President Jackson that he hoped he would wear a proper suit in meeting a lady. Over time he became overweight and fussier about his dress. He wore the formal clothes from the early years of the century with a high white collar, a white tie, and black dress coat, which set off his nimbus of white hair. He favored white silk handkerchiefs and white silk stockings. He was self-conscious about his small feet and wore black patent leather shoes.

His tastes were epicurean. He enjoyed fine food and good vintages. He famously drank copious amounts of champagne, whiskey, sherry, wine, and Madeira. After downing two bottles of cognac, finished off with rye whiskey, his longtime associate John W. Forney observed, "There was no headache, no faltering steps, no flushed cheek. Oh, no! All was as cool, calm and cautious and watchful as in the beginning." But Buchanan's consumption of alcohol gave him gout.

He appeared hale and hearty in company, though his health was generally not good. He grew polyps in his nose and on his neck, which he had removed by rudimentary surgery. He suffered from heart disease and hardening arteries, which likely intensified his inflexibility, vanity, and petulance when others objected to his indeterminacy or hesitantly reached decisions. From his long experience in government he was confident in his judgments, becoming dogged when challenged and obstinate when overrun by events. His vacillation would be finally followed by paralysis. He would treat his cabinet, members of the Congress, and other political figures as subordinates. "Behind his back they called him 'the Squire,' in half-jocular recognition of his success in imposing this inferiority upon them," wrote the historian Roy Franklin Nichols.

Senator John Slidell of Louisiana, indeed sly, strategic, and avaricious, guided Buchanan's every step to his nomination. Slidell wrote the script, a series of tableaux vivant of Buchanan posing as a statesmanlike icon. "Mr. Slidell," recalled Forney, "was a man of the world and a scheming politician, yet never a statesman. He had some reputation as a lawyer, but not as an advocate or pleader. Few men had more influence over James Buchanan, and none did so much to mislead that ill-starred President. His rule was implacable hostility to all who did not agree with him. He was faithful to those who followed him, but his prejudices always dominated his friendships. He had undoubted courage, but his mistake was a belief that the best way to adjust a dispute was by an appeal to the 'code of honor.'" Slidell, according to W.H. Howard, the correspondent for the London *Times,* was "a man of

iron will and strong passions, who loves
the excitement of combinations . . . and
who in his dungeon . . . would conspire
with the mice against the cat sooner than
not conspire at all."

Slidell was born a New Yorker but left
to find his fortune in New Orleans, where
he established a lucrative law practice and
ruthlessly pursued a political career. His
law partner, Judah P. Benjamin, just as
cunning, became the other senator from
Louisiana. Slidell's niece, Caroline Slidell
Perry, was the daughter of Commodore
Matthew Perry, who opened trade to
Japan. Her husband, August Belmont,
was the Wall Street agent of the Roth-

John Slidell

schild banking interests and a Democratic Party funder. Slidell served as his
political mentor.

In 1853, Slidell proposed a bill for the invasion and seizure of Cuba. At
the same time he lined up Belmont in the bond markets to making a financial killing on the policy. He corresponded with Buchanan, who was behind
the Ostend Manifesto of 1854, a parallel document that would threaten Spain
with war if it failed to relinquish Cuba, but which the Pierce administration
scuttled. Slidell broke with Pierce over his refusal to provoke Spain. (Slidell
had been Polk's plenipotentiary to Mexico and helped manipulate events that
led to war.) The rupture turned bitter when Pierce ousted Slidell's ally as the
U.S. attorney in New Orleans who prosecuted Pierce's appointed postmaster
for corruption.

In October 1854, a month before the Democratic defeats in the midterm
elections, Slidell launched plans for the Buchanan candidacy. "We have
abundant time to clear the wreck and repair damages before the presidential
election," he wrote Buchanan. He coaxed a reluctant Buchanan to run, told
him how long to stay in London, when to return to the United States, what
to say, and when to say it.

At Slidell's direction Buchanan circulated a letter on the eve of the convention emphasizing his credentials. His politics were frozen to the point in
time when he had left for his post in England. He was still on record in favor
of the Missouri Compromise, which was repealed by the Kansas-Nebraska

Act. Now he wrote, "I have written and spoken more than any man now alive in favor of the just Constitutional rights of the South over their slaves." He added that "the Morning Advertiser, a British liberal paper . . . more than once expressed its regret that I was such 'a strong pro slavery man.'" Buchanan was touted as "the strongest northern man sound on Southern principles," according to Congressman J. Glancy Jones, chief of the Democratic political machine in Pennsylvania.

On the convention's eve a rumor swept through the political salons of Washington that Douglas and Pierce had conspired to drop out in favor of another candidate, perhaps Senator Robert M.T. Hunter of Virginia or Senator Thomas Jefferson Rusk of Texas. Douglas had offered Hunter the chance to be his vice president in the 1852 nomination struggle. The banker W.W. Corcoran, who had been a source of funds for Douglas's political and financial projects, but was now with Buchanan, told the rumor to Bright. Buchanan's complacent handlers rushed to Cincinnati.

The Buchaneers, as they called themselves, consisted of four senators— Slidell, Benjamin, James A. Bayard of Delaware, and Jesse Bright. They set up camp at the house of Samuel Latham Mitchill Barlow, at the age of thirty one of the wealthiest and most influential Wall Street lawyers, who had temporarily established himself in the Queen City to arrange the completion of the Ohio and Mississippi Railroad. Though a native of Massachusetts, Barlow was a proslavery Democrat. When he was not in Ohio, he lived in a luxurious double brownstone on the corner of Madison and Forty-third Street where he collected art and Democrats. Through his connections he was at that moment securing a strategic job for a former army officer, George B. McClellan, as the superintendent of the Illinois Central Railroad, which Barlow intended to link to the Ohio and Mississippi line. It was the beginning of a relationship that would culminate in McClellan's 1864 candidacy against President Lincoln.

Breaking down Douglas began with Indiana. He thought he had it wrapped up. But at the delegation meeting on the Saturday night before the convention Bright enforced his fiat. Buchanan had 16 votes to Douglas's 10. Bright imposed the unit rule and they all went for Buchanan. "Indiana is all gone—and wrong," Congressman William Richardson of Illinois, Douglas's convention manager, telegraphed him. "To Bright's indomitable energy we are indebted for . . . the *coup d'état* which gave us the vote of Indiana in convention," wrote Forney. After the election, when the jobs began to be doled out and his influence was dismissed, Douglas discovered the full depth of Bright's treachery. Just as he betrayed Pierce, he too was betrayed. His embittered collision with Buchanan was therefore set into the foundation of Buchanan's rise.

Next came the demolition of Douglas's bulwark of New York. Two delegations, one of the Softs and one the Hards, presented themselves. Barlow wrote that "it was evident that if the New York delegation, represented by Mr. Dean Richmond and his associates, who were known as the 'Softs,' secured seats, that the nomination of Mr. Douglas was inevitable." The Buchaneers packed the galleries by gaining control of the visitor's passes and got one of their own, Senator Bayard, appointed as chairman of the credentials committee. The majority report recommended that the Softs be given most of the delegate seats; the minority report suggested an even division. Bayard moved for the minority report, which narrowly carried. New York was neutralized. The Buchaneers had destroyed Douglas before the first ballot. "Every move that was made emanated from some one of the gentlemen there present," recalled Barlow, "and but for their presence and active cooperation, there is little doubt that Mr. Douglas would have been nominated upon the first ballot after organization."

From the first ballot Buchanan had the lead with 131½ votes, to 118 for Pierce, 33 for Douglas, and 4 for Cass. After the fourteenth ballot when Douglas reached 63 and Pierce 75, the Pierce forces threw their votes to Douglas. But there was a crucial defection of Tennessee. Douglas's main support, apart from Illinois and the Softs of New York, came from Southern delegations. Buchanan swept those from Northern, Northwest, and border states. After the sixteenth ballot Richardson rose to withdraw Douglas. "Don't withdraw Doug! Stop!" shouted his supporters. "But I feel I have imposed upon me a duty to—" "Damn the duty, sit down there." Richardson waved a telegram from Douglas. "I shall withdraw Douglas from this contest," he said, and he read the message pleading "harmony."

In the battle for the vice presidency, Douglas's man, Congressman Thomas L. Harris of Illinois, nominated John A. Quitman, the former governor of Mississippi, who Douglas might have taken as his own running mate. But the Louisiana delegation controlled by Slidell nominated Congressman John C. Breckinridge of Kentucky, who won in a stampede. "Then again the convention resolved itself into a carnival," reported Halstead. Breckinridge took the podium to acclaim Buchanan: "Reserved to a green old age he has lived down detraction, and time has destroyed calumny."

Douglas's withdrawal left a bitter taste in the mouths of a number of

Democrats who believed that he had staged an elaborate charade, according to Benjamin F. Butler, a pro-Southern Pierce delegate from Massachusetts, who would later change his political spots to Republican. In Butler's telling, Douglas's men duplicitously promised Pierce's that when Pierce was withdrawn in favor of Douglas he would continue "until a compromise candidate could be brought forward acceptable to all as in the case of Mr. Polk and Mr. Pierce himself." But as Butler surmised, Douglas intended to pull out all along in order to better position himself with Buchanan and for the nomination in 1860. "Was not the whole matter a ruse to bring in the friends of Mr. Pierce to the support of Douglas, so that he might have the merit of withdrawing as the only competing candidate?"

Never leaving the bucolic surroundings of his beloved Wheatland, Buchanan sent letters written at the direction of his handlers to announce the theme of his campaign as a crusade to save the Union. "The Union is in danger and the people everywhere begin to know it," he wrote in June. "The Black Republicans must be, as they can be with justice, boldly assailed as disunionists, and this charge must be reiterated again and again."

Buchanan did not bother to send any letters to Pierce or Douglas. They were now beneath him. But Douglas delivered speeches in city after city on Buchanan's behalf. He sold some of his Chicago real estate property, spending $42,000 on the campaign. He hoped for patronage and other advantages in the future. Buchanan carefully kept his distance and silence.

Outwardly, Douglas sustained his enthusiasm. But the *Illinois State Journal,* Lincoln's newspaper, accidentally caught up with him in an unguarded moment and glimpsed an augury of what was to come. "On the train of cars which conveyed Senator Douglas to Galena, a vote, as usual now-a-days, was taken. The canvassers did not know Douglas, and when they came to him, while going through the cars, the following conversation took place: Canvasser. Who do you vote for, sir—Buchanan or Fremont? Douglas (angrily looking up from the perusal of the Chicago Times)—Vote for the Devil! The result of the canvass was as follows: Fremont 117. Buchanan 15. Fillmore 17. The Devil 1."

CHAPTER FIFTEEN

THE FORBIDDEN WORD

ive days after the Bloomington convention the scene was set for a triumphant homecoming for its hero. "We got out large posters," recalled
Herndon, "had bands of music employed to drum up a crowd &c. The
court house was the place of the meeting. As the hour drew near I lit up the
Court with many blazes and many lights—blowed horns and rang bells, &c.
What do you think the number of the People was—? How many? Three
persons—namely John Pain"—the courthouse janitor—"W H Herndon
and A Lincoln."

Herndon's description of the forlorn event may well have been apocry-
phal or misremembered. There is no other record of such a meeting, but
it's also possible that Herndon failed to notify
anyone that Lincoln was speaking. Whether
or not this was a phantom rally, another
one took place at the courthouse on June 10
that was packed. The *Register* querulously
claimed that one third of the crowd consisted of curious Democrats who had come
to observe Lincoln's "gyrations." It reported
that before the mostly Old Whig assemblage
"he would soften his remarks to a supposed
palatable texture. . . . His timidity before the
peculiar audience he addressed prevented

Millard Fillmore

earnest advocacy with the power and ability he is known to possess." In another dispatch, the *Register* claimed, "Mr. Lincoln's remarks were received with coldness. . . . He was evidently laboring under much restraint, conscious that he was doling out new doctrine to the old whigs about him . . . however . . . his niggerism has as dark a hue as that of Garrison or Fred Douglass."

The *Journal* countered by praising Lincoln for "the most logical and finished argument against the evils to be apprehended from the continued aggressions of the slave power, that it has ever been our good fortune to listen to," but reported almost apologetically that Lincoln preferred "rather to appeal to the reason than to excite the feelings of his hearers."

Lincoln had successfully stage-managed the convention, but the party statewide remained to be organized. The coming campaign would be its crucible. Lincoln carefully avoided using the fraught word "Republican" to refer to what was the Republican Party, but called it the "People's Party." The "Republican" label frightened many of Lincoln's former Whig friends. The prominence of abolitionists in the Republican coalition filled many Old Whigs with disgust. Those drawn to the Know Nothings spurned the German immigrants, a new and large voting group that altered the balance of Illinois politics. To win over the Old Whigs Lincoln had to get them to submerge their nativism in the greater antislavery struggle. He had to make their Know Nothingism a way station to the destination of Republicanism. These were, after all, men he had known well and worked closely with for decades. His focus was rooted in friendships, loyalties, and identity, now shaken and divided.

The Know Nothings were more than skeletons rattling in the Old Whig closet. They had their secret lodges, oaths, and handshakes, but the Know Nothings were not a secret. They were self-proclaimed "the Americans," claiming to speak exclusively for native-born Protestant Americans, a political party mustering in the field with the last Whig president Millard Fillmore as its candidate.

"I don't sympathize with that black Republican movement, in any way, shape, manner, or form," declared Edwin Bathurst "Bat" Webb. "Its permanent success would surely end in the dissolution of this Union." Webb had served in the state legislature with Lincoln as a stalwart Whig, had even courted Mary Todd, and was the Whig nominee for governor in 1852 in a campaign that smashed the Whig Party but in which he respectably carried Sangamon County, the Whig stronghold. Webb, who was Virginia born, lived in a southern Illinois county that might as well have been located in Kentucky for its hostility to the new party.

Joseph Gillespie, who had also served in the legislature with Lincoln and was among his closest political friends, had signed the call for the Bloomington convention, but had second thoughts. Lincoln's loss of the Senate seat the year before had embittered Gillespie against the Whigs' perennial rival. He was too mistrustful of the antislavery Democrats to join with them. Instead, he clung to the old banner and turned to the last Whig president, Millard Fillmore, and the Know Nothings as his last hope. "I have my fears that the so-called Democrats at the Bloomington Convention are going for Buchanan and that it will turn out to be a clean sell of the Whigs and true conservative men of the State," he wrote Lincoln on June 6. "If this is the game, I am for a thorough organization for Fillmore and [Andrew] Donelson [his running mate] whether we sink or swim. They are honest and conservative men and it would be more creditable to fail fighting under that banner than to triumph in such company as I fear some of the wire workers at Bloomington are. I am tired of being dragooned by some half dozen men who are determined to either rule or ruin. I am out of all temper with, and have no faith in the honesty of, men who insist that ten Whigs shall go with one Democrat because they cannot in conscience vote for a Whig. Though I am well satisfied with Trumbull, yet his five particular friends who would rather see the country go to the Devil than to vote for a Whig are not at all to my taste. I have made up my mind that henceforth I can be as reckless as they are, and, so help me God, they shall find out that I am one as well as either of them."

James H. Matheny had been the best man at Lincoln's wedding and had known him since they worked together in the New Salem post office. Douglas referred to him as "Mr. Lincoln's especial confidential friend for the last twenty years." Matheny developed a conspiracy theory that justified his support for the Know Nothings—a theory that Douglas would throw at Lincoln in their 1858 debates and which Lincoln would insist was untrue. The way Matheny saw it, the Whigs, dissident Democrats, and abolitionists made a secret deal in which Trumbull would be supported for the Congress, the abolitionists would get State House patronage jobs, and Lincoln would be backed for the Senate. "But, in the most perfidious manner, they refused to elect Mr. Lincoln," said Matheny, "and the mean, low-lived, sneaking Trumbull succeeded, by pledging all that was required by any party, in thrusting Lincoln aside and foisting himself, an excrescence from the rotten bowels of the Democracy, into the United States Senate: and thus it has ever been, that an *honest* man makes a bad bargain when he conspires or contracts with rogues."

Matheny swore that "he was a whig and nothing else" and that Whigs should not be "sold out" to the Republicans. Disgruntled Old Whigs began holding county conventions and nominated a statewide ticket, which merged with the American Party or Know Nothing slates. Matheny became the Whig/American candidate for Congress in Springfield and Gillespie a presidential elector for Fillmore. At a rally for Fillmore in Springfield, John Todd Stuart, Lincoln's first law partner, one of his earliest mentors, assailed "black republicanism" and charged "the result, if not the design of their movement, was to array the north against the south."

John M. Palmer, a Democrat turned Republican who presided over the Bloomington convention, wrote that "the dog howl of Abolitionism-Black Republicans" made Old Whigs in southern Illinois "feel that they are called specially to the patriotic duty of 'saving the Union' which can be done by throwing their votes away on Fillmore." Benjamin S. Edwards, an Old Whig and Springfield lawyer related to Lincoln through his brother, Ninian Edwards, Jr., Lincoln's brother-in-law, moved uneasily into the Republican Party, wary of the abolitionists. He wrote Trumbull: "You need . . . vindication against the charges of abolition, and opposition to the Union which however unfounded they may be are yet made, and must be met."

Certain prominent Democrats who attended the Bloomington convention were hard to shepherd. "John Wentworth roars like a bull whenever the Republican Party is mentioned and swears that he's a Democrat," observed a friend. It was not until after the campaign of 1856 was waged that most members of the party were willing to abandon their long attachments and hazard wearing the scorned label of Republican—"Black Republicans," as Douglas always called them.

The most intimate defector, however, was located within Lincoln's household. No one was more devoted to his ambition than his wife, Mary. When he was elected to the state legislature in 1854, she forced him to quit in order to run for the Senate. Returning to his old haunts was not good enough for her husband by her lights. She understood his inner insecurities and would not tolerate him settling for anything but the highest office he could attempt to reach. She was embittered when he lost the Senate race and shunned her old friend Julia Trumbull, wife of Lyman Trumbull to whom Lincoln threw his votes to stop Douglas's ally from gaining the seat through bribery. After

Lincoln at last shed the dead skin of the Whig Party his wife wrapped herself in it like a protective covering to shield herself from his new association with the discreditable Republicans.

She had been raised as a Whig through and through. Her father, Robert S. Todd, had been Henry Clay's business partner and political ally, and as a girl Mary gained a reputation as "a violent little Whig." She was unusual among the ladies for her willingness to voice her strong political opinions in mixed company. She referred to her marriage as "our Lincoln party." It began with the two of them. In the 1856 campaign she was no less opinionated, but they were not opinions that helped her husband. She disliked the people Lincoln was trying to bring together. She disdained abolitionists, demeaned immigrants, and wanted nothing to do with those Democrats around Trumbull who she felt had robbed her husband of his rightful place. "Fusionism" was not for her. She remained wedded to the Whig Party.

Mary wrote her younger half sister Emilie Todd Helm, living in Kentucky, a fanciful letter about the election. "Altho' Mr L- is, or was a Fremont man, you must not include him with so many of those who belong to that party, an Abolitionist." The idea that Lincoln was a reluctant Republican, of course, was simply untrue. Mary disclosed her own political desire. It was the figure of Millard Fillmore. "My weak woman's heart was too Southern in feeling, to sympathize with any but Fillmore," she wrote. Mary, who treated her Irish maids poorly, felt an affinity for the anti-immigrant movement. "I have always been a great admirer of his, he made so good a President and is so just a man and feels the necessity of keeping foreigners, within bounds. If some of you Kentuckians, had to deal with the 'wild Irish,' as we housekeepers are sometimes called upon to do, the south would certainly elect Mr. Fillmore next time." Mary's idolatry of Fillmore and bias against immigrants was completely at odds with Lincoln, who ignored her pride and prejudice and soldiered on.

By the time Millard Fillmore sailed with flags flying into New York Harbor on June 22 from a Grand Tour of Europe, his strategy for a return to power was in tatters. His plan had been to present himself as the reassuring figure from the past who could preserve the Union, saving it from division as he had done by forging the Compromise of 1850. Only yesterday's man could bring back yesterday. He was the man of the past for those longing for the past. His promoters let it be known that he had taken the secret oath of the Know Nothings: "America only for Americans." Nativism provided the motif for purification, restoration, and nostalgia. Hatred of immigrants distracted from the conflict over slavery, whose controversy was solely blamed on agitators. Standing firmly against the winds of change, Fillmore promised he could sweep it all away. But in order for his plan to work, the existing parties, including the new Republican one, would have to collapse to clear room for the Americans. His strategy was passive at heart, dependent on lucky events. According to the plan, when a candidate from the Pierce-Douglas wing of the Democrats would be nominated, the Hards of New York would be alienated while Old Whigs, repelled by abolitionists, would flee from the Republican Party. But Buchanan foiled the scheme. He was another version of yesterday's man personifying complacency yet seemingly fresher, thereby canceling out Fillmore's foremost credential. Still, Lincoln worried about Fillmore's appeal to Old Whigs.

Fillmore was more than the sum of his minuses, neither this nor that. His campaign was a suggested center that played on the margins. His supporters rejected not only Northern abolitionists and Southern fire-eaters, but also Republicans and Democrats. They wanted everything back in its proper place as it was in 1850. They wished immigrants to go back to where they came from. They could not explain why their golden age of stability had yielded instability. But the Fillmore campaign was based on more than wishful thinking. It had a geographic base—the border slave states that wanted to banish slavery as an issue from national debate. It also had a political base—Southern Whigs unmoored from their old party and unwilling yet to join the Democrats. And now it had a nationally recognized candidate.

Millard Fillmore offered no ideas, vision, or memorable words. There was nothing about the bland, tired, and gray figure that captured anyone's imagination. There had never been a glimmer of excitement or inventiveness about him. He had been a factotum of the New York State Whig Party, achieved the office of state comptroller, and was named as vice president in 1848 as a sop to the embittered Henry Clay, who had been frustrated from attaining the presidential nomination again and intended Fillmore's selection of running mate to thwart the ambition of Fillmore's former patron Seward to be appointed secretary of state. (By tradition only one representative from a state was chosen for the cabinet and the vice presidency. Fillmore and Seward were both New Yorkers. Putting Fillmore on the ticket negated Seward.) But Vice President Fillmore was shunted aside until the sudden death from cholera of President Zachary Taylor. Fillmore ascended as His Accidency II. (His Accidency I was John Tyler, the first vice president to assume the presidency on the death of his predecessor.) He inspired no movement, ideology, or affection. After passage of the Compromise of 1850, handled by Douglas, the unloved incumbent was denied his party's nomination in 1852. His latter-day Know Nothingism was thin and bloodless. "I am an American," he said, "and with the Americans." He followed its bandwagon in the hope that it would follow him. He had no instinct for arousing passions of any kind. Nobody marched for Fillmore. Fillmoreism was an oxymoron. He was against all "isms."

Lincoln, the Old Whig turned Republican, focused on Old Whigs supporting either Buchanan or Fillmore. As they flew off in all directions he wondered how he might neutralize them or bring them into the orbit of the new party. Lincoln's political calculus was based largely on previous Illinois election results, refreshed by the intelligence he received from political people he knew around the state. In the presidential election of 1852 Pierce won by ten points. In the midterm elections for the Congress in 1854 candidates opposed to the Kansas-Nebraska Act gained four seats, but the Democrats still controlled six. Lincoln understood that the newly organized Republican Party commanded less allegiance than the dissolved Whig Party. Throughout central and southern Illinois the centrifugal force of Whig disintegration was accelerating—and not to the benefit of the Republicans regardless of what they called themselves. Even in Sangamon County, which had been the Whig core in the state, the Old Whigs held out from the Republicans. The Know Nothings there amounted to the Old Whig Party in nativist clothing. Lincoln could see the politics slipping away from the Republicans, failing to become a coherent force while the Know Nothings held the Old Whigs and the Democrats prevailed once again. Lincoln felt the Republicans losing not gaining ground. But his finely attuned frame of reference was based on the old balances of power. His arithmetic metrics of addition and subtraction from the existing parties projected a zero-sum game that was radically in flux.

At the beginning of June, he did not anticipate the upsurge of enthusiasm for the Republicans or factor in the tangible reality of the explosive growth of Chicago. Though Lincoln took on many railroad cases, he was just grasping how profoundly the industrial revolution would politically transform Illinois. In 1850, the population of Chicago was 28,269 and one railroad passed through it. By 1855, the population had nearly tripled to 83,500 and it was the hub for ten railroads, the crossroads between East and West. Stephen A. Douglas, the sponsor of the Illinois Central Railroad, had become a Chicagoan, moved his residence to the new metropolis, and champion of its industrial development. Lincoln came and went occasionally from Chicago and could see the extraordinary change with his own eyes. Neither Douglas nor Lincoln, however, fully understood that just as Douglas was a founding father of the city of Chicago he was also creating the basis for the Republican Party. The world that was coming into being had only surfaced in vague outline.

At the Republican Party organizing meeting on February 22, 1856, Lincoln had stated there could be no hope to "resurrect the dead body of the old Whig party." But even after the Bloomington convention, the situation remained so delicate he couldn't safely utter the word "Republican."

CHAPTER SIXTEEN

VICE PRESIDENT LINCOLN

T he news of Buchanan's nomination came yesterday," Lincoln nervously
wrote Trumbull on June 7, "and a good many Whigs, of conservative
feelings, and slight pro-slavery proclivities, withal, are inclining to go for
him, and will do it, unless the Anti-Nebraska nomination shall be such as to
divert them."

Lincoln was fixated on his former
party mates. "Now there is a grave question to be considered. Nine tenths of the
Anti-Nebraska votes have to come from
old Whigs. In setting stakes, is it safe to
totally disregard them? Can we possibly
win, if we do so? So far they have been
disregarded. I need not point out the instances." But Lincoln proposed a solution—a candidate—a man who would
have an appeal to the Old Whigs. "The
man to effect that object is Judge Mc-
Lean"—Supreme Court Associate Justice John McLean—"and his nomination
would save every Whig, except such as
have already gone over hook and line"—
and Lincoln reeled off a list of defectors

Supreme Court Associate
Justice John McLean

who "will heartily go for McLean, but will every one go for Buchanan, as against Chase, Banks, Seward, [Frank] Blair [Jr.] or Fremont." Lincoln the former surveyor laid out the limits of political possibility as he saw it. "I think they would stand Blair or Fremont for Vice-President—but not more." He was thinking of them as running mates for his candidate.

Lincoln had been chosen as a delegate to the Republican convention but was committed to cases on the judicial circuit. Trumbull had also been selected. Lincoln's letter convinced him that he should go. "Your letter just received decides the question," he wrote Lincoln on June 15. "I will go in the morning, and do what I can to have a conservative man nominated and conservative measures adopted. I have no personal feeling about candidates, but want the strongest man whose sentiments are right, and that Judge McLean is that man, all things considered, I have very little doubt."

John McLean, seventy-one years old, had an impressive appearance; his "features resembled those of George Washington," according to one historian. He was reserved, dignified, and learned. A contemporary chronicler noted "the diligent labors of his energetic and cultivated mind." He considered himself in the tradition of John Marshall and Joseph Story, a firm supporter of federal authority, not a strict constructionist of the states' rights school. He was the only justice on the Supreme Court with antislavery sentiments. But time and again, to the consternation of abolitionists, he had ruled in favor of existing laws upholding slavery. In 1842 he upheld the constitutionality of the federal Fugitive Slave Act of 1793 in *Prigg v. Pennsylvania* and the following year ruled in *Jones v. Van Zandt* against a poor white Ohio farmer who sheltered a runaway slave. "[I]f convictions . . . of what is right or wrong are to be substituted as a rule of action in disregard of the law, we shall soon be without law and protection," he wrote. The Van Zandt case became a celebrated cause for abolitionists. Salmon Chase, assisted by William Seward, argued for the defense. Harriet Beecher Stowe had transparently fictionalized the figure of the saintly Van Zandt as a martyr in *Uncle Tom's Cabin.* McLean's adherence to the rule of abhorrent law continued in the 1853 case *Miller v. McQuerry* in which he decided that the Fugitive Slave Act of 1850 was constitutional and remanded a fugitive to his Kentucky master. Yet McLean was opposed to the extension of slavery in the territories. He also believed that blacks in free states were free, the issue at stake in the impending Dred Scott case. He had already written his decision, though the court was still deliberating. Frustrated that he could not make his decision public, he published a letter in the *National Intelligencer,* the traditional Whig newspaper in Washington, laying out his argument that "Congress has no power to institute slavery in the Territories," and therefore could not exist there. McLean's complex positions made him a conflicted political character. Radical abolitionists denounced him for his constitutional decisions on the legality of slavery while he was an outlier on the court for opposing slavery's extension.

McLean was more than a jurist on the high bench; he was an ambitious politician beneath his black robe. John Quincy Adams wrote in his diary in April 1833 that McLean "thinks of nothing but the Presidency by day and dreams of nothing else by night." A decade later, in April 1843, Adams recorded his view of McLean's bid for the Democratic presidential nomination: "McLean is but a second edition of John Tyler—vitally Democratic, double-dealing, and hypocritical." Adams's harsh opinion of McLean, who was a former cabinet member of his administration, was a scar from McLean's decades in political wars.

McLean climbed the rungs of a lengthy political ladder to attain his eminence. He began as the publisher of a newspaper in Lebanon, Ohio, which he translated into a job at the U.S. Land Office in Cincinnati, which within a year became his platform for becoming a congressman, which in turn within two years lifted him to a seat on the Ohio Supreme Court, which he used to campaign for James Monroe for president, who appointed him commissioner of the Public Land Office and after another year postmaster general. President John Quincy Adams in the spirit of the nonparty Era of Good Feelings retained McLean in his office. When the election of 1828 came around, McLean displayed his nonpartisanship to a fault, pointedly refusing to use his political office to political effect for Adams—behaving "perfidiously," as Secretary of State Henry Clay told Adams. The new president, Andrew Jackson, who believed in the dictum "To the victor belong the spoils," was appreciative of McLean's active indifference to Adams during the campaign, but would not dare reappoint him. McLean had signaled to Jackson a year earlier, "I am the servant of the people, not the administration. The patronage placed in my hands is to be used for the public benefit." Jackson feared McLean might take his high-mindedness seriously beyond damaging Adams. So he named the serious man to the serious position of associate justice on the Supreme Court, which Jackson thought the least consequential branch of government and would cause the least trouble.

From the sanctuary of the court McLean ran for president in every cycle, putting his name forward five times before four different parties publicly and one party surreptitiously. He first tried for the nomination of the Anti-

Masonic Party, gravitated to the Whigs, and then sought elevation as the candidate of the Free Soil Party in 1848. After abandoning the Whigs he could not return to them in 1852, but in early 1853, just after the landslide election of 1852 that buried them, Orville Hickman Browning, an Old Whig and Lincoln ally, wrote McLean, telling him that the Illinois Whigs were searching for a candidate who could unite "all the elements of the Whig party," and that the growing opinion was that he was that man.

It was more than a little ironic that McLean, the Democratic warhorse who remade himself into a man above politics as he avidly pursued it and was distrusted as a bounder by Whigs when he made his initial attempt at the Whig nomination in 1836, was touted as the last refuge for Old Whigs within the new Republican Party. After the Know Nothings strongly emerged in the 1854 elections, McLean thought his opportunity might lie in gaining its nomination. The Know Nothings, after all, seemed to be the strongest new party and was drawing the Whigs to it. Its antipolitical and antiparty claims against the decadent existing parties also appealed to McLean's long-standing pretense. He "obsequiously showered letters on Know Nothings in New York, Pennsylvania, Ohio, and Michigan," according to the historian Michael Holt, "praising their organization as 'the party of the people' that could save the government from 'cliques,' 'demagogues,' and 'political traders and gamesters,' and warning them to 'suffer not the political hacks of any party to enter into your organization or to control your action.'" But McLean was too cautious and calibrated and the Know Nothings turned to Fillmore.

McLean's ambiguity placed him more or less where Lincoln thought the center ought to be in the Republican Party in order to attract the Old Whigs. When he was a young man Henry Clay was his "beau ideal," but he did not back him for the nomination in 1840 or 1848 because he thought military heroes with less substance but broader appeal were stronger candidates. McLean, said Lincoln in 1848, was "not a winning card." In 1855 Lincoln watched McLean perform in the Manny case and came away distinctly unimpressed. "Judge McLean is a man of considerable vigor of mind but no perception at all," he told Whitney. "Point your finger at him and also a darning needle, he would not know which was the sharpest." Lincoln still thought he had the best chance to win, or if not to take the prize certainly to win over Old Whigs. Browning held the same view. "We have many, very many, tenderfooted Whigs, who are frightened by ugly names, that could not be carried for Fremont, but who would readily unite with us upon McLean," he wrote Trumbull on May 19, 1856, about the candidacy of Senator John C. Fremont of California.

"The fact is," wrote Murat Halstead, "that the McLean movement is an attempt made by the antediluvian Whigs who have been placed in Congress by the Republican movement, to reorganize the defunct Whig Party under a thin disguise of Republicanism, to consist solely of talk about the Missouri Compromise." But McLean's support was broader than that and his organization weaker. The abolitionist congressman Joshua Giddings and the *National Era* editor Gamaliel Bailey were for McLean. These men were Ohioans, knew McLean and Chase, whom they were decidedly not endorsing. McLean's candidacy fatally undercut Chase's in Ohio, and by the same token Chase's weakened McLean's. Without control over their state's delegation neither stood a realistic chance of gaining the nomination.

The natural candidate for the Republican nomination of 1856 decided not to enter the field. Thurlow Weed had advised William Seward it was not his year. The Republicans would not win, and he should reserve himself for the next time. According to Weed's memoir, "It was with difficulty that he prevailed upon his friends to bide their time until the next national canvass. He reasoned that the Know Nothings, were Mr. Seward nominated, would ensure the election of Mr. Buchanan. Even as against any other Republican, Mr. Buchanan was almost sure to be elected, and, if elected, Mr. Weed thought, absolutely certain to make so many mistakes that nothing could prevent Republican ascendancy in 1860. It was only four years to wait, and under the circumstances nothing was to be gained by precipitancy." Of the other possibilities Weed was opposed to Chase and McLean. Weed told one associate that McLean was a " 'white-liver'd hollow-hearted Janus-faced rascal.' . . . I think he prefixed 'd——d.' "

The Republican convention opened on June 17 at the Musical Fund Hall in Philadelphia, an "immense hall . . . crowded in every corner," reported Halstead, but "badly ventilated; the air outside was sultry, and the heat within soon became terrible." Francis P. Blair, the man usually behind the scenes, wandered visibly among the delegates as the conductor of the candidacy of John C. Frémont. "He is a little old gentleman," Halstead observed of Blair, "thin, slender and feeble in appearance, yet moving about with considerable activity . . . his head is too big for his body, and his hat too big for his head. He is treated with distinguished consideration, and the mention of his name is invariably followed by uproarious applause."

Blair had originally tried to recruit Thomas Hart Benton, his old Jacksonian "Kitchen Cabinet" intimate, for the nomination, but the cantankerous Benton was determined to fight out his own Missouri war with his enemies within the Democratic Party to the bitter end. So Blair decided that the best man was Benton's son-in-law, the youthful and dashing idol of the West, Colonel John C. Frémont, famed for his expeditions, accompanied by his legendary scout Kit Carson, exploring the Rocky Mountains, the Sierra Nevada, the Oregon Trail, reaching San Francisco Bay, which he called the Golden Gate. An officer of the Corps of Topographical Engineers, Frémont was a mathematician, artist, and scientist, who identified new plant species, and was awarded "the great golden medal" for his research by Alexander von Humboldt on behalf of the King of Prussia and received a tribute from the Royal Geographical Society of London. His best-selling account of his adventures published before the California Gold Rush redefined the Great American Desert as El Dorado. He led the Bear Flag Revolt of 1846 to conquer California, became extremely wealthy from his ownership of mines, and was elected the new state's U.S. senator.

Frémont carried the aura of a romantic military hero, riding in on clouds of glory, not the creature of dank political party clubhouses. He was "the Pathfinder," given the sobriquet by the newspapers, lifted from James Fenimore Cooper's 1840 novel of that title about Natty Bumppo, also known as Leatherstocking, Hawk Eye, and at last "the Pathfinder," Fenimore Cooper's natural man of the American wilderness. " 'Fear nothing, young woman,' said the hunter. . . . I am a man well known in all these parts, and perhaps one of my names may have reached your ears. By the Frenchers and the redskins on the other side of the Big Lakes, I am called La Longue Carabine; by the Mohicans, a just-minded and upright tribe, what is left of them, Hawk Eye; while the troops and rangers along this side of the water call me Pathfinder, inasmuch as I have never been known to miss one end of the trail, when there was a Mingo, or a friend who stood in need of me, at the other."

Frémont fulfilled the dreams of Democrats for another Jackson and Whigs for another proto-Jackson in the winning tradition of William Henry Harrison and Zachary Taylor. His time as senator was fortunately brief and his record negligible. Horace Greeley observed "a candidate must have a slim record in these times," and he moved the *Tribune* behind Frémont's candidacy on the convention's eve. Weed and Seward jumped on board. So did Henry Wilson and Nathaniel Banks of Massachusetts. The bandwagon was rolling. Frémont was more than the available man. At forty-three years old the youngest man ever to run for the presidency, he had more than a seemingly clean slate to gain support from factions trailing the baggage of their past. He was a new man for a new party. He was brilliant and intrepid, a scholar and a soldier in the battle on the frontier for limitless progress. "His manner was refined and dignified," John Bigelow, editor of the *New York Post,* recalled. That Frémont was also without political instinct, arrogant, impetuous, vainglorious, self-seeking, thin-skinned, financially shady, and incapable of working cooperatively went unexplored in the euphoric moment. Frémont appeared on the horizon as a shining mythic icon. In any case, Blair was his manager. Before the balloting began it was apparent that Frémont "had a clear majority," according to Halstead.

The platform was the first order of convention business. To universal acclaim, citing the Declaration of Independence, it denied any authority to establish slavery in the territories, called for Kansas to be admitted as a free state, and declared "the imperative duty of Congress to prohibit in the Territories those twin relics of barbarism—Polygamy, and Slavery." As a point against Buchanan for his passive collusion in in the botched scheme to seize Cuba from Spain, the Ostend Manifesto, a resolution stated, "That the highwayman's plea, that 'might makes right,' embodied in the Ostend Circular, was in every respect unworthy of American diplomacy, and would bring shame and dishonor upon any Government or people that gave it their sanction." "The reading of the resolution referring to the Ostend circular was interrupted by boisterous laughter, and when silence was restored there were loud cries of 'Read it again,'" reported the *New York Herald*. The phrase "might makes right" would remain in Lincoln's mind until he addressed it at the Cooper Union in 1860.

Then suddenly there was dissension. The issue that had threatened to tear apart the Illinois Republican Party at its organizing meeting was raised again by precisely the same person who had brought it up there. George Schneider, the editor of the German language *Illinois Staats-Zeitung,* proposed a resolution against nativism that duplicated every word of the one that had been agreed upon by the Illinois party under the guidance of Lincoln, who went unmentioned, was unknown to the Republican throng, and not consulted by Schneider. "There is no people more in favor of freedom than the German population of Illinois," Schneider assured the delegates. His resolution immediately met stiff resistance from McLean's supporters, especially from Pennsylvania, a state heavily influenced by the Know Nothings and which was solid for McLean. They preferred a policy of silence on nativism, seeking to attract the Know Nothings, not to condemn them.

Their leader was a former Know Nothing and Pennsylvania's most fervent antislavery politician. Thaddeus Stevens had to retire from his seat in the Congress in 1852 because of his abolitionism. He did more than introduce petitions for the repeal of the Fugitive Slave Act. At the trial of two Quakers charged with no less than treason for refusing to assist U.S. marshals in the Christiana Riot that resulted in the killing of a slave owner trying to capture his runaways Stevens served as a defense counsel and won their acquittal. He had been born with a clubfoot to a poverty-stricken family in Vermont. His father deserted. The boy rose through a fierce determination to educate himself, graduating from Dartmouth. He suffered a rare disease that left him hairless and he wore an ill-fitting wig, another mark of disfigurement. He moved to Gettysburg, where he became a successful attorney, the chairman of the City Council, the largest landowner, president of the Gettysburg Railroad, and founder of the Caledonia Iron Works factory. In 1821, Stevens represented a slave owner seeking to repossess a fugitive slave, and was overcome with self-revulsion. His antislavery activity dated from that incident. But his physical disabilities undoubtedly gave him a profound empathy toward the oppressed. He joined the Anti-Masonic Party, promoting John McLean for its presidential nomination. Elected to the state legislature, Stevens sponsored the law establishing a free public education system. He was now a Whig. After the Panic of 1837, he moved to a house in Lancaster only two miles from that of James Buchanan. The two men were diametric opposites, open enemies since the presidential campaign of 1840, and in 1856 Stevens described Buchanan as "a bloated mass of political putridity." While Stevens's law practice was lucrative, he also represented fugitive slaves. He lived openly with his mulatto housekeeper, Lydia Hamilton Smith, for all intents and purposes his common-law wife whom he brought to social occasions. Their house was a stop on the Underground Railroad with a secret hiding place for runaways. Stevens's burning hatred of slavery was matched by his ruthless pragmatism. He joined the intolerant Know Nothings, which included many former Anti-Masons, out of the belief they would be his allies against slavery. He was elected a delegate to the Republican convention at a joint Pennsylvania convention consisting of Old Whigs, Know Nothings, and abolitionists.

Stevens rose at the convention to offer the only objection to any resolution. He wished to strike out certain of Schneider's words: "we oppose all proscreptive legislation," which was interpreted as an implicit rebuke of the Know Nothings. Stevens, the *New York Herald* reported, "thought this would be read as a direct assault upon the largest party in Pennsylvania"—the Know Nothings. "It contained nothing, he admitted, but what was right; but it at the same time contained what would be misunderstood and tortured." David Wilmot, of Pennsylvania, chairman of the resolutions committee, suggested substituting the word "impairing" for "proscriptive," and the controversy was avoided. Stevens could not have known that the words he had excised were originally Lincoln's. Yet, even in its amended form, the first Republican Party platform included a version of the resolution Lincoln had engineered in Illinois.

Thaddeus Stevens

Stevens's editing of the resolution was the only victory for the McLean forces. They spent the day trying to convince delegates that McLean should be nominated for president with Frémont as his running mate, which they promised "pretending to be from authoritative sources," according to Halstead, and a gambit that would lead to Fillmore's withdrawal. "The McLean men were hot last night—in fact, almost desperate, and threatened combustion and explosion if their demands were not complied with." The next morning delegates were presented with a circular: "You are divided between McLean and Fremont. Why not unite their names on one ticket? It would be invincible." But McLean's doom was apparent. Before the voting was about to begin, his manager, Judge Rufus P. Spalding, a Free Soiler and founder of the Republican Party of Ohio, took the floor. He unfurled a letter from McLean withdrawing his name from consideration, "without a struggle in the Convention." His supporters were stunned at the abruptness of the end. Stevens vainly objected. Then Chase's name was withdrawn. An Ohio delegation divided could not stand for one favorite son. Only Frémont was left.

Before the final vote for the presidential nomination, after McLean's letter of withdrawal was read, a McLean delegate from New York, Dewitt Clinton Littlejohn, declared that the Know Nothings "had this Republican movement at heart, and the convention should act liberally with them, and give them at least one of the candidates." Littlejohn, the former Speaker of the New York State Assembly, was both a Know Nothing and an ally of

Thurlow Weed, who himself was backing Frémont. But Owen Lovejoy, of Illinois, "opposed any action conciliating the North Americans. If they did so, the Prince of Iniquity—Stephen A. Douglas—would use it to seduce away the foreign vote." If the motion had stood the slightest chance, the mention of Douglas's name banished it to a netherworld.

The formal vote proceeded with just one live candidate. The chairman called: "All who are in favor of nominating John C. Fremont as the candidate of this convention for the presidency, will signify the same by giving three cheers!" "And," reported Halstead, "three times three perfect Davy Crockett war-whoops, with a touch of the buffalo bull and the wild cat, were given with stunning effect." But some McLean men were bewildered that the McLean-Frémont arrangement had been summarily rejected, "and thought it very strange and hard that such a compromise was not acceptable."

"On being defeated as to Mr. McLean for whom I did my best, I felt badly and at dark after the nomination of Mr. Fremont, I resolved to name you for Vice-President regardless of whom they might name," William B. Archer, an Illinois delegate, wrote Lincoln after the convention. Like Lincoln, Archer was Kentucky born, founded the town of Marshall, from which he was elected to the state legislature, where he served with Lincoln. An Old Whig, Archer joined the Know Nothings, who nominated him as their candidate for governor, which he declined because he believed it would only help elect the Democrat. At the convention Archer stayed up all night with a small group from Illinois trying to round up support for Lincoln's nomination. The favorite candidate of the Frémont forces for vice president was former U.S. senator William Dayton of New Jersey, an Old Whig who was already considered "a concession" to the "McLean men," reported Halstead.

The next day, June 19, Archer took the floor. According to the account in the *New York Tribune*: "Said he was acquainted with Mr. Lincoln, and had known him over thirty years. He was a native of Kentucky, and had always been a Clay Whig and a firm friend of this Republic. He had no fear of the North of Illinois, but the South was inhabited by emigrants from Kentucky and Tennessee, but with Lincoln on the ticket Illinois would be safe for Fremont, [cheers], and he believed it would be safe without him, [loud cheers and laughter], but doubly safe with him." Judge Spalding, Chase's manager, called out, "Will Lincoln fight?" "Col. Archer (jumping at least eighteen inches from the floor, and gesturing emphatically with his arms), YES, SIR. *He is a son of Kentucky* [Loud and prolonged laughter and cheers]."

When the roll was called Dayton won 253 votes, Lincoln 110. It was an unusual showing for an unknown, described by Halstead as "Colonel Lincoln" in his report, apparently thinking that if he was from Kentucky he must be a colonel. The Lincoln tally was more a vote for the importance of Illinois and the lingering resentment of the hard-core McLean supporters than it was for the obscure Lincoln. "I think you will pardon me for the move. I had a strong hope and felt disposed to make the effort," Archer wrote Lincoln.

Lincoln was in Urbana at a session of the Circuit Court of Champaign County. "The weather was dry and hot: our surroundings were not conducive to comfort, and I don't recollect to have ever attended a more uninteresting term of court," recalled Whitney. The traveling entourage of lawyers and Judge Davis stayed at the American House, a "primitive hostelry," whose owner, John Dunaway, beat a gong to summon the guests to meals, "and thereby causing us great annoyance." One evening Dunaway went to bang away but the gong was gone. "When I had reached the room I was in the presence of the culprit. Lincoln sat awkwardly in a chair tilted up after his fashion, looking amused, silly and guilty, as if he had done something ridiculous, funny and reprehensible. The Judge was equally amused; but said to him: 'Now, Lincoln, that is a shame. Poor Dunaway is the most distressed being. You must put that back.'" Lincoln restored the gong and "bounded up the stairs, two steps at a time."

The next day the coterie gathered shortly after noon as they did every day for the arrival of a copy of the *Chicago Tribune*. It reported the nomination of Frémont. And the next day they assembled to read the news about his running mate. "The convention then proceeded to an informal ballot for Vice-President . . ." To everyone's surprise, the gong prankster had been nominated and finished second. "Davis and I were greatly excited," wrote Whitney, "but Lincoln was phlegmatic, listless and indifferent: his only remark was: 'I reckon that ain't me; there's another great man in Massachusetts named Lincoln, and I reckon it's him.'"

But Lincoln brightened when he wrapped up his cases and collected his meager fees. "I do not remember to have seen him happier than when he had got his little earnings together, being less than $40, as I now recollect it, and had his carpet-bag packed, ready to start home."

CHAPTER SEVENTEEN

THE BIRTHER CAMPAIGN

I MMENSE ENTHUSIASM," ran the front-page headline of the *New York Times* story reporting Frémont's nomination. At the moment the convention made it unanimous, a large banner with "JOHN C. FREMONT, for President of the United States" was unfurled behind the platform while in front of it was hung an American flag with the candidate's name inscribed. The slogan, "Free Soil, Free Labor, Free Men, Fremont," was immediately taken up. "'The Path-Finder of the Rocky Mountains,' the chivalric John C. Frémont, the type and embodiment of the spirit of Young America, was yesterday afternoon nominated. . . . Such a degree of unanimity and enthusiasm as this, has had no example in the political history of the country. . . . Though the nominee of the Republican Party has never been identified with any great political movement, and is the youngest man who has ever been nominated for the Presidency, he is so well known, and his romantic history is so familiar to the people of the whole country, that no one, on hearing his name now, will say, as they did of Pierce, 'Who is he?'"

John C. Frémont

Frémont's legend had been printed, but the statesmanship was yet to come. His "romantic history" romanticized the worrisome parts of his history to the vanishing point. He was made new by becoming a man scrubbed of much of his past. His bleached slightness lifted him momentarily above politics and party, his scandals receding from view until his balloon was abruptly pulled back to earth.

"There is no mistake about the effect of Fremont's nomination on the politicians," warned the Washington correspondent of the *New York Herald*. "The Democrats are taken all aback by it. All sorts of stories are trumped up against him. . . . It is reported here on the best authority that a great effort will shortly be made to crush Fremont and blast his prospects forever."

The Republican campaign had the aura of a great awakening, a moral crusade, and a social movement. While Republicans were summoned to rescue democracy and "free soil" from the "Slave Power," and to struggle for the "free labor" system that gave all men an equal chance, the Democrats and Know Nothings raised the cry to save the nation from the Republicans. One common point of the attack was that Frémont and the Republicans were fanatical sectionalists in the grip of abolitionists. "The Union is in danger and the people everywhere begin to know it," Buchanan declared. "The Black Republicans must be, as they can be with justice, boldly assailed as disunionists, and this charge must be reiterated again and again."

Fillmore, for his part, desperately followed a strategy for ruin and rule. His far-fetched scheme was to win over the Southern Whigs, break the Northern Republicans, and discredit Frémont to create a political stalemate in the Electoral College that would throw the election into the House of Representatives, where by some miracle he would be chosen president as the saving middle course. He asserted his centrality by wishfully claiming to hold the balance of power. Campaigning against conflict and partisanship, he created chaos as a spoiler. The bleaker his prospects, the harsher became his campaign.

Fillmore said not a word about Kansas. He said nothing about the extension of slavery. He said nothing about the Know Nothing platform. On June 26, a week after the Republican convention, he delivered a major speech in which he warned that if the Republicans were to win the South would have just cause for secession. "Alas! threatened at home with civil war," he said. The clear and present danger was the existence of the Republican Party itself. "We see a political party presenting candidates for the Presidency and Vice-Presidency, selected for the first time from the free States alone, with the avowed purpose of electing those candidates by suffrages of one part of the Union only, to rule over the whole United States. Can it be possible that those who are engaged in such a measure can have seriously reflected upon the consequences which must inevitably follow, in case of success? Can they have the madness or the folly to believe that our Southern brethren would submit to be governed by such a chief magistrate?"

But the question of illegitimacy was raised about more than the "Black Republicans." While Fillmore tarnished the Republican Party as provocateur of civil war, his operatives spread stories that Frémont, who was an Episcopalian, was actually a Catholic. The Catholic smear, that Frémont was not a true American but the covert agent of a Vatican plot to seize the country, resonated with the paranoid Know Nothing cosmology. Those susceptible to the lie were also susceptible to an extensive Catholic fear-mongering literature, including sexually graphic best-selling novels about rapacious priests preying on innocent Protestant girls. The *New York Express,* a newspaper edited by the Know Nothing candidate for governor, Erastus Brooks, a former Whig state senator, filled its pages with stories about Frémont's secret papist identity. Lincoln would have been familiar with the other chief propagandist, Nathan Sargent, a clever former Whig newspaper correspondent, who had been among Lincoln's boardinghouse mates during his stint in the Congress. "Fremont's Romanism Established," a widely circulated pamphlet, apparently written by Sargent, alleged "the most foul combination" directed by Archbishop John Hughes, the Catholic prelate in New York, in league with "Abolitionists and the Foreigners," and William H. Seward, who had supposedly conspired to deliver the Republican nomination to Frémont in the interest of the Vatican. Sargent wrote Fillmore that the Catholic question was "the battery which proves most effective in thinning his ranks."

The nativist pamphleteers charged that proof of Frémont's Catholicism was irrefutable: Frémont's father was a French Catholic immigrant, Frémont was a bastard, and Frémont and his wife, who had hastily eloped, were married in a civil ceremony by a Catholic priest. Citing bogus sources that Frémont rejected a Protestant Bible from a friend and maintained a Catholic chapel in his home, the case was clinched: "He goes to a Roman Catholic Church in Washington, crosses himself with so-called holy water at the door, and makes the sign of the cross when he goes into his pew."

Frémont's illegitimacy extended to more than his suspect religion. He was assailed as literally illegitimate, the child of a mother who was not divorced from her first husband. "The question arises," editorialized the *Richmond Dispatch,* "could there have been a legitimate marriage without a divorce?"

About Frémont's father, the paper wrote, "The life of the progenitor of the free-soil candidate of the Presidency, shows that he was at least a disciple of Free-love, if not of Free-soil." For good measure, Frémont was also accused of murder; adultery; cannibalism; faking his explorations as "a fancy amateur tourist" and "over-grown schoolboy playing mountaineer" (*New York Daily News*); and according to a trapper quoted in the *Missouri Republican* "a very young beaver" and "a cold-hearted, selfish devil." He was rumored to own seventy-five slaves and denounced as an abolitionist. The *Richmond Enquirer* mocked the Republican slogan: "Free niggers, free women, free land, and Fremont." In San Francisco, Democrats marched in an anti-Frémont parade under the banner "Fremont: Free Niggers and Frijoles."

Frémont's wife worked closely with John Bigelow, of the *New York Evening Post,* to provide the candidate with claims to a legitimate family background. Bigelow's campaign biography was a classic fairy tale of a poor young man revealed to be truly of noble descent.

His mother's father was the brother of Catharine Whiting, the grand aunt of George Washington. Colonel Thomas Whiting was "one of the most wealthy and prominent men of his day," a member of the Virginia House of Burgesses, a king's attorney, member of the naval board. But the father died, the daughter Ann sent to live with evil relatives was dispossessed and forced into an unhappy marriage with an old landowner, Major Pryor, who "lacked refinement and sensibility, and was in every respect repulsive to the young creature, who was sacrificed to him." After they divorced she married Charles Frémont, a French immigrant who was "a man of superior accomplishments and high breeding, spoke English fluently, and was a welcome guest in the best society." He died when their son, John Charles Frémont, was five years old. The boy was confirmed in the Episcopal Church of his mother, graduated from Charleston College, joined the U.S. Corps of Topographical Engineers, and set off on his famous adventures.

Frémont, in fact, was illegitimate. His father, Louis-Rene Fremon, a French-

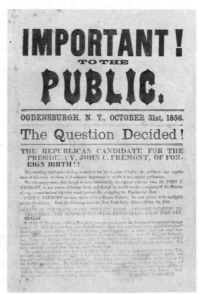

"John C. Fremont . . . shown to be a Roman Catholic . . . inelligible [*sic*] for the Presidency"

Canadian schoolteacher and dance instructor, who called himself Charles, ran off with the married Anne Whiting Pryor, whose divorce was never granted. John Charles Fremont, born in Savannah and raised in Charleston, later changed the family name, adding the "t" and an accent mark. He was raised Protestant, like his mother. But, above all, he was well married.

By creating a personal counter-narrative, Frémont's wife intervened in an effort to save him as she had throughout his entire career. Jessie Benton Frémont, educated from the cradle in the political arts, was the most formidable female political figure of mid-nineteenth-century America. She lent him legitimacy in drawing rooms and smoke-filled rooms. The country's most celebrated individualist counted on her as his "second mind," as he called her. Even when he was roaming the wilderness or European capitals alone or with his sidekick Kit Carson, she was indispensable as his protector and promoter, organizer of his thoughts and writing, manager of his campaigns, and dealing with party bosses, senators, and presidents without the slightest bit of deference but as an equal. None of their political lineages compared to hers, except the Blairs, who were also her family.

Jessie was the favorite of Thomas Hart Benton's six children and protégé, "his consort and collaborator, his apprentice and creation," according to her biographer Sally Denton. He took her everywhere with him in St. Louis and Washington, educated her in the classics, resting her for long periods amid Thomas Jefferson's six thousand books at the Library of Congress, and taught her to speak several languages. She was brought literally to sit at the knee of President Jackson during conferences at the White House while the president played absentmindedly with her hair. She studied birds with her father's friend John James Audubon, heard stories from Washington Irving, and discussed exploration of the West with frequent houseguest William Clark (of Lewis and Clark fame). While in her teens, President Martin Van Buren, a widower, proposed marriage. Benton, champion of Manifest Destiny, brought a trail of scientists and explorers to dinner, and it was there that sixteen-year-old Jessie was introduced to twenty-seven-year-old Lieutenant John C. Frémont, fresh from surveying the region between the Mississippi and Missouri Rivers. They were instantly infatuated with each other, but her father disapproved of the match with the young man of little means, so they eloped, hastily securing a Catholic priest to perform the wedding ceremony.

Some years earlier, Benton and Francis Preston Blair had informally agreed on an arranged marriage between Benton's daughter and Blair's son Francis Jr. That way, Blair told Benton, the two men would "be blended together when we have left the stage of life in history." Blair hero-worshipped Benton as the personification of Western democracy. The two families were raised together, virtually one and the same. The Benton children called Blair "Father Blair" and his children their "cousins." They were, in fact, distant cousins by shared lineage through the Preston family of Virginia. (Jessie's great-grandfather on her mother's side was General Francis Preston.) Montgomery and Frank apprenticed in St. Louis in the law under Benton's tutelage. Benton called Frank "Young Ajax." Elizabeth Blair, the Blair daughter, was Jessie's closest friend. The night Jessie met Frémont, she said, "At last I've met a handsomer man than Cousin Preston." Jessie and Frémont named their first son Francis Preston.

Jessie was as much a trailblazer as her husband. She anonymously coauthored his thrilling account of his expeditions, traveled across the Panama Isthmus in 1849 to meet him in California, and tried to protect him from perils, most of his own making. During the Bear Flag Revolt, Frémont refused to take orders from his superior officer, General Stephen Kearny, and challenged him for the title of military governor of California. During the struggle for power, Frémont circumvented regular channels by dispatching his wife to intervene with President James K. Polk. Jessie considered the martinet Kearny an upstart who had gained his commission through the influence of her father. On June 7, 1847, armored in a green cashmere dress, in the company of her husband's scout Kit Carson, she belted down a drink before heading to the White House. "Mr. Carson and Mrs. Fremont," she announced to the happily surprised mountain man, "will now have a glass of sherry before going into battle."

Jessie handed the president a letter from Frémont proclaiming his innocence. "Doesn't Colonel Fremont's course seem reasonable in this case?" she demanded. Polk, polite to a member of the Benton family, did not reply. In his diary, he wrote: "Mrs. Fremont seemed anxious to elicit from me some expression of approbation of her husband's conduct, but I evaded [making any]. In truth, I consider that Col. Fremont was greatly in the wrong when he refused to obey the orders issued to him by Gen'l Kearney. . . . It was unnecessary, however, that I should say so to Col. Fremont's wife, and I evaded giving her an answer." Frémont was court-martialed for mutiny, Polk declined to intervene, Frémont resigned in dishonor, Jessie fumed at the president, but Frémont returned as senator from California, vindicated by an adoring public that forgave his failings as the envy of rivals.

In 1855, Jessie launched Frémont's covert presidential campaign for the nomination of the newly formed Republican Party by writing an appeal for assistance to "Father Blair," asking him also to help mitigate Benton's jealous resentment of his son-in-law. Together Jessie and Blair acted as stage-managers of Frémont's meteoric rise to the top of the Republican ticket.

Jessie ran the campaign with Blair from headquarters at her 56 West Ninth Street residence in New York City. The open involvement of women as activists was among the campaign's novelties. Women already were at the center of the abolitionist cause, and feminism grew out of abolitionism. In 1856, Jessie became its symbol. "The Frémont campaign marked the first time in American history when women were drawn into the political process, the zeal for Jessie unparalleled," wrote historian Sally Denton. "The 'Fremont and Jessie' campaign, as it immediately became known, inspired thousands of women to take to the street. Widely seen as a full-fledged partner in her husband's pursuits, Jessie became an overnight heroine to women. . . . She straddled the boundaries of Victorian society—outspoken but polite, irreverent but tactful, opinionated but respectful—a woman so far ahead of her time that other women flocked to her." Jessie was conscious that as a woman in politics she, too, was a pathfinder. "I can say as Portia did to Brutus, 'Should I not be stronger than my sex, Being so Fathered and so Husbanded?'" she wrote. Before Frémont won the nomination, but when his name was already being floated, Jessie observed, "Just now I am quite the fashion—5th Avenue asks itself, 'Have we a Presidentess among us—'" "What a shame women can't vote!" wrote Lydia Maria Child, the abolitionist and feminist. "We'd carry 'our Jessie' into the White House on our shoulders."

Jessie called the campaign "a trial by mud." Perhaps the worst blow was her father's endorsement of Buchanan—a "Brutus stab," she called it. Frémont could not cope with the innuendoes. The harsher the smears, the more he withdrew. His daughter, Lily Fremont, recalled, "my father's nature was such that he could not have withstood its bitterness. He was used to life in the open and wanted a square fight, not one filled with petty innuendoes and unfounded recriminations." He left the campaign, including tracking the details of his murky parentage, to his capable wife. She hid the newspapers and correspondence from him to preserve his equipoise while she handled things. He spent much of his time riding and fencing. Jessie, according to Bigelow, could "look into the political cauldron when it was boiling without losing . . . [her] head."

Republican leaders were confounded that the religious falsehood against

Frémont gained credence. Protests against it had a perversely confirming effect. If Frémont were not really a Catholic and part of a Vatican conspiracy of course he would deny it; but if he did deny it he would be seen as dissembling. Meanwhile, attempts to refute the big lie helped circulate it, gave it more importance, and suggested that the Republicans protested too much because they were covering up. Thurlow Weed warned, "the Catholic story is doing much damage." A worried group of several dozen men attended a hasty meeting with Frémont at Astor House, the Broadway luxury hotel where Weed maintained his headquarters in Room 11. Francis P. Blair and Horace Greeley were opposed to making any statement in the belief that it might offend Catholic voters. Frémont refused to dignify the accusation and was averse to dealing with private matters that might be true or half-true. It was decided that a letter under Frémont's signature disclaiming his reputed Catholicism would do more harm than good. Surrogates were enlisted to debunk the smear. In a pamphlet, "Col. Fremont's Religion. The Calumnies Against Him Exposed By Indisputable Proofs," Henry Ward Beecher, the most famous Northern Protestant pastor, insisted," Col. Fremont never was, and is not now, a Roman Catholic. . . . It is a gratuitous falsehood, utter, barren, absolute and unqualified. The story has been got up for politics effect, it is still circulated for that reason, and, like other political lies, it is a sheer unscrupulous falsehood from top to bottom, from the core to the skin, and from the skin back to the core again. In all it ports, in pulp, tegument, rind, cell and seed, it is it thorough and total, untruth, and they who spread it bear false witness."

Neither facts nor clerical authority could undo the damage. Seward wrote his wife, "Fremont, who was preferred over me because I was not a bigoted Protestant, is nearly convicted of being a Catholic." Greeley decried antislavery men who would vote against Frémont in the fear he "would give us all over to the tender mercies of the Pope!" Congressman Schuyler Colfax of Indiana wrote Blair: "These Catholic reports must be extinguished or we shall lose Pa, N.J., Inda., Conn. And the Lord knows how many more states." Thaddeus Stevens lamented that the accusation of Catholicism "lost us the Nation." "It had the most effect," concluded Thurlow Weed.

But more ominous than the cynical and paranoid attacks on Frémont's birth and religion were the consequences of the "disunionism" theme. Originally intended to besmirch the "Black Republicans" as divisive and unpatriotic it assumed a life of its own.

Governor Henry A. Wise of Virginia, who anointed Buchanan "as reliable as Mr. Calhoun himself," announced in September he would call up 150,000 troops to resist Frémont if he were elected. "Tell me if the hoisting of the black flag over you by a Frenchman's bastard, while the arms of civil war are already clashing, is not to be deemed an overt act and a declaration of war?" he said, fusing the birther and disunionist themes.

Wise called for a meeting of Southern governors to prevent Frémont from taking office and to prepare for secession. "The South could not, without degradation, submit to the election of a Black Republican President," he stated at a rally. "To tell me we should submit to the election of a Black Republican, under circumstances like these, is to tell me that Virginia and the fourteen Slave States are already subjugated and degraded, that the southern people are without spirit, and without purpose to defend the rights they know and dare not maintain." Only two governors showed up to Wise's meeting. It was more a tactic than a strategy. His threat of secession was rhetorical. He anticipated that Buchanan would win. But he and others were laying a predicate to act on in the future. If a Republican won the presidency, secession was the logical response.

The *Richmond Enquirer* argued the case on August 29 in an editorial entitled "Fremont and Disunion."

> In voting for Fremont, a portion of the North tenders to the South the issue of this Union or unconditional submission. If Fremont be elected, he comes in as the professed enemy of the South. No Southerner, without treachery to his section of the Union, can become a member of his cabinet. . . . We do not believe that any portion of the South will submit to his administration. . . . Disunion then, in event of his election is inevitable. . . . Let Pennsylvania, New Jersey, Indiana and Illinois, see whether their interests will not be best promoted by uniting with the Southern confederacy. Let California, too, study well the question. . . . But let no one indulge the fatal delusion that Fremont may be elected and yet the Union preserved.—There is not one single possibility of such result. It is hard to keep it together even now. Then, it would fall to pieces without even a struggle to preserve it.

John Minor Botts, a prominent Old Whig from Virginia, enlisted as a Fillmore presidential elector, protested the cynical siren calls for secession, stating that the South would honor the results of the election even if Frémont were to be elected. The *Richmond Enquirer* urged him to flee the state. "Do not wait for the honors or ostracism nor provoke the disgrace of *Lynching* . . .

the best atonement for the treason you have committed, will be to hurry North—and never more."

Several days after Botts was threatened with lynching, Senator James M. Mason of Virginia sent Secretary of War Jefferson Davis a private letter, informing him of Wise's pre-secession plans, for "your most private ear." Mason passed on Wise's secret request in case of a Republican victory, "to exchange with Virginia, on fair terms of difference, percussion for flint muskets" for the state militia. "If so, would it not furnish good reason for extending such facilities to the States? Virginia probably has more arms than the other Southern States, and would divide in case of need. In a letter yesterday to a committee in South Carolina, I gave it as my judgment, in the event of Fremont's election, the South should not pause, but proceed at once to 'immediate, absolute, and *eternal* separation.'" Mason added his hope that Wise's view that "Old Buck" would be elected was "not delusive." In not one Deep South state and only four border states did Frémont's name appear on the ballot.

Throughout the North vast crowds materialized for the Frémont campaign, the likes of which had not been seen before—60,000 people led by fifty bands in Indianapolis, 25,000 in Cleveland, a parade that was six miles long in Michigan. In Beloit, Wisconsin, 30,000 staged a "celebration" with floats, including one with "thirty-two beautiful young ladies" under the banner "Opposition to Old Bachelors." In city after city, the prettiest young woman was chosen for parades to represent the "Queen of Hearts," "Our Jessie." In New York City, a rally at the Academy of Music was packed "from pit to dome," reported the *New York Tribune*.

Walt Whitman, fired from his job as editor of the *Brooklyn Eagle* for supporting the Free Soil Party in 1848, felt inspired to compose an exhortatory essay, "The Eighteenth Presidency!" addressed to *"to each Young Man in the Nation, North, South, East, and West."* The year before, in 1855, he self-published a book of poetry he titled *Leaves of Grass.* Now Whitman wrote of Franklin Pierce, "The President eats dirt and excrement for his daily meals, likes it, and tries to force it on The States. The cushions of the Presidency are nothing but filth and blood. The pavements of Congress are also bloody." He derided Buchanan and Fillmore as "relics and proofs of the little political bargains, chances, combinations, resentments of a past age, having nothing in common with this age." He imagined the coming of "the Redeemer President of These States, [who] is to be the one that fullest realizes the rights of individuals, signified by the impregnable rights of The States, the substratum of this Union. The Redeemer President of These States is not to be exclusive, but inclusive." He appealed to "young men" of the South: "How much longer do you intend to submit to the espionage and terrorism of the three hundred and fifty thousand owners of slaves? Are you too their slaves, and their most obedient slaves?" And Whitman wondered how and when the future would bring an inevitable cataclysm. "What historic denouements are these we are approaching? On all sides tyrants tremble, crowns are unsteady, the human race restive, on the watch for some better era, some divine war. No man knows what will happen next, but all know that some such things are to happen as mark the greatest moral convulsions of the earth. Who shall play the hand for America in these tremendous games? A pretty time to put up two debauched old disunionist politicians, the lees and dregs of more than sixty years! A pretty time for two dead corpses to go walking up and down the earth, to guide by feebleness and ashes a proud, young, friendly, fresh, heroic nation of thirty millions of live and electric men!"

CHAPTER EIGHTEEN

THE GREAT AWAKENING

J udge David Davis, the imperious ruler of the Eighth Judicial Circuit, from his great mansion in Bloomington reflected upon the proceedings of the Republican convention at Philadelphia and was not pleased. "The Judge thinks Fremont a very unfit person to be run for President, and that if elected the Union will not last through his administration," Browning wrote in his diary on June 14. Davis "had no hope of good coming from Fremont's election—that he had no qualifications for the office—that money and corruption had been freely used to procure his nomination, and that he was in the hands of, and would be controlled, by Blair, Greely, Wilson, Thurlow Wead [*sic*] &c all of whom were corrupt. That Buchannan was a man of ability, and considerable states-manship, but that he was timid—lacked nerve & would probably fall under the influence of the ultra pro slavery men of the South." The judge preferred the last Whig president Fillmore, but despaired. "He had more confidence in Fillmore than either of the others, but there was no chance for his election, and upon a

Owen Lovejoy

survey of the whole ground he had but little hope for the future of our Country."

Davis was used to his judgments going unchallenged and was perplexed that he could not command the political tides. He was a conflicted figure trying to hold the elements together, a Southern-raised man of Northern sympathy who had discovered his center of gravity in the Whig Party. Born into a slaveholding Maryland family, his father, a physician, died when he was a boy, and he was passed from household to household until he was shuffled off to boarding school. Educated at Kenyon College in Ohio, founded by Philander Chase, the antislavery Episcopal bishop and uncle of Salmon P. Chase, he moved as a young man to Illinois, began a law practice and real estate business that would eventually make him the largest landowner in the state. He was a stalwart Whig, who instinctively disliked Douglas and warmed to Lincoln. Davis's judgeship was an elected position. He had started out in the legislature. He was the party power of Bloomington, but his party had disintegrated. He had complained that Springfield was "overrun with Foreigners," but disdained the Know Nothings. He was opposed to the extension of slavery, but considered abolitionists "wild and disorganizing." He believed that Know Nothings and abolitionists were disruptive forces that would enable Douglas and the Democrats to win. Davis saw in the defeat of McLean for the Republican nomination the final rejection of Old Whiggism and a projected version of himself.

Davis believed that the election in Illinois would turn upon the crucial swing congressional district centered on Bloomington. Northern districts would vote Republican, the southern districts Democratic. The balance of power rested in the thirteen counties in and around Bloomington, a north-south split that reflected the division within the state itself. Davis placed his hope on the nomination for Congress of a young lawyer from the coterie of the Eighth Judicial Circuit, Leonard Swett. On July 2, in the town of Ottawa, a Republican convention was held that on its first ballot gave Owen Lovejoy 25 votes, Swett 18, and Jesse O. Norton, the incumbent, a Whig, 9. The Swett and Norton men hastily called for a recess. After twenty minutes the two candidates dropped out and threw their support to another Old Whig, Churchill Coffing. But the gambit backfired. Lovejoy gained five more votes, winning the nomination.

"We learned yesterday," chortled the *DeWitt Courier,* a pro-Douglas Democratic newspaper, "that the Republican Convention for this District resulted in the nomination of the Rev. notorious Abolition-Banner-Trailing-Union-

Sliding-Lovejoy to the utter discomfiture of Leonard Swett, and divers other good and worthy aspirants." Davis, angered over the loss of McLean, was furious. "I subscribe to everything you say relative to the nomination of Love-joy," an Old Whig and former member of the legislature, J.C. Pugh, wrote him. "I can see and almost feel its disastrous and deplorable effects every-where."

The split over Lovejoy between the Old Whigs and the abolitionist wings that Lincoln had finessed at the Bloomington convention threatened to tear apart the infant party. But Lincoln refused to join in a factional battle of re-sentment. Leaving Springfield on or near the date of the district convention that chose Lovejoy, he arrived at Princeton, Lovejoy's hometown, for a July 4th rally. He was surprised to find before him a sea of about ten thousand people. Lincoln delivered a brief history lesson about the Declaration of In-dependence, the Ordinance of 1787, the Missouri Compromise, and Doug-las's Kansas-Nebraska Act, taking his seat to "loud and enthusiastic cheers," according to the local newspaper, followed on the platform by Lovejoy, who held Douglas up to ridicule, comparing the "Little Giant" to a louse. The final speaker was "Old Joe" Knox, a well-known attorney, who recounted the gallantry in the Mexican War of William Bissell, the Republican candi-date for governor, and how "Bissell the Lion Hearted" faced down Jefferson Davis, forcing him to withdraw his challenge of a duel, a story which "so thrilled the audience," according to an eyewitness.

The Princeton event was the first great rally Lincoln attended after the Bloomington convention. Here there were not dozens of the curious, or even a couple hundred dutiful adherents, but thousands of people committed to a crusade. For the first time Lincoln saw for himself the spontaneous upsurge for Lovejoy and the Republicans. This excitement could not be artificially produced. It was not the result of old party men. Nor was it like the past campaigns of mass interest he had been part of before, like the first Whig one in 1840 for William Henry Harrison, based on slogans, "Tippecanoe and Tyler, Too" and "Hard Cider and Log Cabin," and which avoided all issues. Now the intensity came from a cause. It was not an abolitionist meeting. It was larger and broader than that. It was the sudden organic appearance of the Republican Party and the cause it represented. What Lincoln witnessed at Princeton was the beginning of a great awakening sweeping the North.

Upon his return after sharing the podium with Lovejoy, Lincoln learned of the plot of disappointed Old Whigs to break with the Republicans to launch an independent candidate against Lovejoy in the general election.

The signers of the call for a bolters' convention at Bloomington were friends of Lincoln. One was Henry Clay Whitney. Another was Asahel Gridley, a former state senator and the wealthiest man in Bloomington infamous for his irascible outbursts. (Lincoln would successfully defend him from an accusation of slander in 1859 with the argument "that the people generally know you to be impulsive and say things you do not mean, and they do not consider what you say as slander.") Another signer was Isaac Funk, a former legislator, founder of Funk's Grove and one of the richest men in McLean County, for whom Lincoln was attorney. This rump group intended to nominate T. Lyle Dickey, one of Davis's close friends, as their candidate. "We are in the midst of a political tornado," Dickey explained in a letter to his son. "The Congressional convention of Fremont men met at Ottawa on the 2d of this month nominated for Congress Rev. Owen Lovejoy, a rank old-fashioned Abolitionist. About half the delegates bolted the nomination and called another convention to nominate another candidate who would not only oppose the introduction of slavery into Kansas, but would at the same time be true to the acknowledged rights of the South under the Constitution, embracing their right to recapture runaway slaves and who in general would exercise a spirit of fidelity and fraternity to the people of the South and avoid all unnecessary cause of difference."

Lincoln wasted little time in writing Davis. His letter of July 7 played to Davis's sense of outrage in order to coax him away from supporting the bolters. "Dear Judge," he wrote, "When I heard that Swett was beaten, and Lovejoy nominated, it turned me blind. I was, by invitation, on my way to Princeton; and I really thought of turning back. However, on reaching that region, and seeing the people there—their great enthusiasm for Lovejoy—considering the activity they will carry into the contest with him—and their great disappointment, if he should now be torn from them, I really think it best to let the matter stand. It is not my business to advise in the case; and if it were, I am not sure I am capable of giving the best advice; but I know saying what I do, will not be offensive to you. Show this to Gridley and other friends, or not, just as you may judge whether it do good or harm." With all due deference, Lincoln put the burden of ripping apart the Republican Party on Davis. "Lincoln had a way of excepting with so much grace and deference, and so apologetically, that the Judge was rather flattered by it," wrote Whitney. Two days later, on July 9, Lincoln sent a similar letter to Whitney: "It turned me blind when I first heard Swett was beaten, and Lovejoy nominated; but after much anxious reflection, I really believe it is best to let it stand. This, of course, I wish to be confidential." He put the weight on Whitney, too.

Lincoln's attitude was obliquely but apparently expressed in the *Illinois State Journal,* more or less his personal vehicle, which on July 7 mocked the *Illinois State Register,* Douglas's paper. Under the headline, "Don't Like It," the *Journal* editorialized, "The Register does not like the nomination of Hon. Owen Lovejoy, by the anti-Nebraska party of the Third Congressional District. Having been utterly unsuccessful heretofore in pleasing our fastidious neighbors, our friends need not feel greatly disappointed that they are still as far as ever from accomplishing that result."

Another friend of Lincoln, Jesse W. Fell, shared his open view on Lovejoy. Fell had originally backed Swett, too, but he was not prepared to let the nascent Republican Party be broken by the bolters. Fell had been responsible for Davis settling in Bloomington. He had sold his thriving law practice to him, became wealthy through real estate and railroads, founded the neighboring town of Normal, the state university, philanthropies, was an early environmentalist, the publisher of the *Bloomington Weekly Pantagraph* newspaper, and a Quaker who participated in the Underground Railroad. "Fell had more energy and force of character, Davis later declared, than any man he had ever known," wrote Davis's biographer Willard L. King. Fell was ceaseless from 1854 onward in promoting Lincoln's political career. He urged Lincoln to stalk Douglas in order to force him to debate and he would not relent in his insistence that there should be Lincoln-Douglas debates. (Fell's great-grandson, Adlai E. Stevenson, became governor of Illinois and was twice nominated as the Democratic candidate for president.)

The bolters' convention met at Bloomington on July 16. Dickey was duly nominated and delivered a speech "much the same as he would have addressed the Supreme Court on a law question," according to a report. Gridley took the platform to stir up the crowd, calling Lovejoy "a nigger thief," adding that he wished Lovejoy had been present when Brooks assaulted Sumner. "Yes sir, with the addition that Lovejoy and Brooks had then cut each other's throats." Suddenly and surprisingly, Lovejoy stepped forward. He had been quietly informed to attend the meeting by Fell. "I have never spoke to his gentleman," Lovejoy said to Gridley. "I have never injured him in thought, word or deed, and yet the best wish he has for me is that a Southern bully may cut my throat." Replying to the accusation of being "a nigger thief," he said, "If it is meant by that that I go to Kentucky or Missouri to entice slaves to run away, it is not true. It is not necessary for me to do that. But if you mean by that charge that when a man or woman comes to my door and asks for a cup of water and a crust of bread and that I point them to the North star, if that is what you mean, and I have had such women come to my door as white as your wife or mine, if that is what you mean, then I plead guilty." He paused and asked, "And who of you would not do the same thing?" The meeting ended with three cheers for Lovejoy. "He killed the bolting convention movement so completely that it never wriggled after that night," according to Ezra M. Prince, the historian of McLean County.

Two days later a ratification meeting of Lovejoy's nomination was held in Bloomington. Gridley spoke against him, Fell for him. Lovejoy was overwhelmingly approved. On July 23, the *Bloomington Pantagraph* published its ringing endorsement: "We want in Congress men of ability and eloquence who may be relied on with perfect confidence to resist the extension of slavery. Nobody doubts that on this question OWEN LOVEJOY will be as true as steel."

Dickey's candidacy cratered. The delicate task of persuading him to face its reality fell to his friend Davis. "I did not dream that you would have taken the nomination for Congress," he wrote Dickey on July 18, two days after Lovejoy stole the thunder at the bolters' convention. "The readiness with which many persons support Lovejoy is surprising." He attributed the cause to the "outrages in Kansas" and "the attack on Mr. Sumner," which "have made abolitionists of those, who never dreamed they were drifting into it." Davis conceded, "I think the grand reason of it all is that his views and opinions are becoming the views and opinions of a majority of the people." He urged Dickey to quit. "We, the old Whig party, will be stricken down during this campaign. Had we not better bide our time, brush up our armor for future operations?" Stubbornly, Dickey held out until September 13, and Davis resumed surreptitious plotting against Lovejoy. On October 31, the Republican committee of Vermilion County sent a letter to the DeWitt County committee declaring its members were "mortified to know" that Davis was at the center of a "clique" "for the avowed purpose" of having Old Whigs "embittered against Mr. Lovejoy."

Throughout the drama over Lovejoy, Lincoln attempted to find a way for the Republicans to ally with the Know Nothings without actually uniting with them. He revived a scheme from the time before the establishment of the Whig Party, in the 1836 presidential election, when the various candidates running against the Democratic ticket pledged to throw their support in the Electoral College to the one who received the most popular votes. According to Lincoln's calculation the Republicans would outpoll the Know Nothings and ultimately be the beneficiary. He tossed the idea around with an Old Whig turned Know Nothing, James Berdan, a railroad attorney with literary polish as the friend of Henry Wadsworth Longfellow and relation by marriage to Washington Irving. "A union of our strength, to be effected in some way, is indispensable to our carrying the State against Buchanan," Lincoln wrote him on July 10. "The inherent obstacle to any plan of union, lies in the fact that of those Germans which we now have with us, large numbers will fall away, so soon as it is seen that their votes, cast with us, may *possibly* be used to elevate Mr. Fil[l]more." Lincoln suggested "one small improvement": "Let Fremont and Fillmore men unite on one entire ticket, with the understanding that that ticket, if elected, shall cast the vote of the State, for whichever of the two shall be known to have received the larger number of electoral votes, in the other states." But Lincoln's notion was inherently quixotic. Berdan lacked the influence over the other Know Nothings to make a deal. Those running the Fillmore campaign had no intention of surrendering. Meanwhile, Douglas was covertly stoking antagonism between Republicans and Know Nothings by secretly directing Democratic funds to the *Weekly Native Citizen,* the state's principal Know Nothing newspaper, which promoted Fillmore.

Lincoln was aware of the rumors of payoffs to Know Nothings and Old Whigs. He felt certain his old mentor John Todd Stuart and his friend James Matheny "and the leading Fillmore men in this section were bribed by the Buchanan corruption fund," he told Herndon, "said that he believed that the Fillmore party, i.e., leaders of it through the State, were bought and sold like hogs are sold in the market."

Lincoln, however, kept devising new means of reaching out to Old Whigs who were for Fillmore. From his contacts across the state he obtained the names and addresses of key Fillmore men and sent them a "confidential" letter that made a tortuous argument of why they should vote for Frémont. "I understand you are a Fillmore man," he wrote. "Let me prove to you that every vote withheld from Fremont, and given to Fillmore, *in this state,* actually lessens Fillmore's chance of being President. Suppose Buchanan gets *all* the slave states, and Pennsylvania, and *any other* one state besides; *then he is elected,* no matter who gets all the rest. But suppose Fillmore gets the two slave states of Maryland and Kentucky; *then* Buchanan *is not* elected; Fillmore goes into the House of Representatives, and may be made President by a compromise. But suppose again Fillmore's friends throw away a few thousand votes on him, in *Indiana* and *Illinois,* it will inevitably give these states to Buchanan, which will more than compensate him for the loss of Maryland and Kentucky; will elect him, and leave Fillmore no chance in the H.R. or out of it." He concluded his incongruous appeal: "This is as plain as the adding up of the weights of three small hogs." The *Register* got hold of a copy of the letter and ridiculed the supposedly "confidential" document. "We pity Mr. Lincoln," the paper wrote, "for verily his abolition taskmasters are requiring dirty work at his hands." Lincoln was undeterred and kept sending the same "confidential" letter to dozens of Fillmore supporters almost to Election Day.

The diehard Whigs maintained a rump party apart from the Know Nothings, mounted a statewide ticket, and published a campaign newspaper called *The Conservative,* which repeatedly savaged Lincoln. "Shortly after his return from the Bloomington Convention, we heard him," the paper editorialized in a tone of mock sorrow. "We were not only surprised but sorry. . . . Surprised that a man of his acknowledged ability would indulge so thin and bold a piece of sophistry and sorry that a man, of his dignity of character, would descend to such pettifogging demogogueism. . . . These thoughts and feelings we shared in common, with all Mr. Lincoln's old and long tried friends, those who stood by him in the days of his early struggle; those who had 'breathed into him the political breath of life,' those who had delighted at all times and everywhere to do him honor." But now they excommunicated him. Lincoln looked for friends elsewhere.

The Germans were more than another stumbling block to the Lincoln-Berdan plan. They were a rising group that could swing Illinois to the Republicans—decisive in numbers, well-educated, and committed to the antislavery cause. The 1856 campaign marked the beginning of Lincoln's extensive relationship with German Americans and the exiled revolutionary Forty-Eighters, who became some of his most important allies, friends, and closest confidants, including his private secretary John Nicolay (who met him at the Bloomington convention), the future governor Gustave Koerner, and Carl Schurz, the journalist, soldier, and politician. Schurz first encountered Lincoln during his 1858 campaign for the Senate. "I had seen, in Washington and in the West, several public men of rough appearance; but none whose looks seemed quite so uncouth, not to say grotesque, as Lincoln's," Schurz recalled. "When, in a tone of perfect ingenuousness, he asked me—a young beginner in politics—what I thought about this and that, I should have felt myself very much honored by his confidence, had he permitted me to regard him as a great man. But he talked in so simple and familiar a strain, and his manner and homely phrase were so absolutely free from any semblance of self-consciousness or pretension to superiority, that I soon felt as if I had known him all my life and we had long been close friends."

Alongside Lincoln, the state party convention at Bloomington had designated one other delegate at large to head its slate of presidential electors: Friedrich Hecker, "perhaps the most influential German in America," according to the *Chicago Democratic Press*. In 1848 he had led an uprising for democracy in Baden crushed by Prussian troops in which the youthful Friedrich Engels served as a soldier in his army and Carl Schurz had been a supporter. Karl Marx criticized Hecker for prematurely attempting to overthrow the old regime. Gustave Koerner, a leader of the Illinois Germans, who was present at the convention, called Hecker "a great orator," with a "profound and comprehensive knowledge of jurisprudence and of history," and "a man of genius," but given to emotional outbursts. Having once trained his artillery against German authoritarian rule, Hecker's polemics now were directed against Stephen A. Douglas, whom he derided as "Master Douglas."

After the Bloomington convention passed its plank against nativism, Hecker urged Germans, with the "history of two continents" guiding them, to join the party, which he said stood for the "principles of all true republicans of all times." "Every German man who loves freedom is inclined to recognize Hecker as his leader and serve under him, certainly never against him," declared the *Iowa Staats-Zeitung*. Hecker launched on a speaking tour, but had to suspend it when his house burned down, possibly an act of arson. "I am solidly convinced that the fire was set," he wrote. "Kansas seems to have moved eastwards." "The smoking ruin of this house should be a lasting sign of what they can expect from the party of slaveholders to all German citizens," wrote the *Illinois Staats-Zeitung,* the newspaper edited by George Schneider, an ally of Lincoln. Lincoln raised funds for Hecker to rebuild his house. "We cannot dispense with your services in this contest," he wrote him on September 14, "and we ought, in a peculiar way, to give you some relief in the difficulty of having your house burnt." With Lincoln's help, Hecker resumed his campaign speeches.

Lincoln launched himself on to the campaign trail, delivering about fifty speeches, mostly in towns in southern and central Illinois, determined to the end to try to win over the Old Whigs. He often found himself facing hostile crowds. At Petersburg, outside Springfield, Henry B. Rankin, Lincoln's law clerk, observed Lincoln being escorted by a "corporal's guard" under a large banner bearing Frémont's profile, to the courthouse steps.

> Around the platform, louder and louder, arose hurrahs for Buchanan and for Fillmore. No voice for Fremont rang out through the crisp air to cheer the coming orator. Lincoln could hardly have had less political sympathy that day if he had entered Charleston or Richmond for that purpose. . . . Rude fellows of the rowdy sort had boasted, "No d—d abolition speeches could be made in Menard County this campaign." Had any other Republican than Lincoln stood before those Menard people, he would not have been heard. Several rushes toward the colours and banners were made, with the evident purpose of tearing them down. Cat-calls, whistles, and tin horns added to the din. Shouts of "Abolitionist," "Nigger equality," with snatches of obscene ballads and campaign songs, made a bedlam of the court-house yard and the surrounding public square. At intervals, and shrill above all such sounds, came the conflicting huzzahs for Buchanan and equally loud shouts for Fillmore. No slogans for the Republican standard-bearer, Fremont, came from the excited crowd of voters.

Lincoln stood silent for a half hour until there was a lull for him to speak. "And here," reported the *Register,* "quietly vanished away the *post mortem* candidate for the vice presidency of the abolition political cock-boat, the depot master of the underground railroad, the great Abram Lincoln. He left no traces of his appearance, and has now 'gone to be seen no more,' leaving behind him, in Menard [County], half a dozen poor souls, to mourn the political death-knell of John C. Fremont in next November."

Noah Brooks, a young journalist working for the Republican cause, who would later become a Lincoln confidant, met him at a rally in Dixon in northern Illinois. "As he reasoned with his audience," Brooks recalled, "he bent his long form over the railing of the platform, stooping lower and lower as he pursued his argument, until, having reached his point, he clinched it (usually with a question), and then suddenly sprang upright, reminding one of the springing open of a jack-knife blade."

After Lincoln spoke he and Brooks discussed the Republicans' prospects that year. "We crawled under the pendulous branches of a tree, and Lincoln, lying flat on the ground, with his chin in his hands, talked on, rather gloomily as to the present, but absolutely confident as to the future. I was dismayed to find that he did not believe it possible that Fremont could be elected. As if half pitying my youthful ignorance, but admiring my enthusiasm, he said: 'Don't be discouraged if we don't carry the day this year. We can't do it, that's certain. We can't carry Pennsylvania; those old Whigs down there are too strong for us. But we shall, sooner or later, elect our president. I feel confident of that.'"

"Do you think we shall elect a Free-soil president in 1860?" Brooks asked. "Well, I don't know," Lincoln replied. "Everything depends on the course of the Democracy. There's a big anti-slavery element in the Democratic party, and if we could get hold of that, we might possibly elect our man in 1860. But it's doubtful—*very* doubtful. Perhaps we shall be able to fetch it by 1864; perhaps not. As I said before, the Free-soil party is bound to win, in the long run. It may not be in my day; but it will in years, I do really believe."

After turning down requests for him to speak in Iowa and New York, Lincoln accepted an invitation to speak at Kalamazoo, Michigan, on August 27, where he addressed a mass rally of ten thousand people, the only time he left Illinois that year. His speech was a fervent defense of free labor over slavery, but more daringly an open defense of abolitionists as Republicans. "The question of slavery, at the present day, should be not only the greatest question, but very nearly the sole question. . . . There could be no middle way." Slavery, Lincoln explained, had enormous economic power that translated into political power. "Slavery is looked upon by men in the light of dollars and cents. The estimated worth of the slaves at the South is $1,000,000,000, and in a very few years, if the institution shall be admitted into the territories, they will have increased fifty per cent in value. . . . Slavery is to be made a ruling element in our government." He explained the insidious influence by which slavery would establish itself in the territories. "We will suppose that there are ten men who go into Kansas to settle. Nine of these are opposed to slavery. One has ten slaves. The slaveholder is a good man in other respects; he is a good neighbor, and being a wealthy man, he is enabled to do the others many neighborly kindnesses. They like the man, though they don't like the system by which he holds his fellow-men in bondage. And here let me say, that in intellectual and physical structure, our Southern brethren do not differ from us. They are, like us, subject to passions, and it is only their odious institution of slavery, that makes the breach between us. These ten men of whom I was speaking, live together three or four years; they intermarry; their family ties are strengthened. And who wonders that in time, the people learn to look upon slavery with complacency? This is the way in which slavery is planted, and gains so firm a foothold."

Lincoln took issue with the leading theoretical argument propounded by a Southern ideologue against the very ideas of democracy and equality. They were made in a book by George Fitzhugh, the chief editorial writer for the *Richmond Enquirer, Sociology for the South, or The Failure of Free Society,* that "aroused the ire of Lincoln more than most pro-slavery books, according to Herndon. "Men are not born entitled to 'equal rights!'" wrote Fitzhugh, dismissing the Declaration of Independence. "I have noticed in Southern newspapers, particularly the Richmond Enquirer, the Southern view of the Free States," said Lincoln. "They insist that slavery has a right to spread. They defend it upon principle. They insist that their slaves are far better off than Northern freemen. What a mistaken view do these men have of Northern laborers! They think that men are always to remain laborers here—but there is no such class. The man who labored for another last year, this year labors for himself, and next year he will hire others to labor for him. These men don't understand when they think in this manner of Northern free labor. When these reasons can be introduced, tell me not that we have no interest in keeping the Territories free for the settlement of free laborers."

Then Lincoln grabbed the sharp end of the knife wielded against the Republicans. The cutting tactic that both Democrats and Know Nothings used to divide Republicans, throw them on the defensive and drive Old Whigs away was to raise the visibility of abolitionists within their ranks. Now Lincoln embraced the abolitionists as fellow party men and put the challenge to the Democrats. "They tell us that we are in company with men who have long been known as abolitionists," he said. "What care we how many may feel disposed to labor for our cause? Why do not you, Buchanan men, come in and use your influence to make our party respectable?" A newspaper account recorded the audience reaction: "(Laughter.)" Lincoln had crossed a Rubicon. And he would appear on platforms in Illinois with Lovejoy.

Douglas, too, was out on the campaign trail. He spoke at a Springfield rally of thousands on September 18. "Shout after shout followed the home-thrusts and happy hits he made at the abolition enemy," reported the *Register.* "He tore off their hypocritical mask, and exposed to his hearers the corruption of the tricksters who trade in negro sympathy and Kansas roorbacks." Theodore Parker, traveling in the state, happened to see Douglas speak at Galesburg in late October. "He was considerably drunk, and made one of the most sophisticated and deceitful speeches I ever listened to," he wrote Senator John P. Hale. "It was mere brutality in respect of morals, and sophistry for logic, in the style and manner of a low blackguard. His enemies said he seldom or never did so ill. But there is a good deal of rough power in his evil face. I never saw him before."

The results of the Electoral College vote in which Buchanan won 174 votes, Frémont 114, and Fillmore 8 did not capture the underlying weakness of the Democratic Party, the potential for the Republicans, and doom of the Know Nothings. Buchanan was elected to face the coming crisis with a fragile mandate. Not just one of the candidates was "sectional." The country itself was in the process of polarizing along sectional lines. As a presidential party, the Democrats faltered across the upper North, from New England to New York to Ohio to Iowa, which Frémont swept. Buchanan was the first candidate since the parties were formally organized to win only by a plurality, not a majority. He barely won five free states. He was dependent on a solid South, where Frémont was kept off the ballot. In three border states where voters were allowed to vote for Frémont, the Republican won 514 in Kentucky, 281 in Maryland, and 291 in Virginia. In Buchanan's home state of Pennsylvania, his majority was only 627 votes against his two challengers. His worst winning state was Illinois, where he lost the popular vote to the two opposing parties by 28,278 votes. It was obvious that if a marginal number of Know Nothings in New Jersey, Pennsylvania, Illinois, Indiana, and California voted for the Republican candidate in 1860, whoever he might be, he would likely be elected. The Republicans' hope directed them strategically to the lower North.

Fillmore, who had railed against the sectionalism of the Republican Party, turned out to be a purely sectional candidate. He won 48 percent of the vote of the border South, 43 percent of the middle South, 41 percent of the lower South, but only 11 percent in the North. The only state he won outright was Maryland. He was the last gasp of the remnant of Southern Whigs, most on their way to realigning as Democrats. His loss was fatal to the Know Nothings. His failure to displace the debate over slavery with nativism removed the rationale for a nativist party.

The essence of Fillmore's candidacy was yearning for a return to the status quo ante—the time when Fillmore was president and had supposedly settled the question of slavery. It was a reactionary sentiment clothed as moderation. After the 1856 election, Fillmoreism would morph into another third party, the Constitutional Union Party, created by many of the same key political operatives who were behind Fillmore's American Party and whose presidential candidate in 1860, John Bell, a former senator from Tennessee, had endorsed Fillmore. Fillmore's legacy was further embodied in the pro-slavery compromises advanced during the secession crisis by Senator John J. Crittenden, of Kentucky, Fillmore's attorney general, a Know Nothing, who had campaigned for Fillmore. Fillmoreism, if there were such a thing, also evolved into Kentucky's determination during the war to remain within the Union as a slave state, exemplified by prominent former Know Nothings, such as George D. Prentice, editor of the *Louisville Journal,* who opposed emancipation with a vehemence he had previously reserved for immigrants. Fillmore in 1856 was an evanescent figure, but his candidacy was the beginning of a complex political conundrum that would plague Lincoln until he signed the Emancipation Proclamation and by that act, end it.

The fire-eating *Charleston Mercury* saw the handwriting on the wall in Buchanan's precarious victory, "elected because the enemies of the south could not agree among themselves." The *Richmond Enquirer,* however, editorialized that the result "is another striking evidence of the growing popularity of negro slavery, to show that negro slavery and the Union must stand or fall together, and that in talking of disunion, in event of Fremont's election, we were but pointing out its inevitable consequence and administering salutary warning."

The 1856 results predicted a future in which Illinois would be the Democrats' weakest link and the Republicans' greatest opportunity. In eight southern Illinois counties Frémont's totals were like those in border states. He received only 50 votes, "cast by preachers, teachers, and eastern people," according to John Moses, a Republican activist, delegate to the Bloomington convention, and later an Illinois historian. Frémont's vote in central Illinois was also not strong. In Springfield, Buchanan carried 912 votes, Frémont 549, and Fillmore 403. Frémont did worse in Sangamon County as a whole. Yet the Republican ticket won every statewide office and Bissell was elected governor with Know Nothing votes. But the Republican victory on the state level also proved the explosive potential of the northern part of the state and the German vote. If Frémont had received the same percentage of votes as Bissell, just a slight marginal improvement, he would have won Illinois.

After the election, the Republicans of Illinois were in a buoyant mood. The first time their party was in the field it had gained power in a state that previously had voted for a Democrat for governor with only one exception since it was admitted to the Union. On December 10, Republicans held a celebratory banquet at the Tremont House in Chicago, a palatial hotel, to be addressed by Lincoln. He was already looking to the Senate race in two years against Douglas. On the stump, Lincoln had made it a point to be introduced as the next Senator from Illinois. His keynote was the beginning of another campaign.

"Our government rests in public opinion," Lincoln said. "Whoever can change public opinion, can change the government, practically just so much." Public opinion, according to Lincoln, was not an immutable god, but itself changeable, subject to political effect, and once transformed would create a new direction in the government. The proof was in the Republican victories in Illinois and the emergence of a Republican North. Lincoln had begun the campaign uncertain whether the new party would be able to cohere at all. He had wandered from car to car on the train to the Bloomington convention in search of Old Whigs from southern Illinois. Six months later, the rigors of the campaign brought together more than a new coalition, but also forged a new political identity. In Illinois, it required the finesse of Lincoln, Fell, and Lovejoy to thwart the lure of the Old Whigs' resentment and avoid the beatific martyrdom of radical posturing. Frémont served his larger purpose as an icon, despite having nothing memorable to say. The attack on his origins was an attempt to abort the birth of the Republican Party. Exploitation of his vulnerabilities projected fear of Republican strengths. His limitations as a politician were not decisive to the final outcome in any case and suggested the void to be filled next time. The passive Frémont had succeeded through his defeat. It was not an ordinary campaign. Unlike the Whig campaigns of the past, it was fought around a set of clearly defined issues and principles. Now representing the public opinion of the North, the Republicans had built their party on a solid foundation.

"Public opinion, on any subject, always has a *'central idea,'* from which all its minor thoughts radiate," Lincoln told the Republican crowd. "That 'central idea' in our political public opinion, at the beginning was, and until recently has continued to be, 'the equality of men.' And although it was always submitted patiently to whatever of inequality there seemed to be as matter of actual necessity, its constant working has been a steady progress towards the practical equality of all men."

Lincoln described the campaign as an early battle in a war for that idea. "The late Presidential election was a struggle, by one party, to discard that central idea, and to substitute for it the opposite idea that slavery is right, in the abstract, the workings of which, as a central idea, may be the perpetuity of human slavery, and its extension to all countries and colors."

He explained how the word "equality" was being twisted on behalf of slavery, by its advocates and for Buchanan. "Less than a year ago, the Richmond Enquirer, an avowed advocate of slavery, regardless of color, in order to favor his views, invented the phrase, 'State equality,' and now the President, in his Message, adopts the Enquirer's catch-phrase, telling us the people 'have asserted the constitutional equality of each and all of the States of the Union as States.' The President flatters himself that the new central idea is completely inaugurated; and so, indeed, it is, so far as the mere fact of a Presidential election can inaugurate it. To us it is left to know that the majority of the people have not yet declared for it, and to hope that they never will."

"State equality" was the latest rhetorical permutation of the doctrine of John C. Calhoun that the South must always be equal in political power to the North in order to preserve and extend slavery. It was a nonnegotiable demand for the rule of the minority—the rule of slaveholders—over the government. Lincoln appealed to the implicit majority of 1856 to become an even more conscious and focused public opinion to overthrow the tyranny of the minority. "All of us who did not vote for Mr. Buchanan, taken together, are a majority of four hundred thousand. But, in the late contest we were divided between Fremont and Fillmore. Can we not come together, for the future?"

Lincoln returned to his critique of Fitzhugh's proslavery ideological tract, *The Sociology for the South, or The Failure of Free Society,* to urge that antislavery men rise above factionalism. "Let every one who really believes, and is resolved, that free society is not, *and shall not be,* a failure, and who can conscientiously declare that in the past contest he has done only what he thought best—let every such one have charity to believe that every other one can say as much. Thus let bygones be bygones. Let past differences, as nothing be; and with steady eye on the real issue, let us reinaugurate the good old 'central ideas' of the Republic. We *can* do it."

For the Republicans after their first national campaign Lincoln offered more than a strategy combining principle and pragmatism. He cut through the rhetoric not only of the proslavery Calhounites, but also that of Douglas's vapid popular sovereignty. "We shall again be able not to declare, that 'all States as States, are equal,' nor yet that 'all citizens as citizens are equal,' but to renew the broader, better declaration, including both these and much more, that 'all *men* are created equal.'"

Lincoln could not know that in his ringing peroration he was arguing against the Dred Scott decision of the Supreme Court that would soon deepen the lines of political battle he had laid out. But even if he did not know the exact shape of events to come his mind was racing toward them. On the eve of Buchanan's inauguration, he wrote a note for himself, drawing a map of how far the recent campaign had gone and charting where the politics would go. At the campaign's start he avoided mentioning the charged word "Republican," but as its end openly called the "Republican organization" an "army," and committed himself to the "work," as he called it, from which he could not "turn away."

Upon those men who are, in sentiment, opposed to the spread, and nationalization of slavery, rests the task of preventing it. The Republican organization is the embodiment of that sentiment; though, as Fragment yet, it by no means embraces all the individuals holding that sentiment. The party is newly formed; and in forming, old party ties had to be broken, and the attractions of party pride, and influential leaders were wholly wanting. In spite of old differences, prejudices, and animosities, its members were drawn together by a paramount common danger. They formed and maneuvered in the face of the disciplined enemy, and in the teeth of all his persistent misrepresentations. Of course, they fell far short of gathering in all of their own. And yet, a year ago, they stood up, an army over thirteen hundred thousand strong. That army is, today, the best hope of the nation, and of the world. Their work is before them; and from which they may not guiltlessly turn away.

CHAPTER NINETEEN

THE WHITE MAN

Pennsylvania was the reason James Buchanan was president. It had sustained his long career; it was why he became the Democratic nominee; and it was the only Northern state that gave him a majority, a mere 1,211 votes. Pennsylvania had tipped the scales for him. The Keystone State was the foundation on which he stood to embark on his mission as national savior. Restoring harmony and destroying the Republican Party were for him one and the same end. "The great object of my administration will be, if possible, to destroy the dangerous slavery agitation at the North, and to destroy sectional parties," he wrote a month after his election to his friend John Y. Mason, an ardent proslavery Virginian, who as minister to France had collaborated with Buchanan on the ill-fated Ostend Manifesto. Even before taking office, he contemplated himself triumphant over his enemies.

The Sage of Wheatland, a habitually disappointed secondary character, was now the cynosure of power. Political pilgrims came and went to his Lancaster

Chief Justice of the Supreme
Court Roger Taney

home seeking his blessing. He was the victor whose task it was to dispense the spoils. He felt put upon by job seekers and banished them from visiting. Operating in secrecy in a vain attempt to shield himself from the pressure, he was nearly overcome as faction battled faction, clique attacked clique, and ambition clashed with ambition.

Buchanan had always been a semidetached political figure who removed himself from the heat of conflict, letting others do his fighting on his behalf, resentful when he was passed over, and complacent when he advanced. He was not particularly grateful for the sacrifice others made for him; nor was he much interested in their motives or needs. Once they became dependent on his position he expected them to work for his next one. He believed his part mainly involved displaying his distinguished personage. When others would not do whatever he wished would gain him whatever office he wanted he would often throw fits threatening to quit. His prima donna scenes usually occurred on a quadrennial basis. "Should there be even the appearance of a serious division in Penna., I shall make my bow and retire," he wrote in 1841 about the presidential race he was painstakingly planning to make in three years. He operated on the force of passive aggression.

Buchanan had never been a master of Pennsylvania politics, but he had survived them. Now finally ascended to his long sought after Olympus, he myopically lost sight of the foothills. His local enemies were beneath him, but they had not dispersed. Buchanan's failure to reward his most faithful servants gave them the opportunity to overwhelm and humiliate him. At last he was president-elect, and as his first act he lost control in Pennsylvania.

John W. Forney, above all others in Buchanan's entourage, had acted as his constant promoter, defender, and handler. He was as impetuous and colorful as Buchanan was stodgy and dull. Born in Lancaster, Pennsylvania, Forney became the owner and editor of the *Lancaster Intelligencer* in 1840 at the age of twenty. His great and persistent cause was the political fortune of James Buchanan. From the *Intelligencer* he rained arrows on any critic. After wielding his pen at the *Washington Union* for Pierce, he returned to his natural home to assist Buchanan in his campaign. As the chairman of the Democratic State Committee, Forney was a whirlwind of organization, directing the publication of newspaper articles and pamphlets, sending speakers to every corner, and speaking himself to the point of exhaustion. He parked his wife and five children at Wheatland for the duration. Time and again, the beneficent Buchanan promised him his heart's desire—editorship of the *Washington Union* as the voice of the administration and a lucrative government printing contract. Governor Henry Wise, of Virginia, protested. Jefferson Davis was said to be "mad as fury." Forney was unreliable and irascible, and he had violently opposed Senator Robert M.T. Hunter of Virginia (and the F Street Mess) for the cabinet. "Against him we shall wage war to the knife and the knife to the hilt," Forney wrote. Under Southern pressure Buchanan denied the prize to his most loyal follower. In his letter to Wise, Buchanan paid Forney a tribute: "Of all men in this State, it is admitted he did the most to secure the Triumph of our ticket both at the State and Electoral election." But he rejected him anyway.

An enraged and alcohol-fueled Forney insisted that Buchanan compensate his loss with either a cabinet post or endorse him for the open U.S. Senate seat. Southerners protested against giving him a cabinet appointment. Buchanan had wanted to award the Senate seat either to his friend Judge Jeremiah Black or his other friend Congressman J. Glancy Jones, but he reluctantly agreed that Forney was owed it since he could not name the temperamental journalist to the cabinet, which would also close off appointing anyone else from Pennsylvania. Buchanan's formal nod enabled Forney to shove aside the former congressman Henry D. Foster, a popular figure from western Pennsylvania, who before the intervention had the nomination wrapped up. But the nomination delivered at the Democratic convention did not guarantee that the Senate seat would be delivered. Buchanan had never exercised much influence within the legislature and he did not use the enormous patronage that would soon be at his fingertips. His enemies instantly filled the vacuum.

Simon Cameron, known as "The Great Winnebago Chief" for gaining a fortune as the federal commissioner settling the claims of the tribe and "The Czar of Pennsylvania" for his ownership of banks, railroads, factories, and newspapers, had once been a Democrat and an ally of Buchanan. He had succeeded him in the U.S. Senate in 1845, but drifted to become a Know Nothing and by 1856 was a Republican. Cameron was ruthless, wily, and corrupt. He believed in winning either through battering or buying those in his way. Buchanan loathed Cameron and blamed him for denying him the Democratic presidential nomination in 1848. "Cameron," he wrote, "after having betrayed me at the Baltimore convention, has been moving heaven and earth to destroy me."

Thaddeus Stevens loathed Buchanan, but only hated Cameron. He had denounced him for bribery after Cameron won the Know Nothing nomination for the U.S. Senate seat in 1855 in a caucus in which he got one more vote than the number of people present. But now that Cameron was a Republican, Stevens backed him for this Senate seat. When the vote was taken three Democratic legislators defected to hand it to Cameron. "My God, what a scene of public corruption and wholesale bribery it was," cried Forney.

The Democratic caucus accused Cameron of using "corrupt and unlawful means." Howell Cobb, of Georgia, whom Buchanan appointed secretary of the treasury, lamented, "Simon Cameron, an abolitionist, was elected. . . . It is a hard blow not only upon Forney but upon Mr. Buchanan and the democratic party. I have never felt more deeply a result than I do this." "To him," the *New York Tribune* wrote about Forney, "more than any other fifty men in the State, is Mr. Buchanan indebted for the vote of Pennsylvania . . . instead of saving him, as he could have done with his boundless patronage, he left him to carry the crushing weight his interference provoked without using his vast power to sustain him. Thus was Col. Forney defeated—thus was Mr. Buchanan defied on the very threshold of his power." "Thus Forney lost the third position he had reason to expect from the Buchanan administration, and both he and Buchanan were profoundly mortified and humiliated by the action of the Legislature," wrote Alexander K. McClure, the Pennsylvania politico.

Buchanan cast around for substitutes to offer Forney, naval officer of Philadelphia or the consulship at Liverpool, which he declined. Instead he bought a newspaper, the *Philadelphia Press,* to establish his independence. In front of "a large company," Buchanan went out of his way to demean Forney, "So, sir," mocked Buchanan, "I find you are trying to make a cabinet for me." The fiasco "opened a chasm between us," Forney recalled, and launched his odyssey of alienation from his patron. "We were all trying to make J.B. President twenty-five years before we got him in, and a pretty mess we made of it," he wrote. "Buchanan had a great many enemies in his own State. He had none of the ways of making people like him." He was, Forney concluded, "cold and formal," and "never awakened real affection."

Embarrassed by his show of political ineptitude, Buchanan was anxious to engage in backstage string pulling before the start of his presidency to settle the central issue of slavery. If he were able to have others do it for him, it would be a spectacular coup. He would not have to perform the messy and inevitably dirty work during his presidency. He would enter as a statesman to mount an unblemished white marble pedestal.

The anticipation of Buchanan's arrival in Washington aroused no great expectations that he would be able to tamp down the conflict. After dithering over his cabinet he filled it with Southerners—from Virginia, Georgia, Tennessee, Kentucky, and Mississippi—and a proslavery Democrat, Isaac Toucey, from Connecticut; the doughface Lewis Cass of Michigan (who was largely incapable of performing the job of secretary of state); and his friend from Pennsylvania Jeremiah Black (who was by contrast highly competent). To Buchanan, these appointments occupied the center and moderate ground, situated against abolitionists and fire-eaters alike, exemplified by complacent Howell "Fatty" Cobb, owner of one thousand slaves. But his unveiled cabinet did little to soothe tensions.

Washington still seethed. Duff Green, the old Jacksonian turncoat who had defected to Calhoun and made a fortune in railroads and real estate in Georgia, was in close touch with the Southern powers-that-be in the capital, the F Street Mess and their acolytes. He warned they were "dissatisfied and hostile," and "Calhoun in his grave was no less potent than in his senatorial chair." On February 17, Edmund Ruffin, the Virginia fire-eater, after dining at the F Street Mess, wrote in his diary that Buchanan had "very little of the respect or the confidence of the men from the South by whose support alone he was sustained and elected. I anticipate for him a reign that will bring him but little of either pleasure or honor."

Virginia Clay, wife of Senator Clement Clay of Alabama and mistress of Jefferson Davis, among the fashionable ladies of the capital, wrote her father at the approaching dawn of President Buchanan: "Everything is excitement and confusion. I tell you Fusion reigns in truth, and Southern blood is at boiling temperature all over the city, and with good cause, too. Old Giddings, Thurlow Weed, Sumner, Seward, Chase (who is here for a few days prior to his inauguration) are daily taunting and insulting all whom they dare . . . there is a Black Republican at every corner of our political fence, and if ever the gap is down we are gone. I wish you could be here to witness the scenes daily enacted in the halls of Congress, to hear the hot taunts of defiance hurled into the very teeth of the Northerners by our goaded but spirited patriots." Late at night during a snowstorm, a "mysterious visitor" wrapped in a large overcoat and hat appeared at the Clay door. Throwing off his coat he revealed himself to be President Franklin Pierce. " 'Lock that door, Clay!' he said, almost pathetically, 'and don't let a soul know I'm here!' " The fugitive president on his way out of office could not wait to leave. " 'Ah, my dear friends!' said Mr. Pierce, leaning forward in his arm-chair and warming his hands as he spoke; 'I am so tired of the shackles of Presidential life that I can scarcely endure it!' "

The Southerners' sense that the walls were closing in on them, even though a Democratic president was about to take the oath of office, was matched by the dread of the antislavery Northerners that they walked in the shadow of Sumner. Senator Henry Wilson of Massachusetts painted the grim scene for the abolitionist Lydia Maria Child. "He told me I could form no idea of the state of things in Washington. As he passes through the streets in the evening, he says the air is filled with yells and curses from the oyster shops and gambling saloons, the burden of which is all manner of threatened violence to Seward and Sumner and Wilson and Burlingame. While he was making his last speech, the Southern members tried to insult him in every way. One of them actually brandished his cane as if about to strike him, but he ignored the presence of him and his cane, and went on with his speech. He says he never leaves his room to go into the Senate without thinking whether he has left everything arranged as he should wish if he were never to return to it alive."

One man appeared to have a reputation above suspicion. "Who doubts the integrity or the learning of the distinguished Chief Justice? If we cannot trust the power there, where, in Heaven's name, shall we repose it?" asked Samuel Phelps, who had been a Whig senator from Vermont. Breaking with the precedent that only posthumous Supreme Court justices should be memorialized with official busts, Seward proposed a bill to honor the living Roger Taney.

Taney was yet another breathing relic of the age of Jackson. He had been Jackson's attorney general, a member of his Kitchen Cabinet, who, in the Bank War against the "money power," ordered the withdrawal of federal funds from the Second Bank of the United States, an act that destroyed it. In a triumphal gesture, Jackson nominated Taney to be secretary of the treasury, and the Senate rejected it. So, in a defiant gesture, Jackson appointed him to the Supreme Court. Opposed by the triumvirate of Clay, Webster, and Calhoun to his elevation as chief justice, Taney was nonetheless approved. He replaced John Marshall and his broad federalism with strict constructionism. Yet on commercial issues he ruled for states' regulation of corporations and deferred on certain national economic issues to the federal government. As attorney general and chief justice, however, his decisions were consistently proslavery. In 1832 he advised Jackson that "the African race" was "a separate and degraded people," never to be "included by the term citizens," and never to be allowed to claim the natural rights of "life, liberty, and pursuit of happiness" proclaimed in the Declaration of Independence. In the 1843 case of *Prigg v. Pennsylvania,* he more than upheld the federal fugitive slave law, but also insisted that the Constitution made its enforcement a positive duty of the states.

Taney was the first Catholic in the cabinet and the first one on the high court. He came from a wealthy slaveholding family in Maryland that owned a tobacco plantation. That he freed many but not all of his own slaves even as he ruled for slavery he did not consider a paradox. His views on slavery constricted along with his arteries. He despised abolitionists, was alarmed at the emergence of the Republican Party, and felt the antislavery movement was a threat to the Constitution, Southern society and therefore the nation. He was not outspoken publicly on the subject. But his private opinions hardened at every Republican advance. His authorized biographer, Samuel Tyler, writing after Taney's death and a decade after the Civil War, described his calcifying attitude. "Abolition, and its aiders and abettors, gloated over a contest which they hoped was the forerunner of a crusade for the extirpation of slavery in the States, and the humiliation of the slave-owners."

Taney had an exalted position not only from his stature as chief justice. He was tactful, charming, and dignified. His personal life was virtuous, he was religious, his habits were austere, his devotion to his family pure, and he had recently, in 1855, been stricken by an almost unimaginable tragedy that inspired widespread sympathy. His wife and beautiful daughter were both afflicted with yellow fever on their vacation and died. He moved alone into spare rented rooms near the Capitol.

Eighty years old, Taney's long hanging hair fell across his deeply creased face, dripping sorrow. He had once been quick and nimble, but he seemed almost too exhausted to shuffle through his duties. "He was an extremely plain-looking man," recalled the Southern hostess Virginia Clay, "with frail body, which once rose tall and erect, but now was so bent that one always thought of him as small, and with a head which made me think of a withered nut. Swarthy of skin, but greyhaired, Judge Taney was a veritable skeleton, 'all mind and no body'; yet his opinion settled questions that agitated the nation, and his contemporaries agreed he was the ablest man who had ever sat upon the Supreme Court bench."

With the advent of 1857, on the eve of the new administration, the capital was swept with talk of a momentous decision to be handed down from the Supreme Court. James Pike, the well-informed correspondent of the *New York Tribune,* reported on January 5: "The rumor that the Supreme Court has decided against the constitutionality of the power of Congress to restrict slavery in the Territories has been commented upon in the most un-reserved manner at this metropolis. It is very generally considered that the moral weight of such a decision would be about equal to that of a political stump speech of a slave-holder or a doughface." But Pike remained uncertain. "Many have expressed the opinion that the question would not be met by the Court, and numbers are still of that way of thinking."

Dred Scott v. John Sanford was the case on the docket (reported by the Supreme Court clerk in a spelling error as "Sandford"). It was a case that began like a number of similar ones about whether a slave who had resided in a free state was free, but it evolved to reflect the hardening attitude toward slavery in Missouri, winding its way into the federal courts, which brought it to the center of national political quandary.

The man in the vise did not know when he was born, signed his name with an "X," and had been the property of four owners. Dred Scott became the most famous invisible man of his time. The country divided over the case bearing his name, but only the bare outline of his picaresque frontier life was known. He filled in few details. His eloquence consisted of his "X" on his lawsuit asking for his freedom. There was no record of his birth sometime between 1795 and 1809. He grew up on the Virginia plantation of Peter Blow, who took him with his wife, seven children, and five other slaves to raise cotton in Alabama in 1820 and to open the Jefferson Hotel in the bustling town of St. Louis in 1830. Just before his death Blow sold Scott in 1833 to Dr. John Emerson, an army surgeon. Scott may or may not have been listed as a slave named "Sam" who may or may not have tried to run away. Emerson was posted to Fort Armstrong in northern Illinois and in 1836 to Fort Snelling near what became St. Paul, Minnesota, but was then part of the Louisiana Territory. Though slavery was prohibited there according to the Missouri Compromise, Emerson came into the possession of another slave, a young woman named Harriet Robinson, when she married Dred Scott. Robinson belonged to Major Lawrence Taliaferro, an Indian agent and justice of the peace, who insisted on performing a formal wedding ceremony, which was highly unusual for slave couples. Scott may or may not have had a previous wife who may or may not have been sold. Taliaferro did not sell Robinson to Emerson but gave her as a kind of gift without payment and without emancipating her. Emerson was assigned to Fort Jesup in Louisiana, taking his slaves from free territory to a slave state. Dred and Harriet had four children, two of whom survived. When Emerson was sent to Florida during the Seminole War the Scotts were hired out to various people in St. Louis. At the

war's end in 1842, Emerson was honorably discharged from the military, returned to St. Louis to establish a private practice, but died suddenly within a
year. His widow, Irene Emerson, inherited his estate, whose inventory did
not bother to mention the Dred Scott family. She had already hired out Dred
and Harriet as servants to her brother-in-law, Captain Henry Bainbridge, an
officer at the St. Louis Jefferson Barracks, where he was friendly with Captain Ulysses Grant. Scott may or may not have accompanied Bainbridge to
Texas during the Mexican War. Dred and Harriet had another child. Mrs.
Emerson hired them out to a St. Louis grocer in March 1846. Scott may have
sought to purchase his freedom. He and Harriet may or may not have feared
they and their children would be sold and separated. Mrs. Emerson may
have refused his offer. On April 6, 1846, they each filed suits against her
claiming that they were in fact free based on previous residence in a free state
and free territory. "He is entitled to his freedom," read Dred Scott's petition
to the Missouri Circuit Court.

The Dred Scott case was another of the unintended consequences of the
assassination in 1837 of the antislavery editor and minister Elijah P. Lovejoy
in the Mississippi River town of Alton, Illinois, across from St. Louis. Harriet
Scott had joined the congregation of the Second African Baptist Church of
St. Louis whose pastor was Reverend John Richard Anderson. Anderson had
been a slave, belonging to the sister of Edward Bates (who would become
Lincoln's attorney general), but bought his freedom. He was the typesetter for
Lovejoy's antislavery paper, the *Alton Ob-*
server, and among the band of defenders
of its new printing press in the warehouse
stormed by the mob that murdered Lovejoy. Inspired by his martyrdom Anderson
became a minister and encouraged slaves
to apply for their legal freedom. Through
Anderson the Scotts were undoubtedly
introduced to the attorney who would
take on their case, Francis B. Murdoch.
Anderson clearly would have known
Murdoch from Alton, where he was the
city attorney who prosecuted the mob
that was acquitted by a jury unwilling to
punish anyone for killing the abolitionist.
The antislavery Murdoch, like Anderson,

Dred Scott

had moved to St. Louis, and he filed the papers in the case charging Mrs. Emerson with trespass and false imprisonment.

Dred Scott began his long journey through the courts accompanied by a shifting cast of lawyers. There had been perhaps a dozen suits that slaves had won in Missouri claiming their freedom for residence in a free state. But in *Scott, a Man of Color v. Emerson* the Scotts lost the first round on an absurd technicality that they must remain Mrs. Emerson's slaves because nobody could provide legal proof that they were her property. In the second trial, however, they won. They were nominally free but in the custody of the St. Louis sheriff, who hired them out. Mrs. Emerson appealed to the Missouri Supreme Court. The case attracted almost no attention even in St. Louis. In the meantime, about 1849 or 1850 Mrs. Emerson moved to Springfield, Massachusetts, to live with her sister. In a whirlwind romance she married a local physician, Calvin C. Chaffee, who was an abolitionist and friend of Charles Sumner. Chaffee was elected as an antislavery Know Nothing to the House of Representatives in 1854 in the wave against the Kansas-Nebraska Act and apparently was unaware that his wife owned slaves.

By the time the Missouri Supreme Court ruled on the case the relatively tolerant tenor toward slaves who had lived in free states had been swept aside. Politics in the state was in the grip of a death struggle between the titanic Thomas Hart Benton, who had become an antislavery crusader, and David Rice Atchison, the president pro tempore of the Senate and central figure of the F Street Mess. Allies of Atchison now dominated the court. On March 22, 1852, the majority issued its decision, which emphasized its political imperative. "Times are not now as they were when the former decisions on this subject were made," it read. "Since then, not only individuals but States have been possessed with a dark and fell spirit in relation to slavery, whose gratification is sought in the pursuit of measure, whose inevitable consequence must be the overthrow and destruction of our Government. Under such circumstances, it does not behoove the State of Missouri to show the least countenance to any measure which might gratify this spirit."

Mrs. Emerson transferred control of Dred Scott and the case to her brother, John Sanford, a wealthy businessman who lived in New York. Scott sued for his freedom in the federal circuit court. On May 15, 1854, it found in favor of Sanford, that Scott and his wife were "lawful property." Scott appealed to the Supreme Court on the grounds of diversity jurisdiction, that a suit spanning two states required federal resolution. Prominent attorneys took up their lances on each side. Senator Henry S. Geyer of Missouri, who had defeated Benton in 1850, and Senator Reverdy Johnson of Maryland, the former attorney general, volunteered for Sanford. Montgomery Blair, the son of Francis P. Blair and protégé of Thomas Hart Benton, who had been a leading lawyer in St. Louis before moving to Washington, represented Scott without fee. Through Francis P. Blair, Gamaliel Bailey, editor of the antislavery *National Era,* funded the court costs. *Dred Scott* was slowly becoming a national controversy.

Montgomery Blair assumed that the decision would be made on the narrow basis of the specific case involving the individual plaintiff. Appearing before the Supreme Court on February 11, 1856, he argued in favor of the "once free, always free" precedent that had previously been upheld in Missouri, that Scott having lived in Illinois fell under its rule, and that he had a right to sue as other slaves had indeed done. Geyer and Johnson abandoned defending the particular merits and instead transformed the case into a platform to challenge the constitutionality of the Missouri Compromise, which had already been repealed. But their line of attack was intended to establish that it was not superseded and irrelevant but had always been wrong, that prohibiting slavery was not a constitutional power ever given to the Congress, and that therefore slavery could not be restrained from any territory. Their argument burnished the principle that John C. Calhoun had insisted was the vindication of the "peculiar institution" and refuted the "great principle" of popular sovereignty that Stephen A. Douglas claimed would allow a territory to choose to be free or slave.

The justices descended into confused colloquy for months. Three wanted to reopen the question of Scott's legitimacy to sue while four others just wanted to proceed to decide on the merits of the case. Justice Benjamin Curtis of Massachusetts wrote his uncle on April 8 that "the court will not decide the question of the Missouri compromise line,—a majority of the judges being of opinion that is it not necessary to do so." It was clear that Justice John McLean would issue a strong dissent in favor of freeing Scott, a statement that might advance his candidacy for the Republican nomination. But that possibility was thwarted when the court announced on May 12 that the case would be reargued in December on the issues of jurisdiction and Scott's right to sue. Postponing the case removed it from the contention of the campaign and scheduled it to coincide with the arrival of the new president.

The court reconvened on December 15. By now public attention was fixed on the case. The *Washington Union,* the main Democratic newspaper, stated, "Seldom, if ever has there been a case before this high tribunal of greater importance, or one in which such a general and deep interest is felt." Blair submitted a supplementary brief to prove the constitutionality of the Missouri Compromise, citing numerous instances of congressional power over slavery in territories. He added that "non-white male citizens" had been recognized by an act of the Missouri legislature in 1845. That salient fact, he argued, should settle the questions of jurisdiction and right to sue. His plea was for judicial restraint.

The next day Senator Geyer opened the argument for Sanford by declaring that "true blacks are not citizens" and the "so-called compromise" had been forced under threat upon the South, which had put loyalty to the Union above the Constitution. Reverdy Johnson spoke on the 18th, delivering rhetoric in which he reverse-engineered the closing line of the most famous speech against the proslavery states' right version of the Constitution, Daniel Webster's oration of 1830 in which he proclaimed, "Liberty *and* Union, now and forever, one and inseparable!" Johnson instead argued that slavery and Union were one and inseparable. Not only was property in man constitutional, but the Union could rightly exist only to preserve it. "Slavery promises to exist through all time, so far as human vision can discover," he said. The Missouri Compromise must be ruled unconstitutional or the Union itself would dissolve. "The extension of slavery on this continent is the only thing which will preserve the constitutional freedom we now enjoy." Thus, the case went to the court.

The Southern justices, still in an excited state from the campaign and feeling defiant in the face of the unexpectedly solid showing of the Republicans in the North, were already in touch with certain Southern politicians who may have exerted pressure. On the day of the second argument, December 15, Congressman Alexander Stephens, in contact with Justice James Wayne of Georgia, wrote his brother, "I have been urging all the influence I could bring to bear upon the Sup. Ct. to get them no longer to postpone the case on the Mo. Restriction before them, but to decide it." At Stephens's prodding, Wayne urged Taney to write the decision.

President-elect James Buchanan decided that he would venture to Washington before his inauguration to shake off the scent of humiliation from the Forney debacle. Behind the curtains, Forney was plunging knives into various backs. Buchanan would establish his newfound prestige, receive notable men as supplicants, and begin to reorder the hierarchy of the capital's status with himself at its apex. Having tried to isolate himself from fierce cross-currents of lobbying for cabinet positions, he was still juggling. He was impatient to claim his privilege and could not wait for his hesitant appointments to catch up with the calendar. On January 26 Buchanan checked into the National Hotel, owned by a friend from Lancaster. The capital was buried in a blizzard of more than a foot of snow and temperatures near zero. Plumbing froze in the hotel, sewage backed up, the kitchen was contaminated, and guests stricken with dysentery. Buchanan was afflicted for weeks. He retreated back to Wheatland. His nephew, Eskridge Lane, who accompanied him, became deathly ill and died on March 27.

He had been fiddling with writing his inaugural address for more than a month, unsure of his theme. His seclusion at home while he suffered from "National Hotel disease" concentrated him more than ever on his upcoming speech. From his visit to Washington he learned that the entire burden of the slavery issue in all its complexity could be lifted from his responsibility and neatly resolved in one stroke by the Supreme Court. He spoke about the progress of the Dred Scott case to his old friend, Justice John Catron, of Tennessee, and others.

Catron was among the cadres of original Jacksonians, a Tennessee mountaineer who had fought with Jackson at the Battle of New Orleans, encouraged by Jackson to settle in Nashville to establish a law practice, rose through the party ranks to a state judgeship, and appointed to the Supreme Court on Jackson's last day in office. His wife was of the socially prominent Childress family and her first cousin was married to President Polk, of Tennessee. Catron and his wife were childless, but he was not. He had a secret mistress named Sally, a slave who worked in a Nashville laundry. Their son James P. Thomas was born in 1827 and to be sold as a child of seven, but Sally arranged a payment through a friendly planter to buy him so that he stayed with her though he remained a slave. In 1851 Thomas's legal owner emancipated him and he opened a barbershop. "Now my own father," Thomas wrote in his autobiography, "was the Hon C and filled chairs of distinction. He presided over the Supreme Court ten Years (of Tennessee) but he had no time to give me a thought. He gave me twenty five cents once. If I was correctly informed that was all he ever did for me." Catron referred to free blacks as "indolent," "thieving," and "depraved."

On February 3, Buchanan wrote Catron a letter to inquire whether the Dred Scott case would be decided before the inauguration on March 4. Catron replied on February 6 that Taney had not yet moved, but he assured Buchanan he would inform him "whether and when" it would be taken up. He wrote again on February 10: "The Dred Scott case will be decided next

Saturday [February 14] but it is not at all probable that you will be helped by the decision in preparing your Inaugural. Some of the judges will not touch the question of [congressional] power, others may, but that it will settle nothing, in my present opinion." Buchanan was receiving information from other informed sources, too. On the 14th, J. Glancy Jones wrote him, "The Supreme Court will give their decision soon and the reasoning of the opinion will cover Squatter Sovereignty. To anxious inquirers on this subject in your inaugural I have answered I believe you would rest on the decision of the Supreme Court." Five days later, Catron wrote again with encouraging news. "You may say in your inaugural that the constitutionality of the Compromise is now before the tribunal, and you may add, 'It is due to its high and independent character to suppose that it will settle and decide a controversy which has so long and uselessly agitated the country, and which must ultimately be decided by the Supreme Court." He explained that the Southerners on the court had been triggered by the provocation of Justices Curtis and McLean, who wrote sharp dissents they were determined to release that would uphold the Missouri Compromise and justify a black's right to sue. "A majority of my brethren will be forced up to this point by two dissentients." Five Southern justices reacted angrily by tossing out the straitjacket of restraint and moving that the chief justice write the opinion that would wrap up all the issues including pronouncing the Missouri Compromise unconstitutional. Justice Wayne, who proposed the motion in conference, believed "it was practicable for the Court to quiet all agitation on the question in the Territories by affirming that Congress had no constitutional power to prohibit its introduction."

Catron asked Buchanan for a helping hand with one of his closest friends and neighbor, Justice Robert C. Grier of Pennsylvania. When Buchanan had turned down a Supreme Court appointment from Polk, the seat was given to Grier. He had presided over the case arising from the Christiana Riot, *United States v. Hanway,* in which the Quaker abolitionist Castner Hanway was acquitted to his dismay, which prompted Grier to denounce abolitionists as "infuriated fanatics and unprincipled demagogues." Ruling in *Moore v. Illinois* in 1852, he upheld the state law that punished those shielding fugitive slaves.

If Grier as a Northerner were to join the majority in the Dred Scott decision, it would have the appearance of a national consensus, not simply the view of only Southern justices. "Will you drop Grier a line, saying how necessary it is—and how good the opportunity is, to settle the agitation by an affirmative decision of the Supreme Court, the one way or the other?" Catron wrote Buchanan, who promptly wrote the letter. Grier was impressed to have received a confidential request from the president-elect. He had been unaware of the maneuvers of his fellow justices but once informed leaped into action. He raced with Buchanan's letter in hand to Taney and Wayne, pledging to Taney that he would work with Wayne to win over the others on the court, not alert that they were already in agreement. Grier wrote back to Buchanan on February 23 to thank him for pushing the court. "We fully appreciate and concur in your views as to the desirableness at the time of having an expression of the opinion of the Court on the troublesome question." He confided that six justices "will decide the compromise law of 1820 to be of non-effect." He praised Buchanan's intervention as the tipping point in deciding the case on the broadest basis. "We have thought it due to you to state to you in candor and confidence the real state of the matter."

Buchanan was anxious over the slow pace in disclosing the ruling. He wanted it released before his inauguration in order to give his benediction to the fait accompli in his address. On February 21, he wrote Catron to hurry: "I want Grier speeded." But Grier needed no prodding. He was enthusiastic. Catron told Buchanan the opinion would be released on March 3, the day before the inauguration. But the aged Taney labored over the fine points of his decision and would not meet the deadline.

Buchanan's meddling was crucial in producing a ruling supported by both Northern and Southern members of the court. If he had not delivered Grier to a broad decision the Southerners would have felt it a more precarious path to take and may have reconsidered issuing it on a purely sectional vote, which would have obviously lacked the ring of legitimacy. For all intents and purposes, Buchanan was a coauthor of Taney's opinion. Before taking the oath of office as president he had made himself the tenth justice.

Buchanan left his home in a private train with stained glass windows depicting his Wheatland idyll and patriotic icons. He arrived in Washington vacillating over a number of unfilled cabinet appointments, still unsteady from "National Hotel disease," for which his personal physician was in constant attendance, and compelling Buchanan to skip a banquet in Baltimore, but secretly knowledgeable about the forthcoming decision of the Supreme Court.

At noon on March 4 the procession to take Buchanan and John C. Breckinridge down Pennsylvania Avenue was stalled when it was discovered that President Pierce had been forgotten and left behind. The doctor gave Buchanan a shot of brandy to fortify him. Before being seated at the East Portico of the Capitol, he spoke briefly with Taney, an encounter that would soon become a matter of intense controversy.

After throat clearing about "the God of our fathers" and "love of the Constitution," Buchanan signaled in his address that he knew of the imminent judgment that would result in "the settlement of the ques-

The Inauguration of James Buchanan

tion of domestic slavery in the Territories." It was, he said, "a judicial question, which legitimately belongs to the Supreme Court of the United States, before whom it is now pending, and will, it is understood, be speedily and finally settled. To their decision, in common with all good citizens, I shall cheerfully submit, whatever this may be, though it has ever been my individual opinion that under the Nebraska-Kansas act the appropriate period will be when the number of actual residents in the Territory shall justify the formation of a constitution with a view to its admission as a State into the Union."

All sides understood Buchanan's message as telegraphing the court's opinion, "pointed and distinct," reported the *New York Tribune*'s James S. Pike the next day. "It is the closing in of an Arctic night in our history. . . . We said, when the Kansas-Nebraska bill passed, 'The revolution is accomplished, and Slavery is king.' We point to Mr. Buchanan's Inaugural and the coming decision of the Supreme Court as the coronation of that power."

Two days later, on the morning of March 6, in the vaulted chamber of the court in the Capitol basement, Taney unfurled the fifty-five pages of his opinion on the long desk and read for nearly three hours in a barely audible voice. His conclusions were sweeping, that the Missouri Compromise was unconstitutional, that Congress could not prohibit slavery in the territories, and that Dred Scott was not a citizen, could never be a citizen, and was henceforth and forever a slave. He reached his decision through tortuous logic, distorted history, and blinkered principles. His argument depended at every point on flat claims of white supremacy, racial purity, and sexual spotlessness. Taney used the word "white" thirty-six times, "mulatto" twenty-one times, "race" fifty-eight times, and the phrase "no rights" four times.

Taney cited "historical facts" about "the men who framed the Declaration of Independence and established the State Constitutions and Governments" that "show that a perpetual and impassable barrier was intended to be erected between the white race and the one which they had reduced to slavery, and governed as subjects with absolute and despotic power, and which they then looked upon as so far below them in the scale of created beings, that inter-marriages between white persons and negroes or mulattoes were regarded as unnatural and immoral, and punished as crimes, not only in the parties, but in the person who joined them in marriage. And no distinction in this respect was made between the free negro or mulatto and the slave, but this stigma, of the deepest degradation, was fixed upon the whole race."

Taney insisted on "showing the fixed opinions concerning that race" in order to demonstrate that "the rights of man and the rights of the people" did not "include them, or to give to them or their posterity the benefit of any of its provisions." He declared that the Declaration of Independence "is equally conclusive." "All men are created equal" did not mean "the whole human family." "But it is too clear for dispute, that the enslaved African race were not intended to be included. . . . The unhappy black race were separated from the white by indelible marks, and laws long before established, and were never thought of or spoken of except as property."

But Taney cited no modern pseudoscientific studies to justify his laws of racial superiority and inferiority. He did not refer to the *Essay on the Inequality of the Human Races,* by the French reactionary Arthur de Gobineau, which posited the existence of a white Aryan race as the bastion of aristocracy and sexual race mixing as the downfall of civilization, a book that Southern ideologues translated and popularized in 1856. Nor did Taney refer to passages in the Bible justifying slavery, a common form of argument made by Southern theologians and politicians. He simply offered his version of the founders for his rationale of an eternal condemnation of the damned race. "No one, we presume, supposes that any change in public opinion or feeling, in relation to this unfortunate race, in the civilized nations of Europe or in this country, should induce the court to give to the words of the Constitution a more liberal construction in their favor than they were intended to bear when the instrument was framed and adopted."

In his stream of racial reasoning he framed his most memorable words— "no rights which the white man was bound to respect." The slaves had been, he explained, "regarded as beings of an inferior order, and altogether unfit to associate with the white race, either in social or political relations; and so far inferior, that they had no rights which the white man was bound to respect."

There was nothing more to be said about that inferiority from the perspective of history or law. "This opinion was at that time fixed and universal in the civilized portion of the white race. It was regarded as an axiom in morals as well as in politics, which no one thought of disputing, or supposed to be open to dispute; and men in every grade and position in society daily and habitually acted upon it in their private pursuits, as well as in matters of public concern, without doubting for a moment the correctness of this opinion."

Taney presented his judgment as the unchallengeable wisdom of the ages. "Upon these considerations, it is the opinion of the court that the act of Congress which prohibited a citizen from holding and owning property of this kind in the territory of the United States north of the line therein mentioned, is not warranted by the Constitution, and is therefore void; and that neither Dred Scott himself, nor any of his family, were made free by being carried into this territory; even if they had been carried there by the owner, with the intention of becoming a permanent resident."

When Taney finished his reading and sank into his chair nearly exhausted, concurring opinions were read, including one from Justice Catron. "Just as well might Congress have said to those of the North, you shall not introduce into the territory south of said line your cattle or horses, as the country is already overstocked," he stated. Catron's son born into slavery would later write, "The southerners always claimed that the peculiar institution was of divine origin. . . . But one of the finest pieces of Engineering was getting the Dred Scott Case before Judge Taney. The Negro has no rights that the white man was bound to respect. . . . White man first. Ingun [sic] next. Dog next. Nigger last." (After the Civil War, James P. Thomas would become one of the most successful businessmen in St. Louis, among the wealthiest blacks in America, and the leader of St. Louis black society.)

Justice McLean read his dissent, which he had wanted to release during the 1856 campaign, but instead had to wait until the day. He denied that slavery was a national institution, but only had protection within the states, expressing the "freedom national" principle of leading antislavery advocates. Congress indeed had a right to legislate against slavery. Dred Scott having resided out of slavery should have been declared free. "A slave is not a mere chattel," McLean stated. "He bears the impress of his Maker, and he is amenable to the laws of God and man."

Justice Benjamin R. Curtis, of Massachusetts, from the Webster wing of the Old Whig Party and a student at Harvard of Justice Joseph Story, spoke next. His dissent was a devastating critique that left all of Taney's arguments knocked down by irrefutable citation of precedent and his historical claims eviscerated with facts. Curtis's masterful opinion revealed Taney's to be banal, incoherent, and false. The invidious comparison would not escape the thin-skinned chief justice, who had believed his decision was a tour de force, the capstone to his illustrious career. Curtis proved that free blacks were in fact citizens of the United States in five states at the time of the ratification of the Articles of Confederation and the Constitution. Nor did the Constitution proscribe blacks from citizenship. Nor would it be "just" to the founders, "nor true in itself, to allege that they intended to say that the Creator of all men had endowed the white race, exclusively, with the great natural rights which the Declaration of Independence asserts." Moreover, the Congress had eight times excluded slavery from the territories and had the full power to continue to do so. Slavery had no national basis in the Constitution. "Slavery, being contrary to natural right, is created only by municipal law."

Taney was enraged that McLean's and Curtis's dissents were published at once in Northern newspapers rather than being withheld until they were buried in the later official court publication. In response to Curtis, Taney secretly made eighteen pages of revisions to his opinion before he permitted it to appear in print. Learning of Taney's changes, Curtis requested that Taney share them before they entered the record according to the usual custom of the court. Taney defiantly refused. He sent Curtis a nasty little note accusing him of conspiring with "irresponsible reporters, through political and partisan newspapers, for political and partisan purposes." Out of ire, Taney sent another letter complaining about "gross misrepresentations in the newspapers." Then he sent yet another one railing about "the truth of the historical facts and principles of law asserted by the court in the opinion delivered from the bench, but which were denied in the dissenting opinions." Stunned at Taney's lack of comity and his charge that he was somehow guilty of misconduct, Curtis resigned from the court on September 1 giving as his reason his sudden attraction to private practice. Taney wrote former president Pierce about criticism of his decision, that "the war is waged upon me in the same spirit and by many of the same men" and "by the unscrupulous means to which they resorted" in the Bank War against Jackson.

"We believe it is settled, and that henceforth sectionalism will cease to be a dangerous element in our political contests," editorialized the *Washington Union,* the administration's organ. "Of course, it is to be expected that fanaticism will rave and clamor against the decision of the Supreme Court."

Taney's decision remanding Dred Scott to slavery also attempted to remand the Republican Party beyond the pale. Its reason for existence, opposition to the extension of slavery in the territories, was ruled to have no basis in the law. If Republicans heeded Taney, they should dissolve their party. The opinion at the same time nullified Douglas's doctrine of popular sovereignty that would grant a territory the right to determine whether it would be free or slave. In withdrawing ambiguity, Taney destroyed the always shaky ground on which Douglas stood. Dred Scott was an instrument of judicial power for multiple political ends.

The individuals involved in the case were soon overshadowed by events and receded from view. John Sanford in a New York insane asylum died two months after the decision was handed down. Calvin Chafee, the Republican congressman from Massachusetts and husband of Irene Emerson, was startled to discover about a month before the case was argued that he was actually the legal owner of Dred Scott. He transferred title to the son of the original owner, Taylor Blow of St. Louis, who emancipated Scott and his family on May 26. Scott worked as a porter at Barnum's Hotel in St. Louis but died of tuberculosis in 1858. Nobody knew how old he was.

The Kansas-Nebraska Act had been an earthquake that repealed the Missouri Compromise, shook apart the established political parties, launched a civil war on the plains, whose violence entered into the chamber of Senate with the assault on Charles Sumner, and led to the rise of the Republican Party. The Dred Scott opinion was a cataclysm that shattered the authority of the Supreme Court in its effort to silence "agitation," a counterrevolution by judicial fiat, but instead of turning the Republican Party into a demeaned, shunned, and hunted band its cause became more urgent than ever.

The day after Taney read his opinion, Horace Greeley wrote in the *New York Tribune* that it was "entitled to just as much moral weight as would be the judgment of a majority of those congregated in any Washington barroom." "Nothing left but resistance," wrote Pike of the *Tribune.* Every New England state legislature passed a resolution denouncing the decision and declaring any slave within its borders free. The New York state legislature proclaimed blacks citizens and slavery a felony. Thomas Hart Benton, "face to face with death," spent his dying energy writing a brief against Taney's Dred Scott decision, one old Jacksonian battling another. The decision, wrote Benton, had its origins in Calhoun's schemes of nullification, "a measure of defense" for slavery that had become "offensive—that is to say, to commence the expansion of slavery, and the acquisition of territory to spread it over, so as to overpower the North with new slave States, and drive them out of the Union. . . . Accidents and events have given this party a strange pre-eminence. Under Jackson's administration proclaimed for treason; since, at the head of the Government and of the Democratic Party."

Among Republicans the sense was widespread that there had been collusion between Buchanan and the Supreme Court in wiring the final decision. A year after Dred Scott, on March 3, 1858, Seward delivered a speech on the floor of the Senate accusing Buchanan of conspiring with Taney.

> The day of inauguration came—the first one among all the celebrations of that great national pageant that was to be desecrated by a collation between the executive and judicial departments to undermine the National Legislature and the liberties of the people. The President, attended by the usual lengthened procession, arrived and took his seat on the portico. The Supreme Court attended him there, in robes which yet exacted public reverence. The people unaware of the importance of the whisperings carried on between the President and the Chief Justice, and imbued with veneration for both, filled the avenue and gardens far away as the eye could reach. The President addressed them in words as bland as those which the worst of all the Roman Emperors pronounced when he assumed the purple. He announced (vaguely, indeed, but with self-satisfaction) the forthcoming extra-judicial exposition of the Constitution, and pledged his submission to it as authoritative and final. The Chief Justice and his associates remained silent.

It was likely that Buchanan and Taney had just exchanged pleasantries on the inaugural stand, though it was also entirely possible that Buchanan may have said something about the coming of the opinion and Taney briefly replied. Seward never knew the true story, which went beyond Buchanan's foreshadowing and was far more damaging than the conjecture. Not until the twentieth century did historians begin to piece together the collusion centrally involving Buchanan from the letters of Catron and Grier. How it had happened was kept hidden at the time.

Reverdy Johnson, the defense attorney in Dred Scott, took the lead in denouncing Seward in a widely published letter for having "desecrated the Senate chamber by virtually threatening the South with early practical subjugation. . . . Never was there a more direct incentive to servile insurrection. Could the slaves of the South hear such teachings, and be as mad and reckless as the speaker, many a homestead would swim in blood." Johnson accused Seward of "libel" with "not, I know, a word of truth in his direct charges." That the justices had "acted extra-judicially" was "groundless." Taney had been the victim of "a slander so gross and revolting, that . . . it cannot but ultimately, if not at once, disgust the public mind."

Southerners embraced Taney's ruling as fervently as Northerners rejected it. In their view, the Republicans should have respectfully accepted the court's judgment and folded their tent. Retrospectively, Jefferson Davis blamed Northern criticism as one of the causes of the war. "Instead of accepting the decision of this then august tribunal—the ultimate authority in the interpretation of constitutional questions—as conclusive of a controversy that had so long disturbed the peace and was threatening the perpetuity of the Union, it was flouted, denounced, and utterly disregarded by the Northern agitators, and served only to stimulate the intensity of their sectional hostility. What resource for justice—what assurance of tranquility—what guarantee of safety—now remained for the South?"

Years later, after the Civil War, Taney told his authorized biographer that "if Mr. Seward had been nominated and elected President instead of Mr. Lincoln, he should, if requested, as was customary, have refused to administer to him the official oath, and thereby proclaim to the nation that he would not administer that oath to such a man."

CHAPTER TWENTY

ALL THE POWERS OF EARTH

James Buchanan was renowned among his friends for writing letters with impeccably beautiful penmanship finished with his large signature adorned with flourishes and curlicues. He decided he would send a thank-you note to Stephen A. Douglas, who had sold Chicago property to raise funds for Buchanan's campaign, spoke before numerous rallies on his behalf, and carried Illinois for him by his "super-human efforts," according to Trumbull. The note was misaddressed in his inimitably careful handwriting to "The Hon. Samuel A. Douglas."

Slave market in New Orleans

When Buchanan visited Washington on his pre-inaugural foray, Douglas called on him at his suite in the National Hotel. Douglas prepared for his encounter by meeting beforehand with friends and allies in New York City to draw up a list of patronage positions he expected to be his reward. He believed that he ought to have a representative on the cabinet, be involved in the selection of other cabinet secretaries, and control the federal jobs in Illinois as well as having influence over those in other Northwest states. But no slight had been forgotten, no suspicion lessened, and no vindictive impulse stayed. Douglas was to remain the once and future rival. Senator John Slidell advised Buchanan against naming "in your cabinet any decided partisan of Douglas." The three choices Douglas proposed for the cabinet, including his lieutenant congressman William A. Richardson, were denied. (Richardson was appointed governor of Nebraska and at first did not want to accept the lowly appointment until Douglas pressured him.) Douglas received crumbs here and there, but on important jobs was shut out.

From Buchanan, Douglas immediately gained the "irresistible" impression that "patronage for the Northwest had been disposed of before the nomination," under the thumb of Senator Jesse Bright of Indiana, who had betrayed him at the convention. Douglas's reaction was to take immediate affront. "If this purpose is carried out," Douglas wrote a friend, "and I am the object of attack, I shall fight all my enemies and neither ask nor give quarter. . . . At present I am an outsider. My advice is not invited nor will my wishes probably be regarded, I want nothing but fair play. I ask nothing for myself. I want only a fair share for my friends. I desire the bold true men who fought the battle to be sustained. If this can be done I am content. If, on the contrary, the power of the Administration is to be used either for plunder or ambition," he would retaliate.

Slidell wrote Buchanan that Douglas "assumes that he is the proper representative not only of Illinois, but of the entire Northwest. He is just now in a very morbid state of mind, believing or affecting to believe that there is a general conspiracy to put him down." He was, Slidell warned, "ready to run amok like a maddened Malay." Buchanan stiffened himself. He took Douglas's demands and disappointment as an attempt at usurpation. "I trust in Heaven I may be President myself," he wrote, "and think I shall be."

"He is a stubborn old gentleman very fond of having his own way," remarked Jeremiah Black, the new attorney general, about his friend Buchanan, "and I don't know what his way is."

The clash between Buchanan and Douglas extended beyond politics into society, where Buchanan had clear preferences. The old bachelor cultivated the company of married women of powerful men, loved to gossip and to have young ladies fluttering around his periphery. His niece, Harriet Lane, twenty-six years old when he entered the White House, for whom he had been the legal guardian since she was orphaned at the age of eleven, acted as his first lady. She had early accepted her uncle's intimate friend William R. King as another uncle. (Later she burned the correspondence between the two men.) Well-educated and poised, she served Buchanan as his hostess in London when he was minister to England, where Queen Victoria befriended her and decreed that "dear Miss Lane" be awarded the rank of spousal ambassadorial consort. As the first woman to adopt the title of first lady, she was a style setter and grand hostess who invited artists to the White House, and she was responsible for the creation of the National Gallery of Art. But she had to endure the overbearing criticism of how the food was cooked and the selection of wine at her uncle's dinners that publicly embarrassed her in front of guests. She enjoyed dancing and playing cards, pleasures he forbad. He invaded her private correspondence, forcing her to devise surreptitious methods of hiding it from him. Flirtatious with young men, she spurned the suitors he attempted to thrust on her. "Miss Lane served to keep the surface of society in Washington serene and smiling, though the fires of a volcano raged in the under-political world," wrote her friend Virginia Clay. Sara Pryor, the wife of Roger Pryor, a diplomat, editor, and Southern fire-eater, recalled, "Always courteous, always in place, silent whenever it was possible to be silent, watchful, and careful, she made no enemies, was betrayed into no entangling alliances, and was involved in no contretemps of any kind."

Just before Buchanan's inauguration, one of the coquettish young women in town for whom Buchanan had developed a distant affection, Adele Cutts, the twenty-two-year-old grand-niece of Dolley Madison, and a classmate of Harriet Lane at the Georgetown Visitation School for Girls, married the forty-four-year-old widower Douglas in an elaborate wedding on November 20, 1856, the social event of the season. Douglas's sudden elevation in status distinctly irritated Buchanan. It was a marriage made in Washington heaven. He had position, power, and money. She had youth, beauty, and social station.

The early years of Adele Cutts were spent in the glow of her great-aunt, the *ne plus ultra* doyen of Washington society, with whom she was casually introduced to presidents and senators, the good and the bad. Adele lived in a mansion on Lafayette Square across from the White House. She attended her first party there at the age of seven. Her mother, Ellen O'Neal, of an old Maryland family, was a "brilliant" social figure. Her aunt, Rose Greenhow, held sway as a prominent hostess of a Southern social and political salon. Her father, James Madison Cutts, the cherished nephew of President Madison, had risen to no more than second comptroller of the treasury.

Adele's lineage made her "the belle of Washington," according to her friend Sara Pryor. "She did not impress one as having what we call 'depth of character'. . . a woman to assume to lead and teach other women. . . . But she was beautiful as a pearl, sunny-tempered, unselfish, warmhearted, unaffected, sincere."

In the three years since the death of his first wife Douglas's alcoholism often raged out of control and his dress was disheveled. His vices had not gone unnoticed. Some of Adele's friends counseled against the match. The Southern aristocracy that dominated the social scene, especially the women, regarded Douglas with a mixture of condescension and contempt. "The dirty speculator and party trickster," wrote Varina Davis, Jefferson Davis's wife, "broken in health by drink, with his first wife's money, buys an elegant well-bred woman because she is poor and her Father is proud." But tended by his new wife Douglas no longer appeared unshaven and his clothes ceased to be seedy. "She was very attentive to her 'little giant,'" wrote Sara Pryor. "When he made those terribly long speeches in the Senate . . . she would wait in the gallery and hurry down to wrap his overcoat around him, as he stood in the hall dripping with perspiration. She imbibed enough political lingo to rally and amuse him."

Douglas commissioned the building of three grand townhouses near the Capitol that became known as Douglas Row. He and his new wife took the corner one, four stories tall, with twenty high-ceiled rooms inlaid with walnut paneling. He sold the one next door to John C. Breckinridge and the other to Senator Henry Rice of Minnesota, both investors in his real estate speculations. In this large house, which Douglas called "Mount Julep," after his favorite cocktail, Adele Douglas entertained on a luxurious scale, providing her husband with a social life to match his ambition, "with the regal manner of a princess," according to Virginia Clay.

Douglas's marriage rankled Buchanan. He resented Douglas's capture of the adorable Adele. Buchanan was not and could not be a rival suitor, but he was jealous that a man he thought of as a political rival had her. The president relied on his power over the spoils to try to spoil it. Though he granted other Democratic senators influence over federal appointments in their states, he gave Douglas little other than the Chicago postmaster. Against the advice of his cabinet and without Douglas's knowledge, Buchanan promoted Adele's father, James Madison Cutts, from his midlevel position within the Treasury Department to a high and well-paid auditorship. The appointment cast Douglas in a bad light. It made it seem that he had sought the plum job for his father-in-law while neglecting to secure jobs for people from Illinois. With the patronage ploy Buchanan had created a little scandal of perceived nepotism and drove a stake into the heart of Douglas's family. Douglas wrote him an angry letter demanding that Buchanan rescind the offer, "that any appointments you may make, or persons you may retain in office—no matter how near and dear they may be to me—must not be considered as any compensation for the omission to appoint such Democrats as I, in common with the rest of the [Illinois] delegation, have or may recommend." Buchanan sent back a cutting reply. "Should I make the appointment . . . it will be my own regard for Mr. Cutts and his family, and not because Senator Douglas has had the good fortune to become his son-in-law." The warfare that was political had turned viciously personal. Cutts stayed in the job.

When the Congress adjourned in late May 1857, Douglas returned to Springfield to deliver his views on the Dred Scott decision. It was his most important speech since he had introduced the Kansas-Nebraska Act three years earlier. Senator Jesse Bright might have been handed the federal patronage of the Northwest, but he could never be more than the rough beast he was. Douglas was the still rising star of the Northwest. Buchanan was just beginning his term, but Douglas was the apparent successor. The results of the 1856 campaign underlined that the Democratic Party required a Northerner at its head to win the presidency. The Southerners controlled the party but could not nominate one of their own and expect to win. Douglas's speech had to prepare him to face three future contests, the immediate one for reelection to the Senate in 1858, followed by a struggle for the party nomination, and then for the presidency itself. His conundrum was that Taney had eviscerated his doctrine of popular sovereignty, which he had invented to justify the Kansas-Nebraska Act. Taney declared no territorial government could prohibit slavery because that authority could only flow from the Congress, whose power to limit slavery was unconstitutional. The Taney opinion struck down

Adele Cutts Douglas

both the Republicans and Douglas in a single blow. Douglas had to find a path through that seemingly implacable obstacle. On June 12 he strode to the podium of a packed Hall of the House of Representatives in Springfield. "We were pleased to see in attendance Col. W.H. Herndon, the Hon. A. Lincoln," reported the *Illinois State Register.*

Douglas began by defending Taney's honor against Republicans' criticism. He reduced their objections to their harsh attacks on Taney personally while presenting himself as the champion of dignity who would never descend to ad hominem smears of "partisan malice." "The moment that decision was pronounced," Douglas said, "and before the opinions of the Court could be published and read by the people, the newspaper press, in the interest of a powerful political party in this country, began to pour forth torrents of abuse and misrepresentations not only upon the decision, but upon the character and motives of the venerable chief justice and his illustrious associates on the bench."

The Republicans, he said, must either accept the court's decision or by resisting it strike "a deadly blow at our whole republican system of government" that would "place all our rights and liberties at the mercy of passion, anarchy, and violence." Douglas put the Republicans on the side of anarchy—"a distinct and naked issue between the friends and the enemies of the constitution—the friends and the enemies of the supremacy of the laws."

He avoided discussing Taney's legal reasoning, instead upholding his bowdlerized history of the founders as proslavery absolutists and seized upon his dictum that the Declaration of Independence was the charter for white supremacy. Once Douglas claimed that ground as his own he exposed the Republicans' true and hidden agenda of sexual deviancy. If the Declaration "really means what the Republican or Abolition party assert it does mean, in declaring that a negro was created by the Almighty equal to a white man . . . we shall certainly be compelled, as conscientious and just men, to go one step further—repeal all laws making any distinction whatever on account of race and color, and authorize negroes to marry white women on an equality with white men." If, on the other hand, "the opponents of the Dred Scott decision shall refuse to carry out their views of the Declaration of Independence and negro citizenship, by conferring upon the African race all the rights, privileges and immunities of citizenship, the same as they are or should be enjoyed by the white, how will they vindicate the integrity of their motives and the sincerity of their profession?" Douglas pronounced the Republicans caught in this "inconsistency," a political trap they could not escape. "But so long as they quote the Declaration of Independence to prove that a negro was created equal to a white man, we have no excuse for closing our eyes and professing ignorance of what they intend to do, so soon as they get the power."

Taney's opinion stated that slaves could not be forbidden in any territory or to be brought into free states and that the Congress could make no law otherwise. Douglas made the decision seem as though it had acquitted his position rather than refuted it. Distorting Taney's slanted version of slanted history to make it seem that the chief justice was vindicating popular sovereignty, he proclaimed it had been the underlying principle of the American Revolution and the Constitution all along, and only applicable to white men. "The history of the times clearly shows that the negroes were regarded as an inferior race, who, in all ages, and in every part of the globe, and under the most favorable circumstances, had shown themselves incapable of self-government. . . . It is on this principle that in all civilized and Christian countries the government provides for the protection of the insane, the lunatic, the idiotic, and all other unfortunates who are incompetent to take care of themselves."

The founders, Douglas insisted, were without exception unabashed racists in order to "preserve the purity" of the white race and "prevent any species of amalgamation." He offered a brief history of the founders as race men based on their ethnographic repellence. "They had witnessed the sad and melancholy results of the mixture of the races in Mexico, South America and Central America" and the "demoralization and degradation" that "operated as a warning to our revolutionary fathers to preserve the purity of the white race. . . . They understood that great natural law which declares that amalgamation, between superior and inferior races, brings their posterity down to the lower level of the inferior, but never elevates them to the higher level of the superior race."

Douglas ended triumphantly with a challenge. "The Supreme Court of the United States has decided that, under the constitution, a negro is not and cannot be a citizen. The Republican or Abolition party pronounce that decision cruel, inhuman and infamous, and appeal to the American people to disregard and refuse to obey it. Let us join issue with them and put ourselves upon the country for trial."

Douglas played a deck of race cards. He carefully raised every fear of racial equality, asking his audience to imagine blacks "at the polls, in the jury box, on the bench, in the executive chair, and in the councils of the nation,"

until "the African race" was joined "in the domestic circle." Douglas's ultimate race card was sexual panic.

Douglas had always practiced the politics of race as it suited him, calculating and commonplace. He freely used the word "nigger," even on the
floor of the Senate. He was a native Vermonter, but had transformed himself into a Westerner, appealing to the Kentuckians who populated Illinois
and wanted nothing to do with blacks. He knew that Illinois had the most
draconian laws restricting free blacks of any Northern state. He understood
that his tarring of the "Black Republicans" tainted them. These politics had
never failed him in Illinois. With popular sovereignty as his platform Douglas had been able to play the issue of slavery both ways and at the same time
remain above it. He left the question of whether the territory he had opened
up under the repeal of the Missouri Compromise would be slave or free to
whoever the phantom people that inhabited it might be. The difference between Douglas's repeal and Taney's ruling that the Missouri Compromise
was unconstitutional, however, was fundamental. Taney, emphatic that
slavery could not be prohibited, demolished Douglas's cultivated ambiguity.
Douglas's response was to embrace the Dred Scott decision as though it said
nothing of the kind and ratified his views. While feigning that Taney concurred on popular sovereignty he scurried to stand on that part of the opinion stating blacks had no rights. Through his sleight of hand Douglas had
performed more than a clever trick. It was more than his usual demagogy
trying to force his opponents to spend their time defending themselves from
convoluted smears. He replaced the equivocality of popular sovereignty with
the certitude of white supremacy. After Dred Scott revealed his claim about
popular sovereignty as artifice, his appeal to racism in all its forms from the
political to the sexual became his central theme. As the leader of the Northern wing of the Democratic Party and its presumptive candidate for president, he put the party firmly on the basis of "the purity of the white race."
"Is it true that the negro is our equal and our brother? The history of the
times clearly show that our fathers did not regard the negro race as any kin
to them, and determined so to lay the foundations of society and government
that they should never be of any kin to their posterity."

"The curtain of 1860 is partially lifted, and we have a peep behind the
scenes," reported the *New York Herald*.

We have here the open sesame of Mr. Douglas to the White House. It is the
clearly foreshadowed position of Mr. Douglas as a favorite of the Southern

ultras, and his extraordinary movement for the Southern inside trade for the succession, in direct hostility to the just and conciliatory policy of Mr. Buchanan's administration. . . . And this is the Southern bid of Mr. Douglas for the next Presidency. Such a speech and such a purpose are not the results of accident. . . . As a democratic Presidential aspirant, Mr. Douglas is now without a rival in the great Northwest. . . . In securing Mr. Douglas, therefore, the Southern ultras, would seem, have secured a good foothold for undermining the administration and for controlling the whole democratic party. . . . Mr. Douglas is with them, and is doubtless fully informed of the good will of Mr. Senator Hunter, Mr. Jefferson Davis and their colleagues.

But, first, Douglas had to retain his Senate seat in 1858. Now it was Lincoln's turn to weigh in. On the evening of June 26, carrying a pile of books under his arm, he walked to the podium in the Hall of Representatives before a sparse crowd, perhaps half the size that had come to hear Douglas. He began in a lawyerly frame of mind. "Judge Douglas does not discuss the merits of the decision; and, in that respect, I shall follow his example, believing I could no more improve on McLean and Curtis, than he could on Taney." Without relitigating the details of the case Lincoln aligned himself with the dissenters and consigned Douglas as Taney's clerk. It was argument by subtle condescension.

"He denounces all who question the correctness of that decision, as offering violent resistance to it. But who resists it? Who has, in spite of the decision, declared Dred Scott free, and resisted the authority of his master over him?" To explain the absurdity of Douglas's accusation Lincoln offered a legal lesson. "Judicial decisions have two uses—first, to absolutely determine the case decided, and secondly, to indicate to the public how other similar cases will be decided when they arise. For the latter use, they are called 'precedents' and 'authorities.' We believe, as much as Judge Douglas, (perhaps more) in obedience to, and respect for the judicial department of government. We think its decisions on Constitutional questions, when fully settled, should control, not only the particular cases decided, but the general policy of the country, subject to be disturbed only by amendments of the Constitution as provided in that instrument itself. More than this would be revolution. But we think the Dred Scott decision is erroneous. We know the court that made it, has often over-ruled its own decisions, and we shall do what we can to have it to over-rule this. We offer no *resistance* to it."

Lincoln systematically laid out how the division of the court deprived the decision of unchallengeable legitimacy.

If this important decision had been made by the unanimous concurrence of the judges, and without any apparent partisan bias, and in accordance with legal public expectation, and with the steady practice of the departments throughout our history, and had been in no part, based on assumed historical facts which are not really true; or, if wanting in some of these, it had been before the court more than once, and had there been affirmed and re-affirmed through a course of years, it then might be, perhaps would be, factious, nay, even revolutionary, to not acquiesce in it as a precedent. But when, as it is true we find it wanting in all these claims to the public confidence, it is not resistance, it is not factious, it is not even disrespectful, to treat it as not having yet quite established a settled doctrine for the country. But Judge Douglas considers this view awful.

Though Lincoln said he would not discuss the merits of the case he homed in on Taney's fallacious history. "I have said, in substance, that the Dred Scott decision was, in part, based on assumed historical facts which were not really true; and I ought not to leave the subject without giving some reasons for saying this; I therefore give an instance or two, which I think fully sustain me. Chief Justice Taney, in delivering the opinion of the majority of the Court, insists at great length that negroes were no part of the people who made, or for whom was made, the Declaration of Independence, or the Constitution of the United States."

Lincoln turned to Curtis's dissent for factual refutation. "On the contrary, Judge Curtis, in his dissenting opinion, shows that in five of the then thirteen states, to wit, New Hampshire, Massachusetts, New York, New Jersey and North Carolina, free negroes were voters, and, in proportion to their numbers, had the same part in making the Constitution that the white people had. He shows this with so much particularity as to leave no doubt of its truth." Lincoln quoted Curtis's own words on the historical evidence to repudiate Taney's faulty assertion, which he also quoted.

Lincoln made a new argument that Curtis had not in order to deny Taney's history. Taney, he said, "does not directly assert, but plainly assumes, as a fact, that the public estimate of the black man is more favorable *now* than it was in the days of the Revolution. This assumption is a mistake. In some trifling particulars, the condition of that race has been ameliorated; but, as a whole, in this country, the change between then and now is decidedly the other way; and their ultimate destiny has never appeared so hopeless as in the last three or four years." Lincoln offered as proof Taney's mangling of the Declaration of Independence to justify white supremacy and the advent of new oppressive laws in the states against restricting slavery. "In those days, our Declaration of Independence was held sacred by all, and thought to include all; but now, to aid in making the bondage of the negro universal and eternal, it is assailed, and sneered at, and construed, and hawked at, and torn, till, if its framers could rise from their graves, they could not at all recognize it." Lincoln's framers were not Taney's or Douglas's.

Then Lincoln took flight beyond the law into poetry. His precise mind escaped into metaphor to capture the captivity of the slave.

> All the powers of earth seem rapidly combining against him. Mammon is after him; ambition follows, and philosophy follows, and the Theology of the day is fast joining the cry. They have him in his prison house; they have searched his person, and left no prying instrument with him. One after another they have closed the heavy iron doors upon him, and now they have him, as it were, bolted in with a lock of a hundred keys, which can never be unlocked without the concurrence of every key; the keys in the hands of a hundred different men, and they scattered to a hundred different and distant places; and they stand musing as to what invention, in all the dominions of mind and matter, can be produced to make the impossibility of his escape more complete than it is.

The jailer was only one of a hundred men, the low man in the chain of slavery. He was performing his task prescribed by the philosopher of slavery, the preacher of slavery, and the politician of slavery. Lincoln portrayed the dark scene from inside the depths of the prison from the point of view of the prisoner. He inhabited through empathy the terror of hopelessness. Slavery was not only physical but metaphysical. The slave stripped of all resources could not free himself. He did not have the key, much less a hundred keys, "no prying instrument." Lincoln's slave was condemned to isolation but a representative figure of millions equally isolated in their common powerlessness. Lincoln's tactile rendering of the door, the bolt, and the key made for a picture of crushing power. It was an absolute power but not a simple power. It was a complex system of power controlled by concurrent keys held by many men. It was an arrogant and confident power. It was an overwhelming power. It held power over the slave so complete that it could not envision any escape. Lincoln projected into the inner thoughts of the men of slavery "musing as to what invention, in all the dominions of mind and matter" could tighten its oppression. The Slave Power was the ultimate political power that Lincoln contemplated. If "all the powers of earth" were against the slave they were also arrayed against those against slavery. It was not only the slave held captive but the country. He had set himself on the path to discover the "prying instrument," the "invention, in all the dominions of mind and matter" of emancipation. Lincoln's mission was to create such a power that would overthrow "all the powers of earth." That power "of mind and matter" must be his "invention."

Lincoln returned back to earth to answer the immediate charge that Douglas flung at him, that Republicans, if they believed the Declaration of Independence proclaimed that "all men are created equal" did not exclusively apply to white men, they also necessarily favored "amalgamation" of the races. Douglas had extended Taney's definition of the Declaration from the historical to the sexual. He intertwined the two questions and Lincoln felt duty bound to unwrap them. In Douglas's case, the sexual was the cynical.

> There is a natural disgust in the minds of nearly all white people, to the idea of an indiscriminate amalgamation of the white and black races; and Judge Douglas evidently is basing his chief hope, upon the chances of being able to appropriate the benefit of this disgust to himself. If he can, by much drumming and repeating, fasten the odium of that idea upon his adversaries, he thinks he can struggle through the storm. He therefore clings to this hope, as a drowning man to the last plank. He makes an occasion for lugging it in from the opposition to the Dred Scott decision. He finds the Republicans insisting that the Declaration of Independence includes ALL men, black as well as white; and forthwith he boldly denies that it includes negroes at all, and proceeds to argue gravely that all who contend it does, do so only because they want to vote, and eat, and sleep, and marry with negroes! He will have it that they cannot be consistent else. Now I protest against that counterfeit logic which concludes that, because I do not want a black woman for a *slave* I must necessarily want her for a *wife*. I need not have her for either, I can just leave her alone. In some respects she certainly is not my equal; but in her natural right to eat the bread she earns with her own hands without asking leave of anyone else, she is my equal, and the equal of all others.

Lincoln's deflection replied only to Douglas's sexual claim. He was silent by omission on Douglas's political claim that Republicans believed blacks could have the right to vote. In his defense of the Declaration, however, Lincoln suggested by inference that they might have that right. He pointed out that both Taney and Douglas "argue that the authors of that instrument did not intend to include negroes, by the fact that they did not at once, actually place them on an equality with the whites. Now this grave argument comes to just nothing at all, by the other fact, that they did not at once, *or ever afterwards,* actually place all white people on an equality with one or another. And this is the staple argument of both the Chief Justice and the Senator, for doing this obvious violence to the plain unmistakable language of the Declaration."

In Lincoln's account, the framers did not designate all men equal in every characteristic but in their rights.

> I think the authors of that notable instrument intended to include *all* men, but they did not intend to declare all men equal *in all respects.* They did not mean to say all were equal in color, size, intellect, moral developments, or social capacity. They defined with tolerable distinctness, in what respects they did consider all men created equal—equal in "certain inalienable rights, among which are life, liberty, and the pursuit of happiness." This they said, and this meant. They did not mean to assert the obvious untruth, that all were then actually enjoying that equality, nor yet, that they were about to confer it immediately upon them. In fact they had no power to confer such a boon. They meant simply to declare the *right,* so that the *enforcement* of it might follow as fast as circumstances should permit. They meant to set up a standard maxim for free society, which should be familiar to all, and revered by all; constantly looked to, constantly labored for, and even though never perfectly attained, constantly approximated, and thereby constantly spreading and deepening its influence, and augmenting the happiness and value of life to all people of all colors everywhere.

Lincoln defined the Declaration as a document intended for the future, a charter to expand rights and a shield against tyranny. "The assertion that 'all men are created equal' was of no practical use in effecting our separation from Great Britain; and it was placed in the Declaration, nor for that, but for future use. Its authors meant it to be, thank God, it is now proving itself, a stumbling block to those who in after times might seek to turn a free people back into the hateful paths of despotism. They knew the proneness of prosperity to breed tyrants, and they meant when such should re-appear in this fair land and commence their vocation they should find left for them at least one hard nut to crack."

To Lincoln, the Declaration was not fundamentalist scripture decreed from olden times to be used as a bludgeon to limit rights according to a warped understanding of original intent. "I had thought the Declaration contemplated the progressive improvement in the condition of all men every-where," he said, and quoted Douglas following Taney to mock them. "But no, it merely 'was adopted for the purpose of justifying the colonists in the eyes of the civilized world in withdrawing their allegiance from the British crown, and dissolving their connection with the mother country.' Why, that object having been effected some eighty years ago, the Declaration is of no practical use now—mere rubbish—old wadding left to rot on the battle-field after the victory is won."

The Fourth of July was a little more than a week after Lincoln's speech. "I understand you are preparing to celebrate the 'Fourth,' tomorrow week," he continued.

> What for? The doings of that day had no reference to the present; and quite half of you are not even descendants of those who were referred to at that day. But I suppose you will celebrate; and will even go so far as to read the Declaration. Suppose after you read it once in the old fashioned way, you read it once more with Judge Douglas' version. It will then run thus: "We hold these truths to be self-evident that all British subjects who were on this continent eighty-one years ago, were created equal to all British sub-jects born and *then* residing in Great Britain." And now I appeal to all—to Democrats as well as others,—are you really willing that the Declaration shall be thus frittered away?—thus left no more at most, than an interesting memorial of the dead past? thus shorn of its vitality, and practical value; and left without the *germ* or even the *suggestion* of the individual rights of man in it?

Sliding past the natural peroration of his speech, Lincoln could not help him-self from attempting another answer to the "amalgamation" accusation. He openly exposed the sexual truth that would not speak its name without in-curring a caning. Few other Northern politicians were willing to talk about the predatory sexual exploitation of female slaves by slaveholders. When Charles Sumner insisted on discussing this sordid reality he provoked his an-tagonists to a violent boiling point. "Let us see," said Lincoln. "In 1850 there were in the United States, 405,751, mulattoes. Very few of these are the off-spring of whites and *free* blacks; nearly all have sprung from black *slaves* and white masters. . . . In 1850 there were in the free states, 56,649 mulattoes; but for the most part they were not born there—they came from the slave States, ready made up. In the same year the slave States had 348,874 mulattoes all of home production. . . . These statistics show that slavery is the greatest source of amalgamation; and next to it, not the elevation, but the degeneration of the free blacks. Yet Judge Douglas dreads the slightest restraints on the spread of slavery, and the slightest human recognition of the negro, as tending horribly to amalgamation."

Lincoln did not stop at his sociological inventory of the source of mulattoes through "home production." He used the Dred Scott decision as no one had yet done. Lincoln spoke about the rape culture of slavery. He unmasked the unexamined sexual consequence of Taney's decision. "Dred Scott, his wife and two daughters were all involved in the suit. We desired the court to have held that they were citizens so far at least as to entitle them to a hearing as to whether they were free or not; and then, also, that they were in fact and in law really free. Could we have had our way, the chances of these black girls, ever mixing their blood with that of white people, would have been diminished at least to the extent that it could not have been without their consent. But Judge Douglas is delighted to have them decided to be slaves, and not human enough to have a hearing, even if they were free, and thus left subject to the forced concubinage of their masters, and liable to become the mothers of mulattoes in spite of themselves—the very state of case that produces nine tenths of all the mulattoes—all the mixing of blood in the nation."

Lincoln's speech was not tightly organized with every subject arranged in its proper place. He returned to issues he had already dealt with in order to inject a new idea as if it just occurred to him. He even wandered off into a discussion of colonization.

His poetic description of the imprisonment of the slave vindicated the humanity of the captive from Taney's dehumanizing words. Lincoln again took up that theme to answer Douglas's demeaning of the "Black Republican Party." "The Republicans," said Lincoln, "inculcate, with whatever of ability they can, that the negro is a man; that his bondage is cruelly wrong, and that the field of his oppression ought not to be enlarged. The Democrats deny his manhood; deny, or dwarf to insignificance, the wrong of his bondage; so far as possible, crush all sympathy for him, and cultivate and excite hatred and disgust against him; compliment themselves as Union-savers for doing so; and call the indefinite outspreading of his bondage 'a sacred right of self-government.'"

The *Illinois State Register,* Douglas's newspaper, observed that "black republicans" present at Lincoln's speech looked "woebegone." Douglas, it reported, "did not know or care whether Mr. Lincoln had any opinion at all or not." Would "a single individual" who heard both speeches be "willing to supersede Judge Douglas with Mr. Lincoln?" When Lincoln argued for black equality "all right thinking men" must regard him as "contemptible." On Lincoln's conjecture about the possible rape of Dred Scott's daughters, "Comment is unnecessary." Lincoln's understanding of the founders and the Declaration of Independence was "idle ranting of insane fanaticism." It was madness to think that they believed the "universally acknowledge inferior . . . to be their equal." Lincoln had reduced "a band of patriots" to "a band of hypocrites." Lincoln's claim that the condition of blacks was worse than ever, the *Register* blamed on antislavery agitators. "The white man, in self defense, was forced to impose restrictions upon the negro." The oppression of the slave was "wholly attributable to Mr. Lincoln and his associates."

Lincoln's imagery in the part of his speech about the imprisoned slave was not abstract to him. Just weeks before he had intervened to rescue a black man held captive behind an iron door in a bolted cell to be sold as a slave. He had not mentioned the incident in his speech.

In Springfield, Lincoln was intimately familiar with the free black community, frequenting a black barber, the Haitian-born William de Fleurville, also known as Florville, but commonly called "Billy the Barber," whom he first met in New Salem and helped bring along to Springfield, sending his friends to him as clients to cut their hair, and representing him when he bought property. ("Billy the Barber" would be one of Lincoln's pallbearers.) In early 1855, a free black woman named Polly Mack, who had been married to one of Florville's barbers, appeared at the office of Lincoln & Herndon with a tale of woe. Her son, John Shelby, had hired himself as a hand on a steamboat on the Mississippi, as Lincoln had done years ago, but when he reached New Orleans without "free papers" he was arrested under the black code and fined. By then his boat had left. Unable to pay his fine he was to be sold into slavery to defray his expenses. He had no means to escape.

The case was a perversely refracted version of Dred Scott. Through a series of unfortunate circumstances, the free black from a free state would become a slave. Shelby had made the mistake of landing in New Orleans during a scare in the aftermath of the presidential campaign that free blacks would incite slaves to run away or revolt. The *New Orleans Times Picayune* called "free negroes" an "evil," a "plague and a pest," who would be a source of "mischief to the slave population."

Learning of the imminent danger to John Shelby, Lincoln was "very much moved," according to one of Lincoln's early biographers Josiah G. Holland. Lincoln appealed to Governor William Bissell, whom he been instrumental in electing as the first Republican in the office, but Bissell told him he had no legal authority over the matter in another state. Lincoln appealed to the governor of Louisiana, who also rejected his request. Lincoln returned to Bissell to see if anything could be done and again he was denied. "Lincoln rose from his chair, hat in hand," Herndon recalled, "and exclaimed with some emphasis: 'By God, Governor, I'll make the ground in this country too hot for the foot of a slave, whether you have the legal power to secure the release of this boy or not.'"

But there was someone in New Orleans who had a connection to Lincoln, Benjamin Jonas, the brother of Abraham Jonas, "one of my most valued friends." Abraham Jonas was indeed Lincoln's closest and most prominent Jewish friend. Their careers ran parallel and intersected. Jonas was born into a Jewish family in Portsmouth, England, and emigrated to the United States in 1819, settling in Cincinnati, where he founded its first synagogue. After his wife and daughter died suddenly he moved to Kentucky, where he opened a general store, was elected to the state legislature, and was a friend and ally of Henry Clay. Seeking opportunity in the West, he moved again in 1842 to Quincy, Illinois, and studied the law under Orville Hickman Browning. As a lawyer and a Whig, he entered into Lincoln's circle. Gustave Koerner, the German leader, attorney, and later governor, described Jonas as "perhaps the best debater and the best politician on the Whig side." Jonas was the leading Whig in Quincy, serving as the town postmaster through patronage appointment. When the Kansas-Nebraska Act was enacted, he recruited Lincoln to come to Quincy to support the local Whig candidate for the Congress and to speak against Douglas "while the little giant is here." In 1856, Jonas was listed along with Lincoln as a Republican presidential elector.

Abraham Jonas's brother Benjamin was a lawyer living in New Orleans, who assumed the role of Lincoln's agent. Communicating with him, Lincoln discovered the price for Shelby's release and told him to "charge the expense incurred to him." "Lincoln drew up a subscription-list, which I circulated," Herndon wrote, "collecting funds enough to purchase the young man's liberty." They raised only $19. Lincoln provided the rest himself. He sent $69.30 to Benjamin Jonas in New Orleans, who acknowledged receipt in a letter dated June 4, "in the matter of the colored boy John Shelby." He informed Lincoln, "I should never have ventured to trouble you, had not the boy mentioned your name, as that of one, who would take an interest in his behalf." It was Lincoln's name that was the key to his freedom.

Abraham Jonas

THE WIZARD OF MISSISSIPPI

B uchanan assumed that the troubles in Kansas were a thing of the past, as he told a small group of friends and neighbors gathered at Wheatland with an air of blithe confidence: "Peace has been restored to Kansas.... We shall hear no more of bleeding Kansas," he promised. "... this Kansas question is one of the most absurd of all Proteus-like forms which abolition fanaticism has ever assumed to divide and distract the country." He would soon have the power to wave away the distraction with his appointment of a new governor.

Robert J. Walker

The parade of presidentially appointed territorial governors in Kansas had been a record of squalid betrayal. The first, Andrew Reeder, a regular Democrat and railroad lawyer from Pennsylvania, arrived with complacent benign intentions and a generous spirit to the proslavery forces, and left in the disguise of a hobo on the run from an arrest warrant issued by the proslavery legislature for his efforts to stop the violence and fraudulent elections. The second, Wilson Shannon, the former Democratic governor of Ohio, entered delivering warm greetings to the proslavery camp and departed a hapless figure hated on all sides after the sacking of Lawrence, with the free state leadership fleeing charges of treason, and John Brown hacking men to death. "Poor man!" wrote Sara Robinson, the wife of the free state governor Charles Robinson. "He feared for his own safety. He was despised by both parties, and a curse to himself. There was a look of utter weariness, of inability to do anything, of incapacity to know what to do."

The next governor, John W. Geary, on his way into Kansas by chance encountered Shannon on his way out. "The ex-governor was greatly agitated," recalled Geary's assistant, John H. Gihon. "He had fled in haste and terror from the territory, and seemed still to be laboring under an apprehension for his personal safety. His description of Kansas was suggestive of everything that is frightful and horrible. Its condition was deplorable in the extreme. The whole territory was in a state of insurrection, and a destructive civil war was devastating the country. Murder ran rampant, and the roads were everywhere strewn with the bodies of slaughtered men. No language can exaggerate the awful picture that was drawn; and a man of less nerve than Governor Geary, believing it not too highly colored, would instantly have taken the backward track, rather than rush upon the dangers so eloquently and fearfully portrayed."

Geary was not a man to be easily intimidated. Six feet six inches tall, he was a Mexican War hero wounded ten times leading troops into battle, joined the Gold Rush to San Francisco, and as the city's first mayor as well as its judge he was law and order personified. He came to Kansas a partisan Democrat devoted to popular sovereignty, suspicious of the free state men, and as governor he did not hesitate to deploy federal troops to end the running battles, invasions, and guerrilla warfare.

Geary's peace, however, was short-lived. His crisis came soon after Buchanan was elected. The proslavery Kansas legislature, elected by means that the previous governors and an investigating congressional committee had declared the product of force and fraud, and dubbed the "bogus legislature" by the competing free state one, moved to establish an undemocratic process by which Kansas would enter the Union as a slave state. It was obvious that the free state forces were a clear majority growing in numbers and that the proslavery camp believed they must not be permitted to express their will. In the proslavery capital of Lecompton, John Calhoun, the surveyor general and head of the federal land office, originally from Springfield, Illinois, held sway. He owed his appointment under Pierce to Douglas, who thought he would be his man on the ground to do his bidding. Calhoun built his own empire, controlling virtually all the patronage of hundreds of positions, and gathering around him a rough gang that coordinated with the Ruffian militias. He worked in tandem with Chief Justice Samuel Lecompte and Judge Sterling G. Cato, who ran the kangaroo courts, and a motley group of sheriffs, who suppressed opposition.

On February 15, 1857, Geary vetoed a bill of the Lecompton legislature that would create a census for election of delegates to a constitutional convention but would deny a referendum. "The crowning act of the legislature was the passage, near the close of its session, of what is called the 'Census Bill,'" wrote Gihon, Geary's assistant. "This was the most infamous scheme to rob thousands of freemen of their right of the elective franchise, that has ever been devised in this or any other country. The bill was created with much care and cunning, by certain prominent United States senators at Washington, and sent to Lecompton. . . . The census takers and judges of election are the sheriffs and other officers appointed by the pro-slavery party, and bound to its interests."

The legislature overrode his veto. Geary called it the "felon legislature," and tried to oust Chief Justice Lecompte as "utterly disqualified for the impartial discharge of his duties," but Pierce kept him in office. Judge Cato promptly arrested seven members of the free state legislature. Geary's intelligence was accurate that the members of the Lecompton cabal were in communication with Southern leaders in Washington. Since Buchanan's election Calhoun and the others received guidance from Senator Slidell and Jacob Thompson (soon to be named to Buchanan's cabinet).

Calhoun traveled to Washington, where Secretary of War Jefferson Davis enabled him to gain Pierce's ear. Pierce denied Geary command of federal troops in Kansas and withheld funds, even his salary, on the claim that the appropriations from the Treasury were depleted. Calhoun's deputy physically attacked Geary's assistant and spat upon Geary at a public meeting before pulling out his pistol and being shot dead in a fracas. Geary, threatened with assassination, announced his resignation to take effect on March 4, the day of Buchanan's inauguration.

The free state convention meeting at Topeka on March 10 declared a boycott of the forthcoming election of delegates. It castigated the constitutional convention as "a creature of fraud," the Lecompton assembly unauthorized to "pass an enabling act," and "the whole machinery pertaining to the election in the hands of pretended officers not elected by the people." That same day Geary fled the territory packing two pistols. He surfaced within the week in St. Louis, where he gave an interview to the antislavery *Missouri Democrat*. "In our humble opinion," he said, "the Kansas question has never worn the ominous aspect and the colossal proportions which it is now beginning to assume. It is impossible to conceive that the people of the North will acquiesce in the final triumph of a system of fraud, violence, and ruthless tyranny—equally impossible to conceive that the slavery extensions will forego their purposes; and therefore the prompt and vigorous intervention of the President is demanded by the most serious consideration."

Geary traveled to Washington to brief the new president and his cabinet, but Buchanan had scant interest in his warnings. Kansas seemed to him far away, peripheral and an artificially stirred up commotion. Just as he believed that the controversy over slavery would be swept away in a single stroke with the Dred Scott decision he felt certain that "Bleeding Kansas" would be transformed into a fair and pleasant land with his appointment of the right man as governor. He had already named Geary's successor, "who only waited the consent of his wife to accept," according to the *New York Evening Post*.

Robert J. Walker was overqualified for the position. The one job for which he was not overqualified but suited was president. By experience, temperament, and judgment he was perhaps the only Democrat on the national scene at the time fit to maneuver through the difficult times ahead. While both the reactive and fussy Buchanan and the inert and fumbling Lewis Cass, whom Buchanan appointed secretary of state, had compiled more distinguished résumés, Walker's record outshined them in comparison. In politics and government Walker's intellect, skill, and ruthlessness were renowned. He was a sharp tactician and a far-seeing strategist, expedient and visionary. Maker of presidents and creator of empires, no one could claim to have accomplished more. Barely five feet tall, weighing about one hundred pounds and suffering from lung disorders, he was universally acknowledged as a dynamo.

The *New York Times* correspondent in Washington, reporting on Walker's appointment, called him "a thinking machine . . . his power, industry, and discrimination, keen insight into the motives of men, and laudable ambition to stand well before the country cannot be questioned. I urged in conversation today with a gentleman who stands high in Mr. Buchanan's confidence, his identification with the ultra-Southern interests, as an objection to his appointment. 'You do not know,' said he, 'of whom you are talking.' I predict that if Mr. Walker goes to Kansas, he will unravel the whole Atchison web, and pave the way for the admission of Kansas as a free State in such a manner that the mouths of those who have hitherto sympathized with border ruffianism will be effectually and forever stopped."

After conferring with Walker, Seward wrote his son on March 30, 1857, "Mr. Robert J. Walker and his secretary, Mr. F.P. Stanton, are uncommon men, independent, self-seeking, and quietly ambitious. They don't mean to play parts subordinate and ministering to the ambition of Cass, Buchanan, Marcy, Douglas, or other aspirants, as their predecessors have, but to establish a power of their own. Walker sees his way through the Governorship of Kansas to the Senate, and through the Senate to the Presidency."

Walker's rise had been unbroken, and he could see his path finally to the top. His large ambitions had been more than matched by his self-confidence and ability. He was born into a prominent Pennsylvania family, his father a judge on the Supreme Court of Pennsylvania. After graduating near the top of his class at the University of Pennsylvania, Walker studied the law, and became a leading corporate attorney in Pittsburgh. He married Mary Bache, the great-granddaughter of Benjamin Franklin, the granddaughter of Alexander J. Dallas, secretary of the treasury under President James Madison, and the niece of George M. Dallas, the mayor of Philadelphia and U.S. senator, who would become Polk's vice president. Walker used his Pennsylvania connections to become chairman of the state Democratic Party and supported Andrew Jackson for president in 1824. Jackson did not win, but Walker was established as the "original Jackson man" in the state. Despite his entrenched social position, political preeminence, and financial security, he had a streak for adventure.

Walker moved to the Southern frontier town of Natchez, Mississippi, following his older brother Duncan to set up the lucrative law firm of Walker and Walker in order to take advantage of the gold rush in real estate and slaves. Walker befriended the lords of the plantations, banks, and railroads, such as Joseph Davis, of Natchez, the master of a new fortune and older brother of Jefferson Davis. When fifteen thousand square miles of fertile territory grabbed from the Choctaw tribe were about to be auctioned to the public, Walker organized a real estate syndicate of two hundred of the leading men to control the price and divvy up the land, a grouping that became the dominant power of Mississippi with Walker at its head.

Walker's initial political mentor in Mississippi, U.S. senator George Poindexter, president pro tempore of the Senate, had been Jackson's mainstay, but in the battle over nullification and states' rights Poindexter aligned against him and with Vice President John C. Calhoun. As chairman of the Committee on Private Land Claims, Poindexter launched an investigation into the corruption surrounding the sale of the Choctaw land. Walker's allies divided that land into new counties chartered to elect state legislators, who voted to oust Poindexter. In his place the new U.S. senator elected in 1836 was R.J. Walker, dubbed "The Wizard of Mississippi," "the first of modern bosses." His first speech was against emancipation in the District of Columbia. "Our peculiar institution," he said, "will yield only at the point of the bayonet." He was a close adviser of the new president, Martin Van Buren.

Under Walker's guidance a tower of financial speculation was built in Mississippi. The state borrowed more than the already astronomical sum of $10 million to loan to members of his syndicate and other wealthy planters on the security of mortgages and derivatives based on the price of slaves. Walker himself plunged into the pool to profit from the market manipulation. The Panic of 1837 nearly wiped them all out. Walker advised the legislature to repudiate the debt. Personally, he relied on credit from President Van Buren, who did not recover politically from the economic depression. The Whig landslide of 1840 deterred Walker from the inner councils of power only for a brief month, the length of William Henry Harrison's tenure before dying of pneumonia and the elevation of his vice president, John Tyler, a states' rights Democrat from Virginia. Walker quickly proclaimed the legitimacy of Tyler to accede to the presidency in the first instance of an incumbent's death, and Tyler adopted him as a friend, adviser, and his floor leader in the Senate.

Walker stridently demanded the annexation of Texas. He was speculating in Texas bonds, land, and slaves, along with others in the close circle of Tyler's advisers and cabinet members. In February 1844, after the Democratic Party of Kentucky contrived to nominate him for vice president, Walker replied by publishing his "Letter" in favor of annexation intended to sway uncertain Northern voters. He sounded the false alarm against England seizing Texas and argued the bizarre theory that the territory would serve as a "safety-valve" for slavery, drawing slave owners out of the South into Texas, from where, after slavery failed there through bankruptcy, the planters would wander into Mexico along with all their slaves, who would somehow be gradually emancipated, eliding the fact that Mexico abolished slavery in 1829. His "Letter" was widely circulated and highly effective in moving public opinion for annexation.

Walker played kingmaker at the Democratic convention of 1844, thwarting the return of his former creditor Van Buren by pushing through the two-thirds rule required for nomination and crowning James K. Polk for president and George M. Dallas, his wife's uncle, for vice president. Polk asked him to be attorney general, but Walker said he would prefer to be secretary of the treasury. Within the cabinet he was first among equals, overshadowing the secretary of state, James Buchanan, who he essentially turned into his clerk. Walker devised a bold new tariff and handled the financing of the Mexican War without a deficit. With the back of his hand still moving pieces in Mississippi he installed Jefferson Davis, his old friend's younger brother, into a congressional seat.

After the Polk administration, Walker settled into Washington in the familiar backstage role of lobbyist, attorney, and investor exploiting his contacts from California to England. One of his protégés, Jefferson Davis, Pierce's secretary of war, modeled himself on Walker's example as the power behind the throne. Walker turned down Pierce's offer of minister to China as a ticket to obscurity. During Buchanan's 1856 campaign he participated in the chief Wall Street fundraising group called the New York Hotel Committee. An alliance of Wall Street financiers and politicos, lower South politicians, including Jefferson Davis, and Douglas pressed the president-elect to appoint Walker secretary of state. He would be the premier of the administration, the great expansionist of empire southward into the Caribbean, inevitably a slave empire, piling wealth upon wealth, tightening the bond of the banks of the North with the plantations of the South, the vision of "Young America" and ultimate Manifest Destiny. Buchanan was wary of giving Walker preeminence to surpass him again. He would be president of his own administration. After he assembled his cabinet he decided there was a place for Walker's gifts.

When Buchanan appeared on his doorstep to ask him to go to Kansas, Walker was neither surprised nor eager. He made Buchanan play the supplicant. The president twice begged him in person and wrote him an importuning letter. "The last person whom the President sent to me on this subject, to urge me to go, was Judge Douglas," Walker recalled. "You must go, Bob," Douglas said. "I feel intensely on this. The whole success of the Kansas-Nebraska Act in that Territory is to a great extent dependent on your consenting to go. I beg it of you."

Douglas desperately needed Kansas to be settled on a basis that would be perceived as vindicating his idea of popular sovereignty. He had been dealt a defeat with Dred Scott, but as he pointed out it was a judicial decision that required the federal government and the states to enforce. The proof for him rested on the practical resolution in Kansas. In his June 12 speech on

Dred Scott, Douglas also gave wishful credence to the rigged constitutional convention, which he "believed to be just and fair in all its objects and provisions." Looking forward through a rosy lens, he declared, "The Kansas question being settled peacefully and satisfactorily . . . slavery agitation should be banished from the halls of Congress and cease to be an exciting element in our political struggle."

Walker was Douglas's deus ex machina. The "Wizard" and the "Little Giant" had a happy relationship. Walker had turned down the presidency of the Illinois Central Railroad on Douglas's advice because it came from a business group connected to rival politicians in Illinois. Once Douglas sorted out the ownership of the railroad, Walker was chosen to negotiate a European loan. Then he proposed Walker for secretary of state. Douglas was apparently unworried that he might be a rival for the presidential nomination. First, Walker could solve Douglas's immediate crisis, which would clear his path to an easy reelection and then the nomination.

Walker's condition of taking the job was "perfect concurrence between the Presidency and myself upon the policy," and that policy was "that the constitution itself should be submitted to the vote of the people." Walker told Buchanan that his wife's opposition to his going was the final obstacle to be overcome, so Buchanan paid her a visit with Walker perched beside her. The president impressed her, Walker said, with the "peculiar reasons why I was the person, who more than all others . . . might perhaps save the country by preventing this impending revolution, and securing the peaceable settlement of that question." Mr. and Mrs. Walker both agreed to accept his flattery and the position. After Walker wrote out his inaugural address Buchanan came to his house again to review it and give his stamp of approval. He modified "only a single sentence." Walker had won the guarantees he sought. He believed he would prevail. His prospect ran from the plains to the presidency. "Mr. Walker," stated *Harper's Weekly,* "may be regarded as the foster-father of Texas; may he be equally fortunate with Kansas . . . what reward would be too high for such a man?"

Walker had his own strategic imperatives. He could see far into the future. Kansas was the royal road to a new Manifest Destiny. Even if it were admitted as a free state Walker saw how its existence could augment the power of the slave states. The success of democracy in Kansas would be the beginning of a new burst of imperialism.

"I should have preferred that a majority of the people of Kansas would have made it a slave state," he stated. "I never disguised my opinions upon this subject, and I especially reiterated the opinion that I was thus in favor of maintaining the equilibrium of the government by giving the south a majority in the Senate, while the north would always necessarily have a majority in the House of Representatives, which opinion I have entertained ever since the Missouri compromise, avowing it at that time and on a great many public occasions ever since, especially in my efforts to make two slave states out of Florida, and six slave states out of Texas."

Walker said "the only plan" was to bring in Kansas as a "democratic State," in which the free state Democrats would somehow join with "the pro-slavery party" against "the violent portion of the Republicans." Then Kansas would support the larger objectives of the slave states for empire, always Walker's lodestar.

In a letter to Buchanan on June 28, Walker explained "we must have a slave state out of the south-western Indian Territory, and then a calm will follow; Cuba be acquired with the acquiescence of the North; and your administration, having in reality settled the slavery question, be regarded in all time to come as a re-signing and re-sealing of the Constitution. . . . I shall be pleased soon to hear from you. Cuba! Cuba! (and Porto Rico, if possible) should be the countersign of your administration, and it will close in a blaze of glory."

Frederick P. Stanton, Walker's deputy, arrived in Kansas before the new governor, in early May. He was a former Democratic congressman from Tennessee, proslavery as a matter of course, but committed to a fair process. Like Shannon and Geary before them, Stanton and Walker were convinced that the free state men were the source of the trouble. Stanton came to Lawrence to tell them they must accept the laws of the "bogus legislature." "Never, never!" they shouted. He recited to them from Longfellow's *Song of Hiawatha*: "I am weary of your quarrels, Weary of your wars and bloodshed, Weary of your prayers for vengeance . . ."

On his way west, Walker stopped in Chicago to confer with Douglas, show him the text of his inaugural address with Buchanan's handwriting on it, and receive his encouragement. Arriving in Kansas, he delivered his speech at Lecompton on May 27 to a roughneck proslavery crowd, telling them his views "express the opinion of the President." While he denounced "the treason and fanaticism of abolition," he declared that "in no contingency will Congress admit Kansas as a slave state or free state, unless a majority of the people shall first have fairly and freely decided this question for themselves by a direct vote on the adoption of the Constitution, excluding all fraud or violence." He compounded this anathema with the heresy that there was a natural "isothermal line" that made cold climates like Kansas inhospitable to slavery.

That evening John Calhoun held a banquet for Walker where the whiskey flowed freely. Calhoun's deputy, A.L. Maclean, rose to deliver a toast. "And do you come here to rule over us?—you, a miserable pigmy like you? You come here with ears erect, but you will leave with your tail between your legs. Walker, we have unmade governors before; and by God, I tell you, sir, we can unmake them again!"

The Lecompton legislature conducted a skewed census, gerrymandered the districts, and arranged polling only for proslavery towns. Walker came before the free state convention on June 8 to urge them to participate. He promised that if the constitution was not submitted to a referendum of the actual settlers he would join in their opposition and so would the president. But they decided to protest the fraud. Districts with thousands of voters were effectively disenfranchised. The proslavery sheriffs and judges took no census in nineteen counties and prepared no lists of voters in fourteen. Not a single free state candidate ran in the election on June 15. Only about 2,200 voters cast ballots in an electorate of eligible voters of perhaps 30,000 total and 9,251 on the registry. The proslavery convention was elected.

Walker's attempt at evenhandedness marked him as a betrayer of the South. Judge Thomas W. Thomas of Georgia wrote his friend Congressman Alexander Stephens on June 15, "I have just read Walker's inaugural in Kansas and if the document I have seen is genuine it is clear Buchanan has turned traitor. I have read and reread, I have thought over and turned the thing in my mind every way, and there is no way to escape the damned spectre. It stands there and glares upon us. *We are betrayed.*" Judge Thomas chaired a Georgia State Democratic Convention that demanded Walker's removal.

Stephens wrote Howell Cobb, of Georgia, now the secretary of the treasury, who replied on June 17, "From what you write and what I see in the papers I fear that Walker's inaugural address is to do us harm in the South." Cobb began slowly moving within the cabinet against Walker.

Congressman Robert Toombs, of Georgia, closely aligned with Stephens, wrote on July 11, "Was there ever such folly as this Walker has been playing in Kansas? Everything was quiet, going on smoothly, to some decision and determination, and the country was quite indifferent what that should be, when he puts in, and merely to give himself consequence and to seem to settle what was rapidly settling itself, raises the devil all over the South. And this is not the worst of it. Buchanan intends to sustain him, and thereby ruin himself and his administration. . . . His 'isothermal' and 'thermometrical' arguments and follies I suppose simply means that Kansas is too cold for 'niggers.'"

Senator Jefferson Davis condemned his early mentor as treacherous and chaired a Mississippi State Democratic Convention that issued a denunciation. The *Richmond South,* a new fire-eating newspaper, editorialized that Walker had "delivered Kansas into the hands of the abolitionists." An editorial in the *Richmond Enquirer* stating that Walker had "abused" his authority and "perfidiously violated instructions" called for his dismissal. Tellingly, the editorial was reprinted in the *Washington Union,* the administration's mouthpiece, on June 27.

Despite the gale of criticism, Buchanan wrote Walker on July 12 not to back down. "The point on which your and our success depends is the submission of the constitution to the people of Kansas. . . . On the question of submitting the constitution to the *bona fide* resident settlers of Kansas, I am willing to stand or fall. In sustaining such a principle we cannot fall. It is the principle of the Kansas-Nebraska bill; the principle of popular sovereignty, and the principle at the foundation of all popular government. . . . Should you answer the resolution of the latter (Mississippi), I would advise you to make the great principle of the submission of the constitution to the *bona fide* residents of Kansas conspicuously prominent. On this you will be irresistible."

Walker pledged he would not bend, writing Buchanan on July 20 that he might reply to the attacks. "If these most unmerited attacks upon me and my policy by the extremists of the South should continue, I cannot speak with entire confidence of the result, although my efforts shall be unrelaxed up to the last moment, inasmuch as I believe the existence of this government may depend upon the peaceful and proper adjustment of this question. It may be necessary for me to answer the southern ultras in a published address; if so, it will be made upon my own responsibility, and the administration will be answerable for it in no respect."

Congressman Laurence M. Keitt, of South Carolina, Preston Brooks's accomplice in the caning of Charles Sumner, wrote a letter on August 3 to the State Rights Democrats holding a banquet in his honor. He denounced "treacherous concession, and huckstering compromises." He described Walker as "a man of broken fortunes and sullied name: a needy adventurer. . . . What was his first act? To debauch Kansas from allegiance to the

South, and deliver her into the hands of Free Soil fanatics. . . . If the cause of the South is lost in Kansas, it is lost through the base betrayal of a perjured minion of federal appointment." He ended with a stirring call. "The South must maintain her rights, though she turn a deaf ear to the appealing shrieks of shivering Cabinets, of hysterical Presidents, and dissolving parties. . . . There should be no dissension in the Southern camp, and I trust there will be none, when the hour arrives in which loyalty to party will be treason to the South."

By the end of July, the Southern members of the cabinet had reached a consensus against Walker along with two Northerners, Attorney General Jeremiah Black and Secretary of State Lewis Cass. Cobb, Stephens, and Toombs were in constant communication with each other about the Georgia State Democratic Convention that condemned Walker, whose strings they pulled and strategy they dictated. On July 31, Cass sent Buchanan a letter, undoubtedly at the behest of the cabinet directorate warning him that Walker's ambition threatened him. "We all fear that Governor Walker is endeavoring to make a record for the future, but while we hope otherwise, we are satisfied that, in any contingency, your record will be found fully satisfactory. The plan which you have adopted is the only true plan." On August 2, Cass forwarded a letter to Buchanan from Toombs threatening to quit the party if he didn't dismiss Walker.

Walker relied upon Buchanan as his bulwark and wrote him on August 3 about the campaign against him. "These attacks of the southern ultras, with every possible exaggeration, are circulated with great activity among the people from the insurgent presses, which are very numerous, by their orators in public addresses, and even by messengers throughout the territory, and at points where I have no adequate means of counteracting these calumnies."

Walker had failed in his first effort to persuade the free state men to participate in an election. He had to navigate through the bramble of its factions. Radical abolitionists were allied with racist Jacksonian Democrats against any compromise over admission of Kansas under anything but their Topeka Constitution. Walker insistently applied his skills and charm on the main leadership, which was at least open to hearing him. After lengthy conversations the free state governor, Charles Robinson, became convinced that Walker "intended to act in good faith." On August 25, a free state convention at Grasshopper Falls resolved that Walker had "repeatedly pledged himself that the people of Kansas should have a full and fair vote," and, despite the noisy dissent of a fraction of the more militant groups, it was agreed to go to the polls to elect a congressional delegate and territorial legislature. There had not yet been a fair election.

On September 7, the proslavery delegates to the Kansas constitutional convention at Lecompton met to elect John Calhoun its president and adjourn until after the legislative elections. On October 5 and 6, the free state men turned out at the polls in force. The antislavery congressional delegate won by more than four thousand votes, an indisputable result, but somehow, at the same time, voters elected a proslavery legislature. That result appeared to be swayed by McGee County, which was Cherokee land settled by less than one hundred voters, but which recorded 1,266 proslavery ballots, and the town of Oxford, occupied by perhaps thirty people but which returned 1,628 votes. Walker investigated. If the results stood the legislature would be proslavery and if they were overthrown it would be antislavery. He discovered the "Indian reserve . . . not yet subject to settlement" and Oxford "a village of six houses, including stores, and without a tavern." He tossed out the fraudulent returns and declared the free state contingent the majority in the legislature. He rode into Lawrence, gathered a large crowd, flourished the lengthy paper rolls of voters from Oxford, and revealed that most of the proslavery names were copied in order from *Williams' Cincinnati Directory* of inhabitants. The belligerent former sheriff Samuel J. Jones rounded up those claiming to have been elected as proslavery members of the legislature in the chamber of Judge Cato, a Lecompton stalwart, who issued a ruling that Walker and Stanton must certify their election or be imprisoned. Walker denied the judge's writ, and Cato simply gave up in the face of his authority. Jones marched into Stanton's office to demand he certify him and the others, but Stanton brushed him aside. A group of free state men suggested to hang Jones, which they said would "give them such deep gratification," but Stanton declined their offer. Walker armed himself with a pistol, recruited Stanton, and the two men called on the saloons on Lecompton's main street to demonstrate undaunted fearlessness.

Back in Washington, conversations soon revolved around the turn of events in Kansas, particularly among Buchanan's cabinet, certain members of which were also the core of his social circle. Howell Cobb was his favorite. A generation younger, only forty-one at the beginning of the administration, he had already been Speaker of the House and governor of Georgia. One of the wealthiest men from the South, master of one thousand slaves, and married to a Lamar, one of the most politically powerful and richest families in Georgia, he was naturally conservative, opposed to Calhoun and nullification, and excoriated by the Southern Rights faction for supporting the Compromise of 1850 as the leader of the Union faction. He was always sensitive to criticism from the Southern Rights flank. With Buchanan he "occupied closer relations toward him than any other member of his Cabinet," according to Cobb's contemporary biographer, "and Mr. Cobb was really the prime minister of the Administration." He held lavish parties in his Washington mansion, dined with the President when his wife was in Georgia, and provided convivial company. He believed that slavery was more than constitutionally protected but also divinely ordained. In 1856 he wrote a tract entitled *A Scriptural Examination of the Institution of Slavery* in which he explained that "African slavery is a punishment, inflicted upon the enslaved, for their wickedness," and "beneficial to the slaves," citing the Bible as "our authority." All Northerners opposed to slavery "are denominated abolitionists," and abolitionism "is not a political question; it is a religious delusion." These were quite ordinary views among men of his place and class.

The other frequent guests around Buchanan's White House table were Attorney General Jeremiah Black, his friend from his home state, and Jacob Thompson, of Mississippi, his secretary of the interior. Buchanan especially liked Thompson's young and charming Southern belle of a wife from a wealthy planter family to whom Thompson was engaged when she was fourteen and had sent to Paris for four years for finishing school before marriage. Thompson had been born in North Carolina, his father a doctor,

Howell Cobb

and after graduating from the university there went to the frontier of Mississippi to make his fortune, which flowed from his father-in-law, Peyton Jones. Thompson built the largest mansion in Oxford on his 2,400-acre plantation, tended with formal gardens and displaying a gallery of paintings collected from his extensive travels. He was the political power of northern Mississippi, elected to the Congress in 1838, and a founder of the University of Mississippi. At its opening, he delivered a speech dedicating the school as a place where "the hearts of our young men should be kept in the right place, and it is verily a sin against our children to send

them into that circle of fanaticism, which surrounds our northern colleges."
He was part of the delegation from the 1852 Democratic convention to inform Franklin Pierce personally of his nomination. Offered the consulship to
Cuba, he declined, waiting to run for the U.S. Senate but narrowly edged out
by Jefferson Davis. In 1856, Buchanan rewarded him with a cabinet appointment. Thompson was a force in his own right in his own state and in the
cabinet represented the lower South. He had achieved a high station he felt
was due him. He was ambitious about money, politics, and the trappings of
high culture—and vindictive. There was one man among the many men he
contended with that he particularly hated. After Polk's election, Thompson
lobbied the president-elect to name Walker to his cabinet. When Walker vacated his Senate seat, the governor handwrote his appointment of Thompson
to succeed Walker. Walker brought the commission with him to Washington
to present to the Senate once he assumed his cabinet post, but he withheld
Polk's signed paper appointing Thompson. The seat was instead filled by
Henry S. Foote, an ally of Walker. Thompson never forgave Walker for his
duplicity. "I never could tolerate Walker," he wrote. "He was true to a friend
only so far as that friend could serve him in his designs."

Throughout September and October, Cobb, Stephens, and a few others
were in frequent communication on what to do about Walker. In a letter of
October 9, Cobb wrote Stephens, agreeing to his plan to make Kansas a slave
state by passing a constitution "to say nothing" about slavery, create a new
registration of voters for a referendum, and appear to be "carrying out the
will of the majority." The suggestion that the stamp of a popular vote would
lend legitimacy to a Lecompton Constitution was soon carried to Kansas.

Cobb summoned John J. McElhone, an official reporter for the House of
Representatives, to dictate a letter to him laying out the idea and to have it delivered to the vice president of the Lecompton convention, Hugh M. Moore,
a contact of Cobb's originally from Georgia. Shortly afterward, a clerk in the
Land Office of the Interior Department, Henry L. Martin, of Mississippi,
was called to the home of Jacob Thompson, who instructed him to go to
Kansas. According to Martin, Thompson spoke to him "as to how the constitution might be shaped to protect the rights of slave owners of the slaves
then there . . . and indicated that all fair-minded men to be willing to go a
step further than that . . . all men ought to be willing to allow them to bring
such servants to Kansas and keep them"—the Dred Scott ruling in action.
Thompson himself testified in 1860 before a congressional committee, "I had
much discussion about that time with various individuals as to the manner

in which the slavery clause should be drawn. There were private conversations in which great difference of opinion existed. My object was to secure the question of slavery, and yet secure the cooperation of the free State and pro-slavery Democrats. On this subject I expressed my opinions freely with Mr. Martin, so much as to the form and manner in which the clause should be drawn." Then Martin went to see Cobb, who vouchsafed "to my care a letter to Hugh M. Moore."

For weeks before the Lecompton convention Martin participated in the meetings to make sure "we had a majority." While Walker moved to overturn the fraudulent election results from McGee and Oxford and make possible a free state legislature, the convention reopened on October 19 urgently determined to preempt the consequences of the only free election in the territory. Martin sat constantly at Calhoun's side through the proceedings giving advice. It was a rump of a convention. Of the sixty elected delegates only forty-three showed up, and most of the sessions were conducted without a quorum. The slavery section was approved by only twenty-eight votes. It read: "The right of property is before and higher than any constitutional sanction, and the right of the owner of a slave to such slave and his increase is the same and as inviolable as the right of any property whatever. The legislature shall have no power to pass laws for the emancipation of slaves without the consent of the owners, or without paying the owners, previous to their emancipation, a full equivalent in money for the slaves so emancipated. They shall have no power to prevent emigrants to the state from bringing with them such persons as are deemed slaves by the laws of any one of the United States or territories, so long as any person of the same age or description shall be continued in slavery by the laws of this state."

The difficult part was how to frame this proslavery document that codified Dred Scott into a question for a referendum. Martin drafted a provision. The whole constitution would not be submitted to an up-or-down vote. Instead it would be passed one way or another on the choice of "constitution with slavery" or "constitution with no slavery," which meant in fact acceptance of slavery as it existed and might exist through bringing in slaves. "I drew it up myself," Martin recalled later. At midnight, in a candle-lit room, the intoxicated delegates voted to approve the referendum. The "schedule" contained other provisions: Walker was to be ousted on December 1, and his power would devolve to a provisional government headed by John Calhoun, who would oversee the election on December 21. Martin returned to Washington to report directly to Thompson.

Calhoun paid a visit to Walker to dangle before him the largest bribe of all. If Walker would concur with the referendum, Calhoun suggested, he would be made the next president of the United States. Walker failed to inquire if anyone had authorized Calhoun to speak in the name of the administration and to offer him support for the presidency. "I said that that was impossible," Walker recalled, "and showed Mr. Calhoun this letter of Mr. Buchanan to me of the 12th of July, 1857. He [Calhoun] said that the administration had changed its policy. I told him I did not believe it. . . . I never would change or modify my views on that question in the slightest respect; that I would fight it out to the end, be the consequences to me personally or politically what they might. Mr. Calhoun continued to insist that I ought to go with the President upon this subject. I denied that he had any right to speak for the President." Walker told him he had a letter from the president backing him and demanded to know if Calhoun had one countermanding it. "He said he had not, but that the assurance came to him in such a manner as to be entirely reliable"—that is, from the leading Southerners of the cabinet, Howell Cobb, Jacob Thompson and Secretary of War John B. Floyd—a Southern Directorate—that claimed the authority to speak in the president's name. Walker told Calhoun that the framing of the referendum denied those opposed to the constitution as a whole any way to have a fair vote on it. "Therefore, I considered such a submission of the question a vile fraud, a base counterfeit, and a wretched device to prevent the people voting even on that question. I said to him that not only would I not support it, but I would denounce it, no matter whether the administration sustained it or not."

Walker was anything but naive about the pulling of strings that traversed half a continent back to Washington. He took neither Calhoun's professions of good faith nor his claim to represent the administration at face value. Walker himself intended to see Buchanan, whom he believed must stand by his word or open the floodgates of the deluge. Walker packed his trunks, boarded a steamer, and headed toward Washington on November 17.

Rolling down the Missouri River to St. Louis on the first part of his voyage, Walker did not know that the bell had tolled for him. The *Washington Union* of November 18, in an editorial written by Attorney General Black and approved by the Southern Directorate within the cabinet, crowed about the turn of events in Kansas as a conclusive triumph. "The vexed question is settled—the problem is solved—the dead point of danger is passed—all serious trouble about Kansas affairs is over and gone. . . . The black republican politicians had all their capital staked on the chances of disorder and confusion in Kansas. The enterprise has failed, and they are ruined. . . . They had their day when their tools and hirelings in Kansas were filling the Territory with alarms and agitating the whole country. . . . Those were the days of 'bleeding Kansas,' and then abolitionism waxed mighty." But the Lecompton referendum "will consign it again to its original nothingness."

Reading the editorial, Buchanan was befuddled. He wrote Black praising him for his "excellent" article, but expressed concern, "I deeply regret to observe that the notice of Governor Walker has been stricken out, whilst the praises of the Convention remain. What is the reason for this? It will give just cause for offence to Governor Walker's friends; and I confess I am much worried myself at the omission."

For months, Buchanan had been trying in vain to create a wave of favorable publicity for Walker but was being stymied. In September, Buchanan asked two Kansans he knew who happened to be visiting Washington to write a letter to be printed in the *Union* that would provide key points in Walker's support. Word of the letter, set in type to be published in the paper, leaked from the editors to the Southern Directorate. Cobb passed back an order to spike the letter; it never ran. Walker heard about the suppression of the letter and wrote Buchanan, "My friends here all regard now the Union as an enemy." Buchanan replied on October 22, praising Walker: "The whole affair is now gliding along smoothly." He added that it was an "injustice" to blame the *Union*'s editor for killing the piece, that Cobb had done it out of "proper" motives to help Walker, "under a firm conviction that they would injure both yourself and the Administration." He ended with a message from Mrs. Walker, who "sends her love." On October 30, the Washington correspondent for the Associated Press, close to Cobb and Thompson, reported that Walker would soon be removed. Buchanan issued a statement that it was a false story. He confronted the A.P. reporter, who refused to reveal his source. Buchanan raised the curious incident with his cabinet and either Cobb or Thompson, or both, freely confessed, and told the president he had already agreed to Walker's firing, which he had not. When a friend asked why Buchanan seemed preoccupied, Cobb replied. "Oh, not much; only Old Buck is opposing the administration."

More than confusion about who was in charge—the president or his cabinet—was in the air. The entire atmosphere suddenly filled with panic. On August 24, the Ohio Life Insurance and Trust Company announced it was suspending all payments, an event described as reverberating like a "cannon shot." The firm was more than the financial agent for the state of Ohio; it was among the largest blue-chip Wall Street banks. When its speculative railroad investments turned to losses, it became apparent its chief financial officer had been embezzling funds. The Ohio Life was a creditor to most of the great New York banking houses, which were forced to call in their loans, which sent shock waves through finance and industry. The crash was not simply an American problem. It was a crisis of the global economic system. For a year the Crimean War had been driving interest rates high on the London exchange, prompting the shedding of American equities and bonds, while pumping up a market bubble in American grain, which, at the war's end, collapsed. Investors rushed to liquidate securities. The boom in Western land, railroads, and agriculture went bust. The Dred Scott decision was among the underlying factors contributing to stalling investment in Western railroads. Banks closed, railroads shut, farmers were dispossessed, and workers thrown out of work. The London correspondent for the *New York Tribune,* Karl Marx, wrote an article explaining that "the American crisis had begun to bear upon England," created a global "panic," the "contagion" spread to Europe, and "the present convulsion bears the character of an industrial crisis." He began taking notes for a larger work.

Buchanan blamed the depression on the evils of paper money and banks, repeating the old formulas of the Jackson period. His grasp of the dynamics of the modern economy and its international dimensions was slight. He was "the Squire" in more than his country residence. Buchanan's understanding of the economy was a study in backwardness and underdevelopment. His solution was to increase silver and gold coinage (called specie), cut government expenditures, and, in response to his home-state Pennsylvania manufacturers, modestly raise tariffs, which put him at odds with his Southern Directorate for whom low tariffs were a matter of doctrinal faith and felt to be essential to the cotton trade. Cobb issued a report openly rebuking Buchanan's position. The economy recovered fairly quickly, unlike in the Panic of 1837, whose effects dragged it down for a decade, but the administration never managed to have any coherent policy. Buchanan expressed his helpless passivity in his December 8 message to the Congress, ". . . it is the duty of the Government, by all proper means within its power, to aid in alleviating the sufferings of the people occasioned by the suspension of the banks and to provide against a recurrence of the same calamity. Unfortunately, in either aspect of the case it can do but little." His homily to bear the worst was a forerunner of his paralysis on secession. The South was less affected by the crisis, though its banks also suspended payments and credit, cotton and tobacco prices dived, and railroads went into receivership. Jefferson Davis blamed New York for its "extravagance," and Southern spokesmen generally took the depression as evidence of the natural superiority of slave society, "solid substance," as the *Richmond Enquirer* put it.

"The revulsion in the business in the country," Buchanan wrote Walker on October 22, "seems to have driven all thoughts of 'bleeding Kansas' from the public mind." But Kansas had not been driven from Buchanan's mind. He was in a crisis of political capital. While Walker steamed back to Washington, Buchanan crumpled under pressure. Up to that point he believed or convinced himself he had been a stalwart supporter of Walker. His wife and Mrs. Walker were social friends. Buchanan, who had spent a lifetime in the trenches of politics, seemed strangely innocent of the movements of his own cabinet's actions to manipulate him. Senator Henry S. Foote of Mississippi, a supporter of Walker, recalled, "It was unfortunately of no avail that these efforts to *reassure* Mr. Buchanan were at that time essayed by myself and others; he had already become thoroughly *panic-stricken*; the howlings of the bulldog of secession had fairly frightened him out of his wits, and he ingloriously resolved to yield without further resistance to the decrial and vilification to which he had been so acrimoniously subjected." Soon "the first significant foreshadowings appeared of the President's determination to go over—horse, foot, and dragoons—to the secession faction."

"The President was informed in November, 1857, that the States of Alabama, Mississippi, and South Carolina, and perhaps others would hold conventions and secede from the Union if the Lecompton constitution, which established slavery, should not be accepted by Congress," wrote the Washington correspondent of the *New Orleans Picayune,* who added, "The President believed this."

John Forney, who established the *Philadelphia Press* newspaper in August, met with his old patron. "He said he had changed his course because certain southern States had threatened that if he did not abandon Walker and Stanton they would be compelled either to secede from the Union or take up arms against him." "Well," Buchanan pled to Forney, "cannot you change too? If I can afford to change, why can't you? If you, Douglas, and Walker will unite in support of my policy, there will not be a whisper of this thing. It will pass by like a summer breeze." Forney demurred, invoking Andrew Jackson, the byword for presidential decisiveness. "Sir," a defensive and flustered Buchanan answered, "I intend to make my Kansas policy a test." "Well, sir," Forney replied, "I regret it; but if you make it a test with your officers, we will make it a test at the ballot box." It was the final break; Forney abandoned Buchanan, and his newspaper became a hotbed of criticism.

Almost every Northern Democratic newspaper defected from Buchanan. Douglas's paper, the *Chicago Times,* led the pack, more than a weathervane but a leading indicator of Douglas's future movements. Under the headline "The Democracy must Submit the Constitution or be Damned," it editorialized, "The country elected him to the office of President, and has sustained his administration since then under the assurance that the privilege of voting for or against the CONSTITUTION would never be denied the people of Kansas. Upon any other ground Mr. Buchanan would never have been nominated at Cincinnati, or, if nominated, WOULD NEVER HAVE BEEN ELECTED."

Walker met on November 26 with Buchanan at the White House and was rebuffed. Buchanan felt it was Walker's responsibility to support the changeable president, not the other way around. Walker should change, too. The Southern Directorate had angled Buchanan into their corner. Without his nod or knowledge, his cabinet had made him the standard-bearer of their plot to undermine his emissary. Buchanan had been usurped without a ripple of resistance. If he were to sustain Walker, he would have to confront his cabinet, possibly replace them, their states in rebellion, and the reigning wing of the Democratic Party. Walker had once been the guiding hand behind a president, and now a president was guided against him. Walker had once been the tribune of Southern expansion, but in the cockpit of Kansas had surprisingly come down on the free state side as had the three governors before him. Kansas was not his yellow brick road to the presidency but to oblivion.

Walker left behind his deputy, Frederick P. Stanton, as the acting governor, who on December 7 convened the newly elected legislature with its free state majority, which launched an investigation into the McGee and Oxford frauds, set the date of January 4, 1858, for a vote on the Lecompton Constitution as a whole, and rejected participation in the referendum of December 21 on the terms of the Lecompton convention as "a farce and a swindle." On December 11, Stanton was dismissed, the fifth territorial governor to fall to presidential betrayal.

Walker formally resigned on December 15. "The idea entertained by some," he wrote, seeming to refer to Buchanan, "that I should see the federal constitution and the Kansas-Nebraska bill overthrown and disregarded, and that, playing the part of a mute in a pantomime of ruin, I should acquiesce by my silence in such a result, especially where such acquiescence involved, as an immediate consequence, a disastrous and sanguinary civil war, seems to me most preposterous." He did not leave without describing how he had been subverted behind Buchanan's back. If Buchanan did not understand how events had been turned, Walker did. "Nor was it until my southern opponents interfered in the affairs of Kansas, and, by denunciation, menace, and otherwise, aided at a critical period by several federal office-holders of Kansas, including the surveyor-general, (the president of the convention,) with his immense patronage, embracing many hundred employees, intervened, and, as I believe, without the knowledge or approbation of the President of the United States, produced the extraordinary paper called the Lecompton constitution."

"So disappears from the stage, and is lost in the crowd supporting this Administration, Robert J. Walker," observed *The National Era,* the capital's antislavery paper, drawing a shroud over him.

Not quite.

THE UNMAKING OF THE PRESIDENT

After meeting with the president, Walker raced to Douglas, who was in Chicago, to give him a blow-by-blow account of his disastrous encounter at the White House. Even before the inevitable clash Douglas was irate. "By God, sir, I made Mr. James Buchanan, and by God, sir, I will unmake him!" Douglas exclaimed to Charles H. Ray, editor of the *Chicago Tribune,* an ally of Lincoln, on November 24. "Douglas has stood by and justified for years far greater outrages in Kansas than any committed by Lecompton Convention," the *Tribune*'s Washington correspondent wrote, "Until he commits himself here in the face of the South, I cannot have full confidence in his private professions made at Chicago."

Douglas was in an aggressive, expansive, and unguarded mood. He believed his graceful concession at the 1856 Democratic convention, his stump speaking during the campaign, and financial support at considerable personal expense

Stephen A. Douglas

had made possible Buchanan's rise to the presidency. Douglas thought he deserved credit for delivering a united party at the start of Buchanan's presidency. Douglas had extended favor to Buchanan to receive favor. But on the ledger Douglas counted only debits. Patronage in Illinois had been wiped away, there was no representative of Illinois in the cabinet, no suitable name Douglas suggested was accepted for any prominent appointment, and insult was added to injury with the gratuitous appointment of Douglas's new father-in-law to an elevated post in the Treasury that was contrived to expose Douglas to the charge of nepotism. Douglas long ago had taken the measure of Buchanan as a flighty lightweight, inveterate gossip, and vengeful weakling. When, during the 1852 battle for the nomination, Douglas's agent, George N. Sanders, editor of the *Democratic Review,* had tagged Buchanan along with the other weary contenders in the field as "old fogies," Douglas asked that Sanders cease and desist because of the ill-will he was fostering, but not because Douglas disagreed with the characterization. Later, in 1860, after Lincoln's election, he "launched out into a kind of tirade on Mr. Buchanan's duplicity and cowardice" to a correspondent for the *New York Times.* "If there is such a rumor afoot," he said, "it was put afoot by him, sir; by his own express proceeding, you may be sure. He likes to have people deceived in him—he enjoys treachery, sir, enjoys it as other men do a good cigar—he likes to sniff it up, sir, to relish it!"

Douglas's platform of popular sovereignty now floated on nothing but thin air. Dred Scott had obliterated his proposition, which he tried to elide through obfuscation. He had depended on Walker to vindicate him, but Walker was eviscerated. In the court and in the territory, in theory and practice, popular sovereignty was rendered moot. Douglas's principle was vacated first by Taney, then by Calhoun, his once presumed agent. The Lecompton convention was the spirit of the law of which Dred Scott was the letter. With or without Douglas, the Northern Democratic Party was in revolt and the party as a whole divided. Douglas could thrust himself into the forefront of the revolt or fall into the ranks behind Buchanan, whom he despised. If he followed the president, he would put his chance at reelection to the Senate, which was the prerequisite of his next presidential campaign, at jeopardy. "To admit Kansas as a Slave State would be destructive of everything in Illinois; we could never recover from it," James W. Sheahan, editor of the *Chicago Times,* Douglas's newspaper. "Remember that the *only* fight of 1858 will be in Illinois."

Norman B. Judd, chairman of the Illinois Republican State Committee, had already picked up political intelligence about Douglas. Judd, a former Democrat close to Trumbull, informed him on November 21, 1857, that Douglas was telling his friends in Chicago that the Lecompton convention had been devised "by certain members of the Cabinet to ruin him," that Buchanan wasn't part of their plot, but was helpless before them. If Douglas failed to fight them, Judd wrote Trumbull, he "has not the ghost of a chance of being re-elected to the Senate, and without he can maintain himself in the State his hopes of the Presidency are all gone."

Lincoln first raised his concern about Douglas's difficult position within the Democratic Party in a letter on November 30. "What think you of the probable *'rumpus'* among the democracy over the Kansas constitution?" Lincoln wrote Trumbull. "I think the Republicans should stand clear of it. In their view both the President and Douglas are wrong; and they should not espouse the cause of either, because they may consider the other a little the farther wrong of the two."

Before he set off for Washington Douglas called several Republican leaders to his Chicago home to inform them he was about to do battle with Buchanan. He wanted them to stop criticizing him, and to split or neutralize them. "He really made some of their eyes stick out at his zeal," Judd wrote Trumbull. In Washington anticipation preceded him like that before a prizefight. On the evening of his arrival supporters gathered at his home to serenade him. The *Chicago Tribune* correspondent, after being briefed "personally" by Walker, reported, "The message, of course, is ready. Mr. Buchanan is as punctual, neat, and trim about such a matter as an old maid."

On December 3, Douglas was ushered into the White House. He introduced his conversation telling Buchanan that he had come as his friend to give him constructive advice, a stilted and rehearsed opening. He urged Buchanan to reject the Lecompton referendum. Buchanan refused his demand. He said he would accept it. "If you do, I will denounce it the moment your message is read," Douglas declared. "Mr. Douglas," Buchanan replied, "I desire you to remember that no Democrat ever yet differed from an administration of his own choice without being crushed." He raised the specter of cautionary examples of men who had dared to cross Jackson and suffered the consequences. "Beware the fate of Tallmadge and Rives," he warned. Yet his history was misremembered. Senator Nathaniel P. Tallmadge of New York had broken with Jackson's successor, Van Buren, and switched to the Whigs, who reelected him. William Cabell Rives, Jackson's minister to France, was elected after Jackson's term three times to the Senate, the last as a Whig. But

Douglas did not bother to engage Buchanan in a dialogue on the nuances of their careers. "Mr. President," he said, "I wish you to remember that General Jackson is dead."

Douglas returned to the White House once more. "Mr. Douglas," said Buchanan, "how are we to allay the contention and trouble created by this strife over the Lecompton Constitution?" "Why, Mr. President," replied Douglas, "I do not see how *you* should have any trouble in the premises. The Constitution says, '*Congress* shall make all needful rules and regulations respecting the Territories,' etc., but I cannot recall any clause which requires *the President* to make any." Douglas, of course, was chairman of the Committee on Territories. In short, the president should defer to him. Buchanan advised him that he was on a course that would end with his departure from the Democratic Party and the smashing of his hopes. "Mr. Senator, do you clearly apprehend the goal to which you are now tending?" "Yes, sir," said Douglas, "I have taken a through ticket, and checked all my baggage." Leaving the White House, Douglas did not return again while Buchanan lived there.

He quietly went to see Alexander Stephens, who had been a catalyst of the Southern Directorate that brought about the crisis. "I have seen Douglas twice," Stephens wrote his brother on December 4. "He is against us: decidedly, but not extravagantly, as I had heard. He puts his opposition on the ground that the Kansas Constitution is not fairly presented. He looks upon it as a trick, etc. His course, I fear, will do us great damage. The Administration say they will be firm. He and they will come into open hostility, I fear."

On December 8, in his first annual message to the Congress, Buchanan formally endorsed the Lecompton referendum, which he claimed would restore the "peace and quiet of the whole country." On whether slaves could be brought into Kansas, he referred to the Dred Scott ruling. "This point has at length been finally decided by the highest judicial tribunal of the country, and this upon the plain principle that when a confederacy of sovereign States acquire a new territory at their joint expense both equality and justice demand that the citizens of one and all of them shall have the right to take into it whatsoever is recognized as property by the common Constitution."

The same day, Douglas rose before the Senate, the galleries packed, to proclaim on Buchanan and Lecompton, "I entirely dissented." He compared the referendum to "Napoleon's idea of a fair and free election of himself as First Consul. . . . If you vote for Napoleon, all is well; vote against him, and you are to be instantly shot. That was a fair election. This election is to be equally fair." Upholding the "great principle" of popular sovereignty, Douglas carefully underlined his indifference to slavery. "It is none of my business which way the slavery clause is decided." He concluded, "But if this constitution is to be forced down our throats, in violation of the fundamental principle of free government, under a mode of submission that is a mockery and insult, I will resist it to the last. I have no fear of any party associations being severed." The galleries burst into "loud applause," prompting Senator Mason of Virginia sitting in the chair to declare, "The offenders against the peace and decorum of the Senate should be expelled. I move that the galleries be cleared."

On the Senate floor, reported the *New York Tribune,* a Southern senator "congratulated" Senator Henry Wilson of Massachusetts, "on the ascension of Mr. Douglas to the Republican party," "You have a new leader, who will lead you to the devil, as he has led us." "You are the only man . . . whom we can elect in 1860," Forney wrote Douglas.

The nefarious plot of Douglas to destroy Buchanan—"this coup d'etat"—was laid out in an article on December 15 in the *New York Herald* headlined: "The Great Conspiracy to Rule or Ruin Mr. Buchanan's Administration." According to this account, while Buchanan was making his cabinet, "a very mysterious effort was made by the Southern fire-eaters in behalf of Robert J. Walker as Premier. We now understand that Mr. Senator Douglas had a very long finger in that pie. . . . The experiment failed; but, not suspecting any trick in the matter, and desirous of conciliating all sides of the party, Mr. Buchanan, as a compromise to the fire-eating Walker clique, offered him the Governorship of Kansas. . . . Mr. Douglas has formally opened the war. . . . It is enough that this coup d'etat of Walker and Douglas involves an issue of life or death to the administration and the democracy. . . . One party or the other must go to the wall—the President or Mr. Douglas."

About a week after his speech Douglas secretly summoned two Republican members of the House, Schuyler Colfax of Indiana and Anson Burlingame of Massachusetts. According to a private memorandum, Colfax recorded that Douglas "was convinced that Jeff Davis and others of the Southrons were really for Disunion, and wished an opportunity to break up the Union; that they hoped and worked to unite the South; that their efforts must be resisted; that their course in the end might compel the formation of a great constitutional Union party. . . . He said our true policy was to put the Disunionists in such a position that when the breach was made, as it would be, they would be in the position of insurgents, not we, as they desired should be the case; so that, they being the rebels, the army and the power of the nation would be against them." Colfax concluded that he "believed that Douglas would be forced out of his party if he persisted in his present course." Colfax shared his memo with the editors of the *Chicago Tribune* and Horace Greeley.

Just as the Buchanan administration excoriated Douglas, certain leading Eastern Republicans suddenly embraced him. Horace Greeley of the *New York Tribune* decided to jump on Douglas's bandwagon. He had condemned him before he embraced him. He had once called him "a criminal." In private he continued to call him "a low and dangerous demagogue" puffed up with "enormous self-conceit." Now Douglas's heresy inspired Greeley's latest enthusiasm. "His course has not been merely right," he wrote, "but conspicuously, courageously, eminently so." The editor's career had been marked by erratic twists and turns and curdled political ambitions of his own. Now he rushed to Washington to plot strategy with Douglas. In a stream of adulatory editorials, he urged that Douglas be returned to the Senate "with substantial unanimity." No newspaper exceeded the *Tribune* in its glowing coverage. "The speech of Senator Douglas today is universally admitted to be a great speech, perhaps the greatest he has ever made. It is admired by all aides for it compact force and plain solid strength . . . masterly skill . . . bold . . . defiant . . . brave . . . great energy." Greeley said "a million copies should be distributed among Democrats by Republicans." Greeley, who had made a practice of holding politicians to his high standard, said, "The Republican standard is too high; we want something practical." The result of 1856 had impressed upon Greeley that Republicans could not elect a president strictly on their own strength and he seemed to believe that Douglas would be an ally of the Republicans if not become one. Somehow Greeley might have thought that his promotion of Douglas would thwart Seward. He could never forgive Seward and Weed for failing to slate him for lieutenant governor of New York. Seward meanwhile joined in praising Douglas, imagining that he might use him to further his own presidential ambition. Douglas was obviously the strongest possible Democratic candidate for president in 1860. Lending him encouragement would accelerate the Democratic split and might lead to denial of Douglas's nomination. The *New York Times,* the newspaper closest to Seward, published speculative columns that Douglas's apostasy might lead to the creation of a new political party combining Douglas Democrats and Republicans.

The *Chicago Tribune*'s Charles Ray never trusted Douglas's motives. "I think I see his tracks all over our State; they point only in one direction; not a single toe is turned toward the Republican camp. Watch him, use him, but do not trust him—not an inch." Yet Ray encouraged Colfax in a letter on December 22 to continue cultivating him. "But if Douglas falters in this crisis, he is a dead man. Now is his time to make a ten-strike, and redeem the great blunder he made three years ago"—the Kansas Nebraska Act. "Tell him, and rub in the idea."

Douglas invited more Republicans for secret conclaves to share his confidences: Congressmen Nathaniel Banks of Massachusetts, Galusha Grow of Pennsylvania, and Senator Wilson. His charm offensive seemed to be making some headway. Colfax, Burlingame, and Congressman Frank Blair, the youngest son of Francis P. Blair, urged their colleagues not to criticize him in the hope he might even leap to the Republicans. Wilson was especially excited at the prospect of Douglas switching parties. "He is as sure to be with us in the future as Chase, Seward, or Sumner," he wrote Theodore Parker. "I leave motives to God, but he is to be with us, and he is today of more weight to our cause than any ten men in the country." Douglas's courting of the Republicans played on both cynicism and wishful thinking that he could be used for their ends and that he was not using them for his. "Don't fear him," advised Senator Henry Wilson. "He will sink the Democratic Party."

As Douglas performed for the Republicans, news from Kansas crashed in waves as though scripted to heighten the drama. Two days after he spoke in the Senate, acting governor Stanton was fired. Then Walker issued a scathing statement and quit his post entirely. On December 21, the referendum on the Lecompton Constitution delivered a vote of 6,226 for "constitution with slavery" and 569 "constitution with no slavery." Free state men boycotted. Commissioners appointed by the free state legislature to investigate the fraudulent vote that had elected the Lecompton convention delegates extended their mandate to include a probe of this dubious election. They unearthed 2,720 illegal ballot-stuffed votes, at least the number they could determine. On January 4, 1858, the free state legislature conducted another referendum. This time the result was 10,226 "against the Lecompton constitution," 138 "for the Lecompton constitution with slavery," and 24 "for the Lecompton constitution without slavery."

At the dawn of the New Year, Colfax observed that the Buchanan-Douglas feud was in its opening scenes. "It looks as though the Democratic Party was going to be hopelessly divided and blown to atoms. . . . The split may be healed, but I don't see how, for the Administration has already commenced

war on him, and he has a perfect appetite for fighting those who fight him."
The Washington correspondent of the *Chicago Tribune* reported, "It is agreed
by all that Douglas' position toward the Administration is daily growing
more defiant, and that all sides have ceased to think that his opposition is a
mere game. . . . A well informed and discreet Senator says that the President
is taking steps to make war upon him by striking at his friends in Illinois. . . .
Another says, 'Buchanan declares openly that Douglas has fallen into the
hands of his enemies, and indicates by his manner that he is determined to
have his blood.'"

On February 2, Buchanan sent a message to the Congress, announcing he
had received the election results certified from "J. Calhoun, Esq., President of
the late constitutional convention of Kansas," and submitted the Lecompton
Constitution for approval to admit Kansas as a slave state. "A great delusion
seems to pervade the public mind in relation to the condition of parties in
Kansas," he stated. The "dividing line" was not between "two violent political parties in that Territory, divided on the question of slavery," but "between
those who are loyal to this government and those who have endeavored to destroy its existence by force and by usurpation." The Lecompton convention and
the vote it conducted was loyal and legal while the free state legislature and its
election was "treasonable" and illegal. He proclaimed he was in favor of accepting Kansas into the Union under the Lecompton Constitution. "Kansas is
therefore at this moment as much a slave State as Georgia or South Carolina."

Just before Buchanan sent his message, Alexander Stephens came to the
White House to advise him. "At my suggestion he made three very important modifications." Stephens thought Buchanan was near a breaking point.
"The conclusion I came to is that Mr. Buchanan really means to do right.
What he most needs is wise and prudent counsellors. He is run down and
worn out with office-seekers, and the cares which the consideration of public
affairs has brought upon him. He is now quite feeble and wan. I was struck
with his physical appearance; he appears to me to be failing in bodily health."

Congressman Thomas Harris of Illinois, a close ally of Douglas, wrote
the editor of the *Illinois State Register,* Douglas's paper, Charles H. Lanphier,
"Rough times ahead. . . . The Pres is mad—crazy."

Rough times manifested themselves first in Congress. Harris served as
Douglas's floor leader in the House on a proposition to refer the Lecompton Constitution to a select committee that would be instructed to investigate the underlying election fraud. Knowing they were in the minority, the
anti-Lecompton representatives stalled, refusing to yield the floor. Late into

the night of February 5, Pennsylvania Republican Galusha Grow wandered across the aisle to chat with a Democratic colleague from his state. John A. Quitman of Mississippi demanded an explanation. Grow said he was objecting to speeches out of order. As Grow returned to his seat, Keitt, Brooks's accomplice, shouted belligerently, "Why don't you go over on your own side, God damn you, if you want to object? What business have you over on this side, anyhow?" Grow, "quietly and coolly," according to the *New York Times* correspondent, replied, "This is a free hall, and I have a right to object from any part, when I choose." And he withdrew his objection. "What did you mean by that answer which you gave me just now?" Keitt asked "in a ruffianly tone." "I meant precisely what I said—that this is a free hall, and I will object from whatever part of it I see fit," said Grow. The ghost of Sumner loomed. "I'll show you, you damned Black Republican puppy!" threatened Keitt. "You may think me what you please, Mr. Keitt," answered Grow, "but let me tell you that no nigger-driver shall come up from his plantation to crack his lash about my ears." "We'll see about that," said Keitt, lunging to grab Grow's throat. Grow threw off his hand. Reuben Davis of Mississippi tried to interpose himself, but Keitt leaped at Grow to strangle him. Grow punched him in his head, "which sprawled him fairly upon his face on the floor." Grow stood back while Keitt dusted himself off and stumbled out of the chamber under the care of "some friends who sponged his bruises." Keitt's knockout was a signal for about a dozen Southern members to rush the Republicans. William Barksdale of Mississippi, a friend of Keitt, who had stood at Brooks's side when he caned Sumner, attacked Grow. John F. Potter of Wisconsin stunned him with a sharp blow. Thinking that he had been hit by Elihu Washburne of Illinois, Barksdale wound up to land a haymaker. Washburne's brother, Cadwallader Washburn (a different spelling), of Wisconsin, grabbed Barksdale by the hair. The *Times* reported: "Horrible to relate, Mr. Barksdale's wig came off in Cadwallader's left hand—and his right fist expended itself with tremendous force against the unresisting air." The fighting instantly ceased as congressmen on both sides gawked at the wig, "and its effect was heightened not a little by the fact that in the excitement of the occasion Barksdale restored his wig wrong side foremost." The House adjourned.

In early February, John Calhoun surfaced in Washington claiming to possess the physical ballots of the January 4 legislative election and refusing to certify them. The *National Intelligencer* greeted his appearance by publishing an exposé of the frauds that the pro-Lecompton forces had committed. Back in Kansas, the free state legislature's investigative committee received information about stolen ballots, obtained a search warrant, and discovered them buried in a candle box under a wood pile at the home of Calhoun's chief clerk in the town of Delaware Crossing. Calhoun had been avoiding Douglas, his old sponsor, since he had arrived in the capital, but the senator summoned him to his house. "What about Delaware Crossing?" he demanded, and like a lawyer questioning a false witness he flourished depositions proving the fraud that he pulled from his desk drawer. "Then how about this evidence?" Calhoun quaked and left. "Why Does He Not Decide?" ran the editorial in the *Intelligencer* about his continuing stonewalling on certifying the election results. On March 2, a member of the Kansas investigating committee brought the actual ballots to Washington. Calhoun reluctantly felt compelled to certify them. He was so thoroughly discredited that for his safety Buchanan had to relocate his office from Lecompton to Nebraska City.

Douglas opened his offensive against the administration's position on Lecompton with a proposal on February 4, demanding to see the communications between executive departments and Kansas officials. It was a precision strike aimed at the Southern Directorate of the cabinet in order to expose their control of Calhoun. Counterattacking, the Democratic caucus expelled him from its meetings on the grounds that no senator opposed to Lecompton could attend.

Jefferson Davis rose in the Senate on February 8 to defend Buchanan's position on Lecompton as "the sentiment of a patriot." With Pierce gone, Davis began a new phase in his career. On the morning of Pierce's last day in office, he confided to Davis, who had been his guiding hand, "I can scarcely bear the parting from you, who have been strength and solace to me for four anxious years and never failed me." Pierce departed from Washington never to return, but Davis entered the Senate.

In the winter of 1858, Davis suffered one of his periodic recurrences of herpes simplex, a venereal disease that afflicted his eyes with hundreds of black growths causing temporary blindness and enervation for several weeks before receding. He also caught what his wife, Varina, described as "a very severe cold," probably pneumonia. "He lay speechless and blind," she wrote, "only able to communicate his thoughts by feeling for the slate and writing them, more or less intelligibly, for four weeks." Every day Davis received a visit from William Seward, who came to tell him of the "passing show." "Your man out-talked ours," he said about the ongoing debates. "You would have liked it, but I didn't."

Still weak, Davis's speech on behalf of Lecompton was an act of will, his resurrection from a deathbed. He applied illness as metaphor to a senatorial critic as the shadow of death. "It ill becomes such a man to point to Southern institutions as to him a moral leprosy, which he is to pursue to the end of extermination, and, perverting everything, ancient and modern, to bring it tributary to his own malignant purposes." Davis spoke as an innocent victim pushed to the edge of an abyss. "Sir, we are arraigned day after day as the aggressive power," he said. "What Southern senator during this whole session has attacked any portion or any interest of the North?" The South was being forced into an existential struggle. "You have made it a political war. We are on the defensive. How far are you to push us?" He concluded in an outpouring of self-pity and morbid nostalgia to compose his epitaph, regretting the passing of the Pierce administration and foreseeing his own. "I think I have given evidence, in every form in which patriotism is ever subjected to a test, and I trust, whatever evil may be in store for us by those who wage war on the Constitution and our rights under it, that I shall be able to turn at least to the past and say, 'Up to that period when I was declining into the grave, I served a Government I loved, and served it with my whole heart.'"

On February 15, Buchanan, feeling besieged, sent a self-justifying letter of blind optimism to Robert Tyler, who had been private secretary to his father, President John Tyler. "The Kansas question brightens daily," he wrote. "Everybody with the least foresight can perceive that, Kansas admitted, and the Black Republican party are destroyed; whilst Kansas rejected, and they are rendered triumphant throughout the Northern States."

On March 3, Seward, Davis's constant visitor and political adversary, delivered his speech on Lecompton, opening with an accusation and ending with a challenge. It was in this speech that Seward charged Buchanan with corruptly conspiring on the inaugural stand with Taney about the Dred Scott decision. The incident, he pointed out, was part of a fundamental conflict. "The question of slavery involves a struggle of two antagonistical systems, the labor of slaves and the labor of freemen, for mastery in the Federal Union. Such a struggle is not to be arrested, quelled, or reconciled, by temporary expedients or compromises." On one side, free labor stood as "the ruling idea" of the nation; on the other, loomed the vampire slavery. "To attempt to aggrandize a country with slaves for its inhabitants, would be to try to make a large body of empire with feeble sinews and empty veins." For his role in siding with slavery Buchanan would be condemned to historical ignominy. "A pit deeper and darker still is opening to receive this Administration, because it sins more deeply than its predecessors." Seward could foresee the storm coming. "The nation has advanced another stage; it has reached the point where intervention by the Government for slavery and slave States will no longer be tolerated. Free labor has at last apprehended its rights, its interests, its power, and its destiny; and is organizing itself to assume the government of the Republic." He offered a prophecy. "The interest of the white race demands the ultimate emancipation of all men." How emancipation would occur "is all that remains for you to decide."

The next day, Senator James Henry Hammond, of South Carolina, answered Seward with a speech that was as grandiose as Davis's had been funereal. "If we never acquire another foot of territory for the South, look at her. Eight hundred and fifty thousand square miles. As large as Great Britain, France, Austria, Prussia and Spain. Is not that territory enough to make an empire that shall rule the world?" In Davis's account, the South was being pushed to the wall. In Hammond's, slavery was the wave of the future.

Hammond gave a disquisition on the wealth of the South as "the wealth of a nation," superior in land mass to the North, able to muster a million men in "a defensive war," and endlessly rich in cotton. "But if there were no other reason why we should never have war, would any sane nation make war on cotton? Without firing a gun, without drawing a sword, should they make war on us we could bring the whole world to our feet. . . . What would happen if no cotton was furnished for three years? I will not stop to depict what every one can imagine, but this is certain: England would topple headlong and carry the whole civilized world with her, save the South. No, you dare not make war on cotton. No power on earth dares to make war upon it." Then he uttered his memorable phrase, which became a rallying cry: "Cotton is king."

Hammond threw Seward's challenge back at him. Slavery, not freedom, was the best system. "But, sir, the greatest strength of the South arises from the harmony of her political and social institutions. This harmony gives her a frame of society, the best in the world, and an extent of political freedom, combined with entire security, such as no other people ever enjoyed upon the face of the earth. Society precedes government; creates it, and ought to control it."

Class domination, inequality, and hierarchy were the foundation of the South's "harmony." Aristocracy required subservience. "In all social systems there must be a class to do the menial duties, to perform the drudgery of life. That is, a class requiring but a low order of intellect and but little skill.

Its requisites are vigor, docility, fidelity. Such a class you must have, or you would not have that other class which leads progress, civilization, and refinement. It constitutes the very mud-sill of society and of political government; and you might as well attempt to build a house in the air, as to build either the one or the other, except on this mud-sill. Fortunately for the South, she found a race adapted to that purpose to her hand."

The black slaves of the South were "elevated" as a "mud-sill" class. Talk of "free soil" and "free men" was mere hypocrisy. "The Senator from New York said yesterday that the whole world had abolished slavery. Aye, the name, but not the thing; all the powers of the earth cannot abolish that. . . . your whole hireling class of manual laborers and 'operatives,' as you call them, are essentially slaves. The difference between us is, that our slaves are hired for life and well compensated. . . . Why, you meet more beggars in one day, in any single street of the city of New York, than you would meet in a lifetime in the whole South. We do not think that whites should be slaves either by law or necessity. Our slaves are black, of another and inferior race. The status in which we have placed them is an elevation. They are elevated from the condition in which God first created them, by being made our slaves. . . . Yours are white, of your own race."

If, as Seward threatened, the North was "to take the Government from us; that it will pass from our hands into yours," the North would be ruined by Southern secession. "The South have sustained you in great measure. You are our factors. You fetch and carry for us. . . . Suppose we were to discharge you; suppose we were to take our business out of your hands;—we should consign you to anarchy and poverty."

Hammond's rise as governor of South Carolina, U.S. senator, and ideologue of slavery, heir to John C. Calhoun, proved the rule of oligarchy. But his picture of the harmonious South, "our glory," was a screen drawn over his chaotic life. Surviving letters from his days at South Carolina College appear to document a homosexual relationship with a fellow student. He entered into the upcountry elite through marriage into a wealthy family. His wife inherited ten thousand acres and 150 slaves. His wife's sister married Wade Hampton II, scion of one of the richest and most powerful families of the planter class. When as governor Hammond dismissed Preston Brooks as a feckless aide he was himself under stress. He had been sexually molesting his four teenaged Hampton nieces for years. He took an eighteen-year-old slave for a mistress and later took her twelve-year-old daughter, apparently the only one of her children not his, as another mistress, with whom he believed he had other offspring. Between 1831 and 1841, seventy-eight slaves died on his plantation. Discovering his affairs, his wife fled, the appalled family treated him as a pariah, and his brother-in-law Wade Hampton II circulated papers about his sex life. Hammond's hope for a Senate seat in 1844 was destroyed and he was socially shunned. He feared that the "impression" had been created "very extensively that I was a *Monster*." But with the death of Senator Andrew Butler in May 1857, he emerged as a compromise candidate to succeed him. The stains of his personal life by then seemed to matter only to the Hamptons.

Following his early idol John C. Calhoun, Hammond had rallied behind nullification. Then the ambitious young man had called Calhoun a "stumbling block" to secession; but Hammond proved insufficiently militant for the fire-eaters, who defeated him in gubernatorial and Senate races. "Cotton is king" was his new banner. It was taken up across the South, emblazoned in the headlines of newspaper editorials as a contemptuous rebuff to Northern agitation. Lecompton became his political linchpin. Within the hotbed of South Carolina, it positioned him as a moderate. In private he wondered, "But if Kansas is driven out of the Union for being a Slave State, can any Slave State remain in it with honor?"

Douglas's speech on March 22 dramatically concluded the formal Senate debate over the Lecompton controversy. "I have no defense to make of my Democracy," he declared. "The insinuation that I am acting with the Republicans, or Americans, has no terror, and will not drive me from my duty or propriety." The next day, Crittenden introduced a substitute bill that called for the Lecompton Constitution to be submitted to a popular vote and if rejected a new constitution to be written. The Crittenden measure was easily defeated; on the motion for admission of Kansas under the Lecompton Constitution thirty-three senators voted in favor and twenty-five opposed.

The action turned to the House. Douglas prowled the aisles and cloakroom badgering members to support the Crittenden bill, which was cosponsored

James Henry Hammond

by Congressman William Montgomery of Pennsylvania. It passed on April 1 by 120 to 112. Twenty-two northern Democrats, following Douglas's lead, defected from the administration. The bill went back to the Senate, which promptly rejected it again. But the Crittenden substitute had served its purpose as a murder weapon—the Lecompton bill was dead.

Alexander Stephens, floor manager in the House, working hand-in-glove with Howell Cobb, took control. He recruited William H. English, an ambitious congressman from Indiana, a protégé of Senator Jesse Bright who had nonetheless been close to Douglas, to propose a bill that would admit Kansas as a slave state with sixteen million acres if the Lecompton Constitution were accepted, but that if it were rejected the territory would be reduced to four million acres and Kansas could not qualify to become a state until the population on land was enough to elect a representative to the House. Senator Henry Wilson called it "a conglomeration of bribes, menaces, and meditated frauds. It goes to the people of Kansas with a bribe in one hand and a penalty in the other." Seward termed it "an artifice, a trick, a legislative legerdemain."

Full-scale bribery began in earnest. A slush fund disbursed checks through a House clerk, a government printer, and other agents to anti-Lecompton Democrats in amounts ranging from $500 to $20,000. Federal contracts were dangled, to build engines for navy ships, for example. Appropriations in key districts were held up until commitments from members on the bill were secured. Senator Slidell offered an entire township of land to one congressman. Cobb, Thompson, and Floyd of the War Department plied their influence with a bank of favors. Buchanan sent Cobb to lobby the House. Newspapers in the districts of swing congressmen were paid "to change their tone on the subject of Lecompton," according to a witness. Individual reporters were handed cash. No expense was spared.

Under the weight of corruption Douglas's support in the Congress buckled. Democrats who had opposed Lecompton could use the English bill to maintain their partisan bases in their districts and curry favor with the administration while enriching themselves. On April 24, Douglas conferred in Washington with Walker, Stanton, and Forney, all disaffected from Buchanan but in agreement that the English bill was something Douglas should support. He was caught between political imperatives for his senatorial race and his presidential hope. He faced a series of imponderables. If he voted against the English bill would he split his base, alienate loyal Democrats, and lose his Senate seat? But if he voted for it could he claim credit for a new referendum in Kansas and victory for his principle of popular sovereignty? If he voted against it would he estrange the South from his presidential bid? But if he voted for it could he make peace with Buchanan to his advantage? As Walker made the case for his voting for the English bill, Douglas paced the room nervously while sweat dripped from his forehead—"they were almost drops of blood." Torn and wavering, Douglas at last deferred to the expedient wisdom of the "Wizard of Mississippi."

Before he issued his statement, Douglas met the next day with his diehard anti-Lecompton group to inform them of his momentous decision. Senator David C. Broderick, of California, an Irish immigrant who had been a stone-cutter, had been angered by Hammond's denigration of working men. He was staking his political career against Lecompton. "I can't understand you, sir," he railed at Douglas. "You will be crushed between the Administration and the Republicans. I shall denounce you, sir. You had better go into the street and blow out your brains!" His heated remarks received approval around the room. Sweating blood again, Douglas switched once more. He would stand against the English bill.

Speaking to the Senate, Douglas echoed Henry Wilson, saying the bill offered "intervention with a bounty on the one side and a penalty on the other." On April 30, the English bill passed by 112 to 103 in the House and 31 to 22 in the Senate. But when the referendum was held in Kansas on August 2, the vote against accepting the Lecompton Constitution was overwhelming, 11,812 to 1,926. Neither Dred Scott nor the English bill could force slavery there. The fiasco belonged to Buchanan and the split party to Douglas.

"I expected that Douglas would oppose the settlement of the Kansas difficulties under the Lecompton Constitution. I won a bet on that from Governor Cobb," recalled Alexander Stephens. "Afterwards I urged both Buchanan and Cobb not to wage war upon Douglas, but I could exert no influence upon either."

Buchanan moved to decapitate Douglas's organization in Illinois, removing his key men from positions of importance. Isaac "Ike" Cook had once been a Douglas man in Chicago, a financial backer of the *Chicago Times,* but quarreled with its editor and irritated Douglas, who had him fired as the Chicago postmaster. Buchanan ousted Douglas's postmaster and inserted Cook back in the job. He also appointed other Douglas enemies as the collector of the Port of Chicago and the U.S. attorney of northern Illinois. Yet another enemy was named a mail agent whose task was to travel around the state firing postmasters in town after town who were Douglas loyalists. Douglas's papers, the *Chicago Times* and the *Illinois State Register,* were deprived of government printing, a lucrative subsidy. Editors were bribed with postmaster appointments. Buchanan met with two Illinois editors at the White House and "told them he would remove every man in Illinois who had opposed him and his policy. . . . A general sweeping out is determined on." "We are all to be struck down, if possible," Congressman Thomas Harris, a Douglas loyalist, wrote to Lanphier, editor of the *Register*. One desperate pro-Douglas officeholder tried to keep his job by claiming he had named his children after James Buchanan and Howell Cobb. Led by Cook, the anti-Douglasites formed a counter-organization within the party dubbed the "National Democrats," declaring as their motto: "Fealty to Senator Douglas is treason to Democracy." Douglas called them "Danites," after a secret band of Mormon assassins. Slidell "openly confessed" to Senator Foote "that he had used money freely in Illinois for the overthrow of Douglas, avowing at the same time his anxiety to see Lincoln elected over him."

Under Cook, the National Democrats mustered about fifty delegates at the Illinois state Democratic convention on April 21, staged a walkout, and called for a new convention. Pro-Douglas speakers referred to them as "spaniels," "hounds," and "janizeries," but still voted down "in the most cowardly manner" resolutions taking an "emphatic stand against the Administration" in the language that Douglas had transmitted, reported the *Illinois State Journal*. The National Democrats held their own convention on June 9 to nominate a slate of statewide candidates, though not a Senate candidate, in order to undercut Douglas. Their strategy was to win a few seats in the state legislature so that there would be no majority for Douglas, a stalemate that would allow a third candidate to emerge. It was a version of the scenario that had led to the election of Trumbull over Lincoln in 1855.

Buchanan's interference in Illinois against Douglas left him as embittered as Douglas's opposition to Lecompton had left Buchanan. The *Washington Union* of May 27 tainted Douglas and "the anti-Lecompton democracy of the north" as a "revival" of the Barnburners, the Softs of New York, who defected from the Democratic Party in 1848 to form the Free Soil Party. The administration paper predicted "their movement will degenerate . . . into unadulterated abolitionism . . ." and virtually read Douglas out of the party: ". . . no man can consistently be recognized as a member of the democratic party who refuses to acquiesce."

Douglas girded himself for the battle to retain his seat upon which his future depended. The road to the presidency lay through Illinois. He mortgaged his Chicago property for $80,000 and took loans for campaign funds.

His health was again "impaired," according to Horace White, the Chicago newspaper reporter. He had to drag himself out of a sickbed to vote against the Lecompton bill. His wife, Adele, suffered a miscarriage. He was drinking, not sleeping, and filled with anxieties. Defeat for the Senate would end his career. He expected a hard campaign. "I shall have my hands full," he told Forney about Lincoln. "He is the strong man of his party,—full of wit, facts, dates,—and the best stump speaker, with his droll ways and dry jokes, in the West. He is as honest as he is shrewd; and if I beat him my victory will be hardly won."

A HOUSE DIVIDED

Lincoln's law partner, reading the news dispatches, was gleeful. "The Buchanan faction here will kill him for the Senatorial seat," Herndon wrote his abolitionist idol Theodore Parker on December 19, 1857. He could not help admitting some grudging admiration for Douglas's break with Buchanan. "Douglas is more of a man than I took him to be: he has got some nerve at least," he wrote Trumbull on December 16, 1857. But Herndon judged him only to be "a policy educated Devil," in a letter to Charles Sumner, on January 28, 1858, mainly motivated by the calculus of presidential politics, and so trying to unite the North behind him for the Democratic nomination in 1860. Douglas's fate was sealed, Herndon wrote Trumbull on February 27: "the Devil will get him: he is lost and gone."

Abraham Lincoln, 1858

Lincoln, however, was less certain than his law partner about the foreordained doom of his lifelong rival. He was agitated by the Eastern Republican flirtation with Douglas as an unwarranted intervention by powerful members of his party and feared that powerful members of his party outside Illinois might use influence to brush him aside. Lincoln sounded out Trumbull for intelligence. On December 25, 1857, Trumbull wrote him about Douglas, "He himself does not know where he is going or where he will come out."

Lincoln nervously wondered what had gotten into the Eastern Republicans. He replied on December 28: "What does the New York Tribune mean by its constant eulogizing, and admiring, and magnifying [of] Douglas? Does it, in this, speak the sentiments of the Republicans at Washington? Have they concluded that the Republican cause, generally, can be best promoted by sacrificing us here in Illinois? If so we could like to know it soon; it will save us a great deal of labor to surrender at once. As yet I have heard of no Republican here going over to Douglas; but if the Tribune continues to din his praised into the ears of its five or ten thousand republican readers in Illinois, it is more than can be hoped that all will stand firm. I am not complaining. I only wish a fair understanding. Please write me at Springfield."

Through early 1858, Lincoln brooded over the Eastern Republicans' promotion of Douglas. "I think Greeley is not doing me right," he told Herndon. "His conduct, I believe, savors a little of injustice. I am a true Republican and have been tried already in the hottest part of the anti-slavery fight, and yet I find him taking up Douglas, a veritable dodger—once a tool of the South, now its enemy—and pushing him to the front. He forgets that when he does that he pulls me down at the same time. I fear Greeley's attitude will damage me with Sumner, Seward, Wilson, Phillips, and other friends in the East." Herndon recalled that Lincoln's complaint was "so much of mingled sadness and earnestness." Once again, he worried he would suffer defeat, but this time at the hands of his own party. Shortly before noon, "gloomy and restless" over Greeley's enthusiasm for Douglas, Lincoln wandered out of his law office to play chess with Illinois Supreme Court justice Samuel Treat, an old friend and his regular chess partner—and that day "did not return again," wrote Herndon.

On December 28, the day Lincoln wrote Trumbull about Greeley, he composed some notes for a speech. Since Douglas opposed Lecompton, Lincoln wrote he was "accosted by friends of his with the question, 'What do you think now?' Since the delivery of his speech in the Senate, the question has been varied a little. 'Have you read Douglas's speech?' 'Yes.' 'Well, what do you think of it?' In every instance the question is accompanied with an anxious inquiring stare, which asks, quite as plainly as words could, 'Can't you go for Douglas now?' Like boys who have set a bird-trap, they are watching to see if the birds are picking at the bait and likely to go under." If the Republicans were to be "haltered and harnessed, to be handed over to him," they would abandon their reason for existence. "His whole effort is devoted to clearing the ring, and giving slavery and freedom a fair fight. With one who considers slavery just as good as freedom, this is perfectly natural and consistent. But have Republicans any sympathy with such a view? They think slavery is wrong; and that, like every other wrong which some men will commit if left alone, it ought to be prohibited by law. They consider it not only morally wrong, but a 'deadly poison' in a government like ours, professedly based on the equality of men. Upon this radical difference of opinion with Judge Douglas, the Republican party was organized. There is all the difference between him and them now that there ever was. He will not say that he has changed; have you?"

Lincoln traced the history of "popular sovereignty," from Lewis Cass in the 1848 campaign, "as a political maneuver to secure himself the Democratic nomination for the presidency. It served its purpose then, and sunk out of sight. Six years later Judge Douglas fished it up, and glossed it over with what he called, and still persists in calling, 'sacred rights of self-government.' Well, I, too, believe in self-government as I understand it; but I do not understand that the privilege one man takes of making a slave of another, or holding him as such, is any part of 'self-government.'"

Lincoln wrote out the words of his answer: *A house divided against itself cannot stand.*

"I believe the government cannot endure permanently half slave and half free. . . . I do not expect the Union to be dissolved. I do not expect the house to fall; but I do expect it will cease to be divided. It will become all one thing or all the other. Either the opponents of slavery will arrest the further spread of it, and put it in course of ultimate extinction; or its advocates will push it forward till it shall become alike lawful in all the States, old as well as new. Do you doubt it?"

Lincoln filed this fragment of writing away in a drawer. Herndon, who "pondered a good deal over Lincoln's dejection," came up with a plan. He decided that he would undertake a fact-finding tour of the East, meet with the great men with whom he had corresponded but never encountered face-to-face, and for the first time see the marble federal buildings of Washington, walk the crowded streets of New York, and climb Beacon Hill in Boston. At Washington, Lincoln's scout met with Trumbull, who confided that while Douglas had no intention of switching parties there was among some Republicans "a DISPOSITION to sell out Illinois" by backing Douglas for the Senate. Herndon was alarmed, "astonished . . . and thunder stuck." Meeting with Senators Seward and Wilson, Herndon confirmed what Trumbull had told him about the drift toward Douglas. But Seward also said that Republicans would never support "so slippery a man as Douglas."

Herndon proceeded to see Douglas himself, who was ill but nonetheless seemed pleased to usher him into his Washington home and give him a cigar. "He is not in anybody's way, not even in yours, Judge Douglas," Herndon assured him about Lincoln. And Douglas returned the sentiment by saying he was not in Lincoln's way. "Give Mr. Lincoln my regards," he said, "when you return, and tell him I have crossed the river and burned my boat." What did he mean by that cryptic remark? Not that he would abandon his party, but that he would not reverse his course against the Buchanan administration on Lecompton.

In New York, Greeley granted Herndon a twenty-minute audience during which he lectured him on the greatness of Douglas. Apparently, he did not know that his visitor was Lincoln's law partner. "He talked bitterly— somewhat so—against the papers in Illinois, and said they were fools," Herndon reported in a letter to Lincoln on March 24. "I asked him this question 'Greeley, do you want to see a third party organized, or do you want Douglas to ride to power through the North, which he has so much abused and betrayed?' and to which he replied, 'Let the future alone; it will all come right. Douglas is a brave man. Forget the past and sustain the righteous.' Good God, righteous, eh!"

In Boston, Herndon met at the State House with Governor Nathaniel Banks, who assumed the bearded rustic from the hinterlands would naturally support the conventional wisdom of Eastern political circles. "He asked me this question 'You will sustain Douglas in Illinois won't you?' and to which I said 'No, never!'" Herndon wrote Lincoln that Banks "affected to be much surprised" at his answer. Herndon added, "The northern men are cold to me—somewhat repellent."

On his Boston sojourn, Herndon dropped in on his constant correspondent and revered hero, Theodore Parker, who cut him short when Herndon began babbling about philosophy. But Herndon's admiration was undimmed, their correspondence continued unabated, and upon his return to Springfield, after a side trip to see the wonder of Niagara Falls, he brought a copy of Parker's collected sermons and lectures for Lincoln, which included "The Effect of Slavery on the American People." According to Herndon, Lincoln "liked especially the following expression, which he marked with a pencil: 'Democracy is direct self-government, over all the people, for all the people, by all the people.'"

Back in Springfield, Herndon briefed the Illinois Republican leaders on the Eastern collaboration with Douglas and scheme to dump Lincoln. He told a tale never substantiated of a secret meeting Douglas held in the late fall of 1857 in Chicago, after he decided to oppose the Lecompton Constitution, with Greeley, Seward, and Thurlow Weed. "Illinois," Herndon wrote Elihu Washburne on April 10, "was to be chaffered for, and huckstered off without our consent, and against our will. . . . Illinois is not for sale. We here are not willing to be sacrificed for a fiction—national maneuvers." On April 19, "Long John" Wentworth, the mayor of Chicago, who also harbored his own not so secret ambition for the Senate, wrote Lincoln, "I fear, Lincoln, that you are sold for the Senate by men who are drinking the wine of Douglas at Washington."

"We want to be our own masters," Herndon wrote Greeley on May 7, "and if any politician wants our respect, confidence, or support now or hereafter, let him stand aloof and let us alone." "Friend Herndon," Greeley replied on May 29, "I have not proposed to instruct the Republicans of Illinois in their political duties, and I doubt very much that even so much as is implied in your letter can be fairly deduced from anything I have written." Then he made "one prediction," that Douglas's close associate, Congressman Thomas Harris, "will beat you badly." Greeley signed off, "Now paddle your own dugout." (Harris, however, suffering from consumption, died in November.)

There were some defections of local Republicans in Illinois to Douglas, gestures of support for his reelection to the Senate, but these only stoked the rising anger of state party leaders against the arrogance and condescension of the Eastern Republicans. "Are our friends crazy?" wrote Jesse Dubois to Trumbull on April 8. Greeley wrote an angry letter to Joseph Medill, editor of the *Chicago Tribune,* "You have repelled Douglas, who might have been conciliated and attached to our side. . . . You know what was the almost unanimous desire of the Republicans of other states; and you spurned and insulted them. Now go ahead and fight it through. You are in for it." "There seems to be a considerable notion pervading the brains of political wet-nurses at the East, that the barbarians of Illinois cannot take care of themselves," editorialized the *Tribune* in reply.

Lincoln monitored the situation closely, writing Washburne on April 26 that an informant had told him of a rumor, that a Republican congressman sent private letters of support on behalf of Douglas, identifying Washburne as the turncoat, and that a number of Chicago Republicans had also communicated to Lincoln as well that Washburne was the culprit, but that Lincoln believed no such thing. "I am satisfied you have done no wrong," he wrote. If Washburne was promoting Douglas, there was no more evidence of the effort from him or another mysterious congressman. On May 27, Lincoln wrote Washburne again, reporting that Herndon had gotten information from Medill, expressing "great alarm at the prospect of North Republicans going over to Douglas." Lincoln, however, couldn't assess exactly what Douglas was calculating. "There certainly is a double game being played some how," he wrote. But he added, "Unless he plays his double game more successfully than we have often seen done, he cannot carry many Republicans North, without at the same time losing a larger number of his old friends South."

Another of Lincoln's regular informants was Charles L. Wilson, editor of the *Chicago Journal,* who on May 31 sent him a clipping of an article reporting that some supporters of Seward were backing Douglas. In reply, on June 1, Lincoln evaluated the motives and actions of the Eastern Republicans: "I have believed—I do believe now—that Greeley, for instance, would be rather pleased to see Douglas reflected over me or any other Republican; and yet I do not believe it is so because of any secret arrangement with Douglas. It is because he thinks Douglas's superior position, reputation, experience, ability, if you please, would more than compensate for his lack of a pure Republican position, and therefore his reflection do the general cause of Republicanism more good than would the election of any one of our better undistinguished pure Republicans. . . . He denies that he directly is taking part in favor of Douglas, and I believe him. Still his feeling constantly manifests itself in his paper, which, being so extensively read in Illinois, is, and will continue to be, a drag upon us. I have also thought that Governor Seward, too, feels about as Greeley does."

Lincoln did more than gather political intelligence. He had always favored party conventions since he had tried to win his first nomination for the Congress in 1843. Now he devised a plan to use the crucible of party politics as an instrument of innovation. Senators, of course, were chosen by state legislatures, and campaigns, such as they were, were conducted behind the scenes and within its chambers after popular election of its members. Douglas's shape-shifting after coming out against the Lecompton Constitution, the cavalier interference of Eastern Republicans, and the reaction against them from Illinois Republicans prompted Lincoln to set in motion a daring new process—a public campaign for senator before the state legislature was elected. The effect would be to turn the legislature into a sort of Electoral College, ratifying the voters' choice.

"My judgment is that we must never sell old friends to buy old enemies," Lincoln wrote one of his most loyal political allies, the Illinois secretary of state, Ozias M. Hatch, on March 24. "Let us have a State convention, in which we can have a full consultation: and till which, let us all stand firm, making no committals, as to strange and new combinations." Soon, meeting in Chicago, the state Republican Party central committee ratified Lincoln's idea and fixed the event for June 16 in Springfield. Nearly every one of the state's one hundred counties held conventions proclaiming support for Lincoln and electing delegates. Herndon raced from county to county, convention to convention. (Among those helping behind the scenes was Hatch's young elections clerk, a former newspaper editor, John Nicolay, who would become Lincoln's assistant in the White House.)

Douglas staged a convention of his own in Springfield on April 21, establishing his control over his state party in an internecine battle with Buchanan loyalists, but also signaling he would not switch parties. Thirty Republicans leaders from the far corners of the state met immediately afterward in Springfield to affirm their support for Lincoln. "A word about the conventions," Lincoln wrote Washburne on April 26. "The democracy parted in not a very encouraged state of mind. On the contrary, our friends, a good many of whom were present, parted in high spirits. They think if we do not triumph the fault will be our own, and so I really think."

The factional divisions between Old Whigs and abolitionists that had plagued the Republican Party since its creation two years earlier, however, suddenly flared again. Judge David Davis was never reconciled to the election of Owen Lovejoy to the Congress. He and his coterie on the Eighth Judicial Circuit, Lincoln's inner circle, plotted against Lovejoy. Their justification was that Lovejoy would alienate Old Whig voters in the central part of the state and cost Lincoln the election. Yet if they succeeded in ousting Lovejoy they might cost Lincoln the election by alienating voters in the northern part. Lincoln, learning of his friends' plans, confidentially warned Lovejoy. "I have just returned from court in one of the counties of your District, where I had an inside view that few will have who correspond with you; and I feel it rather a duty to say a word to you about it," he wrote on March 8. "Your danger *has been* that democracy would wheedle some republican to run against you without a nomination, relying mainly on democratic votes. I have seen the strong men who could make the most trouble in that way, and find that they view the thing in the proper light, and will not consent to be so used. But they have been urgently tempted by the enemy; and I think it is still the point for you to guard most vigilantly. I think it is not expected that you can be beaten for a nomination; but do not let what I say, as to that, lull you." He added a request for secrecy. "Now, let this be strictly confidential; not that there is anything wrong in it; but that I have some highly valued friends who would not like me any the better for writing it."

In May, Lyle Dickey's son-in-law, W.H.L. Wallace, announced he would run against Lovejoy. He believed that he could win enough county conventions to topple the incumbent. Judge Davis decided that he should explore the possibility of becoming a candidate against Lovejoy himself. He dispatched Ward Hill Lamon, one of Lincoln's closest friends, to Champaign County to survey the political ground. Old Whigs encouraged Davis to run. But word leaked out. The *Chicago Tribune* lambasted his stealth campaign. "Judge Davis . . . has no more sympathy with the vitalizing principle of the Republican party than an Egyptian mummy. He was among the bolters in '56 and refused to vote for Lovejoy." Davis's hopes quickly died when the McLean County Republican convention, his own county, rejected him for Lovejoy. "I believe the whole country is fast going to the Devil," Lamon wailed to Lincoln. "Judge Davis is, of course, out of the field." Lincoln replied to Lamon on June 11 that his view "remains unchanged that running an independent candidate against Lovejoy, will not do—that it will result in nothing but disaster all round." He explained that the anti-Lovejoy gesture would only backfire. "In the first place whoever so runs will be beaten, and will be spotted for life; in the second place, while the race is in progress, he will be under the strongest temptation to trade with the democrats, and to favor the election of certain of their friends to the Legislature; thirdly, I shall be held responsible for it, and Republican members of the Legislature, who are partial to Lovejoy, will, for that, oppose me; and lastly it will in the end lose us the District altogether." He urged Lamon and the others to support Lovejoy. To ameliorate the damage to Davis, Lincoln wrote an anonymous article for the *Chicago Tribune* under the pseudonym of "A Republican," who was identified as his friend "for many years." "I am certain that no plot or movement against Lovejoy's re-nomination was led on by him, or that he was cognizant of anything of the kind. . . . I believe he did not vote for Lovejoy in 1856. . . . As to the approaching canvas, Judge Davis expects Lovejoy to be nominated, and intends to vote for him, and has so stated without hesitation or reserve." Lincoln quoted Davis, "the substance if not the exact words": " 'No, gentlemen,' said the Judge, 'I will not lend my sanction to any such movement. If Mr. L. is nominated it is the duty of all good republicans to give him their support.' " On June 7, Davis wrote W.H.L. Wallace on "our failure." "The Abolition element is successful here and very proscriptive. They are entirely in the ascendency. . . . Is there any hope? . . . If it were not for saving Lincoln for United States Senate a pretty great outbreak would follow. I don't believe Lovejoy can be beaten if nominated and there is no use of bolting."

Lincoln began work on his acceptance speech for the convention, scratching out fragments and phrases on scraps of paper and the back of envelopes, stuffing some of them into his stovetop hat for safekeeping. Spreading his notes on his desk, he carefully composed his text. When Jesse Dubois dropped in the office and asked Lincoln what he was doing, he was shooed away. "I'll not let you see it now," Lincoln said. He wanted more than to preserve his unbroken concentration. Dubois was among Lincoln's more conservative friends and Lincoln did not want to hear a preemptive negative comment. In early June, he called Herndon into his office, locked the door and drew the curtain over the glass window. Then he read his speech, stopping at the end of his first paragraph, waiting for the reaction.

This is the paragraph Lincoln read to him: "If we could first know where we are, and whither we are tending, we could better judge what to do, and how to do it. We are now far into the fifth year since a policy was initiated with the avowed object and confident promise of putting an end to slavery agitation. Under the operation of that policy, that agitation has not only not ceased, but has constantly augmented. In my opinion, it will not cease until a crisis shall have been reached and passed. *'A house divided against itself cannot stand.'* I believe this government cannot endure permanently half slave and half free. I do not expect the Union to be dissolved; I do not expect the house to fall; but I do expect it will cease to be divided. It will become all one thing, or all the other."

"It is true, but is it wise or politic to say so?" Herndon replied. Lincoln knew his partner's political leanings and that he was likely to approve. Indeed, on June 1, Herndon had written Parker, "I will do all I can to hold the leader's hands up." But upon hearing Lincoln say, *"A house divided against itself cannot stand,"* Herndon hesitated and wondered aloud whether Lincoln was being prudent. Selected as Lincoln's audience of one for this rehearsal, he should have known that Lincoln was determined to utter that phrase. Herndon knew that was not the first time Lincoln had inserted it into a speech. Lincoln had first used the biblical injunction of "a house divided" fifteen years earlier, in 1843, in a Whig circular, warning against party disunity. Lincoln had tried the phrase "half slave and half free" on the conservative Old Whig Judge T. Lyle Dickey in 1854, shortly after Douglas introduced his Kansas-Nebraska Act, early one morning, when they shared a bedroom on the court circuit. "Oh, Lincoln," Dickey admonished, "go to sleep." He had written the Kentucky judge, George Robertson, on August 15, 1855, "Can we, as a nation, continue together permanently—forever—half slave, and half free?" He had used the line "a house divided, half slave, half free," in his rousing Bloomington convention speech, according to Dickey, who was present.

Now Lincoln told Herndon he would not be stopped from using the provocative phrases. "That expression is a truth of all human experience, 'a house divided against itself cannot stand,' and 'he that runs may read,'" he said. "The proposition also is true, and has been for six thousand years. I want to use some universally known figure expressed in simple language as universally well-known, that may strike home to the minds of men in order to raise them up to the peril of the times. I do not believe I would be right in changing or omitting it. I would rather be defeated with this expression in the speech, and uphold and discuss it before the people, than be victorious without it."

In a speech in Cincinnati, on September 17, 1859, he attributed "the enviable or unenviable distinction of having first expressed that idea" to an editorial published on May 6, 1856, in the *Richmond Enquirer,* a paper that Lincoln clipped and whose lead editorialist, George Fitzhugh, wrote a proslavery tract, *Sociology for the South, or The Failure of Free Society,* published in 1854, that particularly antagonized him. The *Enquirer* editorial stated, "Social forms so widely differing as those of domestic slavery and (attempted) universal liberty cannot long co-exist in the Great Republic of Christendom. They cannot be equally adapted to the wants and interests of society. Two opposite and conflicting forms of society cannot, among civilized men, coexist and endure. The one must give way and cease to exist; the other become universal. If free society be unnatural, immoral, unchristian, it must fall, and give way to slave society—a social system old as the world, universal as man." This Southern version of "a house divided" was a proslavery polemic.

The parable of a "house divided" had its origins in the Gospels of Matthew, Mark, and Luke. In the biblical prophecies the house divided "cannot stand," "is laid waste," and "falls." According to Matthew, Jesus' presence creates the division: "He that is not with me is against me; and he that gathereth not with me scattereth abroad." In Mark, Jesus divides his family into those that follow him and those that do not. In Luke, Jesus sets fathers against sons and mothers against daughters, and that verse is preceded by Jesus' warning: "Suppose ye that I am come to give peace on earth? I tell you, Nay; but rather division."

Lincoln knew the King James Bible as well as he knew Shakespeare. He clarified what he meant by the "house divided" in the lines he read next to Herndon: "Either the opponents of slavery will arrest the further spread of it, and place it where the public mind shall rest in the belief that it is in the course of ultimate extinction, or its advocates will push it forward till it shall become alike lawful in all the States, old as well as new, North as well as South."

Lincoln had quoted Fitzhugh since the publication of his book in 1854 to make his point that proslavery forces did not have limited aims but intended to transform the whole nation into a slavery society. After Taney's decision in Dred Scott, Lincoln had more than a book and newspaper editorials to underscore his argument; he had a Supreme Court ruling to illustrate the boundless design of the Slave Power. So, he read Herndon his next line: "Have we no tendency to the latter condition?"

Just before the convention, Lincoln held a rehearsal, inviting about a dozen of his advisers and friends to the law library at the State House. Upon finishing his reading, they were unanimous—Lincoln must not give the speech. One gently told him it was "ahead of its time." Another, less kindly, called it a "damned fool utterance." Lincoln turned to Herndon. "Lincoln," Herndon said, "deliver that speech as read and it will make you president." Lincoln stood up from his chair and, according to Herndon, declared, "Friends, this thing has been retarded long enough. The time has come when these sentiments should be uttered; and if it is decreed that I should go down because of this speech, then let me go down linked to the truth—let me die in the advocacy of what is just and right." Whether through the prism of Herndon's memory this was an accurate rendering of Lincoln's words, though two other witnesses claim they were, Lincoln was set on delivering the speech.

The Republican convention gathered in Springfield on June 16 to nominate its full slate of candidates. Charles L. Wilson, editor of the *Chicago Jour-*

nal, also a delegate, submitted a resolution "greeted with shouts of applause, and unanimously adopted: Resolved, That Abraham Lincoln is the first and only choice of the Republicans of Illinois for the United States Senate, as the successor of Stephen A. Douglas."

The next night, before perspiring delegates packed into the Hall of the House of Representatives, who "all felt like exploding . . . with electric bolts, shivering what we struck," according to Herndon, Lincoln spoke deliberately in his high-pitched voice, stressing key words he had underlined. His speech had a familiar timbre to his listeners. Its opening and closing echoed the language, including a number of the same words, of one of the best-known orations of the day, Daniel Webster's "Second Reply to Hayne," the Massachusetts senator's speech in 1830 in defense of the federal union and American nationalism against Senator Robert Y. Hayne of South Carolina's advocacy of states' rights. One account of Lincoln's "Lost Speech" at Bloomington reported that he had ended by directly quoting Webster's ringing conclusion: "Liberty *and* Union, now and forever, one and inseparable!" (In his speech, Webster also referred to "the people's Constitution, the people's government, made for the people, made by the people, and answerable to the people.")

Once he had uttered the words of a "house divided" and explained their meaning as the limitless ambition of slavery, Lincoln laid out an overarching political history since 1854 that placed Douglas at the center of intrigue. "Let any one who doubts, carefully contemplate that now almost complete legal combination—piece of *machinery* so to speak—compounded of the Nebraska doctrine, and the Dred Scott decision. Let him consider not only *what work* the machinery is adapted to do, and *how well* adapted; but also, let him study the *history* of its construction, and trace, if he can, or rather *fail,* if he can, to trace the evidences of design, and concert of action, among its chief bosses, from the beginning."

Lincoln started his story with Douglas's Kansas-Nebraska Act, which "opened all the national territory to slavery; and was the first point gained." Buchanan's election was "the second point gained," but "not overwhelmingly reliable and satisfactory" because he failed to win a popular majority of the votes. The Dred Scott decision immediately followed. Douglas endorsed it. Buchanan and Douglas, however, fell into "a squabble" over Lecompton, centered "on the *mere* question of *fact,* whether the Lecompton constitution was or was not, in any just sense, made by the people of Kansas; and in that squabble the latter declares that all he wants is a fair vote for the people, and that he *cares* not whether slavery be voted *down* or voted *up*." Douglas's indifference to slavery, his "care not policy, constitute the piece of machinery, in its *present* state of advancement. This was the third point gained." Douglas throughout, despite his quarrel with Buchanan, was consistent in his political motive "to *educate* and *mould* public opinion, at least *Northern* public opinion, to not *care* whether slavery is voted *down* or voted *up*. This shows exactly where we now *are*; and *partially* also, whither we are tending."

Lincoln raised the suspicion of collusion surrounding the Dred Scott case that Seward had framed. "Why the delay of a reargument? Why the incoming President's *advance* exhortation in favor of the decision?" The incident was merely one in a series. He explained that the events of the past few years were not random or coincidental but could in hindsight be understood as planned.

> We cannot absolutely know that all these exact adaptations are the result of preconcert. But when we see a lot of framed timbers, different portions of which we know have been gotten out at different times and places and by different workmen,—Stephen, Franklin, Roger and James, for instance,—and when we see these timbers joined together, and see they exactly make the frame of a house or a mill, all the tenons and mortises exactly fitting, and all the lengths and proportions of the different pieces exactly adapted to their respective places, and not a piece too many or too few—not omitting even scaffolding—or, if a single piece be lacking, we see the place in the frame exactly fitted and prepared yet to bring such piece in—in such a case, we find it impossible not to believe that Stephen and Franklin and Roger and James all understood one another from the beginning, and all worked upon a common plan or draft drawn up before the first lick was struck.

Lincoln had a subtle and practical political mind with an insight into human nature and an aversion to grand theories. He underplayed the factors of personality he knew inflected the politics—Douglas's overweening ambition and reckless risk taking, Pierce's pathos and malleability, Taney's choleric and sclerotic rigidities, and Buchanan's pomposity and vanity. To be sure, there was collusion, more than was known at the time, such as Buchanan's intervention with the Supreme Court on Dred Scott. But in his willingness to propound his conspiracy theory, Lincoln proved something else, that most Republicans also believed in it.

Lincoln explained the endgame of all the planning, the ultimate goal to be "gained," was the transformation of the whole of the United States into a slave nation. If Douglas were to be followed that is how the "house divided" would become "all one thing, or the other." "We shall lie down pleasantly dreaming that the people of Missouri are on the verge of making their State free," said Lincoln, "and we shall awake to the reality instead that the Supreme Court has made Illinois a Slave State. To meet and overthrow the power of that dynasty is the work now before all those who would prevent that consummation. That is what we have to do. How can we best do it?"

Standing before his most ardent supporters, Lincoln spoke beyond them to the Eastern Republicans who "yet whisper us softly, that Senator Douglas is the aptest instrument." Douglas could not possibly be their champion, for he did not believe in their case at all. "Judge Douglas, if not a dead lion, for this work is at least a caged and toothless one. How can he oppose the advances of slavery? He don't care anything about it. His avowed mission is impressing the 'public heart' to *care nothing about it*." Lincoln acknowledged that a man might change his position, but Douglas had not done that except by "vague inference," and that was hardly a principled basis for embracing him.

Lincoln drew a line in the sand that was a moral test for the Eastern Republicans. "But clearly, he is not now with us—he does not pretend to be—he does not promise ever to be." Lincoln would not allow the Eastern Republicans to define Republicanism. He would set the standard for them. Had they fought to become Republicans only to surrender "our great cause" for the false promise of a false leader?

Lincoln's peroration was as literary and political in his sources as his opening was biblical. He appealed to Republicans as Henry V did to his band of brothers in Shakespeare's St. Crispin's Day speech. He called on "hands" and "hearts," tropes that run through Shakespeare's romances and tragedies. He summoned "the four winds," the four humors of Shakespeare's storms, and held up "fire" as the element for forging a new army. He borrowed from Webster's "Second Reply to Hayne" the words "dissevered," "discordant," and "belligerent"—Webster in his grandeur who described the nightmare of "the broken and dishonored fragments of a once glorious Union; on States dissevered, discordant, belligerent; on a land rent with civil feuds, or drenched, it may be, in fraternal blood!"

"Our cause, then," Lincoln said, "must be entrusted to, and conducted by, its own undoubted friends—those whose hands are free, whose hearts are in the work, who *do care* for the result. Two years ago the Republicans of the nation mustered over thirteen hundred thousand strong. We did this under the single impulse of resistance to a common danger, with every external circumstance against us. Of strange, discordant, and even hostile elements, we gathered from the four winds, and formed and fought the battle through, under the constant hot fire of a disciplined, proud and pampered enemy. Did we brave all then, to falter now,—now, when that same enemy is wavering, dissevered and belligerent? The result is not doubtful. We shall not fail; if we stand firm, we *shall not fail*. Wise counsels may accelerate, or mistakes delay it, but sooner or later, the victory is sure to come."

Immediately after concluding his speech to the "wildest enthusiasm," he handed his text to the *Chicago Journal*'s correspondent, Horace White, for publication, joining him later that evening in the *Illinois State Journal*'s composing room to correct page proofs, and regaling him with the story of how his friends had tried to get him to leave out his statement about a "house divided." Newspapers across the state printed the speech in full. "Masterly," the *Chicago Tribune* called it. The Republican State Committee circulated thousands of copies as a pamphlet. And, a week after Lincoln delivered the speech, the *New York Tribune* published it in its entirety under the headline: "REPUBLICAN PRINCIPLES." Greeley stopped promoting Douglas's Senate bid.

But John L. Scripps of the *Chicago Tribune* warned Lincoln on June 22 that his talk of a "house divided" and the "ultimate extinction" of slavery put off conservative voters. "Some of my Kentucky friends who want to be Republicans, but who are afraid we are not sufficiently conservative, who are also somewhat afraid of our name, but who hate 'Locofocoism' {democrats} most cordially, have objected to the following on the ground of its 'ultraism.'" Scripps suggested to Lincoln it would be "advisable" to tell those voters he was not for "political warfare under legal forms against slavery in the States."

A few weeks later, Norman Judd conferred with Lincoln about printing the speech. "Well Lincoln," he said, "had I seen that speech I would have made you strike out that house divided part." "You would—would you Judd," Lincoln replied.

"The first ten lines of that speech defeated him for the Senate," insisted Leonard Swett. "It was a speech made at the commencement of a campaign and apparently made for the campaign. Viewing it in this light, nothing could have been more unfortunate or inappropriate. It was saying the wrong thing first, yet he saw it was an abstract truth, and standing by the speech would ultimately find him in the right place."

Swett recalled, "In the Summer of 1859 when Lincoln was dining with a party of his intimate friends at Bloomington the subject of his Springfield speech was raised. We all insisted it was a great mistake, but he justified himself, and finally said, 'Well Gentlemen, you may think that Speech was a mistake, but I never have believed it was, and you will see the day when you will consider it was the wisest thing I ever said.'"

But opinion at the time was divided.

THE HIGHER OBJECT

The Little Giant staged his heroic return to Chicago to launch his campaign on July 9. He proudly wore the badges of an infidel, apostate, and heretic. He bore the *Washington Union*'s labels of "traitor" and "renegade." "Kill him off," editorialized the pro-administration *Indianapolis Sentinel,* an organ of Jesse Bright. "Neither the frowns of power nor the influences of patronage will change my action, or drive me from my principles," Douglas told the Senate on March 22. Though nearly endorsing the English bill—a spectacular bribe of millions of acres in land grants to settlers only if the proslavery Lecompton Constitution was accepted—a moment of private indecision that few knew about, he decided his best strategy was to run on defiance.

Abraham Lincoln, 1858

"The whole thing was of course 'spontaneous,'" reported the pro-Lincoln *Chicago Tribune,* "the program having been advertised for several days in the columns of a newspaper and a special train having been chartered to add to the enthusiasm of the masses." Douglas arrived in the evening at the central depot to the firing of artillery, and then proceeded in a carriage drawn by six horses in a grand procession led by bands and two companies of militia, under banners strung across the streets lighted with extra gas lamps, to the downtown Tremont House, where he mounted the balcony to address the crowd. "I regard, therefore," he declared about the struggle over Lecompton, "the great principle of Popular Sovereignty as having been vindicated and made triumphant."

Douglas turned to the task at hand, cutting apart his opponent. "In the first place," he said, "he sets out in his speech to say, quoting from Scripture, that a house divided against itself cannot stand. . . . He advocates, boldly and clearly, a war of sections—a war of the North against the South—of the free States against the slave States—a war of extermination to be continued relentlessly until the one or the other shall be universal, and all the States shall either become free or become slave."

Douglas also charged that his opponent "goes for a warfare upon the Supreme Court of the United States, because of their Judicial decision. . . . He objects to the Dred Scott decision because it does not put the negro in possession of the rights of citizenship on an equality with the white man. I am utterly opposed to negro equality with white men. I repeat, that this nation is a nation of white people, a people composed of European descendants, a people that have established this government for themselves and their posterity, and I am in favor of preserving not only the purity of their blood, but the purity of the government from all mixed races or amalgamations."

Lincoln's talk of "a house divided" had "totally misapprehended the great principle upon which our government rests." Lincoln was proposing "that all States must be free or all must be slave," which would be "despotism." Lincoln would destroy the idea that "this Government of ours is founded on a white basis. It was made by white men for the benefit of white men, to be administered by white men in such a manner as they should determine"—a government of white men, for white men, by white men.

Lincoln, who had accused Douglas of being at the center of a conspiracy, was the perpetrator of a conspiracy—"an unholy, unnatural alliance . . . with men who are trying to divide the Democratic Party for the purpose of electing a Republican senator in my place, are just as much the agents and tools of the supporters of Mr. Lincoln."

"Thus," said Douglas, "you have the outline of the propositions which I intend to discuss before the people of Illinois during the coming campaign."

As soon as he left the balcony, a few shouts from the crowd rang out.

"Lincoln! Lincoln!" Lincoln was there, standing amidst the throng, listening to Douglas's stem-winding speech. In Chicago that day to argue a case before the federal court, Lincoln positioned himself beneath the hotel balcony to listen to Douglas. While Lincoln may have turned up by coincidence it had long been his custom to stalk Douglas. His tactic was to take advantage of crowds that had been initially attracted by Douglas. Once again, this was his plan. "My recent experience shows that speaking at the same place the next day after D. is the very thing," Lincoln explained later that year. Just before he began speaking, Douglas spotted him and invited him to sit near him. Lincoln demurred. He would speak tomorrow. The band played the "Marseillaise," barrels of tar were ignited that shot up flames, and fireworks set off, spelling in the sky: "POPULAR SOVEREIGNTY."

Embattled on all sides, at war with the administration, and challenged by a rival raised from the political dead, the campaign was a referendum on Douglas. The leading man of his party, fighting for his political life, basked in his controversy. Douglas loved drama, being the center of attention at dinner parties or in crowds, talking, backslapping, deal-making, eating, drinking, storytelling. Drawing a worthy opponent only magnified the Little Giant's stature.

Every faction on every side understood that the game was about the succession to the White House. All played with the intensity of a presidential contest. Local politics were waged for national stakes. Both candidates confronted a politics of contradictions. Douglas sought to hold his base within his fractious party and at the same time soften Republican ranks through his antagonism with Buchanan, while also winning over Old Whigs still upset at the rise of abolitionists among the Republicans. Lincoln sought to split off Buchanan Democrats who hated the enemy within more than the one at the gates at the same time he solidified the Republican coalition by unmasking Douglas as unprincipled on slavery. Even before Douglas began his campaign to defend his seat, he rose in the Senate to charge that he was the target of "an unscrupulous coalition" of Buchanan Democrats and Republicans. He had reason to fear such an alliance.

In early July, Lincoln met with Colonel John Dougherty, the National Democratic candidate for state treasurer, and told him, "If you do this the thing is settled—the battle is fought." Herndon served as intermediary to the "Buchaneers," connected through his brother Elliott Herndon, who was editor of the *Illinois State Democrat* in Springfield, and his father, Archie

Herndon, also an influential Buchanan Democrat. Everyone involved understood the value of compartmentalized knowledge. "Lincoln," Herndon wrote Trumbull on June 24, ". . . does not know the details of how we get along. I do, but he does not."

Douglas's paper, the *Chicago Times,* launched its first salvo at Lincoln, who had criticized the Mexican War when he was a congressman a decade earlier. The *Times* falsely stated he pledged to "refuse to vote one dollar to feed, clothe, or minister to the wants of the sick and dying volunteers from my own State, who are suffering in Mexico. Let them die like dogs!" Another Democratic newspaper called Lincoln "a friend of the 'greasers' " and "apologist of Mexico" who "pandered to [the] greasers' profit and advantage." The *Register* picked up the smear that Lincoln gave "aid and comfort" to the enemy. Lincoln gave the *Chicago Tribune* information on his consistent votes for military appropriations in order to rebut the "intense meanness." Henry C. Whitney told him the accusation was "the most potent and dangerous weapon that can be used against you in the rural districts."

The day after Douglas's conquering entrance into Chicago, on July 10, Lincoln spoke from the same hotel balcony. Point by point he sought to answer Douglas, starting with the accusation that there was an alliance between Buchanan Democrats and Republicans. It "depends," Lincoln said, "upon what may be a right definition of the term 'alliance.' " After critiques of popular sovereignty and the Lecompton Constitution, Lincoln defended his use of the phrase "house divided," reading the whole section. "I am quoting from my speech"—and referring back and forth to Douglas's criticisms. "In this paragraph which I have quoted in your hearing, and to which I ask the attention of all . . ."

Justifying his "house divided" speech, Lincoln self-deprecatingly presented himself as Douglas's inferior. "I am not master of language," he said. "I have not a fine education; I am not capable of entering into a disquisition upon dialectics, as I believe you call it; but I do not believe the language I employed bears any such construction as Judge Douglas put upon it. But I don't care about a quibble in regard to words. I know what I meant, and I will not leave this crowd in doubt, if I can explain it to them, what I really meant in the use of that paragraph."

He argued defensively, repeating himself. "I am not, in the first place, unaware that this government has endured eighty-two years, half slave and half free. I know that. I am tolerably well acquainted with the history of the country, and I know that it has endured eighty-two years, half slave and half free." And then in the next line his speech moved to another plane: "I *believe*—and that is what I meant to allude to there—I *believe* it has endured because, during all that time, until the introduction of the Nebraska Bill, the public mind did rest, all the time, in the belief that slavery was in course of ultimate extinction."

Lincoln explained himself clearly without hesitation. "I have always hated slavery, I think as much as any Abolitionist. I have been an Old Line Whig. I have always hated it, but I have always been quiet about it until this new era of the introduction of the Nebraska Bill began. I always believed that everybody was against it, and that it was in course of ultimate extinction."

He protested Douglas's distortion of his position. "Judge Douglas has heard me say it—if not quite a hundred times, at least as good as a hundred times; and when it is said that I am in favor of interfering with slavery where it exists . . ." Lincoln's position for not intervening against slavery in the South was the same as virtually every political antislavery advocate from Seward to Chase, from Sumner to Hale.

Lincoln put Douglas in a special category of moral vacuity. He engaged Douglas on the ground where Douglas never ventured—slavery as a moral question.

> He looks upon it as being an exceedingly little thing—only equal to the question of the cranberry laws of Indiana—as something having no moral question in it—as something on a par with the question of whether a man shall pasture his land with cattle, or plant it with tobacco—so little and so small a thing, that he concludes, if I could desire that anything should be done to bring about the ultimate extinction of that little thing, I must be in favor of bringing about an amalgamation of all the other little things in the Union. Now, it so happens—and there, I presume, is the foundation of this mistake—that the Judge thinks thus; and it so happens that there is a vast portion of the American people that do *not* look upon that matter as being this very little thing. They look upon it as a vast moral evil; they can prove it is such by the writings of those who gave us the blessings of liberty which we enjoy, and that they so looked upon it, and not as an evil merely confining itself to the States where it is situated; and while we agree that, by the Constitution we assented to, in the States where it exists we have no right to interfere with it because it is in the Constitution and we are by

both duty and inclination to stick by that Constitution in all its letter and spirit from beginning to end.

Then he held Douglas up to ridicule for his sexual hysteria, "his passion for drawing inferences that are not warranted. I protest, now and forever against that counterfeit logic which presume that because I do not want a negro woman for a slave, I do necessarily want her for a wife."

In the midst of a description of the patriotic celebration of the Fourth of July, Lincoln made his most memorable public statement against nativism. He had always been opposed to the Know Nothing Party, but he had expressed his strong sentiments privately. In the founding of the Illinois Republican Party he had been instrumental in passing resolutions against nativism, but he had not shown himself acting in front of the curtain. After the election of 1856 in which the Republican Party cohered, the Know Nothings mostly fragmented and dissolved organizationally. Yet nativism remained a virulent strain coursing through politics. He remained fixed on bringing the Know Nothings into the Republican coalition. He also wanted to appeal to the immigrants, especially the Germans, who had become a significant and essential constituency for the Republicans. Lincoln had been subdued on the subject, but now he spoke. Commemorating the Fourth of July and the Declaration of Independence required, he said, including the immigrants.

> We have besides these men—descended by blood from our ancestors— among us perhaps half our people who are not descendants at all of these men, they are men who have come from EuropeGerman, Irish, French and Scandinavian—men that have come from Europe themselves, or whose an- cestors have come hither and settled here, finding themselves our equals in all things. If they look back through this history to trace their connec- tion with those days by blood, they find they have none, they cannot carry themselves back into that glorious epoch and make themselves feel that they are part of us, but when they look through that old Declaration of Inde- pendence they find that those old men say that 'We hold these truths to be self-evident, that all men are created equal,' and then they feel that that moral sentiment taught in that day evidences their relation to those men, that it is the father of all moral principle in them, and that they have a right to claim it as though they were blood of the blood, and flesh of the flesh of the men who wrote that Declaration, and so they are. That is the electric

cord in that Declaration that links the hearts of patriotic and liberty-loving men together, that will link those patriotic hearts as long as the love of freedom exists in the minds of men throughout the world.

But that was not his conclusion. He carried the logic of the Declaration of Independence through the immigrants to the slaves, from a refutation of nativism to a condemnation of slavery.

> Those arguments that are made, that the inferior race are to be treated with as much allowance as they are capable of enjoying; that as much is to be done for them as their condition will allow. What are these arguments? They are the arguments that kings have made for enslaving the people in all ages of the world. You will find that all the arguments in favor of king-craft were of this class; they always bestrode the necks of the people, not that they wanted to do it, but because the people were better off for being ridden. That is their argument, and this argument of the Judge is the same old serpent that says you work and I eat, you toil and I will enjoy the fruits of it. Turn in whatever way you will—whether it come from the mouth of a King, an excuse for enslaving the people of his country, or from the mouth of men of one race as a reason for enslaving the men of another race, it is all the same old serpent, and I hold if that course of argumentation that is made for the purpose of convincing the public mind that we should not care about this, should be granted, it does not stop with the negro.

"My friend has said to me that I am a poor hand to quote Scripture." But Douglas's position would allow the creation of "one universal slave nation. He is one that runs in that direction, and as such I resist him."

Lincoln closed with an appeal to equality. "My friends, I have detained you about as long as I desired to do, and I have only to say, let us discard all this quibbling about this man and the other man—this race and that race and the other race being inferior, and therefore they must be placed in an inferior position—discarding our standard that we have left us. Let us discard all these things, and unite as one people throughout this land, until we shall once more stand up declaring that all men are created equal."

Lincoln looked to the crowd for a reaction but the crowd had turned completely quiet. There was no applause. Lincoln's talk of race and equality, sounding like that of a radical abolitionist, had reduced his audience to silence. So, he declared, he had reached his end. "My friends, I could not, without launching off upon some new topic, which would detain you too long, continue tonight."

"Disgusting," declared the *Chicago Times.* The *New York Herald* described Lincoln as Douglas's "nigger worshipping competitor" speaking the "most repulsive disunion nigger equality principles and doctrines." The *Register* stated, "Lincoln takes bold and unqualified ground with Lovejoy and ultra-abolitionism." The abolitionist *Chicago Congregational Herald,* however, called him "a champion." The *New York Times* and the *New York Tribune* reprinted the speech in full from the *Chicago Tribune,* Lincoln's greatest national exposure. A number of Republicans worried he had gone too far. "The only trouble will be (as I told him)," Norman B. Judd wrote Trumbull, "he will allow Douglas to put him on the defensive." Joseph Gillespie, an old Lincoln friend, who had belonged to the Know Nothings, running now as a Republican for the legislature, wrote Lincoln a "doleful letter" that he was "scared" the Know Nothings were going for Douglas. "Don't fail to check the stampede at once," Lincoln urged.

Douglas began a triumphant procession from Chicago to Springfield in a private train car bedecked with banners and flags and accompanied by his wife, aides, Democratic officials, and members of the press. Douglas's luxurious train car was provided courtesy of one his enthusiastic supporters, the Illinois Central's superintendent, George B. McClellan. Douglas stopped in Joliet and then Bloomington, where he gibed at Lincoln for asserting that blacks were equal "under the law," which he claimed proved his point about "amalgamation." Lincoln was divisive, while Douglas stood for national unity. "I tell you, my friends, it is impossible under our institutions to force slavery on an unwilling people."

Lincoln took the same train from Chicago but sat in a common car. "Lincoln was perhaps the only Lincoln man on the train," recalled the *Chicago Times* editor James Sheahan. He was following Douglas as a tactic to get him to "divide time," to debate him from the same platform. At Bloomington, Lincoln stood in the crowd on the railroad platform, but visibly identifiable, and was given a spot up front by Douglas. He joined Douglas's train the next day as a passenger, still stalking him. When the train pulled into Springfield, Douglas disembarked to address a large crowd, to deliver his developing stump speech deriding Lincoln and proclaiming his faith in popular sovereignty. Lincoln, carrying his suitcase and umbrella, went off to prepare his response in a speech that evening.

On July 17, Lincoln delivered another stem-winder that began with yet another self-deprecating comparison of himself with Douglas—Douglas "of world wide renown; Douglas who looked upon "certainly, at no distant day, the President of the United States"; Douglas "in his round, jolly, fruitful face, post offices, land offices, marshalships and cabinet appointments, chargeships and foreign missions, bursting and sprouting out in wonderful exuberance ready to be laid hold of" by the "greedy hands" of his supporters; Douglas, who was given "marches, triumphal entries and receptions . . ." And then there was, alas, Lincoln. "On the contrary nobody has ever expected me to be President. In my poor, lean, lank, face, nobody has ever seen that any cabbages were sprouting out." He drew a laugh from the crowd. "These are disadvantages all, taken together, that the Republicans labor under. We have to fight this battle upon principle, and upon principle alone."

The *Chicago Times* compared Lincoln's "poor, lean, lank" self-pity to that of Dickens's figure of unctuous hypocrisy Uriah Heep. The *Illinois State Register* was so delighted it published Lincoln's speech in full next to Douglas's and asked readers to compare the two to Douglas's advantage.

The Republican State Committee summoned Lincoln to an emergency meeting in Chicago on July 22. Lincoln's campaign manager and party chairman, Norman B. Judd, was receiving reports from around the state that Lincoln's support was faltering. His gambit of trailing after Douglas diminished him. Douglas was succeeding in tainting him as a proponent of "negro equality." Lincoln's recent speeches, taking Douglas's bait, had made him vulnerable, as though he were an abolitionist. Judd was determined to put Lincoln under the State Committee's "intellectual guardianship," monitoring "every word, every thought, every argument he utters." The members of the State Committee had not liked his "house divided" statement from the start.

The day of the State Committee meeting, the *Chicago Tribune,* the committee's sounding board, ran an editorial advocating a series of candidate debates. Before Lincoln had arrived to discuss the matter, it was settled for him. On July 24, Lincoln wrote Douglas proposing the idea. "Will it be agreeable to you to make an arrangement for you and myself to divide time, and address the same audiences during the present canvass?"

Douglas was hesitant. "The whole country knows me and has me measured," he wrote a friend. "Lincoln, as regards myself, is comparatively unknown, and if he gets the best of this debate—and I want to say he is the ablest man the Republicans have got—I shall lose everything. Should I win, I shall gain but little. I do not want to go into a debate with Lincoln." Despite his reservations, Douglas soon agreed, perhaps out of pride, self-confidence, and the need to appear fearless. But rather than accepting Lincoln's proposal, which might have meant dozens of debates, perhaps fifty, he proposed only seven.

Even then, still nervous about Lincoln operating alone, the Republican State Committee summoned Senator Trumbull from Washington to reverse the momentum they felt had been lost as a result of Lincoln's speeches. Trumbull had authority as a senator that Lincoln lacked—and firsthand knowledge of Douglas's record in the Senate. On August 7, Trumbull spoke in Chicago. He offered a corrective to any misimpressions that Lincoln might have created. "The charge that we want to have anything to do with negroes is utterly untrue. It is a false clamor, raised to mislead the public mind. Our policy is, to have nothing to do with them. . . . I want to have nothing to do either with the free negro or the slave negro. We, the Republican Party, are the white man's party."

Not once did Trumbull bother to mention the Republican candidate's name or refer even obliquely to him. Instead he accused Douglas of hypocrisy, that he had been central to a "plot" against "popular sovereignty." Trumbull revealed that when a provision to a bill proposed by Senator Robert Toombs had been proposed to provide for a vote in Kansas on a constitution, free or slave, on June 25, 1856, Douglas as chairman of the Committee on Territories stripped the measure of the referendum. "It is preposterous," said Trumbull, "it is the most damnable effrontery that man ever put on, to conceal a scheme to defraud and cheat a people out of their rights, and then claim credit for it." Douglas was enraged, calling Trumbull "the miserable, craven-hearted wretch," but the charge could not be refuted for the simple reason that it was true. "I will cram the truth down his throat, till he shall cry enough," said Trumbull.

Douglas was rattled. His surrogates attempted to obscure the cynical sleight of hand Trumbull had exposed, but they could not deny it. Trumbull cut to the heart of his pretense to principle. Without consistency on popular sovereignty, Douglas stood exposed as opportunistic, wavering, and untrustworthy. It also cast a harsh light on his conflict with Buchanan, making it appear less a brave struggle than a raw contest for political primacy. Douglas was determined to even the score in the first debate with Lincoln at the small north-central town of Ottawa on August 21.

In preparation for the contest, Lincoln sat at his desk, undoubtedly in his law office, to compose a fragment of thought. He would not use the words in the debates. He spoke them neither in public nor in intimate conversation. Nobody later reported hearing him utter them. His fragment was unknown until it was discovered decades later. It revealed his deepest motives, the objects of his fierce ambition, his sense of himself engaged in a transatlantic movement, his description of the character of his opponents, and his premonition for an undefined future. "I have never professed an indifference to the honors of official station; and were I to do so now, I should only make myself ridiculous. Yet I have never failed—do not now fail—to remember that in the republican cause there is a higher aim than that of mere office." He would not appear "ridiculous" even to himself about his striving; he had no need for false humility looking in the mirror. But he was dedicating himself to something higher.

"I have not allowed myself to forget that the abolition of the Slave-trade by Great Brittain, was agitated a hundred years before it was a final success; that the measure had it's open fire-eating opponents; it's stealthy 'dont care' opponents; it's dollar and cent opponents; it's inferior race opponents; its negro equality opponents; and its religion and good order opponents; that all these opponents got offices, and their adversaries got none." Lincoln had distinct people in mind in setting out these categories of opponents to emancipation—Southern fire-eaters, Douglas, Northern financial interests, Douglas, Douglas, and proslavery Southern theologians. They might prevail in the present, but were doomed in history. "But I have also remembered that though they blazed, like tallow-candles for a century, at last they flickered in the socket, died out, stank in the dark for a brief season, and were remembered no more, even by the smell."

Lincoln invoked the names of the British emancipationists as his aspirational models. "School-boys know that Wilbe[r]force, and Granville Sharpe [*sic*], helped that cause forward; but who can now name a single man who labored to retard it?" William Wilberforce was the member of Parliament who joined with the small group of English abolitionists, among them Granville Sharp, to end the slave trade through the Slave Trade Act of 1807 and emancipate slaves in the British Empire through the Slave Abolition Act of 1833. The story of his extraordinary struggle may not have been common knowledge to schoolboys in the United States, but it was to Lincoln. He read far and wide, proslavery editorials and tracts, abolitionist literature, and English journals, and was well acquainted with the transatlantic connections of abolitionism. "Remembering these things I can not but regard it as possible that the higher object of this contest may not be completely attained within the term of my natural life. But I can not doubt either that it will come in due time. Even in this view, I am proud, in my passing speck of time, to contribute an humble mite to that glorious consummation, which my own poor eyes may not last to see."

It is possible that Lincoln was familiar with Wilberforce's famous speech of April 18, 1791, commencing his long battle to break the chains of slavery. "Let us not despair; it is a blessed cause, and success, ere long, will crown our exertions. Already we have gained one victory; we have obtained, for these poor creatures, the recognition of their human nature,

William Wilberforce

which, for a while was most shamefully denied. This is the first fruits of our efforts; let us persevere and our triumph will be complete."

Lincoln echoed Wilberforce's approach that insisted on the humanity of slaves as the first and most important step toward reaching emancipation; that the struggle would demand the commitment of patience; that it would require many steps; and that it would prevail. But Lincoln had to win an election.

At about the same time that Lincoln wrote this fragment he also filled a sheet with campaign strategy. The outcome of the Senate race, of course, would depend on the result of state legislative contests: the legislative was the senatorial. Based on the vote tallies from the 1856 election, Lincoln calculated where to concentrate, which candidates to help, and which were beyond help. District by district, he gamed the election. "By this, it is seen, we give up the districts numbered," he wrote, figuring those amounted to "22 representatives." "We take to ourselves, without question . . . 27 representatives." "Put as doubtful, and to be struggled for . . . 26 representatives." By different formulas, he adjusted for and against. "Taking the joint vote of Fremont & Fillmore against Buchanan as a test; and the 21.22.25.26.27.&33. with 9 representatives are brought over to our side—raising us to 48 & reducing our adversary to 27." That was the best-case scenario.

THE MORAL LIGHTS

No one had more faith in the ability of Lincoln than Herndon. But facing the Little Giant in seven debates was a challenge unlike any other. Herndon wrote Theodore Parker on July 24 that "we Republicans have a clever villain to combat. Douglas is an ambitious and an unscrupulous man; he is the greatest liar in all America; he misrepresents Lincoln throughout, and our people generally are not logical enough to see the precise manner, point and issue of the deception."

Lincoln had spent more than twenty years yearning for his chance to take on Douglas. His envy that Douglas soared above him made him feel diminished and left behind. He had debated Douglas beginning in 1840 on behalf of William Henry Harrison while Douglas took up the side of Martin Van Buren. Lincoln wrote hundreds of anonymous newspaper editorials over the years criticizing Douglas in the *Journal*. He futilely followed Douglas around trying to get him to "divide time" to debate the Kansas-Nebraska Act in 1854. He almost joined Douglas in the Senate in 1855 but threw the election

Abraham Lincoln, 1859

to Trumbull rather than let Douglas's candidate win. His wife and friends thought Trumbull had the place that was meant for him. He was fixed on the Senate race against Douglas since then. Greeley and other Eastern Republicans considered Lincoln an insignificant speck to be brushed aside so the party could align with Douglas in his battle with Buchanan. Lincoln's advisers except Herndon believed he had stumbled out of the gate with his "house divided" speech. They felt he needed to be handled.

Douglas's agreement to engage in a series of debates was unprecedented. Fighting for his political life against a host of enemies became the most riveting spectacle in the country and the national press covered the race as a sensational drama. Lincoln was overnight catapulted into prominence, but only because he was shadowing Douglas. Suddenly, his speeches were reprinted in the great Eastern newspapers. He was gaining the beginnings of a national reputation. But he had no sense that this was the first round of an even greater contest with Douglas. He was not playing on a future chessboard. He was attempting to end Douglas's career in Illinois and dash all of Douglas's hopes for higher office. Neither Lincoln nor the Illinois Republicans had a glimmer of his presidential nomination as they pursued the Senate campaign. If Douglas beat him for the Senate seat, Lincoln did not conceive of any future political match with him. At the state convention in June, the *Daily Missouri Republican* newspaper conducted an informal poll of the delegates and "passengers on the train," producing a lopsided "preference for the Presidency" in 1860 for Seward with 139 votes, followed by Frémont at 32, McLean with 13, Trumbull 7, Chase 6, W.H. Bissell 2, and "Scattering" 26. Nobody mentioned Lincoln.

Lincoln's strategy for the election centered on winning the Fillmore voters of 1856, almost all Old Whigs. He targeted the central counties within eighty miles of Springfield, where the Fillmore voters were concentrated. He knew that the Democratic-controlled legislature had shaped the districts to give Douglas a likely majority. Instead of reapportioning the districts to account for the explosive growth in the northern part of the state, the legislature left the districts untouched, "by the gerrymandering of the State seven hundred Democratic votes were equal to one thousand Republican votes." For Lincoln to wait on the sidelines until the elections were resolved and lobby the legislature would be a passive and self-defeating exercise. He had to make the legislative races turn on the Senate race. The legislative had to become the senatorial.

His attention to political detail was like that of a master tailor. He did not miss a stitch. He contacted his old friend Joe Gillespie, running for the State

Senate in Madison County, a crucial swing district located centrally along the Mississippi River. Alton, where Elijah Lovejoy was murdered, was its biggest town. Lincoln had served in the legislature with Gillespie, a Whig who had been a Know Nothing but was now a Republican. Lincoln wrote him on July 16 with political intelligence that "specimens of Douglas democracy" had been in Springfield, "making very confident calculation of beating both you, and your friends for the lower House in that county." Lincoln advised, "If they do so, it can only be done by carrying the Fillmore men of 1856." He listed columns of votes in the district from 1856. "By this you will see, if you go through the calculation, that if *they* get one quarter of the Fillmore votes and *you* three quarters, they will beat you 125 votes. If they get one *fifth* and you four fifths, you beat them 179. In Madison alone if our friends get 1000 of the Fillmore votes, and their opponents the remainder—658, we win by just two votes. This shows the whole field, on the basis of the election of 1856." He added a note of deference and a caution, "Of course you, *on* the ground, can better determine your line of tactics, than any one off the ground; but it behooves you to be wide awake, and actively working. Don't neglect it; and write me at your first leisure."

Suffering the defection of some of his closest allies, Lincoln felt the Old Whig problem intimately, not just as election numbers on a ledger. John Todd Stuart, from whom he had learned the law and logrolling in the legislature, was vociferously backing Douglas. Stuart had run against Douglas for the Congress in 1838, debated him often, and won by thirty-six votes. But he was outraged that Lincoln met with abolitionists to form the Republican Party. In 1856, he campaigned for Fillmore, railing at rallies against "Black Republicanism," whose "movement" would "array the north against the South." According to Herndon, "Between Lincoln and Stuart from 1843 to 1865 there was no good feeling of an honest friendship. Lincoln hated some of the ways of Stuart. Lincoln felt no jealousy toward Stuart, Stuart did toward Lincoln. Stuart in his heart hated Lincoln."

Stuart's law partner, Benjamin Edwards, was a member of Lincoln's extended family, the brother of Lincoln's brother-in-law, Ninian Edwards, Jr., and Lincoln's co-counsel on hundreds of cases. Edwards had required coaxing to go along with the Republicans in 1856, but he felt too uneasy about the abolitionist element to stay. Edwards introduced Douglas at a rally on July 17 at Edwards Grove, his land in Springfield, where "a vast crowd" assembled, bands played, and Douglas spoke for hours. "His friends pronounced it the best speech of his campaign," recalled Gustave Koerner, the German American leader, a former Democrat turned Republican, who was there. Lincoln appeared, too, but left before Douglas's remarks. The *Journal* claimed in its report that the band played over Edwards's speech. Lincoln came on the train from Bloomington to Springfield with Douglas and his entourage. Leonard Volk, the sculptor, who was a member of Douglas's party, recalled seeing him disembark. Lincoln "stalked forward alone, taking immense strides . . . carpetbag and an umbrella in his hands, and his coat-skirts flying in the breeze. I managed to keep pretty close in the rear of the tall, gaunt figure, with the head craned forward, apparently much over the balance, like the Leaning Tower of Pisa, that was moving something like a hurricane across the rough stubble-field! He approached the rail-fence, sprang over it as nimbly as a boy of eighteen, and disappeared from my sight."

Rumor reached Lincoln that Douglas was preparing to announce the endorsement that would be most devastating to Lincoln's prospects. Lincoln wrote a letter to Senator John J. Crittenden of Kentucky, who represented in the public mind the model of the Old Whig. Not only was he Clay's successor and had served as the last Whig attorney general but also had been the best man at the second marriage of Lincoln's father-in-law, Robert S. Todd, Clay's ally and business partner. Crittenden had abandoned the Whigs for the Know Nothings but still carried the Clay mantle. On July 7, Lincoln wrote him an imploring letter of quiet desperation:

> I beg you will pardon me for the liberty in addressing you upon only so limited an acquaintance, and that acquaintance so long past. I am prompted to do so by a story being whispered about here that you are anxious for the reelection of Mr. Douglas to the United States Senate . . . and that you are pledged to write letters to that effect to your friends here in Illinois, if requested. I do not believe the story, but still it gives me some uneasiness. . . . You have no warmer friends than here in Illinois, and I assure you nine tenths—I believe ninety-nine hundredths—of them would be mortified exceedingly by anything of the sort from you. When I tell you this, make such allowance as you think just for my position, which, I doubt not, you understand. Nor am I fishing for a letter on the other side. Even if such could be had, my judgment is that you would better be hands off! Please drop me a line; and if your purposes are as I hope they are not, please let me know. The confirmation would pain me much, but I should still continue your friend and admirer.

Crittenden replied on July 29, assuring Lincoln that though it was "highly gratifying to me" that Douglas joined with him in opposing the Lecompton

Constitution he had no plans to endorse him. "Since the adjournment of Congress I have not written a single letter to anyone in Illinois." While Crittenden's assurance may have been true, it was not the whole truth. Thomas L. Harris, the Democratic candidate for governor of Illinois, wrote Douglas that Crittenden had told him "that he would do anything we desired—he would write to anybody," and that a letter from Crittenden would "control 20,000 American {Know-Nothing} and Old Whig votes in the center and south."

Two days after misleading Lincoln, on August 1, Crittenden wrote a letter to Judge T. Lyle Dickey, Lincoln's Old Whig friend who previously had talked him out of using the "house divided" phrase and now was operating as a go-between for the Douglas campaign with Crittenden. Indeed, a week later, on August 9, Dickey openly endorsed Douglas. In Dickey's letter, which he addressed to Benjamin Edwards, he quoted Crittenden praising Douglas for his "courage and patriotism," for acting "gallantly," and for "heroism." He added that he did not want to be perceived as "intermeddling" in the election.

Lincoln's paper, the *Illinois State Journal,* wrote, "The letter is very appropriately addressed to B.S. Edwards, Esq., of this place, also a recent and miraculous convert to the principles of Democracy. Dickey, like Edwards, has been for a long time itching for political honors, and not finding the Whigs or Republicans willing to gratify him in his wishes, has been looking out for an excuse to lop over to the enemy." The turncoats had stabbed Lincoln in the back, but Crittenden made the deeper thrust to draw blood.

Since Lincoln's Chicago speech of July 10, Douglas had traveled around the state flaying him for his remarks on racial equality: ". . . let us discard all this quibbling about this man and the other man—this race and that race and the other race being inferior, and therefore they must be placed in an inferior position—discarding our standard that we have left us. Let us discard all these things, and unite as one people throughout this land, until we shall once more stand up declaring that all men are created equal." Douglas would not let Lincoln forget those words, which he repeatedly raised as Lincoln's major gaffe. He pasted into a small notebook Lincoln's "house divided" statement, which he read at every stop as the trigger for his attack lines.

In Bloomington, Douglas sneered, "If the divine law declares that the white man is the equal of the negro woman, that they are on a perfect equality, I suppose he admits the right of the negro woman to marry the white man." In Springfield, on July 17, at Edwards Grove, he ridiculed Lincoln's citation of the Declaration of Independence's credo that "all men are created equal," "He thinks that the negro is his brother. I do not think that the negro is any kin of mine at all." He derided "nigger equality." And: "We must preserve the purity of the race not only in our politics but in our domestic relations." In the town of Havana on August 13, Douglas lost his temper, calling Lincoln "a liar, a coward, a wretch and a sneak." Horace White of the *Chicago Tribune* reported, "It would be difficult for me to give an adequate idea of the littleness, meanness and foulness of Douglas' harangue here today. . . . He returned to his vomit half a dozen times with a new volley of bar-room phrases for Lincoln and Trumbull. . . . In the 'attacking' part of the speech I heard nothing but negro equality and amalgamation—amalgamation and negro equality—with a slight tincture of blackguardism against the Declaration of Independence." When Lincoln appeared at Lewistown on August 17, the Democrats posted a large sign: "Lincoln declares the negro his equal."

Lincoln argued that Douglas had "no claim to the support of the Old Line Whigs of Illinois" in light of being a "life-long enemy" of Henry Clay, who spoke of the "ultimate emancipation of the slave." "Douglas's position was as opposite to it as Beelzebub to an Angel of Light." As he had in Chicago, Lincoln exposed the moral hollowness at Douglas's core. "All others have said either that it is right and just, and should therefore be perpetuated, or that it is wrong and wicked, and should be immediately swept from civilized society, or that it is an evil to be tolerated because it cannot be removed. But to Judge Douglas belongs the *distinction* of having never said that he regarded it either as an evil or a good, morally right or morally wrong." Unlike "all others," Douglas "was the only statesman of any note or prominence in the country who had *never said to friend or enemy whether he believed human slavery in the abstract to be right or wrong.*"

In fact Douglas never had made a public statement against slavery. Nor had he defined it as a "positive good," as John C. Calhoun had. He defended it as constitutionally mandated and protected. He praised the founders for establishing a charter that permitted slavery. He defined slavery as the freedom of property. He diminished the Declaration of Independence as applying only to white men. He commended the Dred Scott decision for denying rights to blacks, even though the ruling demolished his pretext of popular sovereignty. (Reverdy Johnson, an Old Whig and the attorney who in the Dred Scott case argued for his enslavement, eagerly endorsed him.) Douglas harped on sexual fear of interracial marriage. He warned against pollution of blood purity. He had used these ploys in one way or another over his career.

Now he deployed all these gambits to appeal to the Old Whigs and Know Nothings. He usually began by claiming the founders as proslavery, but sexual panic was always his closing argument. These were his salient wedges. There was a method to his mendacity.

Before the debates, while Lincoln was stalking Douglas town to town, George Fitzhugh, Lincoln's ideological nemesis and chief editorialist for the *Richmond Enquirer,* described the clash in Illinois as the most significant national political event. "The canvass between the Black Republicans and the Democracy is fairly opened. . . . Mr. Lincoln, the Black Republican candidate . . . took the broadest, and most radical abolition grounds which have ever been occupied by Giddings, Lloyd Garrison or Wendell Phillips. He proclaimed the doctrine, that 'a house divided against itself, cannot stand.' . . . On the question of negro citizenship, Mr. Douglas was particularly emphatic. He maintains that our Government was founded upon the white basis, that it was established by white men for the benefit of white men, to be administrated by white men and their posterity. . . . In short, the issue . . . is the most direct and radical that has ever been made in this country, involving the great question of State rights and State sovereignty on the one hand, and consolidation and despotism on the other."

From his placid summer White House at a resort in Bedford Springs, Pennsylvania, Buchanan angrily observed the progress Douglas was making with Old Whigs by raising the specter of the "Black Republicans" and tarring Lincoln as the proponent of "nigger equality." He ordered his attorney general, Jeremiah Black, to write new editorials in the *Washington Union* excoriating Douglas. "Judge Douglas ought to be stripped of his pretensions to be the champion of Popular Sovereignty," wrote Buchanan on August 5. Black replied that Douglas should be "wiped as a man wipeth a plate, turning it over and wiping it."

Douglas had choreographed his arrival at campaign events as an imperial entrance. "He came like some great deliverer, some mighty champion, who had covered himself with imperishable laurels, and saved a nation from ruin," reported the *Philadelphia Press,* Forney's newspaper. It was especially important for Douglas to stage a conspicuous display of his popularity and power coming into the site of the first debate, Ottawa, a heavily Republican northern town, on August 21, before he spoke a word. Dressed in an expensive suit, fancy shirt, and wearing a broad hat, he was escorted by a reception committee of local notables from the nearby town of Peru, from where he rode in a magnificent carriage drawn by four horses to be met by a waiting group of hundreds assembled with a blaring band to lead the way into the streets festooned with flags and banners, and pushing through a crowd of about ten thousand people, "a vast smoke house," according to the *Chicago Tribune,* the sounds of more bands and peddlers hawking their wares from the corners, to the wooden platform constructed in the public square, his appearance triumphantly announced with the firing of two brass cannon. Lincoln came by the Rock Island Railroad to the depot without fanfare.

The debate format consisted of sequential speeches, an hour speech followed by a ninety-minute response followed by a thirty-minute rebuttal and conclusion. There was no moderator. Douglas and Lincoln alternated debate after debate in making the first statement. They appeared on an open-air wooden platform constructed for the occasion, standing when speaking and seated while their opponent took the stage. Behind them on the platform sat their chosen friends and supporters. Thousands clustered around to listen, cheer and hoot.

In his opening speech, Douglas cut straight to the chase; in one long breath he expressed all the points he would ever make against Lincoln in different forms and forums. He began with a history of the country and the political parties, a nation that by 1854 had secured peace over the question of slavery with both parties standing "on the same platform." He had proposed his Kansas-Nebraska Act, not to extend slavery but to extend popular sovereignty, and "every Whig and every Democrat in the House voted in the affirmative," with only abolitionists opposed.

But the Union had been disrupted by a conspiracy of two men willing to destroy their parties for the ulterior motive of abolition. Lincoln the Whig and Trumbull the Democrat made a bargain "to dissolve the old Whig party on the one hand, and to dissolve the old Democratic party on the other, and to connect the members of both into an Abolition party, under the name and disguise of a Republican party." Their base motive was to help each other secure Senate seats. Lincoln, under false colors, "went to work to Abolitionize the old Whig party all over the State, pretending that he was then as good a Whig as ever."

Lincoln and Trumbull's true plan was supposedly contained in protocols of abolitionists at a meeting in Springfield in October 1854. Douglas brandished his exposé. "I have the resolutions of their State Convention then held, which was the first mass State Convention ever held in Illinois by the Black Republican party, and I now hold them in my hands and will read a part of them."

Douglas read the entire document, its preamble borrowed from the Declaration of Independence and its resolutions calling for overturning the Fugitive Slave Act, stopping the extension of slavery, and ending slavery in the District of Columbia. He flung the challenge to Lincoln: Did he support these positions? Douglas promised to pose these questions even in the southernmost part of the state. "My principles are the same everywhere." Douglas was the man of principles, Lincoln the opportunist.

He then offered a malignant account of Lincoln's career. Douglas's life of Lincoln began inaccurately with his subject as a grocery clerk whose "business enabled him to get into the legislature." Lincoln was a joke-teller, who loved common sports and "could ruin more liquor than all of the boys of the town together," though Lincoln was well known as a virtual teetotaler and temperance advocate. Douglas praised him for a reputation gained in lowlife pursuits—"the dignity and impartiality with which he presided at a horse-race or fist-fight excited the admiration and won the praise of everybody that was present and participated." They had served together in the legislature, but Lincoln "subsided, or became submerged, and he was lost sight of as a public man for some years." He emerged again as the "Abolition tornado swept over the country," got elected to the House, where he opposed the Mexican War, "taking the side of the common enemy against his own country." Then, Douglas said, "when he returned home he found that the indignation of the people followed him everywhere, and he was again submerged or obliged to retire into private life, forgotten by his former friends." But the obscure loser, seeing his chance, "came up again in 1854, just in time to make this Abolition or Black Republican platform"—Douglas referred eight times in this speech to "Black Republicans."

Douglas turned to Lincoln's "house divided" speech, reading the whole paragraph containing that quotation, mocking him for being "destructive of the existence of this Government." Lincoln was against the principles of the founders, who "made this Government divided into Free States and Slave States, and left each State perfectly free to do as it pleased on the subject of slavery."

Douglas came to the heart of his appeal.

I ask you, are you in favor of conferring upon the negro the rights and privileges of citizenship? ("No, no.") Do you desire to strike out of our State Constitution that clause which keeps slaves and free negroes out of the State, and allow the free negroes to flow in, ("never") and cover your prairies with black settlements? Do you desire to turn this beautiful State into a free negro colony, ("no, no.") in order that when Missouri abolishes slavery she can send one hundred thousand emancipated slaves into Illinois, to become citizens and voters, on an equality with yourselves? ("Never," "no.") If you desire negro citizenship, if you desire to allow them to come into the State and settle with the white man, if you desire them to vote on an equality with yourselves, and to make them eligible to office, to serve on juries, and to adjudge your rights, then support Mr. Lincoln and the Black Republican party, who are in favor of the citizenship of the negro. ("Never, never.") For one, I am opposed to negro citizenship in any and every form. (Cheers.) I believe this Government was made on the white basis. ("Good.") I believe it was made by white men for the benefit of white men and their posterity forever, and I am in favor of confining citizenship to white men, men of European birth and descent, instead of conferring it upon negroes, Indians, and other inferior races. ("Good for you." "Douglas forever.")

Douglas ridiculed Lincoln as a fellow traveler of abolitionists,

following the example and lead of all the little Abolition orators, who go around and lecture in the basements of schools and churches, reads from the Declaration of Independence, that all men were created equal, and then asks, how can you deprive a negro of that equality which God and the Declaration of Independence awards to him? He and they maintain that negro equality is guaranteed by the laws of God, and that it is asserted in the Declaration of Independence. If they think so, of course they have a right to say so, and so vote. I do not question Mr. Lincoln's conscientious belief that the negro was made his equal, and hence is his brother, (laughter,) but for my own part, I do not regard the negro as my equal, and positively deny that he is my brother or any kin to me whatever. ("Never." "Hit him again," and cheers.) Lincoln has evidently learned by heart Parson Lovejoy's catechism. (Laughter and applause.) . . . he is worthy of a medal from Father Giddings and Fred Douglass for his Abolitionism. (Laughter.) He holds that the negro was born his equal and yours, and that he was endowed with equality by the Almighty, and that no human law can deprive him of these rights which were guaranteed to him by the Supreme ruler of the Universe. Now, I do not believe that the Almighty ever intended the negro to be the equal of the white man. ("Never, never.") If he did, he has been a long time demonstrating the fact.

Electing Lincoln would lead to nothing less than the end of the Republic and civil war. "I believe that this new doctrine preached by Mr. Lincoln and his party will dissolve the Union if it succeeds. They are trying to array all the Northern States in one body against the South, to excite a sectional war between the Free States and the Slave States, in order that the one or the other may be driven to the wall." With that portentous warning, casting the contest between Lincoln and himself as between doom and salvation, Douglas sat down.

Lincoln's reply was almost wholly defensive against the "very gross" misrepresentation of his record. He denied helping found the Republican Party in Illinois, pointing to Owen Lovejoy in the crowd, who could verify that he wasn't even in town then. As for "abolitionizing the old Whig Party," Lincoln put on his glasses to read paragraph after paragraph from his Peoria speech of 1854 against the Kansas-Nebraska Act in which he declared slavery "wrong . . . wrong . . . wrong," the "covert real zeal for the spread of slavery, I cannot but hate," and "I hate it because of the monstrous injustice of slavery itself." But he quoted himself saying, "I have no prejudice against the Southern people," and that he could not "admit" to make the slaves "politically and socially our equals," that "the great mass of white people will not," but that he was for some form of "gradual emancipation."

Lincoln attempted to blunt Douglas's sharpest point by neutralizing it, so he elaborated.

> Now, gentlemen, I don't want to read at any greater length; but this is the true complexion of all I have ever said in regard to the instruction of slavery and the black race. This is the whole of it; and anything that argues me into his idea of perfect social and political equality with the negro, is but a specious and fantastic arrangement of words, by which a man can prove a horse chestnut to be a chestnut horse. I will say here, while upon this subject, that I have no purpose, directly or indirectly, to interfere with the institution of slavery in the States where it exists. I believe I have no lawful right to do so, and I have no inclination to do so. I have no purpose to introduce political and social equality between the white and the black races. There is a physical difference between the two which, in my judgment, will probably forever forbid their living together upon the footing of perfect equality; and inasmuch as it becomes a necessity that there must be a difference, I, as well as Judge Douglas, am in favor of the race to which I belong having the superior position.

And yet, Lincoln added, "I hold that, notwithstanding all this, there is no reason in the world why the negro is not entitled to all the natural rights enumerated in the Declaration of Independence,—the right to life, liberty, and the pursuit of happiness. I hold that he is as much entitled to these as the white man."

He defended his "house divided" speech through a new metaphor, calling slavery "the apple of discord," making it into the enticing apple of original sin in the Garden of Eden, and asserting, "I believe we shall not have peace upon the question until the opponents of slavery arrest the further spread of it, and place it where the public mind shall rest in the belief that it is in the course of ultimate extinction." This, he claimed, was the true belief of the founders. The stages from stopping the expansion of slavery to "ultimate extinction," he did not explain because he could not. He had no idea other than ship- ping the slaves, supposedly peacefully freed by their Southern taskmasters, perhaps compensated, to Liberia. Agreeing with Douglas's conclusion that ending the "house divided" required civil war would have been politically suicidal. But it was a common thought. Lincoln begged the question in his "house divided" speech. Douglas used it as a weapon against Lincoln. Only abolitionists and secessionists were free to voice it.

Finally, near the end of his reply Lincoln rounded back to his own thrust against Douglas. "Then what is necessary for the nationalization of slavery? It is simply the next Dred Scott decision. It is merely for the Supreme Court to decide that no *State* under the Constitution can exclude it, just as they have already decided that under the Constitution neither Congress nor the Territorial Legislature can do it. When that is decided and acquiesced in, the whole thing is done."

Douglas's denial of the humanity of the slave also denied the basis of the American experiment. "When he invites any people, willing to have slavery, to establish it, he is blowing out the moral lights around us. When he says he 'cares not whether slavery is voted down or voted up,'—that it is a sacred right of self-government—he is, in my judgment, penetrating the human soul and eradicating the light of reason and the love of liberty in this Amer- ican people."

Partisans on each side hailed their champion's performance. The most important judgment for Lincoln was from the impetuous Greeley, who had been avidly for Douglas and reluctantly for Lincoln. Now he wrote that Lincoln had made the race "a contest for the Kingdom of Heaven or the Kingdom of Satan—a contest for advance or retrograde in civilization." By contrast, Greeley wrote about Douglas that "sympathy is diminished by the manner in which he has chosen to conduct the canvass, which reminds us more of the wild and unscrupulous athlete of his earlier days than of the noble displays of last Winter . . . we think Mr. Lincoln has decidedly the advantage. Not only are his doctrines better and truer than those of his antagonist, but he states them with more propriety and cogency, and with an infinitely better temper." Greeley called the debates "a mode of discussing political questions which might well be more generally adopted." The *New York Tribune* published full transcripts of the debates, like congressional debates. Just as the debates were novel, so was their publication in the national press. In the pages of the metropolitan broadsheets, Lincoln's reputation was being built. On the Lincoln side the *Chicago Tribune* assigned its own stenographer and on the Douglas side the *Chicago Times*. Both cleaned up Douglas's language, substituting "negro" when he had said "nigger."

Lincoln in private worried how to parry Douglas's torrent of falsehoods. He told his friend Clifton H. Moore, a lawyer on the circuit with him for decades, "Douglas will tell a lie to ten thousand people one day, even though he knows he may have to deny it to five thousand the next." It turned out that the Springfield Republican platform of 1856 Douglas cited was not from the Springfield gathering at all, but from a district meeting at the time in Aurora about which Lincoln had nothing to do. But Horace White of the *Chicago Tribune* later told Jesse W. Weik, who assisted Herndon with his biography of Lincoln, that the dangerous lie was not about the platform but about Lincoln's drinking.

> The fact I had in mind when I spoke of Douglas's unveracity in stump speaking was a statement he made at the Ottawa joint debate in which he said that Lincoln as a young man "could ruin more liquor than all of the boys in town together." This was said in order to draw Lincoln into a personal controversy. Everybody who knew Lincoln knew that he never used liquor or tobacco at all. He said to me once that he had never taken a drink of any alcoholic beverage in the past twenty years. That he should have been a drunkard before 1838 is impossible. Not only was Douglas's statement essentially false as to Lincoln, but it would have been a true description of himself (Douglas) at the time of the Ottawa debate. The fact was that Douglas at that time was drinking himself to death—an end which he reached three years later. The pen of the historian has not touched upon that fact as yet. I have no doubt whatever that Douglas made that false statement about Lincoln to get a denial from him that he was a drinking man, in which event he would have enlarged upon it and given particulars which he could

easily have invented and would have assured Lincoln that he did not wish to injure him, etc., leading off the debate into a personal quagmire as was his habit when he was getting the worst of it. But Lincoln was too smart. He never noticed the charge at all. So Douglas never repeated it.

Post-debate Republican newspapers hailed Lincoln as David slaying Goliath, but his defensive performance dispirited Republican leaders, who fell to fighting among each other over what to do next. "This campaign has not been managed right," David Davis said on August 18 to the State Committee treasurer Ozias M. Hatch. He organized a rally in what ought to have been safe political territory and hardly anyone turned out. "No enthusiasm," said Davis. The State Committee members thought Lincoln was making things worse. Norman Judd complained that by "repelling the charges . . . that he was an 'Abolitionist,' in favor of 'negro equality,' and 'amalgamation'" Lincoln only succeeded in raising them again.

The Douglas team believed that the first debate was all that counted. "The fate of Lincoln was sealed by the discussion at Ottawa," wrote Sheahan, "and nothing but a special interposition of Providence could have elected a Legislature favorable to his election to the Senate."

On the night before the next debate, Judd and others on the state committee caught up with Lincoln, at two in the morning barging into his hotel room, waking him up and trying to shake him up to take the fight to Douglas. Lincoln stubbornly wanted to keep to answering Douglas's questions to him at Ottawa. But the newspapermen had devised a series of questions for Lincoln to pose to Douglas. "Don't be defensive at all," Joseph Medill and Charles Ray, the coeditors of the *Chicago Tribune,* wrote him. ". . . be bold, defiant and dogmatic . . . in other words, give him hell . . . put a few ugly questions at Douglas." Charles Wilson of the *Chicago Journal* wrote him questions, too. The point of these questions was to drive a wedge between Douglas's and Buchanan's followers. Judd said that Lincoln "listened very patiently . . . but he wouldn't budge an inch from his well studied formulas." Yet he absorbed the advice.

The town of Freeport, near the Wisconsin border, was as solid a Republican district as could be found in Illinois, represented in the Congress by Elihu Washburne and in the State Senate by John Addams (whose daughter Jane would become one of the great Progressive Era reformers, founder of the settlement house movement). Fifteen thousand people crowded into the town on August 27 to witness the debate, "a vast audience as strongly tending to Abolitionism as any audience in the State of Illinois," as Lincoln described it. While Douglas made a grand entrance in an elegant carriage, dressed in ruffled shirt, fine coat with shiny buttons, light colored pants, a plantation hat, and well-polished shoes, Lincoln's handlers paid for him to be drawn in on a plain buckboard wagon accompanied by farmers.

In rapid-fire succession Lincoln shot out answers to the questions put to him in the last debate. Then he issued four questions of his own to Douglas, the second of which was the most carefully calculated to catch him in controversy, trapping him between Douglas Democrats and Buchanan Democrats, between popular sovereignty and the Dred Scott decision. "Can the people of a United States Territory," asked Lincoln, "in any lawful way, against the wish of any citizen of the United States, exclude slavery from its limits prior to the formation of a State Constitution?" The "in any lawful way" part of the question was crafted to pit Douglas against the Dred Scott ruling to expose his contradictions if not hypocrisy.

He dispatched Douglas's claim in the Ottawa debate that he was party to a supposed Republican Party platform of 1854, when, in fact, Lincoln disclosed, the document Douglas had flourished was not the state Republican platform at all, but a proclamation of a Kane County organization. "I am just as responsible for the resolutions at Kane County as those at Springfield, the amount of the responsibility being exactly nothing in either case," he said, "no more than there would be in regard to a set of resolutions passed in the moon."

Douglas replied with exasperation to Lincoln's questions. "I answer emphatically, as Mr. Lincoln has heard me answer a hundred times from every stump in Illinois, that in my opinion the people of a Territory can, by lawful means, exclude slavery from their limits prior to the formation of a State constitution. Mr. Lincoln knew that I had answered that question over and over again."

Douglas quoted again from the "house divided" speech, read yet more resolutions passed by Republican organizations, and called Lincoln the tool of abolitionist advisers. Douglas picked out one man to personify Lincoln's subversive political association, his subversive belief in racial equality, leading naturally to "racial amalgamation." That man was Frederick Douglass, a former fugitive slave, famed as the author of his autobiography, a forceful speaker on the abolitionist circuit, and founder of the splinter Radical Abolition Party. Douglass admired Lincoln's "house divided" speech, and said of it, "Well and wisely said."

Douglass was a foil for Douglas to stereotype as the black man ostentatiously surrounded with the accoutrements of wealth and white women serving his pleasure, the symbol of amalgamation and Lincoln's intent. Douglas's paper the *Register* had foreshadowed the attack line with an article on August 7: "Another Ally of Lincoln—The Nigger Chief Out for Him." "The last time I came here to make a speech," said Douglas, "while talking from the stand to you, people of Freeport, as I am doing today," Douglas said about an appearance in 1854,

> I saw a carriage—and a magnificent one it was—drive up and take a position on the outside of the crowd; a beautiful young lady was sitting on the box-seat, whilst Fred Douglass and her mother reclined inside, and the owner of the carriage acted as driver. I saw this in your own town. All I have to say of it is this, that if you Black Republicans, think that the negro ought to be on a social equality with your wives and daughters, and ride in a carriage with your wife, whilst you drive the team, you have perfect right to do so. I am told that one of Fred Douglass's kinsmen, another rich black negro, is now traveling in this part of the State making speeches for his friend Lincoln as the champion of black men. All I have to say on that subject is, that those of you who believe that the negro is your equal and ought to be on an equality with you socially, politically, and legally, have a right to entertain those opinions, and of course will vote for Mr. Lincoln.

Douglas expressed contempt for Lincoln's factual correction of his confusion of the 1854 Kane County platform for the Springfield one. "Mr. Lincoln makes a great parade of the fact that I quoted a platform as having been adopted by the Black Republican party at Springfield in 1854, which, it turns out, was adopted at another place. Mr. Lincoln loses sight of the thing itself in his ecstasies over the mistake I made in stating the place where it was done. He thinks that that platform was not adopted on the right 'spot.'" Douglas used his error to demean Lincoln as unpatriotic on the Mexican War, referencing a speech at the time that led to Lincoln being derisively nicknamed "Spotty," and conflate his position with abolitionism. "Lincoln and his political friends are great on '*spots.*'" (Renewed laughter.) "In Congress, as a representative of this State, he declared the Mexican war to be unjust and infamous, and would not support it, or acknowledge his own country to be right in the contest, because he said that American blood was not shed on American soil in the '*right spot.*' ('Lay on to him.') And now he cannot answer the questions I put to him at Ottawa because the resolutions I read were not adopted at the '*right spot*.'" Even if Douglas was wrong on the particular, he claimed to be right in general. So he would not stop making exactly the same point. "When I get into the next district, I will show that the same platform was adopted there, and so on through the State, until I nail the responsibility of it upon the back of the Black Republican party throughout the State. ('White, white, three cheers for Douglas.' A voice—'Couldn't you modify and call it brown?' Laughter.) Not a bit. I thought that you were becoming a little brown when your members in Congress voted for the Crittenden-Montgomery bill, but since you have backed out from that position and gone back to Abolitionism, you are black and not brown. (Shouts of laughter, and a voice, 'Can't you ask him another question.')"

Over and over again Douglas derisively baited the largely Republican crowd as "Black Republicans," deliberately seeking to stir their anger so he could posture as the brave statesman taking his stand against mob rule. When he said, "Black Republicans," he elicited from the crowd cries of "White, White!" Having provoked the audience, he answered it: "I wish to remind you that while Mr. Lincoln was speaking there was not a Democrat vulgar and blackguard enough to interrupt him. But I know that the shoe is pinching you. I am clinching Lincoln now, and you are scared to death for the result. I have seen this thing before. I have seen men make appointments for joint discussions, and the moment their man has been heard, try to interrupt and prevent a fair hearing of the other side. I have seen your mobs before, and defy your wrath."

Lincoln, in posing his question to Douglas, knew that he had answered it "a hundred times from every stump." He wanted him to repeat it in the most prominent setting and in the most damaging way so that it would receive the widest possible circulation. His goal was get Douglas to further alienate the Buchanan Democrats. The immediate effect altered the debates' dynamic. In pressing Douglas, Lincoln went off the defensive and onto the offensive, galvanizing his campaign. Some in retrospect believe that Lincoln's question, what became known as the "Freeport Doctrine," was advanced with the 1860 election in mind, but the evidence for that hypothesis consists of likely bogus quotes from Lincoln, who did not have the presidency in mind.

The long-term effects on Douglas were lasting and devastating. Southerners could disagree with Douglas on Lecompton as a matter of policy, but not on doctrine. His assent that slavery could be excluded "in any lawful way" defied the Dred Scott decision, seemed to agree that Congress could legislate slavery's prohibition and permanently thwart any expansion of slavery, tilting the majority of political power in the future toward "ultimate extinction." That was the connotation of Lincoln's question. Jefferson Davis, in a speech in Vicksburg, called Douglas's Freeport admission "worse than even the Wilmot Proviso," and Douglas's view "as objectionable as those of his adversary, Mr. Lincoln. They were both equally destructive of the rights of the South, both at war with the Constitution . . . he would have been glad if they had made a Kilkenny fight of it, and neither had been left to proclaim a victory."

"It is impossible that confidence thus lost can be restored," said Senator Judah P. Benjamin of Louisiana on May 22, 1860, on Douglas's Freeport position. Benjamin said of Douglas in the 1858 campaign that "he went home, and under the stress of a local election, his knees gave way; his whole person trembled."

The "Freeport Doctrine" was hardly the first or final factor that fractured the Democratic Party, but it contributed to its rupture to the extent that it made Douglas more toxic to Buchanan Democrats and to the South. "Judge Douglas Repudiates the Dred Scott Decision," headlined the *Washington Union,* Buchanan's voice. "Judge Douglas," the paper wrote, "in the early part of his present canvass in Illinois, took great pains to tickle the ears of the South with encomiums upon the Dred Scott decision," but at Freeport "backs out from the doctrine of the Nebraska-Kansas bill, abandons the Cincinnati platform, and repudiates the Dred Scott decision; and that he does so by reasserting the odious squatter-sovereignty doctrine in its most radical and obnoxious form."

Jonesboro, located deep in southern Illinois, in the most conservative part, in the region known as lower Egypt, populated by Southerners, hosted the third debate on September 15. It was the most sparsely attended debate, witnessed at most by 1,400 people. Jonesboro was more a test for Douglas than Lincoln. Lincoln was not going to win many votes there. Douglas feared that support for Buchanan would strip votes from him. He brought in former Tennessee governor and senator James C. Jones, a former Whig, to stump on his behalf, and by Election Day "no less than 41 slave holders" from out of state campaigned in southern Illinois for him, according to the *Chicago Democrat.*

The tenor of the place gave Douglas a receptive audience for projecting Frederick Douglass as the star in Douglas's very own minstrel show. "Why, they brought Fred Douglass to Freeport, when I was addressing a meeting there, in a carriage driven by the white owner, the negro sitting inside with the white lady and her daughter. ('Shame.') When I got through canvassing the northern counties that year, and progressed as far south as Springfield, I was met and opposed in discussion by Lincoln, Lovejoy, Trumbull . . . (Laughter.) Father Giddings, the high-priest of Abolitionism, had just been there, and Chase came about the time I left. ('Why didn't you shoot him?') I did take a running shot at them, but as I was single-handed against the white, black and mixed drove, I had to use a shot gun and fire into the crowd instead of taking them off singly with a rifle. (Great laughter and cheers.)"

Once again, Douglas ridiculed Lincoln's "house divided" speech before pivoting to the core of his message.

> I hold that a negro is not and never ought to be a citizen of the United States. ("Good, good," and tremendous cheers.) I hold that this Government was made on the white basis, by white men, for the benefit of white men and their posterity forever, and should be administered by white men and none others. I do not believe that the Almighty made the negro capable of self-government. I am aware that all the Abolition lecturers that you find traveling about through the country, are in the habit of reading the Declaration of Independence to prove that all men were created equal and endowed by their Creator with certain inalienable rights, among which are life, liberty, and the pursuit of happiness. Mr. Lincoln is very much in the habit of following in the track of Lovejoy in this particular, by reading that part of the Declaration of Independence to prove that the negro was endowed by the Almighty with the inalienable right of equality with white men. Now, I say to you, my fellow-citizens, that in my opinion, the signers of the Declaration had no reference to the negro whatever, when they declared all men to be created equal.

Lincoln spent his time trying to answer again Douglas's original interrogatories and clarify the facts. Fending off Douglas's charge that Lincoln and Trumbull had made a secret pact dividing offices between them, he said, "there is not a word of truth in it." He talked about the founders as antislavery, how Douglas's repeal of the Missouri Compromise was the source of the problem, and most of his already stated positions. Lincoln's conclusion expressed his feeling of having lived too long in Douglas's shadow and unwilling to be belittled by him any longer. "The Judge has set about seriously trying to make the impression that when we meet at different places I am literally in his clutches—that I am a poor, helpless, decrepit mouse, and that I can do nothing at all. This is one of the ways he has taken to create that impression. I don't know any other way to meet it, except this. I don't want to quarrel with him—to call him a liar—but when I come square up to him I don't know what else to call him, if I must tell the truth out."

Nothing new was said; nothing was resolved. The most unusual fireworks were provided by the appearance of Donati's Comet streaking across the night sky. Lincoln gazed at it for an hour. But Lincoln's remarks on his relation to Douglas and resistance to his demeaning methods were the most psychologically revealing statements of the debates.

After the Jonesboro debate, Douglas ramped up his attack on Lincoln for supporting "negro equality." His paper, the *Register,* mocked a free black from Chicago, H. Ford Douglas, who spoke in a church for Lincoln, "much to the edification and delight of his abolition Republican brethren, who seem in duty bound, according to the philanthropic ideas inculcated by Parson Lovejoy, to swallow every greasy nigger that comes along. . . . It is perfectly right that he should take a nigger to his bosom."

Under the headline "Negro Equality," the *Chicago Tribune* explained on September 28 that Douglas exploited the issue "to obscure the magnitude of his own misconduct. . . . If by much drumming and repeating he can fasten the odium of 'Negro Equality' upon his enemies, he thinks he can escape the fate which overtook his assistants in the Nebraska job, and slide back into the Senate." The *Tribune* pointed out that there were only six thousand "colored inhabitants of Illinois (of all hues) among a million and a half of Caucasians," who "earn their own bread. . . . Yet will no argument, not even that of self-respect, deter Mr. Douglas from vociferating 'nigger equality' to the end of the chapter. His followers in the central and southern portions of the State make it the beginning, middle and end of all their harangues. Put the question to five of them taken at random anywhere south of Bloomington, why they are supporting Douglas, and four of them will tell you 'Because he goes against nigger equality.' Ask them what man, woman or child in the whole State is in favor of negro equality, and the reply will be 'Oh, Lincoln and all the Black Republicans.'"

The fourth debate took place in Charleston, in Coles County, the heart of conservative Old Whig territory, populated mainly by Kentuckians. Lincoln's father had settled there and his stepmother still lived on the farm Lincoln had bought for them. Lincoln had long practiced law in the county. One of the attorneys to whom he was close, Thomas A. Marshall, was the nephew of Henry Clay, an Old Whig who had become a Republican. Lincoln managed to coax Marshall into running for the State Senate. Marshall advised him on Fillmore men who might be swayed and warned that to persuade them he must not endorse "negro equality." "Our enemies are preparing for a desperate fight," Marshall wrote him on July 22. "We must go into it with as little weight as possible. Unless they succeed in exciting some strong prejudices against us we are safe in the [this] quarter."

Both candidates entered Charleston on September 18 in elaborate parades of bands, wagons, and floats. Lincoln's carriage was followed by a float decorated as the "Ship of State," carrying thirty-two young women in flowing white dresses holding flags with the names of the states, and one riding on a white horse bore a banner reading, "Kansas, I Will Be Free." On the side of the float was the motto: "Westward the Star of Empire Takes its Way, Our Girls Link-on to Lincoln, Their Mothers were for Clay." When the parade entered Charleston, Lincoln saw his stepmother, stopped, kissed her, and got back in his carriage.

Just as the debate was about to begin a group of Douglas partisans shoved their way to the front of the crowd near the platform carrying a banner with a crude caricature of Lincoln with a black woman under the words "Negro Equality." Two of Lincoln's local supporters, who were on the platform, jumped off to scuffle with the Douglas men and tear down the banner.

Lincoln's opening statement took Marshall's talking points as his text. He sought to separate himself from the taint of the "negro equality" stigma to win over the wavering Fillmore and Old Whig votes. He had said most of it before, lately at the Ottawa debate, but this was his most encyclopedic and compact summary in order to present himself as a conservative Old Whig. "While I was at the hotel today," he said,

> an elderly gentleman called upon me to know whether I was really in favor of producing perfect equality between the negroes and white people. While I had not proposed to myself on this occasion to say much on that subject, yet as the question was asked me, I thought I would occupy perhaps five minutes in saying something in regard to it. I will say then that I am not, nor ever have been, in favor of bringing about in any way the social and political equality of the white and black races, that I am not, nor ever have been, in favor of making voters or jurors of negroes, nor of qualifying them to hold office, nor to intermarry with white people; and I will say in addition to this that there is a physical difference between the white and black races which I believe will forever forbid the two races living together on terms of social and political equality. And inasmuch as they cannot so live, while they do

remain together there must be the position of superior and inferior, and I as much as any other man am in favor of having the superior position assigned to the white race. I say upon this occasion I do not perceive that because the white man is to have the superior position the negro should be denied everything. I do not understand that because I do not want a negro woman for a slave I must necessarily want her for a wife. My understanding is that I can just let her alone. I am now in my fiftieth year, and I certainly never had a black woman for either a slave or a wife. So it seems to me quite possible for us to get along without making either slaves or wives of negroes. I will add to this that I have never seen, to my knowledge, a man, woman, or child who was in favor of producing a perfect equality, social and political, between negroes and white men. I recollect of but one distinguished instance that I ever heard of so frequently as to be entirely satisfied of its correctness, and that is the case of Judge Douglas's old friend Col. Richard M. Johnson.

Richard Mentor Johnson, a hero of the War of 1812, said to have killed the Native American chief Tecumseh, and senator from Kentucky, had been Martin Van Buren's vice president. He married a slave, an octoroon, living with her openly, by whom he had two daughters, whom he freely acknowledged. Upon his wife's death, he took another slave as his mistress, and when she fled into the arms of a lover he hunted her as a fugitive slave and sold her, after which he lived with another slave mistress. In 1840, Johnson insisted on retaining his position as vice president, throwing the Democrats into tumult, and Van Buren decided to run without a running mate, the first and only time in American political history. Though Johnson died in 1850, Lincoln revived him as his own counter to Douglas's race baiting.

Douglas's response was an attempt to reclaim his hold on the "negro equality" issue. "I am glad," he said, "that I have at last succeeded in getting an answer out of him upon this question of negro citizenship and eligibility to office, for I have been trying to bring him to the point on it ever since this canvass commenced."

Then he bashed Lincoln and Trumbull, from the Mexican War to their alleged conspiracy to destroy the political parties, from Frederick Douglass to the depravities of the "house divided" speech. He lampooned the "Black Republicans" and Lincoln as hypocritical. "Their principles in the north are jet-black, in the center they are in color a decent mulatto, and in lower Egypt they are almost white. Why, I admired many of the white sentiments contained in Lincoln's speech at Jonesboro, and could not help but contrast them with the speeches of the same distinguished orator made in the northern part of the State."

"I am told that I have but eight minutes more," Douglas said near his end.

I would like to talk to you an hour and a half longer, but I will make the best use I can of the remaining eight minutes. Mr. Lincoln said in his first remarks that he was not in favor of the social and political equality of the negro with the white man. Everywhere up north he has declared that he was not in favor of the social and political equality of the negro, but he would not say whether or not he was opposed to negroes voting and negro citizenship. I want to know whether he is for or against negro citizenship? . . . Lincoln maintains there that the Declaration of Independence asserts that the negro is equal to the white man, and that under Divine law, and if he believes so it was rational for him to advocate negro citizenship, which, when allowed, puts the negro on an equality under the law. . . . I say that this Government was established on the white basis. It was made by white men, for the benefit of white men and their posterity forever, and never should be administered by any except white men.

Lincoln noticed that his old friend Orlando B. Ficklin was seated on the platform to support Douglas. Ficklin, a Democrat, had served together with the Whig Lincoln in the legislature and the Congress, and they were involved in many cases on the circuit. Without warning Lincoln called on Ficklin to step forward to vouch that Lincoln had voted for military appropriations for the Mexican War. Ficklin did not tell a lie. "Mr. Lincoln voted for that resolution." Lincoln's theatrics turned the trick on Douglas. "I take it these people have some sense," he said to the crowd, "they see plainly that Judge Douglas is playing cuttlefish, [Laughter] a small species of fish that has no mode of defending itself when pursued except by throwing out a black fluid, which makes the water so dark the enemy cannot see it, and thus it escapes. [Roars of laughter.] Ain't the Judge playing the cuttlefish?" Lincoln had the crowd rolling with him in debunking Douglas. "Why does he stand playing upon the meaning of words, and quibbling around the edges of the evidence?" On he went, citing Euclid, "If you have ever studied geometry, you remember that by a course of reasoning, Euclid proves that all the angles in a triangle are equal to two right angles. Euclid has shown you how to work it out. Now, if you undertake to disprove that proposition, and to show that it is erroneous, would you prove it to be false by calling Euclid a liar? [Roars of laughter and enthusiastic cheers.]"

"Republicans saw it, democrats realized it, and 'a sort of panic seized them, and ran through the crowd of up-turned faces,'" recalled Isaac N. Arnold, a Republican lawyer from Chicago who was present. Douglas "walked rapidly up and down the platform, behind Lincoln, holding his watch in his hand, and obviously impatient for the call of 'time.'" He held up his watch and shouted, "Sit down, Lincoln, sit down. Your time is up." "They tell me that my time is out, and therefore I close." "Yes," loudly remarked a Lincoln supporter on the platform, "Douglas has had enough, it is time you let him up."

Lincoln's pandering on "negro equality" left the most lasting impression in historical accounts of the Charleston debate. He was also criticized by a religious abolitionist publication for having "planted himself on low prejudice." But his victory over Douglas, who was reduced to frustration and anger, was the conclusion of those who observed it. Lew Wallace, an Indiana state senator, the future Civil War general and author of *Ben-Hur,* was a Douglas supporter who came to cheer his champion. He described Lincoln wearing a suit from "a slop-shop," and "a more unattractive man I had never seen."

> Now, not having been blessed with a vision of the events to come, which were to set this uncouth person in a niche high up alongside Washington, leaving it debatable which of the two is greatest, I confess I inwardly laughed at him; only the laugh was quite as much at the political manager who had led him out against Mr. Douglas. Nevertheless, I gave him attention. Ten minutes—I quit laughing. He was getting hold of me. The pleasantry, the sincerity, the confidence, the amazingly original way of putting things, and the simple, unrestrained manner withal, were doing their perfect work; and then and there I dropped an old theory, that to be a speaker one must needs be graceful and handsome. Twenty minutes—I was listening breathlessly, and with a scarcely defined fear. I turned from him to Mr. Douglas frequently, wonderin'; if the latter could indeed be so superior to this enemy as to answer and overcome him. Thirty minutes—the house divided against itself was looming up more than a figure of speech. My God, could it be prophetic!

It was three weeks to the next debate. Douglas was drinking heavily. His speech, the *Chicago Journal* reported, "was observed to be very difficult, as though his tongue was much swollen." The *Chicago Tribune* taunted him in a piece headlined "Poor Little Dug!" "Douglas grows fainter and weaker as he progresses. His one act comedy is losing interest with all sorts of hearers. . . . His voice is growing hollow and husky, his temper is bad, and his whole appearance jaded and worn."

The debates turned north. The town of Galesburg was described by Democratic newspapers as "the Abolition nest," "nest of nigger thieves," and "the center of abolitiondom in this State." George Washington Gale, a Presbyterian minister from upstate New York, founded the town as an ideal Christian colony and Knox College in 1837. Residents of Galesburg and trustees of Knox College provided much of the leadership in the formation of the Illinois Anti-Slavery Society, the state Liberty Party, and Free Soil Party. Gale was indicted for hiding fugitive slaves. Knox College enrolled black students, including, as Lincoln would have known, Varveel Florville, the son of his barber.

The candidates marched into town on October 7 with bands, cavalcades, and banners. "Small-fisted Farmers, Mud Sills of Society, Greasy Mechanics, for A. Lincoln," read one mocking Senator Hammond's "Cotton is King" speech denigrating free labor. A bevy of young women paraded for Douglas, their dresses embroidered with the slogan: "White Men or None." A large crowd ranging from 10,000 to 25,000, according to newspaper estimates, gathered on a raw autumn day on the grounds of Knox College.

Douglas was physically struggling, his voice hoarse, popping lozenges, wearing an overcoat to guard against the cold, and "very hard to listen to," according to a spectator. He accused Lincoln, who "has no hope on earth, and has never dreamed that he had a chance of success," of forging "an unholy and unnatural combination" with the Buchanan administration "to beat a man merely because he has done right." He accused Lincoln of hypocrisy. "In the extreme Northern part of Illinois he can proclaim as bold and radical Abolitionism as ever Giddings, Lovejoy, or Garrison enunciated, but when he gets down a little further South he claims that he is an old line Whig, (great laughter,) a disciple of Henry Clay, and declares that he still adheres to the old line Whig creed, and has nothing whatever to do with Abolitionism, or negro equality, or negro citizenship. ('Hurrah for Douglas.')" He quoted as an accusation from Lincoln's Chicago speech—"let us discard all this quibbling about this man and the other man—this race and that race and the other race being inferior"—but "operating under an alias" in lower Egypt. He quoted the "house divided" speech as an accusation that Lincoln's "doctrine" would have enabled the slaveholding state to establish slavery "throughout the American continent."

Douglas invoked Jefferson, the author of the Declaration of Independence, as a slaveholder who was not a hypocrite.

I tell you that this Chicago doctrine of Lincoln's—declaring that the negro and the white man are made equal by the Declaration of Independence and by Divine Providence—is a monstrous heresy. The signers of the Declaration of Independence never dreamed of the negro when they were writing that document. They referred to white men, to men of European birth and European descent, when they declared the equality of all men. I see a gentleman there in the crowd shaking his head. Let me remind him that when Thomas Jefferson wrote that document, he was the owner, and so continued until his death, of a large number of slaves. Did he intend to say in that Declaration, that his negro slaves, which he held and treated as property, were created his equals by Divine law, and that he was violating the law of God every day of his life by holding them as slaves? . . . I say to you, frankly, that in my opinion, this Government was made by our fathers on the white basis. It was made by white men for the benefit of white men and their posterity forever, and was intended to be administered by white men in all time to come.

Lincoln seized Jefferson from Douglas's hands to render him in his complexity and in his shadow to diminish Douglas.

I believe the entire records of the world, from the date of the Declaration of Independence up to within three years ago, may be searched in vain for one single affirmation, from one single man, that the negro was not included in the Declaration of Independence; I think I may defy Judge Douglas to show that he ever said so, that Washington ever said so, that any President ever said so, that any member of Congress ever said so, or that any living man upon the whole earth ever said so, until the necessities of the present policy of the Democratic party, in regard to slavery, had to invent that affirmation. And I will remind Judge Douglas and this audience, that while Mr. Jefferson was the owner of slaves, as undoubtedly he was, in speaking upon this very subject, he used the strong language that "he trembled for his country when he remembered that God was just"; and I will offer the highest premium in my power to Judge Douglas if he will show that he, in all his life, ever uttered a sentiment at all akin to that of Jefferson.

Lincoln dismissed the charge of hypocrisy as misleading sophistry. "Perhaps by taking two parts of the same speech, he could have got up as much of a conflict as the one he has found. I have all the while maintained, that in so far as it should be insisted that there was an equality between the white and black races that should produce a perfect social and political equality, it was an impossibility. This you have seen in my printed speeches, and with it I have said, that in their right to 'life, liberty and the pursuit of happiness,' as proclaimed in that old Declaration, the inferior races are our equals."

Then, in one long breath, in a single paragraph Lincoln called slavery "wrong" sixteen times.

> Judge Douglas declares that if any community want slavery they have a right to have it. He can say that logically, if he says that there is no wrong in slavery; but if you admit that there is a wrong in it, he cannot logically say that any body has a right to do wrong. He insists that, upon the score of equality, the owners of slaves and owners of property—of horses and every other sort of property—should be alike and hold them alike in a new Territory. That is perfectly logical, if the two species of property are alike and are equally founded in right. But if you admit that one of them is wrong, you cannot institute any equality between right and wrong. . . . Now, I confess myself as belonging to that class in the country who contemplate slavery as a moral, social and political evil, having due regard for its actual existence amongst us and the difficulties of getting rid of it in any satisfactory way, and to all the Constitutional obligations which have been thrown about it; but, nevertheless, desire a policy that looks to the prevention of it as a wrong, and looks hopefully to the time when as a wrong it may come to an end.

Douglas rejoindered by repeating his accusation of hypocrisy, protesting that Lincoln was making equality "a moral question" in one place and not another. "I said that I did not care whether they voted slavery up or down, because they had the right to do as they pleased on the question, and therefore my action would not be controlled by any such consideration. ('That's the doctrine.') Why cannot Abraham Lincoln, and the party with which he acts, speak out their principles so that they may be understood? Why do they claim to be one thing in one part of the State and another in the other part?"

Douglas's anger grew as he spoke. A number of reporters noted that he foamed at the mouth and shook his fists as he raged that Lincoln was guilty of making false charges. "His grand manner was gone," said one observer.

Quincy was a town on the Mississippi that had originally been Douglas's home, had tilted Democratic against Whigs, gone for Buchanan in 1856, but had a sizable German population, in short, the sort of swing district Lincoln needed. On October 13, he opened by replying again to well-worn accusations. Talking about misrepresentations of what Lincoln said where and the different platforms of the Republican Party was becoming tired theater. Then he got to slavery itself. He called slavery "wrong" thirty-three times. "I suggest that the difference of opinion, reduced to its lowest terms, is no other than the difference between the men who think slavery a wrong and those

Bas relief, Lincoln-Douglas debate at Quincy, by Loredo Taft

who do not think it wrong. The Republican party think it wrong—we think it is a moral, a social and a political wrong. We think it as a wrong not confining itself merely to the persons or the States where it exists, but that it is a wrong in its tendency, to say the least, that extends itself to the existence of the whole nation. Because we think it wrong, we propose a course of policy that shall deal with it as a wrong. We deal with it as with any other wrong, in so far as we can prevent its growing any larger, and so deal with it that in the run of time there may be some promise of an end to it."

Douglas would not engage Lincoln on the moral wrong of slavery. He immediately accused him of slander. "I regret that Mr. Lincoln should have deemed it proper for him to again indulge in gross personalities and base insinuations in regard to the Springfield resolutions." He went through his old arguments in elaborate detail, again accused Lincoln of hypocrisy and quoted the Chicago speech. "Did old Giddings, when he came down among you four years ago, preach more radical abolitionism than that? ('No, never.') Did Lovejoy, or Lloyd Garrison, or Wendell Phillips, or Fred Douglass, ever take higher Abolition grounds than that? . . . He knew that I alluded to his negro-equality doctrines when I spoke of the enormity of his principles, yet he did not find it convenient to answer on that point." Then he cited the "house divided" speech, ridiculing Lincoln. "How then does Lincoln propose to save the Union, unless by compelling all the States to become free, so that the house shall not be divided against itself? He intends making them all free; he will preserve the Union in that way, and yet, he is not going to interfere with slavery anywhere it now exists. How is he going to bring it about? Why, he will agitate, he will induce the North to agitate until the South shall be worried out, and forced to abolish slavery. . . . and it does not become Mr. Lincoln, or anybody else, to tell the people of Kentucky that they have no consciences, that they are living in a state of iniquity, and that they are cherishing an institution to their bosoms in violation of the law of God. Better for him to adopt the doctrine of 'judge not lest ye shall be judged.'"

Lincoln replied that Douglas defied the founders on "the institution of slavery." "Judge Douglas could not let it stand upon the basis which our fathers placed it, but removed it, and *put it upon the cotton-gin basis.*"

Quickly, he moved on to the Dred Scott ruling as the refutation of Douglas's popular sovereignty. "The truth about the matter is this: Judge Douglas has sung paeans to his 'Popular Sovereignty' doctrine until his Supreme Court, co-operating with him, has *squatted* his Squatter Sovereignty out. But he will keep up this species of humbuggery about Squatter Sovereignty. He has at last invented this sort of *do-nothing Sovereignty*—that the people may exclude slavery by a sort of 'Sovereignty' that is exercised by doing nothing at all. Is not that running his Popular Sovereignty down awfully? Has it not got down as thin as the homeopathic soup that was made by boiling the shadow of a pigeon that had starved to death?"

Lincoln defended his belief in equality as he had stated it at Chicago. Douglas, he said, "thinks that is a terrible subject for me to handle. . . . The Judge has taken great exception to my adopting the heretical statement in the Declaration of Independence, that 'all men are created equal,' and he has a great deal to say about negro equality. I want to say that in sometimes alluding to the Declaration of Independence, I have only uttered the sentiments that Henry Clay used to hold." And he quoted Clay approving of the sentiment. Lincoln finished by standing on his charge of conspiracy. "I won't withdraw the charge in regard to a conspiracy to make slavery national," he said. He went into the "certain matters of fact," brushing aside whether Buchanan was "in the country at that time" and who owned Dred Scott and what their politics were in order simply to state it was "a made up case, for the purpose of getting that decision." And then: "But my time is out and I can say no more."

Carl Schurz met Lincoln for the first time on the train to Quincy. Schurz, the exiled German liberal, had run unsuccessfully for lieutenant governor in Wisconsin the year before and volunteered as a speaker for Lincoln's campaign. He admitted to being "somewhat startled by his appearance."

On his head he wore a somewhat battered "stove-pipe" hat. His neck emerged, long and sinewy, from a white collar turned down over a thin black necktie. His lank, ungainly body was clad in a rusty black dress coat with sleeves that should have been longer; but his arms appeared so long that the sleeves of a "store" coat could hardly be expected to cover them all the way down to the wrists. His black trousers, too, permitted a very full view of his large feet. On his left arm he carried a gray woolen shawl, which evidently served him for an overcoat in chilly weather. His left hand held a cotton umbrella of the bulging kind, and also a black satchel that bore the marks of long and hard usage. His right he had kept free for handshaking, of which there was no end until everybody in the car seemed to be satisfied. I had seen, in Washington and in the West, several public men of rough appearance; but none whose looks seemed quite so uncouth, not to say grotesque, as Lincoln's.

Schurz was equally surprised at Lincoln's platform performance. "His voice was not musical, rather high-keyed, and apt to turn into a shrill treble in moments of excitement; but it was not positively disagreeable. It had an exceedingly penetrating, far-reaching quality. The looks of the audience convinced me that every word he spoke was understood at the remotest edges of the vast assemblage. His gesture was awkward. He swung his long arms sometimes in a very ungraceful manner. Now and then he would, to give particular emphasis to a point, bend his knees and body with a sudden downward jerk, and then shoot up again with a vehemence that raised him to his tip-toes and made him look much taller than he really was—a manner of enlivening a speech which at that time was, and perhaps still is, not unusual in the West, but which he succeeded in avoiding at a later period."

Douglas appeared to Schurz as Lincoln's opposite in looks, manner, and sympathy. "No more striking contrast could have been imagined than that between those two men as they appeared upon the platform. By the side of Lincoln's tall, lank, and ungainly form, Douglas stood almost like a dwarf, very short of stature, but square-shouldered and broad-chested, a massive head upon a strong neck, the very embodiment of force, combativeness, and staying power. I have drawn his portrait when describing my first impressions of Washington City, and I apprehend it was not a flattering one. On that stage at Quincy he looked rather natty and well groomed in excellently fitting broadcloth and shining linen. But his face seemed a little puffy, and it was said that he had been drinking hard with some boon companions either on his journey or after his arrival. The deep, horizontal wrinkle between his keen eyes was unusually dark and scowling."

In Schurz's telling, Lincoln's last half hour "seemed completely to change the temper of the atmosphere. He replied to Douglas's arguments and attacks with rapid thrusts so deft and piercing, with humorous retort so quaint and pat, and with witty illustrations so clinching, and he did it all so good-naturedly, that the meeting, again and again, broke out in bursts of delight by which even many of his opponents were carried away, while the scowl on Douglas's face grew darker and darker. Those who by way of historical study now read the printed report of that speech and of its pointed allusions to persons then in the public eye, and to the happenings of those days, will hardly appreciate the effect its delivery produced on the spot."

Two days later, on October 15, about 125 miles downriver from Quincy, the final debate was held at Alton, just across the Mississippi from St. Louis, where Elijah Lovejoy had been killed twenty-one years earlier by an anti-slavery mob. Five thousand people assembled to listen, cheer, and jeer. This was Douglas's chance to hammer his nails. "The issue thus being made up between Mr. Lincoln and myself on three points, we went before the people of the State." Those three points were: "First, that this Government could not endure permanently divided into free and slave States, as our fathers made it; that they must all become free or all become slave; all become one thing or all become the other, otherwise this Union could not continue to exist. I give you his opinions almost in the identical language he used. His second proposition was a crusade against the Supreme Court of the United States because of the Dred Scott decision; urging as an especial reason for his opposition to that decision that it deprived the negroes of the rights and benefits of that clause in the Constitution of the United States which guaranties to the citizens of each State all the rights, privileges, and immunities of the citizens of the several States." And third, as Lincoln said in his Chicago speech: "that the Declaration of Independence having declared all men free and equal, by Divine law, also that negro equality was an inalienable right, of which they could not be deprived."

Douglas asked the audience to engage in a thought experiment about Lincoln as a founding father. "Imagine for a moment that Mr. Lincoln had been a member of the Convention that framed the Constitution," he said. And imagine he had said, "A house divided against itself cannot stand." With an adroit twist, Douglas explained that given the reaction Lincoln would have been the founding father of universal slavery. "You see that if this abolition doctrine of Mr. Lincoln had prevailed when the Government was made, it would have established slavery as a permanent institution, in all the States."

Douglas recounted the "warfare" conducted against him for opposing the Lecompton Constitution and how he had bravely defied Buchanan for his principle of popular sovereignty. "They now tell me that I am not a Democrat, because I assert that the people of a Territory, as well as those of a State, have the right to decide for themselves whether slavery can or cannot exist in such Territory." He quoted Buchanan in favor of popular sovereignty, then Jefferson Davis, Congressman James Orr of South Carolina, and Alexander Stephens. Douglas dramatized himself as the man in the arena, alone against all the powers that be. "It is the principle on which James Buchanan was made President. Without that principle he never would have been made President of the United States. I will never violate or abandon that doctrine if I have to stand alone. ('Hurrah for Douglas.') I have resisted the blandishments and threats of power on the one side, and seduction on the other, and have stood immovably for that principle, fighting for it when assailed by Northern mobs, or threatened by Southern hostility."

Just as he stood against Buchanan and the others, he also took his stand against Lincoln for his abolitionist heresy. "But the Abolition party really think that under the Declaration of Independence the negro is equal to the white man, and that negro equality is an inalienable right conferred by the Almighty, and hence that all human laws in violation of it are null and void. With such men it is no use for me to argue. I hold that the signers of the Declaration of Independence had no reference to negroes at all when they declared all men to be created equal. They did not mean negro, nor the savage Indians, nor the Fejee Islanders, nor any other barbarous race. They were speaking of white men." But the peace was disturbed by "these ambitious Northern men," who "wished for a sectional organization"—the Republican Party—and "formed a scheme to excite the North against the South."

It was Lincoln's turn, and within ten seconds he completely shifted the tone, opening with praise for Douglas "gradually improving in regard to his war with the Administration. [Laughter, 'That's so.'] At Quincy, day before yesterday, he was a little more severe upon the Administration than I had heard him upon any occasion, and I took pains to compliment him for it. I then told him to 'Give it to them with all the power he had'; and as some of them were present, I told them I would be very much obliged if they would *give it to him* in about the same way. [Uproarious laughter and cheers.] I take it he has now vastly improved upon the attack he made then upon the Administration. I flatter myself he has really taken my advice on this subject. All I can say now is to re-commend to him and to them what I then commended—to prosecute the war against one another in the most vigorous manner. I say to them again—'Go it, husband! Go it, bear!' [Great laughter.]"

Defending himself against the charges thrown at him, the statements in Chicago and elsewhere, Lincoln stepped through the bramble of accusations to a higher plane with the vantage point and clarity of history. Finally, he spoke in sharp concise sentences to express the thought he had been forging for years.

At Galesburg the other day, I said in answer to Judge Douglas, that three years ago there never had been a man, so far as I knew or believed, in the whole world, who had said that the Declaration of Independence did not include negroes in the term "all men." I reassert it to-day. I assert that Judge Douglas and all his friends may search the whole records of the country, and it will be a matter of great astonishment to me if they shall be able to find that one human being three years ago had ever uttered the astounding sentiment that the term "all men" in the Declaration did not include the negro. Do not let me be misunderstood. I know that more than three years ago there were men who, finding this assertion constantly in the way of their schemes to bring about the ascendancy and perpetuation of slavery, *denied the truth of it*. I know that Mr. Calhoun and all the politicians of his school denied the truth of the Declaration. I know that it ran along in the mouth of some Southern men for a period of years, ending at last in that shameful though rather forcible declaration of [Senator John] Pettit of Indiana, upon the floor of the United States Senate, that the Declaration of Independence was in that respect "a self-evident lie," rather than a self-evident truth. But I say, with a perfect knowledge of all this hawking at the Declaration without directly attacking it, that three years ago there never had lived a man who had ventured to assail it in the sneaking way of pretending to believe it and then asserting it did not include the negro. I believe the first man who ever said it was Chief Justice Taney in the Dred Scott case, and the next to him was our friend, Stephen A. Douglas. And now it has become the catch-word of the entire party.

Lincoln quoted Clay at length on the Declaration, as he had at Quincy, but Lincoln went beyond his Clay quotations to state himself, "And when this new principle—this new proposition that no human being ever thought of three years ago—is brought forward, I *combat* it as having an evil tendency, if not an evil design. I combat it as having a tendency to dehumanize the negro—to take away from him the right of ever striving to be a man. I combat it as being one of the thousand things constantly done in these days to prepare the public mind to make property, and nothing but property, of the *negro in all the States of this Union."*

He quoted Clay again: "I desire no concealment of my opinions in regard to the institution of slavery. I look upon it as a great evil." "But when Mr. Clay says that in laying the foundations of societies in our Territories where it does not exist, he would be opposed to the introduction of slavery as an element, I insist that we have *his warrant*—his license for insisting upon the exclusion of that element which he declared in such strong and emphatic language *was most hateful to him*. [Loud applause.]"

Lincoln went to the root, to the language of the Constitution. "Again, the institution of slavery is only mentioned in the Constitution of the United States two or three times, and in neither of these cases does the word 'slavery' or 'negro race' occur; but covert language is used each time, and for a purpose full of significance. . . . And I understand the contemporaneous history of those times to be that covert language was used with a purpose, and that purpose was that in our Constitution, which it was hoped and is still hoped will endure forever—when it should be read by intelligent and patriotic men, after the institution of slavery had passed from among us—there should be nothing on the face of the great charter of liberty suggesting that such a thing as negro slavery had ever existed among us. [Enthusiastic applause.] This is part of the evidence that the fathers of the Government expected and intended the institution of slavery to come to an end."

Lincoln now turned the founders on Douglas. His betrayal was not just in his interpretation. By flouting their understanding, he violated their intention and introduced on his own an extension of slavery. He had not been neutral or passive. He had not stood back to appeal to the principle of popular sovereignty. He had acted himself as the agent of chaos.

It is not true that our fathers, as Judge Douglas assumes, made this Government part slave and part free. Understand the sense in which he puts it. He assumes that slavery is a rightful thing within itself—was introduced by the framers of the Constitution. The exact truth is, that they found the institution existing among us, and they left it as they found it. But in making the Government they left this institution with many clear marks of disapprobation upon it. They found slavery among them, and they left it among them because of the difficulty—the absolute impossibility of its immediate removal. And when Judge Douglas asks me why we cannot let it remain part slave and part free, as the fathers of the Government made it, he asks a question based upon an assumption which is itself a falsehood; and I turn upon him and ask him the question, when the policy that the fathers of the Government had adopted in relation to this element among us was the best policy in the world—the only wise policy—the only policy that we can ever safely continue upon—that will ever give us peace unless this dangerous element masters us all and becomes a national institution—*I turn upon him and ask him why he could not let it alone.* [Great and prolonged cheering.] I turn and ask him why he was driven to the necessity of introducing a *new policy* in regard to it?

But the responsibility did not simply belong to Douglas. It was a power, the Slave Power, deeply entrenched, grasping for more power, overriding politicians and parties, dividing churches, a power they required another power to stop it, not the indifference of a Douglas.

But is it true that all the difficulty and agitation we have in regard to this institution of slavery springs from office seeking—from the mere ambition of politicians? Is that the truth? How many times have we had danger from this question? Go back to the day of the Missouri Compromise. Go back to the Nullification question, at the bottom of which lay this same slavery question. Go back to the time of the Annexation of Texas. Go back to the troubles that led to the Compromise of 1850. You will find that every time, with the single exception of the Nullification question, they sprung from an endeavor to spread this institution. There never was a party in the history of this country, and there probably never will be, of sufficient strength to disturb the general peace of the country. Parties themselves may be divided and quarrel on minor questions, yet it extends not beyond the parties themselves. But does *not* this question make a disturbance outside of political circles? Does it not enter into the churches and rend them asunder? What divided the great Methodist Church into two parts, North and South? What has raised this constant disturbance in every Presbyterian General Assembly that meets? What disturbed the Unitarian Church in this very city two years ago? What has jarred and shaken the great American Tract Society recently, not yet splitting it, but sure to divide it in the end? Is it not this same mighty, deep-seated power that somehow operates on the minds of men, exciting and stirring them up in every avenue of society—in politics, in religion, in literature, in morals, in all the manifold relations of life? [Applause.] Is this the work of politicians? Is that irresistible power which for fifty years has shaken the Government and agitated the people to be stilled and subdued by pretending that it is an exceedingly simple thing, and we ought not to talk about it? [Great cheers and laughter.] If you will get every body else to stop talking about it, I assure you I will quit before they have half done so. [Renewed laughter.] But where is the philosophy or statesmanship which assumes that you can quiet that disturbing element in our society which has disturbed us for more than half a century, which has been the only serious danger that has threatened our institutions—I say, where is the philosophy or the statesmanship based on the assumption that we are to quit talking about it, [applause] and that the public mind is all at once to cease being agitated by it? Yet this is the policy here in the north that Douglas is advocating—that we are to care nothing about it! I ask you if it is not a false philosophy? Is it not a false statesmanship that undertakes to build up a system of policy upon the basis of caring nothing about *the very thing that everybody does care the most about*? ['Yes, yes,' and applause]—a thing which all experience has shown we care a very great deal about? [Laughter and applause.]

For Lincoln the moral issue was entwined with the constitutional issue, which could only be resolved as a political issue. Here he came to the heart of the matter, beyond caviling over his various statements, at last reaching the culmination of his decades' long contest for primacy with Douglas, which Douglas had always won, to demonstrate, as Lincoln adduced from Euclid, a geometry against tyranny and slavery.

"The Democratic policy in regard to that institution will not tolerate the merest breath, the slightest hint, of the least degree of wrong about it," he said.

Try it by some of Judge Douglas's arguments. He says he "don't care whether it is voted up or voted down" in the Territories. I do not care myself in dealing with that expression, whether it is intended to be expressive of his individual sentiments on the subject, or only of the national policy he desires to have established. It is alike valuable for my purpose. Any man can say that who does not see anything wrong in slavery, but no man can logically say it who does see a wrong in it; because no man can logically say he don't care whether a wrong is voted up or voted down. He may say he don't care whether an indifferent thing is voted up or down, but he must logically have a choice between a right thing and a wrong thing. He contends that whatever community wants slaves has a right to have them. So they have if it is not a wrong. But if it is a wrong, he cannot say people have a right to do wrong. He says that upon the score of equality, slaves should be allowed to go in a new Territory, like other property. This is strictly logical if there is no difference between it and other property. If it and other property are equal, his argument is entirely logical. But if you insist that one is wrong and the other right, there is no use to institute a comparison between right and wrong. You may turn over everything in the Democratic policy from beginning to end, whether in the shape it takes on the statute book, in the shape it takes in the Dred Scott decision, in the shape it takes in conversation, or the shape it takes in short maxim-like arguments—it everywhere carefully excludes the idea that there is anything wrong in it.

That is the real issue. That is the issue that will continue in this country when these poor tongues of Judge Douglas and myself shall be silent. It is the eternal struggle between these two principles—right and wrong—throughout the world. They are the two principles that have stood face to face from the beginning of time; and will ever continue to struggle. The one is the common right of humanity and the other the divine right of kings. It is the same principle in whatever shape it develops itself. It is the same spirit that says, 'You work and toil and earn bread, and I'll eat it.' No matter in what shape it comes, whether from the mouth of a king who seeks to bestride the people of his own nation and live by the fruit of their labor, or from one race of men as an apology for enslaving another race, it is the same tyrannical principle. I was glad to express my gratitude at Quincy, and I re-express it here to Judge Douglas—*that he looks to no end of the institution of slavery.* That will help the people to see where the struggle really is. It will hereafter place with us all men who really do wish the wrong may have an end. And whenever we can get rid of the fog which obscures the real question—when we can get Judge Douglas and his friends to avow a policy looking to its perpetuation—we can get out from among that class of men and bring them to the side of those who treat it as a wrong. Then there will soon be an end of it, and that end will be its "ultimate extinction."

Lincoln reached the crescendo of the seven debates, its dramatic climax, but he was informed he had ten more minutes, so he filled in mostly on Dred Scott.

Douglas's response began by melding his principle of popular sovereignty with his theme against "negro equality." "I care more for the great principle of self-government, the right of the people to rule, than I do for all the negroes in Christendom," he said. (He did not use the word "negroes.") Then he went to Lincoln's traitorous position on the Mexican War, which he claimed was equivalent to his opposition to Douglas. "That a man who takes sides with the common enemy against his own country in time of war should rejoice in a war being made on me now, is very natural." Lincoln also made war on Henry Clay. "Who got up that sectional strife that Clay had to be called upon to quell? I have heard Lincoln boast that he voted forty-two times for the Wilmot proviso, and that he would have voted as many times more if he could. (Laughter.) Lincoln is the man, in connection with Seward, Chase, Giddings, and other Abolitionists, who got up that strife that I helped Clay to put down. (Tremendous applause.)" He scorned Lincoln for talking about the extinction and evil of slavery. "His idea is that he will prohibit slavery in all the Territories and thus force them all to become free States, surrounding the slave States with a cordon of free States and hemming them in, keeping the slaves confined to their present limits whilst they go on multiplying until the soil on which they live will no longer feed them, and he will thus be able to put slavery in a course of ultimate extinction by starvation. (Cheers.) He will extinguish slavery in the Southern States as the French general exterminated the Algerines when he smoked them out. He is going to extinguish slavery by surrounding the slave States, hemming in the slaves and starving them out of existence, as you smoke a fox out of his hole. He intends to do that in the name of humanity and Christianity, in order that we may get rid of the terrible crime and sin entailed upon our fathers of holding slaves. (Laughter and cheers.)"

Douglas continued his mockery and ridicule. "He says that this slavery question is now the bone of contention. Why? Simply because agitators have combined in all the free States to make war upon it. Suppose the agitators in the States should combine in one-half of the Union to make war upon the railroad system of the other half? They would thus be driven to the same sectional strife. Suppose one section makes war upon any other peculiar institution of the opposite section, and the same strife is produced. The only remedy and safety is that we shall stand by the Constitution as our fathers made it, obey the laws as they are passed, while they stand the proper test and sustain the decisions of the Supreme Court and the constituted authorities." And on that defense of Taney's reputation in the Dred Scott decision the great debates ended, the last exchange on the same stage between Lincoln and Douglas.

Since Douglas was appointed to his first political office, state's attorney of Morgan County, in 1834, he had systematically accumulated power in Illinois. He rose from office to office, from the state legislature to Springfield Land Office to secretary of state, from the Illinois Supreme Court to the House of Representatives, and to the Senate, his platform for his ultimate ascension to the presidency. He had come up as a loyal member of the party devoted to Jackson, the dominant party of the state. Swiftly, he took over the Democratic Party, imposing a convention system and placing his loyalists in strategic positions. His achievements in Washington as the central actor in the Compromise of 1850, the Illinois Central Railroad Act, and the Kansas-Nebraska Act, whatever the criticism, made him into a titanic figure, especially compared to puny Illinois politicians. All this power was projected through his personal energy, his ferocity in political combat, his kinetic speeches punctuated by sweat, shouts, and ripping of shirts. He stood more than his own ground against the great men of the Senate and with presidents. Douglas produced around himself a magnetic field of awe. But facing Lincoln in seven debates, one after another, the Little Giant shrank in stature. He put Lincoln on the defensive at the start, but he could not intimidate, humiliate, or embarrass him. Lincoln's use of logic, history, and moral appeal finally elevated him above Douglas. Failing to overawe Lincoln, the awe of Douglas dimmed. Douglas was still the senator and still the front-runner for the Democratic nomination for president, but an essential and intangible part of his power was spoiled. The damage was apparent in his physical appearance.

"I was really shocked at the condition he was in," recalled Gustave Koerner.

His face was bronzed, which was natural enough, but it was also bloated, and his looks were haggard, and his voice almost extinct. In conversation he merely whispered. In addressing his audience he made himself understood only by an immense strain, and then only to a very small circle immediately near him. He had the opening and conclusion. His speech, however, was as good as any he had delivered. Lincoln, although sun-burnt, was as fresh as if he had just entered the campaign, and as cool and collected as ever. Without any apparent effort he stated his propositions clearly and tersely, and his whole speech was weighted with noble and deep thoughts. There were no appeals to passion and prejudice. The Alton speech contained, by general admission, some of the finest passages of all the speeches he ever made. When Douglas's opening speech had been made, he was vociferously cheered. When, after Lincoln's speech, which made a powerful impression, Douglas made his reply, there was hardly any applause when he closed.

Douglas signaled to T. Lyle Dickey to launch his missile. Four days after the Alton debate, on October 19, at a rally in Decatur, Dickey took the platform to read the full letter from which he had previously quoted Crittenden's endorsement of Douglas. It was promptly published in the Democratic newspapers. Douglas seized upon it as a club to batter Lincoln for having "betrayed Henry Clay." "Isn't he a pretty man to be claiming Old Line Whig support?"

A week after the last debate, in Rushville on October 20 Douglas supporters greeted Lincoln by raising a black flag atop the county courthouse and a black doll swinging from an upstairs window draped with a banner "Hurrah for Lincoln!" On October 23, he was met in Dallas City with a huge painted canvas hung across the main street of a black man above whose head was encircled the word "Equality."

Douglas traveled in luxury by private train, but the rigors of the campaign exhausted him, his voice cracking and his words often inaudible. In Rock Island, on October 29, Douglas's final campaign event, supporters paraded before him with banners reading: "This Country Was Made For White Men" and "Down With Negro Equality."

"The planting and the culture are over; and there remains but the preparation, and the harvest," said Lincoln in his last speech of the campaign, on October 30, in Springfield. "I have said that in some respects the contest has been painful to me," he confessed. "Myself and those with whom I act have been constantly accused of a purpose to destroy the Union; and bespattered with every imaginable odious epithet; and some who were friends"—obliquely referring to Dickey—"as it were but yesterday have made themselves most active in this."

On November 1, the *Chicago Tribune* published an exposé of Douglas's Mississippi plantation, "Mississippi or Illinois—Which?" Douglas, in fact, was a slave owner, inheriting from his first wife a large Mississippi cotton plantation. For political purposes the paperwork put it in the names of his two young sons for whom he was guardian and executor of their estate. "If the slaves, the use and benefit of whom Mr. Douglas enjoys, were planted down on some prairie in Illinois, where they could be seen by the Senator's constituents; if their backs seared by the lash, their bodies pinched by hunger, their limbs beat by excessive overwork, were exposed where they could be gazed upon by the free men of this State, his chances of representing free Illinois in the councils of the Nation would be hopelessly destroyed." The information in the *Tribune* originated with Buchanan's close adviser Senator John Slidell, himself the owner of a Louisiana plantation, who delivered it on a July trip to Chicago to an anti-Douglas Democrat, Dr. Daniel Brainard, who in turn passed it on to the newspaper. James Sheahan, editor of the *Chicago Times,* defended Douglas, calling the incident "the most violent . . . the last paroxysm of abolition regard for the moral and physical condition of 'Douglas' plantation of human chattels," and a "total failure." He denounced Slidell for having "sought the election of Lincoln, with his negro equality doctrines, by the defeat of Douglas." Slidell claimed he had nothing to do with the story, but the *Tribune* produced documentation that the "authority given for these alleged facts . . . was the Hon. John Slidell, of Louisiana." (In 1872, Douglas's sons unsuccessfully sued the federal government for compensation for the Union army's 1863 expropriation and burning of their plantation's cotton.)

Election Day was November 2, the Republican legislative vote was greater than it had ever been for the Whigs in Illinois, polling 190,468, more than the 166,374 for the Douglas Democrats. But receiving the returns on election night, "dark, rainy, and gloomy," said Lincoln, "I had been reading the returns and had ascertained that we had lost the legislature." Knowledgeable about the districts around the state, he immediately determined that they were going Democratic. The legislature was still apportioned according to the 1850 census and gerrymandered on the basis of 1852, tilted toward the Democrats, giving the victory to Douglas. Lincoln's party won 53 percent of the vote, Douglas's 47, but awarded 53 percent of the electoral vote. If the election had been held on the popular vote, the Republicans would have won forty-four seats to the Democrats' forty-one. Despite having lost the popular vote, the champion of popular sovereignty was returned to his seat in the Senate.

Had the Republicans carried three more of the Old Whig districts in central Illinois, they would have prevailed. Douglas's "negro equality" attack had succeeded in making Lincoln unacceptable to enough Old Whigs. Crittenden's letter had been a fatal stab in the back. And the Buchanan Democrats that fielded their own slate only gained a pathetic 5,071 votes. The *Illinois State Journal* reported that the "Fillmore vote . . . which both the other parties struggled to secure . . . went for the Douglas candidates." Of the twenty-two counties in which Fillmore had won 30 percent or more of the vote in 1856, the Democrats won all but two in 1858. Of the fourteen legislative districts in which the Know Nothings had a significant presence, the Democrats carried eleven. Of the legislative seats held by Know Nothings, the Democrats won all six. Across the state, Know Nothings flocked to the Democrats and were repelled by the Republicans. The Know Nothings and Southern-born Old Whigs held the balance of power. They voted for Douglas despite his open hostility to the Know Nothings. Racism trumped nativism. The farther south the district in the state, the greater Douglas's gains. Thirteen counties, all in southern Illinois, registered particularly heavy increases from the 1856 vote for Democrats of over 15 percent for Douglas. The Democrats even picked up two legislative seats in Sangamon County. But the Republicans won the seats in Coles County.

Late on election night, wandering home through Springfield's streets, Lincoln tripped on the dark, wet path, a final indignity. "A slip, not a fall," he later recalled.

Lincoln's friends were embittered and fed his gloom. Davis wrote him on November 7 a letter filled with rage against Dickey's act of subversion: "The Pharisaical old Whigs in the Central counties, who are so much more righteous than other people, I can't talk about with any patience—The lever of Judge Dickeys influence has been felt—He drew the letter out of Mr. Crittenden & I think, in view of everything, that it was perfectly outrageous in Mr Crittenden to have written anything—Some of you may forgive him, & Gov Seward & Mr. Greeley but I cannot—It was very shameful in my opinion for Dickey, to have kept that letter from 1st Augt & then published it a week before the election—This portion of the state has been almost the only part doing well."

Lincoln's greatest chance had dissolved into another defeat. He offered his own analysis of the election results to his old friend and doctor Anson G. Henry. "As a general rule, out of Sangamon, as well as in it, much of the plain old democracy is with us, while nearly all the old exclusive silk-stocking whiggery is against us. I do not mean nearly all the old whig party; but nearly all of the nice exclusive sort. And why not? There has been nothing in politics since the Revolution so congenial to their nature, as the present position of the great democratic party."

He felt no regret but was tinged with despair. "I am glad I made the late race. It gave me a hearing on the great and durable question of the age, which

I could have had in no other way; and though I now sink out of view, and shall be forgotten, I believe I have made some marks which will tell for the cause of civil liberty long after I am gone."

Within a week, Lincoln was calculating vote numbers to project the future strength of the party. "But let the past as nothing be," he wrote Norman Judd on November 15. "For the future my view is that the fight must go on. . . . We have some hundred and twenty thousand clear Republican votes. That pile is worth keeping together. It will elect a state trustee [treasurer?] two years hence. In that day I shall fight in the ranks, but I shall be in no one's way for any of the places. I am especially for Trumbull's reelection."

"The fight must go on," he wrote on November 19 to Henry Asbury, a friend in Quincy, the law partner of Abraham Jonas. "The cause of civil liberty must not be surrendered at the end of *one,* or even, one *hundred* defeats. Douglas had the ingenuity to be supported in the late contest both as the best means to *break down,* and to *uphold* the Slave interest. No ingenuity can keep those antagonistic elements in harmony long. Another explosion will soon come. Yours truly A. LINCOLN."

Lincoln may have said he had no political future, but he was laying the groundwork for one if it might come into view. On his own he moved forward to arrange the publication of the debates. "I wish to preserve a Set of the late debates (if they may be called so) between Douglas and myself," he wrote Charles Ray of the *Chicago Tribune.* "To enable me to do so, please get two copies of each number of your paper containing the whole, and send them to me by Express; and I will pay you for the papers & for your trouble. I wish the two sets, in order to lay one away in the raw, and to put the other in a Scrap-book. Remember, if part of any debate is on *both* sides of one sheet, it will take two sets to make one scrap-book."

Lincoln tried to rouse Ray from his dejection. The melancholic Lincoln, seemingly defeated for his last time, was remarkably resilient. "I believe, according to a letter of yours to [Ozias] Hatch you are 'feeling like h—ll yet.' Quit that. You will soon feel better. Another 'blow-up' is coming; and we shall have fun again. Douglas managed to be supported both as the best instrument to *put down* and to *uphold* the slave power; but no ingenuity can long keep these antagonisms in harmony. Yours as ever A. LINCOLN."

Within a month, Lincoln had collected transcripts of the debates from the *Chicago Tribune* and *Chicago Times* in order to make an authoritative version. John Nicolay, the twenty-six-year-old German-born former editor of the *Pike County Free Press* and clerk for Secretary of State Ozias Hatch, was helping him as an assistant. By March 1859, he sent them out to publishers. By the fall, Lincoln signed a contract with Follett, Foster & Co., of Columbus, Ohio. The debates would not fade into memory.

On January 6, the Illinois legislature convened to elect Douglas along a strict party line vote. Charles H. Lanphier, editor of the *Register,* telegraphed the victorious results to Douglas: "Glory to God and the Sucker Democracy, Douglas 54, Lincoln 41. Announcement followed by shouts of immense crowd present. Town wild with excitement. Democrats firing salute. . . . Guns, music and whisky rampant." Back over the wires from Washington to Springfield flashed the laconic comment of the victor, "Let the voice of the people rule."

On the day of Douglas's election, Henry Clay Whitney found Lincoln alone in his law office, "gloomy as midnight . . . brooding over his ill-fortune," and reflecting that people "are always putting me in the place where somebody has to be beaten and sacrificed for the welfare of the party or the common good."

But a clerk in the Lincoln-Herndon law office, Charles S. Zane, recalled Lincoln in a different mood. "In January, 1859, while the Democrats were celebrating the election of Stephen A. Douglas to the United States Senate, Archibald Williams . . . came into Lincoln's office and finding him writing said: 'Well, the Democrats are making a great noise over their victory.' Looking up, Lincoln replied: 'Yes, Archie, Douglas has taken this trick, but the game is not played out.'"

THE PHOENIX

———— ✦ ————

Four days before the election, after speaking to a large rally at Petersburg, twenty miles outside Springfield, Lincoln was driven to the station to catch a train home. There he found a young journalist, Henry Villard, who wrote for the German language newspaper *New Yorker Staats-Zeitung*. "The train that we intended to take for Springfield was about due," Villard recalled.

After vainly waiting for half an hour for its arrival, a thunderstorm compelled us to take refuge in an empty freight-car standing on a side track, there being no buildings of any sort at the station. We squatted down on the floor of the car and fell to talking on all sorts of subjects. It was then and there he told me that, when he was clerking in a country store, his highest political ambition was to be a member of the State Legislature. "Since then, of course," he said laughingly, "I have grown some, but my friends got me into *this* business. I did not consider myself qualified for the United States Senate, and it took me

Lincoln, October 1858

a long time to persuade myself that I was. Now, to be sure," he continued, with another of his peculiar laughs, "I am convinced that I am good enough for it; but, in spite of it all, I am saying to myself every day: It is too big a thing for you; you will never get it. Mary insists, however, that I am going to be Senator and President of the United States, too." These last words he followed with a roar of laughter, with his arms around his knees, and shaking all over with mirth at his wife's ambition. "Just think," he exclaimed, "of such a sucker as me as President!"

Mary Todd Lincoln never wavered in her faith that her husband should become president. She had proclaimed as a girl to Henry Clay that she would marry a president. She saw as no one else did the diamond in the rough that was Lincoln, marrying him against the wishes of her family, who dismissed him as socially unsuitable, a lowly "plebe." The mingling of their ambitions was the foundation of "our Lincoln party," as she called their enterprise long before there was a Republican Party. Her sharp differences with him in their politics and social attitudes—her nativism, harsh treatment of her Irish maids, disdain for her husband's easy relationships with free blacks, her refusal to support Frémont's candidacy in 1856—made not the slightest difference in her unstinting devotion to his rise and her resentment toward anyone who might impede it. She was equally intolerant of his underlying insecurities. "His ambition was a little engine that knew no rest," said Herndon. But when it slowed at the bottom of a hill, she provided the push. She had no patience for his undervaluing of himself. When he was elected to the state legislature in 1854, she insisted the position was beneath him and that he must immediately run for the Senate. She never forgave her friend, Julia, Lyman Trumbull's wife, after Lincoln sacrificed his candidacy to elect Trumbull. (Even after Lincoln's death, Mary wrote that Julia "would not be received—She is indeed 'a whited Sepulchre.'") Lincoln knew that any backtracking would meet Mary's wrath.

Trumbull, who was the beneficiary of Lincoln's selfless calculation, his ally and yet held a residue of rivalry, tried to measure the ambiguities of Lincoln's ambition for decades. Trumbull had known Lincoln since they served in the legislature together. "We were both opposed to the spread of slavery, and from the foundation of the Republican party till his death we were in political accord," he wrote. "I do not claim to have been his confidant, and doubt if any man ever had his entire confidence. He was secretive, and communicated no more of his own thoughts and purposes than he thought would subserve the ends he had in view. He had the faculty of gaining the confidence of others by apparently giving them his own, and in that way attached to himself many friends. I saw much of him after we became political associates, and can truthfully say that he never misled me by word or deed. He was truthful, compassionate, and kind, but he was one of the shrewdest men I ever knew. To use a common expression he was 'as cunning as a fox.' He was a good judge of men, their motives, and purposes, and knew how to wield them to his own advantage." But Trumbull thought that Lincoln was eerily passive in making his progress. "He was not aggressive. Ever ready to take advantage of the public current, he did not attempt to lead it." On the other hand, Trumbull wrote, "Mr. Lincoln was by no means the unsophisticated, artless man many took him to be. . . . Another popular mistake is to suppose Mr. Lincoln free from ambition. A more ardent seeker after office never existed. From the time when, at the age of twenty-three, he announced himself a candidate for the legislature from Sangamon County, till his death, he was almost constantly either in office, or struggling to obtain one. Sometimes defeated and often successful, he never abandoned the desire for office till he had reached the presidency the second time." Yet Trumbull could not help feel that Lincoln was "a follower." "Without attempting to form or create public sentiment, he waited till he saw whither it tended, and then was astute to take advantage of it." Trumbull remained fixed on the riddle of Lincoln's paradoxical transparent and enigmatic character.

To others who knew Lincoln, his acute sense of the possible in any particular moment was not about vacillating on the path of least resistance but mysteriously related to his prescience. David R. Locke, then the editor of the Bucyrus, Ohio, *Journal,* who first encountered Lincoln during the 1858 campaign, received his analysis on the outcome of the election before it occurred. "At the time, he said he should carry the State on the popular vote, but that Douglas would, nevertheless, be elected to the Senate, owing to the skillful manner in which the State had been districted in his interest. 'You can't overturn a pyramid, but you can undermine it; that's what I have been trying to do.' He undermined the pyramid that the astute Douglas had erected, most effectually. It toppled and fell very shortly afterward."

A year later, in 1859, Locke met Lincoln in Columbus, Ohio. "By this time his vision had penetrated the future, and he had got a glimmering of what was to come. In his soul he knew what he should have advocated, but he doubted if the people were ready for the great movement of a few years later. Hence his halting at all the half-way houses.

" 'Slavery,' said he, 'is doomed, and that within a few years. Even Judge Douglas admits it to be an evil, and an evil can't stand discussion. In discussing it we have taught a great many thousands of people to hate it who had never given it a thought before. What kills the skunk is the publicity it gives itself. What a skunk wants to do is to keep snug under the barn—in the daytime, when men are around with shot-guns.' "

Two years later, in 1860, just days after his election to the presidency, Lincoln reminded Joseph Medill of the *Chicago Tribune* about the Freeport Doctrine in the Lincoln-Douglas debates. "He bent his head down to my ear and said in low tones, something like this: 'Do you recollect the argument we had on the way up to Freeport two years ago over my question that I was going to ask Judge Douglas about the power of squatters to exclude slavery from territories?' And I replied—that I recollected it very well. 'Now,' said he, 'don't you think I was right in putting that question to him?' I said: 'Yes Mr. Lincoln, you were, and we were both right. Douglas' reply to that question undoubtedly hurt him badly for the Presidency but it re-elected him to the Senate at that time as I feared it would.' Lincoln then gave me a broad smile and said—'Now I have won the place that he was playing for.' We both laughed and the matter was never again referred to." But Lincoln at the time did not know that was the game he was playing for. Yet he intended to damage Douglas not only in the Senate campaign but also in his campaign to come for president. He was playing a long game against Douglas. He didn't know it was for himself. But what he had done dawned on him.

Two days after the election, on November 4, Jeriah Bonham, editor of the *Illinois Gazette* of Lacon, a town near Peoria, published an editorial entitled, "Abraham Lincoln for President in 1860." Bonham was a Whig turned Republican who had known Lincoln since 1844 and spoke with him during the recent campaign about how to win over Old Whigs. Bonham's editorial declared that Douglas's election though losing the majority thwarted "the popular voice." In 1860, Lincoln "should lead the hosts of freedom" against Douglas. "Who has earned the proud position as well as he?" Bonham recalled discussing his percipient article with "personally strong friends of Mr. Lincoln" in the county who "thought his time 'was not yet,'" that he might be ready to run for governor in 1858, then the Senate once more, and perhaps "for the presidency, if ever, some ten to fourteen years ahead—either for 1868 or 1872."

On November 5, Horace White of the *Chicago Press and Tribune* wrote Lincoln a letter. "I don't think it possible for you to feel more disappointed than I do, with this defeat, but your popular majority in the state will give us the privilege of naming our man on the national ticket in 1860—either President or Vice Pres't. Then, let me assure you, Abe Lincoln will shall be an honored name before the American people. I am going to write an article for the Atlantic Monthly to further that object." White signed it: "Your friend in distress." He added, "I believe you have risen to a national reputation & position more rapidly than any other man who ever rose at all."

Jesse W. Fell, who had originated the notion to challenge Douglas to debate, was the first person to present a plan to Lincoln for a campaign for the presidency. Within Lincoln's circle Fell was unusual as a successful businessman with broad social interests and political shrewdness who lacked envy or resentment and was a fount of constructive ideas. During the Senate campaign Fell was absent from Illinois, traveling on business in the East. Following Lincoln through the newspapers, which reprinted the debates, "an impression began to form, that by judicious efforts he could made the Republican candidate for presidency in 1860," he recalled. Shortly after the election, at the end of December, when Lincoln was in Bloomington, attending Judge Davis's court, "I espied the tall form of Mr. Lincoln emerging from the court-house door." Fell brought him to his brother's nearby law office and "in the calm twilight of the evening" told him, "Lincoln, I have been East," and "everywhere I hear you talked about. . . . Being, as you know, an ardent Republican and your friend, I usually told them we had in Illinois *two* giants instead of one; that Douglas was the *little* one, as they all knew, but that you were the *big* one, which they didn't all know." He explained that he had built a national reputation as an antislavery advocate and "you can be made a formidable, if not a successful, candidate for the presidency."

"Oh, Fell," Lincoln replied, "what's the use of talking of me for the presidency, whilst we have such men as Seward, Chase and others, who are so much better known to the people, and whose names are so intimately associated with the principles of the Republican party. Everybody knows them; nobody, scarcely, outside of Illinois, knows me."

Fell was hardly deterred by Lincoln's reticence. "The men you allude to, occupying more prominent positions, have undoubtedly rendered a larger service in the Republican cause than you have," he said, "but the truth is, they have rendered *too much* service to be available candidates. Placing it on the grounds of personal services, or merit, if you please, I concede at once the superiority of their claims. Personal services and merit, however, when incompatible with the public good, must be laid aside. Seward and Chase have both made long records on this slavery question, and have said some very radical things which, however just and true in themselves, and however much these men may challenge our admiration for their courage and devotion to unpopular truths, would seriously damage them in the contest, if nominated."

Fell had given thought to the kind of winning candidate the Republicans should field. "We must bear in mind, Lincoln, that we are yet in a minority; we are struggling against fearful odds for supremacy. We were defeated on this same issue in 1856, and will be again in 1860, unless we get a great many new votes from what may be called the old conservative parties. These will be repelled by the radical utterances and votes of such men as Seward and Chase. What the Republican party wants, to insure success, in 1860, is a man of popular origin, of acknowledged ability, committed against slavery aggressions, who has no record to defend and no radicalism of an offensive character to repel votes from parties hitherto adverse. Your discussion with Judge Douglas has demonstrated your ability and your devotion to freedom; you have no embarrassing record; you have sprung from the humble walks of life, sharing in its toils and trials; and if we can only get these facts sufficiently before the people, depend upon it, there is some chance for you."

Fell had the idea that he would use his connections in Pennsylvania to plant articles "manufacturing sentiment in your favor" as a potential candidate. He explained to Lincoln that Republicans in Pennsylvania would run Simon Cameron as a favorite son, but that he was unacceptable "and will be dropped." He asked Lincoln to tell him the details of his life story for publication. "Won't you do it?"

"Fell, I admit the force of much that you say, and admit that I am ambitious, and would like to be President. I am not insensible to the compliment you pay me, and the interest you manifest in the matter; but there is no such good luck in store for me as the presidency of these United States; besides, there is nothing in my early history that would interest you or anybody else; and, as Judge Davis says, 'it won't pay.' Good night." Fell accepted Lincoln's rejection of "my pet scheme" for the moment, but not as final. "I notified him, however, as his giant form, wrapped in a dilapidated shawl, disappeared in the darkness, that this was not the last of it; that the *facts* must come."

On November 24, Congressman Thomas L. Harris, Douglas's indispensable ally who represented the Sangamon County district, died after a long battle with tuberculosis. He had been bedridden, spitting up blood for weeks—"this melancholy event has been anticipated for some months," reported the *Illinois State Journal*. Trumbull encouraged Lincoln to run for the vacant seat. "It would certainly be a great triumph and have a most happy effect in the future if you could be returned from the district right on the eve of a four thousand majority against us," he wrote. Lincoln had no interest in launching himself into a campaign he might well lose, nor in lowering his sights at once from the Senate to the House. "I have not the slightest thought of being a candidate for Congress," he replied to Trumbull on December 11. Lincoln's friend, James C. Conkling, with whom he had served years ago in the legislature and was a member of the Republican State Committee, was slated as the party's candidate, and was defeated on January 4, 1859.

On the evening of January 5, 1859, the eve of Douglas's foreordained election by the legislature the next day, an inner group of Republicans met with Lincoln in the capitol's law library to discuss how to "keep the party afloat," according to Henry Clay Whitney. They were especially upset "in view of the defection of Greeley—the endorsement of Douglas." Lincoln, of course, was there. So were state auditor Jesse K. Dubois, John M. Palmer (a former state senator who had presided over the Bloomington convention), Joe Gillespie, state senator Norman Judd, Ebenezer Peck (just elected to the legislature), Jackson Grimshaw (a Quincy lawyer and old Lincoln friend), Secretary of State Ozias Hatch, Whitney, and perhaps some others. "I am decidedly in favor of maintaining the party, and I see no valid reason for discouragement," said Palmer to general agreement. At the conclusion of Dubois's remarks, he added, "And I am also in favor of putting Lincoln up for a place on the ticket, either for President or Vice-President—one or the other." According to Whitney the "sentiment was cheered," Lincoln gave "a modest speech, which ended, 'As to the matter of my name on the National ticket'—when he was stopped by several of us; and he subsided." According to another account from R.W. Miles, a Republican from Knox County, who sat in "the secret caucus meeting," Lincoln responded to the call for his candidacy by rising to his feet and exclaiming, "For God's sake, let me alone! I have suffered enough!" But according to Judge Davis, after various names of possible presidential contenders were raised, Lincoln spoke up. "Why don't you run me?" Lincoln asked. "I can be nominated, I can be elected, and I can run the government." David Davis was surprised. "We all looked at him and saw that he was not joking," he said later.

Shortly after the election, at a reception given by Governor Bissell, "Mr. Lincoln was standing near the center of the room, entirely alone, with his usual sad countenance, and apparently unnoticed by anyone," recalled Elijah M. Haines, a legislator and Lincoln supporter. "I said to my wife, 'Here is

Mr. Lincoln; he looks as if he had lost all his friends; come and have an introduction to him, and cheer him up.'" Lincoln invited Mrs. Haines to dance.
"He had occasion during their conversation to refer to his age, remarking
incidentally that he was almost fifty years old; whereupon, as if suddenly
reflecting that his age was a good part of a man's life, and as if unwilling to
relinquish his hold upon the future, he suddenly braced himself up, and said,
'But, Mrs. Haines, I feel that I am good for another fifty years yet.'"

A few months later, that spring, Haines recalled another conversation
with Lincoln. "It would seem that the original intention of Lincoln's friends
had been to bring him out as a candidate for the Vice-Presidency," he wrote.
Haines sought to encourage Lincoln, "referring to his growing reputation, I
remarked to him that I did not know that we would be able to make him
President, but perhaps we could do the next best thing, and make him
Vice-President. He brightened up somewhat, and answered by a story which
I do not clearly recall, but the application of which was that he scarcely considered himself a big enough man for President, while the Vice-Presidency
was scarcely big enough office for one who had aspired to a seat in the Senate
of the United States."

At the onset of the Senate campaign Illinois Republicans were overwhelmingly inclined to support Seward for the presidential nomination in
1860. After the campaign they were infuriated at Eastern Republicans for
flirting with Douglas and looking for an alternative of their own. Only a
month before the election Seward seemed a simple number one choice to
Herndon writing to Theodore Parker on October 4: "you say you are, 1st, for
Seward; 2nd, for Chase, and 3rd, for Senator Trumbull, if, etc.; and in answer
to this, I say 'we of the West have no choice—we do not care who it is, so
that he is a good Republican.'" Even then, Herndon was irritated at Greeley.
"Greeley is acting a great dog, is he not? Just look at the power of his great
paper, with its world-wide circulation, and does he state who he is for, what
he wants, what Illinois is doing, what freedom is struggling for, and how,
with intensity, etc.? Nothing of the kind. He does not seem to know there is
such a man as Lincoln, such a struggle as 1858–9, and such a State as Illinois.
Does he keep his own people 'posted'? Who would know by Greeley's paper
that a great race for weal or woe was being fought all over the wide prairies
of Illinois? Who would? It is strange indeed!"

Just days after Lincoln's loss the Illinois Republican deference to Seward
turned into a rage. Herndon wrote Parker on November 8: "Greeley never
gave us one single, solitary, manly lift. On the contrary, his silence was his

opposition. This our people felt. We never got a smile or a word of encouragement outside of Illinois from any quarter during all this great canvass. The East was for Douglas *by silence.* This silence was terrible to us. Seward was against us too."

Herndon's conflation of Greeley and Seward was more than a little ironic given their bad blood. Greeley had been hailing Douglas in his paper while Seward operated quietly in the Senate cloakroom and Washington drawing rooms encouraging Douglas, but he endorsed neither him nor Lincoln. Seward's game was played behind the scenes to enhance Douglas's destruction of Buchanan, widen the split within the Democratic Party, making Douglas's nomination and election that much more difficult, and Seward's that much more likely. The *New York Times,* read by Illinois Republicans as close to Seward, described the "Triumph of Douglas" as "one of the most wonderful personal victories ever achieved by a public man . . . against the Republicans on the one hand and the Administration on the other, with the greatest firmness and self-reliance."

Toward the end of the campaign, on October 25, before a sympathetic audience in Rochester, Seward delivered the most consequential speech he ever made. He was not running for reelection, but he addressed a double purpose, one local, to heighten the antislavery message while diminishing the nativists in New York, and one national, to assert his primacy as the preeminent voice of the Republican Party and by that the presumptive presidential nominee. "Our country is a theater," he said, "which exhibits in full operation two radically different political systems—the one resting on the basis of servile or slave labor, the other on the basis of voluntary labor of freemen. . . . Shall I tell you what this collision means? They who think that it is accidental, unnecessary, the work of interested or fanatical agitators, and therefore ephemeral, mistake the case altogether. It is an irrepressible conflict between opposing and enduring forces, and it means that the United States must and will, sooner or later, become either entirely a slave-holding nation or entirely a free-labor nation." He further declared, "It is the failure to apprehend this great truth that induces so many unsuccessful attempts at final compromise between the slave and free States, and it is the existence of this great fact that renders all such pretended compromises, when made, vain and ephemeral."

In New York, the speech was instrumental in solidifying his base. Seward described his dramatic effect to James Watson Webb, editor of the *New York Courier* and Enquirer, a longtime supporter who had even named a son after Seward. "I saw a reserve Republican power of 70,000 to 80,000 in state in the rural districts who had slept two years since the last Presidential Campaign, betraying the state to the Democratic party last year, needing to be roused with a battle cry that they could respond to." The Republicans swept the state, winning for governor, a large majority in the legislature, and all but four congressional seats. But Seward's statement of an "irrepressible conflict" indelibly marked him as a radical, an easy target of Southerners, and vulnerable to future divisive events. He never escaped his phrase.

Seward's speech conversely was used to rouse the Southern Ultras. The fire-eating Senator Alfred Iverson of Georgia, looking forward to the 1860 election, announced that Seward's "irrepressible conflict" speech was an incitement to secession. "The election of a Northern President, upon a sectional and anti-slavery issue, will be considered cause enough to justify secession. Let the Senator from New York, or any other man avowing the sentiments and policy enunciated by him in his Rochester speech, be elected President of the United States, and, in my opinion, there are more than one of the Southern States that would take immediate steps toward separation. And, sir, I am free to declare here, in the Senate, that whenever such an event shall occur, for one, I shall be for disunion!"

Senator Hammond of South Carolina warned, "The South is to be Africanized and the elections of 1860 are to decide the question . . . it is to be emancipation or disunion after 1860, unless Seward is repudiated."

Herndon, while angry about Seward to Parker, wrote a praiseworthy letter to Seward on December 18, observing the parallel to Lincoln's "house divided" speech and appearing to boost Seward's presidential candidacy, urging him to "seize some golden opportunity." Herndon was trying to ingratiate himself with the man he still regarded as the Republican candidate. Seward replied with a nice little perfunctory letter: "No one can regret more than I do the failure of Mr. Lincoln's election." Giving Lincoln no more mind, complacent about his inevitability, Seward left on a Grand Tour of Europe and the Middle East from which he did not return until December 1859.

The fury in Illinois against the Eastern Republicans hardly abated, but burned to a white heat, especially against Greeley. The *Chicago Press and Tribune,* on February 2, 1859, published a lead editorial ripping "the criminal folly of the *New York Tribune* in still clinging to the coat tails of that politician"—Douglas. "While the Illinois election was pending we looked for the hostility of the Tribune against the Republican candidates, though we did not look for it in the back-door, round-the-corner fashion in which it came. . . . But now that the election is passed and Mr. Douglas has avowedly returned to his vomit, it is amazing beyond all things that the Tribune should still hang to his skirts." The Chicago voice for Lincoln warned that the Senate race was not the end of the contest. "Our complaint lies here; that having helped to do serious harm to the Republican cause in the West, his obstinacy will not suffer him to retrace a step nor even to pause midway in his wild career. It is quite as consistent to give aid and comfort to Mr. Douglas now, while he is turning the crank of the pro-slavery machine, as during the campaign when he was only promising to . . . whoever embarks in the enterprise of sneering down the Republican creed of this State or the Republican candidate for the Senate, will find blows to take as well as blows to give while we remain in the management of newspaper columns."

Lincoln returned to his law practice. He had lost a good deal of business during his campaign and depleted his funds. "This year I must devote to my private business," he wrote declining an invitation to give a speech at a distant agricultural fair. So, he took on cases of debt collection, railroads, and murder. But his eye was fixed on politics. Just as he attended to his clients he did not neglect political business near and far. His situation was the opposite of what it had been a decade earlier, in 1849, when he came back from Washington after his single term in the Congress bearing unpopularity for being against the Mexican War, feeling the political world closed to him, and despairing he was trapped. Now Lincoln politely refused to acknowledge he was running for any office, much less the presidency, while intervening strategically to position the state and national Republican Party for the 1860 election. The rumors about him were extremely helpful. It was highly unlikely he might gain the nomination, but he might be named the running mate, and, no matter what, the publicity kept alive his prospect of challenging Douglas for the Senate in 1864. He was the leading man of the Illinois party determined to play out the role.

Lincoln always maintained his focus on Douglas. His competition never ended. He considered his rival no less unscrupulous, ruthless, and wily, his slipperiness not necessarily grasped even by those Southern Democrats who despised him. A month after the election, on December 11, Lincoln laid out scenarios to Trumbull about Douglas through 1860 in which he would wreak damage on naive Republicans after feckless Democrats failed to subdue him. "Since you left," Lincoln wrote,

Douglas has gone South, making characteristic speeches, and seeking to re-instate himself in that section. The majority of the democratic politicians of the nation mean to kill him; but I doubt whether they will adopt the aptest way to do it. Their true way is to present him with no new test, let him into the Charleston [Democratic] Convention, and then outvote him, and nominate another. In that case, he will have no pretext for bolting the nomination, and will be as powerless as they can wish. On the other hand, if they push a Slave code upon him, as a test, he will bolt at once, turn upon us, as in the case of Lecompton, and claim that all Northern men shall make common cause in electing him President as the best means of breaking down the Slave power. In that case, the democratic party go into a minority inevitably; and the struggle in the whole North will be, as it was in Illinois last summer and fall, whether the Republican party can maintain its identity, or be broken up to form the tail of Douglas' new kite. . . . The truth is, the Republican principle can, in no wise live with Douglas; and it is arrant folly now, as it was last Spring, to waste time, and scatter labor already performed, in dallying with him.

On March 1, Lincoln spoke to a rally of Republicans in Chicago on the eve of a city election, his first speech since the Senate election, to call for caution against the fatal danger Douglas posed to the cause, "so long as we all agree that this matter of slavery is a moral, political, and social wrong, and ought to be treated as a wrong, not to let anything minor or subsidiary to that main principle and purpose make us fail to cooperate." The siren song of the Eastern Republicans that urged the embrace of Douglas, he declared, would lead to the destruction of the new party. "I have believed," said Lincoln, "that in the Republican situation in Illinois, if we, the Republicans of this State, had made Judge Douglas our candidate for the Senate of the United States last year and had elected him, there would to-day be no Republican party in this Union. I believed that the principles around which we have rallied and organized that party would live; they will live under all circumstances, while we will die. They would reproduce another party in the future. But in the meantime all the labor that has been done to build up the present Republican party would be entirely lost, and perhaps twenty years of time, before we would again have formed around that principle as solid, extensive, and formidable an organization as we have, standing shoulder to shoulder to-night in harmony and strength around the Republican banner."

Lincoln constantly found new ways to restate why Republicans must never allow themselves to be seduced by Douglas. "The Republican principle, the profound central truth that slavery is wrong and ought to be dealt with as a wrong, though we are always to remember the fact of its actual existence amongst us and faithfully observe all the constitutional guarantees—the unalterable principle never for a moment to be lost sight of that it is a wrong and ought to be dealt with as such, cannot advance at all upon Judge Douglas' ground—that there is a portion of the country in which slavery must always exist; that he does not care whether it is voted up or voted down, as it is simply a question of dollars and cents. Whenever, in any compromise or arrangement or combination that may promise some temporary advantage, we are led upon that ground, then and there the great living principle upon which we have organized as a party is surrendered."

Again and again, he hammered at his ultimate point of the conflict between right and wrong, between principle and Douglas. "I do not wish to be misunderstood upon this subject of slavery in this country. I suppose it may long exist, and perhaps the best way for it to come to an end peaceably is for it to exist for a length of time. But I say that the spread and strengthening and perpetuation of it is an entirely different proposition. There we should in every way resist it as a wrong, treating it as a wrong, with the fixed idea that it must and will come to an end. If we do not allow ourselves to be allured from the strict path of our duty by such a device as shifting our ground and throwing ourselves into the rear of a leader who denies our first principle, denies that there is an absolute wrong in the institution of slavery, then the future of the Republican cause is safe and victory is assured."

A gathering of Republicans in Boston invited him to attend a commemoration of Thomas Jefferson's birthday on April 13. Lincoln had been appropriating the founder of the Democratic Party, the author of the Declaration of Independence, and the prime mover behind the Ordinance of 1787 prohibiting slavery in the Northwest Territory, for his own cause since he spoke against Douglas's Kansas-Nebraska Act in 1854. Lincoln intended to remove the heart of Jefferson from the Democrats, to separate Jefferson from slavery, to expose the Democrats' betrayal of their true heritage, and to wrap the Republicans in the legitimacy of Jefferson. He sought to wrest Jefferson from his distorted reduction into a doctrine of pro-slavery states' rights defined as liberty.

Lincoln could not attend the Boston event, but instead sent a message, noting that "it is both curious and interesting that those supposed to descend politically from the party opposed to Jefferson, should now be celebrating his birth-day in their own original seat of empire, while those claiming political descent from him have nearly ceased to breathe his name everywhere. Remembering too, that the Jefferson party were formed upon their supposed superior devotion to the *personal* rights of men, holding the rights of *property* to be secondary only, and greatly inferior, and then assuming that the so-called democracy of to-day, are the Jefferson, and their opponents, the anti-Jefferson parties, it will be equally interesting to note how completely the two have changed hands as to the principle upon which they were originally supposed to be divided. The democracy of to-day hold the *liberty* of one man to be absolutely nothing, when in conflict with another man's right of *property*. Republicans, on the contrary, are for both the *man* and the *dollar*; but in cases of conflict, the man *before* the dollar."

Lincoln offered a humorous anecdote to describe the realignment of parties in which the core principles of democracy had been transferred from their original source. "I remember once being much amused at seeing two partially intoxicated men engage in a fight with their great-coats on, which fight, after a long, and rather harmless contest, ended in each having fought himself *out* of his own coat, and *into* that of the other. If the two leading parties of this day are really identical with the two in the days of Jefferson and Adams, they have performed about the same feat as the two drunken men. But soberly, it is now no child's play to save the principles of Jefferson from total overthrow in this nation."

Lincoln had long been upset by the contempt shown by proslavery advocates and the contemptuous indifference of Douglas to the "self-evident" truth that "all men are created equal." "The principles of Jefferson are the definitions and axioms of free society," said Lincoln. "And yet they are denied, and evaded, with no small show of success. One dashingly calls them 'glittering generalities'; another bluntly calls them 'self evident lies'; and still others insidiously argue that they apply only to 'superior races.' These expressions, differing in form, are identical in object and effect—the supplanting the principles of free government, and restoring those of classification, caste, and legitimacy. They would delight a convocation of crowned heads, plotting against the people. They are the vanguard—the miners, and sappers—of returning despotism. We must repulse them, or they will subjugate us. This is a world of compensations; and he who would *be* no slave, must consent to *have* no slave. Those who deny freedom to others, deserve it not for themselves; and, under a just God, cannot long retain it."

Lincoln ended by claiming Jefferson's first principle and the very cause of the American Revolution for his party. "All honor to Jefferson—to the man who, in the concrete pressure of a struggle for national independence by a single people, had the coolness, forecast, and capacity to introduce into a merely revolutionary document, an abstract truth, applicable to all men and all times, and so to embalm it there, that to-day, and in all coming days, it shall be a rebuke and a stumbling-block to the very harbingers of re-appearing tyranny and oppression."

Lincoln's stupendous ideological reinvention of the Jeffersonian tradition was not the idle work of someone who expected to be spending the years ahead in small claims courts. In turning down the invitation of Thomas J. Pickett, editor of the *Rock Island Register,* to speak at Rock Island, Lincoln observed on April 16, "As to the other matter you kindly mention, I must, in candor, say I do not think myself fit for the Presidency. I certainly am flattered, and gratified, that some partial friends think of me in that connection; but I really think it best for our cause that no concerted effort, such as you suggest, should be made." Whether someone who confidently challenged Douglas, who was the leading Democratic candidate for president, truly thought himself as just "a sucker" was at least a deflection. His advice not to wage a "concerted effort" was at least a matter of strategy.

The Republican State Central Committee had met in Bloomington on April 7 to discuss Lincoln's presidential candidacy among other matters. According to Gustave Koerner, "it was agreed that the best policy for the party in our State was to keep Lincoln in the background for the present, or at least not to push his claims to any extent. The friends of Seward, Bates, Cameron and Chase, would fight against each other, and necessarily damage the candidates they upheld. Lincoln, being out of the struggle in a measure, would be let alone, and, when brought forward at the proper time, would meet with no embittered enemies." Lincoln was almost certainly a proponent of this approach. None of it leaked publicly.

On April 20, William Osborn Stoddard, the youthful writer for the *Central Illinois Gazette,* published in Champaign, wrote an editorial entitled "Party Principles," in which he dismissed as Republican presidential candidates "second rate men, 'compromise men' and sapless political sticks," suggesting instead "the man who for years stood alone on the floor of the United States Senate, the only champion of free labor against the encroachments of the slave oligarchy, to the gallant son of Illinois who won so proud a wreath of laurels I the last senatorial campaign"—Seward and Lincoln. A week later, on April 27, Lincoln, in town representing clients, happened to drop by Stoddard's office. "We had the pleasure of introducing to the hospitalities of our sanctum a few days since," he wrote, "the Hon. Abraham Lincoln. Few men can make an hour pass away more agreeably. We do not pretend to know whether Mr. Lincoln will ever condescend to occupy the White House or not. . . . No man in the west at the present time occupies a more enviable position before the people or stands a better chance of obtaining a high position among those to whose guidance our ship of state is to be entrusted." (Stoddard would become one of Lincoln's private secretaries in the White House.)

Throughout the spring German Americans organized rallies across the country against a proposed law in the Massachusetts legislature that would deny the vote to foreign-born citizens for two years after their naturalization. Carl Schurz spoke at Faneuil Hall in Boston on April 18, the eve of the anniversary of the Battle of Lexington and Concord, against the bill and for "True Americanism," the "ideal mission of this country," "the Republic of equal rights." German language newspapers served as the main advocates of the anti-nativist movement. In Springfield, Republicans held a meeting on May 14 to "protest" the Massachusetts act and uphold "Liberty and Equality to all the American citizens." Theodore Canisius, an exiled German revolutionary turned Republican, who had lately edited a newspaper called the *Freie Presse* in Alton that had backed Lincoln for the Senate, was the principal organizer of the assembly. The chief speaker was Herndon, delivering a speech that was undoubtedly edited by Lincoln, which denounced the nativist bill as "impolitic," "wrong and unjust," and "cruelly or wickedly despotocratic."

Days after the Springfield protest, both the *Illinois State Journal* and the *Chicago Press and Tribune* published a letter Lincoln wrote to Canisius opposing the Massachusetts bill. "I am against its adoption in Illinois, or in any other place, where I have a right to oppose it," he wrote. "Understanding the spirit of our institutions to aim at the *elevation* of men, I am opposed to whatever tends to *degrade* them. I have some little notoriety for commiserating the oppressed condition of the negro; and I should be strangely inconsistent if I could favor any project for curtailing the existing rights of *white men,* even though born in different lands, and speaking different languages from myself."

Immediately after Lincoln's letter was widely published, he became the secret owner of a German language newspaper and installed Canisius as editor. Through Canisius, Lincoln bought the title to the *Staats-Anzeiger* with the proceeds of a $500 legal fee. "Herndon," he told his partner, "I gave the

Germans $250 of yours the other day." Lincoln also attempted to secure some funding from the Republican State Central Committee, but Norman Judd did not trust Canisius. "I can only say in confidence," he wrote Lincoln, ". . . that Canisius is a leech. He sucked more blood from you at Springfield and from the "Com[mittee], than the whole establishment was worth." Yet Lincoln managed to get a small sum. Lincoln handwrote the contract on May 30 with his banker and chief political funder, Jacob Bunn, noting that he "bought the press, types &c . . . with my money," appending a provision that Canisius as editor would edit the paper "in political sentiment" in line with "Republican platforms," and not publish "any thing opposed to, or designed to injure the Republican party." The *Illinois Staats-Anzeiger* began appearing in July. If any incident marked the beginning of Lincoln's campaign for the presidency it was his purchase of this newspaper, which advanced him in contrast to the other German paper, the *Illinois Staats-Zeitung* of Chicago, whose editor, George Schneider, though friendly to Lincoln, was promoting Seward for president. In July, Lincoln sent personal letters to German Republicans asking them, as he wrote one, "I think you could not do a more efficient service than to get it a few subscribers, if possible." (Lincoln sustained the *Staats-Anzeiger* until December 6, 1860, after which he appointed Canisius consul to Vienna.)

During the 1848 campaign, the Whigs had sent Lincoln on a speaking tour in New England to make the case to antislavery voters not to cast ballots for the Free Soil Party. Though he appeared on the same platform as Seward in Boston, he referred to himself as a "hayseed." He was a little remarked upon curiosity. After his invisible congressional career, until the Whig Party expired, not a single national newspaper solicited his opinion. During the 1856 campaign, the farthest east he traveled to speak and the largest crowd he attracted was at Kalamazoo, Michigan. Until his Senate contest with Douglas he was a minor provincial character without any reason to demand wider attention. Now, anticipating the 1860 race, he felt self-possessed in his reputation to inform influential men in the party where they were in error. He presumed to instruct them on how to frame a Republican center around a winning strategy, which required Illinois. Holding the Illinois party together was paramount to him, but it was a means to a larger end.

Without personal familiarity, he sent Salmon Chase a letter on June 9 to explain to him the snare the Ohio party had just created for the 1860 campaign. Lincoln knew well that Chase was a leading candidate for president.

"Please pardon the liberty I take in addressing you, as I now do," Lincoln began politely before instantly dropping his deference. "It appears by the papers that the late Republican State convention of Ohio adopted a Platform, of which the following is one plank, 'A repeal of the atrocious Fugitive Slave Law.'" Lincoln himself considered it "ungodly," as he said privately. But he was speaking to harsh political imperatives. "This is already damaging us here. I have no doubt that if that plank be even *introduced* into the next Republican National convention, it will explode it. Once introduced, its supporters and its opponents will quarrel irreconcilably. The latter believe the U.S. constitution declares that a fugitive slave *'shall be delivered up'*; and they look upon the above plank as dictated by the spirit which declares a fugitive slave *'shall not be delivered up.'* I enter upon no argument one way or the other; but I assure you the cause of Republicanism is hopeless in Illinois, if it be in any way made responsible for that plank. I hope you can, and will, contribute something to relieve us from it."

Chase wrote back on June 13 telling Lincoln that the Ohio party's position was of a piece with his "house divided" speech. "The reliance you put in my discretion and in my disposition to avoid all extremes which may endanger the success of the Republican Party gratifies me much, and it will be my study to deserve it. That the avoidance of extremes however, is not at all inconsistent with the boldest & manliest avowal of our great principles & views your own example is that noble speech of yours at Springfield which opened the campaign last year in Illinois makes evidence enough." He added, like a teacher to a pupil, "I trust that our friends in Illinois will, if not already prepared to take the same ground, soon be educated up to it."

Lincoln replied on June 20, "My only object was to impress you with what I believe is true, that the introduction of a proposition for repeal of the Fugitive Slave law, into the next Republican National convention, will explode the convention and the party. Having turned your attention to the point, I wish to do no more." So ended their first exchange.

Lincoln was horrified at the Fugitive Slave Act. But he gave it nominal support to show his support for the rule of law. Having done that, he went on to make his overarching argument that the founders were antislavery and the Constitution an antislavery document, despite the federal fugitive slave provision. He also sought to deprive the Democrats of a wedge issue to divide and isolate the Republicans. His immediate political assent did not mean either his personal assent or his intention for slavery's "ultimate extinction."

In July 1857, Frederick Clements, a fugitive slave, was arrested and jailed in Springfield, the first fugitive slave case in Illinois after the Dred Scott decision. Clements was represented at the hearing before the federal commissioner by the law firm of Lincoln and Herndon with Herndon as the acting attorney. On the basis of the Dred Scott ruling, Clements was remanded to his owner in Kentucky. "The poor negro was tried and sent south—could not prevent it," Herndon wrote Theodore Parker. "You cannot do any good when the iron-chain logic is around the man and fetters are on his limbs." He pointed out that the commissioner received $10 from the government for declaring Clements a slave, whereas he would have got $5 if he had decided he was free.

In September 1859, a slave named Jim Gray escaped from his master in Missouri to Illinois, where he was captured. At his hearing in Ottawa, where Lincoln and Douglas had begun their debates a year earlier, local abolitionists physically intervened and whisked Gray away. He fled to Chicago and then to freedom in Canada. John Hossack, the leading industrialist in Ottawa, a prominent Republican who had sat on the platform of the debate as a Lincoln man, and whose mansion was a station in the Underground Railroad, was arrested for blocking police and enabling Gray to escape. He was represented at his trial in 1860 by Isaac Newton Arnold, a Chicago lawyer, founding member of the Republican Party, and legal associate of Lincoln. Hossack delivered a stirring speech to the jury. "Great God! Can these things be? Can it be possible? What country is this?" The *Chicago Times,* Douglas's paper, played up the trial to equate Lincoln with lawbreaking. Hossack was sentenced to ten days after which John Wentworth, Chicago's mayor, held a large banquet in his honor. A.J. Grover, a Springfield lawyer and friend of Lincoln, told him he would have done what Hossack had. "Constitutional or not, I will never obey the Fugitive Slave Law." Grover recalled Lincoln's reply, "and I shall never forget his earnestness as he emphasized it by striking his hand on his knee, 'it is ungodly! it is ungodly! no doubt it is ungodly! but it is the law of the land, and we must obey it as we find it.'"

Out of the blue, on June 13, 1859, Lincoln heard from an old friend, Josiah Lucas, who had once edited a Whig paper in Jacksonville, Illinois, gone to Washington as a clerk in the Land Office, and tried to help Lincoln secure appointment as head of the Land Office in early 1849. Lucas wrote Lincoln on June 13 that he would soon hear from "our old friend," Nathan Sargent, an Old Whig journalist known as "Oliver Old School" and former clerk of the House of Representatives, who had been one of Lincoln's boardinghouse mates in Washington, and "with your humble servant as tutor has got to believe that you would not make a bad Candidate for the White House." Sargent had more recently worked as recorder of the Land Office under Fillmore, joined the Know Nothings, and been a publicist for Fillmore in 1856. "Sargent belongs to the Fillmore school,—in other words, he was a prominent 'K. N.' but always a Whig and bears towards the Locos [Democrats] an undying hatred. There are many old Whigs in friend Sargent's fix who are anxious to have a chance to help in driving the Spoilers from power, if they can get a plank to stand upon."

Sargent was at the center of a movement to create a new third party on the ruins of Fillmore's campaign and the Know Nothings, an attempted Fillmore redux to displace the Republicans, remove the antislavery position from national politics, and edge aside the Southern Ultras. Working with A.H.H. Stuart, Fillmore's secretary of the interior, a Know Nothing state senator in Virginia, Sargent reached out to border state leaders such as John Bell of Tennessee and Crittenden of Kentucky and held an organizing conference in late 1858, which led to Opposition Party state conventions in Virginia, North Carolina, and Kentucky. Eventually, the Opposition Party would mutate into the Constitutional Union Party in 1860, the recasting of the American or Know Nothing Party and last gasp of Old Whigs who could not give up the ghost.

Lincoln heard from Sargent at once. "How do you do? my worthy & esteemed old friend. You are having an easy time compared with what you had last year. Well, that year has gone, & this is going: but another is coming full of importance; & what are to be its results? Shall we, like a parcel of fools quarrel & lose all? or shall we, like men of common sense, let minor matters go, & unite to whip the enemy?" Sargent confessed he was not a Republican, still an "Old Whig" and "an American," in other words, a Know Nothing, and wanted to co-opt Lincoln to his politics. He proposed a bare-bones program of opposition to reopening the slave trade and corruption as the way to gain Southern support.

Lincoln's response on June 23 was scathingly dismissive. He had no intention of abandoning the Republican Party or his opposition to the extension of slavery to chase the chimera of Old Whiggery.

> You state a platform for such union in these words "*Opposition to the opening of the Slave-trade; & eternal hostility to the rotten democracy.*" You add, by way of comment "I say, if the republicans would be content with this,

there will be no obstacle to a union of the *opposition*. But this should be distinctly understood, before Southern men are asked to join them in a National convention." Well, I say such a platform, unanimously adopted by a National convention, with two of the best men living placed upon it as candidates, would probably carry Maryland, and would certainly not carry a single other state. It would gain nothing in the South, and lose everything in the North. . . . Last year the Republicans of Illinois cast 125,000 votes; on such a platform as yours they cannot cast as many by 50,000. You could not help perceiving this, if you would but reflect that the republican party is utterly pow[er]less everywhere, if it will, by any means, drive from it all those who came to it from the democracy for the sole object of preventing the spread, and nationalization of slavery. Whenever this object is waived by the organization, they will drop the organization; and the organization itself will dissolve into thin air. Your platform proposes to allow the spread, and nationalization of slavery to proceed without let or hindrance, save only that it shall not receive supplies directly from Africa. Surely you do not seriously believe the Republicans can come to any such terms.

Lincoln had crafted much of his rhetoric in his debates with Douglas and charted his travels around the state to winning over the Old Whigs. He still worried about alienating them as his letters to Chase showed. But there were red lines he would not cross. In his letter to Sargent, he cut off his overture for Republicanism to collapse into the American Party of Fillmore or now the Opposition Party of Crittenden. Bitter about Crittenden's intervention against him in the Senate race, Lincoln had not the slightest intention of suddenly abandoning everything he had done to create the Republican Party for his betrayer's new mock party. He had never before been so explicit about the uselessness of the Old Whig position. Lincoln had given it up long ago, but his letter put into words goodbye to all that. He could not know his conflict with Old Whiggery and its various posthumous incarnations was in its early stages and would last until he signed the yet unimagined Emancipation Proclamation.

On the Fourth of July Congressman Schuyler Colfax of Indiana came to Springfield to meet with other Republican leaders and coordinate for the coming national campaign but missed seeing Lincoln. Lincoln wrote him a letter on July 6 communicating his main thought, which explained the coherence of his actions over the past few months. "My main object in such conversation would be to hedge against divisions in the Republican ranks generally, and particularly for the contest of 1860," he wrote. "The point of danger is the temptation in different localities to '*platform*' for something which will be popular just there, but which, nevertheless, will be a firebrand elsewhere, and especially in a National convention. As instances, the movement against foreigners in Massachusetts; in New-Hampshire, to make obedience to the Fugitive Slave law, punishable as a crime; in Ohio, to repeal the Fugitive Slave law; and squatter sovereignty in Kansas. In these things there is explosive matter enough to blow up half a dozen national conventions, if it gets into them; and what gets very rife outside of conventions is very likely to find its way into them. What is desirable, if possible, is that in every local convocation of Republicans, a point should be made to avoid everything which will distract republicans elsewhere. . . . In a word, in every locality we should look beyond our noses; and at least say *nothing* on points where it is probable we shall disagree."

Colfax wrote back to Lincoln on July 14 to acknowledge the difficulty of the political task ahead in combining conservatives and radicals. "How this mass of mind shall be consolidated into a victorious phalanx in 1860 is the great problem—I think of our eventful times. And he who can could accomplish it, is worthier of fame than Napoleon or Emanuel." He concluded, "And I can assure you if you will lead in this work, you will find me a faithful follower of your counsel."

Colfax was not the only Republican leader from another state drawn to Lincoln. On July 23, he received a long letter from Samuel Galloway, a former Republican congressman from Ohio. The state party was wracked with division over a case in which Judge Joseph Swan, chief justice of the Ohio Supreme Court, a Republican, felt compelled to uphold the ruling of a federal court that found an abolitionist guilty under the Fugitive Slave Act. Swan was not renominated for his position, which was elective. Galloway laid out the treacherous politics to Lincoln:

> We made a great blunder in Ohio, at our recent Convention, in dishonoring Judge Swan by not renominating him for the Sup. Judgeship—He is very capable, honest & popular. . . . He would have been pleased to decide otherwise—but could not do so, conscientiously, with his intelligence of decisions of our Courts upon that subject—Our radicals clamored for a repudiation of all existing adjudications . . . and hence they resolved upon his defeat and presented the degrading alternative—reject Swan or we will repudiate & defeat the ticket—Our trading politicians and political prostitutes for the

sake of harmony (falsely so called) alarmed at the threat, agreed to sacrifice Swan & propitiate the fanatics—The result will be, I am apprehensive that our Republican ticket will be beaten in Ohio—Many of us who despise the Fugitive Slave Law, and who would labor and have labored to have it modified or repealed, equally despise all attempts to overthrow it by lawless & revolutionary measures.—We cannot consistently denounce the efforts to reopen the slave trade, by overriding the Constitution & laws—and yet act similarly in regard to a plain provision of the Constitution as to the recapture of "fugitives from labor"—unless we in Ohio can purge ourselves from this stain upon our Republicanism; and we cannot engage in the battle for 1860, with hope of success—To be brief, and to jump to my conclusion—we cannot have Salmon P Chase, or any man representing his ultra ideas as our Candidate for 1860. Chase and I are personally friendly—and in this matter I have no one friend to reward nor enemies to punish—The object is too great to be sacrificed either to partialities or prejudices—

Galloway observed that other hopeful candidates also carried similar burdens. "The Objections to Seward and [Nathaniel] Banks are quite as formidable as those which may be noted against Chase I will not at present specify or discuss them—The truth and my idea upon this point are not to be disguised—We must take some man not hitherto corrupted with the discussion upon Candidates." Galloway raised two more names as possibly acceptable, Trumbull and Senator William P. Fessenden of Maine, but confessed, "I would cheerfully adopt any one of you but I am candid to say you are my choice—and that preference is well known by many of my intimate friends—Your programme of principles as set forth in your discussions with Judge Douglass—will suit all Republicans—and especially those of the old Whig stamp—"

Lincoln replied on July 28 to Galloway's "flattering" letter. He agreed with Galloway's reflections on the political situation in Ohio but added a warning against Douglas: "another thing our friends are doing which gives me some uneasiness. It is their leaning towards 'popular sovereignty.'" Lincoln did not mention to Galloway his own correspondence with Chase. "As to Gov. Chase, I have a kind side for him. He was one of the few distinguished men of the nation who gave us, in Illinois, their sympathy last year. I never saw him, suppose him to be able, and right-minded; but still he may not be the most suitable as a candidate for the Presidency." He finished with his usual demurral. "I must say I do not think myself fit for the Presidency."

Yet he urged Galloway to keep writing. "I shall look for your letters anxiously."

Jesse Fell, who had first raised the idea of Lincoln's presidential candidacy to him, meanwhile quietly traveled the state as secretary of the Illinois State Central Committee organizing Republicans for his "big idea." "He found occasion, moreover, in perfecting the state organization, to visit most of the counties, where the people as a rule were eager to see 'Abe' Lincoln a presidential candidate," wrote Fell's biographer. "There was no need, apparently, to urge Lincoln's name to Illinoisans. It was in other states that the Lincoln propaganda must be pushed."

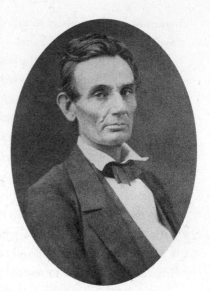

Abraham Lincoln, 1859

ICARUS

James Buchanan had accepted the devastating losses of the Democrats in the 1858 midterm elections with "much philosophy." "Well! we have met the enemy . . . & we are theirs," he wrote his niece Harriet Lane. "This I have anticipated for three months, and was not taken by surprise, except as to the extent of our defeat. . . . Yesterday . . . we had a merry time of it, laughing among other things over our crushing defeat. It is so great that it is almost absurd."

"There is no such entity as a democratic party," concluded the *Washington States,* a Democratic newspaper in the capital, in an editorial after the elections. "Have we a Democratic Party among us?" asked the pro-administration *Washington Union,* answering that the party would certainly "achieve victory" in 1860 under "the banner of its time-honored principles." In another article, the newspaper assailed Douglas as a heretic for his Freeport Doctrine in his debates with Lincoln.

There was, at least, not much left of the Northern wing of the Democratic Party. Hardly any supporters of the Bu-

Stephen A. Douglas

chanan administration survived in Northern state legislatures. Of the remaining Democrats, most were anti-Lecompton Douglas Democrats. Barely any Democrats remained in New England. Republicans were ascendant in Ohio, Indiana, Pennsylvania, and New York; Democrats were routed throughout the upper Midwest. Yet the elections ratified the Democrats' hold across the South as universal with no Republicans and a few pockets of latter-day Know Nothings. The greater the Republican gains in the North, the more precarious Southerners felt their hold on federal power.

In the House of Representatives, the Democrats lost 35 seats; the Republicans gained 26. They declined from a 133 to 90 majority to a Republican near majority of 116 to 98 Democrats, with 5 seats held by Know Nothings and 8 by Democrats aligned with Douglas. Only 33 Northern Democrats remained; only 25 supported the administration. Every Democratic seat in the North that was lost—27—was lost to the Republicans. Every loss in the South was to the Opposition Party. The Know Nothings melted down from 9 seats to 5, but the Opposition Party, Know Nothings by another name, gained 19. In the Senate, the Democrats' majority shrank from 42 to 20 majority to 39 to 25, all the Republican gains in Northern states.

Douglas believed his victory had put him on a sound footing for going forward to the nomination. His sense of security rested on illusion. In Illinois he had won only through gerrymandered districts and lost the popular vote. The Northern Democratic Party was hollowed out. His enemies in the Northwest such as Jesse Bright were waiting to ambush him. But Douglas took his reelection as a victory over Buchanan, who had done all he could to sabotage him. His bravado gave him a false belief he had the upper hand. "I have nothing to ask for or grant in that quarter," he told Charles Ray of the *Chicago Tribune*. "He made the war; and by God! He shall make peace if peace is to be made at all." Douglas thought his supposedly inherent strength would force Buchanan to sue for peace, the Southerners to fall in line, and his march to the nomination proceed as a stately affair.

In late November 1858, Douglas and his wife left Chicago for a grand triumphal political tour. He headed down the Mississippi River "to try the pulse of the Southern people," landing at St. Louis, Memphis, and New Orleans, where he regaled crowds with reprises of highlights of his campaign against Lincoln—extolling popular sovereignty and assailing the "house divided." Douglas in New Orleans on December 6 called Lincoln "unscrupulous" for "declaring the doctrine that the Union cannot continue to exist half slave and half free." He attacked Lincoln's upholding the Declaration of

Independence's statement that "all men are created equal" as the "Abolition Catechism." "By this specious, but sophistical argument, they have succeeded in imposing on some weak-minded men, and some old women and children, until they have educated a generation who really believe that the negro is their brother." He repeated his refrain from the debates that "this Government was made by white men, for the benefit of white men and their posterity forever, to be administered by white men, and none others," and that "the negro race" should be regarded like "the deaf and dumb, or the insane."

Douglas appealed to the "glorious destiny which the Almighty has marked out," pointing to the acquisition of Cuba, which Southerners, if not the Almighty, had marked out for the expansion of slavery. "It is our destiny to have Cuba, and it is folly to debate the question," Douglas proclaimed. With that flourish, his steamer headed for Havana, where he delivered a rousing speech envisioning the manifest destiny of gaining Cuba and bought a stockpile of two thousand cigars. In Baltimore, on January 5, 1859, he declared, "It is none of our business whether you have slaves or not. . . . When you get into those hot climates, it is not a struggle between the negro and the white man, but a struggle between the negro and the crocodile." He pushed on to New York, welcomed as a conquering hero by thousands at City Hall, then to Philadelphia, where he was greeted with a two-hundred-gun salute and feted with a dinner at Independence Hall, before arriving for the reopening of the Congress in December.

Buchanan's blithe spirit about the midterm losses in his letter to Miss Lane was pretense. He was bitter, angry, and vengeful, his hostility concentrated on his nemesis. Howell Cobb spoke for the administration: "If Judge Douglas had done as he promised . . . all of us ought to have sustained him. Such has not been his course. Publicly he attacks the administration. . . . Privately he indulges in the coarsest abuse of the President. Under these circumstances to ask our support is in my opinion asking too much. . . . [Douglas is] determined to break up the Democratic party . . . to unite with anybody and everybody to defeat us."

Buchanan's war on Douglas intensified. Having failed to defeat him in Illinois he was determined to destroy him for the nomination. Every federal job and contract was denied to any potential Douglas delegate and dangled before any against him. The entire government was geared into a patronage operation to damage Douglas for the convention. "If Douglas is to be defeated nothing should be left in doubt," George Plitt, one of Buchanan's oldest friends, wrote Howell Cobb. "Even a single delegate from New England might turn the scale one way or the other." Buchanan even made an effort to reconcile with Robert J. Walker to entice him to enter as a candidate to save the party from both Douglas and the Southern Ultras. No secondary hatred was allowed to deter from the principal hatred.

While Douglas was steaming to Cuba, the Democrats on the Senate Committee on Committees, directed by Slidell, stripped him of his chairmanship of the Committee on Territories. In a stroke his power base in the Senate was destroyed and he was for all intents and purposes excommunicated from the Democratic caucus. One after another Southern senator urged that Douglas be read out of the Democratic Party for his Freeport "heresy," as Senator Clement C. Clay of Alabama put it. "How can any true state rights Southern man maintain that he should have been retained as an exponent of the Democratic party?" Douglas's key ally on the committee, Senator David C. Broderick of California, was excluded from the kangaroo court that evicted him.

The *Chicago Press and Tribune* reported, "the political remains of Mr. Douglas were formally interred by the Senate . . . the Douglas party in the Senate is brought down to the accumulation of zeros. . . . The brethren had divided Joseph's coat among them, the administrators had distributed the assets of the defunct's estate. It seems more Douglas men have been detected in office. They must go out, and it is now confidentially announced that execution will be immediately done. . . . As regards the approaching Presidential contest, Mr. Douglas might as well never have been a member of the Democratic party; and . . . he might as well leap into a cauldron of living fire, as to submit his fortune to the Charleston Convention."

Upon returning to Washington, Douglas withheld comment about the deprivation of his lost chairmanship. He stepped back onto the Senate floor on January 12. "The demeanor of his colleagues generally was studiously cold and distant," reported the *New York Times*. "A few of them approached to welcome him back to the Chamber—but many more avoided him altogether." In early February 1859, he and Adele opened the social season with a "grand ball" at their mansion, inviting 1,200 notables, asserting his status as the future leader of the party and the next president. Every member of the Buchanan cabinet sent regrets.

Douglas was cut by more than coldness. Several apparent attempts were made in January to ensnare him in quarrels that would provoke duels to kill him. "There are men here who will not spare him . . . are keen for his blood," said Senator Hammond. When Douglas protested against Slidell over planting the story about Douglas's Mississippi plantation in the *Chicago Tribune* during the Senate campaign it seemed to Douglas's people that Slidell wanted to push him into a duel. *Harper's Weekly* warned, "Senator Slidell is a well known fire-eater, to whom personal encounters and duels are matters of course. He is doubtless highly skilled in the use of dueling weapons. Senator Douglas is not likely to know any thing about pistols. If Senator Slidell persuades his colleague to 'go out' with him, the chances are that the latter will be killed." "Soon it was whispered that it had been determined at a caucus at Cobb's home that John Slidell should insult Douglas in the Senate bar, force the quarrel and shoot him down," wrote Douglas's biographer, George Fort Milton. A sympathetic newspaper reporter, George Alfred Townsend, sent Douglas a note, "If you are pushed to the wall send for Tom Hawkins, of Louisville." Hawkins was a famous gunslinger and duelist. There may or may not have been a plot to pull Douglas into a duel, but Douglas felt himself under physical threat. He had witnessed what had happened to Sumner. He hired Tom Hawkins as a personal bodyguard to accompany him around Washington. Dealing with Slidell, Douglas stopped his surrogates from responding and the matter died out.

The Slidell affair was instantly followed by another clash. After Douglas denounced Buchanan's shadow party in Illinois of National Democrats working against him, Senator Graham N. Fitch of Indiana, who owed his seat to Bright's machine, accused Douglas of a personal affront because Fitch's son was among those who had received a patronage appointment in Illinois. On January 21, Douglas responded to Fitch's insults. "Today, in secret session of the Senate, you offered me an affront so wanton, unprovoked, and unjustifiable that I am obliged to infer it must have been the impulse of momentary passion, and not of deliberate premeditation." Douglas demanded "retracting the offensive language which you thus gratuitously and unwarrantably applied to me." His notes were hand delivered by Tom Hawkins. Fitch wrote him the next day of his "determination to defend the honor and character of my son." Douglas finally sent a letter that his remarks did not include his son. Fitch withdrew his challenge and Douglas accepted. "I am averse to prolonging this controversy." The *Washington Union* published in full Douglas's and Fitch's letters to highlight the bad blood.

On February 23, the Senate of the 35th Congress convened for one of its last orders of business—the Southern claim for protection of slavery in the territories in the Democratic platform. It was raised not for any legislative

purpose, but entirely to derail Douglas
on his road to the presidential nomination. Senator Albert Gallatin Brown of
Georgia demanded, "We have a right
of protection for our slave property in
the Territories. The Constitution, as ex-
pounded by the Supreme Court, awards
it. We demand it and we mean to have it."
Without it, he said, "the Constitution is a
failure, and the Union a despotism, and
then, Sir, I am prepared to retire from the
concern." "I would never vote for a slave
code in the Territories by the Congress,"
replied Douglas. "We are not, without
eyes open, to be cheated," said Jefferson
Davis.

Senator Jefferson Davis of Mississippi

Davis had risen from the near dead. For months in 1858, during the
Lecompton debate, he had been wracked with fever, chills, and blindness,
suffering his worst bout with the effects of the venereal disease that chron-
ically afflicted him for years. He was confined to a darkened room, gripped
with pain, his left eye filled with pus. He appeared in the Senate for debates "a pale ghastly-looking figure, his eye bandaged with strips of white
linen over the head," according to a reporter for the *Washington Union*. He
never regained sight in his left eye. Clouded and discolored, he could see only
light and darkness. He posed for photographs in the future showing only his
right side. The year before, in July 1857, he and his family went on a recu-
perative holiday for months to Maine. He spoke in Boston defending both
slavery and the Union, the latter emphasis opening him to denunciations
from fire-eating newspapers, the *Charleston Mercury* and the *New Orleans
Delta,* as a traitor. His rival in Mississippi, Albert Gallatin Brown, saw the
moment as a chance to seize the banner of Southern Rights from him. Davis
corrected the record with a public letter stating he did not mean the Union
could not be dissolved.

Davis delivered a formal speech before the Mississippi legislature on November 16, 1858, casting a malediction on Douglas. He declared there was
no difference between Douglas and Seward, whom he called the "master
mind of the so-called Republican Party." "I cannot be compelled to choose
between men, one of whom asserts the power of Congress to deprive us

of a constitutional right, and the other only denies the power of Congress, in order to transfer it to the territorial legislature. Neither the one nor the other has any authority to sit in judgment on our rights under the Constitution."

Then Davis laid down the conditions for secession in the event an antislavery candidate would be elected president. "Whether by the House or by the people, if an Abolitionist be chosen President of the United States, you will have presented to you the question of whether you will permit the government to pass into the hands of your avowed and implacable enemies. Without pausing for your answer, I will state my own position to be that such a result would be a species of revolution by which the purposes of the Government would be destroyed and the observance of its mere forms entitled to no respect. In that event, in such manner as should be most expedient, I should deem it your duty to provide for your safety outside of a Union with those who have already shown the will, and would have acquired the power, to deprive you of your birthright and to reduce you to worse than the colonial dependence of your fathers."

In his speech on February 23 in the Senate, Davis chose the metaphor of blindness to describe Douglas, whom he personally despised, and compare him with Seward, whom he personally liked. "If I have to choose between the two, I could forgive more to the blindness of the man who warred upon a constitutional right, and who I hoped was ignorant of its existence, than to the man who admitted it and withheld from me every possibility of its enjoyment."

Douglas piped up. "I recognize slave property as being on an equality with all other property, and apply the same rules to it," he protested. But Davis would not accept Douglas's explanation. He called popular sovereignty "a siren's song . . . a thing shadowy and fleeting, changing its color as often as the chameleon . . . a delusive gauze thrown over the public mind" (referencing his failing eyesight), and declared that Douglas had committed "a fatal blunder" and was "full of heresy." He accused Douglas of creating "a squabble by which men seek to build up a political reputation by catering to the prejudice of a majority to exclude the property of the minority. It is that upon which I set my feet with scorn and indignation."

James M. Mason of Virginia rose to revile Douglas as a false messiah: "You promised us bread, and you have given us a stone; you promised us a fish, and you have given us a serpent; we thought you had given us a substantial right; and you have given us the most evanescent shadow and delusion." "I have no idea of leaving," Douglas said defiantly. "I intend to stand here in my place."

The Senate floor on that date, February 23, was the opening of Douglas's abyss. His gestures at conciliation and candidacy were summarily rejected. His motives were censured as purely selfish and lacking any principle. He had misjudged that he would be treated with some modicum of deference as the presumptive candidate, that the Southerners would approach him as the coming power, and they would adjust to him. Douglas was always attempting to re-create the moment of his greatest success, when he burst onto Washington in 1850, taking command of passage of the Compromise and enacting the Illinois Central Railroad Act. But he had been easily shunted aside for the nomination in 1852 after offending nearly everybody. Four years later, in 1856, his championing the Kansas-Nebraska Act in 1854, which he calculated would more than replicate his 1850 feat, did not carry the nomination for him. He was again denied as Southern support went to an eternal Northern man of Southern sympathy. Douglas supposed his concession at the convention and his political and financial contributions to Buchanan's campaign would smooth his nomination in 1860, when he would have earned his turn after all. But the Southerners were resolved to resist him to the end. His own mechanism, constructed for his victory, the Kansas-Nebraska Act, inexorably ground down his hopes. Lecompton forced him to choose his doctrine or the fraud his doctrine had fostered. His ambition was posed against his ambition. He could either lose Illinois and his reelection, the North and his nomination certainly, or much of the South and the nomination possibly. In 1858 he had no choice except for Illinois, and Lincoln drove him into a corner with the Freeport Doctrine. Lincoln understood what Douglas did not, that his opposition to Lecompton was unforgivable, his Freeport Doctrine fatal. Lincoln the fatalist, a believer in the cause and effect of circumstances, also believed in intervening when he felt he could hasten the process. After Douglas's reelection, his opportunism, which had been intended to meet the Southerners halfway, was repulsed with utter contempt. His vapid nostrums about popular sovereignty to establish a middle ground within his party were taken as an ill wind. His rote attacks on Lincoln's "house divided" speech did him little good with those who classified him as menacing as Lincoln. Pointedly indifferent to slavery, he could not grasp the consequences of the central question for his own political future. Attempting to evade the issue, he made himself vulnerable. Trying to control events, he was consumed by them. He was both the cause and the effect.

He was no longer suspended in midair. Douglas could not see that flying toward the sun he would be incinerated.

It had become a truism since 1852 that the Democrats could not win the presidency without a Northern candidate, and Douglas was the only logical, preeminent, and viable one. He dispatched a host of agents far and wide to gather endorsements, delegates and gin up newspaper support. Many dark horses were touted, but no other candidate had a campaign remotely competitive. His *Chicago Times* editor, James W. Sheahan, was assigned to write the campaign biography from Douglas's own outline. Douglas had an idealized portrait painted by the renowned artist George P.A. Healy, depicting him in the pink of health, rosy cheeked, with a slender silhouette. Douglas had it reproduced as a photograph and widely distributed it. One of his key men, A.D. Banks, editor of the *Southside Democrat* newspaper in Virginia, toured through the West and South and reported in person to Douglas that his support was "overwhelming and resistless." Forney, working hand in glove with Douglas, plagued Buchanan in the *Philadelphia Press* with columns of embarrassing incidents while organizing Pennsylvania delegates. Even the mercurial George N. Sanders, who had defected for the main chance with Buchanan in 1856, was back on board. Reverdy Johnson wrote Douglas in March that Buchanan would pay the price for opposing him. "What a bankrupt Administration we have. To differ with the President is treason and he who does is reviled. I wonder if the fool will ever discover that in this he only makes his own course the more odious."

Visiting Chicago, J.B. Dorr, editor of the *Dubuque Daily Express and Herald* of Iowa, reported to Sheahan disquieting news about fraying support. He urged Douglas to announce his candidacy at once. On June 22, Douglas wrote a letter to Dorr intended as a public declaration. He stated that his platform would be exactly that of the party's platform of 1856, which had endorsed popular sovereignty as a sop to him. On that basis, he would reject "new issues as the revival of the African slave trade, or a Congressional slave code for the Territories," and "in such an

Stephen A. Douglas, portrait by George Peter Alexander Healy event I could not accept the nomination if tendered to me." With that he drew his own line in the sand beside the one Jefferson Davis and the other Southerners had drawn. Both Douglas and the Southerners were now agreed on the grounds for division. But Douglas gained more confidence. Delegations shaped up for him. While fire-eating Southern newspapers abused him, no other major candidate stepped forward. When, in Alabama, John Forsyth, editor of the *Mobile Register,* one of Douglas's stalwarts, defeated an Ultra for a State Senate seat on the Douglas platform, Ultraism seemed in retreat.

The Douglas bandwagon appeared to be rolling along. In New York, the campaign was under the firm direction of Dean Richmond, a corporate genius, first vice president of the New York Central Railroad, and chairman of the Democratic State Committee. Unexpectedly, the state convention to choose delegates in August turned into a maelstrom. The ancient enmities of New York's internecine wars between the Hards and Softs resurfaced. Mayor Fernando Wood of New York City, boss of Tammany Hall, and favorite of the Five Points gangs that were both criminal and political organizations like the Dead Rabbits, stirred up trouble encouraging the Hards. Senator Daniel S. Dickinson, hardest of the Hards, advanced himself as a favorite son candidate. Governor Henry A. Wise of Virginia, who had until then presented himself to Douglas as a staunch supporter and unbending friend, leaked to the *New York Herald* a letter intended to devastate him during the New York convention and declared his own far-fetched candidacy. "The South cannot adopt Mr. Douglas' platform," Wise wrote. "It is a short cut to all the ends of black republicanism. He then will kick up his heels. If he does or don't he can't be nominated, and the main argument against his nomination is that he can't be elected if nominated. If he runs an independent candidate and Seward run, and I am nominated at Charleston I can beat them both. Or, if squatter sovereignty is a plank of the platform at Charleston and Douglas is nominated the South will run an independent candidate on protection principles and run the election into the House. Where, then, would Mr. Douglas be? The lowest candidate on the list." The Hards emerged from the chaos with about one third of the thirty-five delegates, a reprise of the split of 1848 between Hunkers and Barnburners, a reprise of their split of 1848 with the Softs, which would prove disastrous to Douglas at the Charleston convention.

Buchanan's peevishness, not only at Douglas, increased over the months. "In the privacy of the White House he became more irritable, impatient, fussy, and dictatorial," wrote his biographer Philip Klein. Upon the death of his postmaster general, A.V. Brown, after Buchanan failed to get funding for his department's deficit before the 35th Congress adjourned, Forney's newspaper, the *Philadelphia Press,* reported, "Mr. B. is delighted at the idea that any member of his Cabinet should get sick, and is in the habit of saying every day, 'I never was in better health in my life; I can take my glass of Old Monongahela, dine heartily, indulge in Madeira, and sleep soundly, and yet my Cabinet is always dilapidated.'" His obsessive overbearing need for petty control drove away his devoted niece Harriet Lane, who had been serving as first lady. "I can do very well without her," he said. His private secretary and nephew, James Buchanan Henry, quit, moved to New York, and married. Buchanan did not attend the wedding or give a gift. He insisted that cabinet members spend their evenings with him. Jacob Thompson's wife, Kate, referred to him as "Old Gurley," partly after the Reverend Phineas Gurley, the Senate chaplain, and partly as a double entendre. Behind his back, cabinet members and their wives referred to "Old Buck" as "Old Venison." In late July Buchanan went on his regular summer vacation to the resort of Bedford Springs, bringing along a companionable "grass widow," a Mrs. Bass from Virginia, and her three children. Buchanan was aggravated that his room was near that of Simon Cameron, his old enemy, and exasperated when Mrs. Bass's slave girl fled, allegedly encouraged by Cameron.

Refreshed from his summer vacation, Buchanan insistently defended his purge of any and all Douglas supporters on the grounds of the Dred Scott decision. "I cannot retain in an important position any man who practices rebellion against the Supreme Court of the United States," Buchanan wrote in a letter to a friend. Douglas, of course, incoherently upheld Dred Scott, and Buchanan stated that "Douglas and his followers resist it on the ground that a Territorial Legislature possess this right" to "prohibit slavery." Buchanan's delusional political strategy was staked on Dred Scott, which was toxic in the North. "The issue in 1860," he wrote, "beyond all question will be between the Republicans who refuse to yield obedience to the decision, and the Democrats who sustain it and in doing so will sustain the cause of law, property and order. On this line we shall win."

Douglas decided to publish a brief for popular sovereignty to establish its historical, constitutional, and political legitimacy. The September issue of *Harper's Monthly* gave over most of its pages to his article, "Popular Sovereignty in the Territories: The Dividing Line Between Federal and Local Authority," a pedantic and turgid piece, replete with bowdlerized quotes, which attached unreadable paragraph to unreadable paragraph like freight cars coupled in a train yard. Douglas's essential argument was that the founding fathers were earlier versions of Stephen A. Douglas in their view of slavery as a matter of popular sovereignty in the states and territories, or as he infelicitously put it, "every distinct political Community, loyal to the Constitution and the Union, is entitled to all the rights, privileges, and immunities of self-government in respect to their local concerns and internal polity, subject only to the Constitution of the United States."

The most important lasting effect of his article was to serve as a text for Lincoln to refute in his Cooper Union speech five months later. But the immediate impact was to further alienate Southerners. John B. Floyd, Buchanan's secretary of war, hoped the article "will finally extinguish him." Attorney General Jeremiah Black published a lengthy response on September 10 in the *Washington Constitution* newspaper (successor to the *Union*). "The style of the article is, in some respects, highly commendable," he wrote. "It is entirely free from the vulgar clap-trap of the stump, and has no vain adornment of classical scholarship. But it shows no sign of the eloquent Senator; it is even without the logic of the great debater. Many portions of it are very obscure. . . . We do not deny, that the article in Harper is extremely difficult to understand. Its unjointed thoughts, loose expression, and illogical reasoning, have covered it with shadows, clouds, and darkness. But we will not admit that it has no meaning at all." Black proceeded easily to deconstruct Douglas's confusedness, particularly on Dred Scott, which Douglas endorsed but claimed allowed for popular sovereignty, which it did not. But soon the back-and-forth controversy over abstruse theoretical points was superseded with news of a sensational killing.

On September 13, one of Douglas's closest allies in the Senate, David C. Broderick of California, was shot dead in a duel. They had the same enemies and the bullet might as well have been for Douglas, who had avoided being provoked into duels earlier in the year. The rough-and-ready Broderick, an orphaned stone mason's apprentice and New York fireman, joined the Gold Rush, and climbed his way to become lieutenant governor of California and political boss of San Francisco. He was an antislavery yet partisan Democrat. Elected to the Senate in 1856, displacing the proslavery John B. Weller, a friend of Buchanan, Broderick cut a deal to divide patronage with the other California senator, William M. Gwin. Under their terms Broderick would control the federal jobs and Gwin the state ones. But Gwin complained to the Southern Directorate of Buchanan's cabinet and Broderick was completely shut out. His isolation served Buchanan's pique for having defeated Weller. He favored Gwin in any case.

Gwin was Broderick's antagonist and antithesis. Fabulously wealthy from a gold mine and the owner of a Mississippi plantation, originally from Tennessee, and a private secretary to President Jackson, Gwin led what was proudly called the Chivalry faction of the California Democratic Party, aligned with Southern Ultras. In Mississippi, he had been instrumental as a power broker in the election of Robert J. Walker to the Senate and his business partner. He also befriended the young Jefferson Davis. Gwin moved on to Texas, where he grabbed half a million acres of land, and then as a speculator to California, where he literally hit gold. Gwin's Southern manners extended to fighting one duel and threatening another against Senator Henry Wilson of Massachusetts. Broderick had tried to block Gwin's reelection in 1857, which Gwin finessed by combining forces with the Know Nothings. Gwin derided Douglas for his removal as chairman of the Committee on Territories because of his Freeport Doctrine, publicly quoting Howell Cobb against Douglas. Douglas replied that Gwin's "frank avowal" revealed Buchanan's hand in his ouster.

The antislavery Broderick bucked up Douglas to maintain his opposition against Lecompton. Unlike Douglas, he was not of the "don't care" school on slavery. When Hammond delivered his "Cotton is King" speech, Broderick took to the Senate floor to condemn his "mudsill" theory of free labor, brandishing his common background, disdainful of slavery, and offending the Southern members. For months in 1859, David Terry, the chief justice of the Supreme Court of California, a violent proslavery Know Nothing close to Gwin, and who had stabbed a man and been defeated for reelection, tried to provoke Broderick to a duel with vicious taunts. Broderick eventually succumbed to the challenge. Terry provided the pistols, one of which was on a hair trigger and was deliberately handed to Broderick. It prematurely discharged into the ground and left him standing as a target. After Broderick's murder, Edward D. Baker, Lincoln's old friend, now the Republican senator from Oregon, eulogized him as a martyr before a crowd in San Francisco of tens of thousands. Broderick's killing, he said, was "a political necessity, poorly veiled under the guise of a private quarrel" and "the consequence of intense political hatred." He proclaimed what he said were Broderick's last words: "They have killed me because I was opposed to the extension of slavery and a corrupt Administration." Broderick's death and Baker's oration had a revolutionary effect on California politics, the beginning of the end of the pro-Southern Chivalry faction, that rippled through public opinion in the North, rolling the tide toward the Republicans. In Washington, a number of pro-Douglas congressman armed themselves coming and going around town, joining the already armed Republicans and Southerners. Senator Hammond remarked, "the only persons who do not have a revolver and a knife are those who have two revolvers."

When Broderick was struck down by a bullet to the lung, Douglas was campaigning in Ohio for the state Democratic ticket to prove his coattails. All the state offices were on the ballot. On the day Douglas's schedule had been announced, William T. Bascom, secretary of the Ohio Republican State Central Committee, invited Lincoln to Ohio "to head off the little gentleman." He followed up after Lincoln accepted. "Your despatch came duly to hand; and created a sensation in our City. I at once telegraphed to Cincinnati, and have since written to the leading men to prepare for you. We shall get up a large meeting here. Which day will you come? What time will you arrive? Do not fail us. We depend much upon you. There is no man who can do so much good in this State just at this time as yourself."

Before Lincoln went on the speaking tour in Ohio, he wrote notes for himself. He sketched out a political scenario in which the Southern Ultras trying to destroy Douglas instead played into his cynical hands to shatter the Republicans. His notes reflected his fears from the Senate campaign and his anxiety over betrayal by Eastern Republicans. In late December, Greeley had appeared in Bloomington while Lincoln was there and invited him to meet at his hotel, but Lincoln, still too angry over his touting of Douglas, refused. "What will Douglas do now?" Lincoln wrote to himself. "He does not quite know himself. Like a skillful gambler he will play for all the chances." Lincoln gamed out Douglas's possible moves to survive, which depended in the end on tricking the Republicans. "His first wish is to be the nominee of the Charleston convention, without any new test. The democratic party proper do not wish to let it go just that way. They are thinking of getting up a Slave code test for him. They better not. Their true policy is to let him into the convention, beat him then, and give him no plausible excuse to bolt the nomination. But if they press the Slave code test upon him, he will not take it; but, as in the case of Lecompton, will appeal to the North on his bravery in opposing it. True the logic of his position, as an endorser of the Dred Scott decision imperatively requires him to go the Slave code. Honestly believing in that decision, he cannot, without perjury, refuse to go the Slave code. But he will refuse."

After decades of close observation Lincoln defined the essence of Douglas's political character that made him so dangerous. "He never lets the logic of principle, displace the logic of success." Lincoln felt that Eastern Republicans never really grasped what he did about Douglas. "And then, when he thus turns again to the North, we shall have the Lecompton phase of politics reproduced on a larger scale. It will then be a question whether the Republican party of the Nation shall make him President, in magnanimous gratitude for having opposed a Slave code, just as it was, last year, a question whether the Illinois Republicans should re-elect him Senator, in magnanimous gratitude for having opposed Lecompton. Some larger gentlemen will then have a chance of swallowing the same pill which they somewhat persistently prescribed for us little fellows last year. I hope they will not swallow it. For the sake of the *cause,* rather than the *men,* I hope they will not swallow it."

Lincoln understood that flirting with Douglas would compromise and cripple the Republican cause. "The Republican cause cannot live by Douglas' position. His position, whether for or against a slave code, for or against Lecompton, leads inevitably to the nationalizing and perpetuity of slavery, and the Republican cause cannot live by it. Dallying with Douglas is, at best, for Republicans, only loss of labor, and loss of time. Wander with him however long, at last they must turn back and strike for a policy, which shall deal with slavery as a wrong, restrain its enlargement, and look to its termination."

In his private jottings, Lincoln felt free to give vent to his frustration over the Eastern Republican embrace of Douglas, whose exploitation of the issue of "Negro equality" was sheer exploitation. "Fudge!! How long, in the government of a God, great enough to make and maintain this Universe, shall there continue knaves to vend, and fools to gulp, so low a piece of demagougeism as this." The *New York Times,* still promoting Douglas, published his speeches in Ohio at length.

Lincoln again stalked Douglas, city after city in Ohio through September, appearing a day or two after Douglas had spoken, trailing after his presence and refuting his arguments. Lincoln's shadowing of Douglas was the sequel to their Senate campaign. When the campaign had first begun Lincoln was a little-known figure, but the debates had attracted national attention and elevated him into Douglas's natural counterpart. Now they reprised their battle, testing their strength for their parties in another state and in another national spectacle. Drawing on his assembled "Scrap-Book" of the debates, Lincoln recapitulated all his points against Douglas, "only a continuation of the Illinois debates of the year before," recalled David R. Locke, the *Bucyrus Journal* editor, who caught up with Lincoln in Columbus. Offstage, on the intermarriage of blacks and white, Lincoln told Locke, "I shall never marry a negress, but I have no objection to anyone else doing so. If a white man wants to marry a negro woman, let him do it—*if the negro woman can stand it.*"

In Ohio Lincoln introduced several new elements into his criticism of Douglas. On his impenetrable *Harper's* article, in Columbus, on September 16, Lincoln said, "He has a good deal of trouble with his popular sovereignty. His explanations explanatory of explanations explained are interminable." The *Chicago Press and Tribune,* covering "Mr. Lincoln in Ohio," reported, "The review is comprehensive, and complete, riddling the Douglas-Harper essay from stem to stern. . . . Mr. Lincoln's remarks on the omissions and falsifications in the patented essay—particularly in the omission of the Jeffersonian ordinance of 1787—are exceedingly pointed and forcible."

Lincoln leveraged the icon of Jefferson for the Republicans. He held up Jefferson as not only the paradigm of democracy but also antislavery sentiment. Douglas, he said, "ought to remember that there was once in this country a man by the name of Thomas Jefferson, supposed to be a Democrat—a man whose principles and policy are not very prevalent amongst Democrats to-day, it is true; but that man did not take exactly this view of the insignificance of the element of slavery which our friend Judge Douglas does. In contemplation of this thing, we all know he was led to exclaim, 'I tremble for my country when I remember that God is just!' We know how he looked upon it when he thus expressed himself. There was danger to this country—danger of the avenging justice of God in that little unimportant popular sovereignty question of Judge Douglas. He supposed there was a question of God's eternal justice wrapped up in the enslaving of any race of men, or any man, and that those who did so braved the arm of Jehovah—that when a nation thus dared the Almighty every friend of that nation had cause to dread His wrath." Six years later, Lincoln would distill his thinking on divine wrath over slavery into his Second Inaugural Address. Now, he posed it as a contest between the founder of the Democratic Party and its would-be standard-bearer. "Choose ye between Jefferson and Douglas as to what is the true view of this element among us."

Taking off from his expropriation of Jefferson, he turned the argument against Douglas's demagoguery over "negro equality," retooling his rhetoric from their debates. "Did you ever five years ago, hear of anybody in the world saying that the negro had no share in the Declaration of National Independence; that it did not mean negroes at all; and when 'all men' were spoken of negroes were not included? I am satisfied that five years ago that proposition was not put upon paper by any living being anywhere. I have been unable at any time to find a man in an audience who would declare that he had ever known anybody saying so five years ago. But last year was not a Douglas popular sovereign in Illinois who did not say it. Is there one in Ohio but declares his firm belief that the Declaration of Independence did not mean negroes at all? I do not know how this is; I have not been here much; but I presume you are very much alike everywhere. Then I suppose that all now express the belief that the Declaration of Independence never did mean negroes. I call upon one of them to say that he said it five years ago."

Since Douglas had gone on his post-campaign Southern tour, he had adopted as regular trope the denigration of blacks as swamp creatures on the level of crocodiles. Few things Douglas said bothered Lincoln more than this reduction of men into reptiles. He saw it as a systematic corruption of public opinion aimed at degrading American ideals and democracy, the application of a big lie technique, in which the lie is repeated until it was believed, with this particular lie used insidiously to drive a larger agenda of inequality, beginning with the dehumanization of blacks. "They are taking him down, and placing him, when spoken of, among reptiles and crocodiles, as Judge Douglas himself expresses it."

Lincoln challenged his audience. "Is not this change wrought in your minds a very important change? Public opinion in this country is everything. In a nation like ours this popular sovereignty and squatter sovereignty have already wrought a change in the public mind to the extent I have stated. There is no man in this crowd who can contradict it. Now, if you are opposed to slavery honestly, as much as anybody I ask you to note that fact, and the like of which is to follow, to be plastered on, layer after layer, until very soon you are prepared to deal with the negro everywhere as with the brute. If public sentiment has not been debauched already to this point, a new turn of the screw in that direction is all that is wanting; and this is constantly being done by the teachers of this insidious popular sovereignty. You need but one or two turns further until your minds, now ripening under these teachings will be ready for all these things, and you will receive and support, or submit to, the slave trade; revived with all its horrors; a slave code enforced in our territories, and a new Dred Scott decision to bring slavery up into the very heart of the free North."

Lincoln reached back to the crescendo of his debates with Douglas, declaring that to achieve these ends "they must blow out the moral lights around us; they must penetrate the human soul and eradicate the love of liberty; but until they did these things, and others eloquently enumerated by him, they could not repress all tendencies to ultimate emancipation."

Again, he reprised himself. "I ask attention to the fact that in a pre-eminent degree these popular sovereigns are at this work; blowing out the moral lights around us; teaching that the negro is no longer a man but a brute; that the Declaration has nothing to do with him; that he ranks with the crocodile and the reptile; that man, with body and soul, is a matter of dollars and cents. I suggest to this portion of the Ohio Republicans, or Democrats if there be any present, the serious consideration of this fact, that there is now going on among you a steady process of debauching public opinion on this subject. With this my friends, I bid you adieu."

On his way to Cincinnati Lincoln stopped for a brief speech at the railroad depot at Hamilton, accompanied by Congressman John A. Gurley, "a very short man, and as these gentlemen emerged from the car, a great laughter went up from the multitude present." "My friends," said Lincoln, pointing to himself, "this is the long of it," and putting his hand on Gurley's head, "this is the short of it." Then, according to a local historian, he "tore the argument of Hon. Stephen A. Douglas on popular sovereignty to shreds." The Democratic newspaper in Hamilton described him, "Ugliness predominates," but conceded "he is no slouch at wit."

That night in Cincinnati, September 17, he adopted the rhetorical device of addressing the Kentuckians in the audience and those across the Ohio River. First, he used this gambit to depict Douglas as proslavery.

I say, then, in the first place, to the Kentuckians, that I am what they call, as I understand it, a "Black Republican." (Applause and laughter.) I think Slavery is wrong, morally, and politically. I desire that it should be no further spread in these United States, and I should not object if it should gradually terminate in the whole Union. (Applause.) While I say this for myself, I say to you, Kentuckians, that I understand you differ radically with me upon this proposition; that you believe Slavery is a good thing; that Slavery is right; that it ought to be extended and perpetuated in this Union. Now, there being this broad difference between us, I do not pretend in addressing myself to you, Kentuckians, to attempt proselyting you; that would be a vain effort. I do not enter upon it. I only propose to try to show you that you ought to nominate for the next Presidency, at Charleston, my distinguished friend Judge Douglas. (Applause.) In all that there is a difference between you and him, I understand he is as sincerely for you, and more wisely for you, than you are for yourselves. [Applause.] I will try to demonstrate that proposition. Understand now, I say that I believe he is as sincerely for you, and more wisely for you, than you are for yourselves.

Then, Lincoln issued a portentous warning to the Kentuckians and Southerners generally. "I often hear it intimated that you mean to divide the Union whenever a Republican, or anything like it, is elected President of the United States," he said. He baited them. "Are you going to split the Ohio [River] down through, and push your half off a piece? Or are you going to keep it right alongside of us outrageous fellows? Or are you going to build up a wall some way between your country and ours, by which that moveable property of yours can't come over here anymore, to the danger of your losing it?"

Lincoln told them that no matter how fiercely they fought for slavery they would lose to the overwhelming power of the North. "Will you make war upon us and kill us all? Why, gentlemen, I think you are as gallant and as brave men as live; that you can fight as bravely in a good cause, man for man, as any other people living; that you have shown yourselves capable of this upon various occasions; but, man for man, you are not better than we are, and there are not so many of you as there are of us. (Loud cheering.) You will never make much of a hand at whipping us. If we were fewer in numbers than you, I think that you could whip us; if we were equal it would likely be a drawn battle; but being inferior in numbers, you will make nothing by attempting to master us."

While Southerners and proslavery Northern Democrats blamed the division in the country on antislavery "agitation," Lincoln blamed slavery itself. "We believe that the spreading out and perpetuity of the institution of slavery impairs the general welfare. We believe—nay, we know, that that is the only thing that has ever threatened the perpetuity of the Union itself. The only thing which has ever menaced the destruction of the government under which we live, is this very thing. To repress this thing, we think is providing for the general welfare. Our friends in Kentucky differ from us. We need not make our argument for them, but we who think it is wrong in all its relations, or in some of them at least, must decide as to our own actions, and our own course, upon our own judgment."

Lincoln's Cincinnati speech was widely circulated, printed in the *Cincinnati Daily Gazette,* reprinted in the *National Intelligencer* in Washington, and produced as a pamphlet by the Ohio Republican State Central Committee. But it received its greatest circulation through a stealth effort by Douglas, who arranged to have fifty thousand copies published under the title, "Douglas an enemy to the North," and distributed in the South, cynically using Lincoln to counter Southern hostility against him.

On his way home to Springfield, Lincoln addressed a crowd in Indianapolis. He traveled to Milwaukee on September 30 to speak at the state fair, where he denounced Hammond's "mud-sill theory" of labor. In notes to himself, he wrote, "*Equality,* in society, alike beats *inequality,* whether the lat[t]er be of the British aristocratic sort, or of the domestic slavery sort. . . . Free labor has the inspiration of hope; pure slavery has no hope." He spoke in Beloit and Janesville. Within two weeks, from mid-September to early October, Lincoln delivered eleven speeches.

Lincoln wrote Chase a letter regretting they had not met when he had been in Ohio. He warned him against any leaning toward Douglas. "It is useless for me to say to you (and yet I cannot refrain from saying it) that you must not let your approaching election in Ohio so result as to give encouragement to Douglasism. That ism is all which now stands in the way of an early and complete success of Republicanism; and nothing would help it or hurt us so much as for Ohio to go over or falter just now."

On October 13, the Republicans swept Ohio, winning formidable majorities in the legislature and the governorship. They also swept Iowa, Minnesota, and Pennsylvania, humiliating Buchanan. "Is not the election news glorious?" exulted Lincoln. "We all think that your visit aided us," Samuel Galloway wrote him. "You have secured a host of friends among Republicans." Nominating Chase for president, Galloway wrote, "would sink us. . . . Your visit to Ohio has excited an extensive interest in your favor. Whilst I would desire to have you remain as you are unobtrusive; at the same time, tis my . . . advice that you treat kindly and respectfully all requests for the use of your name."

William T. Bascom wrote Lincoln, "These are splendid results, and we feel very much satisfied at them. We think they dispose of all the hopes of Douglas in Ohio. Squatter sovereignty is dead here. We feel that some of the credit of this result is due to you, and in behalf of our Republican friends I again return you our most grateful thanks. In the future of the Republican Party in Ohio your visit to the Buckeye State will be held in grateful remembrance." Lincoln clubs began to appear in Ohio.

The reenactment of the Lincoln-Douglas debates throughout Ohio damaged Douglas and enhanced Lincoln. Douglas's party went down to defeat, Lincoln's to victory. Just a year earlier, cannons boomed for Douglas's reelection and he strode forward as the inevitable candidate. Lincoln, who had slipped into the mud in a seemingly final indignity, now wore the laurels. Pursuing Douglas again served his purposes. Douglas's flaming ambition revived him.

The day before the Ohio results, on October 12, Lincoln received a telegram from James A. Briggs, the head of the Ohio State agency in New York. Briggs had been a Cleveland attorney, counsel to railroads, newspaper publisher and editor, founder of Cleveland's public high schools, and Free Soiler, friend to both Giddings, Lincoln's old abolitionist boardinghouse mate, and Chase. The telegram was addressed to "Hon. A. Lincoln," and it read: "will you speak in Mr Beechers church Broo[k]lyn on or about the twenty ninth (29) November on any subject you please pay two hundred (200) dollars." Briggs represented an influential group of Republicans interested in the 1860 Republican presidential campaign. Beecher was, of course, the Reverend Henry Ward Beecher of the most famous theological family in the country that also included his sister, Harriet Beecher Stowe, author of *Uncle Tom's Cabin*. From the pulpit of Beecher's Plymouth Church, renowned as the "Grand Central Station of the Underground Railroad," Beecher had thundered for resistance to slavery in Kansas.

Lincoln "came rushing into the office one morning, with the letter from New York City," recalled Herndon. "Billy, I am invited or solicited to deliver a lecture in New York. Should I go?" "I advised Mr. Lincoln I thought

Invitation to Lincoln to speak in New York

it would help open the way to the Presidency—thought I could see the meaning of the move by the New York men—*thought* it was a move against Seward—thought Greeley had something to do with it—think so yet—*have no evidence*. The result . . . was a profound one, as I think." Lincoln accepted, but the date and the venue would change.

At 7:05 in the morning of October 17, a passenger train conductor of the Baltimore and Ohio Railroad sent a telegram to the main office: "Express train bound east, under my charge, was stopped this morning at Harper's Ferry by armed abolitionists. They have possession of the bridge and the arms and armory of the United States. . . . The leader of those men requested me to say to you that this is the last train that shall pass the bridge either East or West . . . you had better notify the Secretary of War at once." By afternoon, President Buchanan ordered Marines under the command of Lieutenant Colonel Robert E. Lee to the town.

THIS GUILTY LAND

In early May of 1858 a peculiar man knocked on the door of William Seward's home in Washington. "He began with a story of great personal distress, involving himself and family, and stated that he had come to me on that account," Seward recalled to the Senate Committee investigating John Brown's raid at Harpers Ferry. "I supposed that the object of his visit was to solicit charity. I allowed him to go on with his story without interruption. I found it very incoherent, very erratic, and thought him a man of an unsound or very much disturbed mind."

Hugh Forbes, a Scotsman of about forty-five years old, who called himself a colonel, had been a silk merchant in the Tuscan city of Sienna, fought with Garibaldi in the failed Italian revolution of 1848, fled to Paris, married and fathered children, only to leave them behind when he sailed for New York, where he was editor of an Italian language newspaper, the *European,* from which he was fired, lived in an apartment on the Lower East Side on Delancey Street next to a brothel, advertised as a fencing coach, and worked as a

John Brown, 1859

translator for the *New York Tribune*. Through another Scot, James Redpath, a former reporter for the *Tribune,* he was introduced to John Brown, who was on a disappointing fundraising foray to Manhattan in March 1857. Redpath had attached himself to Brown as his chief publicist. Brown was fascinated with Forbes's credentials as an exotic military expert in revolutionary warfare and hired him at $100 a month with a $600 advance. For the penniless soldier of fortune, Brown offered the promise of both soldiering and fortune. He saw stars and dollars in his eyes. He would be the "general in the revolution against slavery" and paid royally by the wealthy benefactors he learned were bankrolling Old Brown. His first call was on Horace Greeley, who forked over $700, and then visited the most munificent donor of them all, Gerrit Smith, whom he hit up for an additional $150, which the eternally credulous Smith wrote would "prove very useful in our sacred work in Kansas" and that "if Federal troops fight against" the cause "we must fight against them." For months Forbes ignored Brown's urgent plaints to come west and instead dallied over his translation of a guide to guerrilla warfare entitled *Manual of the Patriotic Volunteer*. When he showed up at last at Brown's miserable little camp at Tabor, Iowa, he discovered there was no army or armory, just Brown's sad-sack son Owen, whom Brown assigned Forbes to drill in marching and target practice. Relative peace had broken out in Kansas as the political struggle over the Lecompton Constitution heated up. Forbes wrote a stilted two-page tract, "The Duty of the Soldier," referring to ancient republics and appealing to U.S. soldiers to desert. Brown presented it to donors and requested $500 to $1,000. Some disapproved, but Gerrit Smith sent $25.

During the long boring days and nights in camp Brown confided to the untrustworthy Forbes his latest and most grandiose version of his Subterranean Pass Way. He intended to lead twenty-five or fifty men "to beat up a slave quarter in Virginia" and gathering two hundred or five hundred slaves who would "swarm" to him, of whom he would take "100 or so of them" to capture the Harpers Ferry federal armory, escaping with its weaponry into "three, four or five distinct parties," to "beat up other slave quarters," drawing more into his invincible army. Entrenched in the Allegheny Mountains after "liberating" Virginia he would advance through Tennessee and Alabama, and "his New England partisans would in the meantime call a Northern Convention, restore tranquility and overthrow the pro-slavery administration."

Isolated and broke, with a bounty on his head for the Pottawatomie murders, Brown spun an ever more elaborate vision in which he saw himself as the general of a slave army, seizing one Southern state after another, and leading to the overthrow of the U.S. government by the Transcendentalists of Boston.

Forbes proposed an alternative to Brown's fantastical scheme. Raiding parties operating on the Virginia and Maryland border would swoop down to free small groups of slaves "once or twice a month" and send them to Canada. Even a single failure would not "compromise" the whole enterprise. If it could sustain itself, Forbes wrote, "Slave property would thus become untenable near the frontier . . . and it might reasonably be expected that the excitement and irritation would impel the proslaveryites to commit some stupid blunders." But Brown wasn't interested in Forbes's small-scale idea; nor could he continue to pay him. After only a month with Brown, Forbes told him he was returning to New York for a brief time on personal business. He had decided to expose Brown as a dangerous charlatan.

Forbes showed Seward his guerrilla warfare manual. He claimed he had been hired to help free state settlers defend themselves. He said he had "suggested the getting up of a stampede of slaves secretly on the borders of Kansas, in Missouri, which Brown disapproved," and that "Brown did not pay him anything." "He said Brown was a very bad man, and would not keep his word; was a reckless man, an unreliable man, a vicious man." Seward sent him away, telling him that while he was "touched" by his story about his family's privations, as a Senator he could not give him advice about Kansas.

Seward said Forbes gave no inkling of the attack on Harpers Ferry and that the meeting "passed out of my memory." "All kinds of erratic and strange persons call on me with all manner of strange communications and applications."

Soon after visiting Seward, Forbes went to the Senate chamber to find Senator Henry Wilson sitting at his desk on a Saturday. "I had never before heard of him," recalled Wilson. Forbes explained that Brown had employed him to drill men "for the defense of Kansas," had not paid him, and that Brown's financial backers "were under obligations to pay him." "He seemed to be in a towering passion, greatly excited . . . that Brown was not a fit man to have arms, that they ought to be got out of his hands." Then he disappeared. When Wilson saw his friend Gamaliel Bailey, editor of *The National Era,* the next evening at his house Bailey asked him if he had seen Forbes. Bailey had spoken to him, too. He told Wilson that Brown's backers in Massachusetts, whom Wilson well knew, "ought to get those arms out of Brown's hands, and that I had better write to some of them to that effect."

After Forbes defected, Brown attracted a nucleus of misfits to serve as his phalanx—a naive idealist who was also a killer, a petty thief, a former lover of Lord Byron's widow, a mercenary, an attempted murderer who had lived among Indians, a crusading journalist, a lost teenager, and a fugitive slave. In December 1857, Brown instructed them that the departed Forbes would train them for their mission to liberate slaves, "a successful insurrection in the mountains."

For a month, from January 28, 1858, through most of February, Brown felt safe, like a fugitive slave himself, in Frederick Douglass's home in Rochester, where he composed a Provisional Constitution on behalf of "We, the citizens of the United States, and the oppressed people, who, by a recent decision of the Supreme Court, are declared to have no rights which the white man is bound to respect" that denounced slavery as "a most barbarous, unprovoked, and unjustifiable war of one portion of its citizens upon another portion" against the spirit of the Declaration of Independence. Brown's constitution established a government for the land within the country he expected to occupy. In forty-nine articles he laid out three branches, stipulated every citizen must "labor in some way for the general good," removal from office for "intoxication," outlawed "swearing, filthy conversation," provided for the sharing of "captured or confiscated property" including watches and jewelry for "the common benefit" or an "intelligence fund," and that deserters would be "put to death." Brown talked day and night about his constitution until "it began to be something of a bore to me," Douglass confessed. "Once in a while, he would say he could, with a few resolute men, capture Harper's Ferry," Douglass wrote, but added, "I paid but little attention to such remarks."

Brown wrote his Boston benefactors about "BY FAR the most important undertaking of my whole life," and asked for money. On February 22, he divulged his "whole outline" to Gerrit Smith and Franklin Sanborn, the youthful director of the Massachusetts Kansas Aid Committee, at Smith's house in Peterboro, New York, "to the astonishment and almost the dismay of those present," recalled Sanborn. He and Smith suggested "difficulties; but nothing could shake the purpose of the old Puritan." He told them, quoting the Book of Romans, "If God be for us, who can be against us?" And the money he requested, he pled, was only a "small sum." Smith informed Sanborn, "You see how it is; our dear old friend has made up his mind to this course, and cannot be turned from it. We cannot give him up to die alone; we must support him."

Sanborn raced to Boston to arrange meetings for Brown in his room at the American House hotel for the group that with Smith and Sanborn became known as the "Secret Six." George L. Stearns, descended from an old Puritan family, was a wealthy manufacturer, married to the niece of the abolitionist writer Lydia Maria Child, and a chief funder of the Emigrant Aid Society. Thomas Wentworth Higginson, a Unitarian and Transcendentalist minister, disciple of Theodore Parker, married to the niece of William Ellery Channing, theological founder of Unitarianism and Moral Philosophy, had stormed the Boston courthouse where the fugitive slave Anthony Burns was imprisoned in 1854 in a vain effort to release him. Samuel Gridley Howe, physician and reformer, founder of the first school for the blind, had spent six years as a surgeon organizing relief efforts and fighting in the Greek War of Independence under the spell of Byron, whose verses he freely recited. He saw himself as a Byronic hero, a romantic breaking the bonds of oppression. He bought Byron's self-designed plumed battle helmet at a Greek auction and hung it in the hallway of his Boston home. The King of Greece decorated him a Chevalier of the Order of St. Saviour. His friends and wife half-jokingly referred to him as "Chev." Higginson called him "a natural crusader or paladin . . . in whom every call to duty took a chivalrous aspect." He had like Higginson been a member of Parker's Boston Vigilance Committee to shield runaways and been involved in shepherding slaves to Canada. And like Higginson he had gone to Kansas to witness the struggle firsthand. He gave Brown the gift of "a little walnut box with a fine Smith & Wesson revolver in it," recalled Howe's daughter.

And there was Parker himself, the moral center of the Transcendentalists, stricken with tuberculosis, who would leave the country in early 1859 in search of a cure he knew he would not find. From Rome, on November 24, 1859, after receiving word of Brown's death sentence, Parker wrote, "wishing I was at home again to use what poor remnant of power is left to me in defence of the True and the Right." Spitting up blood constantly from his diseased lungs, he wrote, "Slavery will not die a dry death." He prophesied that "the negroes will take their defence into their own hands, especially if they can find white men to lead them." Like almost all radical abolitionists except for a very few individuals, Parker believed in the natural inferiority of blacks. "No doubt the African race is greatly inferior to the Caucasian in general intellectual power, and also in that instinct for liberty which is so strong in the Teutonic family, and just now obvious in the Anglo-Saxons of Britain and America. . . . But there is a limit even to the negro's forbearance."

He could not help but return to the trauma of Sumner's caning and the revenge that would be visited upon the South. "One of the legitimate products of her 'peculiar institution,' they are familiar with violence, ready and able for murder. Public opinion sustains such men. Bully Brooks was but one of their representatives in Congress. . . . She cries . . . 'Hurrah for Brooks!' . . . The South must reap as she sows; where she scatters the wind, the whirlwind will come up. . . . The fire of vengeance may be waked up even in an African's heart, especially when it is fanned by the wickedness of a white man: then it runs from man to man, from town to town. What shall put it out? *The white man's blood!*"

Brown represented a stab at slavery beyond mortality. All of the Secret Six saw Brown as the purest of Puritans. Higginson said that Brown reminded him of Cromwell or a "high-minded, unselfish, belated Covenanter; a man whom Sir Walter Scott might have drawn." Julia Ward Howe, Howe's wife, described Brown as "a Puritan of the Puritans, forceful, concentrated, and self-contained." Four of the Secret Six had been close to Sumner, aiding his rise to the Senate, and Higginson a rapt admirer. Sumner's near death snapped a bond to practical politics. Their friendships with him focused on his difficult effort to regain his health and composure. His removal from the day-to-day political saga sent them reeling in another direction. In Brown they found an idol for revenge. The Secret Six had become a sect bound with religious intensity that Brown's crackpot scheme was the eschatological culmination of the Puritan City on a Hill, the American Revolution and the struggle for emancipation. With the precise accounting of a State Street banker, Stearns, the "Treasurer of the Enterprise," kept track of every penny. They called it "the wool business."

On May 8, 1858, Brown held a convention in Chatham, Canada, of thirty-four black men who he believed would recruit the soldiers for his revolutionary army. None of the invited white abolitionists nor any of the Secret Six attended. He explained his plan for the insurgency in his opening address. He told the convention "all the free negroes in the Northern States would immediately flock to his standard," "all the slaves in the Southern States would do the same," and so would "many of the free negroes in Canada." He would be so "successful" that some Southern states would recognize his organization and agree to emancipation. He read his Provisional Constitution, which would govern his occupied territory. Brown was elected commander-in-chief and various followers elected secretary of state and secretary of the treasury and so on. To his disappointment, the black leaders at the convention failed to recruit anyone for his operation. Only one man present, a free black from Pennsylvania, Osborne Perry Anderson, a printer by trade, working in Chatham, went along with Brown.

Even while Brown recited his Provisional Constitution to the delegates of the Chatham convention, Hugh Forbes wandered around Washington knocking on doors. Senator Wilson, alarmed at what he heard, sent Dr. Howe a letter on May 9, not knowing of the Secret Six but of his previous relationship with Brown. "I write to you to say that you had better talk with some few of our friends who contributed money to aid old Brown to organize and arm some force in Kansas for defence, about the policy of getting those arms out of his hands & putting them in the hands of some reliable men in that Territory. *If they should be used for other purposes, as rumor says they may be, it might be of disadvantage to the men who were induced to contribute to that very foolish movement.* If it can be done, get the arms out of his control and keep clear of him at least for the present." Howe wrote back, "No countenance has been given to Brown for any operation outside of Kansas by the Kansas Committee." It was a duplicitous answer. The Kansas Committee had not given Brown approval, but the Secret Six had.

Sanborn was already frantically writing Higginson to warn him of Forbes's sudden entrance onto the scene. Brown had not told the Secret Six about Forbes, though he had told Forbes about them. Fearful of Forbes's disclosures, Brown grew a flowing white beard and adopted the pseudonym of "Nelson Hawkins." "H.F. is Hugh Forbes," Sanborn wrote Higginson on May 7, "an Italieo English hothead whom N.H. [Brown] last year in an evil hour admitted to his councils . . . he is now at Washington where he can do great harm." Howe, who received three "ill-natured and spiteful" letters from Forbes, burned them. Higginson wrote Parker that he was opposed to postponement of Brown's attack. "I regard as any postponement as simply abandoning the project." Parker replied, "If you knew all we do about 'Col.' F. you would think differently." Sanborn wrote Higginson that "the opinion of P.H. & S. [Parker, Howe, and Smith]—and G.S. [George Stearns]—who are such large stockholders, will prevent them raising money now." Smith wrote Sanborn a letter, which he forwarded to Higginson, "I never was convinced of the wisdom of this scheme. But as things now stand, it seems to me it would be madness to attempt to execute it." On May 14, Stearns sent Senator Wilson's cautionary letter to Howe on to Brown, ordering him, "You will recollect that you have the custody of the arms alluded to, to be used for the defence of Kansas, as agent of the Massachusetts State Kansas Aid Committee. In consequence of the information thus communicated to me [by Dr. Howe and Senator Wilson], it becomes my duty to warn you not to use them for any other purpose, and to hold them subject to my order as chairman of said committee."

Brown arrived in Boston on May 30, where, after conferring with his secret board of directors, he agreed to postpone his revolution "till next winter or spring," according to Higginson. Brown "considered delay very discouraging," disparaged the other members of the Secret Six to Higginson—"they were not men of action"—called Stearns "a timid man," and said of him and Parker "he did not think abounded in courage."

Brown's expedition was on ice, his backers skittish and his followers behaving like a herd of scattering cats. He remained anxious about Hugh Forbes's influence with his donors and dispatched one of his aides on a mission to counter him. Richard Realf, twenty-four years old, had been dubbed secretary of state of Brown's Provisional Government at Chatham possibly because he was English. The precocious author of a volume of high-flown poetry entitled *Guesses at the Beautiful,* he had an affair with Lady Anne Isabella Noel Byron, fell swiftly into her disfavor, and found himself singing for shillings on street corners until he emigrated to New York, soon seeking adventure in Kansas with John Brown's unmerry band. After Forbes had forced the delay of the insurrection, Brown read aloud to Realf Senator Wilson's letter to Howe and sent him to New York, to "somehow or other procure an introduction to Forbes; and he being an Englishman and I being an Englishman, he thought we might presently establish mutual good relations; that by ingratiating myself into his esteem, I might ultimately be able to possess myself, acting for Brown, of that obnoxious correspondence held by Forbes, written by Brown to him, in which Brown had developed his plans." However implausible this scam was to pry the damaging letters from Forbes, it was more conceivable than invading Virginia. But Realf never saw Forbes. He went to Boston bearing a letter of cognizance from Brown to gain the trust of the Secret Six. He told them he would go to England to raise "at least $2,000" for Brown's undertaking. "I was a protege of Lady Noel Byron, Charles Kingsley [a famous Anglican priest, novelist, and friend of Charles Darwin], and others of the aristocracy and literati," he said. On "my simple word," they gave him $250 for his voyage. Realf disappeared for nearly a year in England, claiming to visit his parents and explore conversion to Catholicism, to return via New Orleans and never contacting Brown again. It's possible he collected funds in England, but Brown never saw a penny if there was one. "I was not collecting money for them in England, or that if I did, they did not get it; which, so far as implicating me is concerned, amounts to about the same thing," he later testified. (The peripatetic poet missed Harpers Ferry but turned up bravely carrying the flag of the 88th Illinois infantry in the charge down Missionary Ridge at Chattanooga, writing copy for the *Pittsburgh Commercial* newspaper, and winding up a down-and-out suicide in San Francisco.)

Brown resurfaced at a hotel in Lawrence, Kansas, on June 25, wearing his full beard as a kind of mask. "Yet many persons who had previously known him did not penetrate his patriarchal disguise," wrote James Redpath, the journalist, who was there. Brown referred to himself as "the old Abolitionist 'mit de' white beard on," his only known self-deprecating joke. Low on funds, he played with the idea of writing a best-selling book of his adventures in Kansas. He had warmed up with a lecture at Chatham advertised: "Horrors Perpetrated . . . by the Missouri Border Ruffians & Pro-Slavers from the South . . . PILLAGE—INCENDIARISM—BASE OUTRAGES &C &C." The book would be styled along the lines of one of his favorite biographies, Joel Tyler Headley's *The Life of Oliver Cromwell,* a stirring defense of the Puritan revolutionary published in 1848. Ironically, the most moving scene in Headley's Cromwell was his scene of Charles I's composure and dignity at his execution. But Brown never wrote a sentence. His mind was concentrated on his own revolution to begin at Harpers Ferry. When Richard Hinton, the journalist, visited, his aide-de-camp, John Henry Kagi, revealed "the glory of the grand ideas." Hinton told him the plan was suicidal. But Brown argued, "Nat Turner with fifty men held a portion of Virginia for several weeks." Of course, Nat Turner was captured and executed.

For months, Brown suffered from "ague" and was listless and even crankier. He repeatedly wrote the Secret Six for money. "Do let me hear from you at this point," he wrote in July. "It now looks as though but little business can be accomplished until we get our mill into operation," he wrote in September, using the wool business cover story. He attempted to interject himself into some passing trouble involving the indictment of a free state militia leader, but his offer of militant support was rejected. He scorned the free state movement, which was on the verge of success. "Abortion!—yes, that's the word," he said about the entire effort. He talked about "answering the call of the Lord," and told Hinton, "The hour is very near at hand, and all who are willing to act should be ready." But the Secret Six would not send him funds until the following spring.

Hearing that a slave and his family at a farm in Missouri were to be sold to a Texas slave owner, Brown "hailed it as heaven-sent," and announced he would "carry the war into Africa." His raiding party hit several farms in Vernon County, Missouri, on the night of December 20, captured eleven slaves, took horses, mules, oxen, saddles, bedding, wagons, bacon, looted personal belongings, held two whites as prisoners, and killed a man. He sent the slaves along lines of the Underground Railroad to Canada. Missouri's governor put a $3,000 price on Brown's head. President Buchanan set a reward for $250. Brown's action aroused near unanimous condemnation from the free state forces. James Lane, leader of one of the free state militias, volunteered to arrest him. Charles Robinson, the free state governor, turned against him. George A. Crawford, founder of the free state town of Fort Scott, sought out Brown. "I protested to the Captain against this violence," he wrote Eli Thayer, creator of the Emigrant Aid Society in Massachusetts. "We were settlers, he was not. He could strike a blow and leave." Crawford explained to Brown "the facts that we were at peace with Missouri; that our Legislature was then in the hands of the Free-State men . . . even in disturbed counties . . . we were in a majority. . . . I think the conversation made an impression on him, for he soon after went to his self-sacrifice at Harper's Ferry." William Hutchinson, a reporter for the *New York Times,* recalled a sleepless and excited Brown holding forth all night about "my work, my great duty, my mission."

Brown slipped into Lawrence to sell his stolen goods including watches. He summoned William A. Phillips, a correspondent for the *New York Tribune* and free state activist, to his hotel room, with the message "he was going away, and might never see me again." Brown despised politics and politicians of whatever stripe. The truce in Kansas that brought politics to the forefront closed the space for violent bands of men. But Brown saw a wider field for his operations. "And now," Brown told Phillips, "we have reached a point where nothing but war can settle the question." According to Phillips, he talked about the possibility of secession if a Republican was elected president, though Brown rarely offered commentary on politics except to disdain it. "All this has a strangely prophetic look to me now; then it simply appeared incredible, or the dream and vagary of a man who had allowed one idea to carry him away." Phillips doubted that war was inevitable. "Our best people do not understand the danger," replied Brown. "They are besotted. They have compromised so long that they think principles of right and wrong have no more any power on this earth."

He launched into the history of Spartacus and his slave revolt against Rome. Phillips pointed out that Spartacus and his soldiers were "warlike people" and even then "crushed" by the Roman legions. "You have not studied them right," said Brown. He insisted that the slaves of the South would rise in a spirit of ferocious vengeance like Spartacus's followers. With the example of Spartacus before him, Brown would avoid his fate. Instead of "wasting his time in Italy until his enemies could swoop on him, [he] should have struck at Rome; or, if not strong enough for that, he should have escaped to the wild northern provinces, and there have organized an army to overthrow Rome." Phillips told him, "I feared he would lead the young men with him into some desperate enterprise, where they would be imprisoned and disgraced." Brown replied, "when your household gods are broken, as mine have been, you will see all this more clearly." Determined to wear the crown of the gladiator chief, Brown would ignore the tactical lesson he claimed to have learned from Spartacus.

Brown's fixation on the crucified warrior assigned the noblest motive to his suicidal impulse. "Certainly the cause is enough to *live* for, if not to—for," he had written Sanborn on February 24 from Peterboro, where he disclosed his plot. Brown left blank a space for the obvious missing word "die," which emphasized it like the name of God as something holy. "I have only had this one opportunity, in a life of nearly sixty years; and could I be continued ten times as long again, I might not again have another equal opportunity. . . . I expect nothing but to 'endure hardness'; but I expect to effect a mighty conquest, even though it be like the last victory of Samson." Samson, who brought down the temple on himself, died like Spartacus in his cause. After invoking the biblical suicide, Brown confessed his attraction to death. "I felt for a number of years, in earlier life, a steady, strong desire to die; but since I saw any prospect of becoming a 'reaper' in the great harvest, I have not only felt quite willing to live, but have enjoyed life much; and am now rather anxious to live for a few years more." Now he could trace his rendezvous on a map to a destination if not a destiny.

Brown's raid into Missouri thrilled the Secret Six. "Do you hear the news from Kansas? Our dear John Brown is . . . pursing the policy which he intended to pursue elsewhere," declared Gerrit Smith. On February 1 Brown left Kansas for good, headed east. The funds began to flow again. Howe wrote John Murray Forbes, one of the wealthiest men in Boston, his fortune made in the China trade, introducing him to Brown. "He is of the stuff of which martyrs are made," Howe wrote. Brown stopped at Peterboro in New

York to see Smith on April 11 and arrived in Concord, Massachusetts, to speak at the Town Hall on May 8 before an audience of Emerson, Thoreau, and Bronson Alcott, who recalled that Brown's new beard "gives to the soldierly air the port of an apostle. . . . I think him about the manliest man I have ever seen—the type and synonym of the Just."

He came to Boston on May 9. He met alone with Howe, who objected to his kidnapping of whites and stealing personal property. Brown rejected his plea. Howe sent him to J.M. Forbes (no relation to Hugh Forbes), who invited him to tea at his Milton estate. Brown struck him as having "a little touch of insanity" and treated "almost with scorn" any belief in electoral politics. Still, perhaps out of respect for Howe, whose charity for the blind he funded, he pledged $100.

Brown strangely appeared at the meeting of the power brokers of the Massachusetts Republican Party. Someone, probably Stearns, likely on June 1, brought him to the regular lunch at the Parker House hotel of the Bird Club, a convivial yet serious-minded gathering of the politicians, lawyers, industrialists, and journalists to discuss Republican electoral campaigns, the latest political news, and how to advance their agenda within the state legislature and the U.S. Congress. Henry Wilson recognized Brown at once despite the foliage of his newly grown beard and acknowledged him as the menace that Hugh Forbes had identified. "I understand you do not approve of my course," Brown said to him. "I understand from some of my friends here you have spoken in condemnation of it." Wilson's recollection was that he was referring either to his letter to Howe about Hugh Forbes's revelations or "his going into Missouri and getting slaves and running them off." Wilson told him, "I believed it to be a very great injury to the anti-slavery cause; that I regarded every illegal act, and every imprudent act, as being against it." Brown said "he thought differently, and he believed he had acted right, and that it would have a good influence, or words to that effect."

That night Brown had dinner with Stearns and possibly one or two others at the Parker House. He fell into a reverie about himself as Moses leading his people out of bondage but not reaching the Promised Land. He handed Stearns the gift of a bowie knife which he had stolen from one of his victims at Pottawatomie, William "Dutch Bill" Sherman, before slitting his throat and cutting off his hand. "I think it probable that we may never meet again in this world," said Brown, "and I want to give to you in token of my gratitude an article which may have, at a future time, some little historic value." He falsely explained it was a "spoil of war" he had picked up in a clash at

Black Jack. Stearns was clearly touched. Brown left Boston on June 4 with $800 from a variety of sources and $2,000 from Stearns.

On about July 12, Brown bought a small farm for his base of operations five miles outside Harpers Ferry. He took a new alias, Isaac Smith. Slowly the members of his party trickled in, until there were twenty-one including five black men, three of his sons, one of his daughters, and one of the men's wives. Upstairs he stored 198 Sharps rifles, 200 revolvers, and 950 pikes; downstairs, they cooked, ate, and slept on the floor. Brown referred to his activity as "mining operations." He dictated "A Declaration of Liberty," dated—4th, 1859. "When in the course of human events, it becomes necessary, for an Oppressed People to Rise," it began. On it went quoting the Declaration of Independence on the equality of men, the consent of the governed, and the right of revolution. "Clanish Oppressors; who wickedly violate this sacred principle; oppressing their fellow Men, Will bring upon themselvs that certain & fearful retribution, which is the Natural, and Necessary penalty of evil Doing. . . . The history of Slavery in the United States, is a history of injustice & Cruelties inflicted upon the Slave in every conceivable way, & in barbarity not surpassed by the most Savage Tribes. It is the embodiment of all that is Evil, and ruinous to a Nation; and subversive of all Good." Against "the People" were arrayed "*Our President* & other Leeches . . . swarms of Blood Suckers, & Moths." He concluded, quoting Jefferson from his 1781 *Notes on the State of Virginia* on slavery: " 'I tremble for my Country, when I reflect; that God is Just; And that his Justice; will not sleep forever.' Nature is mourning for its Murdered, and Afflicted Children. Hung be the Heavens in Scarlet."

On August 25, Secretary of War John B. Floyd received an urgent letter explaining in precise detail the plot of "Old John Brown" to "strike the blow in a few weeks" at Harpers Ferry. Floyd ignored the warning, later claiming the letter "confused me a bit" and that Brown's scheme was beyond his comprehension. The authorship of what became known as the "Floyd letter" remained a mystery for thirty-six years. David J. Gue, twenty-three years old, a Quaker living in Iowa, had learned of Brown's plan from a friend at the town of Springdale, where Brown spent a couple of weeks on his way east from Kansas. Gue believed that betraying Brown would prompt the army to increase the guard at Harpers Ferry, thwart the plan, and save Brown's life. He "anxiously" scanned the papers for news that his letter had achieved his aim. (Gue would become a New York artist and paint Grant's portrait.)

In early September, Brown told his company of his plan to seize and hold the arsenal at Harpers Ferry. He faced a general revolt. "You know how it resulted with Napoleon when he rejected advice in regard to marching with his army to Moscow," said his son Owen. Brown threatened to resign, but the dissenters caved, and "within five minutes, he was again chosen as the leader." Brown told Owen, "We have here only one life to live, and once to die; and if we lose our lives it will perhaps do more for the cause than our lives could be worth in any other way." His mission was revolutionary suicide.

Brown summoned Frederick Douglass to meet him in an isolated quarry at Chambersburg, Pennsylvania. Brown appeared in the guise of a fisherman with a rod. Sitting among the rocks, he told Douglass, "He had completely renounced his old plan, and thought that the capture of Harper's Ferry would serve as notice to the slaves that their friends had come, and as a trumpet, to rally them to his standard. He described the place as to its means of defence, and how impossible it would be to dislodge him if once in possession." Douglass argued that his plan would be "fatal." He was familiar with the geography of Harpers Ferry, a hub of transportation, with many avenues in and out, the arsenal exposed at a low point and an easy target from above—"a perfect steel-trap and that once in he would never get out alive; that he would be surrounded at once and escape would be impossible," said Douglass. "He was not to be shaken by anything I could say." Brown explained he would take "the best citizens" hostage and "dictate terms." Douglass was astonished at his fantasy and told him, "Virginia would blow him and his hostages sky high." Brown threw his arms around Douglass. "Come with me, Douglass, I will defend you with my life. I want you for a special purpose. When I strike, the bees will begin to swarm, and I shall want you to help hive them." Douglass refused the offer. "Such then," he wrote, "was my connection with John Brown."

The sudden arrival of a windfall of cash served as a preliminary trigger. On October 14, Francis Jackson Meriam, twenty-two years old, frail but volatile, blind in one eye, entered the law office of Alexander K. McClure in Chambersburg asking him to write his will, bequeathing his estate to the Massachusetts Anti-Slavery Society. Meriam was the grandson and namesake of Francis Jackson, a prominent abolitionist devoted to Garrison and nonviolence, Boston city councilor, and wealthy real estate mogul. Meriam was an unstable manic-depressive, "in a state of mental excitement bordering on insanity," said Howe. He had traveled to Haiti with Redpath as a sidekick and was desperate to join Brown's expedition. On the street in Boston he encountered Lewis Hayden, a free black leader, former fugitive slave, recruiting agent for Brown, and privy to the proceedings of the Secret Six, who informed him that Brown was being held up by a lack of funds. Meriam drew $600 in gold from his inheritance and under the direction of Sanborn and Higginson, with the knowledge of Stearns, made his way to Brown's hideout. "I consider him about as fit to be on this enterprise as the devil is to keep a powder house; but everything has its use and must be put to it if possible," Sanborn wrote Higginson, adding "out of the mouths of babes and suckling come dollars by the hundred, and what is wisdom compared to that?" The day before the raid Meriam was inducted into the charmed circle. The articles of the Provisional Constitution were read aloud to him and Brown administered an oath of loyalty and secrecy. (Meriam would remain behind dispensing weapons, manage to flee, and escape with his life. During the war in an unexpected reunion he served as a captain under Colonel Thomas Wentworth Higginson with the South Carolina Colored Volunteers.)

Another trigger appeared to be the information that many of the weapons stored at the Harpers Ferry armory were about to be shipped to forts elsewhere. Brown did not understand that he had picked up the first evidence of Floyd's early orders to shift matériel out of reach of the North to Southern armories in anticipation of an unfavorable result in the 1860 election that would prompt secession. Brown simply wanted to grab the guns.

Some within the company believed that further recruits to "headquarters" would arrive within three weeks. But it's likely that no more volunteers were coming, that their hope was rumor. Brown told them the date for the attack was fixed on October 25, but he had been enigmatically changeable in the past. Osborne P. Anderson, a surviving black member of the party, wrote "the men at the Farm had been so closely confined, that they went out about the house and farm in the day-time during that week, and so indiscreetly exposed their numbers to the prying neighbors." Brown impulsively moved the attack forward against the resistance of most of his men. How much longer could he hold the claustrophobic group without risking exposure? From a rigid preconception he created an internally unstable and unsustainable environment that was combustible. Ultimately, Brown was his own trigger.

Early on Sunday morning, October 16, John Brown roused the men, read Bible verses, and led a prayer for "the liberation of the bondmen." The Provisional Constitution was recited, military commissions formally assigned, and orders given. Eighteen men were to be in the attacking unit and four to handle matters at "headquarters." At eight that evening, Brown said, "Men, get on your arms. We will proceed to the Ferry." He climbed into his wagon filled with weapons and a crowbar, doffed the cap he wore in Kansas, and announced, "Come, boys!"

Upon entering Harpers Ferry, Brown's men cut the telegraph wires, seized two watchmen as prisoners, and easily occupied the armory and arsenal. Meanwhile, six of his men broke into the house several miles away of Lewis W. Washington, great-grandnephew of President Washington. They demanded his guns, Lafayette's pistol, and the sword that Frederick the Great had given as a gift to George Washington. Then they asked for his watch and cash, which Washington refused. "I presume you have heard of Ossawatomie Brown?" he was asked. He had not. "Well," he was told, "you will see him this morning." He and four of his slaves were taken hostage. The entourage moved to the farm of a neighbor, John H. Allstadt, and also took him, his son, and six slaves. To Washington's astonishment they were driven to the armory. Until then he had assumed he was the victim of a robbery. Brown and his men broke the gates to the armory with a sledgehammer and crowbar. "I want to free all the negroes in this state," Brown told the watchman. "I have possession now of the United States armory, and if the citizens interfere with me I must only burn the town and have blood." The captured slaves were handed pikes and ordered to guard their masters and drill holes for shooting. "I presume you are Mr. Washington," said Brown. "I wanted you particularly for the moral effect it would give our cause, having one of your name as a prisoner."

The plan began to unravel from a single isolated incident that soon cascaded out of control. One watchman on the Maryland bridge, Patrick Higgins, escaped, though suffering a superficial scalp wound from a bullet. When the Baltimore and Ohio train pulled into town at 1:25 a.m. he warned the conductor there were dangerous men shooting. The engineer and baggage-master walked out to see for themselves and were fired on. Shepherd Hayward, the porter at the station, a free black, appeared, searching for the missing Higgins. Brown's men shouted for him to halt, but confused or scared he turned to walk back to the station and was shot in the back. He writhed in agony for twelve hours until he died. Thus, the first victim of Brown's liberation of the slaves was a free black man.

The next man killed was Thomas Boerley, a grocer, who wandered out of his home to check on the nighttime racket. He was shot by Dangerfield Newby, a free slave who had joined Brown's band with the dream of freeing his slave wife and seven children. Boerley was shot "without a word of warning . . . with as little compunction as if he had been a mad dog," according to an eyewitness. Then, on High Street, Newby shot dead George Turner, a West Point graduate and well-respected local squire, who came to town because he had heard his friend Lewis Washington had been abducted.

Brown boasted to the train conductor that he had captured Harpers Ferry to free the slaves and inexplicably allowed the train to continue on its route in the morning. When it arrived in Monocacy at seven a.m., the conductor telegraphed the superintendent, and the news spread at lightning speed up a chain of command to Governor Wise and President Buchanan, and quickly down the chain to the Maryland Volunteers, who set out for Harpers Ferry. Meanwhile, the town's physician, John D. Starry, after treating the lightly wounded Higgins and mortally wounded Hayward, observed Brown bringing the hostages into the armory, jumped on a horse, and rode all night, arousing everyone along the way. By the time he reached Charles Town on the morning of the 17th church bells were sounding the alarm and the Jefferson Guards were hurtling toward Harpers Ferry.

Feeling secure within the engine house of the armory, Brown captured more than thirty more prisoners, workers and soldiers coming to the armory as they did every morning. Brown ordered breakfast for forty-five people from the local tavern. Kagi, stationed at the rifle works, urged Brown to flee immediately with his weaponry into the countryside. Townspeople began shooting at the armory. Brown decided he would negotiate with his prisoners about arranging a cease-fire that would allow him to hold the fortified position unmolested. "Hold on a little longer, boys, until I get matters arranged with the prisoners," he told his men, who took the "tardiness of our brave leader," according to Anderson, "to be an omen of evil by some of us." By noon, the Jefferson Guards marched in. Dangerfield Newby was shot through the throat with a six-inch spike. His corpse was dragged through the street, his ears cut off, and pigs herded to feast on his body. Brown was trapped. Hundreds of militiamen from far and wide occupied the heights and started a festive turkey shoot. Jugs of whiskey were passed around. "Kill them, kill them!" they chanted.

Brown sent out one of his raiders, Will Thompson, under a flag of truce with a delusional idea he would negotiate something. Thompson was instantly arrested. Brown sent out two more men under a white flag, Aaron D. Stevens and Brown's son Watson, who were cut down. Stevens was badly wounded. Watson was mortally shot but managed to drag himself back to the engine house. Willie H. Leeman, a frightened teenaged recruit, dashed out of the armory hoping to escape across the Potomac. His brains were blown out and his body rolled into the river where it was used for target practice. Kagi and two others at the rifle works tried to get away. He was killed at once and left in the shallow water. Another was mortally wounded and died the next day. A third was arrested. Fontaine Beckham, the decades-long serving mayor and B&O station agent, closely attached to Heyward Shepherd, and unarmed, was shot dead standing on the depot platform while trying to see what was going on. His death inflamed the militiamen, who dragged Will Thompson to the Potomac, shot him in the head, shoved his body next to Leeman's, and also used it for target practice.

Oliver Brown, another son, caught a bullet while he was firing from the engine house. He asked his father to put him out of his misery. "Oh, you will get over it," said Brown. "If you must die, die like a man." During the cold dark night in the engine house, Oliver Brown curled in a corner and died. When Brown called out to him and he failed to answer, he said, "I guess he is dead." Watson Brown lay in another corner bleeding to death. Two of Brown's men, Dauphin Thompson and Jeremiah G. Anderson, spoke up. "Are we committing treason against our country by being here?" they asked Brown. "Certainly," he replied. "If that is so, we don't want to fight any more," they said. "We thought we came to liberate the slaves and did not know that that was committing treason." Two others, Albert Hazlett and Osborne Anderson, slipped out the back, and managed to get across the river into the hills. (Hazlett was captured and hung. Anderson was guided through the Underground Railroad to Canada and would later join the Union army.) The handful of slaves that had been taken from nearby plantations and armed quietly ran away into the night. Brown sleeplessly walked around inside the engine house wearing the sword of Frederick the Great.

Before midnight, the U.S. Marines arrived under the command of Colonel Robert E. Lee and Lieutenant J.E.B. Stuart. They waited for dawn. Stuart delivered a note from Lee addressed to Brown demanding his surrender and telling him he could not escape. "Well, lieutenant, I see we can't agree," he told Stuart. Lee ordered the building stormed. The door was broken down. Brown's men opened fire, killing two marines. Soldiers bayoneted Dauphin Thompson and Jeremiah Anderson to death. Lieutenant Israel Greene struck Brown with his sword but only wounded him. The troops took eleven prisoners, "the sorriest lot of people I ever saw," said Greene. Apart from the dead, dying, and wounded, the survivors were cold, hungry, and in terror of being killed. As they were brought out, the crowd chanted, "Hang them, hang them!" Brown was taken into the paymaster's office of the armory, his wounds tended, and given food and water. "I recovered the sword," Lewis Washington would testify. "Brown carried that in his hand all day Monday, and when the attacking party came on he laid it on a fire engine, and after the rescue I got it."

Had Israel Greene's sword been sharper and his blow decisive, John Brown would only be remembered for the raid and not the trial and execution. His martyrdom would have been wretched. His mad revolution, his willful incompetence, his defiance of all caution and reason, and his trail of murders, thievery, frauds, and dissembling would have hung his reputation without the last noble chapter to cast a glow. Brown's great good luck was to escape being run through in the engine house. Nothing he planned went right, and his survival was a thing of chance. It was what he was playing for all along, but his death came off better than anything he ever organized.

Brown would not become a new Cromwell and his ragtag band bore no resemblance to the New Model Army, but with his doom foreordained he followed the stations of the cross of Charles I. Brown drew on a familiar text. His self-possession and sympathetic gestures paralleled the description of the monarch awaiting execution in Brown's favorite biography of Cromwell, by Headley, a volume that had once inspired him to contemplate an autobiography casting himself in the role of Cromwell. He failed as Cromwell triumphant, but succeeded as Cromwell defeated, acting out Charles condemned.

Through his self-control, the captive King Charles I gains control. He no longer holds mastery over his realm but of himself in the inexorable circumstances of his death. "I am not afraid," Charles tells a weeping supporter. He refuses plans for escape, blesses his children, and hides his grief. "The last hours of Charles, were his best," wrote Headley, "and he never appeared so much a king, as when he mounted the scaffold. After forgiving his enemies—praying in the presence of the awe-struck multitude, and declaring his confidence that he was going from a corruptible, to an incorruptible, crown, he lay calmly down, and putting aside his clustering hair, himself gave the signal to strike." Confounding his executioners, the "death of the king was compared to the crucifixion of Christ." His saintlike performance removed the burden from his murderous tyranny. The regicides bore the guilt. "So, the execution of Charles, who accounted the rights of his people as nothing, was a damning act. . . . Sympathy, rather than principle, has converted him into a martyr."

Brown brought to his own last act the same zealotry but greater persuasiveness than he had brought to his thirty-six-hour revolution. His ultimate fiasco became his ultimate coup. His failed role as blood-curdling liberator was a rehearsal for his successful curtain call as suffering scapegoat. His invasion of Harpers Ferry was a tragic catastrophe, but his performance as a prisoner was a tragic masterpiece.

On the afternoon of October 19, John Brown lay on his side on the floor of the armory, his face and clothes streaked with blood, his hair matted, his wounds bandaged, exhausted, crushed, two of his sons dead nearby. Standing around him assembled his first questioners, a notable and intimidating panel of Senator James M. Mason of Virginia, who had hurried to the scene from his Winchester home; Congressman Alexander R. Boteler, who represented the district and had witnessed many of the events; Congressman Clement Vallandigham of Ohio, who would later become the leader of the pro-Confederate Copperheads opposed to President Lincoln; Governor Wise; Lieutenant J.E.B. Stuart; a local doctor; and a reporter from the *New York Herald,* who recorded the interrogation. Bedraggled and filthy, Brown rose in stature with every question from those looming above him. His arms had proved ridiculously inadequate in his defense, but his words defeated whatever they fired at him. He summoned a reserve of eloquence more pointed than his pikes. They had him as their prisoner, but they could not escape him. The more they tried to fasten the crime to him, the tighter he bound the chains of their greater guilt around them.

Brown began with a simple lie to cover up for the Secret Six. "Can you tell us who furnished money for your expedition?" asked Mason. "I furnished most of it myself; I cannot implicate others," Brown replied. Then he turned the question to reproach himself for his failure, displaying his honesty. "It is by my own folly that I have been taken. I could easily have saved myself from it, had I exercised my own better judgment rather than yielded to my feelings." Mason badgered him. "If you would tell us who sent you here,—who provided the means,—that would be information of some value." "I will answer freely and faithfully about what concerns myself," Brown said sternly. "I will answer anything I can with honor,—but not about others." Thus the Puritan deflected the line of inquiry invoking the Southern code of honor. "Any questions that I can honorably answer I will,—not otherwise. So far as I am myself concerned, I have told everything truthfully. I value my word, sir."

"What was your object in coming?" asked Mason. "We came to free the slaves, and only that," said Brown. "How do you justify your acts?" Mason demanded, giving Brown his opportunity to condemn him. "I think, my friend, you are guilty of a great wrong against God and humanity,—I say it without wishing to be offensive,—and it would be perfectly right for any one to interfere with you so far as to free those you willfully and wickedly hold in bondage. I do not say this insultingly." "I understand that," Mason conceded. Brown went on. "I think I did right, and that others will do right who interfere with you at any time and at all times. I hold that the Golden Rule, 'Do unto others as ye would that others should do unto you,' applies to all who would help others to gain their liberty."

J.E.B. Stuart the cavalry officer charged in, misjudging the terrain he was on and failing to anticipate being outflanked. "But don't you believe in the Bible?" he demanded. "Certainly I do," answered the great Calvinist. "What wages did you offer?" asked Mason, changing the subject. "None," replied Brown. Stuart wanted to return to his Bible test. "'The wages of sin is death,'" he declared solemnly, quoting from the Book of Romans. "I would not have made such a remark to you if you had been a prisoner, and wounded, in my hands," said Brown. He claimed the mount of humility and mercy, convicting Stuart of the sin of prideful cruelty. Brown was the Christ, Stuart the Roman. With that Brown defeated Stuart on the battlefield of faith.

After brushing off Vallandigham's petty attempts to implicate the Ohio abolitionist congressman Joshua Giddings, Brown was asked, "Do you consider yourself an instrument in the hands of Providence?" "I do," he said. Giving him a further opening, he was asked with incredulity, "Upon what principle do you justify your acts?" "Upon the Golden Rule," he declared. "I pity the poor in bondage that have none to help them: that is why I am here; not to gratify any personal animosity, revenge, or vindictive spirit. It is my sympathy with the oppressed and the wronged, that are as good as you and as precious in the sight of God." He added, "I don't think the people of the slave States will ever consider the subject of slavery in its true light till some other argument is resorted to than moral suasion."

Brown refused to answer question after question that sought to get him to implicate others. "I do not wish to annoy you," said the newspaper reporter, "but if you have anything further you would like to say, I will report it." Brown the prophet replied, "I have nothing to say, only that I claim to be here in carrying out a measure I believe perfectly justifiable, and not to act the part of an incendiary or ruffian, but to aid those suffering great wrong. I wish to say, furthermore, that you had better—all you people at the South— prepare yourselves for a settlement of this question, that must come up for settlement sooner than you are prepared for it. The sooner you are prepared the better. You may dispose of me very easily,—I am nearly disposed of now; but this question is still to be settled,—this negro question I mean; the end of that is not yet."

Governor Wise baited him. "Brown, suppose you had every nigger in the United States, what would you do with them?" "Set them free," he said simply. The questioner became annoyed. "Your intention was to carry them off and free them?" "Not at all." "To set them free would sacrifice the life of every man in this community." "I do not think so." Then the questioner became accusatory. "I know it. I think you are fanatical." Brown flung back the charge. "And I think you are fanatical. 'Whom the gods would destroy they first make mad,' and you are mad." With that, Brown claimed the high ground of reason.

"Mr. Brown," said Governor Wise, "the silver of your hair is reddened by the blood of crime, and you should eschew these hard words and think upon eternity. You are suffering from wounds, perhaps fatal; and should you escape death from these causes, you must submit to a trial which may involve death. Your confessions justify the presumption that you will be found guilty; and even now you are committing a felony under the laws of Virginia, by uttering sentiments like these. It is better you should turn your attention to your eternal future than be dealing in denunciations which can only injure you."

"Governor," Brown answered, "I have from all appearances not more than fifteen or twenty years the start of you in the journey to that eternity of which you kindly warn me; and whether my time here shall be fifteen months, or fifteen days, or fifteen hours, I am equally prepared to go. There is an eternity behind and an eternity before; and this little speck in the center, however long, is but comparatively a minute. The difference between your tenure and mine is trifling, and I therefore tell you to be prepared. I am prepared. You all have a heavy responsibility, and it behooves you to prepare more than it does me."

Brown had lost his battle, but within hours of the smoke settling he had already won the aftermath. No matter how many men they massed against him now, his captors were overmatched. "They are mistaken who take Brown to be a madman," said Wise after the interview. "He is a bundle of the best nerves I ever saw; cut and thrust and bleeding, and in bonds. He is a man of clear head, of courage, fortitude, and simple ingenuousness. He is cool, collected, and indomitable, and it is but just to him to say that he was humane to his prisoners, and he inspired me with great trust in his integrity as a man of truth. He is a fanatic, vain and garrulous, but firm, truthful, and intelligent."

The nation's press descended on the small Charles Town courtroom packed with hundreds of spectators where Brown's trial began on October 25. The entire front page of the *New York Times,* among other newspapers, was given over to transcripts and reports of "The Trial of the Insurgents." The *New York Herald* stated it was "in point of national importance" the most prominent trial in a half century. More than one thousand militiamen from around the state patrolled the town. Brown lay on a cot in the middle of the courtroom rising unsteadily to make his first objection. "Virginians, I did not ask for any quarter at the time I was taken. I did not ask to have my life spared. The Governor of the State of Virginia tendered me his assurance that I should have a fair trial; but, under no circumstances whatever will I be able to have a fair trial. If you seek my blood, you can have it at any moment, without this mockery of a trial." The somber judge, Richard Parker, a former Democratic congressman from an old Virginia family, determined to preside over a fair trial, assigned him two competent attorneys already prepared to take his case. A young Boston lawyer, George H. Hoyt, would soon join the defense table. After a jury of twelve men was empaneled, Brown was arraigned on charges of treason against the Commonwealth of Virginia, incitement of slave insurrection, and murder—"evil and traitorous." One of Brown's lawyers raised an insanity defense, but if Brown were to be declared insane, he could not be executed and his design for martyrdom would be foiled. He stood to object, called it "miserable artifice and pretext . . . and if I am insane, of course I should think I know more than all the rest of the world. But I do not think so. I am perfectly unconscious of insanity." And so that last straw was discarded. Brown explained in a letter to his brother on November 12 his motive "that I am worth inconceivably more to hang than for other purpose." Brown denounced his local attorneys and they quit. His case was left to Hoyt, who was joined by two prominent Northern attorneys quietly arranged by Montgomery Blair. Brown was intent that his lawyers elicit from his former hostages the testimony that he had not harmed them. He believed this would deflect the charges by showing he was a humanitarian. The jury returned a verdict of guilty after forty-five minutes of deliberation. "Not the slightest sound was heard in the vast crowd, as this verdict was returned and read," reported the *New York Herald,* "not the slightest expression of elation or triumph was uttered from the hundreds present. . . . Nor was this strange silence interrupted during the whole of the time occupied by the forms of the court."

Judge Parker asked Brown if he had anything to say before sentencing. He stood erect from his bed on the floor. "I deny everything," he said. His claim of blamelessness was false and argumentative. But in the shadow of his cross he put on the crown of thorns. "This Court acknowledges, too, as I suppose, the validity of the law of God. I see a book kissed, which I suppose to be the Bible, or at least the New Testament, which teaches me that all things whatsoever I would that men should do to me, I should do even so to them. It teaches me, further, to remember them that are in bonds as bound with them. I endeavored to act up to that instruction. I say I am yet too young to understand that God is any respecter of persons. I believe that to have interfered as I have done, as I have always freely admitted I have done, in behalf of His despised poor, I did no wrong, but right. Now, if it is deemed necessary that I should forfeit my life for the furtherance of the ends of justice, and mingle my blood further with the blood of my children and with the blood of millions in this slave country whose rights are disregarded by wicked, cruel, and unjust enactments, I say, let it be done." Parker sentenced him to death, and he was on his way to his Calvary.

Over the next month John Brown in his cell was at the serene center of the universe. He wrote a series of letters, in the plain style of Bunyan's *Pilgrim's Progress,* touching letters to his wife and children, inspiring and courageous ones to his friends, spiritual ones disclaiming any motive of revenge, and unapologetic ones for following God's voice to free the slaves. Every day he met with visitors including proslavery men. "I endeavor to improve them faithfully, plainly, and kindly," he wrote. He found strength in his coming execution. "I think I feel as happy as Paul did when he lay in prison," he wrote. "He knew if they killed him, it would greatly advance the cause of Christ; that was the reason he rejoiced so. On that same ground 'I do rejoice, yea, and will rejoice.' Let them hang me; I forgive them, and may God forgive them, for they know not what they do. I have no regret for the transaction for which I am condemned. I went against the laws of men, it is true, but 'whether it be right to obey God or men, judge ye.'" By the day of his execution he had been transfigured.

On December 2, in the bright light of the late morning, Brown was taken from the jail wearing red carpet slippers, a blue shirt, a vest, and his still blood-stained black suit with cuts in it, his battle raiment now his shroud for crucifixion. He sat in the back of the wagon with his jailor atop his black

The Execution of John Brown, drawing by David Hunter Strother

walnut coffin for the ride through the streets to a field when his gallows had been constructed. "This is a beautiful country," Brown said gazing into the distance at the Blue Ridge Mountains where he thought he would be hiding with his slave army. The wagon drove through ranks of troops standing at attention in a hollow square. "I am sorry citizens have been kept out," he said.

"Brown had his arms tied behind him, and ascended the scaffold with apparent cheerfulness," wrote an eyewitness, Major Thomas Jackson (later known as "Stonewall"), professor of natural philosophy at the Virginia Military Institute, in command of the VMI cadets at the execution. "After reaching the top of the platform, he shook hands with several who were standing around him. The sheriff placed the rope around his neck, then threw a white cap over his head and asked him if he wished a signal when all should be ready—to which he replied that it made no difference, provided he was not kept waiting too long." "You must lead me—I cannot see," said Brown when he was asked to step on the trapdoor. Ten minutes after the trapdoor was opened the rope was cut. "With the fall his arms below the elbow flew up, hands clenched, and his arms gradually fell by spasmodic motions—there was very little motion of his person for several minutes, after which the wind blew his lifeless body to and fro."

"So perish all such enemies of Virginia!" shouted Colonel J.T.L. Preston of VMI. "All such enemies of the Union! All foes of the human race!"

Standing about thirty feet from the scaffold in the line of the Richmond

John Brown's last note, December 2, 1859, the day of his execution

Greys, one militiaman felt faint at the sight of Brown's twisting body. "I would like a good, stiff drink of whiskey," said John Wilkes Booth. He left the scene with the mementos of a piece of the poplar wooden box that had contained Brown's coffin and one of Brown's pikes inscribed "Major Washington to J. Wilkes Booth," a gift from B.B. Washington, great-great-nephew of George Washington, of the Continental Morgan Guard of Winchester. "I may say I helped to hang John Brown," Booth wrote a year later. But he never spoke of him except in a tone of awe. "John Brown was a man inspired, the grandest character of this century!" The lesson he took away was that "open force is holier than hidden craft, the Lion is more noble than the fox."

As John Brown left his jail cell on his way to his execution he handed one of his guards a note: "I, John Brown, am now quite certain that the crimes of this *guilty land* will never be purged away but with *blood. I* had, as I now think vainly, flattered myself that without very much bloodshed it might be done."

WITCH HUNT

John Brown's initial legacy was contained in a carpetbag he left in the attic of the farmhouse he used as his base camp. It was filled with hundreds of letters implicating everyone with whom he communicated. Soldiers under Lieutenant Stuart's command discovered the cache of incriminating and seemingly incriminating documents on the afternoon after Brown's capture. "Had he succeeded, therefore, in gaining the hills and beginning his guer-rilla raids, his enemy would have been in full possession of his purposes and of the names of his confederates in the North," wrote Brown's biographer, Oswald Garri-son Villard. The soldiers also found most of the pikes with which he intended to arm slaves and distributed them to mi-litiamen, townspeople, and hangers-on as souvenirs. Brown's letters were shared with the reporter from the *New York Herald* on the scene and soon published in the newspaper along with those letters obtained for a price from the erstwhile soldier of fortune and insurgency expert Hugh Forbes. "I never dreamed that the most terrible engine of destruction which

Hinton Rowan Helper

he would carry with him in his campaign would be a carpet-bag loaded with 400 letters, to be turned against his friends," Forbes wrote in a note to James Gordon Bennett, editor of the *Herald,* which was prominently featured to highlight an editorial entitled, "The Exposure of the Nigger-Worshipping Insurrectionists." "After Brown and his unfortunate comrades shall have been disposed of, the turn of Seward and the other republican Senators and members of Congress will come," it said. "If they be not impeached and condemned, then neither should a hair of John Brown's head suffer, for he is really less guilty than they."

Seward was on a Grand Tour of Europe, not to return until the year's end, but he immediately became the prime target. He was, after all, the prohibitive front-runner for the Republican presidential nomination. John Brown, who believed he was God-sent, was a godsend to Democrats. He appeared like a lightning bolt to strike down Seward. On October 19, the *New York Herald* published the first news about John Brown's raid alongside "Wm. H. Seward's Brutal and Blood Manifesto," his "irrepressible conflict" speech reproduced in its entirety. Brown's "treason, robbery and murder" was claimed to have been "plotted by that demagogue, Wm. H. Seward." On October 27, Hugh Forbes claimed in the *Herald* he had confided to Seward "the whole matter in all its bearings." "What is Treason?—Who are Traitors?" ran the headline on an editorial two days later. "Let the Senate take Seward and [Henry] Wilson, and every other one of the traitors in its bosom, in hand, and either impeach them or expel them from the chamber. . . . Let justice be done on all the traitors concerned in Brown's treason."

On November 18, the conservative Wall Street Democrats with financial ties to the Southern cotton trade, led principally by S.L.M. Barlow, the lawyer and financier instrumental in the nomination of Buchanan, usually operating politically as the Fifth Avenue Hotel Committee held a meeting under the name of an organization they called the New York Democratic Vigilant Association, a name calculated to mock the abolitionist New York Vigilance Committee, which served as the public face of the Underground Railroad. This Democratic Vigilant Committee was the Fifth Avenue Hotel Committee in another guise. It raised money to "make known to our Southern brethren our condemnation of the instigators of the movement [behind Harpers Ferry]." The group published a pamphlet called *Rise and Progress of the Bloody Outbreak at Harper's Ferry,* featuring on the title page excerpts from Seward's "irrepressible conflict" speech. The committee cited Hugh Forbes's letters to "prove that republican Senators of the United States, were made cognizant of the invasion intended, but concealed the secret within their own breasts, and refrained from divulging it to the public authorities." "John Brown has only practiced what William H. Seward preaches," the committee concluded.

Seward was traveling in Paris with John Bigelow, an editor and co-owner of the liberal antislavery newspaper the *New York Post,* who observed that he was "not disturbed in the least about the Harper's Ferry incident," or the attempt to blame him. But Seward's enemies did not even need Forbes's garbled and uncorroborated account to convict him; they simply cited his "irrepressible conflict" speech as proof. A Richmond newspaper posted an advertisement in which one hundred Virginians pledged "to pay five hundred dollars each ($50,000) *for the head of William H. Seward,* and would add a similar reward for Fred Douglass, but regarding him head and shoulders above these Traitors, will permit him to remain where he now is."

Frederick Douglass had fled to England on the day Brown was captured. Few men had a longer or closer association, or guilt by association, with John Brown. Douglass feared "in what was then the state of the public mind I could not hope to make a jury of Virginia believe I did not go the whole length he went, or that I was not one of his supporters; and I knew that all Virginia, were I once in her clutches, would say 'Let him be hanged.'" He bolted through Canada to catch a ship from Labrador to Liverpool. "I could but feel that I was going into exile, perhaps for life." Governor Wise declared that "could he overtake that vessel he would take me from her deck at any cost." Once in London, Douglass applied to the U.S. embassy for a passport but was refused on the grounds that he was not considered to be a citizen. He went to the French embassy and was issued a visa immediately. Douglass did not return for six months to the United States, where he was stunned "to participate in the most important and memorable presidential canvass ever witnessed in the United States, and to labor for the election of a man who in the order of things was destined to do a greater service to his country and to mankind than any man who had gone before him in the presidential office." But in November of 1859, in flight, again a fugitive, Douglass had no premonition of when or how he might come back, or of Lincoln's nomination.

Gerrit Smith panicked when a *Herald* reporter arrived at Peterboro to interview him about his involvement with Brown. "I am going to be indicted, sir, indicted!" he shouted. The *Herald* correspondent wrote, "I believe that Brown's visit to his house last spring was intimately connected with the insurrection, and that it is the knowledge that at any moment, either by the discovery of papers or the confession of accomplices, his connection with the affair may become exposed, that keeps Mr. Smith in constant excitement and fear." On November 7, Smith's doctor diagnosed him as "quite deranged," and he was committed to an insane asylum. When he was released after more than a month confinement, he denied to his deathbed his complicity with Brown.

Upon hearing that Brown's letters had been discovered, Franklin Sanborn destroyed "the records of our conspiracy" in his possession. He consulted John A. Andrew, a Boston lawyer and Republican, who would in 1860 be elected governor. Andrew's opinion was that he could be "suddenly and secretly arrested and hurried out of the protection of Massachusetts law." That night, on October 20, Sanborn fled to Canada. After Wendell Phillips wrote him that Higginson, Howe, and Ralph Waldo Emerson concurred that there was "no risk" he returned within a week.

The day Sanborn came back Howe and Stearns arrived in exile in Canada. Howe became unnerved when Andrews advised him he could be arrested, and Howe convinced Stearns he was at jeopardy and must join him. Howe sent a denial of his knowledge of Brown's raid to the *New York Tribune*. "That event was unforeseen and unexpected but by me," he wrote. He could not "reconcile" the John Brown he knew with "his characteristic prudence, and his reluctance to shed blood, or excite servile insurrection. It is still to me a mystery and a marvel."

Higginson was infuriated at Howe's disavowal, writing him "it would be the extreme of baseness in as to deny complicity with Capt. Brown's general scheme—while we were not, of course, called upon to say anything to criminate ourselves." Sanborn wrote Higginson to disagree: "What has been prudence is prudence still and may be for years to come." Higginson angrily replied, "Is there no such thing as honor among confederates?" Higginson publicly held meetings in Worcester to defend Brown for "the most formidable insurrection that has ever occurred," while attempting to organize elaborate rescue missions that never got off the ground.

Theodore Parker, dying in Rome, wrote a defense of John Brown in the form of a prophecy. "For it is not to be denied that we must give up DEMOCRACY if we keep SLAVERY, or give up SLAVERY if we keep DEMOCRACY." On the day of Brown's execution, Parker said to his doctor, "I shall be seeing Brown soon. . . . Hold a séance and I shall let you know his answer."

On the morning of Brown's hanging, George Luther Stearns sat by Niagara Falls, on the Canadian side, "listening to the dirge of the cataract," according to his son. "There he repeated the vow he had made at the time of the assault on Sumner, to devote the rest of his life and fortune to the liberation of the slave." In January 1860, he quietly went to North Elba, New York, to Brown's farm, to visit his grave. He endowed and managed a fund for his widow and family, paid for the private education of two of Brown's daughters at the school in Concord where Sanborn was headmaster, and arranged for a mason to carve a tombstone for John Brown. Back in Boston, some people ostracized him, but most of the Bird Club "stood by him."

At two in the afternoon on December 2, about two hours after John Brown was hanged, the leading citizens of Concord crowded into the Town Hall for a Martyr's Service, exalting the legend of John Brown. The first speaker was Henry David Thoreau. After the raid, when nearly all abolitionists scurried to separate themselves, he had delivered on October 30 "A Plea for John Brown," in which he said, "Some eighteen hundred years ago Christ was crucified; this morning, perchance, Captain Brown was hung. These are the two ends of a chain which is not without its links. He is not Old Brown any longer; he is an angel of light." Now he read poetry as a liturgy from Marvell, Wordsworth, and Tennyson. Ralph Waldo Emerson read from Senator Mason's interview with Brown and from Brown's last speech to the court. Emerson, who was the most famous intellectual and sought after lecturer in the country, had electrified controversy on November 8, just after Brown received his sentence, in an address he entitled "Courage," before a packed protest meeting at the Music Hall in Boston, in which he declared Brown "the new saint awaiting his martyrdom, and who, if he shall suffer, will make the gallows glorious like the cross." Bronson Alcott led the Concord congregation in a new "Service for the Death of a Martyr," and ending with the singing of a "Dirge" composed by Franklin Sanborn: "Today beside Potomac's wave, Beneath Virginia's sky, They slay the man who loved the slave, And dared for him to die."

Virginia governor Henry A. Wise's handling of Brown did more to revolutionize Southern opinion than any other factor. John Brown, who had contempt for politics and made a point of knowing almost nothing about it, became a malleable political element for him to twist and turn. Throughout his erratic career, beginning as a Whig, Wise "delighted in his isolation and rioted in the eccentricities of his genius," according to John Forney. Wise had wanted to be the Democratic presidential nominee in 1856 but pledged support to Douglas, whom he betrayed for Buchanan. Raising the flag of rebellion, he proclaimed that if Frémont were elected he would march fifty thousand Virginians on Washington and proposed a preliminary secession conference. In 1858 he promised Douglas he would support him for the nomination in 1860, but betrayed him again. Despite his vehement threats and appeals to honor, he was at constant political war with the Calhoun faction of the Democratic Party in Virginia, which was known as the Chivalry and more radical than its phlegmatic leader Senator Robert M.T. Hunter. Wise decried "the extremists South," while occasionally borrowing their rhetoric in vain efforts to usurp them. In the passion play of John Brown, the high-strung governor played a series of shifting roles from Pontius Pilate to Marc Anthony, from Hamlet to Lord High Executioner. He held Brown for trial in a Virginia court presided over by a fair-minded judge rather than turn him over to a drumhead military tribunal. His hands were washed of guilt, at least for the moment. After personally hectoring Brown, Wise praised him for the courage of his convictions, seeming to rise above vengeance. Then he put Charles Town under martial law to surround the condemned man and prevent an illusory attack to rescue him. Wise refused to commute his death sentence on grounds of insanity, then reconsidered, only to insist Brown was sane. "I therefore say to you firmly that I have precisely the nerve enough to let him be executed," Wise declared. The *Richmond Enquirer,* edited by the governor's son, O. Jennings Wise, editorialized that Brown "may be insane . . . but there are other *criminals,* guilty wretches, who instigated the crimes perpetrated at Harper's Ferry. Bring these men, bring Seward, Greeley, Giddings, Hale, and Smith to the jurisdiction of Virginia, and Brown and his deluded victims in the Charlestown jail may hope for pardon." Three days after Brown's execution, Wise told the Virginia legislature, "If these men were monomaniacs, then are a large portion of the people of many of the states monomaniacs." His tribute to Brown tainted the whole North. It fit with the logic that Brown, who was his own party, was the representative man of all Republicans. This was a campaign theme. Wise was running for the Democratic presidential nomination, hoping to be the latest dark horse candidate. Brown was his horse. Wise also called upon the legislature to impose greater repression on slaves in supposed fear they might be inspired by Brown to rebel. "The most stringent laws are required against all secret and nightly association of negroes, bond or free," he said. That, too, was part of his campaign.

Edmund Ruffin, the Virginia fire-eater, co-founder of the recently formed secessionist League of United Southerners, who had come to Charles Town to join the ranks of the VMI cadets in order to witness the hanging, was an acidulous observer of Wise's antics. "Before the Harper's Ferry affair," he wrote, "he had but little support in Virginia (and none elsewhere) for the presidency, which he was seeking so boldly and shamelessly. But his conduct in and since the affair, though very blameable for indiscretion, has given him more popularity than all he ever acquired for his real worth and ability, or his praiseworthy public services." Ruffin viewed Wise's belligerence as pantomime; Brown's authentic militancy, however, thrilled him. Stuart's soldiers gave him a batch of Brown's pikes to whose wooden handles Ruffin attached a label: "Samples of the favors designed for us by our Northern Brethren." He brought one to Washington to show to Southern senators and shipped others to every Southern governor. He beat the drum for a reopening of the slave trade and boycott of Northern goods.

Wise's handling of the Brown incident dismayed the conservative Virginia Chivalry faction. James Seddon, the former congressman (later Confederate secretary of war), wrote Senator Hunter on December 26 that "the train of events and the course of public conduct and opinion upon them, especially in Va have been injudiciously and alarmingly mismanaged and misdirected, and I hold the unsound judgment, insatiate vanity and selfish policy of our fussy Governor mainly responsible for them." Seddon believed that Wise had committed a political offense in not depicting Brown and his band as "the mad folly of a few deluded cranks branded fanatics" rather than "elevating them to political offenders or making them representatives and champions of Northern Sentiment." Instead, "our Honorable Governor, seduced by the passion of oratorical display, commenced by a picturesque description of them as heroes and martyrs, and, by insisting on holding them as the chiefs of an organized conspiracy at the North, has provoked and in a measure invoked the sympathy and approbation of large masses and of established organs of public opinion at the North." At the same time, by making "these infamous felons grand political criminals" he "roused pride and animosities of both sections against each other, has brought on a real crisis of imminent peril to both."

The Southern reaction to Harpers Ferry went through three stages: first, shock; then, relief and triumph; and, finally, a paroxysm of paranoia, some spontaneous and some cynical. Relief that Brown was so swiftly defeated gave way to exhilaration that the slaves did not rise up. Harpers Ferry was hailed as vindication of slavery. "I take pride in repeating," said Senator Mason, "that the State of Virginia was saved from insurrection among her slaves only by the loyalty of her slaves. That those fields do not now present a scene of incendiarism and blood is owing only to the loyalty of the slaves upon the soil of Virginia." Upon further reflection, Mason decided that Harpers Ferry implicated the entire Republican Party. "John Brown's invasion was condemned [in the North] only because it failed," he said. "But in view of the sympathy for him in the North and the persistent efforts of the sectional party there to interfere with the rights of the South, it was not at all strange that the Southern States should deem it proper to arm themselves and prepare for any contingency that might arise."

Brown's sanctification by some abolitionists, despite the nearly universal condemnation of his action by Republicans, was received as an insult to Southern honor. John S. Wise, the governor's son, wrote, "When it was learned that, in many parts of the North, churches held services of humiliation and prayer; that bells were tolled; that minute-guns were fired; that Brown was glorified as a saint; that even in the legislature of Massachusetts, eight out of nineteen senators had voted to adjourn at the time of his execution; that Christian ministers had been parties to his schemes of assassination and robbery; that women had canonized the bloodthirsty old lunatic as 'St. John the Just'; that philanthropists had pronounced him 'most truly Christian'; that Northern poets like Whittier and Emerson and Longfellow were writing panegyrics upon him; that Wendell Phillips and William Lloyd Garrison approved his life, and counted him a martyr,—then Virginians began to feel that an 'irrepressible conflict' was indeed upon them."

The logic of disunion and the images down to the "bells" precisely echoed those of Christopher G. Memminger, South Carolina's commissioner sent to organize a secession conference of Southern states. "Harper's Ferry is the truthful illustration of the first act of the drama to be performed on a Southern theatre," stated the resolution of the South Carolina legislature that established his office, which also predicted inexorable secession, "The election of a black Republican President will settle the question of our safety in the Union." Memminger, a dignified former state legislator and financier, traveled to Richmond to present his case to the General Assembly on January 27, 1860. "Every village bell," he said, "which tolled its solemn note at the execution of Brown, proclaims to the South the approbation of that village of insurrection and servile war, and the ease with which some of the confederates escaped to Canada proves that much of the population around are willing to abet the actors in these incendiary attempts." Brown's singular act was construed as the will of the North. "The Harper's Ferry invasion with the developments following it, and the now existing condition of the country, prove that the North and the South are standing in hostile array—the one with an absolute majority, sustaining those who meditate our destruction and refusing to us any concession or guaranty, and the other baffled in every attempt at compromise or security. . . . Can any one mistake the roaring of the storm at Washington? Has the column of the Republican party there shown any sign of wavering?" The Virginia legislature rejected Memminger's appeal, but the first secession commissioner was laying the groundwork. The governors of South Carolina, Mississippi, and Alabama began regular communications on plans for a Southern Confederacy. (Memminger would become the first Confederate secretary of the treasury.)

A great fear swept the South. State after state passed more draconian black codes. Slave patrols and lynching increased. Random Northerners—businessmen, salesmen, and visitors—were physically assaulted, tarred and feathered, whipped, and threatened by mobs. Local vigilance committees warned Northerners to leave. The Montgomery, Alabama, *Mail* newspaper suggested that Northern peddlers should be assumed to be John Browns in disguise, arrested and hung. Booksellers and teachers with suspect Yankee accents were driven out. The biracial experimental Berea School in Kentucky established by Cassius M. Clay and run by the minister John G. Fee was ordered by a county committee to shut down or else Fee would be killed. Boycotts of Northern goods were launched. Blacklists of businesses doing business with Northern firms were published. Local groups demanded payment to pronounce Northern businesses clean of abolitionism. "Let Virginia call home her sons!" proclaimed Governor Wise. And 259 medical students from schools in Philadelphia returned home on December 20 to cheering crowds, bands, and a banquet addressed by Wise in Richmond. Militia units across the South, inspired by the spectacle of the soldiers amassed around John Brown in his prison, attracted volunteers and regularly drilled. The three states that responded positively to Commissioner Memminger's circuit riding for secession appropriated large sums for their militias: South Carolina, $100,000; Mississippi, $150,000; Alabama, $200,000. Governor William Gist of South Carolina privately wrote to the state's congressional delegation, "If . . . you upon consultation decide to make the issue of force in Washington, write or telegraph me, and I will have a regiment in or near Washington in the shortest possible time."

On December 5, the Monday following the Friday on which John Brown was hanged, the 36th Congress convened. The Democrats controlled the

Senate, but no one had a majority in the House, where the first order of business was to elect a Speaker. Republicans held 109 seats, Democrats 101, but of these, 12 were anti-Lecompton Democrats who would not organize with the regular Democrats, 26 were Know Nothings, of which only 3 were not from the South. The one stray Whig, John Sherman of Ohio, emerged after one ballot as the Republican consensus candidate for Speaker. He had been a prosperous Whig lawyer in Cleveland aroused by the Kansas-Nebraska Act to run for the Congress. He had led the investigation and written the report on "The Troubles in Kansas." He was also organically connected to the powerful Thomas Ewing, who had been the Whig U.S. senator from Ohio, secretary of the treasury under Harrison and Tyler, and secretary of the interior under Taylor, and most importantly the foster father of Sherman's younger brother, William Tecumseh Sherman, taken in after the death of their father and who married Ewing's daughter. Within the Ohio Republican Party, Congressman Sherman was not a radical like Giddings and Chase, but acknowledged as a moderate. He was now under fierce attack as the equivalent of John Brown.

The day after Republicans unified behind Sherman, on December 6, Congressman John B. Clark of Missouri proposed a resolution unique in congressional history, that any member who had "endorsed and recommended . . . a certain book," whose "doctrine and sentiments" he declared were "insurrectionary" was unfit to be Speaker. The dangerous book in question was

John Sherman of Ohio

The Impending Crisis of the South, written by Hinton Rowan Helper. At the suggestion of Francis P. Blair, the book, which had been published in 1857, was abridged in an edition of 100,000 copies printed by the *New York Tribune* that the Republican Party was circulating. Sherman had lent his name among more than sixty Republicans in its approval as a party document. Clark submitted excerpts for the record and said that those "who design to carry that treason and rebellion into effect, deserve a fate which it would not be respectable for me to announce in this House."

Listening to Clark, Sherman thought his proposal "seemed so ludicrous that we regarded it as manufactured frenzy." Then John S. Millson of Virginia spoke. "One who consciously, deliberately, and of purpose, lent his name and influence to the propagation of such writings is not only not fit to be Speaker, but is not fit to live," he said. Sherman rose to submit a letter from Blair explaining that the edition of the offending book was "expurgated" of many "obnoxious" passages, that Sherman himself had not read the book, and that he was opposed to "any interference whatever by the people of the free States with the relations of master and slave in the slave States." His concessions did not have a calming effect.

Congressman Laurence Keitt of South Carolina, Preston Brooks's accomplice in the caning of Sumner, read at length from Seward's speeches and cited his "irrepressible conflict" speech, to demand of Republicans, "He is now the head of the Republican party. Do you endorse him, or do you repudiate him? . . . We mean now to defend ourselves. All we say to you is elect your candidate. Stand upon your platform, and then let each party fight out its own cause."

This brought Thaddeus Stevens to his feet to offer remarks dripping with sarcasm, that he did not "blame" the "gentlemen from the South" for "the language of intimidation," which "they have tried fifty times, and fifty times they have found weak and recreant tremblers in the North who have been affected by it, and who have acted from those intimidations." Martin J. Crawford of Georgia accused Stevens of deceiving the South "pretending to respect our rights, whilst you never intend to give us peace." "I am not to be provoked by interruptions," coolly replied Stevens. So began the bitter two months long battle over the Speakership.

Hinton Helper, the son of an illiterate dirt farmer from North Carolina who died when he was a child, sought his fortune in the California Gold Rush, and failing at that wrote a devastating economic, sociological, and political critique of the South. Unable to find a publisher, even in New York, he self-published the book. *The Impending Crisis of the South: How to Meet It* was a unique and inarguable statistical handbook of information on how slavery destroyed economic development, invention, education, and enterprise, while promoting poverty, disease, and ignorance. Even more it was the most insightful and scathing exposé ever written by a Southerner of "the entire mind of the South," the mirror of an oligarchy that in its compulsion for "acquiescence with slavery" suppressed freedom of speech and thought and depended upon the "abject servilism" not just of the slaves but of "the non-slave holding whites."

Here was Helper's unforgivable crime, his revolutionary call to poor whites to overthrow slavery in their own interest. "Notwithstanding the fact that the white non-slaveholders of the South, are in the majority, as five to one, they have never yet had any part or lot in framing the laws under which they live. There is no legislation except for the benefit of slavery, and slaveholders. As a general rule, poor white persons are regarded with less esteem and attention than negroes, and though the condition of the latter is wretched beyond description, vast numbers of the former are infinitely worse off. A cunningly devised mockery of freedom is guaranteed to them, and that is all. To all intents and purposes they are disfranchised, and outlawed, and the only privilege extended to them, is a shallow and circumscribed participation in the political movements that usher slaveholders into office."

Helper borrowed a famous phrase of Sumner's to captiously describe slave owners, "the lords of the lash," to designate them as the oppressors of the poor whites. "The lords of the lash are not only absolute masters of the blacks, who are bought and sold, and driven about like so many cattle, but they are also the oracles and arbiters of all non-slaveholding whites, whose freedom is merely nominal, and whose unparalleled illiteracy and degradation is purposely and fiendishly perpetuated. How little the 'poor white trash,' the great majority of the Southern people, know of the real condition of the country is, indeed, sadly astonishing."

Helper's cutting descriptions of "the slave-driving oligarchy" were endlessly creative and rivaled Sumner's in their abuse: a "junto," "vain-glorious, self-sufficient and brutal," "haughty cavaliers of shackles and handcuffs," "insulting to intelligence." His descriptions of slavery were unrestrained as a vampiric "sum of all villainies." "The diabolical institution subsists on its own flesh. At one time children are sold to procure food for the parents, at another, parents are sold to procure food for the children. Within its pestilential atmosphere, nothing succeeds; progress and prosperity are unknown; inanition and slothfulness ensue ; everything becomes dull, dismal and unprofitable; wretchedness and desolation run riot throughout the land; an aspect of most melancholy inactivity and dilapidation broods over every city and town; ignorance and prejudice sit enthroned over the minds of the people; usurping despots wield the sceptre of power; everywhere, and in everything, between Delaware Bay and the Gulf of Mexico, are the multitudinous evils of slavery apparent."

The Slave Power rested on the passivity of the "masses of white people" that "succumbs to its authority." Told what to think and do by slaveholders, "poor whites may hear with fear and trembling, but not speak. They must be as mum as dumb brutes, and stand in awe of their august superiors, or be crushed with stern rebukes, cruel oppressions, or downright violence. If they dare to think for themselves, their thoughts must be forever concealed."

Helper unapologetically called himself an abolitionist, and said every Southerner should be an abolitionist, but his sympathy was not principally with the blacks. He pierced the veil of the ideology of white supremacy that raised the racial identity of poor whites above their inherent class conflict with the slaveholders, calling that ideology "the black veil."

> The black veil, through whose almost impenetrable meshes light seldom gleams, has long been pendent over their eyes, and there, with fiendish jealousy, the slave-driving ruffians sedulously guard it. Non-slaveholders are not only kept in ignorance of what is transpiring at the North, but they are continually misinformed of what is going on even in the South. Never were the poorer classes of a people, and those classes so largely in the majority, and all inhabiting the same country, so basely duped, so adroitly swindled, or so damnably outraged. It is expected that the stupid and sequacious masses, the white victims of slavery, will believe, and, as a general thing, they do believe, whatever the slaveholders tell them; and thus it is that they are cajoled into the notion that they are the freest, happiest and most intelligent people in the world, and are taught to look with prejudice and disapprobation upon every new principle or progressive movement. Thus it is that the South, woefully inert and inventionless, has lagged behind the North, and is now weltering in the cesspool of ignorance and degradation.

The Impending Crisis, which by early 1859 had become the greatest best-seller since *Uncle Tom's Cabin,* was banned from circulation in the South in the spirit of the Gag Rule of the 1830s. Most importantly, it provided a tool for the Democrats to force a crisis on the Republicans. Helper's book became a rallying point for the Democrats, who were just short of a majority, to thwart Sherman's election as Speaker. It was fitted into a forced logic that insisted on a continuum from John Brown to the Republican Party to Seward; now Helper was inserted into the equation. On the day Sherman was nominated, the *New York Herald* connected all the dots in an editorial that set the tone. "'Either slavery must be abolished, or the Union must be dissolved.' That is the argument of the bloody and brutal Rochester manifesto [of Seward]; that is the plain English of Helper's insurrectionary and treasonable book . . . .

Helper and John Brown bring them what they want. . . . John Brown puts Helper's doctrine into execution. Thus the black republican party appears as the direct foe of the Union."

Roger Pryor, the fire-eating editor, now a congressman from Virginia, declared that if Sherman were elected Speaker it would give "to the South the example of insult as well as injury," and "I would walk, every one of us, out of the halls of this Capitol." Helper's book, he said, was circulated "in rebellion, treason, and insurrection, and is precisely in the spirit of the act which startled us a few weeks since at Harper's Ferry." These talking points and words about "treason" and "insurrection" were constantly repeated. Thomas C. Hindman of Arkansas, for example, delivered a stem-winding speech denouncing "the Black Republican Bible, The Helper Book." "The tenets and practices of the Republican party lead to civil war, to bloodshed, to murder, and to rapine. . . . This traitorous, sectional, and bloody Republican party is the one that met us at the threshold of this House, on the first day of the session demanding the Speakership." He added to Sherman's crimes his criticism of the Fugitive Slave Act, which made him "a practical encourager of negro-stealing, and an assistant of the underground railroad." "In other words," replied Sherman, "I am charged with being a Republican. That is my offense; none other."

The *New York Tribune* and Greeley naturally jumped into the fray, acclaiming Helper as more menacing to slavery than Brown. "As 'the pen is mightier than the sword,' so Rowan Helper, armed with facts and figures, calling upon the give millions of non-slaveholders to rise and take possession of the Southern ballot-boxes, is far more to be dreaded by the Slavery Propagandists than a thousand John Browns, armed with pikes and rifles, urging ignorant negroes to escape into the Free States."

Over a biblical forty days and nights, forty-four ballots were taken with Sherman falling just three votes short. Finally, he cut a deal with three Know Nothings to vote for another Republican, one who had not previously endorsed *The Impending Crisis,* William Pennington of New Jersey, which allowed the Republicans to organize the House and claim the chairmanships of the committees.

The game of smearing Sherman had achieved its aim. He was not the actual target. Helper's book was merely the available artifice. The true focus was Seward. "The defeat of Sherman was gall and wormwood to the Seward division of the Blacks [Republicans]," Senator Toombs wrote Alexander Stephens on February 10. "It brought them into national discredit and strengthened the opposition to Seward inside the party."

The controversy over *The Impending Crisis,* however, did not relent. It boiled over on the floor of the House with a speech by Owen Lovejoy on April 5, 1860, in which he called slavery "the sum of all villainy." A mocking voice shouted, "You are joking." As Lovejoy spoke he wandered toward the Democratic side of the chamber. Pryor of Virginia angrily walked to confront him. "It is bad enough to be compelled to sit here and hear him utter his treasonable and insulting language; but he *shall not,* sir, come upon this side of the House shaking his fist in our faces." John F. Potter of Wisconsin, a Republican, stepped toward Pryor. "We listened to gentlemen on the other side for eight weeks, when they denounced the members upon this side with violent and offensive language. We listened to them quietly and heard them through. And now, sir, this side *shall* be heard, let the consequences be what they may." Amid calls for Lovejoy to be seated or to continue, Barksdale of Mississippi, who had acted as Brooks's bodyguard while he beat Sumner, shouted, "Order that black-hearted scoundrel and nigger-stealing thief to take his seat, and this side of the House will do it." Other members and Barksdale again called him a "nigger thief."

Lovejoy declared he had endorsed Helper's book, and if it was "treason," as Pryor had said, "I did it." "You may kill Cassius M. Clay, as you threaten to do; but 'the blood of the martyrs is the seed of the Church,'" quoting the saying of an early Christian theologian that became a credo of English Protestant martyrs. "You may shed his blood, as you shed the blood of my brother on the banks of the Mississippi twenty years ago—and what then?" The blood of his brother, Elijah P. Lovejoy, the first martyr of the abolitionist cause, killed in Illinois for publishing an antislavery newspaper, was his inspiration. "A Republican Party will spring up in Kentucky and all the slave states ere long," he said, an implicit comparison of the Republicans to the early Protestants.

"What is the objection to the book?" Lovejoy went on. "The objection is that a citizen of the United States, an American citizen, addressed himself to his fellow-citizens, in a peaceful way, through the press, and for this you find fault with him and say that he must be hanged. . . . Has not an American citizen a right to speak to an American citizen? I want the right of uttering what I say here in Richmond. I claim the right to say what I say here in Charleston."

"You had better try it," threatened Milledge L. Bonham, who had succeeded Preston Brooks in his seat from upcountry South Carolina. Lovejoy replied that he could question monarchy in England, "but I cannot go into the slave State and open my lips in regard to the question of slavery." "No," interrupted Martin of Virginia, "we would hang you higher than Haman." Yet Lovejoy continued. "You drive away young ladies that go to teach school; imprison or exile preachers of the Gospel; and pay your debts by raising the mad-dog cry of abolition against the agents of your creditors."

"The meanest slave in the South is your superior," sneered Barksdale of Mississippi. Lovejoy wondered if American rights were "less sacred" than the ancient claim of liberty, "I am a Roman citizen." "This is my response to the question why I recommended the circulation of the Helper book." He was interrupted again and again. "And if you come among us, Martin repeated, "we will do with you as we did with John Brown—hang you as high as Haman. I say that as a Virginian." "I have no doubt of it," said Lovejoy.

After Lovejoy finished, Roger Pryor of Virginia challenged John Potter of Wisconsin to a duel, demanding "satisfaction" for his insolence. Potter chose Bowie knives as the weapons. Pryor's second called the knives a "vulgar, barbarous, and inhuman mode." The challenge was withdrawn. Potter was hailed in the Northern press as a hero.

On the day Lovejoy defended free speech of the House floor, Reverend Daniel Worth, a friend of Helper, was convicted in North Carolina for circulating his book. It was the reason that Lovejoy was speaking. Worth had been arrested the previous Christmas for his crime. *The National Era* stated, "We should literally have no room for anything else, if we were to publish all the details of whippings, tar-and-featherings, and hangings, for the utterance of Anti-Slavery opinions in the South." Worth was found guilty of selling the book, a verdict upheld by the North Carolina Supreme Court. After his conviction, the legislature amended the law to make distributing an "incendiary" book a crime punishable by death.

On the same day the House went down the rabbit hole chasing John Sherman for endorsing *The Impending Crisis,* the Senate created a Select Committee to Inquire into the Late Invasion and Seizure of the Public Property at Harper's Ferry. Senator Mason was appointed its chairman and Senator Davis acted as chief prosecutor. Davis announced that the ultimate culprit was his colleague who had faithfully sat by his bedside through his recent illness. "I will show before I am done," declared Jefferson Davis on December 8, "that Seward, by his own declaration, knew of the Harper's Ferry affair. If I succeed in showing that, then he, like John Brown, deserves, I think, the gallows, for his participation in it."

Seward and Wilson were questioned about their encounters with Hugh

Forbes and their advance knowledge of Brown's plans, which they categorically denied. Their appearances nonetheless highlighted their guilt by association. Howe and Stearns testified that they knew nothing beforehand of Brown's raid. "Never," said Howe. "I should have disapproved of it if I had known of it," said Stearns, "but I have since changed my opinion." Jefferson Davis asked him about Brown's visit to the Bird Club at the Parker House. "What kind of a house is this Parker House?" "It is one of the best eating-houses in the town," Stearns replied. Davis's interest in the well-known hotel "excited a good deal of amusement in Boston," wrote Stearns's son. That summer, on a vacation to the White Mountains of New Hampshire, Davis passed through Boston, where he dined at the Parker House "to see what it was like."

After Stearns testified, he and Mason were the last men left in the Senate room. Mason handed him a Sharps rifle. "Doesn't your conscience trouble you for sending these rifles to Kansas to shoot our innocent people?" he asked. "Self-defense," replied Stearns. "You began the game. You sent Buford and his company with arms before we sent any from Massachusetts." "I think," said Mason, "when you go to that down below, the old fellow will question you rather hard about this matter and you will have to take it." "Before that time comes I think he will have about two hundred years of slavery to investigate, and before he gets through that will say, 'We have had enough of this business. Better let the rest go.'" According to Stearns, Mason "laughed and left the room."

As the House was embroiled in its battle over the Speaker, Stephen A. Douglas strode into the Senate to deliver his first formal address to the 36th Congress, entering as the presumptive Democratic presidential candidate, and drawing "a crowd sufficient to have filled the immense galleries several times over," according to the *New York Times*. "The Senator from Illinois!" dramatically announced the president of the Senate.

In his first statement on Harpers Ferry, Douglas offered a proposal to give the Congress authority to "repel invasions" from one state into another. He read a letter from Governor Wise to President Buchanan requesting such aid, which Buchanan rejected. "I would make it a crime to form conspiracies with a view of invading States or Territories to control elections, whether they be under the garb of Emigrant Aid Societies of New England or Blue Lodges of Missouri," he said. Douglas's proposal was nothing less than a far-ranging Sedition Act that would turn the federal government into a police force hounding the Republican Party. The galleries applauded, but

Douglas's bill was dead on arrival. It was transparently contrived as another tactic to besmirch Buchanan.

Harpers Ferry, Douglas went on, was "the logical, natural consequence of the teachings and doctrines of the Republican party," and that in "exciting northern passion, northern prejudice, northern ambition against southern States, southern institutions, and southern people . . . invite the South to assail and abuse and traduce the North." He offered as his proof none other than the words of his recent Republican opponent. "I had to meet this issue of the 'irrepressible conflict,'" said Douglas, and he read at length from Lincoln's "house divided" speech, which was the "same doctrine." "Then," said Douglas, "he goes on to say they must all be one thing or all the other, or else the Union cannot endure. What is the meaning of that language, unless it is that the Union cannot permanently exist, half slave and half free—that it must all become one thing or all become the other? That is the declaration. The declaration is that the North must combine as a sectional party, and carry on the agitation so fiercely, up to the very borders of the slaveholding States, that the master dare not sleep at night for fear that the robbers, the John Browns, will come and set his house on fire, and murder the women and children, before morning." Douglas's ghoulish tale of Lincoln inspiring the nighttime slaying of families was the only time his name was raised. Lincoln was at the forefront of Douglas's mind if no one else's. He was still debating Lincoln.

Douglas's proposal was tabled in less than a week. His anti-Buchanan ploy was especially irritating to Southerners. His fanciful suggestion to put federal military power behind both his anti-Lecompton and anti-abolitionist positions was popular sovereignty played with toy soldiers. Yet Douglas still believed that in taking this approach he could secure Southern delegates to the Democratic convention at Charleston, gain the nomination, and hold the South to win the presidency. "The prospects in the South are improving every day. We will have a strong party in the South when the convention meets," he wrote Lanphier, the editor of the *Illinois State Register,* on October 1, 1859. A week before Douglas's Senate speech attacking Lincoln, his forces were overwhelmed by Southern Ultras in state conventions in Alabama, Georgia, and Oregon, which was as Ultra as Mississippi. At the Alabama convention, the Ultras drew a line in the sand, ordering its delegates to uphold "a platform of principles, recognizing distinctly the rights of the South," particularly "to protect the owner of slaves in the enjoyment of his property in the Territory," or to walk out, in effect, to secede from the Democratic Party as the first step to secede from the Union.

The day after Pennington's election as Speaker, on February 2, Jefferson Davis introduced a number of resolutions into the record with minimal comment affirming the constitutional right to slavery. One of the proposals was more than a doctrinal statement. It was a torpedo launched toward the Democratic convention and intended to explode Douglas. Following the resolution of the Alabama party convention, it declared that neither the Congress nor a territorial legislature could prohibit any citizen from bringing slaves into "the common Territories," a legislative codification of Dred Scott, the establishment of a national slave code. Buchanan, who had withheld his annual message to the Congress until after the selection of a Speaker, also timed its release to Davis's resolution, and "cordially congratulated Congress upon the final settlement of slavery in the territories."

Douglas had already announced he would oppose such a maneuver. Davis, of course, knew that. Douglas understood the obvious purpose was to dictate a platform plank at the convention that would tear apart the party and sink him. He wanted to stand on the 1856 party platform, as though Dred Scott and what it had unleashed had not happened. The avatar of Manifest Destiny was King Canute trying to stop the rolling of the tides. His supporters were filled with alarm. "The platform movement in the Senate is designed to keep down Douglas," Congressman John McClernand of Illinois, a Douglas stalwart, who replaced Thomas Harris in the Springfield seat after his death, wrote Lanphier. "The president is urging it on." Toombs wrote Stephens on Davis's resolutions: "Davis' are those approved by the Pres[iden]t and are in the main good; but I think all of them are wrong. It is the very foolishness of folly to raise and make prominent such issues now. . . . Hostility to Douglas is the sole motive of movers of this mischief. I wish Douglas defeated at Charleston, but I do not want him and his friends crippled or driven off. Where are we to get as many or as good men in the North to supply their places?"

Again, on February 29, the Senate galleries were overflowing to hear a presumptive presidential candidate, this time William H. Seward, at last ready to hold forth in his first speech of 1860. He thought it would "remove all obstacles to his nomination to the Presidency at Chicago," wrote his friend Henry B. Stanton, the former secretary of the American Anti-Slavery Society and New York state senator, and then a correspondent for the *New York Tribune*. "He read it to me before it was delivered, and requested me to write a description for the *New York Tribune* of the scene in the chamber during the delivery, which I did. The description was elaborate, the Senator himself suggesting some of the nicer touches, and every line of it was written and on its way to New York before Mr. Seward had uttered a word in the Senate Chamber."

Though Seward was the cynosure of censure, blamed as the instigator of John Brown, he had not yet uttered a word of his own. "In coming forward among the political astrologers," he began, "it shall be an error of judgment, and not of disposition, if my interpretation of the feverish dreams which are disturbing the country shall tend to foment, rather than to allay, the national excitement."

But Seward had come to allay the excitement. He came to answer his accusers with a statesmanlike address, offering a lofty view of the historical development of political parties, the growth of free labor and slave economies, and promising that the Republican Party "will in this emergency lay aside all impatience of temper, together with all ambition, and will consider these extraordinary declamations seriously and with a just moderation."

He came as an exemplar of civility, disclaiming any antagonism, to plead that the Republicans were not for "negro equality," not a sectional party, "never more patient, and never loved the representation of other sections more, than now," and to declare the party "vindicated against the charge of hostility to the South."

He came to excoriate John Brown. "While generous and charitable natures will probably concede that John Brown and his associates acted on earnest though fatally erroneous convictions, yet all good citizens will nevertheless agree, that this attempt to execute an unlawful purpose in Virginia by invasion, involving servile war, was an act of sedition and treason, and criminal in just the extent that it affected the public peace and was destructive of human happiness and human life."

So, in the interest of conciliation, the first antislavery senator called Brown's antislavery beliefs "erroneous convictions," and the defense attorney for fugitive slaves who with his abolitionist wife still operated at their home a lawbreaking station of the Underground Railroad and had freely given refuge to Harriet Tubman, a fugitive slave, a conductor of the Underground Railroad, and in fact one of John Brown's co-conspirators, called the rising of the "servile" treason.

Seward ended with a pastoral vision of the country in the near future, undoubtedly under his presidency, beyond "all the winds of controversy," "through hazes, mists, and doubtful and lurid lights." "But the appointed end of all this agitation comes at last, and always seasonably; the tumults of the people subside; the country becomes calm once more; and then we find that only our senses have been disturbed, and that they have betrayed us. The earth is firm as always before, and the wonderful structure, for whose safety we have feared so anxiously, now more firmly fixed than ever, still stands unmoved, enduring and immovable."

Seward's peroration was intended to set the capstone on his persona as a great pacifier. He seemed to suggest that the "agitation," the word used by Southerners and their Northern sympathizers to cast anathema on antislavery politics, would end in a miraculous turn of the earth's cycles "seasonably," and all would somehow be well again.

"His speech," reported the *New York Times*, "is a philosophical exposition of the real nature of that controversy, and aims mainly at dissipating the false impressions which misunderstanding on the one hand, and misrepresentation on the other, have created in regard to it." The newspaper printed the whole speech in a special edition under the headline "The Irrepressible Conflict," his most famous or infamous phrase from his most famous speech, whose reminder vitiated his attempt to sidestep it.

"So calm in temper," editorialized the *New York Tribune*, "so philosophic in statement, so comprehensive in grasp, so passionless even in its inculpations, so far-reaching in its views, it must everywhere be recognized as a speech which no other man could have made." The "irrepressible conflict" melted into thin air.

Immediately upon Seward finishing his speech Douglas leaped up to recall an earlier Seward, reading an excerpt from a speech Seward delivered in 1848 declaring the fugitive slave clause of the Constitution "a violation of Divine Law." Douglas tossed aside Seward's current gestures at mollification. "Whatever agitation [against nonintervention on slavery in the territories] has grown out of the question since, has been occasioned by the resistance of the party of which that Senator is the head." Douglas took the opening to repeat his line from his debates with Lincoln, "This government was made by white men, on the white basis, for the benefit of white men." Seward's opportunism was an occasion for Douglas's opportunism.

Then Jefferson Davis rose. "I found rather those generalities not sufficiently glittering to delude," he remarked with acid contempt. His line was an allusion to the condemnation of Republicans for embracing the Declaration of Independence and its claim that "all men are created equal" by Rufus Choate, the Massachusetts Old Whig, in his endorsement of Buchanan's candidacy in 1856. Davis derided Seward's "high-sounding professions of attachment to the Union, and fraternity to its various members," and asked "are we to believe these mere professions of the lips[?]" He answered his question with more questions. "Who has been more industrious, patient, and skillful, as a sapper and miner against the foundations of the Constitution, than the Senator himself? Who has been in advance of him in the fiery charge on the rights of the States, and in assuming to the Federal Government the power to crush and to coerce them?" Davis took to instruct Seward. It was not enough that Seward proposed to leave slavery alone, it was despicable that he compared it invidiously to free labor. "There is nothing . . . which has led men to greater confusion of ideas than this term of 'free States' and 'slave States.'" Seward, according to Davis, "was less informed than I had previously believed him to be. Negro slavery exists in the South, and by the existence of negro slavery, the white man is raised to the dignity of a freeman and an equal. Nowhere else will you find every white man superior to menial service. Nowhere else will you find every white man recognized so far as an equal as never to be excluded from any man's house or any man's table. Your own menial who blacks your boots, drives your carriage, who wears your livery, and is your own in every sense of the word, is not your equal; and such is society wherever negro slavery is not the substratum on which the white race is elevated to its true dignity." But, Davis said, Seward failed to comprehend these basic facts of inequality. "I must suppose him to be as ignorant as his speech would indicate."

Seward was confident his speech had achieved its desired effect. "As he handed me some copies," Henry B. Stanton recalled, "he said, in his liveliest manner, 'Here we go down to posterity together.' He was in buoyant spirits, seeming not to doubt that his nomination was assured."

Seward's tone had been pitched to deflect the image of a radical. "I have had a very strong belief in Mr. Seward's nomination till Mr. Brown visited Virginia," James S. Pike, the *New York Tribune* correspondent, wrote privately. But Seward's effort to escape the shadow lengthened it. He called attention to what he was so obviously avoiding. The consummate politician's aloof pose above politics was unpersuasive. His condescension toward and condemnation of John Brown were compelled by the accusations against himself. His calls for civility blaming both sides in a false equivalence only stirred his enemies to assail him further. Absent in Europe for nearly a year he had lost an intangible touch for the state of play. He had measured the fabric of his speech too short and too long to fit the Republican Party. He did not cut it just right. "So passionless," reported the *Tribune,* intending to be praiseworthy of his statesmanship. He tried to make people forget about "the irrepressible conflict," but "the irrepressible conflict" had not forgotten about him. His February 29 speech, his last important speech as a senator as it would happen, was a miscalculation not only of the political environment of the Republican Party on the eve of its convention but also the beginning of his misjudgment of the impending crisis that would extend until the firing upon Fort Sumter. His faith in experience and expedience would no more gain the nomination than pacify secession. He expected events to run his way on assumptions that were being overthrown. Seward also seemed oblivious or indifferent that two days earlier in New York City a man in an ill-fitting suit had threaded the needle.

CHAPTER THIRTY

RIGHT MAKES MIGHT

The journalist Henry Villard went west to cover miners seeking to strike for their fortunes and on his eastward return over the plains of Kansas, on December 1, 1859, about thirty miles from the town of St. Joseph, "an extraordinary incident occurred," he recalled. "A buggy with two occupants was coming toward us over the open prairie. As it approached, I thought I recognized one of them, and, sure enough, it turned out to be no less a person than Abraham Lincoln: I stopped the wagon, called him by name, and jumped off to shake hands. He did not recognize me with my full beard and pioneer's costume."

They had last seen each other more than a year ago at a campaign rally near Springfield. "When I said, 'Don't you know me?' and gave my name, he looked at me, most amazed, and then burst out laughing. 'Why, good gracious! you look like a real Pike's Peaker.' His surprise at this unexpected meeting was as great as mine. He was on a lecturing tour through Kansas. It was a cold morning, and the

Lincoln, by Mathew Brady, February 27, 1860, the day of the Cooper Union speech

wind blew cuttingly from the northwest. He was shivering in the open buggy, without even a roof over it, in a short overcoat, and without any covering for his legs. I offered him one of my buffalo robes, which he gratefully accepted. He undertook, of course, to return it to me, but I never saw it again. After ten minutes' chat, we separated. The next time I saw him he was the Republican candidate for the Presidency."

Lincoln's invitation to come to Kansas came from Mark Delahay, who wished Lincoln might help make him a U.S. senator, an ambition never realized. Lincoln hoped his presence might help him win support for his stealth presidential campaign from the Kansas delegation to the Republican convention. Delahay was married to the fifth cousin of Lincoln's mother, Nancy Hanks, and when Lincoln rode the legal circuit of Illinois he was part of his entourage in the town of Petersburg. Raised by a Quaker mother to oppose slavery, Delahay had been a nominal Democrat, and migrated to Kansas from Alabama in early 1855. There he purchased the newspaper in Leavenworth and served as one of three secretaries of the Topeka Constitutional Convention. Elected a free state delegate to the Congress, he was never allowed to take his seat in Washington. While Delahay was at a Free State Party meeting in Lawrence, a mob attacked the *Leavenworth Register* office and destroyed his printing press. He provided a regular stream of information to Lincoln on the troubles in Kansas. Some in Lincoln's circle were wary of him, "distressingly impecunious and awfully bibulous," according to Henry C. Whitney. But Lincoln found him useful.

Just hours after he encountered Villard, Lincoln arrived at the town of Elwood, where he entered the dining room of the Great Western Hotel, removed his buffalo robe, and spoke for the first time about John Brown, whose execution was to be the next day. He was careful to judge separately Brown's motive and his means. "It was a violation of law and it was, as all such attacks must be, futile as far as any effect it might have on the extinction of a great evil," he said. "We have a means provided for the expression of our belief in regard to slavery—it is through the ballot box—the peaceful method provided by the Constitution. John Brown has shown great courage, rare unselfishness, as even Governor Wise testifies. But no man, North or South, can approve of violence or crime."

Lincoln reached Atchison on the evening of Brown's hanging. Lincoln turned the law and its inexorable logic used to convict Brown to convict the Southern fire-eaters. "Old John Brown," he said, "has just been executed for treason against a state. We cannot object, even though he agreed with us in

thinking slavery wrong. That cannot excuse violence, bloodshed, and treason. It could avail him nothing that he might think himself right. So, if constitutionally we elect a President, and therefore you undertake to destroy the
Union, it will be our duty to deal with you as old John Brown has been dealt
with. We shall try to do our duty."

Lincoln refused to act defensively about Brown. In Leavenworth, on December 5, he called the Democrats' effort to blame the Republican Party for
Harpers Ferry nothing but a ploy. "The attempt to identify the Republican
party with the John Brown business was an electioneering dodge," he said.
"In Brown's hatred of slavery the speaker sympathized with him," reported
the *Leavenworth Register* (Delahay's paper back in operation). "But Brown's
insurrectionary attempt he emphatically denounced. He believed the old man
insane, and had yet to find the first Republican who endorsed the proposed
insurrection. If there was one he would advise him to step out of the ranks
and correct his politics." But Lincoln put the ultimate blame on slavery itself;
nor would he blame the slaves for rising against it. "But slavery was responsible for their uprisings. They were fostered by the institution. In 1830–31, the
slaves themselves arose and killed fifty-eight whites in a single night. These
servile upheavings must be continually occurring where slavery exists."

The next day he observed the election of state officials conducted under
the free state constitution—in defiance of the Lecompton Constitution recognized by the Buchanan administration. After a week in Kansas, Lincoln
returned to Springfield "delighted with his visit and the cordial reception he
met with from the people of that incipient state," reported the *Illinois State
Journal,* which noted about the election there, "The returns thus far indicate that the Republicans did their whole duty, having made great gains."
Indeed, the Republicans swept the boards, winning 86 of 100 seats in the
legislature. (Delahay soon wrote Lincoln he would manage his presidential
campaign if Lincoln would provide the funds. Lincoln replied he "can not
get, the money," but offered to send Delahay $100 to pay for his expenses if
he were elected a convention delegate. Delahay was not chosen, but Lincoln
sent him the money anyway. Lincoln would not win a single Kansas delegate
at the Republican convention.)

Once he was back home, Jesse Fell again bothered him to submit an autobiography. Hardly anyone outside of Illinois knew Lincoln's story. Even in
Illinois Lincoln had been reticent about revealing his background. Throughout his debates with Douglas and his speeches in Ohio and Kansas, he had
not sought to advance himself by portraying his rise from a log cabin. About

his lowly origins, he was silent. But on December 20 he acceded to Fell's badgering. He decided to provide a "little sketch," a page and a half of the bare facts of his early poverty, political offices, and physical self-description. "There is not much of it," he wrote of his life, "for the reason, I suppose, that there is not much of me." The subject he discussed more than any other in this brief document was education, or lack of it. His father "grew up literally without education." Lincoln wrote of himself that he attended "some schools, so called." "If a straggler supposed to understand Latin, happened to sojourn in the neighborhood, he was looked upon as a wizard. There was absolutely nothing to excite ambition for education. Of course when I came of age I did not know much. Still somehow, I could read, write, and cipher to the Rule of Three; but that was all. I have not been to school since. The little advance I now have upon this store of education, I have picked up from time to time under the pressure of necessity." He was "sort of a clerk in a store," served in the Black Hawk War, elected to the legislature, "studied law," elected to the Congress, and: "Always a Whig in politics, and generally on the Whig electoral tickers . . . I was losing interest in politics, when the repeal of the Missouri Compromise aroused me again. What I have done since then is pretty well known."

Jesse Fell, who conceived the idea that Lincoln should challenge Douglas to debates, had a strategic mind. Before he had come to Illinois as a young man he had grown up in Pennsylvania and maintained a myriad of political contacts there. He knew that Republicans feared a Seward candidacy. He had been at war with the nativists of New York for decades and probably cost Henry Clay the presidency in 1844 as a result, and was unpopular in Pennsylvania, where the Know Nothings had been a controlling force within the legislature and Philadelphia as recently as 1855. Simon Cameron had been elected to the Senate as a Republican in an alliance with the Know Nothing remnant. But Fell understood that Cameron, running as a favorite son candidate for president, could never be nominated with his reputation for corruption. Fell believed that Pennsylvania would be the Keystone State for Lincoln at the convention, swinging for him. His prescience, which would be precisely realized, prompted him to give Lincoln's "sketch" to his old friend, Joseph J. Lewis, a prominent lawyer, a Quaker like Fell, and who had represented the abolitionists in the notorious Christiana Riot case involving the murder of a slaveholder attempting to reclaim his runaway slaves. Lewis burnished Lincoln's short account of his life into an article of several thousand words, published it in the *Chester County Times* in January 1860, and saw that it was widely reprinted in newspapers throughout the state. (Lincoln would appoint him the second commissioner of internal revenue.)

Even as the far-sighted Fell prepared to project Lincoln's reputation to the East, Lincoln was dragged again into the pit of internecine warfare plaguing the Illinois Republican Party. This time he did not have to untangle the hostility of Old Whigs toward abolitionists, but vindictive hatreds going back decades of former Democrats turned Republicans against each other. The ferocity of petty animosities and the poisons of suspicion had the potential of shredding the party and spoiling his candidacy before it was launched. The depth of resentment threatened to draw in virtually the whole Republican Party.

The conflict was a struggle for primacy between two great political beasts from Chicago, "Long John" Wentworth, the mayor, with an ego as large and swaggering as his six feet seven inches height, and Norman B. Judd, the state senator, whom Trumbull described to Lincoln as "the shrewdest politician . . . in the state." According to the journalist Horace White (who became the secretary of the Illinois Republican Central Committee in 1860), Judd was "fertile in expedients . . . a 'trimmer,' sly cat-like, and mysterious, and thus he came to be considered more farseeing than he really was; but he was jovial, companionable, and popular with the boys who looked after the primaries and the nominating conventions." But the rivalry had spun out of control. Judd had declared to run for the Republican nomination for governor and Wentworth was determined to destroy him.

On December 16, Lincoln received a desperate letter from one of his stalwart supporters, urging him to stop "the War of the Roses at Chicago." Nathaniel Niles, a lawyer, judge, and former editor of the *Belleville Advocate,* one of the editors who had summoned Lincoln to the organizing meeting in 1856 of the Illinois Republican Party, wrote, "You can command in this matter—as the acknowledged, indisputable leader of the party you can enforce the peace. It is of some interest to all of us that an unseemly personal warfare should not go on; and it may be of some interest also to the belligerents, to stop it—Please consider this matter and go up to Chicago."

Wentworth and Judd had been enemies since 1844, when Judd encouraged a friend to challenge Wentworth for Congress, and another Judd friend, Ebenezer Peck, a state legislator, chased Wentworth down the street with a cane for allegedly libeling him.

Lincoln was already enmeshed in the conflict. Wentworth and Judd fired accusations at each other through competing newspapers, the *Chicago Dem-*

Norman B. Judd

ocrat, which Wentworth owned, and the *Tribune,* which was aligned with Judd. As early as 1857, Lincoln had signaled his disquiet. "I do not entirely appreciate what the republican papers of Chicago are so constantly saying against Long John," Lincoln wrote Henry C. Whitney. "We cannot afford to lose the services of 'Long John' and I do believe the unrelenting warfare made upon him, is injuring our cause."

Judd, close to Trumbull, had been among the Democratic state senators who had held out for him over Lincoln in the struggle for the Senate seat in 1855. Lincoln's friends, especially David Davis, and above all Mary Lincoln, never forgave Judd. But Judd the Democrat became the chairman of the Republican State Central Committee and was in charge of Lincoln's 1858 Senate campaign. Judd told Lincoln that Wentworth was trying to undermine him because he wanted to grab the Senate seat. After the defeat, his maladroit first gesture to Lincoln was to dun him to cover the party's debt from the race. Wentworth wrote David Davis that Judd was responsible for the loss. "I agree with him religiously," said Davis, believing that the former Democrat had ignored the Old Whig counties. He stirred up opposition to Judd's candidacy for governor. When the *Clinton Central Transcript* published an editorial discussing the upcoming Republican nomination of a candidate for governor, it blamed Lincoln's defeat on "Northerners" in the state—code for Judd—who slated "ultra men"—code for Owen Lovejoy—Lincoln wrote a letter to the editor on July 3, 1859, to protest, "I think this is unjust and impolitic."

In November 1859 the *Chicago Democrat* accused Judd not only of financial corruption and sinking Lincoln's chance for the Senate against Trumbull in 1855, but also secretly plotting to "cheat Lincoln for the third time" by working to nominate Trumbull for president. On December 1, Judd filed a libel suit against Wentworth. The same day he fired off a letter to Lincoln. "I begin to doubt whether there is such a thing as truth in this world. . . . From the representations that are afloat amongst your friends and believed in by some of them I am induced to doubt myself—and think is it true that Lincoln has been cheated by me." The slander was being spread "without any public defense by you or any of your friends." Judd made clear to Lincoln he understood the high stakes. "You have ambitions, high hopes and brilliant prospects, and no man has or will aid you more faithfully than myself—There is no risk in doing right." He suggested a remedy. "There is only one mode of replacing the harmony of the party—and that is John Wentworth is to be driven out or silenced," and his friends and "their lying associates kicked into the kennel with the rest of the curs."

That same day Judd wrote Trumbull a histrionic letter, "I have slaved for L as you know and that I should today be suffering amongst his friends by the charge of having cheated him, and he silent is an outrage that I am not disposed to submit to." The truth was that Judd was bad-mouthing Lincoln. Thomas J. Pickett, editor of the *Rock Island Register,* another member of the small group that issued the original call for the organizing meeting of the Republican Party, and a Lincoln loyalist, recalled Judd dropping by his paper's office. When Pickett volunteered he was for Lincoln for the presidential nomination, he recalled, "Mr. Judd, in a sneering tone said, 'I am not joking; tell me your honest choice.' I repeated, 'Abraham Lincoln.' He quickly responded, 'I am astonished that any one should think of his nomination when we have first class statesmen in our party like Lyman Trumbull, Salmon P. Chase and John M. Palmer.'"

After he returned from his Kansas trip, Lincoln wrote Judd a letter on December 9. "It has a tone of blame towards myself which I think is not quite just," he wrote, but gave Judd what he wanted, stating that the charges against Judd were "false and outrageous." On December 14, Lincoln released a public letter to prevent "a wrong being done to him by the use of my name in connection with alleged wrongs to me." He declared that during the Senate campaign, "I had no more sincere and faithful friend than Mr. Judd—certainly none whom I trusted more." He added carefully, "I have been and still am very anxious to take no part between the many friends, all good and true, who are mentioned as candidate for a Republican gubernatorial nomination." After all, two of Lincoln's friends and former Whigs, Leonard Swett and Richard Yates, were also seeking the nomination.

Wentworth slyly asked Lincoln to represent him in the Judd libel suit. Lincoln instead suggested that he publish an apology and in return Judd would withdraw his suit. He drew up detailed terms for agreement from both parties and used David Davis as a go-between to Wentworth. Davis wrote Lincoln that if they would make the settlement "you will have, politically, accomplished a great result." Judd wrote Lincoln still complaining about Wentworth's libels. "These things unretracted can or ought I to 'eat dirt.' . . . What shall I do[,] write me." But the libel suit disappeared. Without fanfare, Lincoln's settlement had gone into effect.

"I know," wrote Herndon, "the idea prevails that Lincoln sat still in his chair in Springfield, and that one of those unlooked-for tides in human affairs came along and cast the nomination into his lap; but any man who has had experience in such things knows that great political prizes are not obtained in that way. The truth is, Lincoln was as vigilant as he was ambitious, and there is no denying the fact that he understood the situation perfectly from the start. In the management of his own interests he was obliged to rely almost entirely on his own resources. He had no money with which to maintain a political bureau, and he lacked any kind of personal organization whatever."

Only Jesse Fell envisioned the path for Lincoln. Lincoln had created the Illinois Republican Party, but it was not unified behind the idea of his presidential candidacy, which hardly anyone yet thought was plausible. The Old Whigs still hated the abolitionists and were wary of the Democrats, while the Democrats hated the Democrats. But the party was more than a house divided whose rancor he had to calm. Herndon was always willing to do Lincoln's bidding if he was properly directed, but he had detoured into sniping against Judd along with the Davis crowd, which included Mary. For all the publicity attached to Lincoln's campaign against Douglas, he had lost. He had not held office for a decade. No one who had only been a backbench congressman, one-term at that, had ever been nominated much less elected president. There were rumblings for Trumbull as a favorite son. Lincoln needed Illinois, but Illinois had to perceive him as more than Illinois for him to win Illinois.

The *Chicago Press and Tribune* reported on January 10 that the book of the Lincoln-Douglas debates was being published, "a first-rate document for the campaign," and "no trifling compliment to Old Abe." Two days later, the Springfield Young Men's Republican Club announced "the name of this association be and is hereby changed, and be hereafter called the "LINCOLN CLUB." And two days after that the *Illinois State Journal,* the newspaper under Lincoln's influence, issued a ringing endorsement of Lincoln for president, "the favorite son of Illinois." A week later, the paper published the pragmatic case that Illinois and Pennsylvania were the key strategic states. It was the case that Jesse Fell made. "Looking over the whole field, we regard it that the success of the Republicans depends upon those two states, and the Republican nominating Convention should select its candidates with direct reference to the exigency which exists. . . . It is with this view and with the further consideration that the Great West deserves the Presidency, that the Republicans of Illinois present the name of ABRAHAM LINCOLN as their first choice for the nomination."

On the last week of January, when a number of key people from around the state came to Springfield for the sessions of the state Supreme Court and the federal court, a secret group was convened in the office of Lincoln's friend, the Illinois secretary of state, Ozias M. Hatch, to discuss his presidential candidacy. The meeting was called by Jackson Grimshaw, a member of the Republican Central Committee, a lawyer from Quincy, who had run for Congress unsuccessfully in 1858. Judd was there, along with Leonard Swett, Jesse K. Dubois, Ward Lamon, Ebenezer Peck, Nehemiah Bushnell (Orville Browning's law partner and president of the Northern Cross Railroad), and John Whitfield Bunn, the Springfield merchant along with his brother Jacob who financed Lincoln's campaigns. Those present had varied recollections. Grimshaw had initially been promoting the notion of a Cameron-Lincoln ticket. Judd recalled he "strongly opposed this action, saying the proper and only thing to do was to claim the Presidency for him and nothing less." Grimshaw later told Herndon, "We all expressed our personal preference for Mr. Lincoln as the candidate for the presidency and asked him if his name might be used at once in connection with the coming nomination and election. Mr. Lincoln with his characteristic modesty doubted whether he could get the nomination even if he wished it and asked until the next morning to answer us whether his name might be announced as one who was to be a candidate for the office of President before the Republican Convention. The next day he authorized us to consider him and work for him if we pleased as a candidate for the presidency." Grimshaw wondered if he would accept the vice presidency if he could not get the presidential nomination. "No!" Lincoln replied.

Almost all of those in this caucus were Lincoln's longtime Whig friends. Judd, now on board with Lincoln, and his friend Peck were the former Democrats. The obvious missing person was Orville Browning. He was working for Edward Bates as the conservative alternative. The oldest of the candidates at sixty-five, Bates had fought in the War of 1812, served in the Congress for a single term from 1827 to 1829, was a prominent attorney in St. Louis, had freed his slaves, but "always disclaims Republicanism," briefly belonged to the Know Nothings, and was backed by Francis P. Blair on the basis that he could carry border states and Old Whigs. Bates stood as an improved version of Fillmore. (Fillmore had offered him the post of secretary of war, which he declined.) The rationale for Bates's candidacy was that because he was not really a Republican he would attract those who were not Republicans.

He presented the hope of a repressible conflict. The temporizing Bates was also supported by the radical Greeley, who wanted to use him to stop Seward out of revenge. Seward's supporters saw Bates as an anachronism who would "settle nothing," as John Bigelow wrote William Cullen Bryant, the editor of the *New York Post*. Bates would find his "associations" with "men and doctrine" in the Republican Party "uncongenial," and "the end would be that the old Whig party, of which in his person you would have effected the resurrection, would sink back into its grave after a second time betraying the cause of freedom." The coming conflict between Seward and Bates, with Chase in the middle, without another miraculous option, seemed irrepressible.

About two weeks after the secret caucus meeting, Browning came to Springfield. That day the Republican Central Committee fixed a convention in May at Decatur that would nominate state candidates—and give a presidential nod. Lincoln visited Browning that evening at his hotel room. Browning was likely aware of the caucus meeting for Lincoln and that he was excluded because he was for Bates. "We had a free talk about the presidency," Browning wrote in his diary, noting Lincoln's reaction. "He says it is not improbable that by the time the national convention meets in Chicago he may be of opinion that the very best thing that can be done will be to nominate Mr. Bates." The most interesting thing about this entry was not Lincoln's effort to mollify Browning, but his apparent foreknowledge that the convention would be at Chicago, which had not yet been decided. It's possible, though, that Browning wrote after the event based on memory.

Lincoln was alarmed by his meeting with Browning. The next day he wrote Judd for help to advance his candidacy as the return of his favor to him. "I am not in a position where it would hurt much for me to not be nominated on the national ticket; but I am where it would hurt some for me to not get the Illinois delegates," he wrote. "What I expected when I wrote the letter [on your behalf] . . . is now happening. Your discomfited assailants are most bitter against me; and they will, for revenge upon me, lay to the Bates egg in the South, and to the Seward egg in the North, and go far towards squeezing me out in the middle with nothing. Can you not help me a little in this matter, in your end of the vineyard?" This was not the first time he had discussed the convention with Judd. Lincoln had already written him about locating it in Chicago, which would be a coup. "I find some of our friends here, attach more consequence to getting the National convention into our State than I did, or do. Some of them made me promise to say so to you," Lincoln wrote him on December 14, the same day he released his letter exonerating Judd of wrongdoing. "As to the *time,* it must certainly be after the Charleston fandango; and I think, within bounds of reason, the later the better."

A week later, on February 16, the *Chicago Press and Tribune* published a blazing editorial: "The Presidency—Abraham Lincoln," which touted him as the candidate to win the swing states and catalogued his virtues from "unimpeachable purity of private life" to "great acuteness of intellect" to "Right on the record." "Should the Convention give him this position, then the honor which he has not sought, but which his admirers have hoped he might attain, will, like ripe fruit, fall into his hands. Abraham Lincoln will never be President by virtue of intrigue and bargain." "You saw what the Tribune said about you—was it satisfactory?" Judd wrote Lincoln.

On February 22, George Washington's birthday, the Republican National Committee met in New York City at the Astor House, Thurlow Weed's lair. Norman B. Judd was the representative of Illinois. Seward's supporters wanted the convention to be in New York; Chase's in an Ohio city; and Bates's advocates in St. Louis. Judd proposed a neutral city, in a state the party needed to carry, and did not have a serious national candidate of its own. And without mention of Lincoln the Republican National Committee decided on Chicago.

Lincoln left for New York City the next day to speak on "a political subject" at the Plymouth Church in Brooklyn. Since he received the invitation on the eve of John Brown's raid the world had tilted. Lincoln's round of speeches in Ohio in 1859 before Harpers Ferry were versions of what he had said in his debates. John Brown had exposed Douglas's and Seward's vulnerabilities within unstable parties, but they both continued to act on the unspoken assumption that they would be their party's nominees and adjusted to the increasingly charged atmosphere with the general election in mind. Lincoln had spent his entire political career to this point crafting most of his important speeches to counter Douglas. Now he had to think about his speech in the light of Douglas and Seward. Taking on Douglas was familiar territory, but approaching Seward was uncharted. He could rebut Douglas, but not Seward. Lincoln had to present himself to let others draw the contrasts, not only with Seward but also implicitly with Chase and Bates. Lincoln's positioning had to be subtle yet apparent. And there was another unseen presence he could not escape. Like the ghost in a Shakespeare play John Brown was a haunting figure the actor had to address. The phantom of Harpers Ferry loomed over the characters on the stage.

Between law cases and settling feuds Lincoln sequestered himself in the law library of the State Capitol, following his practice with his important speeches since the one he delivered against the Kansas-Nebraska Act in 1854. He took Douglas's article from *Harper's Magazine* in which he argued that the framers of the Constitution were self-consciously indifferent to slavery as an opposing brief. Lincoln had been rebutting Douglas on the "revolutionary fathers" since his 1854 speech. He had pointed out then Jefferson's antislavery sentiments and inspiration for the Northwest Ordinance of 1787 banishing slavery from the territories, which Lincoln considered as integral to the Constitution and proving the intent of the founders. He had repeated these arguments in his debates with Douglas in 1858. Lincoln always believed that Douglas twisted logic and distorted history. Now, determined to make one more overwhelming argument against him, Lincoln's research was prodigious, the greatest scholarly effort in his life. He owned the two volumes of Jonathan Elliot's *The Debates in the Several State Conventions on the Adoption of the Federal Constitution as Recommended by the General Constitution at Philadelphia in 1787,* in which he found the evidence that a large majority of the signers of the Constitution believed the federal government had the authority to regulate slavery. Lincoln consulted James Kent's *Commentaries on the Constitution,* Charles Lanman's *Dictionary of the United States Congress,* the *Annals of Congress,* the *Congressional Globe, The Letters of George Washington, The Autobiography of Thomas Jefferson, The Papers of James Madison,* and biographies. "He probably consulted, too, a life of the Marquis de Lafayette, and likely examined the works of Alexander Hamilton," wrote the historian Harold Holzer. "He reread Benjamin Franklin's petition against slavery. He looked through accounts of the great slave uprisings, including Nat Turner's insurrection in 1831." He scoured old yellowing newspapers and he read *The Impending Crisis of the South.*

"The finished speech grew very slowly," recalled Henry B. Rankin, an occasional clerk in the Lincoln-Herndon law office. "Herndon's patience was tried sorely at times to see him loitering and cutting, as he thought, too laboriously." "He was painstaking and thorough in the study of his subject," Herndon wrote, "but when at last he left for New York we had many misgivings—and he not a few himself—of his success in the great metropolis. What effect the unpretentious Western lawyer would have on the wealthy and fashionable society of the great city could only be conjectured."

Lincoln's sponsor, the Young Men's Central Republican Union, had come into existence to provide a forum for potential alternatives to Seward. Few of its members were actually young men, but rather an assemblage of influential personages, including William Cullen Bryant of the *New York Post,* the distinguished lawyer David Dudley Field, and the ubiquitous marplot Greeley. Many had been Barnburners of the Democratic Party faction that had split in 1848 to form the Free Soil Party and were perennial opponents of Weed's political machine. Far from being the "unpretentious Western lawyer," Lincoln was keenly aware of the political backgrounds of the men he was about to encounter. He had campaigned for the Whigs against the Free Soil Party through New England, appearing on the same Boston platform with Seward, their first meeting. Lincoln had developed strong feelings about Greeley, who had been for Douglas until he wasn't in the Senate race. When Greeley came through Springfield in the aftermath and sent Lincoln a message he would like to meet him, Lincoln spurned him. He knew Greeley was now for Bates. Lincoln also loved Bryant's poetry, especially "Thanatopsis," tolling "the silent halls of death." But Lincoln did not know that Bryant had initiated the invitation for him to come to New York because he was Bryant's choice for the nomination if Seward faltered, but wanted to be able to judge him in person.

Bryant had closely followed the famous debates with Douglas, which were covered in his newspaper, but he also knew about Lincoln firsthand from his four brothers, early settlers of Princeton, Illinois, all abolitionists and Republicans, eminent in science and horticulture. Lincoln stayed at the home of John Howard Bryant, a poet, journalist, and former state legislator, when he came to Bryant's Woods to deliver a Fourth of July address in 1856 denouncing Douglas and the Kansas-Nebraska Act, followed to the stage by Owen Lovejoy. The prosperous Bryant brothers were Lovejoy's principal backers and would almost certainly have been aware of the internal politics surrounding Lincoln's endorsement of Lovejoy over the objections of David Davis. The Bryants were also close to Jesse Fell, Lincoln's indispensable friend. (John Bryant would be an Illinois delegate pledged to Lincoln at the Republican convention in Chicago. President Lincoln appointed him collector of internal revenue.)

According to George H. Putnam, of the publishing family, William Cullen Bryant felt that "if Seward could not be nominated it would be necessary to accept some candidate from the West, and he suggested that this young lawyer in Illinois, who had in his debates with Douglas shown an exceptional grasp of the grave issues pending and a power to influence public opinion, might very possibly prove to be the best man for the purpose if Seward could not be secured. Bryant reminded his friends that he had printed in the Evening Post a full report of the Lincoln-Douglas Debates, and he said that these debates had given him a very high opinion of the clear-sightedness, patriotism, and effective force of the young lawyer. He suggested that they had better send an invitation to Lincoln to give an address in New York in order that they might secure a personal impression of the man and of his methods."

Salmon P. Chase turned down an invitation to speak, feeling his preeminence was already established and that he did not need to condescend to seeking it. The first speaker in the series was the Blair scion, former congressman Francis Preston Blair, Jr. The second was Cassius M. Clay, who devoted much of his speech to praising Helper's book as a call for poor Southern whites to overthrow "the slaveholding interest." Clay and Lincoln encountered each other in New Haven after Lincoln's New York speech. Clay, Henry Clay's flaming abolitionist cousin, who had lived as a university student in Mary Todd's house in Lexington, gave Lincoln "a long talk" on "my arguments in favor of liberation." "Clay," Lincoln replied, "I always thought that the man who made the corn should eat the corn." Clay was for Chase for president and for Seward, "my next choice." But after he read Seward's Senate speech "in favor of Union, with or without slavery . . . I took up Lincoln as a more reliable man."

Lincoln arrived in the city two days early, only to learn from reading a notice in the *New York Tribune* that he would not speak at the Plymouth Church but at the Cooper Union. The next day, on Sunday, the abolitionist editor Henry C. Bowen of the *New York Independent* brought him to the Plymouth Church, where he greeted parishioners, heard Henry Ward Beecher's sermon, and greeted him. "Let Virginia make him a martyr," Beecher had said of John Brown shortly after his raid. "Now, he has only blundered. His soul was noble; his work miserable. But a cord and gibbet would redeem all that, and round up Brown's failure with a heroic success." Sometime after Brown's execution, Beecher delivered a sermon at the Broadway Tabernacle in New York City, where he brandished the chains that had bound John Brown in jail, threw them to the floor, and stomped on them as the symbolic crushing of slavery. After shaking Beecher's hand, Lincoln took a ferry back to the city and returned to his hotel to polish his speech.

On the morning of February 27, several representatives of the host committee met Lincoln at his room at the Astor House. They had put him up at the best hotel in town. "We found him in a suit of black, much wrinkled from its careless packing in a small valise," recalled Richard C. McCormick, an editor at the *New York Post*. "He received us cordially, apologizing for the awkward and uncomfortable appearance he made in his new suit, and expressing himself surprised at being in New York. His form and manner were indeed odd, and we thought him the most unprepossessing public man we had ever met." McCormick, a newspaperman, suggested Lincoln give copies of his speech to the press so it could be printed the next day. "The address was written upon blue foolscap, all in his own hand, and with few interlineations. I was bold enough to read portions of it, and had no doubt that its delivery would create a marked sensation throughout the country."

Lincoln's handler apparently had a little program for him. "During the day," wrote McCormick, "it was suggested that the orator should be taken up Broadway and shown the city, of which he knew but little, stating, I think, that he had been here but once before." The Astor was located on Broadway, across from P.T. Barnum's American Museum, which a month before had added to its exhibits of albinos, mermaids, and stuffed creatures a life-size wax figure of "Osawatomie Brown Himself!" with two pikes.

Lincoln was escorted on a stroll past the store windows for two miles until he reached Bleecker Street. He was taken up a flight of stairs, through glazed glass doors into the studio of Mathew Brady, the photographic portraitist of the great, the celebrated, and the monied who could afford the services of his art. In the reception room, Lincoln encountered one of the illustrious men who had come to sit for a Brady picture. It was ironic that George Bancroft, the diplomat, founder of the Naval Academy at Annapolis as secretary of the navy, and historian, was there by happenstance. He was the intellectual guiding hand behind Douglas's *Harper's* article that Lincoln was prepared to disprove. McCormick recalled, "The contrast in the appearance of the men was most striking—the one courtly and precise in his every word and gesture, with the air of a trans-Atlantic statesman; the other bluff and awkward, his every utterance an apology for his ignorance of metropolitan manners and customs."

Once Lincoln entered into what Brady called "the operating room," the photographer felt challenged at the sight of his subject. "I had great trouble in making a natural picture," he said. Lincoln's neck was too thin and elongated, his suit wrinkled, and one sleeve was shorter than the other. Brady posed him standing next to a false column that suggested statesmanship. He had Lincoln spread his hand on top of two books that symbolized his learning and also hid the longer sleeve. After he made the exposure, Brady and his team worked their magic in the darkroom to iron out some of the wrinkles and lengthen the shirt collar. Lincoln left before he could see the striking image of a self-possessed but determined figure nearing the height of his powers. Only after he was nominated did the photo emerge. Within days, woodcut engravings appeared on the front page of *Harper's Weekly* and tens of thousands of lithographic copies were reproduced to depict the man of destiny. "Brady and the Cooper Institute made me president," Lincoln later remarked.

At eight in the evening, fifteen hundred notables who had paid an admission price of 25 cents gathered under twenty-seven crystal chandeliers in the Great Hall of the Cooper Union, which had just opened the previous year, anticipating the words of the man whose debates with Douglas they had read but whom few of them had ever seen. Bryant's *Post* advertised Lincoln in the morning paper—"birth in a slaver state, personal observation of the effects of slavery, and equal knowledge of the advantages of a state of society in which the laboring population is free."

The audience applauded the entrance onto the stage of the old crusading editor and poet Bryant with his flowing white beard and hair, followed by the serious and plodding figure of David Dudley Field, and finally the speaker, carrying the pages of his speech in his hand, who took a seat "with his legs twisted around the rungs of the chair—he was the picture of embarrassment," recalled a member of the audience, Russell H. Conwell, who was later the founder of Temple University. Bryant stood to introduce "an eminent citizen of the West, hitherto known to you only by reputation . . . a gallant soldier in the campaign of 1856 . . . [a] great champion . . . [i]n the battle we are fighting in behalf of freedom against slavery and in behalf of civilization against barbarism. . . . I have only, my friends, to pronounce the name of"—and after a dramatic pause—"Abraham Lincoln of Illinois!"

Lincoln's hair, neatly combed for Brady, was tousled, and when he opened his mouth the audience was stunned that his voice was high-pitched, "thin" and "squeaky," an eyewitness recalled. "Mr. President and Fellow-Citizens of New-York," he began in a Kentucky twang. Numerous members of the audience described him as "ungainly" and "awkward." His speaking style was unusual, standing stationary, almost motionless in one spot, gesticulating not with his hands but suddenly jerking his head and mop of hair. He began "in a low, monotonous tone," recalled McCormick, and after reading through a few paragraphs he lost his place, "began to tremble and stammer," and turn over his handwritten blue foolscap pages. "He spoke in a high-pitched voice, in which there was not a trace of the smooth-tongued orator," recalled Henry Martyn Field, D.D. Field's brother and a renowned clergyman. "But there was a singular clearness in his style, with a merciless logic which no listener could escape, as he unfolded link after link in the iron chain of his argument." Noah Brooks, the correspondent for the *New York Tribune,* observed that "his face lighted up as with an inward fire; the whole man was transfigured. I forgot his clothes, his personal appearance, and his individual peculiarities. Presently, forgetting myself, I was on my feet like the rest, yelling like a wild Indian, cheering this wonderful man."

Lincoln's speech from its start seemed to be a straightforward, even statistical primer on the constitutional history of slavery; but that was just his predicate. His method was intrinsic to his mission. He had a more subtle and deeper motive than to win the case on the evidence. He intended to assert the primacy of fact to defeat falsehood and of history to expose demagogy. The facts spoke for themselves, but that was not enough for Lincoln. He surgically took apart each and every point that threw the Republicans on the defensive. As he wielded the facts to puncture and deflate his opponents, he answered sweeping questions of who was the true American, who was "sectional," and who was the patriot. Standing on reason he rejected fanaticism even as he acknowledged its righteous springs in the antislavery cause. In a feat of alchemy, he transformed conservatism into the revolution of the saints. In a burst of eloquence, he gave voice to the innermost feelings of those struggling against a greater power and facing vilification and persecution for their beliefs. The wrinkled suit, the disorderly hair, and the hayseed accent were the shock before the recognition. Once he was heard his initially off-putting appearance had a reverse effect of giving a depth of credence to his words. Lincoln vindicated the Republican Party. He stood as its exemplar. He was the standard-bearer.

"The facts with which I shall deal this evening are mainly old and familiar; nor is there anything new in the general use I shall make of them. If there shall be any novelty, it will be in the mode of presenting the facts, and the inferences and observations following that presentation."

Lincoln immediately claimed as his own Douglas's central idea: *"Our fathers, when they framed the Government under which we live, understood this question just as well, and even better, than we do now."* "I fully endorse this, and I adopt it as a text for this discourse," declared Lincoln. Systematically reviewing the records of signers of the Constitution he proved that twenty-one out of thirty-nine supported federal control over slavery in the territories and that of the rest their positions were unknown but likely to be in line with the others. "Among that sixteen were several of the most noted anti-slavery men of those times—as Dr. Franklin, Alexander Hamilton and Gouverneur Morris—while there was not one now known to have been otherwise, unless it may be John Rutledge, of South Carolina."

Lincoln made clear that in appealing to the authority of the "fathers," he was not adhering to a doctrine of original intent. He was emphatically not what would later be called an "originalist," but believed the Constitution was a living document. "Now, and here, let me guard a little against being misunderstood. I do not mean to say we are bound to follow implicitly in whatever our fathers did. To do so, would be to discard all the lights of current experience—to reject all progress—all improvement." Lincoln declared that he believed in "evidence so conclusive, and argument so clear," and that Douglas, who argued that the founders denied power to the federal government to prohibit slavery was engaged in an act of misleading.

> But he has no right to mislead others, who have less access to history, and less leisure to study it, into the false belief that "our fathers, who framed the Government under which we live," were of the same opinion—thus substituting falsehood and deception for truthful evidence and fair argument. If any man at this day sincerely believes "our fathers who framed the Government under which we live," used and applied principles, in other cases, which ought to have led them to understand that a proper division of local from federal authority or some part of the Constitution, forbids the Federal Government to control as to slavery in the federal territories, he is right to say so. But he should, at the same time, brave the responsibility of declaring that, in his opinion, he understands their principles better than they did themselves; and especially should he not shirk that responsibility by asserting that they "understood the question just as well, and even better, than we do now."

After demolishing the false foundation of Douglas's popular sovereignty and Taney's Dred Scott decision, Lincoln swiveled to "address a few words to the Southern people." Of course, Southerners were absent from the bastion of Northern antislavery opinion arrayed before Lincoln. He was not debating Southerners so much as demonstrating to his audience how they could refute them.

"I would say to them:—You consider yourselves a reasonable and a just people; and I consider that in the general qualities of reason and justice you are not inferior to any other people. Still, when you speak of us Republicans, you do so only to denounce us a reptiles, or, at the best, as no better than outlaws. You will grant a hearing to pirates or murderers, but nothing like it to 'Black Republicans.' In all your contentions with one another, each of you deems an unconditional condemnation of 'Black Republicanism' as the first thing to be attended to. Indeed, such condemnation of us seems to be an indispensable prerequisite—license, so to speak—among you to be admitted or permitted to speak at all."

One after another, Lincoln examined the smears against Republicans, debunking them and reversing the accusation on the accusers. With each one, he stated the charge, followed with, "We deny it." By his use of the plural "we," he put himself as the spokesman for the Republican Party.

On sectionalism: "We deny it." "The fact that we get no votes in your section, is a fact of your making, and not of ours." Here Lincoln turned a political condition into an evidentiary one, flourishing "fact." Relying on the authority of history, he cited Washington's letter to Lafayette in favor of the prohibition of slavery in the Northwest Territories. "Could Washington himself speak, would he cast the blame of that sectionalism upon us, who sustain his policy, or upon you who repudiate it?"

On conservatism: "What is conservative?" It was not the Southerners who properly fit the classic definition, but the Republicans. "Not one of all your various plans can show a precedent or an advocate in the century within which our Government originated. Consider, then, whether your claim of conservatism for yourselves, and your charge or destructiveness against us, are based on the most clear and stable foundations."

On "revolutionary": "We deny it. We admit that it is more prominent, but we deny that we made it so. It was not we, but you, who discarded the old policy of the fathers."

The most potentially damaging of the charges was that Republicans were secretly behind John Brown. "You charge that we stir up insurrections among your slaves. We deny it; and what is your proof? Harper's Ferry! John Brown!!" Here Lincoln not only refuted the charge, but used it to describe the political motive behind the "slander," an attempt to influence state elections "near at hand, and you were in evident glee with the belief that, by charging the blame upon us, you could get an advantage of us in those elections." But, he pointed out, the tactic had backfired. "In your political contests among yourselves, each faction charges the other with sympathy with Black Republicanism; and then, to give point to the charge, defines Black Republicanism to simply be insurrection, blood and thunder among the slaves."

Drawing upon history again, Lincoln reminded the Southerners that insurrections were "no more common now than they were before the Republican Party was organized. What induced the Southampton insurrection, twenty-eight years ago, in which, at least, three times as many lives were lost as at Harper's Ferry." Nat Turner's rebellion in Virginia in 1831 required no outside agitator. "You can scarcely stretch your very elastic fancy to the conclusion that Southampton was 'got up by Black Republicanism.'" Slaves had reason to revolt. If they failed to do so, it was not because they loved slavery, but because they were repressed and isolated. "The indispensable concert of action cannot be attained." But the absence of a general slave uprising was not evidence of contentment. "The explosive materials are everywhere in parcels; but there neither are, nor can be supplied, the indispensable connecting trains."

Lincoln stepped back in his argument to view Harpers Ferry as a historical event with a measure of objectivity. "John Brown's effort was peculiar. It was not a slave insurrection. It was an attempt by white men to get up a revolt among slaves, in which the slaves refused to participate. In fact, it was so absurd that the slaves, with all their ignorance, saw plainly enough it could not succeed."

Lincoln compared the psychology of revolutionary virtue of John Brown to his European counterparts. This led him into his longest reflection on the nature of political assassination. "That affair, in its philosophy, corresponds with the many attempts, related in history, at the assassination of kings and emperors. An enthusiast broods over the oppression of a people till he fancies himself commissioned by Heaven to liberate them. He ventures the attempt, which ends in little else than his own execution. Orsini's attempt on Louis Napoleon, and John Brown's attempt at Harper's Ferry were, in their philosophy, precisely the same."

Yet in both cases the target was tyranny. "The eagerness to cast blame on old England in the one case, and on New England in the other, does not disprove the sameness of the two things." Nor would repression solve the issue. "And how much would it avail you, if you could, by the use of John Brown, Helper's Book, and the like, break up the Republican organization? Human action can be modified to some extent, but human nature cannot be changed. There is a judgment and a feeling against slavery in this nation, which cast at least a million and a half of votes. You cannot destroy that judgment and feeling—that sentiment—by breaking up the political organization which rallies around it. You can scarcely scatter and disperse an army which has been formed into order in the face of your heaviest fire; but if you could, how much would you gain by forcing the sentiment which created it out of the peaceful channel of the ballot-box, into some other channel? What would that other channel probably be? Would the number of John Browns be lessened or enlarged by the operation?"

Unable to succeed politically, the Southerners would tear down the Constitution in the name of constitutional originalism. "But you will break up the Union rather than submit to a denial of your Constitutional rights." And yet, Lincoln said, there were no such rights. "When you make these declarations, you have a specific and well-understood allusion to an assumed Constitutional right of yours, to take slaves into the federal territories, and to hold them there as property. But no such right is specifically written in the Constitution. That instrument is literally silent about any such right. We, on the contrary, deny that such a right has any existence in the Constitution, even by implication."

Rising to prophecy, Lincoln foresaw the Southerners' perverse originalism as a thin cover to maintain their oppressive power even unto secession. "Your purpose, then, plainly stated, is that you will destroy the Government, unless you be allowed to construe and enforce the Constitution as you please, on all points in dispute between you and us. You will rule or ruin in all events."

With the election only eight months away, the crisis of American democracy was drawing near. "But you will not abide the election of a Republican President! In that supposed event, you say, you will destroy the Union; and then, you say, the great crime of having destroyed it will be upon us! That is cool. A highwayman holds a pistol to my ear, and mutters through his teeth, 'Stand and deliver, or I shall kill you, and then you will be a murderer!'"

Lincoln turned to his audience as though he had just been speaking beyond it. "A few words now to Republicans." Here in the most condensed section of his speech he attempted his most difficult and paradoxical political task. Just as in ostensibly speaking indirectly to Southerners about Republicans, in speaking directly to Republicans he was appealing for Republicans to adopt a strategic attitude and by implication the strategist.

Lincoln saw through the calls for a false civility, deference to the Slave Power that was simply appeasement. "It is exceedingly desirable that all parts of this great Confederacy shall be at peace, and in harmony, one with another. Let us Republicans do our part to have it so. Even though much provoked, let us do nothing through passion and ill temper." His rhetoric paced from paradox to paradox, from conciliation to defiance. Proposing harmony, "let us calmly consider their demands," but he suggested that nothing, really, would work. "Will they be satisfied if the Territories be unconditionally surrendered to them? We know they will not. . . . Will it satisfy them, if, in the future, we have nothing to do with invasions and insurrections? We know it will not."

He reconsidered the original quandary. "The question recurs, what will satisfy them? Simply this: We must not only let them alone, but we must, somehow, convince them that we do let them alone." Convincing them, he went on, meant conceding everything Republicans believed in. "This, and this only: cease to call slavery wrong, and join them in calling it *right*. And this must be done thoroughly—done in *acts* as well as in *words*. Silence will not be tolerated—we must place ourselves avowedly with them. . . . We must arrest and return their fugitive slaves with greedy pleasure. We must pull down our Free State constitutions. The whole atmosphere must be disinfected from all taint of opposition to slavery, before they will cease to believe that all their troubles proceed from us."

In the interest of fairness, he admitted, "they do not state their case precisely in this way."

But in the interest of frankness he said they could not stop themselves from careening down their reckless course toward their ultimate goal. "Demanding what they do, and for the reason they do, they can voluntarily stop nowhere short of this consummation. Holding, as they do, that slavery is morally right, and socially elevating, they cannot cease to demand a full national recognition of it, as a legal right, and a social blessing."

He moved toward his conclusion in the form of a rhetorical question. "Thinking it right, as they do, they are not to blame for desiring its full recognition, as being right, but, thinking it wrong, as we do, can we yield to them?" In one long breath, through parallel construction, he compactly stated his policy, ending once again in a question that was a challenge to his audience, crafted to arouse them to understand and accept the whole of his strategy. "Wrong as we think slavery is, we can yet afford to let it alone where it is, because that much is due to the necessity arising from its actual presence in the nation; but can we, while our votes will prevent it, allow it to spread into the National Territories, and to overrun us here in these Free States?" And his answer to the aggressive reach of the Slave Power: "If our sense of duty forbids this, then let us stand by our duty, fearlessly and effectively."

Then came Lincoln's peroration in two seamless but distinct paragraphs, the first a succinct and fervent critique of Stephen A. Douglas's demagogy without mentioning his name, the refined acuity of Lincoln's decades of observation and engagement, aimed as well by inference at the leading lights of the Eastern Republicans who had flirted with Douglas in the senatorial contest, some seated in the hall.

Let us be diverted by none of those sophistical contrivances wherewith we are so industriously plied and belabored—contrivances such as groping for some middle ground between right and the wrong, vain as the search for a man who should be neither a living man nor a dead man—such as a policy of "don't care" on a question about which all true men do care—such as Union appeals beseeching true Union men to yield to Disunionists, reversing the divine rule, and calling, not the sinners, but the righteous to repentance—such as invocations to Washington, imploring men to unsay what Washington said, and undo what Washington did.

Finally, unapologetically and unreservedly, liberated from conditional tenses and question marks, no longer speaking to imaginary figments, he issued a crusader's call to battle for Republicans that would have raised the roof on Beecher's Plymouth Church.

He did not mention John Brown, the dragnet for his followers, the smears of Republicans as his aiders and abettors, the Mason Committee, Douglas's call for a sedition act, the near explosion on the floor of the Congress over Lovejoy reminiscent of the near murder of Sumner, the near duel of Pryor and Potter, the duel that killed Broderick, the threats of Jefferson Davis to try Seward for treason, the threats against Cassius Clay, the heated spirit of violence.

> Neither let us be slandered from our duty by false accusations against us, nor frightened from it by menaces of destruction to the Government nor of dungeons to ourselves. LET US HAVE FAITH THAT RIGHT MAKES MIGHT, AND IN THAT FAITH, LET US, TO THE END, DARE TO DO OUR DUTY, AS WE UNDERSTAND IT.

The crowd that had been taken aback ninety minutes earlier by the appearance of the "ungainly" speaker now rose as a body, cheering and cheering again, waving hats and handkerchiefs. As the tumult died down Greeley was summoned to the stage and as Lincoln sat near him the editor who had caused him so much grief in his campaign against Douglas now declared that the people present had witnessed "a specimen of what free labor and free expression of ideas could produce."

Noah Brooks, the correspondent for the *New York Tribune,* said he left the Cooper Union with "my face glowing with excitement and my frame all aquiver." When a friend asked him his opinion of Lincoln after the event, he spontaneously replied, "He's the greatest man since St. Paul."

After a celebratory dinner held by his hosts at the Athenaeum Club on

Fifth Avenue, where he was asked just who might carry Illinois for the Republicans in the election, at about midnight Lincoln went to the Tribune Building to proofread galleys of the text as it would be published in the next day's edition. He insisted on the capitalization of the last sentence. He wandered back to his hotel, leaving his manuscript at the newspaper office, where it was tossed into a wastepaper basket. Four New York newspapers printed his speech in full. Bryant's *Post* filled the front page with headlines of Lincoln's conquest: "The Framers of the Constitution in Favor of Slavery Prohibition. THE REPUBLICAN PARTY VINDICATED. THE DEMANDS OF THE SOUTH EXPLAINED. Great Speech of Hon. Abraham Lincoln, of Illinois, at Cooper Institute."

On his way to visit his son Robert at Exeter Academy in New Hampshire, Lincoln received a flood of invitations to speak throughout New England. Beginning with a reprise of the Cooper Union speech at Providence, he spoke eight more times, swinging back to New York for another nonspeaking appearance at the Plymouth Church. His speeches on tour were improvised from his formal text. His language became more colloquial, sarcastic, and humorous. At Hartford, on March 5, Lincoln said that the Democrats were "pretty generally getting into a system of bushwhackery" and that Douglas "goes into fits of hydrophobia" at Seward's "irrepressible conflict doctrine." "Another species of bushwhacking," he went on, "is exhibited in their treatment of the John Brown and Harper's Ferry affair. . . . The Democracy is still at work upon John Brown and Harper's Ferry, charging the Republicans with the crime of instigating the proceedings there; and if they think they are able to slander a woman into loving them, or a man into voting with them, they will learn better presently."

The *Chicago Press and Tribune* beat the drum for Lincoln in virtually every edition. "The Republicans are delighted with Lincoln's New York speech," wrote Joseph Medill, the paper's Washington correspondent. "The speech has created a sensation through the eastern states such as few speeches have ever done. Bates' stock culminated last week, and is now fast falling. By the time the Convention is held it will be out of the market. The signs now are, that if Seward is not nominated, Lincoln will be." Reading the *Tribune*'s encomiums to Lincoln, an "irritated" Seward called on Medill, "and 'blew me up' tremendously for having disappointed him—'gone back on him'—and preferring that 'prairie statesman,' as he called Lincoln. . . . He dismissed me from his presence, saying that thereafter he and I would no longer be friends."

WALPURGISNACHT

J ames Sheahan, editor of the *Chicago Times,* rushed against his deadline to finish his campaign biography, *The Life of Stephen A. Douglas,* shortening accounts of recent events to get it to the printer before the Democratic convention. Douglas helpfully advised the author that he had "no recommendations of mercy to make in behalf of the administration." *Harper's Weekly* announced the biography would be "their prominent spring book." Large quantities were shipped to Charleston for distribution to delegates. "At this day," Sheahan concluded of Douglas, "he occupies the most extraordinary position of being the only man in his own party whose nomination for the Presidency is deemed equivalent to an election. Friends of other statesmen claim that other men, if nomi-

The South Carolina Institute Hall, site of
the Democratic convention, 1860

nated, may be elected—a claim that admits of strong and well supported controversy; but friend and foe—all Democrats, unite in the opinion that Douglas' nomination will place success beyond all doubt."

"There will be no serious difficulty in the South," Douglas wrote on February 19 to Peter Cagger, a wealthy New York lawyer who was in the inner circle of the group that informally controlled much of the state Democratic Party and known as the "Albany Regency." "The last few weeks have worked a perfect revolution in that section. They all tell me and write that all will be right if our Northern friends will fearlessly represent the wishes and feelings of the Democracy in their own States." Douglas envisioned that the convention would move toward him like clockwork. It would begin by adopting his platform, the same platform that the convention that nominated Buchanan had adopted in 1856, the Cincinnati Platform. By settling controversy at the start, his inevitability would be apparent and he would be nominated on the first ballot. If the voting went to a second ballot he would win on assurances given to his agents. The election itself would be an uncomplicated matter. According to his calculations of the Electoral College, the South would be solid for him, all the border states would follow, and along with California and Oregon he would take his own state and Indiana, needing only New York or Pennsylvania to put him over the top. New Jersey would be in his column, too.

The optimistic signs seemed obvious. Not a single challenger to Douglas for the nomination emerged from the North. From the South, not one could attract delegates beyond their own state. Howell Cobb desperately wanted to succeed Buchanan, but Buchanan would not anoint him. Cobb struggled to control his state's delegation, which humiliated him when its convention refused to name him a favorite son. Toombs was inclined to accept Douglas, though he thought only a Southern Democrat could avert disaster, and Stephens signaled he would be open to becoming Douglas's running mate. "He would like very much to be put on the ticket with you for Vice-President," Douglas's agent reported to him after speaking with Stephens. Senator Hunter and Governor Wise hotly divided Virginia with Hunter forcing an uninstructed delegation that tilted to him. Neither of them, however, was viable. Slidell was a favorite son of Louisiana, but was ferociously opposed by former Senator Pierre Soulé, who was for Douglas, using him to punish his enemy Slidell. James Guthrie, Pierce's secretary of the treasury and president of the Louisville and Nashville Railroad, beat out Vice President John C. Breckinridge in Kentucky, which worked to Douglas's advantage because the youthful Breckinridge had more serious potential as a competitor. In Tennessee, Senator Andrew Johnson had the backing of the old Polk machine but the Douglas people got word that Johnson would go for Douglas on the second ballot. Jefferson Davis put himself forward in Mississippi, privately encouraged by Franklin Pierce, who wrote to praise his former secretary of war as "'the Coming Man,' one who is raised by all the elements of his character above the atmosphere ordinarily breathed by politicians." Andrew Johnson thought Davis "burning up with ambition, is nearer consumed by the internal heat than any man I ever saw. . . . What Jeff will do if he is not nominated God only knows!" But even some Mississippi delegates seemed willing to support Douglas on a second ballot. In Alabama, an Ultra bastion, Douglas's man there, John Forsyth, editor of the *Mobile Register,* wrote him, "Your foes are getting shaky in the knees." And later he reported to Douglas that he was "stronger a thousand times with the Southern people" than anyone imagined. He believed that once the platform was passed, a border state delegation would come out for Douglas and "the Southern spell is broken." Even in South Carolina, former congressman James Orr was allied with Douglas and prepared to swing the delegation for him. Observing the proliferation of Southern favorite sons, Senator Hammond of South Carolina thought they were all self-defeating, "all looking on Douglas as the great bug-a-boo—thereby elevating him at their own expense and equally ready to cut down any other person supposed to look that way." The *New York Herald* estimated there were twenty-six candidates for the Democratic nomination. But there was only one with a national following and a majority within the party.

Before the convention Douglas maintained two busy campaign headquarters with free-flowing bars, one in New York and the other at the National Hotel in Washington. Many Northern delegates stopped in the capital to congregate before setting off for Charleston. On April 16, delegates from twenty-four states staged a Douglas rally at the hotel to show he could claim 155 votes. The Northern states had sixty percent of delegates, and Douglas controlled eighty-four percent of those. Of the 303 total delegates, he could boast a majority even before the convention. But according to rules two thirds were required to nominate. The South had about forty percent of the delegates, so if they nearly held together they could block any nomination. Douglas, however, believed that would be highly unlikely. He had pledges in his back pocket for the second ballot, and precedent, he felt, should favor him when there was no other challenger. He had, after all, conceded graciously to

Pierce and Buchanan. It was his turn to be the recipient of gestures of good-will in the interest of party unity. This time there was no Northern man of Southern sympathy waiting in the wings who could win a Northern state. No Southern candidate could win any. Douglas had sufficient votes to block any challenger. It was clear there was really only one possible candidate. To deny Douglas would be to deny the will of the majority. To reject Douglas would be to reject the party itself.

But Douglas had been mistrusted from the moment he burst into Congress to pass the Compromise of 1850 and then immediately launched his a presidential campaign. He conceived of himself as a singular force, the spirit of the age, "Young America" and Manifest Destiny. But in his self-intoxication he had forgotten to check in with the powers-that-be. His will to power collided with the intent of the F Street Mess. He believed he was an independent actor while all along the Southerners thought of him as useful only as their cat's paw. Even when he advanced their purposes, his need to satisfy Northern voters made him dangerous. The unresolvable problem of his conceit was that he could not ultimately realize his ambition except as a Northerner. They tolerated him when, in his Kansas-Nebraska Act, he helped repeal the Missouri Compromise. But then his abstraction of popular sovereignty intended to be all things to all sections was shattered by the realities of "Bleeding Kansas" and Dred Scott. Taney's decision left no ground for Douglas's doctrine. He pretended he was upheld, but popular sovereignty was swept aside. The Lecompton Constitution exposed his conundrum. Either he stood by his discarded idea or he would face defeat in his Senate race for reelection against Abraham Lincoln. Lincoln drove him to the wall of his political fatality on the Freeport Doctrine. Now, the Alabama delegation came to the convention pledged to bolt if the platform did not support a national slave code. And Jefferson Davis proposed it in the Senate as a nail in the coffin of Douglas's candidacy.

In his biography of Douglas, anticipating his victory, Sheahan wrote that, "in defiance of all the bitterness of his enemies, throughout all coming time the name of DOUGLAS and the great principle of Popular Sovereignty will be so linked in the records of the past, and so closely identified with the memories of the present, that the fame of the former can only perish in the overthrow of the latter—an occurrence only possible in the total destruction of truth itself."

But even as Sheahan's hagiography was being printed, Douglas received worrying reports. Henry B. Payne, one of his chief men in Ohio, a former state senator and gubernatorial candidate, wrote him on March 17 that the Ultras intended "to bring the Southern sentiment to the point of demanding Davis' resolution as a sine qua non, making Congressional protection a test of orthodoxy and proscribing all who dissent." Payne predicted that if the delegates from Oregon and California, already hostile to Douglas, voted for the Alabama Platform then only Pennsylvania, controlled by the Buchanan forces, stood against catastrophe. Unless Douglas could control the platform committee it "would be destruction to us at home." If the Alabama Platform passed, Payne wrote, "Our men will be prepared to retire from the Convention in the contingency above spoken of."

Nothing Douglas could say to denounce either John Brown or Hinton Helper, Abraham Lincoln or William Seward would make his enemies loathe him less. Nothing he could do to conciliate his enemies, even bidding beyond the Ultras—not his bill to suppress antislavery conspiracies—would lead to his acceptance. Jefferson Davis expressed his unvarnished feelings about Douglas's nomination in a letter to Franklin Pierce: "If our little grog drinking, electioneering Demagogue can destroy our hopes, it must be that we have been doomed to destruction."

On January 12, 1860, on the floor of the Senate, Davis and others baited Douglas. They ridiculed his complaint against their removal of him as chairman of the Committee on Territories. They belittled his prospective nomination as the Democratic presidential candidate. They mocked the Little Giant as pathetic and marked him as an outcast. Their contempt was undisguised.

"The Senator magnifies himself when he supposes that there is any combination against him," said Jefferson Davis. "He altogether exalts himself above his level when he supposes there is a combination here to oppress him. He was not in my mind. . . . He may find that he had enough to do when he finishes one man without invoking all the Democracy to stand up together in order that he may kill them at once."

Douglas had ceaselessly attempted over the years to ingratiate himself with Davis. But Davis had followed Calhoun in adamant opposition to the Compromise of 1850 that had made Douglas's career. Davis guided Pierce's hand to sign Douglas's Kansas-Nebraska Act only after the F Street Mess pressured Douglas to repeal the Missouri Compromise, and then Davis still regarded it as a half measure and Douglas an obstacle to his vision of a slave empire encompassing the West. Douglas had attended a dinner with Davis hosted by the former Mississippi governor John Quitman in honor of Preston Brooks after he nearly murdered Sumner at which he was given an honorary cane. But Davis and his wife still thought of Douglas, even after his marriage to Adele Cutts, as vulgar white trash. ("Public sentiment proclaims that the most arrogant man in the United States Senate is Jefferson Davis," editorialized the *New York Tribune* about the time of this encounter. "Nor does there seem to be much doubt that in debate he is the most insolent and insufferable. The offence consists not so much in the words used as in the air and mien which he assumes towards opponents.")

Douglas's public style was never to retreat or apologize, but to trample his opponents. His usual techniques of hollering, threatening, stamping his feet, twisting elbows, or bribery would not, however, work with Davis. Davis stood between Douglas and his prize. He wanted Davis to loosen his grip, to let Douglas take the nomination that was rightfully his, but he could not back down without losing the respect of the entire North and the worshipful galleries. He understood that the underlying difference was one of class. "In regard to the statement of the Senator from Mississippi that I overrate myself," he replied, "I shall institute no comparison between him and me, or the modesty of my bearing and his in this body."

Clement Clay of Alabama, who with his wife belonged to same social set as Jefferson Davis and his wife, entered into the fray. "I do not exactly agree with my friend from Mississippi in thinking it evinces a great deal of egotism," he said about Douglas's performance, "but I think, with due deference, that it may be construed as evincing something worse. It looks, sir, to me, as an invocation of public sympathy on behalf of a persecuted and abused man. It looks at least . . . very much like the conduct of Peisistratus when he ran into the market-house, exhibited the self-inflicted wounds which streamed with his blood, and asked a body-guard for his protection."

Douglas took the back-and-forth insults as part of a concerted effort to deny him the nomination. "He has no right," he said about Davis to Clement Clay, "to claim to the organization and say that he intends to bolt the nominees . . . if he does not extend to me the right hand of Democratic fellowship, I shall survive the stroke. . . . I should like to understand who it is that has the right to say who is in the party and who not." Douglas pointed out that Buchanan in 1856 received two thirds of his popular vote from the North and one third from the South. "Then one third of the Democratic party is going to read out the remaining two thirds? . . . If these tests are to be made, one third will not subdue two thirds. . . . I do not admit the fact there is a better Democrat on earth than I am, or a sounder one of the question of State rights, or even on the slavery question. No, not one. When a man tells me he will vote for me if nominated—wonderful condescension indeed? Vote for me if nominated! As if such a man could for a moment compare records with me in labor the Democratic party."

Davis returned to the issue of Douglas's removal as chairman of the Committee on Territories as a suggested precedent for thwarting him now, tossing in a non sequitur about the Fugitive Slave Act, which Douglas after all had helped pass. "I should object to any man being a district attorney or district judge whose constitutional opinions or whose conscientious feelings would not allow him to execute the fugitive slave law," Davis said.

"Of course," replied Douglas.

"He would be unfit for the place," said Davis. "If he was a gentleman, he would not accept it. . . . It amounts merely to this: that where there is a difference between Democrats in opinion upon a particular point, that marks a particular position to which he is not suited, if a majority of the party differ from him. . . . As for me, I am one of the rank and file."

"So am I," said Douglas.

"Well," Clay concluded, "let it go."

But no one was letting it go. There was, despite Jefferson Davis's claim to the contrary, "a combination" to "oppress" Douglas. It was a coalition of the loathing. No one hated Douglas more than the president of the United States. "Old Buck is determined to rule or ruin us," Toombs wrote on December 4, 1859. "I think he means to continue his own dynasty or destroy the party, and the times are at least favorable to his accomplishing the latter result and the country with it."

Buchanan had issued a statement that he would not run for reelection; nor would he help Cobb to become his successor. Buchanan was a poisoned chalice in any case. Between "rule or ruin," he was left with the decision to ruin. Slidell, his malign spirit, called Douglas's views "an unequivocal declaration of war." Just as Buchanan had used the federal patronage to create an Illinois faction called the National Democrats to harass the apostate Douglas, he deployed his power to pack various state delegations. Buchanan's popularity was depleted, but he could achieve control of most of the delegates from Pennsylvania. Buchanan dangled plums before delegates from New Jersey, which turned anti-Douglas. Jobs were bartered against Douglas throughout the New England states. Delegates from Rhode Island were turned. The battle over Connecticut was bitter. Franklin Pierce prevailed upon the New Hampshire Democratic convention to adopt the Southern slave code platform. When the New Hampshire delegates passed through

Washington on their way to Charleston, Jefferson Davis lectured their leader on "the evil effect of permitting N.H. to be mustered in under the banner of Douglas," Davis reported to Pierce. In Massachusetts, Buchanan named a new collector of the Port of Boston, who used the patronage over delegates if they would oppose Douglas. Douglas's agent in New England set off an alarm that the administration was "raising Heaven and earth" to break down support.

The team that had secured Buchanan's nomination four years earlier was dispatched to Charleston with the mission of undermining Douglas. They had no other candidate in mind, though Jefferson Davis remained an unattainable favorite. Slidell and Bright were not delegates, but they set up headquarters in a mansion rented by the New York financier S.L.M. Barlow. They were joined by Senator James A. Bayard, who controlled the Delaware delegation. Caleb Cushing, who had been Pierce's attorney general, was the key New Englander of the group. He had given the Douglas campaign his private indication that he leaned to Douglas's nomination, but it was a ruse for treachery.

At a Faneuil Hall rally on December 8, 1859, organized to rail against John Brown and the "Black Republican Party," Cushing declared, "The Southern States cannot meekly lie down and be trodden upon by the Northern." He wrote a friend he favored a negotiated secession of the Southern states, "and I exhort them to do so." He spent Christmas in Washington, dining with Buchanan and Jefferson Davis. On New Year's Day, Cushing wrote Franklin Pierce, "We seem to be drifting into destruction before our eyes— in utter helplessness—the administration is unpopular and the President is embarrassed with insoluble questions. Congress is paralyzed by party spirit and everybody seems to despair of any help from men, waiting vaguely for providential intervention." In January 1860, Cushing released a public letter defending slavery and calling criticism "a mere untruth." He "warmly supported the candidacy of Mr. Jefferson Davis," according to Richard Taylor, the son of President Zachary Taylor, who was an influential member of the Louisiana delegation to the convention. Privately, Cushing fantasized taking the second spot on a ticket headed by Davis.

Charleston had been designated as the site for the convention four years earlier. The Northerners on the convention committee chose it in a gesture to party unity. Thomas Dyer, the former mayor of Chicago, traveled to Charleston to secure a hall for Douglas's headquarters, and reported to him on February 29, "Charleston is the last place on Gods Earth where a national convention should have been held." The city of fifty thousand was the Southern crucible of lavish wealth, aristocratic pretension, and nullification. The atmosphere was dominated by the daily press run of the *Charleston Mercury,* filled with screeds from the pen of Robert Barnwell Rhett, the former senator, Calhoun's old associate, who had railed for secession for more than a decade and lately called for the formation of Southern Leagues to replace the national Democratic Party. On April 19, as delegates began to arrive, he wrote an editorial in the *Mercury* to greet them, calling for the dissolution of the party and secession. "The Democratic party, as a party, based upon principles, is dead," he declared. ". . . On every living issue deemed vital to the South, the Northern members, as a body, are against the South, and agree, substantially, with the Consolidationists and Black Republicans. And this result, the South herself has produced by her weakness and timidity. She has now no other alternative, but to raise up the lifeless body of the Democratic party, by restoring to it living principles, and putting it into power, or to dissolve the Union. To stand in her present position in the Union, is to be in the broad road to inevitable ruin, helpless and hopeless."

Douglas urged as many Northern supporters as possible, even if they were not delegates, to flood the town to overwhelm the local hostility. They stepped off their trains and steamers into a charming, quaint, and thoroughly antagonistic environment, scented with azaleas and politically poisoned. Coming from the cool early spring climate of the North, they wore their woolen suits as the thermometer hit one hundred and the humidity wilted them. There were too few hotels; rooms went for astronomical prices. Douglas packed at least three hundred beds into the second floor of the Hibernian Hall, his headquarters, where delegates crammed into numbered cots alongside boxes of Sheahan's *Life of Douglas.* Important Southern delegates, however, were given quarters in the best houses on the Battery, catching the sea breeze from the harbor, where they could glimpse in the distance, on a man-made island, Fort Sumter still under construction. One of Douglas's influential delegates, J.W. Gray, publisher of the Cleveland *Plain Dealer,* curious about slavery, visited a slave auction and found "the strange spectacle of human beings sold like horses was one of the most revolting sights he had ever seen."

Murat Halstead, on the scene for the *Cincinnati Commercial,* acutely observed the conventions of 1860. "The Douglas men came down here from their headquarters in Washington, where whisky flows like a river," he wrote, "—they were full of enthusiasm—rampant and riotous—'hot as monkeys'—and proclaim that the universal world is for the Little Giant.

They have a desperate fight before them, and are brim full of the sound and fury of boastfulness. . . . The principal hotels swarm like hives."

"Imagine a crowded barroom," wrote the reporter from the *New York Herald*. "The weather is hot; the people are thirsty. . . . There are drinkers from the frozen North, drinkers from the crafty East, drinkers from the luxuriant West, drinkers from the fiery South—drinkers from everywhere. . . . They talk and talk—jabber and jabber—bet and bet, and drink and drink!"

A cloud of dread and confusion descended on the opening of the convention. Newspaper headlines flashed the latest revelations from Washington of the investigation of corruption in the Buchanan administration. Immediately after the Democrats had put the Republicans through the prolonged agony of electing a Speaker of the House, the Republicans installed Congressman John Covode of Pennsylvania, sworn enemy of Buchanan, as chairman of the probe. The president believed the evil hand of his personal Judas, John Forney, was behind the whole conspiracy against him. Buchanan denounced the Covode Committee as a "Star chamber" and demanded his impeachment rather than the investigation. "I defy all investigation," he cried. The Covode Committee of the House also provided a drumbeat of stories counter to those emanating from the Mason Committee of the Senate, which was seeking to unearth Republican complicity with John Brown. Covode held hearings uncovering widespread corruption in the War Department in granting naval contracts, building contracts, fraudulent land contracts, and bartered appointments. It exposed the embezzlement of $160,000 by the postmaster of New York, who absconded to Europe just a step ahead of arrest. It revealed payoffs at the Philadelphia Custom House and Navy Yard. It disclosed the exploitation of government printing contracts and jobs in the effort to destroy Douglas and sway congressmen on the Lecompton and English bills. Forney testified about printing bribes for "subserviency to the administration in its Kansas policy," according to the committee report. Secretary of War John Floyd and Attorney General Jeremiah Black were tainted as paymasters of bribery. In the coup de grâce, Robert J. Walker's letter that proved that Buchanan had lied to him about Lecompton, that he approved Walker's policy which he then subverted, was timed for release on the convention's eve.

"The reception of the New York papers, containing the testimony before the Covode Committee and the Buchanan-Walker letter, fell like a bombshell and a half into the Democratic camp," reported the *New York Times*. Douglas's forces rejoiced. The revelations were greeted as vindication of his

Lecompton position and giving him a boost going into the convention. "The testimony of Walker and his production of Mr. Buchanan's letter at this particular moment were designed as a coup d'etat in favor of Douglas," reported the *New York Herald*. "It was all arranged a fortnight ago, and delegates here knew all about it before the Herald arrived. A thousand copies of the Herald containing the evidence were ordered beforehand and were circulated this morning among the delegates."

Yet at the same time the disclosure of the Walker letter angered Southern delegates, reminding them why they hated Douglas. Seven Southern delegations agreed in a meeting that if the Alabama Platform was not endorsed they would walk out. "The sudden weakness of Douglas is found in the fact that seven Southern States have declared their intention of bolting," reported the *New York Herald*. "This determination is partly the result of the fierceness with which Robert J. Walker's testimony before the Covode committee is thrust in every delegate's face, as an evidence that the Southern Lecompton policy was wrong, and Douglas was right in fighting them." The *New York Times* reported about the Southern bolters, "If unsuccessful, they will in high dudgeon and martial array vamoose ye ranche." Slidell used Jefferson Davis's withdrawal of his lifeless candidacy to give the bolters an additional jolt. "Slidell," reported the *Times,* "brought and has exhibited a letter from Jeff. Davis to the Mississippi Delegation, withdrawing his name from the list of candidates, and advising them to withdraw from the Convention in case Douglas is nominated." "The opposition to Mr. Douglas is of the most bitter type," reported the *New York Tribune*.

More than three thousand delegates, hangers-on, journalists, and spectators crowded into the confines of the South Carolina Institute on Meeting Street, around the corner from Calhoun's tomb at the St. Philips Episcopal Church Cemetery. The seats were nailed to the floor, the air stale, and the heat constantly rising. A bizarre fresco was painted as a backdrop to the stage. "Three highly colored but very improperly dressed females are there engaged," wrote Halstead. "One seems to be contemplating matters and things in general. Another is mixing colors with the apparent intention of painting something. The other is pointing with what seems to be a common bowie-knife, to a globe. The point of the dagger is plunged into the Black Sea. It may be held to be according to the proprieties, that the continent which is outlined most conspicuously on this globe is marked 'Africa.'"

On April 23, the opening day of the convention, the Douglas forces felt invigorated by exercising discipline over the credentials committee, excluding upstart delegations from Illinois and New York. By the second day, however, the storm loomed. "There is an impression prevalent this morning that the Convention is destined to explode in a grand row," wrote Halstead. "The best informed and most dispassionate men are unable to see how such a termination of this party congress can be avoided. The Southern delegates last night, in caucus assembled, resolved to stand by the Jeff. Davis resolutions. There is tumult and war in prospect."

The senatorial claque of Slidell and company worked the committee on organization so that the fifteen Southern state representatives joined by their allies from California and Oregon outvoted the sixteen Douglas members to elect Caleb Cushing as permanent chairman of the convention. "But we did not know," wrote J.W. Gray of the Cleveland *Plain Dealer,* "that we had unwittingly elected the veriest toady and tool of the Fire-Eaters." Yet the Douglas forces ended the day with what seemed like a decisive win on the rules. The change allowed imposition of the unit rule on those states whose state conventions prescribed it, which all along had been part of the Douglas strategy and compelled the entire delegations from New York, Indiana, and elsewhere to vote as a unit for his nomination. The rules change also lifted the unit rule from any state whose convention had not required it, thus allowing pro-Douglas delegates who were a minority in Southern delegations to vote for him. Douglas won on the rules by a vote of 198 to 101, which his managers took as a harbinger of ultimate victory.

The coming conflict centered in the platform committee. Douglas proposed adoption of the 1856 Cincinnati Platform, which was intentionally riddled with ambiguities to accommodate that convention. Since that platform preexisted the Dred Scott decision it permitted evasion of any statement on the ruling that might remove ambiguity and lift the veil of popular sovereignty. For all Douglas's careful planning and the solidarity of his delegates, Southerners had gained control of the platform committee assisted by Cushing's rulings from the chair.

"'Bubble, bubble, toil and trouble.' No witches' cauldron, agitated by whatever number of Satan's imps, ever boiled with such fury," stated the *New York Herald.* "The platform will be the touchstone that will either enliven the hopes or turn to dross all the glitter of Mr. Douglas' pretensions."

On April 27, the committee's majority report favored a congressional slave code ("the Jeff. Davis resolutions"), denied that any territorial legislature could exclude or prohibit slavery, and asserted that it "is the duty of the Federal Government to protect, when necessary, the rights of persons and property on the high seas, in the Territories, or wherever else its Constitutional authority extends." The Douglas position consisted of the Cincinnati Platform with a sop to Dred Scott, that the questions of "rights of property in States or Territories" were "judicial" and should be decided by the Supreme Court.

Jefferson Davis had withdrawn as a candidate, but the platform fight was a shadow battle between Davis and Douglas. Davis represented the majority position; Douglas, the minority. "Child's play has ended," reported the *New York Times,* "and all must work with eyes upon the end. . . . Of one thing you may be certain—unless the Convention agrees to the desire of the South in this regard, the Convention will be dissolved, and two candidates be nominated; and in that case no nomination would suit the South so well as Jefferson Davis, of Mississippi, and Fernando Wood, of New York"—the pro-Southern mayor who was head of the anti-Douglas faction of the state's delegation.

The Charleston convention was transformed into a warped version of Kansas with the Douglas camp in the ironic role of the free staters, and the platform, which was the majority report of the committee but supported by a minority of the convention, an equivalent of the Lecompton Constitution. The majority platform could also be seen as an instrument of nullification, Calhoun's revenge, raised in the only national convention ever held in his city, intended to nullify Douglas's nomination. Douglas could not plausibly run as a candidate in the North having abandoned his principle of popular sovereignty or accepted a platform that prescribed a national slave code. "Here, then," wrote Halstead, "is the 'irrepressible conflict'—a conflict between enduring forces."

Both resolutions, both platforms, were sent to the whole convention where Douglas's numbers prevailed. His team faced its dilemma with shifting tactics rooted in wishful thinking. "It was asserted, early in the sitting of the Convention, that it would be impossible for the South to submit to Mr. Douglas as the nominee upon a platform on which it would be possible for him to stand," wrote Halstead. "The Douglas men at first laughed this to scorn. Presently they saw such indications of earnestness, that they paused and considered the matter, and became much more tolerant, and seemed willing to acquiesce in any sort of a platform, provided the South would allow the nomination of Douglas. . . . It became apparent the moment the platform was taken into consideration that there were differences it would be impossible for honest men to accommodate. The Douglas men begged for a chance for ambiguity. They craved and clamored for a false pretense. They begged to be allowed to cheat, and for the privilege of being cheated. They were particularly anxious for success. They were not so particular about principle."

Faced with splitting the convention, the Douglas camp had some months earlier gamed how a Southern walkout could work to its advantage. The *St. Paul Pioneer and Democrat* paper explained the stratagem in January. "This course will throw out of the Convention that class of votes which would be cast against him. . . . It will reduce that much the number of delegates, and of course, the number required to make up a two-thirds majority; while it leaves his strength intact." John Forsyth, Douglas's main backer in Alabama, wrote him in February about William Lowndes Yancey, the Alabama Ultra leader, "my fear is that Yancey . . . will not . . . stand up to the instructions and leave the convention." If a few Southern states walked out it would enable Douglas to reach the two-thirds vote necessary for nomination more easily and allow him to occupy the political center for the general election campaign. "Their game then was, to have three or four States, at most, go out," wrote Halstead. "They wanted a little eruption, but not a great one."

Henry B. Payne, Douglas's trusted man from Ohio, was given the task to defend Douglas's platform position before the convention, calling on Southerners to "put no weights upon the North," and refusing compromise on popular sovereignty. "We never will recede from that doctrine, Sir; *never, never, never,* so help us God."

The Southerners summoned their advocate to the rostrum, William Lowndes Yancey, "the prince of the Fire-Eaters," as Halstead dubbed him, the silver-tongued speaker of the Ultras also known as the "Orator of Secession." The plantation owner, former newspaper editor, and congressman from Alabama was the author of the Alabama Platform, demanding the full extension of slavery into the territories without any interference by half measure compromises like Douglas's popular sovereignty, which he first proposed at the 1848 Democratic convention. When it was overwhelmingly dismissed he walked out accompanied by only one other Alabamian. The fire-eater strategy was never to pass the platform for its own sake, but to break the party apart, catalyze a walkout of Southern delegates, destroy Douglas's candidacy, elect a "Black Republican" as president, provoke secession, and create a Southern Confederacy.

Yancey's motive was more than ideological or economic, but profoundly

William Lowndes Yancey

personal, buried in his wretched past. After his father, a former South Carolina state legislator, died when he was only three, his mother married a Northern Presbyterian minister, Nathan Beman, who had come to Georgia to teach school, and the family moved to Troy, New York. Beman was a cruel and violent stepfather, who physically and mentally abused his wife and children. Beman went on to associate with prominent abolitionists and become president of Rensselaer Polytechnic Institute. Yancey dropped out of Williams College at Amherst, relocated to upcountry South Carolina, and married the daughter of a wealthy planter. Within a year, he moved to Alabama to establish a large cotton plantation. At this news, Beman cast out his wife and sent her south. Yancey associated the North with his stepfather, "cold, austere, forbidding, cruel, and hypocritical," according to his biographer Eric Walther.

In 1838, on a visit to South Carolina, asserting his honor, Yancey murdered his wife's uncle in a petty dispute over something a young cousin had said, and briefly served time in jail for manslaughter, after which he returned to Alabama and was elected to the Congress. The most notable episode during his one term was his duel with Congressman Thomas Clingman of North Carolina, a Whig, over a disagreement about Texas annexation in which neither man received a scratch. The end of his elective career was the beginning of his march from the fevered swamp on the political margins to the podium of the South Carolina Institute.

From 1848 onward, Yancey perennially urged his Alabama Platform on state and national conventions. Robert Barnwell Rhett, of South Carolina, with whom he bonded in the Congress, became his brother fire-eater, the two constituting what other Southerners referred to as a "clique." "Such folly—such madness I never expected from the South," Senator Hammond wrote to William Gilmore Simms, editor of the *Southern Quarterly Review,* in 1859. The fire-eaters were "insuring Seward's election. . . . Neither more nor less. That is what our Rhetts . . . are working for in conjunction . . . all of them, and [Senator Albert Gallatin] Brown, [Jefferson] Davis, [John] Slidell, etc., etc., were recruiting sergeants for Seward and his gang. The infatuated and besotted 'fire-eaters.'"

In anticipation of the election year, Yancey wrote Rhett to publish an editorial asserting that if the Democratic Party failed to accept the Alabama Platform a new Southern party should be formed, and that if the Republican Party won the election the Southern legislatures should recall their states' senators and representatives from the Congress and prepare the "means for their common safety"—secession. Rhett's paper, the *Mercury,* ran the manifesto on October 13, 1859. The timing served to advance Yancey's resolution on November 12 to the Democratic Party of Montgomery, Alabama, which in turn became the platform approved in January by the state convention, and then carried to other Southern states, and to Charleston.

At long last, elevated to the convention podium, Yancey had everybody's attention. He denied that he knew of any Southerners who were "disruptionists," "disunionists," or "factionists." He was present there only "to save the South" and "rescue the country." The South, he said, was a victimized "minority." It was "unsafe in the Union." "Ours is the property invaded; ours are the institutions which are at stake; ours is the peace that is to be destroyed; ours is the property that is to be destroyed; ours is the honor at stake—the honor of children, the honor of families, the lives, perhaps, of all—all of which rests upon what your course may ultimately make a great heaving volcano of passion and crime, if you are enabled to consummate your designs."

The villain of the crime was the prospective nominee. "Mr. Douglas's doctrine is at war with the rights of southern citizens," said Yancey. Douglas was "animated by an ardent and consuming ambition." As though raising a cross against the devil Yancey quoted the inscription on Calhoun's tomb: "Truth, Justice and the Constitution."

Yancey's true audience was the Southerners in the hall and he addressed his closing words to them. "To my countrymen of the South I have a few words here to say. Be true to your constitutional duties and rights. Be true to your own sense of right. Accept of defeat here, if defeat is to attend the assertion of the right, in order that you may secure a permanent victory in whatever contest you carry a constitutional banner. Yield nothing of principle for mere party success—else you will die by the hands of your associates as surely as by the hand of your avowed enemy."

Finally, he bid farewell to the Democratic Party, condemning it for its betrayal of the South, and unmistakably calling for the lynching of its chief betrayer, Stephen A. Douglas. "The people have no interest in parties, except to have them pledged to administer the government for the protection of their rights. The leaders of the masses, brilliant men, great statesmen, may, by ever ignoring the people's rights, still have a brilliant destiny in the rewards of office and the distribution of eighty millions annually; but when those leaders, those statesmen, become untrue to the people, and ask the people to vote for a party that ignores their rights, and dares not acknowledge them, in order to put and keep them in office, they ought to be strung upon a political gallows higher than that ever erected for Haman."

Yancey spoke at twilight, and as darkness fell the gaslights in the hall flickered and flashed, Southerners interrupted with "outbursts of applause," and were filled with "rapturous enthusiasm"—"the speech of the convention," wrote Halstead.

But the vanity of Yancey's gothic lament of Southern victimization at the hands of the Northern wing of the Democratic Party stirred Senator George E. Pugh of Ohio to jump out of his seat and take the podium. "When have we betrayed the South?" he demanded. "When have we broken faith with the South? Put your finger upon the place." He listed Northern state after state where by standing on the Southern position the Democrats had been decimated. "Now, when we come here to debate with you, you commence by telling us that we are an inferior class of beings; that we shall not assume to have or express any opinion; that we shall not call upon you to stand by your plighted faith; that we shall put our hands on our mouths and our mouths in the dust. Gentlemen of the South, you mistake us. We will not do it."

On April 28, Saturday, men on each side amended the clashing resolutions. The Southerners whittled their platform down to its essence of federal protection of slavery in the territories and "wherever else." The Douglas side diluted its platform down to simply allowing the Supreme Court to settle the whole matter. They were prepared to drop popular sovereignty, which was nowhere mentioned, for the nomination. But the Southerners filibustered. The longer the delay, the more momentum ran against Douglas.

On April 29, Sunday, the Douglas camp tried winning support by offering delegates prospective federal jobs that would be forthcoming from the administration of President Douglas. Douglas's old adventurer and adviser, George N. Sanders, who had ruined him in the 1852 campaign, was on the scene acting as a back channel to Buchanan, whom he had assisted in the 1856 campaign. Sanders sent Buchanan a long telegram pleading with him to relent against Douglas. Buchanan was peeved that he personally had to pay the charge of the wire, which cost $26.80.

On April 30, Monday, the competing planks were presented to the delegates. In the instant before the vote, Halstead glanced at Yancey. "Mr. Yancey caught my eye at this 'solemn moment,' as various gentlemen in the Convention insisted upon calling it, and he was smiling as a bridegroom."

While the Douglas majority passed its platform, seven Southern state delegations abstained on every vote. "And now commenced the regular stampede. Alabama led the Southern column. . . . There was a shudder of excitement, an universal stir over the house, and then for the first time during the day, profound stillness." The silence was soon broken with fervent speeches as the delegations declared their withdrawals. "The South Carolinians cheered loud and long, and the tempest of applause made the circuit of the galleries and the floor several times before it subsided. There was a large number of ladies present, and they favored the secessionists with their sweetest smiles, and with nods and glances of approval, a delighted fluttering of fans and parasols, and even occasional clapping of hands."

That night was the Walpurgisnacht of the Democratic Party, the traditional May Day's eve when witches gather for their revels. An hour before midnight, Halstead wandered the streets of Charleston. "The night was beautiful with moonlight, which silvered the live oaks along Meeting Street, and made the plastered fronts of the old houses gleam like marble." He heard the distant music of a band and shouting. "I soon came upon a street full of people in front of the Court House, and heard a thousand throats call for 'Yancey!' 'Yancey!'" And Yancey stepped forward. "He spoke of the seceding delegates as about to form the 'Constitutional Democratic Convention,' and the delegates who remained, as composing the 'Rump Convention.'. . . Every ultra sentiment was applauded with mad enthusiasm. Yancey said that, perhaps even now, the pen of the historian was nibbed to write the story of a new Revolution. At this, some one of the crowd cried 'three cheers for the Independent Southern Republic.'" The Charleston Brass Band played again and the crowd marched to the offices of the *Mercury* to hear Rhett deliver a fire-eating speech.

Late that night Richard Taylor, the son of the late president, made his way to the house where Buchanan's men—Slidell, Bright, and Bayard—had set up their headquarters, "not as delegates, but under the impulse of hostility to the principles and candidacy of Mr. Douglas." Taylor made an urgent case, "pointing out the certain consequences of Alabama's impending action," and he persuaded them. "Mr. Yancey was sent for, came into our views after some discussion, and undertook to call his people together at that late hour, and secure their consent to disregard instructions. We waited until near dawn for Yancey's return, but his efforts failed of success." He had done his job all too well. "Governor [John A.] Winston, originally opposed to instructions as unwise and dangerous, now insisted that they should be obeyed to the letter, and carried a majority of the Alabama delegates with him. Thus, the last hope of preserving the unity of the National Democracy was destroyed, and by one who was its earnest advocate."

In the sober light of day, the townspeople of Charleston were still celebrating but the Douglas camp found itself hungover and surrounded by wreckage. "The Convention Breaking Up," ran the headline on the *Mercury*. "The events of yesterday will probably be the most important which have taken place since the Revolution of 1776," Rhett declared. "The Douglas men look badly this morning, as though they had been troubled during the night with bad dreams," wrote Halstead. But the nightmare was real enough and not over. Almost all of the Douglas supporters from the North, including a number of delegates, left for home. "The attendance at the regular Convention was very slim. The Hall where the seceders were in session was on the contrary crowded," the *New York Times* reported. "Cushing's course is detested by all, North and South."

The certainty and poise of Douglas's entire strategy relied on the solidity of New York, personified in its chairman, Dean Richmond, master of the New York Central, who brought with him to the convention the "Silk Stockings" of Wall Street, including August Belmont, the American manager for the Rothschild bank. They had stood by Douglas through the 1852 convention and been his rock at this one. Richmond had fended off New York City mayor Fernando Wood's rascals of his Mozart Hall faction, established after he was expelled from Tammany Hall. His complete control was guaranteed by the victory on the unit rule. But Douglas's inability to close the deal turned Richmond from bullish to bearish. He quietly wished he could substitute Horatio Seymour, the former governor of New York, for Douglas. He never mentioned it publicly. But now the test came to sustaining Douglas. With the walkout of seven Southern delegations, the question was whether the nominee would be selected by two thirds of those present or two thirds of the whole. Cushing, still in the chair of the convention, ruled that retaining the old rule was valid even though the Southern delegates were phantoms and the motion was laid on the table. New York, under Richmond, was the decisive vote. Breaking with all the other Douglas delegations, New York cast its thirty-five votes as a unit for the old two-thirds rule, which carried by twenty-nine, 141 to 112. It spelled Douglas's doom.

Richmond's faithlessness was the last step in Douglas's march of folly. At first his managers thought winning on the unit rule would assure his nomination. When they lost the vote on the convention chairman they thought Cushing would be at least neutral. Then they thought a walkout of two or three Southern delegations would help Douglas. The final blunder was to count on New York to be unswaying. Now Douglas's name was put into nomination, followed by nominations for James Guthrie of Kentucky, Senator Daniel S. Dickinson of New York, Senator Hunter of Virginia, Senator Johnson of Tennessee, and Senator Joe Lane of Oregon. "After the vote of New York had decided that it was impossible to nominate Douglas, she proceeded, the roll of States being called, to vote for him as demurely as if she meant it," wrote Halstead. "The first ballot for the nomination of a candidate for the Presidency, was taken about dusk, amid the most profound silence. When the name of Douglas was put in nomination, a feeble yelp went up from the North-western delegations. It was not hearty and strong, but thin and spiritless . . . the cold steel of the new construction of the two-thirds rule had pierced their vitals."

After fifty-six ballots Douglas still fell short and his tally was stagnant. The New York delegation announced that if he didn't receive two thirds on the sixtieth ballot it would dump him. On May 3, Douglas's leadership decided that the convention should be adjourned for six weeks, until June 18, where it would meet in Baltimore.

While the regular Democratic convention deadlocked, the bolters, calling themselves the Constitutional Democratic Convention, assembled in the theater of St. Andrew's Hall to act out a moonlight and magnolia dramaturgy of revolution beneath a large portrait of Queen Victoria. Senator Bayard, one of Buchanan's agents, served as chairman, and delivered a ringing denunciation of the regular convention as "the spirit of Black Republicanism that existed there for power and plunder." Yancey, "greeted with the most deafening applause," repeated the section of his speech proclaiming that the ultras were not "disunionists." The slave code platform was unanimously passed. One speaker urged the nomination of a candidate. Jefferson Davis's name was bruited. But there was no nomination. Some thought the regular convention would decide to concede on the platform and invite them back to occupy their delegate seats. Others worried that they would be banished forever from the Democratic Party. The fire-eaters gave speeches calling Douglas men the worst sort of abolitionists. Pretty ladies fluttered in the galleries. When the regular convention adjourned, the counter-convention agreed to reassemble on June 11 in Richmond.

One week after the suspension of the Democratic convention, on May 10, the Constitutional Union convention was held in Baltimore. This assemblage attracted whatever was left from the decayed remnants of the Old Whigs and the Know-Nothings, a reprise of the American Party that had four years earlier nominated Millard Fillmore. The chairman of the convention was Senator John J. Crittenden, given three rounds of three cheers when he entered. The program of the party was to uphold the status quo, "the Constitution as it is," as one speaker said, while resolutely avoiding all issues, especially slavery. "Everybody is eminently respectable, intensely virtuous, devotedly patriotic, and fully resolved to save the country," wrote Halstead. "They propose to accomplish that political salvation so devoutly to be wished, by ignoring all the rugged issues of the day. The expression against platforms was universal and enthusiastic."

Declaring itself the party of principle with a one-line platform—"The Constitution of the country, the union of the States, and the enforcement of the laws"—the delegates nominated a respectable backward-looking ticket of Senator John Bell of Tennessee for president, an Old Whig ("the fossil remains of the old Whig strain of political geology," according to the *New York Herald*), but one of two Southerners (along with Sam Houston) to vote against the Kansas-Nebraska Act, and Edward Everett for vice president, the distinguished and even older Old Whig from Massachusetts. Both had the distinction of serving as short-lived cabinet secretaries in the short-lived administration of William Henry Harrison.

The Constitutional Unionists of course stood no chance of victory, but like Fillmore four years earlier pinned their hopes on a deadlock in the Electoral College that would throw the contest into the House of Representatives where they could be the balance of power. The *New York Times* editorialized that the chief purpose of the party was "primarily the defeat of the Republican ticket." Medill of the *Chicago Press and Tribune* called it a "stupid absurdity" that was "a repetition of the Fillmore swindle of 1856." The Douglas camp believed the Constitutional Unionists might drain off Old Whig votes from the Republicans throughout the lower North, tilting states to the Democrats. From Douglas's point of view, Crittenden's Constitutional Unionists were a distant ally potentially producing an effect similar to what Crittenden's letter did in reducing the Old Whig vote for Lincoln in the Senate race.

In Washington, after the Southern bolt, Senator Milton S. Latham of California, a proslavery Democrat who had succeeded the murdered Broderick, recorded in his diary the spread of rumors sweeping the capital. On May 2, while dining at Senator Hammond's, Sam Ward burst in with astonishing news that "Douglas was withdrawn and Guthrie has 196 votes." (Ward was an extraordinary cosmopolitan of wide influence, the son of a wealthy banker, married to an Astor, the brother of Julia Ward Howe, and friend of Seward, but a Democrat who would become known as "King of the Lobby.") "[John C.] Breckinridge turned *pale* and I could almost hear Mrs. B' heart beat." After dinner, Latham and Senator William M. Gwin, of California, went to Ward's house, who confided he got his information from the White House. Ward rounded up Jefferson Davis and the entourage went to see Buchanan, who told them he hadn't received that news, at which the "countenances of D[avis] and G[win] fell—didn't believe it and off we started for Gov. Cobb." He wasn't at home, but "Mrs. C. had heard no such news. Then we went to Senators Hunter and Mason. Hunter and Cobb out but Mason was in. Mason heard the news, seemed glad of Douglas defeat but not pleased at the idea of having Guthrie for President. By and by Hunter and Cobb came and said 'Douglas 150½ and Guthrie 68, adjourned until tomorrow.' A perfect damper and Gwin retires with 'dam[n] the luck.'"

The next day, May 4, Latham met with Douglas, "who was under the influence of liquor. . . . His eye flashed fire when he spoke of his enemies and called them 'blood hounds after his life &c.' Said 'this controversy has but commenced &c.' I told him there was 'too much fire in his eye, for a great man and he showed too much passion, to keep cool, it would all come right.' He said I would *feel,* when they got after me."

Lincoln's defense of the Republican Party against the charges of both Douglas and the Southerners in his Cooper Union speech proved to be a strange guide to the war between Douglas and the South inside the Democratic Party. Douglas had assailed Lincoln for his "house divided" speech and as a representative of a sectional "Black Republican Party." Yet Douglas was subjected to the same withering attacks from his enemies within. He was the one accused of being the sectional candidate, the one dividing the house, no better than a Black Republican. Just as Lincoln pointed out to Republicans that nothing would satisfy Southerners except agreeing with them on the unrestricted rights of slavery, Douglas faced the same demand of utter capitulation as the only act that would pacify them. Lincoln's speech was a prophecy of Douglas's catastrophe. At Charleston, his brand of popular sovereignty imploded and his impending crisis exploded into the Democrats' irrepressible conflict.

Douglas had devised his "great principle" of popular sovereignty to evade hard choices, create a soft center, and maneuver to preeminence above controversy. But his doctrine had perversely been used to crush him at the convention he thought would crown him. The fights over the platform and the two-thirds rule, which had been enacted in 1844 to secure Southern veto over the presidential nomination, gave substance to popular sovereignty that Douglas never imagined. He believed in the rule of the majority. The Southerners, even many of those who did not bolt, did not believe in it. They did not believe in its application at the Democratic convention; nor did they believe in it within the nation. Since John C. Calhoun, they had sought to find formulas for sustaining minority rule. The Alabama Platform was a pure form of Calhounism. At the convention, the Democratic Party shattered over democracy itself. The churches had already divided over slavery, the Whigs had fragmented, and the Democratic split was the destruction of the last national institution uniting the country.

On the day the Charleston convention was suspended, May 4, the *New York Times* ran an editorial, "The Disruption of the Democratic Party," acknowledging the harsh reality:

> The Charleston Convention has abandoned the attempt to nominate a Democratic candidate for the Presidency. . . . The contest between the two sections of the Union has at last penetrated the Democratic Party, and rendered it impossible for the two wings to agree upon a declaration of principles. When the majority adopted its platform the minority seceded. . . . The result was to give the South the victory. They have controlled the Convention, and prevented the nomination of any candidate. . . . The disruption itself is a fact of very marked importance, not only in the history of political parties but of the country itself. It seems to sever the last link of nationality in the political affairs of the Union. . . . We regard the struggle as one for political power. . . . The Slave States have substantially controlled the policy of the Federal Government for the last fifty years. . . . The time has come when they must relinquish their grasp. Power is passing into the hands of the majority. . . . It is among the inevitable events of political history. . . . The South can either accept it as inevitable and make the best of it,—or plunge the whole country into turmoil, and bring down swift ruin upon its

own borders, in the vain contest against national growth and development.

Alexander Stephens, who if Douglas had won the nomination at Charleston might have been his running mate, reflected to a friend that "men will be cutting one another's throats in a little while. In less than twelve months we shall be in a war, and that the bloodiest in history. Men seem to be utterly blinded to the future. . . . The only hope was at Charleston.

Remains of the South Carolina Institute Hall, 1865

If the party could have agreed there we might carry the election. As it is, the cause is hopelessly lost. . . . Mark me, when I repeat that in less than twelve months we shall be in the midst of a bloody war." From the remove of the turmoil on his estate in Georgia, he wondered, "What amazes me in Douglas is his desire to be President. I have sometimes asked him what he desired the office for."

The Douglas men leaving Charleston were sunk in depression; no gambit, not the resumption of the convention at Baltimore, would put the party back together again. "It is the prevalent impression that the Democratic Party has been done for," wrote Halstead. "Even if it should be possible to patch up a superficial reconciliation, and nominate with a whole Convention, the nomination would be worthless. I hear it stated here a hundred times a day, by the most orthodox Democrats and rampant Southerners, 'William H. Seward will be next President of the United States.'"

THE RAILSPLITTER

On April 29, the sixth day of the Democratic convention, divided over its platform, but with the result unclear, Lincoln wrote Trumbull, "The taste *is* in my mouth a little."

Lincoln's understated line was an unmistakable announcement of his candidacy. It appeared plainly stated, slyly humorous and slightly humble in the Lincoln style. But it was in its simplicity his indirect way of telling Trumbull that he was aware of Trumbull's unannounced national ambitions, that he had precedence over him, and that he would overcome the tangled politics that threatened to sideline him once again.

The *Chicago Press and Tribune* had raised the banner of Lincoln, and it published a pamphlet of his Cooper Union speech. But behind the scenes its editor Joseph Medill tried to keep all avenues open. Just after the Cooper Union speech, and perhaps as a result of Seward's scolding of Medill for his Lincoln enthusiasm, the *Tribune* published an editorial suggesting that Lincoln "would not permit his friends to use his name in rivalry with

Lincoln, *The Railsplitter,* painting, 1860

that of Mr. Seward." The *Illinois State Journal* on March 13 reprimanded the *Tribune*. "Has Mr. Seward, then, such transcendent claims upon the party, that no other man must be mentioned by the side of him? . . . If Mr. Lincoln's name is presented to the Convention, it will not be 'in rivalry' with Mr. Seward, Mr. Bates, or anybody else: but because 'his friends,' as a matter of expediency and choice prefer him as their candidate, and believe that under his leadership the Republican party is sure of the victory."

"The Illinois State Journal will not provoke a controversy with us," the *Tribune* replied on March 15, observing, "The views expressed in that [editorial], we doubt not, are the views of Mr. Lincoln himself." Trying to climb down, the *Tribune* said that while Seward "is unquestionably the choice of a majority of the Republican party," and that Lincoln "would not" consider Seward's nomination "inexpedient," the paper stated, "Mr. Lincoln is our candidate—has been so from the beginning, and will be so until the Convention takes from us the right as partisans to press his claims."

The *Tribune*'s tentative tone revealed its skepticism about Lincoln's chances, even though it endorsed him as a favorite son of Illinois, which gave the paper a modicum of influence. Privately, Medill wrote Trumbull to assay his interest in running as the vice president on a ticket headed by Supreme Court Justice John McLean, whose candidacy had quickly folded in 1856 and who was now seventy-five years old. Medill told Trumbull that "a young, fresh, reliable" running mate would balance McLean. "The judge is old and may not live thro' a term," he wrote encouragingly. He added that to be sure he was still for Lincoln, but just exploring hypothetical possibilities. Trumbull took his suggestion more seriously. He wrote McLean that he was "the only person who can be nominated in Chicago in opposition to Governor Seward," and "I think we could also give you Illinois" in the convention after Lincoln's bid fell apart. The taste was also in Trumbull's mouth a little.

Medill's candidate shopping and Trumbull's interest were complicated by the running feud between "Long John" Wentworth and Norman B. Judd, and by David Davis's siding with Wentworth. Wentworth, just re-elected mayor of Chicago, with Judd's support in the end, was determined to destroy Judd's effort to win the Republican nomination for governor. Judd, the longtime intimate ally of Trumbull, wrote him on April 2 trying to draw him into active participation in the Lincoln campaign, a letter that clearly was crafted in consultation with other members of Lincoln's inner circle and had received Lincoln's approval. "Cannot a quiet combination between the delegates from New Jersey Indiana and Illinois be brought about—including Pennsylvania—United action by those delegates will probably control the convention—Nothing but a positive position will prevent Seward's nomination—The movement for Lincoln has neutralized to some extent the Bates movement in our state. . . . State pride will carry a resolution of instruction through our convention—This suggestion has been made to Mr. L."

Wentworth and Davis engaged in a ploy using Trumbull's flirtation with McLean to turn Lincoln against Judd in order to give Wentworth control with Davis over Lincoln's candidacy. It was a scheme that was completely obvious to Lincoln. On April 21, Wentworth wrote Lincoln, "I enclose you an article (one of many that I see) placing Trumbull in rivalry with you for vice President." He emphasized, "Davis is here. He agrees with me in all things." Judd's work for Lincoln's nomination, he warned, would end badly. "Davis and I shall not call until you are beaten once more," he wrote acidly.

They especially agreed that Judd should be defeated for governor. Judd was "crying and whining," and wanted to exclude Wentworth from the state party convention in Decatur on May 9. Wentworth declared, "I do not intend that he should be Governor under any circumstances!" He concluded, "I shall be at Decatur anyhow and so should you."

Two days later, on April 23, in tandem with Wentworth, Davis wrote Lincoln that Wentworth should replace Judd as his campaign manager. "I am more and more convinced of the wonderful power of John Wentworth— If he had managed the campaign in this State in 1858, I wd have bet half I am worth that you would have been successful." To advance Wentworth to Lincoln, Davis tried to create bad blood between Lincoln and Judd as well as bad blood between Lincoln and Trumbull. Davis cited Wentworth's superior political insight. "He believes that the Tribune clique as he calls them, are devoted to the Elevation of Seward Trumbull and that then going for you is a mere blind—He believes this—There is no mistake about it, and I must confess to sharing his opinion a good deal—He wishes to make you the great man of the State and not Trumbull—No matter what his motive, you could not have a more Effective or efficient friend." Davis relayed Wentworth's gossip that Gustave Koerner, the German American leader, "is not to be relied on" and "really for Seward." Davis urged Lincoln that he must appoint Wentworth one of his delegates to the national convention to take charge of his candidacy. "Wentworth must be appointed one of the delegates at large—I will vouch for his faithfulness. . . . You ought to have got him long ago to 'run you.'" "Write me," Davis finished. Lincoln, however, did not. The episode only increased his mistrust of Wentworth, and Davis's judgment by extension.

The day after Davis's letter was sent, Trumbull wrote Lincoln that he had taken a survey of his political contacts in the key states and concluded that Seward "cannot" and "should not be nominated." Trumbull did not believe Bates could be nominated either. The only option would be McLean. But Trumbull insisted, "I wish to be distinctly understood as first & foremost for you. I want our State to send delegates not only instructed for you, but your friends who will stand by and nominate you if possible, never faltering unless you yourself shall so advise." McLean should "only be taken up as a compromise candidate," and only in "the belief, that it would be better to take him and probable victory than Seward and probable defeat." He finished, "I want to know your views."

To this letter, Lincoln for the first time unequivocally declared his candidacy. Having confessed his interest, he offered his assessment of the state of play. "Now, as to my opinions about the chances of others in Illinois. I think neither Seward or Bates can carry Illinois if Douglas shall be on the track; and that either of them can, if he shall not be." Lincoln's chance as he saw it depended upon Douglas prevailing. If the Democrats were to nominate anyone more favorable to the Southern position than Douglas, then it would be generally felt that any Republican could win. But with Douglas as the Democratic nominee the sense that Seward couldn't match his appeal in the lower North would become a growing factor at the Republican convention.

"A word now for your own special benefit," Lincoln wrote confidentially. "You better write no letters which can possibly be distorted into opposition, or quasi opposition to me. There are men on the constant watch for such things out of which to prejudice my peculiar friends against you. While I have no more suspicion of you than I have of my best friend living, I am kept in a constant struggle against suggestions of this sort."

The election of delegates in Cook County to the state convention on April 28 was a battle royal between Wentworth and Judd. Wentworth used every tool at his disposal including dispatching the Chicago police as precinct workers, but Judd swept the slate winning all forty-seven delegates. ". . . every man is a Lincoln as a first choice," Judd wrote Lincoln on May 2. He advised him that the state ticket should include more than old Whigs, a strong suggestion that Lincoln might support him, an old Democrat. "You must quietly shape the destinies of the party," Judd wrote. He warned that Wentworth had gone to Springfield, and "has probably seen you before this and whispered his poison, it will not effect you—and our friends in the State house must not listen to his suggestions."

Wentworth had in fact already come to Springfield. He repeated to Lincoln his stories about Trumbull, Judd, and the "Tribune clique." "I tell you want, Lincoln," he said. "You must do like Seward does—get a feller to run you." The phrase was exactly the same as the one used by Davis. But Lincoln was not about to adopt Wentworth as his Thurlow Weed.

Lincoln's men moved up the Illinois State Republican Convention to May 9 in Decatur in order to consolidate the state delegation behind him as a phalanx. Most of the counties were for him, the largest under Judd pledged to him, but there were pockets of support for Bates and Seward, and about thirty counties uncommitted. Lincoln's greatest fear was a divided delegation, which would by itself doom his candidacy.

The chief of convention planning, Richard J. Oglesby, a lawyer from Decatur, a Mexican War veteran. and State Senate candidate, was not a delegate, but he was in charge of all arrangements. He directed the construction of a makeshift structure on State Street to house the convention, called "The Wigwam," a wooden frame covered by a large tent he purchased from a traveling circus. Oglesby was fully committed to Lincoln, and wanted to "kill the Seward boom," and had a notion that Lincoln needed an image to depict him as a symbol of free labor. He knew Lincoln's elder cousin, John Hanks, who lived near Decatur, as an old settler, and had heard tales of his exploits on the Illinois frontier, how he and the Lincolns had migrated as one extended family in wagons from Indiana, how he and Lincoln had gone down the Mississippi on a flatboat to New Orleans, and how they had chopped down trees, and split the logs into rails. Oglesby took Hanks in a buggy about twelve miles west of the town to a clearing. Hanks identified a fence. "They are the identical rails we made," he said. They detached two of them, tied them to the rear wagon axle and dragged them to Oglesby's barn.

Thousands of delegates, party men, and onlookers crushed into the hastily built Wigwam. Jackson Grimshaw, a Lincoln man, called the convention to order. Joe Gillespie, Lincoln's old friend, was elected chairman, and before any other business, he turned the convention over to Oglesby. Oglesby said he was "informed that a distinguished citizen of Illinois—and one whom Illinois would ever delight to honor was present, at the meeting, and he wished to move that this body invite him to a seat on the stand." The delegates craned their necks to look to the back of the Wigwam. "Abraham Lincoln!" shouted

Oglesby. "The storm of applause burst forth loud, long and deep," recalled one delegate. "As it subsided—the motion was seconded—and passed." But Lincoln could not make his way forward through the packed meeting. Suddenly he was lifted up, and carried above the heads of the throng, "until he found himself, kicking scrambling—crawling—upon the sea of heads between him and the stand. The enthusiasm was at too high a pitch, for the ludicrousness of the scene. . . . The cheering was like the roar of the sea, hats were thrown up by the Chicago delegation." Lincoln "rose bowing and blushing," smiled, and thanked the delegates for their "manifestations of esteem."

Oglesby calmed the crowd. He declared that "an old Democrat desired to make a contribution to the convention." "Receive it! Receive it!" shouted the crowd. "What is it?" cried others. "All was expectancy and excitement," recalled Oglesby. In walked John Hanks and a local carpenter, each holding an old wooden rail between which was hung a banner: "Abraham Lincoln, the rail candidate for the Presidency in 1860. Two rails from a lot of three thousand, made in 1830, by John Hanks and Abe Lincoln, whose father was the first pioneer of Macon County."

Again, the crowd went wild. "Lincoln! Lincoln!" delegates cheered. "The roof was literally cheered off the building," recalled another delegate, "hats and canes and books and papers were tossed aloft, as men jumped and screamed and howled, until part of the awning over the platform fell on their heads. When the enthusiasm finally subsided the Wigwam was almost a wreck."

"How are you Abe?" John Hanks said to his cousin when he reached the stage. "How are you, John?" Lincoln replied.

"The whole scene was for a time simply tempestuous and bewildering," wrote Ward Hill Lamon, Lincoln's friend and eyewitness. "But it ended at last; and now the whole body, those in the secret and those out of it, clamored like men beside themselves for a speech from Mr. Lincoln." Lincoln, recalled a delegate, "blushed, but seemed to shake with inward laughter." "Gentlemen," said Lincoln, laughing as he spoke, "I suppose you want to know something about those things. I don't know whether we made those rails or not; fact is, I don't think they are a credit to the makers. But I do know this: I made rails then, and I think I could make better ones than these now."

The convention moved directly to balloting on the gubernatorial nomination. Judd ran strongly in front, but was short of a majority. On the fourth ballot, Leonard Swett, who was losing ground, urged his supporters to vote for Richard Yates, who won. Yates, who was a Lincoln protégé in the Whig Party, accepted with an endorsement of Lincoln, which set off another demonstration. Wentworth was ecstatic at Judd's demise, but Judd's composure in defeat and prompt endorsement of Yates was received with acclaim and Wentworth was cast as the spoiler. The *Chicago Press and Tribune,* undoubtedly reflecting Lincoln's point of view, wrote that "many delegates now regret that they did not vote for him [Judd]. His slanderers and back-biters now receive the indignant execrations of those delegates whom their falsehoods deceived. The friends of Mr. Swett attribute his failure to get the nomination for Governor to Wentworth, whom they heartily denounce for his impertinent interference with the Convention, thereby creating a prejudice against the person he advocated."

The next day, the Decatur convention passed a resolution instructing the delegation to vote as a unit for Lincoln: "Resolved: Abraham Lincoln is the first choice of the Republican party of Illinois for the Presidency, and instructing the delegates to the Chicago Convention to use all honorable means to secure his nomination, and to cast the vote of the State as a unit for him." The leader of the Seward delegates, Thomas J. Turner, a former speaker of the Illinois House, from Freeport, rose to object to any instruction. But John M. Palmer, a stalwart Lincoln man, replied, "Is he so blind and so deaf that he cannot see and hear that this Convention is literally sitting on a volcano of its own enthusiasm for Abraham Lincoln, and just aching to give three cheers and a tiger for Old Abe?" Turner was overridden, and the unit rule imposed. Still, Swett later observed, "Our delegation was instructed for him, but of the twenty-two votes in it, by incautiously selecting the men, there were eight who would gladly have gone for Seward." The unit rule turned out to be essential discipline on the delegation. "Every Body for Lincoln," read the headline in the *Press and Tribune.*

After the first day of the convention, Lincoln gathered Judd, Swett, Davis, state senator Burton C. Cook, and other members of the delegate selection committee, and conferred in a nearby park. They carefully went over the list for the national convention. Lincoln as the preferred candidate could name four at-large delegates. He named Judd, the reward for his steadfastness and skill; Davis, who, despite his recent mischievous bungling, was a formidable politico; and Gustave Koerner, a strategic choice to win over the German Americans. He also named Orville H. Browning over the objection of Oglesby. "I know that old Browning is not for me," explained Lincoln, but he "will do more harm on the outside than he could on the inside." Once Bates faded, Browning would prove useful. "When Orville sees this he'll undoubtedly come over to me, and do us some good with the Bates men." Notably left out was "Long John" Wentworth. "His desire to be a delegate to the Chicago Convention or a member of the State Committee," said the *Press and Tribune,* "was treated with utter scorn, and the man whom he sought to blacken stands higher in public estimation than ever before."

As for John Hanks, he kept the original two rails, sold both, one for five dollars, and promptly drove out to collect a wagonload of more, which he stored in Oglesby's barn, doing a booming business at a dollar apiece. "Then," recalled Oglesby, "other people went into the business, and the supply seemed inexhaustible."

THE WIGWAM

T hurlow Weed, confident of his ability to pull the strings for the nomination of Seward, dismissed Lincoln to delegates as "a backwoods lawyer" who was preposterously being pushed forward as a "presidential possibility." Seward was the preeminent man of his party, the former governor of New York, its senator, anointed as a young man by John Quincy Adams, tribune of the antislavery cause, maker of Whig presidential candidates for as long as there was such a party, adviser to Whig presidents, just returned from Europe, where he was treated as the next president.

The center spread of *Harper's Weekly* of "Prominent Candidates for the Republican Nomination" featured a large portrait of Seward surrounded by the lesser lights, with Lincoln relegated to the bottom line, between John C. Frémont, the candidate of the last convention, and John Bell, who was the candidate of the Constitutional Union Party. Cassius Clay, a very dark horse, was in a far corner. Lincoln was shunted below Salmon P. Chase, whose Ohio delegation was hopelessly

Abraham Lincoln, May 20, 1860

"Prominent Candidates For The Republican Presidential
Nomination At Chicago," *Harper's Weekly*

split, wrecking his chances from the start; Speaker of the House William Pennington, who was not a candidate, and whose picture was there apparently to fill in a space; ancient Justice John McLean, who had some old admirers and a small contingent from Ohio lying in wait to undermine Chase; and Senator Simon Cameron, favorite son of Pennsylvania and no place else. Near Seward, on the top line, were a gray-bearded Edward Bates, being handled by the Blairs for their own purposes, the former Know Nothing who advertised himself as not quite a Republican; and Congressman Nathaniel Banks of Massachusetts, another darkest of horses, too closely linked to the Know Nothings. Below Seward was a vista of Washington with the White House in the middle ground. But the convention was in Chicago.

Chicago was Lincoln's city. The explosive growth of the city revolutionized the balance of political power in the state from the south and middle to the north. Chicago made possible the Illinois Republican Party. Lincoln and his men knew it, lived it, and felt it, and the others did not. His wrinkled suit and shrill Kentucky accent that had created initial apprehension at Cooper Union misled the New York audience into thinking of him as a rustic savant, something like the mermaid at P.T. Barnum's American Museum, but come to life before their eyes, moving them to wonder. But Lincoln was not just from Springfield, or a wanderer on the Eighth Judicial Circuit of central Illinois. Even before he came to Chicago in 1847 to attend the River and Harbor

Convention to protest President Polk's veto of internal improvements for its development, he was one of the makers of the city. As the Whig floor leader of the legislature he had engineered passage of the Illinois and Michigan Canal that connected Chicago to the Mississippi River. Lincoln was a "backwoods lawyer" whose driven aspiration was a flight from country life, and who was quite consciously an agent of urbanization, modernity, and industrialism.

The former fur trading post on the lake was a town of ten thousand when Lincoln first saw it. Barely more than a decade later more railroads converged on Chicago than any other city in the world. Overnight it had displaced St. Louis as the gateway between the East and the West. Cyrus Mc-Cormick's manufacturing works produced more than four thousand reapers a year, the harbinger of the assembly line and mass production. Chicago's markets dominated the richest agricultural land on earth. Twelve huge grain silos, the city's early skyscrapers, loomed above the endless urban sprawl. The Chicago Board of Trade created the futures market to set the price of wheat and hogs, the first commodity exchange. Chicago's harbor was the world's largest lumberyard, hundreds of boats arriving by the hour. The great meat-packing operations that occupied miles would soon employ one fifth of the city's workers. Chicago was being feverishly built on free labor, floated on risk, propelled by rail and water, rewarding the inventive and the brash with little time to defer to tradition or authority.

In the counting rooms of Wall Street and Boston's State Street, long established relations with Southern interests still prevailed. In the metropolis on the prairie, cotton was not king. Antislavery sentiment was nearly universal. The Free Soil Party carried the city in 1848. In 1850, the Chicago Common Council voted a resolution: "That the fugitive slave law lately passed by Congress is a cruel and unjust law, and ought not to be respected by an intelligent community, and that this Council will not require the city Police to render any assistance for the arrest of fugitive slaves."

All sorts of Lincoln's friends had close ties to the city, both political and business. Lincoln himself invested in Iowa real estate with Norman B. Judd. John Whitfield Bunn, the Springfield merchant who financed Lincoln's campaigns and was the initial contributor and treasurer of his 1860 effort, along with his brother Jacob Bunn were major investors in a wide array of Chicago-based firms. "Lincoln's political career can be viewed as the first instance in the history of the United States of large-scale corporate interests successfully supporting a Republican candidate for the presidency," wrote the family's historian. But as John Bunn pointed out, he always acted at Lincoln's direction.

The rise of Chicago was entwined with the rise of Lincoln. Lincoln was offered a partnership in a Chicago law firm in 1849, which he turned it down, but tried many cases in its courts. He knew the leading members of the bar, the editors of the newspapers, and the politicians. From the moment he thrust himself back into public life after 1854, he became embroiled in Chicago's fractious politics that threatened his ability to hold together the newly formed Republican Party. He operated behind the scenes in local elections using his agents so his hand would not be detected, especially to upset Douglas on the one hand and the Know Nothings on the other. He addressed crowds at Chicago, raised money, and even brought his young son Willie with him on one trip to stay at the Tremont House hotel. "I had made his acquaintance as early as 1856," recalled John M. Palmer, later a general, Illinois governor, and U.S. senator, "and had, as a young and ardent Republican, frequently occasion to consult with him in regard to political matters while acting as secretary of one of our young Republican clubs." Once, waiting in a Chicago courthouse with Palmer and Judd to appear on behalf of a client, Lincoln sat in on a trial out of curiosity in which a lawyer named Blackwell held forth on the habits of storks in Holland. "That beats me!" said Lincoln. "Blackwell can concentrate more words into the fewest ideas of any man I ever knew. The storks of Holland! Why, they would eat him up before he began to get half through telling that story about them."

In late March of 1860, Lincoln came to Chicago to argue as the lead attorney in the case of *Johnston v. Jones* and Marsh before the U.S. Circuit Court. The so-called "Sandbar" case involved ownership of some of the most valuable lakefront property in the city. The Army Corps of Engineers had dredged a sandbar to create a deep channel where the Chicago River met Lake Michigan for easier access to the harbor. North of the channel the tides washed in the sand and sediment to make a sizable parcel of new land. Today this area is among the most expensive real estate in the city, the northeast land running along Michigan Avenue. William S. Johnston owned a lot adjoining that of William Jones and Sylvester Marsh. Johnston sued Jones and Marsh to eject them from the new land. After four trials, Jones appealed a verdict in Johnston's favor to the federal court, hiring Lincoln as his lawyer. The lead attorney for Johnston was Lincoln's friend, Isaac N. Arnold, already preparing to help advance his nomination at the convention. After an eleven-day trial, Lincoln won the "Sandbar" case. Among the witnesses he called was John H. Kinzie, one of earliest settlers, who had arrived in 1803, when there were one hundred people in Chicago. "I believe," Lincoln told the jury, "he is common law here, as one who dates back to the time whereof the memory of man runneth not to the contrary."

The day after the trial ended, April 5, Lincoln was met at the Chicago train station by Harvey B. Hurd, a Chicago lawyer, professor at the newly founded Northwestern University, and an ardent abolitionist, who was secretary of the local branch of the Kansas Aid Society and had helped shelter John Brown when he passed through on his way east. Hurd was a close friend and later the law partner of Grant Goodrich, the Chicago lawyer who had offered Lincoln a partnership, also active in the antislavery movement and a leader in creating Northwestern. Hurd was one of the founders and real estate developers of the town of Evanston, just north of Chicago, and he escorted Lincoln there. Lincoln had accepted an invitation to visit from Julius White, the harbormaster of Chicago, who was involved in the "Sandbar" case. Many of the townspeople, including the faculty at Northwestern, uniformly Republicans, gathered to hear Lincoln give a little speech from the porch of White's house. (Lincoln would appoint White collector of the Port of Chicago.)

Afterward, Lincoln went back to Chicago for the sole purpose of sitting for a life mask and bust to be cast by the sculptor Leonard Volk. Volk, twenty-three years old, would later become the founder of the Chicago Academy of Design, now the School of the Art Institute. He was related by marriage to Stephen A. Douglas, his wife's cousin. Douglas was Volk's patron, subsidizing his study in Rome and Florence, and Volk named his son in his honor, Stephen A. Douglas Volk. Earlier in the year, Volk had made a mask and statue of Douglas. Volk came by the courthouse during the "Sandbar" case to ask Lincoln if he would do a sitting. He had the idea that Lincoln might be the Republican candidate. Just as Lincoln posed for his photograph taken by Mathew Brady, he decided to be a subject for Leonard Volk. He was interested in exploring depictions of his image. "Mr. Volk," he said, "I have never sat before to sculptor or painter—only for daguerreotypes and photographs. What shall I do?" Lincoln sat quietly for an hour while the plaster cast on his face set. He returned the next few days while Volk worked on the bust. On Sunday, Lincoln told him that a friend had invited him to church, "but I thought I'd rather come and sit for the bust. The fact is, I don't like to hear cut and dried sermons. No, when I hear a man preach, I like to see him act as if he were fighting bees." "And," Volk recalled, "he extended his long arms, at the same time suiting the action to the words."

In January 1861, Volk visited President-elect Lincoln, no longer clean-shaven but with the stubble of a beard, sitting in his parlor at his home in Springfield surrounded by friends and politicians. Lincoln had posed for a bust from another sculptor, but couldn't make out the likeness. "But," he said, "in two or three days after Mr. Volk commenced my bust, there was the animal himself!"

After sitting for Volk, Lincoln returned to Springfield to await the news that would be forthcoming from the convention at Chicago. Chicago was even more of a factor for the Republican convention than Charleston was for the Democratic one. The campaign of the "backwoods lawyer" had the place wired. Chicago was the convention site, after all, because Judd had convinced the Republican National Committee that Illinois would have no favorite son candidate. Now Judd finagled the Illinois Central and Prairie State Railroads to provide half-rate fares to Chicago, flooding the city with Lincoln supporters on a lark to "make history." Tens of thousands of Lincoln men roamed the streets in a holiday mood. The size of the crowds in Chicago dwarfed those of Charleston and made "the little excitement" there seem "insignificant," according to Murat Halstead.

Delegation by delegation entering the city at the Great Union Depot were greeted by salutes and rockets fired by the Chicago Light Artillery. The Wide Awakes, companies of young Republicans in military-like drill wearing caps and capes and carrying oil-lit torches, accompanied by the Light Guard Band, escorted the delegates to their hotels with march music and fanfare.

David Davis arrived in Chicago on Saturday, May 12, "the first on the ground," four days before the convention's start, startled to discover that Judd, who had done so much to arrange matters, had in his preoccupation with his own failed campaign for the gubernatorial nomination neglected to set up a headquarters. Immediately, Davis spoke with a friend, the owner of Tremont House, John B. Drake, the city's leading hotelier, a Republican, and partner in various enterprises in Chicago with Lincoln's backer Jacob Bunn, including the Chicago Secure Depository Company and the Chicago and Alton Railroad. (Drake's sons would establish the Drake and Blackstone hotels, still operating. The Drake, on the "Magnificent Mile," is located on land that was at issue in the "Sandbar" case.) Drake's Tremont hotel was booked, but Davis paid guests in adjoining rooms to leave. A sign was affixed to the door: "Illinois Headquarters." From the window Davis could see a banner hung on the building of the *Chicago Journal* across the street: "SEWARD." "Here without anybody electing him to the position, he at once became the leader of all the Illinois men," recalled Leonard Swett of Davis. "He told me when I arrived there Monday to join his staff and go to work, and if everybody would also work, the nomination could be made."

Davis created a political machine overnight, marshaling the Illinois delegates and alternates; the entourage of the Eighth Judicial Circuit, including Jesse Fell, Leonard Swett, William Herndon, Stephen Trigg Logan, and Ward Hill Lamon; Illinois state officials Ozias M. Hatch, secretary of state; Jesse Dubois, state auditor; and William Butler, state treasurer; editors of the *Chicago Press and Tribune* and other Illinois journalists; and Mark Delahay, Lincoln's distant cousin from Kansas, whose expenses Lincoln personally paid. A close friend of Davis, John Z. Goodrich, a former congressman and newspaper editor from western Massachusetts, and member of the Republican National Committee, moved into the Tremont House to help. Taylor Hawkins, an influential Iowa delegate, the mayor of Keokuk, and an old friend of Lincoln from his childhood in Kentucky, joined the group.

Judd and Davis put aside their antagonism to labor together in common cause. "Long John" Wentworth was the outrider, angry that Lincoln had named Judd and not him as a delegate, and out of resentment and mischief sent the police on raids of the extensive whorehouses to arrest delegates. He loudly talked up Seward in hotel lobbies. Davis, who had been pressing Wentworth on Lincoln, assigned a man to shadow him everywhere to rebut him.

"No one ever thought of questioning Davis' right to send men hither and thither, nor to question his judgment," said Swett. The Illinoisans "worked like Turks for Lincoln's nomination," William A. Jayne, Lincoln's old friend, personal physician, and a state senator, reported to Trumbull. "Judge Davis is furious," Dubois wrote Lincoln. "Never saw him work so hard and so quiet in all my life."

"He seated himself behind a big table in the rooms of the headquarters and organized committees of visitation to the various delegations, and did the other work of the convention," recalled Swett. "For instance, he had Samuel C. Parks, of

David Davis

Logan, who was born in Vermont, organize a delegation of about four, also from Vermont, to visit the delegates from that State; and he had me, from the State of Maine, organize a delegation, and visit my old friends from the Pine Tree State, and every man was to come back and report to him. And so he labored with all, issued his orders to all, and knew the situation of every delegation." Native Kentuckians Logan and Richard Yates, the Illinois Republican candidate for governor, were sent to the Kentucky delegation; Lamon, the native Virginian, to the Virginians. "No men ever worked as our boys did. I did not, the whole week I was there, sleep two hours a night," wrote Swett.

"The gods help those who help themselves," editorialized the *Press and Tribune*. "Illinois is bound by all considerations of self defense to labor for the man who can bring her to the land of promise, and so she will be found laboring in the Chicago Convention." For the benefit of delegates, the paper published the results of the race for the Senate: Lincoln, 125,275 votes; Douglas, 121,190.

"Availability" was the word most frequently bandied about the candidates. It meant electability. The case for Lincoln as the most available man was seemingly paradoxical. He was as principled as Seward on slavery, their positions indistinguishable, and Lincoln's "house divided" statement preceded Seward's controversial "irrepressible conflict" one, but Lincoln was perceived as the moderate and Seward the radical. Lincoln was also not a nativist, unlike Bates, and yet acceptable to nativists, unlike Seward. The *Press and Tribune* spelled out the Lincoln strategy for the convention in two editorials. Under the headline, "The Winning Man—Abraham Lincoln," the paper stated on May 15, "Without a stain of Know-Nothingism on his skirts, he is acceptable to the mass of the American party." In a prescient article the next day on "The Doubtful States," it published the vote totals of Pennsylvania, New Jersey, Indiana, and Illinois from the 1856 presidential election to show that if the Fillmore votes were combined with those for Frémont they would constitute majorities in those states. "A nomination which will drive the Fillmore vote over to John Bell must necessarily prove fatal to the Republican ticket. Who has the hardiness to affirm that Mr. Seward is popular with the Fillmore men? Or that he is the best candidate to secure their support."

Lincoln's team ruthlessly exploited his rivals' vulnerabilities to demonstrate their unavailability. The discrediting of Bates created a vacuum that lifted Lincoln and forced a choice between Lincoln and Seward. In the two-man contest, the availability question became acute and the momentum rushed to the least tainted.

Bates was a dignified and passive candidate taken up by Francis P. Blair and his sons in order to block Seward. Blair, the old Jacksonian Democrat, had viewed Seward, the preeminent Whig, as the partisan enemy for decades. But mostly he thought that in an election that the Republicans ought to win, Seward was the Republican most likely to lose. Blair hoped to make Bates the candidate as he had made John C. Frémont the candidate in 1856. But Frémont had a romantic heroic image, was a member of the Blair extended family through his marriage to Jesse Benton, and had no real opposition for the nomination once Seward decided he would wait for his chance in 1860. Bates had endorsed the opponent of Francis P. Blair, Jr., when he ran for the Congress as a Republican in 1858, but the Blairs were not about to let that slight get in the way of having an available candidate of their own.

"Dined with F.P. Blair Jr.," read Bates's diary for April 27, 1859—"a confidential conference" of "influential leaders" to "adopt me." They "say," Bates recorded, "that Mr. Seward cannot get the nomination of his party, perhaps not because he is not the acknowledged head of the party and entitled to the lead, but because the party is not quite strong enough to triumph alone; and his nomination therefore would ensure defeat."

But Bates's supposed strength was also his weakness. He was raised up as a candidate on his negative capability, being not a Republican, which was touted as his pulling power to unreconstructed Old Whigs, Know Nothings, and the softest of Republicans. Bates's personal politics were those of the Constitutional Unionists, and he even had hoped for their nomination. The flaw in his strategy was that his appeal to nativist prejudice did not cut only one way.

The German Americans were a decisive voting bloc in the swing states; their leadership was highly organized and they drew a red line against Bates. Failing to account for the Germans as potent political actors revealed incomprehensible blindness on the part of the Bates team. His candidacy was headed straight for the rocks. During the two days before the convention, on May 14 and 15, the Conference of the Germans at the Deutsches Haus in Chicago raised an ultimatum that the Republican candidate could not be nativist in any way, shape, or form, and proscribed Bates.

The movement against Bates that lead to the ultimatum at the conference began with the Iowa Republican clubs, which passed resolutions on March 7 reading: "Whereas, therefore, Edward Bates has shown himself to be an approver and supporter of the plans and measures of the Pro-Slavery Know-Nothings, and a disapprover and opponent of the Republican principles. . . . Resolved, that the nomination of Edward Bates as the Republican candidate for the Presidency would imply a desertion from Republican principles and that we, therefore, under no circumstances will vote for the Hon. Edward Bates." The German Republicans of Ohio, meeting in Cincinnati, called for the pre-convention conference.

The Illinois Republican convention at Decatur that endorsed Lincoln had adopted a two-point platform at his direction, one of which was in favor of a Homestead Act and the other against the nativist restrictions against immigrants, specifically the Massachusetts law that denied voting rights to naturalized citizens for two years after they had become Americans. "That we are in favor of giving full and efficient protection to all the rights of all citizens, at home and abroad, without regard to the place of their birth. That our naturalization laws, having been enacted by the Fathers of the Revolution and the Constitution, and being just in principle, we are opposed to any change being made in them intended to enlarge the time now required to secure the rights of citizenship under them, and that the State Legislatures should pass no law discriminating between native born and naturalized citizens in the exercise of the right of suffrage."

The Illinois platform was the high standard for German Republicans. It was well-known among them that it was Lincoln's platform. It was equally well-known to them that the Philadelphia Platform of the 1856 convention was exactly the formula that Lincoln had approved in the founding document of the Illinois Republican Party. The German Republican Club of New York had already called on German Republicans across the country to endorse a common platform based on the principles expressed in Philadelphia. That platform was proposed there by George Schneider of the *Illinois Staats-Zeitung* newspaper. Schneider himself was at the conference at Deutsches Haus; so were other forceful Illinois Germans aligned with Lincoln, including Friedrich Hecker, whose burned house was rebuilt on funds Lincoln had raised, and Gustave Koerner, Lincoln's chosen delegate-at-large. But these pro-Lincoln German connections were invisible to those nativists worried about Seward's long anti-nativist record and who saw Lincoln as more acceptable. Meanwhile, introducing the German factor into the nomination battle would prove devastating to Bates's claim to be the most "available" and sharpened the contest between Lincoln and Seward.

Bates's most visible promoter on the scene was the mercurial Horace

Greeley, mounting his own stop-Seward movement. The editor of the most influential national Republican newspaper was a malcontent, an idealist, and given to enthusiasms that he fooled himself into thinking showed his superior pragmatism. In a rage over not being slated years ago as lieutenant governor by Weed and Seward, passed over for none other than Henry J. Raymond of the *Times,* Greeley was set on revenge and thought of himself as adopting the methods of Weed against Seward. Before the convention he dispatched reporters north and west to spread the word that Seward could not win. Yet he perversely stopped at Weed's house in Albany on his way to Chicago and left the impression he would support Seward. Greeley managed to get himself credentialed as a Bates delegate from Oregon. He was ubiquitous in the hotels and on the streets, arguing as he told the Kansas delegation, "So, to name Seward, is to invite defeat." "He was not idle a moment, and, wherever he happened to be, was surrounded by a gaping crowd," recalled Isaac Hill Bromley, an editor of the *New York Tribune,* who was present in Chicago. Henry J. Raymond, editor of the *New York Times* and a Seward stalwart, wrote, "Mr. Greeley labored harder, and did tenfold more, than the whole family of Blairs . . . and he devoted every hour of the interval to the most steady and relentless prosecution of the main business which took him thither,—the defeat of Governor Seward. He labored personally with the delegates as they arrived,—commending himself always to their confidence by professions of regard and the most zealous friendship for Governor Seward, but presenting defeat, even in New York, as the inevitable result of his nomination." Greeley was effective against Seward, but ineffectual for Bates. "We let Greeley run his Bates machine," said Swett, "but got most of them for a second choice." Bromley observed that as the stooped and bright-eyed Greeley buttonholed delegates, "Some mischievous fellow pinned a Seward badge on his coattail; it amused the crowd for a moment without giving him the slightest disturbance."

Another editor from the *New York Tribune,* Abram J. Dittenhoefer, who traipsed with Greeley among the delegates, concluded

from my intimacy with Mr. Greeley, that the factor which had the most to do with Seward's defeat was the fear of Henry S. Lane, Republican candidate for Governor of Indiana, and of Andrew G. Curtin, Republican candidate for Governor of Pennsylvania, that Seward could not carry these two States. This weakness would not only insure defeat of the Presidential ticket, but would carry down with it the aspirations of these two Gubernatorial candidates. I talked with both of these able politicians on the subject, and the reasons they gave for their opposition to Seward were that he had antagonized the Protestant element of the country and the remnants of the old "Know Nothing party" by his advocacy, in a message to the New York Legislature, of a division of the school funds between Catholic parochial schools and the common or public schools of the States in proportion to the number of Catholics and non-Catholics. How much ground there was for the anxiety of Lane and Curtin I have never been able to settle in my mind. Whether they were unduly alarmed or not, the dissemination of these views among the delegates created a noticeable weakening on the part of Seward's friends.

Neither Indiana nor Pennsylvania was a Republican state. In Pennsylvania, the label of Republican was still too controversial and the party was called the People's Party. Both elections were to be held in October. The combined vote of the Republicans and the Know Nothings in both states exceeded that of the Democrats. Both Lane and Curtin "were looking solely to their own success in October, and their success meant the success of the Republican party in the nation," wrote Alexander K. McClure, a Pennsylvania politician close to Curtin. "I was with Curtin and interested as he was only in his individual success, as he had summoned me to take charge of his October battle in Pennsylvania. The one thing that Curtin, Lane, and their respective lieutenants agreed upon was that the nomination of Seward meant hopeless defeat." Both Lane and Curtin were unbothered that Lincoln might appear radical, even more radical than Seward. The insuperable problem with Seward was that he had proposed state funding of Catholic schools, "on that single question when Governor of New York that made him an impossible candidate for President in 1860."

Indiana was the first target of the Lincoln men, who had a network of contacts in the neighboring state. Lincoln had already begun the process in response to a letter from Cyrus M. Allen, a lawyer from Vincennes and convention delegate, who wrote Lincoln in April with the intelligence that the delegation would be unpledged, arrive early, and open to hearing from him. Lincoln replied that Jesse Dubois and David Davis would meet him in Chicago. As soon as Davis came to the city he launched into private meetings with the Indiana delegation, intensive talks that continued day after day.

"Things are working admirably well now," Delahay wrote Lincoln on Monday, May 14. "The Stock is gradually 'rising.' Indiana is all right. . . .

Penna says we can't give our vote for Seward. N York in return says N York will not go Cameron, and they whisper, that a man with Democratic antecedents can't be nominated for Pres—this all to my mind looks as well as we could wish." William Butler wrote Lincoln that day, "Your chances are brightening, Illinois, Indiana, Iowa Maine and New Hampshire will present a solid front for you as they stand this morning. Ohio and Pennsylvania divided. Ohio inclining for you." Within hours Butler sent another dispatch. "The Pennsylvania and New York delegates are quarreling," he wrote. "The Pennsylvania delegation will not go for Mr. Seward under no circumstances. They tell us to stand fast never go to Mr. Seward they are much excited—The New York men tell us to stand firm, don't go to Mr. Cameron. The respective delegations from New York and Pennsylvania have both proposed to run you for Vice President. We have persistently refused to suffer your name used for Vice President on any ticket. Things yet looks favorable, though I can't tell what things turn it may take. Prospects looks bright for you."

Joseph Medill, editor of the *Chicago Press and Tribune,* told Lincoln biographer Ida M. Tarbell that "half the Indiana delegation had been won for Lincoln on the ground of availability before the convention met." Swett, however, stated Indiana "came to us unitedly" and "acted efficiently with us" by then. Charles H. Ray, publisher of the *Press and Tribune,* claimed that to secure Indiana's support he had traded a cabinet post for Caleb B. Smith and Indian commissioner for William P. Dole. "We are going to have Indiana for Old Abe, sure," he says he told Davis. "How did you get it?" "By the Lord," he explained, "we promised them everything they asked." Jesse Fell, however, said that "a disposition of favors was a good deal spoken of at Chicago, in a quiet way, though of course no improper pledges . . . were asked . . . and [they] could not be given." Caleb Smith, an Old Whig who had served with Lincoln in the Congress, confirmed Fell's account of a suggestive method. "The Republicans of [Indiana] generally supposed that Mr. L. would select some man from this state for a place in his cabinet."

Overly enthusiastic and impatient, Ray wrote Lincoln on the 14th, in a communiqué he marked "Profoundly Private," "Your friends are at work for you hard, and with great success. Your show on the first ballot will not be confined to Illinois, and after that it will be strongly developed. But you need a few trusty friends here to say words for you that may be necessary to be said. Dast you put yourself in the hands of Judd, David Davis, and, if there is no better man, Ray? A pledge or two may be necessary when the pinch comes."

The impulse to cut deals may have been inspired as an attempt to equal the wiles of Thurlow Weed, who held forth in his packed parlor at the Richmond House pouring a bottomless supply of champagne and handing out an endless supply of cigars, surrounded by "a crowd of men, some of whom did not strike me as desirable companions," as Carl Schurz recalled. He came to Weed's suite as a leader of the Wisconsin delegation pledged to Seward and to get direction. "But we did not find there any of the distinguished members of that delegation whom we most wished to see—William M. Evarts, George William Curtis, Henry J. Raymond, Governor Morgan, and others." Instead he discovered a gaggle of New York politicians, "apparently of the lower sort, whom Thurlow Weed had brought with him to aid him in doing his work. What that work consisted in I could guess from the conversations I was permitted to hear, for they talked very freely about the great services they had rendered or were going to render. . . . Among these men Thurlow Weed moved as the great captain, with ceaseless activity and noiseless step, receiving their reports and giving new instructions in his peculiar whisper, now and then taking one into a corner of the room for secret talk, or disappearing with another through a side door for transactions still more secret."

Weed's operation was reinforced with thirteen cars packed with two thousand Seward "irrepressibles" from New York that pulled into the Chicago station "singing songs not found in hymn-books." Murat Halstead, who arrived with the contingent, wrote, "The number of private bottles on our train last night was something surprising. . . . I do not feel competent to state the precise proportions of those who are drunk, and those who are sober."

The New York boosters marched around the streets led by the tall figure of Tom Hyer, the first recognized heavyweight champion boxer, who won his title in a 101-round match in 1841, and although he last held the title in 1851 he was the biggest celebrity at the convention. There was a political reason beyond his pugilistic fame that Weed brought Hyer as the drum major of the Seward parades in Chicago. He was the hero of the nativist gangs of New York, had been a street thug for Seward's sworn enemies, and an enforcer for the Know Nothings. His presence was Weed's symbolic way of signaling to those from states with swing Know Nothing voters that Seward was acceptable. Hyer was spotted towering in any crowd. He had adopted the dress of a dandy complete a silk top hat. (In February 1861, he attended a reception at Astor House in honor of President-elect Lincoln.)

The New York crowd intended to create a clamorous momentum for

Seward had the reverse effect of reminding those wary of Weed of their reservations. James G. Blaine, a member of the Maine legislature and the protégé of Senator William Pitt Fessenden, wrote him "that the Seward force is on the ground and assumes an air of dictation which is at once unwarranted and offensive, and which I think will create a reaction before Wednesday." Before the convention began, Blaine observed, "I do not myself believe that he will be nominated, though a great many here think otherwise. If he is not, I will adhere to the opinion I expressed to you in Portland, that the game lies between Lincoln and yourself—Chase, McLean, Banks, and Bates stand no chance."

The head of the Connecticut delegation, Gideon Welles, a former Democrat and Free Soiler who was the editor of the *Hartford Press,* wrote, "It was the misfortune of Mr. Seward that he was associated with and the candidate of the most offensive lobby combination of that date. He was not accused or suspected of receiving pecuniary benefit himself from the practices of that class of jobbing party lobbyists, but he was thought to be indifferent if not assenting to their practices, and was their candidate. . . . But there was a large element—the result showed a very decided majority—of the Republicans averse to any nomination or movement which would tend to transfer Albany intrigues to Washington, and introduce the debasing practices on the Hudson into our national politics."

Weed invited Henry S. Lane of Indiana to dinner, where, according to Mrs. Lane, who was present, he pleaded with him to direct Indiana to vote for Seward, "saying they would send enough money from New York to ensure his election for Governor." Mrs. Lane later wrote, "His proposal was indignantly rejected."

Then Weed sent Senator Preston King of New York to meet with William Butler to make him an offer he thought he could not refuse. King brought with him a man named "Mr. Street." "Mr. Street," Butler wrote Lincoln on May 15, "soon entered into what he termed a confidential conversation." He said he was "authorized to say if Illinois would consent to have Mr. Lincoln's name placed on the ticket in connection with Mr. Seward, that an arrangement could be made" to pass $100,000, "placed in the proper hands," to "carry Illinois and Indiana." Butler told him that "under no circumstances could your name be used in a second place." He added, "I am a little afraid of this element." Weed offered similar sums to other delegations and to other vice president possibilities. He approached Simon Cameron through Alexander Cummings, editor of the *Philadelphia Bulletin.* "The flood of Seward money promised for Pennsylvania was not without efficacy," wrote Halstead. "The phrase used was, that Seward's friends 'would *spend oceans of money.*'"

Orville Browning arrived later in Chicago than the other old Lincoln friends, on Tuesday, May 15. Formally pledged to Lincoln, he was still pining for Bates. "Oh, if Lincoln would withdraw, as he should do, we could nominate that great statesman, Edward Bates, of Missouri," he told Thomas J. Pickett, editor of the *Rock Island Register,* who was an Illinois delegate and ardent Lincoln man. "But as it is," Browning said, "of course Seward will be nominated." "I saw Browning at Chicago: he was first for Bates," recalled David Davis. "I told him there was no earthly chance for him—Bates." Davis immediately put Browning to work for Lincoln. He brought Browning with him to give speeches on Lincoln's superior "availability" to the Maine, New Hampshire, and Massachusetts delegations. The natural Bates leader in Illinois became the Old Whig testifying for Lincoln as the only candidate who could carry Illinois.

While Weed was promising large piles of cash, Davis received word that the New Jersey delegation was being swept with the suggestion from the Seward campaign that Lincoln should be the number two on the ticket in order to deflate his prospects. "Palmer," Davis instructed John M. Palmer, "you must go with me at once to see the New Jersey delegation." Palmer, a former Democrat, told the key New Jersey delegate, a judge that Davis knew, "'Sir, you may nominate Mr. Lincoln for Vice-President if you please. But I want you to understand that there are 40,000 Democrats in Illinois who will support this ticket if you give them an opportunity. We are not Whigs, and we never expect to be Whigs. We will never consent to support two old Whigs on this ticket. We are willing to vote for Mr. Lincoln with a Democrat on the ticket, but we will not consent to vote for two Whigs." "Will they do as Palmer says?" the judge asked Davis. "Oh," he replied, "oh, Judge, you can't account for the conduct of these old Locofocos," referring to them with the old derogatory name Whigs gave to Jacksonian Democrats. "Certainly. There are 40,000 of them, and, as Palmer says, not one of them will vote for two Whigs." Palmer waited until he and Davis returned to the Tremont House to tell him, "Davis, you are an infernal rascal." "Judge Davis said nothing, but chuckled as if he had greatly enjoyed the joke," Palmer recalled. "This incident is illustrative of the kind of work we had to do. We were compelled to resort to this argument—that the old Democrats then ready to affiliate with the Republican party would not tolerate two Whigs on the ticket—in order to break up the movement to nominate Lincoln for

Vice-President. The Seward men recognized in Lincoln their most formidable rival, and that was why they wished to get him out of the way by giving him second place on the ticket."

"We are quiet but moving heaven and earth," Davis and Dubois wired Lincoln the day before the convention opened. "Nothing will beat us but old fogy politicians. The heart of the delegates are with us." Butler wrote Lincoln with some intelligence: "[Thaddeus] Stevens of Pennsylvania says with Mr. Seward Pennsylvania is lost. [W]ith Mr. Lincoln or Mr. McLean they can carry it by 20,000. Stevens is instructed for Cameron but frankly says it will not do. I must stop everything. All is confusion & noise. I will keep you advised as well as I can."

The proceedings began on Wednesday, May 16, in a brick and wooden structure that could hold at least ten thousand people and was topped on its arch with letters reading: "REPUBLICAN WIGWAM." It was the largest indoor space in the country, built in short order for the event itself, considered a marvel, an example of the will and muscle of Chicago. "Around the front of the gallery," reported the *Press and Tribune,* "are the coats of arms of the States, and between them wreathes of evergreen. The pillars and supports have been painted white, and wreathed with evergreens, and from each to each have been twined draperies in red, white and blue, with artificial flowers and miniature national flags. The pillars supporting roof, which form a continuous row along the front of the platform, bear, on the side to the audience, busts of distinguished men, supported by figures of Atlas. . . . The brick wall at the rear has been painted and divided into arched panels, in which are colossal statuary paintings. Over the center of the state is suspended a large gilt eagle." Above the stage hung a star-studded banner with two blanks: "For President—For Vice-President—."

Just past noon, Norman Judd, on behalf of the host committee, presented the chairman, George Ashmun, a former Whig congressman from Massachusetts, with a gavel made from an oak plank of Commodore Perry's ship and inlaid with ivory and silver. Judd gave a little speech reciting the vessel's motto—"Don't give up the ship"—and Perry's famous utterance—"We have met the enemy, and they are ours." As Judd gazed out on the sea of delegates he could see them seated under their state banners. "I superintended the arrangements of the seats," he later explained. He put New York on the right, with "New England, Wisconsin, Minnesota, and all the strong Seward States around her. On the other side I put Illinois, Pennsylvania, and Indiana, and Missouri, and grouped around these the delegates from the border States,

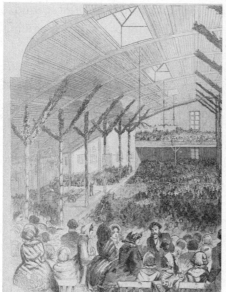

The Wigwam, site of the Republican convention, 1860

and all the small doubtful delegations. The advantage of the arrangement was, that when the active excitement and canvassing in the Convention came on, the Seward men couldn't get over among the doubtful delegations at all to log-roll with them, being absolutely hemmed in by their own followers who were not likely to be swerved from their set preference for Seward." He had anticipated a hard-fought, multiple ballot nomination and insured that Seward's forces would be landlocked, unable to bargain and cajole on the convention floor.

On Thursday morning, May 17, the Seward men wearing their Seward badges massed four abreast behind sporting man Tom Hyer and a brass band playing the popular tune "O Isn't He a Darling?" to tramp in impressive soldierly display through downtown to the Wigwam. "The Pennsylvanians declare, if Seward were nominated, they would be immediately ruined," reported Halstead. "New Jerseyites say the same thing. The Indianians are of the same opinion. They look heart-broken at the suggestion that Seward has the inside track, and throw up their hands in despair. . . . Illinois agonizes at the mention of the name of Seward, and says he is to them the sting of political death. Amid all these cries of distress, the Sewardites are true as steel to their champion, and they will cling to 'Old Irrepressible,' as they call him, until the last gun is fired and the big bell rings."

The bell began to toll for Bates with the passage of the platform. Carl Schurz and George Schneider cosponsored an anti-nativist resolution: "The Republican party is opposed to any change in our naturalization laws, or any State legislation, by which the rights of citizenship heretofore accorded to immigrants from foreign lands shall be abridged or impaired, and is in favor of giving a full and sufficient protection to all classes of citizens, whether native or naturalized, both at home and abroad." The only fireworks over the platform came from the omission of the opening lines of the Declaration of Independence, which had appeared in the 1856 platform, prompting a threatened walkout by Joshua R. Giddings of Ohio, who had been working against Seward, but were added out of respect for his leonine presence and embarrassment over the words' exclusion, and the document was approved unanimously. "A herd of buffaloes or lions could not have made a more tremendous roaring," wrote Halstead.

Throughout the day, the Seward forces had repulsed a series of procedural motions for anything but a majority vote on the nominee. At noon, a hurried caucus convened at the Cameron Hotel in the rooms of representatives of the four "doubtful states," which were panicked about Seward's imminent nomination. Andrew Reeder, of Pennsylvania, the fugitive territorial governor of Kansas, presided as chairman of the meeting. Thomas H. Dudley, the state chairman for New Jersey, proposed to Judd that a working group of three delegates from each of the states try to settle on one candidate. The Committee of Twelve included David Davis and Caleb Smith of Indiana, who was for Lincoln.

"So confident were the Seward men, when the platform was adopted, of their ability to nominate their great leader, that they urged an immediate ballot, and would have had it if the clerks had not reported that they were unprovided with tally-sheets," Halstead reported. An unknown voice shouted, "This convention adjourn until ten o'clock tomorrow morning." The convention adjourned with the Seward men in "high feather," without a "particle of doubt of his nomination in the morning." That evening Weed laid out a banquet at the Richmond House with three hundred bottles of champagne, bands, and Tom Hyer.

Davis and the Illinois men, gathered in their headquarters at the Tremont House, received an urgent message from Lincoln. Down in Springfield, Edward L. Baker, editor of the *Illinois State Journal,* had become alarmed at an article in the *Missouri Democrat*, which was pro-Bates, that stated Lincoln was as radical as Seward. Lincoln wrote on the margin of the paper, "I agree with Seward in his 'Irrepressible Conflict,' but I do not endorse his 'Higher Law' doctrine." He added a line against making hard and fast deals, perhaps in reaction against Ray's self-important letter three days earlier urging him to invest Ray and the others with the power to cut such deals: "Make no contracts that will bind me."

Lincoln placed the newspaper with his handwritten notes into Baker's hand and sent him at once on the train to Chicago. When the messenger appeared at the Tremont House, he was not warmly greeted. "Damn Lincoln!" said Jesse Dubois. Leonard Swett said, "I am very sure if Lincoln was aware of the necessities—" "Lincoln ain't here," said Davis with finality, "and don't know what we have to meet, so we will go ahead, as if we hadn't heard from him, and he must ratify it!" Herndon, who was there, too, wrote that Lincoln did not "appreciate the gravity of the situation," and Davis "went ahead with his negotiations."

Lane of Indiana and Curtin of Pennsylvania were both committed to Lincoln. The rumor was rife that if Seward was nominated, they would not campaign for the ticket. "Henry S. Lane, candidate in Indiana, did say something of the kind," reported Halstead. "He asserted hundreds of times that the nomination of Seward would be death to him, and that he might in that case just as well give up the canvass." The Indiana delegation was working hand in glove with Davis. But the Pennsylvania one was split between Curtin and Cameron, who were enemies. Cameron had defeated Curtin for the U.S. Senate seat in 1855, in a "desperate factional battle" that "left wounds which were yet fresh and inspired the bitterest hostility," recalled Alexander K. McClure, Curtin's campaign manager. After dinner on the 17th, the Indiana and Pennsylvania delegations met at the Cook County Court House to try to work out a common position. It was not a closed meeting and the room was filled with other delegates and Chicagoans.

"The Bates men, having learned of this meeting, appeared there in force, and [Frank] Blair had already commenced making a speech for Bates when word was sent to our headquarters of what was going on," recalled Gustave Koerner. Davis instantly dispatched Koerner and Browning to the scene. When Koerner announced he had come to speak for Lincoln "the cheers almost shook the court house." He pointed out that Bates had presided at the convention in 1856 that nominated Fillmore and was supported by the Know Nothings and had backed the Know Nothings in local St. Louis elections. "I would tell this meeting in all candor that if Bates was nominated, the German Republicans in the other States would never vote for him; I for one would not, and I would advise my countrymen to the same effect." Browning, "from a Whig Standpoint," stepped up to credential Lincoln as an Old Whig who ought to receive Old Whig votes, but "had always opposed Native Americanism. This would secure him the foreign Republican vote all over the country." Koerner wrote, "The delegates then held a secret session, and we soon learned that Indiana would go for Lincoln at the start, and that a large majority of the Pennsylvanians had agreed to vote for him for their second choice."

At the same time, the Committee of Twelve was meeting in the rooms of David Wilmot of Pennsylvania. Most of the New Jersey delegation was still backing its favorite son, William Dayton, who had been the nominee for vice president in 1856. After four hours of indecision, Horace Greeley popped in, learned that there was no resolution, and sent a telegram to his paper: "Chicago, Thursday, May 17—11:40 P.M.—My conclusion, from all that I can gather to-night, is, that the opposition to Gov. Seward cannot concentrate on any candidate, and that he will be nominated. H. G."

But once Greeley left, the crisis point was reached. The men went around the room to reveal their counts if their favorite sons were to drop out. Lincoln was clearly the strongest candidate. Dudley of New Jersey proposed that his delegation would end its support for Dayton and vote for Lincoln on the second ballot if Pennsylvania would do the same. The Pennsylvanians agreed in principle. According to Dudley, they also agreed to offer the vice presidency to Congressman Henry Winter Davis, of Maryland, who had been a Know Nothing and was David Davis's first cousin; but in the morning, he refused the honor.

Even later that night, Davis, Swett, and a few other trusted Lincoln men met at the Tremont House with a negotiating team of Pennsylvanians led by a friend of Cameron's, Judge Joseph Casey. Casey put his cards on the table at the start—secretary of the treasury. Whatever the language, he left the room certain he had an understanding. Casey wrote Cameron: "It was only done after everything was arranged carefully and unconditionally in reference to Yourself—to our satisfaction—and we *drove* the anti-Cameron men from this state into it." Swett would later insist that "no pledges have been made, no mortgages executed." After the meeting, in the Tremont lobby, Davis told the editors of the *Chicago Press and Tribune,* "Damned if we haven't got them." Asked how he had "got them," he replied, "By paying their price." He sent a telegram to Lincoln, "Am very hopeful. Don't be excited. Nearly dead with fatigue. Telegraph or write here very little."

Lane also came and went from the Tremont. "I saw Henry S. Lane at one o'clock, pale and haggard, with cane under his arm, walking as if for a wager, from one caucus-room to another, at the Tremont House," reported Halstead. "He had been toiling with desperation to bring the Indiana delegation to go as a unit for Lincoln. And then in connection with others, he had been operating to bring the Vermonters and Virginians to the point of deserting Seward."

The morning edition of the *Chicago Press and Tribune* featured an urgent plea to nominate the candidate with the greatest "availability" in the "doubtful States." Under the headline addressed to the delegates, Lincoln's paper wrote: "That with a victory within our grasp, if that prudence is exercised which the crisis demands, there should be any number of delegates, who, for the sake of promoting the fortunes and gratifying the ambition of any living man, dare to stake all upon the contingency of a Democratic disruption, rather than throw themselves back upon the certain and reliable strength of the party opposed to the extension of Human Slavery, is too monstrous for belief."

Daylight broke on the last day of the convention, Friday, May 18, the day of the nomination, but the Pennsylvania delegation had not rested. Some delegates had agreed upon a resolution that the whole delegation should vote as a unit on the first ballot for Cameron and then by a majority vote continue to cast its vote as a unit. But a few didn't want to vote for Cameron at all. At a caucus meeting at nine o'clock that morning Curtin, who was Cameron's adversary, gave a passionate speech for the unit rule. It took some time for the delegates to walk to the Wigwam.

The Seward throng gathered bright and early for their march behind Tom Hyer and a brass band to their choice seats in the Wigwam. The Lincoln men were anxious that the best tickets were being monopolized for Seward. The son of Jesse Fell recounted, "Father and the rest of the Committee had a rush meeting, at which it developed that through some underhand work that all the Seward adherents had been furnished tickets of admission and that if they all got in there would be no room for the Lincoln 'rooters.' So father suggested that he would have plenty more tickets printed, and that they would be put in the hands of their friends, at the same time cautioning their friends to be on hand early—which was done. Amongst some of the first New York tickets presented at the door were some that were not regular, and as a consequence, the door-keepers held them back until father could be seen, and meanwhile the Lincoln friends were getting the seats, and had done it so well that they concluded to let technicalities go and admit all those holding tickets." Another Illinois man, Henry M. Russell, who had been head of the delegation from Urbana at the state convention and come to Chicago to assist the Davis group, recalled that he had helped "organize a coup which on bogus visitors' tickets gained 300 Illinois rooters admission to the Wigwam on the last morning of the convention, and at the same time denied entrance to an equal number of jubilant New Yorkers who, after parading the Chicago streets headed by a bass band, planned to march into the hall and shout for Seward." Inside the hall, Davis directed Dick Oglesby, who had invented "The Railsplitter," and had "very stout lungs," to "fill the body of the building where the public were admitted, with a strong-voiced brigade of shouters," according to Leonard Swett.

After the invocation and rap of the chairman's gavel, the Pennsylvania delegation came in through a side door to find their seats occupied by squatting spectators. Once the interlopers were routed, William Evarts of New York arose to declare, "Sir, I take the liberty to name as the candidate to be nominated by this convention for the office of President of the United States, William H. Seward." Halstead recorded the decibel level: "Hundreds of persons stopped their ears in pain. The shouting was absolutely frantic, shrill and wild. No Camanches, no panthers ever struck a higher note, or gave screams with more infernal intensity." Then Judd put Lincoln's name into nomination, the signal for the leather lung shouters. "Imagine all the hogs ever slaughtered in Cincinnati giving their death squeals together, a score of big steam whistles going (steam at 160 lbs. per inch), and you conceive something of the same nature. I thought the Seward yell could not be surpassed; but the Lincoln boys were clearly ahead, and feeling their victory, as there was a lull in the storm, took deep breaths all round, and gave a concentrated shriek that was positively awful, and accompanied it with stamping that made every plank and pillar in the building quiver." Henry Lane jumped on a table, "swinging hat and cane, performed like an acrobat."

On the first ballot, Seward was in first place with 173½, but Lincoln was second at 102, just where the Illinois strategy wanted him to be. Bates had 48, Cameron 50½, Chase 49, Dayton 14, McLean 10, Collamer of Vermont 10, and a few others. Seward's totals in a few key states were less than expected. Indiana went for Lincoln, "a startler"—Caleb B. Smith had seconded his nomination—and it became apparent that the momentum was running against Seward.

On the second ballot, Seward immediately took losses in New Hampshire and Vermont, where he could not afford any depletion, and four of Greeley's "Oregon boys" shifted from Bates to Lincoln. Then Pennsylvania announced 48 votes for Lincoln. "The New Yorkers started as if an Orsini bomb had exploded." The convention secretary declared the results: Seward 184½, Lincoln 181, Bates 35, Chase 42½, Dayton 10, and a few scattered votes. Seward had gained a bit, but the holdouts were inclined to Lincoln. The inevitable suddenly came into clear sight.

Without stop the roll of states was called for the third ballot. "Massachusetts!" Four switched from Seward to Lincoln. "Pennsylvania!" Four more switched to Lincoln. "Maryland!" All four Bates delegates and one for Seward switched to Lincoln. (The hidden hand of the Blairs was moving.) "Ohio!" Chase's vote collapsed, 14 defected from his base and one for McLean shifting to Lincoln. Lincoln was now 1½ short of the nomination. "Greeley saw it," wrote Tarbell, "and a guileless smile spread over his features as he watched Thurlow Weed press his hand hard against his wet eyelids."

Joseph Medill of the *Press and Tribune* had insinuated himself in a seat on the convention floor amid the Ohio delegation, next to the state chairman, David Cartter, and whispered in his ear, "If you can throw the Ohio delegation to Lincoln, Chase can have anything he wants." Cartter paused, called for recognition, and spoke in his stutter. "I-I a-arise, Mr. Chairman, to a-announce the c-change of f-four votes, from Mr. Chase to Abraham Lincoln."

"The deed was done," wrote Halstead. "There was a moment's silence. The nerves of the thousands, which through the hours of suspense had been subjected to terrible tension, relaxed, and as deep breaths of relief were taken, there was a noise in the wigwam like the rush of a great wind, in the van of a storm—and, in another breath, the storm was there. There were thousands cheering with the energy of insanity." Cannons were fired on the roof of the Wigwam. Smoke and the smell of gunpowder wafted in through the open doors. A gigantic charcoal portrait of Lincoln was brought in and hung by the stage. One hundred guns were fired in salute at the Tremont House. "City wild with excitement. From my inmost heart I congratulate you," Jesse Fell wired Lincoln.

Weed was "completely unnerved by the result at Chicago" and burst into tears on the convention floor. He refused to be consulted on the vice presidency, "in a temper that indicated contempt for the action of the convention," recalled McClure. The sentiment was on the side of Cassius M. Clay, but the nomination went to Senator Hannibal Hamlin, of Maine, a former Democrat who had supported Seward, an obvious balance. McClure visited Weed in his rooms and "found him sullen, and offensive in both manner and ex-pression." Curtin saw Weed, too, "very rude, indeed." Weed bitterly accused Curtin of selfishness, "You have defeated the man who of all others was most revered by the people and wanted as President. You and Lane want to be elected, and to elect Lincoln you must elect yourselves."

Seward had expectantly awaited his anointment at his home in Auburn. "On the day when the convention was to ballot for a candidate, Cayuga county poured itself into Auburn," recalled his friend Henry Stanton. "The streets were full, and Mr. Seward's house and grounds overflowed with his admirers. . . . Flags were ready to be raised, and a loaded cannon was placed at the gate, whose pillars bore up two guardian lions." A messenger galloped up with the results of the first ballot. The crowd cheered. The messenger re-turned with the tally of the second ballot. "I shall be nominated on the next ballot," said Seward, and "the throng in the house applauded, and those on the lawn and in the street echoed the cheers." The messenger rode up again with another telegram: "Lincoln nominated. T.W." "Seward turned as pale as ashes. The sad tidings crept through the vast concourse. The flags were furled, the cannon was rolled away, and Cayuga county went home with a clouded brow."

Stanton believed that Seward never truly recovered from the trauma of his loss. "Mr. Seward felt his defeat at Chicago beyond all power of expres-sion, and he never forgave those who had actively contributed to produce it. In incensed moments he accused some men wrongfully, as he subsequently admitted. He was a good hater, and lay in wait to punish." About a year later, Secretary of State Seward raised objections to Lincoln's appointment of Carl Schurz to be minister to Spain. Schurz had been a stalwart Seward man at the convention, but Seward balked that his background as a revolutionary would not make him an effective diplomat to Bourbon Spain. Congressman John F. Potter, of New York, interceded for Schurz, telling him that reject-ing the worthy Schurz would be "a severe disappointment to a good many people." Seward leaped from his chair. "Disappointment! You speak to me of disappointment. To me, who was justly entitled to the Republican nom-ination for the presidency, and who had to stand aside and see it given to a little Illinois lawyer! You speak to me of disappointment!" (Schurz got the appointment.)

While Chicago was delirious in revelry at Lincoln's nomination, Davis and Judd pushed through the crowds in the street to see Weed at his hotel. They found him more sad than angry. He was, "for some purpose," going to

Iowa. They arranged for him to visit Springfield on his way east where they would introduce him to Lincoln. Weed came a week later, on May 24. "Mr. Lincoln and Mr. Weed," recalled Swett, about the two politicians, "naturally 'took to each other' from the very day they met."

Edward Bates received the news of Lincoln's nomination as an affront to his dignity. "Some of my friends who attended the Convention assure me," he wrote in his diary, "that the nomination of Mr. Lincoln took every body by surprise: That it was brought about by accident or trick, by which my pledged friends had to vote against me." He blamed "a few Germans . . . with their truculent boldness, scared the timid men of Ind[ian]a. into submission. Koerner went before the Ind[ian]a. Delegation and assured them that if Bates were nominated the Germans would bolt!" He believed that the Republicans would soon regret they had not chosen him. "I think they will soon be convinced, if they are not already, that they have committed a fatal blunder." Judd sent Browning to see Bates at St. Louis to ask him if he would campaign for Lincoln. Bates declined, explaining that "he thought it would be in very bad taste, and incompatible with the dignity of his character and position." But a month later he wrote an endorsement that was published in the *St. Louis Democrat*—"a great letter," declared Browning.

On the day that the struggle within the Wigwam reached its climax, Lincoln played handball against an alley wall with some boys. "This game makes my shoulders feel well," he said. Then he sat around in the law office of his friend, James C. Conkling, a former state legislator and member of the Republican State Central Committee, who just returned from helping out Davis in Chicago. They killed time speculating about the convention for two hours, before Lincoln remarked, "Well, Conkling, I believe I will go back to my office and practice law." Edward L. Baker, the *Illinois State Journal*'s editor, back from running his errand to Chicago for Lincoln, ran up the stairs to Lincoln's office with the first ballot result. Lincoln decided to get word on the next rounds in the office of the *Journal*. Baker stationed himself at the telegraph office. Soon, a wire arrived: "TO LINCOLN YOU ARE NOMINATED." Baker brought the telegram to the *Journal,* read it aloud, and led three cheers "for the next president." "He [Lincoln] received all with apparent coolness from the expressions playing upon his countenance," recalled a clerk in Lincoln's law office, Charles. "However, a close observer could detect strong emotions within." Lincoln announced he should leave to tell Mary. "I must go home. There is a little short woman there that is more interested in this matter than I am." People hearing of the news had already excitedly begun to gather in front of the newspaper. "Boys," said Lincoln, "you had better come and shake hands with me now that you have an opportunity—for you do not know what influence this nomination may have on me. I am human, you know." "I can see him now as he went away," one of Lincoln's old friends, John Carmody, recalled. "He leaned forward and walked mighty fast. The boy that went with him had to run almost to keep up with him."

Lincoln's Right Hand, cast by Leonard Volk

In the late afternoon Lincoln saw a man walking down the street toward his house and went out to greet him. "His face looked radiant," wrote Leonard Volk, who had already been on the train headed to Springfield while Lincoln was being nominated in the Wigwam. "I am the first man from Chicago, I believe, who has the honor of congratulating you on your nomination for President," he said. Lincoln brought him into the house where Mary gave him a bouquet of roses she was carrying. Volk himself had a present for the Lincolns. It was a small version of the bust that Lincoln had sat for a month earlier.

Volk asked Lincoln if he would allow him to make a full-scale statue and casts of his hands. Two days later, on Sunday morning, he recalled, "I found him ready, but he looked more grave and serious than he had appeared on the previous days." Volk wanted to cast Lincoln's right hand, swollen from shaking hands, grasping an object. "Thereupon he went to the wood-shed, and I heard the saw go, and he soon returned to the dining-room (where I did the work), whittling off the end of a piece of broom-handle." Lincoln pointed to a scar on his hand. "You have heard that they call me a railsplitter, and you saw them carrying rails in the procession . . . well, it is true that I did split rails, and one day, while I was sharpening a wedge on a log, the ax glanced and nearly took my thumb off, and there is the scar, you see."

A FALLEN STAR

Three days after the Democratic convention at Charleston adjourned in shambles, on May 7, Jefferson Davis resumed the battle on the floor of the Senate by reintroducing his national slave code. Even before the Republican convention, he posed the challenge, "If a party hostile to our institutions shall gain possession of the Government, that we shall stand quietly by, and wait for an overt act? Is not a declaration of war an overt act? What would be thought of a country that, after a declaration of war, and whilst the enemy's fleets were upon the sea, should wait until a city had been sacked before it would say that war existed, or resistance should be made? The power of resistance consists, in no small degree, in meeting the evil at the outer gate." Douglas was "the evil" and his nomination "the outer gate."

It took the ill and rankled Douglas a week to reply. "I am no longer a heretic. I am no longer an outlaw from the Democratic Party," he declared to the

Life mask of Stephen A. Douglas, cast by Leonard Volk, 1857

Senate on May 15, claiming that the passage of his platform at the suspended convention that failed to nominate him had vindicated him. But he was unable to finish his speech from physical exhaustion. The next day, he laid out how the Ultra leadership at Charleston had plotted "to divide and destroy the Democratic Party" for years, to "lead, directly, inevitably, to a dissolution of the Union, and the formation of a southern confederacy." He flourished a letter written by Yancey in 1858, urging tactics "precipitating the cotton states into revolution." Document in hand, Douglas accused, "So, it seems, that, in 1858, a well-digested plan had been matured and approved by many of the ablest men of the South; and even in Virginia." The plan "was not to be executed at once," but again quoting Yancey, "at the proper time." That time, Douglas stated, was at the Charleston convention, when "the program was carried out to the letter." Yancey's plan, "published two years ago, is a truthful history of the secession movement at Charleston." Now, accusing Jefferson Davis without uttering his name, Douglas said, "The Yancey platform at Charleston, known as the majority report from the committee on resolutions, was the same as the Senate caucus resolutions; the same as the resolutions now under discussion, and upon which the Senate is called upon to vote." Douglas went out of his way to say he would not accuse any senator of desiring "disunion." But he warned, "that such a platform of principles, insisted upon, will lead directly and inevitably to a dissolution of the Union."

Jefferson Davis rose to the full height of his condescension to ridicule Douglas's delusion that he possessed a particle of authority as the rightful Democratic nominee, the Little Giant hallucinating that he was the Sun King. "The fact that the Senator criticized the idea of the States prescribing the terms on which they will act in a party convention recognized to be representative, is suggestive of an extreme misconception of relative position; and the presumption with which the Senator censured what he was pleased to term 'the seceders,' suggested to me a representation of the air of the great monarch of France when, feeling royalty and power all concentrated in his own person, he used the familiar yet remarkable expression, 'the State, that's me.' Does the Senator consider it a modest thing in him to announce to the Democratic Convention on what terms he will accept the nomination; but presumptuous in a State to declare the principle on which she will give him her vote? It is an advance on Louis Quatorze."

Douglas, according to Davis, was a pathetic narcissist simply seeking the attention of his better. "Nothing but the most egregious vanity, something far surpassing even the bursting condition of swollen pride, could have induced the Senator to believe that I could not speak of squatter sovereignty without meaning him." Sumner had been caned for the similar offense of *lèse-majesté*.

A week later, after the Republicans nominated Lincoln, Senator Judah P. Benjamin, of Louisiana, who was Slidell's law partner and speaking ex cathedra for the administration, took the floor to cast a curse on Douglas. "The causes that have operated on me have operated on the Democratic party of the United States, and have operated an effect which the whole future life of the Senator will be utterly unable to obliterate. It is impossible that confidence thus lost can be restored." Benjamin consigned him to a ring of the Inferno as a betrayer. "We accuse him for this, to wit: that having bargained with us upon a point upon which we were at issue, that it should be considered a judicial point; that he would abide the decision; that he would act under the decision, and consider it a doctrine of the party; that having said that to us here in the Senate, he went home, and under the stress of a local election, his knees gave way; his whole person trembled." Douglas had pledged his fealty to Dred Scott, was a turncoat on Lecompton, and embraced the heresy of the Freeport Doctrine.

Benjamin exalted Lincoln to diminish Douglas. His description of the reversal of fortune was the apotheosis of the lifetime rivalry. "His adversary stood upon principle," said Benjamin, "and was beaten; and lo! he is the candidate of a mighty party for the Presidency of the United States. The Senator from Illinois faltered. He got the prize for which he faltered; but lo! the grand prize of his ambition today slips from his grasp because of his faltering in his former contest, and his success in the canvass for the Senate, purchased for an ignoble price, has cost him the loss of the Presidency of the United States. Here were two men, struggling before the people of a State on two great sides of a political controversy that was dividing the Union, each for empire at home. One stood on principle—was defeated. Today, where stands he? The other faltered—received the prize; but, today, where stands he? Not at the head of the Democratic party of these United States. He is a fallen star."

Benjamin cornered Douglas in his contradictions. He pronounced him guilty of his crimes of ambition. He convicted him of perfidy and duplicity, and he excommunicated him. "We have separated from him. He is right in saying we have separated from him. We have separated from him, not because he held principles in 1856 different from ours. We have separated from him, not because we are intolerant of opposition from anybody. . . . We separated from him because he has denied the bargain that he made when he went home; because, after telling us here in the Senate that he was willing that this whole matter should be decided by the Supreme Court, in the face of his people, he told them that he had got us by the bill; and that, whether the decision was for us or against us, the practical effect was to be against us; and because he shows us now again that he is ready to make use of Black Republican arguments used against himself at home, and to put them forth against the Democratic party in speeches here in the Senate."

The "fallen star" was the fallen angel. Douglas might yet gain the prize, but he would be expelled from paradise. Every protest he made against the injustice directed at him further condemned him. His attempt to assert ultimate authority was a rebellion against true authority. His claim to his rightful place in the seat of power was blasphemous against those in whose name he claimed it. Assailing hypocrisy, his own was exposed. The closer he came to power, the more tragic his fall. In a reversal of Milton's Lucifer, his refusal to serve in hell would deprive him of the redemption of reigning in heaven.

On the eve of the second Democratic convention, staged for his resurrection, Douglas's health was already failing. He had less than a year to live. He was drinking and smoking heavily. He had trouble speaking. His voice was thick and raspy. He breathed with difficulty. He had bronchial attacks. He was bedridden for much of the time. He feared he would have an operation on his throat that would not cure his illness. He was certainly suffering from cirrhosis of the liver, likely heart disease, and possibly throat or lung cancer. He was deeply depressed. His eight-month-old daughter, who had never thrived, died. He had two sons from his previous marriage, but he and Adele were not able to have any children of their own.

After the debacle at Charleston, Douglas loyalists in Alabama, Louisiana, and Georgia ousted the bolters in state conventions. But some of those that had walked out wanted their seats back at the second convention, if only to make more trouble. Douglas refused to accept them, writing in a letter of June 4 that they "openly avow their object to be to bolt again and break up the convention."

On June 18, the Democrats met at the Front Street Theatre in Baltimore. Caleb Cushing, who had presided as the double-crossing chairman at Charleston, was back with the gavel. "The hostile feeling between the factions of the Democracy was even more embittered than at the time of the adjournment at Charleston, and the more the points of difference were caucused, the more intense was the warfare," wrote Halstead. Rival Southern delegations—pro- and anti-Douglas—the newly invested and the bolters—

appeared before the credentials committee. That night in the streets crowds of Southerners yelled "deafening and persistent cries of 'Yancey!' Yancey!'" who stepped forward to entertain them with "one of his handsome silver-toned speeches." The credentials struggle dragged on day after day. The Douglas forces were willing to accept a divided delegation from Georgia, but none of the other bolters. On the fourth day the floor of convention hall collapsed, a physical manifestation of the political situation. "The panic was dangerous," reported Halstead. "Delegates rushed in masses to the windows, and climbed, nimbly as monkeys, over the chairs of the reporters."

On the fifth agonizing day Georgia's bolters were seated. But would the others also be forgiven? "There was no longer any doubt about the disruption of the Convention. It was merely a question of time, and the time short." Rumor swept the convention that Douglas offered to withdraw in the interest of party peace, but Douglas's camp adamantly denied it. In fact, the discouraged Douglas had written such a letter, which was suppressed by his convention manager, William Richardson. Douglas had lost heart. He had hit bottom. It was too late anyway. "The long looked-for 'Crisis' a hundred times postponed, arrived at last," wrote Halstead. His followers were in no mood for compromise; they did not share their champion's loss of nerve. "He had stirred up the storm but could not control the whirlwind," wrote Halstead. The core of the Douglas supporters ran out of patience. Southern implacability standing in the way of the obvious solution had led to rejected overtures, turning into simmering frustration and boiling anger. "The Democracy of the North-west rose out of the status of serfdom. There was servile insurrection, with attendant horrors, and Baltimore became a political St. Domingo." The majority refused to seat Alabama, which would mean admitting Yancey, and refused to seat Louisiana, and refused the others. "The South was amazed to hear its favorite threat of secession despised and hooted at." The chairman of the Virginia delegation stood, "very pale, nervous and solemn," and announced Virginia would walk out. The Virginians "rose in a body, and passing into the aisles, proceeded to leave the theater, shaking hands and bidding personal friends good-by." Then they were followed one after another by North Carolina, Tennessee, Maryland, and the Pacific Coast states in the hands of the pro-slavery sympathizers, California and Oregon, and the next day Kentucky, Missouri, and Arkansas departed. Caleb Cushing left, too. Out of the original 303 delegates assembled fewer than 200 remained. On the sixth day, on the second ballot, Douglas was nominated as the candidate of a party in pieces.

The Southern bolters moved across Baltimore to the Maryland Institute. Caleb Cushing appeared on its podium as chairman. "The leading Southerners of the delegations smiled radiantly," wrote Halstead. "Yancey, who always wears a surface smile, twisted about in his seat with the unrest of intolerable felicity, laid his head first upon one shoulder and then upon the other, and glowed with satisfaction." The convention unanimously nominated its own candidates: John C. Breckinridge of Kentucky, Buchanan's thirty-nine year-old vice president, a passive tool of the Southern Directorate, for president, and Senator Joseph Lane of Oregon as his running mate.

"Yancey! Yancey!" yelled the delegates. Yancey stepped forward to the platform to bury Douglas. "I will let Mr. Douglas rest where his friends have placed him, contending, however, that they have buried him today beneath the grave of squatter sovereignty. The nomination that was made (I speak it prophetically), was made to be defeated and it is bound to be defeated." Often brilliant and compelling, Yancey then veered interminably into byways of Alabama politics, and spoke on and on. Cushing tried to close him down. The climax turned into an anticlimax. Hundreds of spectators clambered toward the exits. "His speech was a disenchanter," wrote Halstead. "He was not calculated to assist his party at all, but rather to place embarrassments in its way." But it did not matter what he said. The breakup of the Democratic Party foreshadowed Democratic defeat. Yancey had achieved his aim, precipitating his revolution.

Late in the evening of June 23, Douglas's supporters welcomed delegates at the Washington train station returning from the Baltimore convention and marched to his home to serenade him. Douglas came out to address them. He had strained every fiber to reach this point. He had at last realized his life's ambition. And his mouth was filled with ashes. "Secession is disunion," he said. "Secession from the Democratic Party means secession from the federal Union."

The close of the two disastrous conventions was hardly the end of the Democratic shambles. Douglas had named Senator Benjamin Fitzpatrick of Alabama as his running mate. Yancey paid him a call to urge him to drop out, which he promptly did. Douglas couldn't hold his ticket together. Finally, he secured Herschel V. Johnson, a former Georgia senator and governor, and Democratic loyalist.

Two days after the Baltimore convention, on June 25, Breckinridge, Toombs, and Cushing dined at Jefferson Davis's house in Washington. Davis proposed that John Bell, the candidate of the Constitutional Union Party,

Douglas, and Breckinridge withdraw in favor of Fitzpatrick, a single unifying candidate in order to beat Lincoln. It's possible that Davis might not have
had Fitzpatrick in mind, but Franklin Pierce or himself, or someone else.
During the Baltimore convention, Davis and Cushing, who had been the
powers behind Pierce's presidency, attempted to convince him to declare his
candidacy to rescue the party from Douglas, but Pierce instructed Cushing
to prevent "even a remote possibility" of that happening. Davis's name was
put into nomination, but he received few votes. After dinner the men all
walked to Breckinridge's house, which was next door to Douglas's, where a
crowd had come to serenade Breckinridge as the somewhat bewildered candidate. Davis, according to his account, proceeded to raise his scheme with
Douglas. "When I made this announcement to Mr. Douglas—with whom
my relations had always been such as to authorize the assurance that he could
not consider it as made in an unfriendly spirit—he replied that the scheme
proposed was impracticable, because his friends, mainly Northern Democrats, if he were withdrawn, would join in the support of Mr. Lincoln, rather
than of any one that should supplant *him* (Douglas); that he was in the hands
of his friends, and was sure they would not accept the proposition." Douglas
was in no mood for conceding to Jefferson Davis.

Davis's far-fetched notion of a fusion candidate had already been attempted behind the scenes at the Baltimore convention. Congressman John
Cochrane, of New York, on the evening before the convention, had dinner at
Toombs's house with Breckinridge and several others. Toombs and Breckinridge took him aside, "accosting me in the hall," to inform him that he should
meet at Baltimore with Slidell. Cochrane brought Dean Richmond, the head
of the New York delegation, with him to call upon Slidell at a private home.
Slidell had a proposal. If the New Yorkers would drop Douglas and support
Horatio Seymour, the former New York governor, Slidell could assure them
that "the seceded states, together with the whole South, would return into
the Convention, and make him the candidate of the party." Richmond seriously considered the proposal. He discussed it with some key members of the
delegation, only to return with the report that it was "impossible." "Negotiations ceased," recalled Cochrane. "Further concessions seemed to be useless."

John Cabell Breckinridge was the heir to a privileged and distinguished
family. His uncle, Robert J. Breckinridge, had been the Speaker of the House,
U.S. senator, and Thomas Jefferson's attorney general. His father, Robert's
brother, Joseph Cabell Breckinridge, was the Kentucky Speaker of the House
and business partner of John J. Crittenden and Robert Todd, the father of

Mary Todd. His mother was the daughter of the founder of Hampden-Sydney College and granddaughter of John Witherspoon, a signer from New Jersey of the Declaration of Independence and founder of Princeton. John C. Breckinridge had played as a boy with Mary and met Lincoln on one of his visits to his wife's hometown of Lexington. Nor was Breckinridge hostile to Douglas. He had been his ally in passing the Kansas-Nebraska Act, and Douglas had arranged loans for him to become his partner in real estate speculations. He had risen quickly and far on the basis of his eminent background, proper conduct, and deference to his elders, who kept rewarding him. John Witherspoon had also been a founder of the Presbyterian Church in the United States and a notable Calvinist theologian. His grandson was imbued with a fatalist sense of obligation to authority that overcame his inner reservations. He was a Unionist who went along with being given the nomination of the breakaway branch of the party, but was not the actor in the most dramatic turn in his life. "My course has been surrounded by difficulties for which I am wholly blameless," he told a friend about accepting the nomination. "We must each pursue what seems to be the path of duty." He confided to Varina Davis, Jefferson Davis's wife, "I trust I have the courage to lead a forlorn hope." Breckinridge was his own lost cause.

As Buchanan's vice president Breckinridge had been viewed as decorative and decorous, and excluded from the councils of the administration's policies and politics. His presidential campaign was run out of the White House by Slidell and company in consultation with Buchanan. Young Breckinridge assumed the role of figurehead on a ship headed for the rocks. "They will spare no effort, therefore, to defeat Douglas," commented the *New York Times,* "and whatever of influence may remain to the Administration will be remorselessly and unscrupulously used in aid of the same object. Mr. Buchanan is not a man of strong passions, but all the hatred of which his cold and clammy nature is susceptible is concentrated upon Mr. Douglas."

The existence of two Democratic parties created conflict and confusion in the states outside the lower South. The Dem-

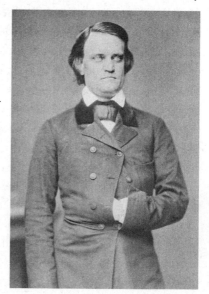

John C. Breckinridge

ocratic National Committee under Douglas's control urged "unequivocal support" for him, but Pennsylvania presented a combined electoral ticket that allowed electors to vote for either Douglas or Breckinridge, which of course sabotaged Douglas. "An amalgamation ticket with the bolters," he said, "would disgust the people and give every northern state to Lincoln." His use of the words "amalgamation" and "disgust" had the connotation of sexual race mixing.

Douglas had expected to run a traditional campaign in which he did not give stump speeches. "It is the first time in my life that I have been placed in a position where I had to look on and see a fight without taking a hand in it," he said. He continued to issue statements against the Breckinridge and Lincoln candidacies, but left open the door to some sort of relationship with the Bell campaign. "We must make the war boldly against the Northern abolitionists and the Southern Disunionists, and give no quarter to either. . . . We can have no partnership with the Bolters."

But he started delivering stem-winding speeches, first in Boston, then Albany and Newport, and receiving harsh criticism and derision from his opponents for venturing out in public, proof of his coarseness. His enemies circulated a broadside: "'Boy' Lost." The National Democratic Executive Committee of the Breckinridge party issued a formal statement calling him a "traveling mountebank." He had trouble raising money, especially from New York interests connected to the Southern trade. August Belmont, agent of the Rothschild bank, his finance chairman, was reduced to dunning local district party organizations for $100, but received little return. At a meeting at his Fifth Avenue mansion, where Belmont and his wife were preparing to entertain the visiting Prince of Wales, he held a conference with the Wall Street donors, who rejected his supplication unless there would be a miraculous fusion with Breckinridge.

Douglas's campaign put out stories that Breckinridge had favored the Whig candidate for president in 1848, signed a petition to pardon John Brown, and was a secessionist. In a speech on September 5 at Lexington, his only major speech of the campaign, Breckinridge called all the charges untrue. He accused Douglas of responsibility for destroying the Democratic Party by victimizing the South at the Baltimore convention. "Whole States were excluded and disfranchised in that Convention, not to speak of individuals," he said. "The most flagrant acts of injustice were perpetrated for the purpose of forcing a particular dogma upon the Democratic organization, and the gentleman who is the representative of that dogma is the representative also of principles which I will be able to show repugnant alike to reason and the Constitution."

Cushing spoke at a Breckinridge rally in Boston on September 12, declaring Douglas would not win a single Northern electoral vote and the Republicans would start a civil war. "The Republican Party," he said, "is a monstrous and ridiculous abortion, a gigantic falsehood, swindle and fraud," and that if Lincoln was elected "the Republicans will have to burst up at once, or to attack the domestic rights of the States."

Dean Richmond of the Albany Regency attempted to create a fusion ticket of Douglas and Breckinridge, but his negotiations fell into a round of mutual accusations and contempt. "There can be no middle ground," read the statement of the pro-Breckinridge party in response to his overture. "Squatter Sovereignty is but another form of Free-Soil Republicanism, and necessarily continues the excitement, strife and bloodshed caused by fanatical emigrant-aid societies with their contributions of Sharp's rifles." The *New York Times* wrote of the Albany Regency's "ruin," its "blunders," the "craziness" of its fusion schemes, its unprincipled alliances with Fernando Wood on the one hand and the Know Nothings on the other, "craven and incompetent," its fate "a sealed fact."

The Constitutional Unionist campaign, the most conservative of the campaigns and the one operating most on magical thinking, circulated letters pledging its signers never to speak about slavery as a public issue. John Bell gave an interview to the *New York Herald* at his Tennessee home on August 8, his major contribution to the debate. "Mr. Bell," the paper reported approvingly, "has a third interest in about four hundred slaves, the balance belongs to his second wife. They are employed in Mr. Bell's iron works. . . . The system by which this large body of slaves is governed is admirable and humane." Bell stated he preferred Douglas over Breckinridge, and so long as his followers "adhered to principle" would be in favor of fusion efforts "to defeat Lincoln," but "he had no apprehensions that Lincoln would be elected." He believed his own "cause is progressing gloriously," and that either he or his running mate Edward Everett "will be President—by the people of the House, or through the action of the Senate."

Douglas had a brief delusional episode that lasted about two weeks after the Baltimore convention. He could not restrain himself from sketching out to Charles Lanphier, editor of the *Illinois State Register,* just how he would win. He would carry the South, except for South Carolina and Mississippi, which would go for Breckinridge, and the border states, which would go for

Bell. Then he would carry the New England states, except for Massachusetts and Vermont. He would carry most of the rest of the North. But if the election were deadlocked and happened to go into the House of Representatives he was certain that Breckinridge had "no show" and he would win there. But by the time Douglas reached Boston in early July, however, his wishful projections had evaporated and he confided to Senator Henry Wilson "his conviction that Lincoln would be elected."

On August 31, in Baltimore, Douglas introduced the charge of conspiracy into the center of the campaign, raising the accusation he had laid out three months earlier in his Senate floor speech. "There is a mature plan throughout the Southern states to break up the Union," he said. "I believe the election of a Black Republican is to be the signal for that attempt and that the leaders of the scheme desire the election of Lincoln so as to have an excuse for disunion." Politically and personally he was closer than Lincoln to the trauma tearing the country apart. Douglas was the target of the Southern Ultras, their immediate enemy and obstacle, within their own party; Lincoln was the "excuse." He experienced the crack-up of the Democratic Party and the nation as one and the same thing. Until the Democratic convention, he could no more envision the party coming apart than he could imagine severing his limbs. He thought he knew the South, the real South—he had married two Southern women, owned a Mississippi plantation—and to him it was not a place that would ever separate from the Union. Haunted by the recent death of his infant daughter and wracked with illness, gasping for breath, his voice described as a "spasmodic bark," he began to speak about his own death—his political death—and relate it to the death of the country. "I am not seeking the Presidency," he said. "I am too ambitious a man to desire to have my death-warrant signed now. . . . My object is to preserve this Union by pointing out what, in my opinion, is the only way in which it can be saved."

Douglas conflated his fate with that of the party and the country, a trinity. Before an audience in Richmond, the day before his Baltimore appearance, he described the Democratic Party as "the only historical party now remaining in the country, the only party that has its northern and southern support firmly enough established to preserve this Union." But Douglas was pleading for a party that had ceased to exist at Charleston and Baltimore. The moment it was finally within the grasp of his leadership was the signal for its dissolution. He had proposed the Kansas-Nebraska Act to win the regard of the South for the purpose of becoming president only to set in motion the events that turned him into an object of obloquy. He was left standing on the ruins of what had been until his nomination the only national party, as much a sectional candidate as the others. Jefferson Davis, back in Mississippi, told a crowd that gallows should be constructed for both Douglas and Lincoln with the difference being their height.

"The sky is dark," Herschel Johnson, Douglas's running mate, wrote Alexander Stephens in mid-July. Following grim results from early elections in Vermont and Maine, Douglas met privately with Johnson on September 11 at the Fifth Avenue Hotel in New York to review strategy. "I told him," said Johnson, "he underestimated the power of Mr. Buchanan's army of office holders, in the Northern States; that although they could not carry a single one for Breckinridge, they would bring him enough votes to give them all to Lincoln, that he (Douglas) would not carry a single Southern State and that I regarded Lincoln's election as certain. I shall never forget the expression of deep sadness, at this announcement. He was silent and thoughtful, for a moment, but rallying said, 'If you be correct in your views, then God help our poor country.'"

In late September, trying to hold back the tide in the Northwest states, Douglas barnstormed by train through Pennsylvania, Ohio, and Indiana, speaking until his voice gave out. At Toledo, before a midnight rally at the station, he ran inside another train that had just come into the depot. He had heard that William Seward was a passenger. Seward, in fact, had gotten over his gloom and was touring the country giving speeches for Lincoln. He was accompanied by Charles Francis Adams, Jr. Chugging from a whiskey bottle in his hand, careening down the aisle, Douglas shouted to Seward, "Come, Governor, they want to see you; come out and speak to the boys!" "How are you, Judge?" Seward replied. "No; I can't go out. I'm sleepy." "Well! if you don't want to you shan't." Douglas left, drinking. "So," recalled Adams, "on this occasion, Douglas, a Presidential candidate, had, more than half drunk, rushed into that car at midnight, whiskey-bottle in hand, to drag Seward . . . out of his sleeping-berth, to show him in a railroad station to his (Douglas's) political heelers!" When Douglas reached Cincinnati, he was too debilitated to address the thousands that had assembled to hear him.

"I'm no alarmist," Douglas said in Chicago at a grand reception on October 5. "I believe that this country is in more danger now than any other moment since I have known anything of public life." On October 8, in Cedar Rapids, Iowa, he received a telegraph from John Forney that Pennsylvania had voted Republican in the early presidential ballot; then he learned that Indiana and Ohio had gone Republican, too. Curtin and Lane, who had staked their elections on Lincoln's nomination, were victorious. "Mr. Lincoln is the next president," Douglas said to his traveling secretary. "We must try to save the Union. I will go South." He told Congressman Edward McPherson of Pennsylvania, "By God, sir, the election shall never go into the House; before it shall go into the House, I will throw it to Lincoln." The *New York Times* reported, "The words thus used were accompanied by a violent gesture, and perhaps an additional oath."

The day after the catastrophic early elections, on October 9, Richmond dangled $200,000 before state candidates on the Breckinridge ticket and worked out an awkward distribution of New York presidential electors favoring Douglas, fusion achieved through payment of a sufficient sum of cash. The deal was cut without Douglas's permission. That, more or less, was the end of the campaign funds.

Douglas went south. He spoke at the levee at St. Louis and boarded a steamer down the Mississippi to Memphis, addressing crowds before heading to Nashville, where Yancey arrived on the same day. "If I have antagonized Mr. Douglas," he told a rally, "it is because he has tied the brand of discord to the tail of the party fox to be turned loose on our Southern fields." On his way to Chattanooga, Douglas's train narrowly avoided a wreck. He was convinced there was a deliberate effort to assassinate him. He was trailed by vituperative editorials. He arrived at Atlanta on October 30, where he was greeted by Alexander Stephens, the only prominent Southern leader other than his running mate willing to campaign with him. They knew he could not win Georgia, but hoped he might throw the state to Bell. But where would that lead? Bell existed only to throw the election into the House. Douglas headed to Alabama. The state was split North and South, between support for him and for Yancey, between the increasingly open division over Union and secession.

On the evening of November 1 Douglas was escorted from the Montgomery train station by a torchlight parade to his hotel, but when he approached the entrance he and his wife were pelted with a barrage of rotten eggs and tomatoes. The next day he appeared at the State Capitol before a large crowd, most of whom were Bell and Breckinridge voters. It was the significant speech of his campaign.

"The Republic is now involved in darkness, and surrounded with those elements of discord which inspire the patriot's hearts with dread," he began. He recapitulated his case for "principle of non-intervention on the subject of slavery," which he claimed the basis of "peace between the North and the South." He depicted himself as a brave defender of Southern rights on the Fugitive Slave Act, being denounced as "a traitor, a Benedict Arnold, a Judas Iscariot," and standing against "the Northern people in a wild frenzy of fanaticism" whipped up by "Seward, Sumner, Chase, Giddings and the Abolition leaders." He described how "the Abolitionists howled" against his Kansas-Nebraska Act. At every turn he said he was also opposed by Jefferson Davis. "Why was there any secession from Charleston and Baltimore? The men who seceded tell the people that they were not willing to endorse Douglas and his squatter sovereignty notions. I believe that is their excuse. The record shows that excuse is not true." He veered into a tangent on how climate determined the presence of slavery. "For instance, suppose we should acquire the Island of Cuba, and I trust we will very soon, and after we acquired it, it should be colonized by Sumner, Seward, Chase, Giddings, Lincoln and men of that class, nobody but Abolitionists going there, do you think they would free the negroes in Cuba? How long would it be before they would each have a plantation?"

He returned to his theme. "Do you think there is a solitary fire-eater in all America who believes that his party can procure an act of Congress protecting slavery, and enforcing its existence, where the people do not want it? I do not think there is one of them who would risk his character by pretending that he did. Then why do they make the demand? . . . What is the inference? The only inference I can draw is, that these men desire a pretext for breaking up this Union."

Finally, he exposed the plot against him and the country, his recognition of the political reality of defeat staring him in the face, and made his plea against secession. "I believe there is a conspiracy on foot to break up this Union," he said. "It is the duty of every good citizen to frustrate the scheme. If Lincoln is elected, he owes it to the Breckinridge men, and then they tell us, after having tried to secure that result by dividing the party, that if he is elected they are going to dissolve the Union. At Norfolk, Virginia, they wanted to know whether, if Lincoln was elected, I would help them dissolve the Union. I told them never on earth."

Douglas defended his stance against secession by laying out a scenario of political tactics. "There is no living man who would do more to defeat Lincoln than myself. There is no man more anxious to defeat him than myself. And I would have no trouble in beating him to death, but for the support given him by the Breckinridge men." Douglas was daydreaming about what might have been if he had not been who he was, the Southerners were not the Southerners, and slavery was not an issue. But then he contemplated the inevitability of Lincoln. "If Lincoln is elected," he said, "he must be inaugurated." He described how he would lead the effort in the Congress to thwart Lincoln from realizing the Republican platform. "And after he is inaugurated," Douglas explained, "if he attempts to violate any man's rights, or the Constitution of the country, we will punish him according to the Constitution, to the extent of the law. Notwithstanding the combination between the Breckinridge men and the Black Republicans at the North, we have already succeeded in ensuring the election of enough Douglas Democrats, united with the South, to outvote the Black Republicans. We shall hold both Houses of Congress against him during his term, if he should be elected." With that vision of Lincoln elected but denied, he pled again to his Southern audience, "I hold that the election of any man on earth by the American people, according to the Constitution, is no justification for breaking up this government."

Among those listening to Douglas was William Lowndes Yancey. He had just spoken in favor of secession in New Orleans, where he called it "the right to save ourselves from despotism and destruction—the right to withdraw ourselves from a government which endeavors to crush us." That night, in Montgomery, Yancey was escorted by city officials and leaders of the Breckinridge Club in a carriage drawn by four white horses through the cheering people in the streets to the "constant firing of cannon and the strains of music," onto the stage of the newly constructed Artesian Basin Theatre, where he was warmly greeted by the justices of the Alabama Supreme Court and the mayor. Then he was introduced, "Three cheers for the greatest orator of the world!"

Another face in the crowd at both Douglas's and Yancey's events was a young actor who was a member of a traveling troupe that had come to Montgomery, where he would play the lead role in *Richard III*. "Booth, Booth, Booth!" read the advertisements, exploiting the most famous family name of the theater. "He was convinced that Douglas was simply a professional politician and a rank opportunist," recalled a stagehand about the reaction of John Wilkes Booth. But Booth had struck up a friendship with Yancey's son, Ben, and walked from his favorite bar with him to hear his father's speech. "Yancey's oratory swept the young actor off his feet and he left the meeting in a delirium of enthusiasm." Afterward, "at every opportunity," he "sought conversation with Ben's father."

The evening of his Montgomery speech, Douglas and Adele boarded a steamboat to take them to Selma for his speech the next day. As he spoke hundreds rushed onto the boat, the floor broke, they tumbled to the deck below, and were badly bruised. Adele stayed behind to recuperate while Douglas hobbled away on crutches to the final stop of his campaign in Mobile.

On November 6, Douglas awaited the election results in the office of the editor of the *Mobile Register,* John Forsyth. The outcome was quickly apparent. Without allowing a moment to lapse, Forsyth showed Douglas an editorial he had already written to be published in the next day's paper calling for a state convention to determine whether Alabama should secede. Douglas opposed printing it, but Forsyth insisted that holding a convention was the only way to try to halt secession. According to Douglas's private secretary, "he returned to his hotel more hopeless than I had ever before seen him." Back in Washington, a month later, Douglas would receive a letter from Forsyth, suddenly transformed from Unionist to secessionist, declaring himself in favor of a civil war rather than "be stripped of 25 hundred millions of slave property and to have turned loose among us 4,000,000 of freed blacks," and concluding, "With your defeat the cause of the Union was lost."

On his way back to Washington, Douglas passed through New Orleans, where he was welcomed with a silk banner with his likeness, reading, "Our Choice in 1864."

WIDE-AWAKE

Lincoln did not campaign. His policy was discretion. He did not leave Springfield, instead receiving a stream of visitors in a room at the State Capitol. He was "bored—bored badly," Herndon reported to Trumbull on June 19. "Good gracious, I would not have his place and be bored as he is—I could not endure it."

The Republican campaign circulated authorized biographies, pamphlets of his speeches, the book of his debates with Douglas, and engravings of Mathew Brady's photograph. The Repub-licans in the Congress flooded the mail with franked copies of the Covode Com-mittee report on the Buchanan adminis-tration's corruption. Surrogate speakers roamed the country on Lincoln's behalf. Chase spoke. Seward went on a whis-tle-stop tour. Orville Browning spoke to the Old Whigs, Owen Lovejoy to the ab-olitionists, Carl Schurz to the Germans, and Cassius Clay galvanized the Wide-Awakes.

The Wide-Awake Clubs were spon-taneously organized in Hartford by five young store clerks to escort the militant

Abraham Lincoln, August 13, 1860

Clay to a rally. By the time the campaign was in full swing they had attracted hundreds of thousands of young men, wearing uniforms of glazed black oilcloth capes and hats, carrying lanterns on poles, and marching at rallies and parades. The Wide-Awakes created a widespread network of Republican activism, partisan newspapers, and crossed class lines, drawing in mechanics and farmers. In almost every town and city the Wide-Awakes drilled in public squares. Unlike the hard cider campaigns of the past, the Wide-Awake clubs stressed the values of temperance and self-discipline, and they organized to turn out the vote and guard the polls. Democrats countered with the "Chloroformers" intended to put the Wide-Awakes to sleep. They also created the Little Giants and Little Dougs clubs; the Bell campaign mounted the Bell Ringers and Clapperites, while the Southern Democrats joined the Breckinridge Clubs. But these groups were a shadow of the Wide-Awakes, which swept the North. Every Lincoln rally was led by phalanxes of marching Wide-Awakes in their capes and bearing their torches. They were a new phenomenon in politics, a fad, and yet more than that. The sudden growth of this quasi-military, coordinated mass movement was a political Great Awakening, a reflexive response to a rapidly polarizing country. A note from an officer of the Beardstown, Illinois, Wide-Awakes to the secretary of the Springfield Wide-Awakes about a forthcoming "grand rally," caught the spirit for "an assembling of the masses at Springfield on the 8th [of August], as shall strike terror to the hearts of all opponents of our worthy standard bearer, 'Honest Old Abe,' and rekindle, within the bosom of his friends, fires of devotion, that shall, in the coming November, sweep from the political arena those twin sisters of iniquity, 'Squatter Sovereignty and Disunion.'" In Galena, Illinois, a former army captain and ostensible Douglas supporter, Ulysses Grant, turned down the invitation to train the "Douglas Guards" and instead drilled the Wide-Awakes. Lincoln didn't need to say a word to arouse them.

"I have observed that those candidates who are most cautious of making pledges, stating opinions or entering into arrangements of any sort for the future save themselves and their friends a great deal of trouble and have the best chance of success," William Cullen Bryant wrote Lincoln on June 16. The editor of the *New York Post,* host to Lincoln at Cooper Union, who had been at the Chicago convention, and was now a Lincoln presidential elector from New York, advised him that reserve was his wisest strategy. "The people have nominated you without any pledges or engagements of any sort; they are satisfied with you as you are, and they want you to do nothing at

Abraham Lincoln's membership certificate in the Chicago Wide-Awake Club

present but allow yourself to be elected. I am sure that I but express the wish of the vast majority of your friends when I say that they want you to make no speeches, write no letters as a candidate, enter into no pledges, make no promises, nor even give any of those kind words which men are apt to interpret into promises."

Lincoln's eyes were open and his mouth shut. "I hesitate to say it, but it really appears now, as if the success of the Republican ticket is inevitable," Lincoln confided in a letter on August 4 to Simeon Francis, the founder of the *Illinois State Journal,* who had moved a year earlier to Oregon to edit the *Oregon Farmer.* Lincoln's admission of the obvious was restricted to private correspondence. He conducted his campaign by reticence. He delivered no speeches, wrote no public letters, and gave no substantive interviews. His silence was more than a matter of following the tradition of maintaining the dignity befitting a statesman and cultivating the sense that the office found the man. Speaking was the sign of the desperate, as Douglas demonstrated daily. Spelling out policy positions in letters was dangerous, as Henry Clay proved in 1844 in letters that alienated his supporters and encouraged his detractors. Lincoln was quiet, but alert and wary.

The crisis had begun. The crack-up of the Democratic Party that made Lincoln's election inevitable was the most obvious sign. In the North the overnight mobilization of the Wide-Awakes was a kind of prerevolutionary upsurge. Lincoln's motionlessness did not mean that he was inert. Nor was he dormant. But the politician believed that politics as usual would ultimately prevail. On August 15, he wrote a friend, acknowledging the letter of John Minor Botts, the Old Whig from Virginia supporting Bell, who advised that "in no probable event will there be any very formidable effort to break up the Union. The people of the South have too much of good sense, and good temper, to attempt the ruin of the government." Lincoln seemed to agree with that assessment. Lincoln saw Douglas's shipwreck, but he was the beneficiary, not its victim. Douglas inhabited the experience that Lincoln could view only from the outside. Douglas was also, unlike Lincoln, a national figure, who knew firsthand all the men of his party and their motives. Lincoln was at a half distance, even personally unfamiliar with many of the leading personalities of his own party. He did not have any relationships with the Southern leaders, except a long-ago tie to Alexander Stephens from the days when he was a young Whig in the Congress working for the election of Zachary Taylor. Lincoln's experience of the South came largely from Kentucky, a border state with a border state of mind. Extrapolating from Kentucky, which was about to vote for Bell and give Breckinridge only about one third of its votes, was a misleading Southern indicator. Certainly, Kentucky in the fall of 1860 did not want "to attempt the ruin of the government," but the same could not be said for South Carolina. Yet in his immobility Lincoln steadfastly refused to move in the slightest from his position against the extension of slavery and in defense of the integrity of the federal government. The pressure on him to back down, fatally compromise, and withdraw from his principles was about to begin, and would build until the firing on Fort Sumter. His silence during the campaign, even if he misjudged the intensity and dynamic of secession, was not indifference, but a principled virtue.

Lincoln did his best to position himself as unthreatening to the South. He used a reporter from the *New York Herald* to attempt to communicate the message. Simon P. Hanscom, the *Herald* correspondent, came to Springfield, which the paper dubbed "The Republican Mecca," in late October. The *Herald* was an unlikely outlet for Lincoln to use. The paper called him "a vulgar village politician," one of its nicer epithets. It regularly peppered its columns with "nigger." Lincoln had made the mistake of speaking too freely in replying to another of its reporters, who asked him if he'd like to visit his home state of Kentucky, that he might be lynched. The paper had a heyday turning the gaffe into a controversy. Hanscom was something of a ringer, a clerk for the Republicans on the House committee on the Kansas troubles, who also wrote for the *New York Tribune*. "In conversation with Lincoln I found him eminently conservative," he wrote, and "the most violent Southern fire-eater will find it difficult to question his patriotism or impartiality." Hanscom also confidently but unreliably reported "with some degree of confidence" that "Mr. Seward will not hold a place in the next administration." He also pointed to Lincoln's comments on his visit to Kansas, undoubtedly directed by Lincoln, in which he spoke about secessionists suffering the same fate as John Brown if they chose to break up the Union.

Lincoln quietly dispatched Medill of the *Chicago Press and Tribune* to negotiate a détente with the *Herald*'s editor, James Gordon Bennett, "His Satanic Majesty." "He can do us much harm if hostile. If neutralized a point is gained," Medill wrote Lincoln. Bennett told Medill on July 5 that Lincoln would be "broken down" by the "radical element," "the first time he said, you caught a runaway nigger, and sent him back to slavery you would raise the d—l in your party, and thereupon the old Satanic laughed loud and boisterously. It was on that rock (the Fugitive law) that Fillmore ship—cracked, and you would dash to pieces on the same rock, he was confident." Bennett was certain Lincoln would be elected, which would cause "the Republicans be split to pieces by being put into power." "When I arose to leave him, he said 'we could beat your man Lincoln, if we would unite, but I think it would be better for the country to let him be elected. I'll not be hard on him.'"

The unscrupulous Bennett instantly broke his promise and was soon comparing Lincoln's "public declarations" to "the bloody acts of John Brown," and warning that Lincoln would impose black equality. What "decent white man," he editorialized, would "vote himself down to the level of the negro race?" (It was a rare use of the proper word "negro" in the *Herald*.) On October 24, the paper reported on the large fusion rally in New York. Bennett himself had been instrumental behind the scenes pushing for the fusion of the Douglas, Bell, and Breckinridge forces in the state. The headlines ran: "Tremendous Uprising of the People. Turn Out of the Conservatives Last Evening. The Wide Awakes Completely Squelched. Bell-Ringers, Little Giants and Breckinridgers Side by Side." The *Herald* prominently printed in featured boxes the mottos of banners held at the rally: "We want none but white men at the helm"; "No niggers allowed in this club"; "I see the nigger peeping through the fence"; "To the memory of Old Abe Lincoln, who died November 6, 1860."

The *Herald* also hyped the "the inconsistency and insincerity of 'honest Abe,'" by featuring the attacks of Wendell Phillips, the radical abolitionist. "Who is this huckster in politics?" asked Phillips in a speech on May 30 in Boston. Lincoln was simply "a country court lawyer, whose only recommendation was that out of the emptiness of his past, lying newspapers could make him any character they pleased." Phillips followed with an article in Garrison's *The Liberator* on June 22 headlined: "Abraham Lincoln, the Slavehound of Illinois."

Phillips's speech was delivered at the Massachusetts state convention of the Radical Abolition Party, which nominated Gerrit Smith for president, who had recently been released from the insane asylum where he committed himself after being exposed as one of the Secret Six behind John Brown. The tiny party would not receive a measurable vote in 1860. But Phillips's attack was the beginning of rising abolitionist criticism of Lincoln as slow, vacillating, and compromising. Phillips's censure also disclosed the factional and schismatic nature of abolitionist politics. William Lloyd Garrison, who insisted on publishing Phillips's article only under his byline in order to separate it from *The Liberator*'s editorial position, considered Gerrit Smith's nomination "extremely farcical." Frederick Douglass endorsed Lincoln a week after the Republican convention as "one of the most frank, honest men in political life," but under the stress of Phillips's and a few others' hostile remarks switched to support Gerrit Smith. Smith himself privately wrote Joshua Giddings about Lincoln, "I feel confident that he is in his heart an abolitionist," and that his election would "be regarded as an Abolition victory." Giddings wrote Lincoln a congratulatory letter and publicly praised him as "honest and faithful," and campaigned strenuously for him as if it was "a sort of jubilee." Two men close to John Brown endorsed Lincoln. Thomas Wentworth Higginson, one of the Secret Six, declined to back the Radical Abolitionists in favor of "the excellence of the Republican nominations." Richard J. Hinton, a journalist who accompanied Brown in Kansas, wrote the first campaign biography of Lincoln, noting that he was not a "radical" though "decidedly opposed to slavery," and not "old" despite being called "Honest old Abe." Sumner endorsed Lincoln, as did Henry Wilson, and others down the list of Republican senators and members of Congress. In the end, almost all the prominent abolitionists supported Lincoln's candidacy, and a few criticized Phillips.

Lincoln was known in New York through his Cooper Union appearance. He was known in New England mainly through his scant biographies, his reputation from the 1858 Senate campaign, and the testimonials of his friends. None of the New England abolitionists had actually met him. Herndon had a worshipful and epistolary relationship with Theodore Parker, but

Parker died in Florence the week before Lincoln was nominated. Herndon visited Garrison in 1858 on his Eastern tour to turn Greeley-influenced Republicans and abolitionists away from supporting Douglas over Lincoln in the Senate race. Herndon explained to Garrison that Lincoln was "all right on slavery." He understood that Garrison was hostile to politics in general and in particular to strategic antislavery politics instead of immediate abolition. "We are as we are," Herndon told Garrison. "You hate Republicanism, but never mind that: it is a midlink," which would, he suggested, help "climb to heaven." His effort to persuade Garrison of the value of both politics and Lincoln to his cause fell, at least in 1860, on deaf ears. The distorted image that Phillips projected for sectarian purposes combined with the antipolitical current that was always present in the abolitionist movement formed a lasting impression of suspicion about Lincoln among them. Three days after Lincoln's election, Garrison wrote in *The Liberator* that "we are warranted in entertaining no confident hopes," and that Lincoln's administration "must be a continual support of slavery."

The Illinois abolitionists, however, knew Lincoln, sought him out to create the Illinois Republican Party, and had come to see him as their political leader, not one of them, but in large part because of that, indispensable. From the moment of his nomination forward, the Illinois abolitionists and preeminently Owen Lovejoy were stalwart regardless of the intensity of criticism from Eastern abolitionists. "I have seen enough of political life to know that it is not altogether a bed of roses," Lovejoy wrote Lincoln in a congratulatory letter after his nomination. He also sent a book to Mary to ingratiate himself with the person closest to Lincoln who was very skeptical of him because he was an abolitionist. Two days earlier, Lincoln had written an anonymous letter in the *Chicago Press and Tribune* in a clear signal to Republicans: "Judge Davis expects Lovejoy to be nominated and intends to vote for him." Davis, in fact, remained dyspeptic on the subject of Lovejoy. "What on earth induced Govr Seward to indorse Lovejoy as he did in his speech," he complained to Lincoln. Lovejoy, freed from internal strife within the party through Lincoln's quiet efforts, was released to campaign far and wide for him. One of Lovejoy's close associates, Ichabod Codding, a member of the small band of original radical founders of the Illinois Republican Party, a minister trained as a speaker against slavery by Theodore Weld in the first organized group of abolitionist circuit riders, worked his heart out for Lincoln, speaking from town to town, and editing *A Republican Manual for the Campaign: Facts for the People, The Whole Argument in One Book,* which began with Lincoln's biography, "With His Opinions on Human Rights and the Slavery Question." Zebina Eastman, who came to Illinois after Elijah P. Lovejoy's murder to crusade as an abolitionist editor, was initially skeptical of Lincoln, but had learned to trust him, and would receive President Lincoln's appointment as consul to Bristol, England. "He is a politician," Eastman later said of Lincoln, "as every man must be who holds an important office, and such men, and only such, can kill slavery, because . . . the life of slavery is its political power."

Lincoln's nomination was taken up as a fervent cause by another group of abolitionists, the German Americans. They raised the Republican banner for Lincoln in the spirit of the Revolution of 1848, whose suppression had sent them to America. Their political leaders' meeting at the Deutsches Haus in Chicago at the convention was instrumental in squelching Bates's candidacy and opening the path for Lincoln. Across the country the German language newspapers were a Republican chorus. Lincoln wrote Carl Schurz on June 18, "I beg you to be assured that your having supported Gov. Seward, in preference to myself in the convention, is not even remembered by me for any practical purpose, or the slightest u[n]pleasant feeling. I go not back of the convention, to make distinctions among its' members; and, to the extent of our limited acquaintance, no man stands nearer my heart than yourself." At Lincoln's invitation, Schurz visited him at Springfield on July 24. After checking into his hotel, Schurz was surprised by a knock at his door. The presidential candidate told Schurz to rest in bed from his trip while for two hours they talked politics. "Men like you," Lincoln told him, "who have real merit and do the work, are always too proud to ask for anything; those who do nothing are always the most clamorous for office, and very often get it, because it is the only way to get rid of them. But if I am elected, they will find a tough customer to deal with, and you may depend upon it that I shall know how to distinguish deserving men from the drones." Lincoln brought him home to dinner with Mary and the boys, and then the Wide-Awakes appeared. "I have never seen so large a torch-light procession. Lincoln insisted on accompanying us, although he had not appeared in public since his nomination. He declared that he must once hear 'that tremendous speaker.' And so the Wideawakes surrounded 'Old Abe' and me; thus arm in arm we marched to the capitol." Schurz spoke first in German, then in English. "Lincoln sat directly in front of me all evening, watched every movement and applauded with tremendous enthusiasm. When I had finished, he came to me and shook hands and said: 'You are an awful fellow! I understand your power now!'" Lincoln gave him a copy of the book of his debates with

Douglas and Mary told him to bring his wife next time. Schurz left in a euphoric state ready to spread the word for Lincoln.

Germans in every city organized for Lincoln through their bunds, or associations. In New York City, after the anti-Lincoln fusion ticket was forged, the garment factories dependent on the Southern cotton trade systematically started to fire workers, most of them Germans, as a consequence of German American support for Lincoln. "German fellow-citizens!" read the leaflet entitled "An Address to the Republican Germans in Williamsburg." "Stand by Lincoln and freedom and do not be intimidated into voting for the Fusion ticket. The lackeys of the slave power tell you that there is so little work now because the firms that work in the clothing industry for the South are fearful of the election of Lincoln. They lie!" The author of the manifesto, who also spoke at a pro-Lincoln workers' rally on October 30, Joseph Weydemeyer, had been a Prussian military officer turned revolutionary, an intimate of Karl Marx and Friedrich Engels, member of the Communist League turned Free Soiler, and was still in touch with Marx and Engels about his American activities, which they encouraged. Weydemeyer, who contributed articles to the *Illinois Staats-Zeitung,* was a delegate at the Deutsches Haus conference. (In the war he would serve as a lieutenant colonel.) He was not the only comrade of Marx laboring for Lincoln. There was also August Willich, another Prussian officer and revolutionary, who became a German language newspaper editor in Cincinnati, and would befriend Lincoln. It is a matter of more than historical curiosity and not ironic, but an aspect of Lincoln's relationship with Germans, that a few good comrades in the New World played roles in his election. The Republican Party is in fact the only American political party that was cofounded by some men personally close to that distant admirer of Lincoln, Karl Marx.

On September 1, Seward's campaign train pulled into Springfield. Lincoln, accompanied by Trumbull, hopped aboard to greet him. Charles Francis Adams, Jr., traveling with Seward, recorded in his diary, "Judge Trumbull I had met before in Washington, and again in St. Louis the previous day; but 'old Abe' was a revelation. There he was, tall, shambling, plain and good-natured. He seemed shy to a degree, and very awkward in manner; as if he felt out of place; and had a realizing sense that properly the positions should be reversed. Seward too appeared constrained." Trumbull introduced Lincoln to Seward. They had met before, speaking together for the Whigs in Boston in 1848. "There was no demonstration; not a pretense of a reception," wrote Adams, who didn't quite know what to make of Lincoln. He observed that he had "a mild, dreamy, meditative eye which one would scarcely expect to see in a successful chief magistrate in these days of the republic." Seward and Lincoln talked for five minutes, Seward gave a short speech to those gathered at the depot, and the train pulled out for Chicago. On October 12, Lincoln wrote him, "It now really looks as if the Government is about to fall into our hands."

On October 20, Major David Hunter, one of the few antislavery Republican officers in the army, stationed at Fort Leavenworth, Kansas, wrote a strange letter to Lincoln, whom he said he had met years ago in Chicago. It was the first warning of an attempt to assassinate him, a story "that a number of young men in Virginia had bound themselves, by oaths the most solemn, to cause your assassination, should you be elected. Now Sir, you may laugh at this story, and really it does appear too absurd to repeat, but I beg you to recollect, that on 'the institution' these good people are most certainly demented, and being crazy, they should be taken care of, to prevent their doing harm to themselves or others." Lincoln replied on October 26 that he had also received a rumor about a coup: "I have another letter, from a writer unknown to me, saying the officers of the army at Fort Kearny have determined, in case of Republican success at the approaching presidential election, to take themselves, and the arms at that point, South, for the purpose of resistance to the government. While I think there are many chances to one that this is a humbug, it occurs to me that any real movement of this sort in the army would leak out and become known to you. In such case, if it would not be unprofessional or dishonorable (of which you are to be judge), I shall be much obliged if you will apprise me of it."

As his election appeared imminent, Lincoln received a letter from one of the most important supporters of John Bell urging him to tell the public that he, Lincoln, intended to behave more or less like John Bell. George D. Prentice, editor of the *Louisville Journal,* wrote that Lincoln should release a public letter "setting forth your conservative views . . . and therefore calculated to assure all the good citizens of the South and to take from the disunionists every excuse or pretext for treason." Prentice was pro-Unionist and proslavery. He had been close to Henry Clay, his biographer, but after the Whigs came apart he became a Know Nothing, publishing vicious anti-Catholic diatribes and provoking an anti-immigrant riot in Louisville in 1855 trying to prevent Germans from voting that left twenty-two people dead. Now Prentice was for order, peace, and civility. Lincoln replied on October 29 that Prentice's idea was "a very worthy one" in theory, but pointed out that "my conservative views and intentions," which were "already in print," were being ignored by

Prentice. Instead, Lincoln wrote, "you . . . busy yourself with appeals to all conservative men, to vote for Douglas—to vote any way which can possibly defeat me—thus impressing your readers that you think, I am the very worst man living. If what I have already said has failed to convince you, no repetition of it would convince you." Lincoln thought Prentice's suggestion would prove counterproductive. "If I do finally abstain, it will be because of apprehension that it would do harm," he wrote. "For the good men of the South—and I regard the majority of them as such—I have no objection to repeat seventy and seven times. But I have *bad* men also to deal with, both North and South—men who are eager for something new upon which to base new misrepresentations—men who would like to frighten me, or, at least, to fix upon me the character of timidity and cowardice. They would seize upon almost any letter I could write, as being an *'awful coming down.'* I intend keeping my eye upon these gentlemen, and to not unnecessarily put any weapons in their hands."

Lincoln would not allow himself to be flattered or intimidated into taking a public position that would eclipse the Republican platform, make him seem too eager or anxious about assuming power, and falsely attempt to resemble John Bell. If he were to adopt Prentice's tactic, he would deprive his candidacy of its purpose, demoralize Republicans, and boost the fusion tickets in the North, the last a desperate ploy to throw the election into the House. Silence was golden.

On November 1, Major Hunter replied to Lincoln. He debunked Lincoln's story about a coup, but had precise information about the "treasonous" shifting of military resources in preparation for secession under the direction of the sitting secretary of war John Floyd, the former Virginia governor. Hunter recorded "the sending by the government of a large number of arms to Charleston, and the ordering of the Engineer officers to have the Forts in that harbor finished, and put in a complete state of defense. I may also add the sending of two companies from this post—one to Augusta Arsenal, Georgia, the other to Fort Smith, Arkansas. These are small affairs, but they tend to show which way the current is running." Hunter continued to send Lincoln information after the election and Lincoln continued to encourage him to send more.

On November 4, a group of Ohio politicos paid Lincoln a visit, including Robert C. Schenck, a former Whig congressman who had been an early supporter, and Donn Piatt, a journalist and former diplomat who had been close to Chase. They put themselves before Lincoln to influence his appointments, which might include them. Piatt warned Lincoln that the portents of secession were serious, but it was an observation and a warning, not a suggestion that he offer any gesture. "He could not understand that men would get up in their wrath and fight for an idea," wrote Piatt. "He considered the movement South as a sort of political game of bluff, gotten up by politicians, and meant solely to frighten the North. He believed that when the leaders saw their efforts in that direction were unavailing, the tumult would subside. 'They won't give up the offices,' I remember he said, and added, 'Were it believed that vacant places could be had at the North Pole, the road there would be lined with dead Virginians.'"

The day before the election, on November 5, Lincoln had another caller, a prominent Boston businessman connected to the Southern trade and representing a host of New England commercial interests. "I have called to see," he said, "if the alarms of many persons in New England engaged in commerce and manufactures cannot by some means be relieved. . . . Our trade has fallen off, our workmen are idle, we get no orders from the South, and with the increasing chances of civil war, bankruptcy and ruin stare us in the face." He requested a statement from Lincoln of "conservative" intentions "to reassure the men honestly alarmed." According to John Nicolay and John Hay, Lincoln's private secretaries, Lincoln "divined at once the mercenary nature of the appeal and it roused him to repel the pressure." "This is the same old trick by which the South breaks down every Northern victory," he replied. "Even if I were personally willing to barter away the moral principle involved in this contest, for the commercial gain of a new submission to the South, I would go to Washington without the countenance of the men who supported me and were my friends before the election; I would be as powerless as a block of buckeye wood." Lincoln did not accept the terms presented to him. "There are many general terms afloat, such as 'conservatism,' 'enforcement of the irrepressible conflict at the point of the bayonet,' 'hostility to the South,' etc., all of which mean nothing without definition. What then could I say to allay their fears, if they will not define what particular act or acts they fear from me or my friends?"

Again, Lincoln explained to his visitor, ""If I shall begin to yield to these threats, if I begin dallying with them, the men who have elected me (if I shall be elected) would give me up before my election, and the South, seeing it, would deliberately kick me out. If my friends should desire me to repeat anything I have before said, I should have no objection to do so. If they required me to say something I had not yet said, I would either do so or get out of the way. If I should be elected, the first duty to the country would be to stand by the men who elected me."

"The South and the Revolutionary Consequences of Lincoln's Election" ran the headline on the lead editorial on Election Day, November 6, in the *New York Herald*. "Active secession proceedings have already been initiated in several of the Southern States in anticipation of the disunion signal of Lincoln's election. . . . Here, then, are the foreshadowed consequences of Lincoln's election—the secession of South Carolina and several other States, and the arming of the border slave States to protect the seceding States from federal coercion. Of course, any attempt by arm on the part of the federal government, under such a state of thing, to coerce the seceding States into submission, would be criminally foolish in the highest degree, for it could result only in a calamitous civil war." Yet another article on the same page reported on "The Secession Movement in the South." "It is the part of madness to ignore all the positive proof that comes to us showing the magnitude of this secession movement. The evidence is irresistible, and if the North still persists in ridiculing it, it will come upon the country like a thunderclap from a serene sky. Wise and patriotic men will strive to avert the pending storm. It can yet be done by defeating Lincoln."

Dawn on Election Day was greeted in Springfield by the firing of a cannon, awakening citizens to their duty to file to the courthouse opposite the capitol, the sole polling place in town. Lincoln spent the day in the governor's office with a view from the window of the voters coming and going, chatting with visitors, until he noticed a thinning of the line across the street, strolled over to vote, tore off the top part of the ballot containing the presidential choice with his name on it to show he had not immodestly voted for himself, and returned to his perch after five minutes. By nightfall, he retreated to the telegraph office with a few friends to watch the ticker. Trumbull burst in at about nine o'clock, arriving on the train from Alton. "We've got 'em; we've got 'em," he kept saying as the returns came in. About ten o'clock, a wire arrived from Cameron: "Pennsylvania 70,000 for you. New York safe. Glory enough." Lincoln felt relaxed enough to have dinner, wandering to Watson's Saloon, taken over by the ladies for the occasion. His entrance was greeted by their voices in unison, "How do you do, Mr. President?" Just as he was about to eat, a runner rushed in with a telegram showing a diminished Democratic vote in New York City, the last hope for the Democrats to win New York and throw the election into the House of Representatives. The throng burst into song: "We're the Lincoln boys! We're the Lincoln boys! Ain't you glad you joined the Republicans? Joined the Republicans—Joined the Republicans!"

Lincoln walked over to the telegraph office, receiving results throughout the night. Near dawn he said he "guess'd he'd go home now." He found Mary asleep. He tried to wake her. "Mary! Mary! We are elected!'"

Lincoln won with less than forty percent of the vote. In the Electoral College, he carried the entire Northeast (except the southern part of New Jersey below the Mason-Dixon line that went to Douglas), the Northwest states, and narrowly won California and Oregon. Breckinridge swept the Deep South, Maryland, and Delaware. Bell held the border states of Virginia, Kentucky, and Tennessee. Douglas barely carried a sharply divided Missouri, but came in second nationally in the popular vote. The Douglas and Bell total in the South in favor of the Union exceeded that for Breckinridge. Lincoln's total in the North exceeded that for Douglas, Bell, and Breckinridge combined. He received not a single vote in ten Southern states; the Republican Party was kept off the ballot. The Democrats kept control of the Senate and clawed back the House, though Republicans and anti-Lecompton Democrats constituted a majority.

For the first time in a presidential election the invincibility of the South on the issue of slavery was broken. A president pledged against its expansion would soon be at the helm of the executive branch, invested with the power of federal patronage, the ability to appoint federal judges and justices of the Supreme Court, and command of the armed forces.

The day after the election, the Stars and Stripes over federal buildings was lowered across South Carolina and State Rights flags, a red star on a white background, and Palmetto State flags were hoisted in their place.

On December 20 the delegates of the secession convention assembled in the South Carolina Institute Hall, thereafter known as Secession Hall, where months earlier the Democratic Party was broken apart. Each man solemnly walked up to the stage to sign the document: "To dissolve the Union between the State of South Carolina and other States united with her under the compact entitled 'The Constitution of the United States of America.'" The ultimate cause stated was "the election of a man to the high office of President of the United States, whose opinions and purposes are hostile to slavery. He is not to be entrusted with the administration of the common Government, because he has declared that that 'Government cannot endure permanently half slave, half free,' and that the public mind must rest in the belief that slavery is in the course of ultimate extinction."

The *Charleston Mercury* published an extra edition: "The Union Is Dissolved!"

ACKNOWLEDGMENTS

———— ◆•◆ ————

During the past few years I have been immersed in the events and personalities of the period in which Abraham Lincoln emerged as a national
leader. But like other Americans I could not avoid having at least one eye
wide awake to the whirlwind that bears more than a passing resemblance
to the gathering storm that led to Lincoln's election. If the house divided,
the manipulations of demagogues, the appeals to anti-immigrant nativism
and racism, a dysfunctional presidency, and the breakup of the old parties
seem familiar, it is because they were Lincoln's central subjects. New facts
and facets remain to be unearthed on Lincoln, held up to the light and that
illuminate both past and present crises.

I appreciated the opportunity that Congressman Jamie Raskin of Maryland extended to me to speak at the Capitol in January 2019 with the incoming Democratic members of the 114th Congress about Lincoln, who
appeared not as an unapproachable marble figure but a politician like them
who had walked the same grounds and confronted what seemed similarly
perplexing problems.

Nearly all of those to whom I am indebted for helping me produce this
volume make recurrent appearances in these acknowledgments for their
well-deserved credit in the two earlier Lincoln ones. First and foremost is
Alice Mayhew, editor nonpareil. Beyond her extraordinary acumen and deep
knowledge, she also has the power to see through a manuscript with X-ray
vision, locate the fracture lines and prescribe the remedy that makes it all
come together. Assisting her operations has been the estimable Stuart Roberts, now elevated to editor in his own right, and his worthy successor, Amar
Deol, whose feats of juggling have ended miraculously with all the elements

in the right place. Once again, Fred Chase has performed the delicate task of copy editing with the most precise attention and bringing to bear his own literary gift. I am grateful to Jonathan Karp, president of Simon & Schuster, for his commitment to the scope of this project. To Robert Barnett, a man you always want on your side.

Andrew Edwards, now on the history faculty at the University of Oxford, has repeated his incredible deed of organizing my notes and bibliography with the same aplomb he showed with the previous volumes.

I should note that I wrote this work, like the previous ones, without research assistants and continue to be responsible alone for any errors.

Sean Wilentz, professor of history at Princeton University, and I have carried on a decades-long conversation on American history, not to mention baseball and music. He has been my coconspirator extending beyond the Lincoln-Douglas debates. Like him, I believe, as he testified before the House Judiciary Committee in 1998: "History will track you down."

The community of scholars of Lincoln, the Civil War, and the Constitution have been generous with their time and discernment, and in directing me to new sources of information. I am grateful to Terry Alford, of Northern Virginia Community College; Michael Burlingame, of the University of Illinois at Springfield; Joan Cashin, of Ohio State University; Allen Guelzo, of Gettysburg College; Harold Holzer, director of the Roosevelt House Public Policy Institute at Hunter College; Ian Hunt, of the Lincoln Presidential Library at Springfield; and Jeffrey Rosen, president of the National Constitution Center.

Throughout these years of concentration occasionally interrupted by days of distraction I have been sustained by the friendship of, among others, David Brock, James Carville, Andrew and Leslie Cockburn, Joe Conason, Bill and Renilde Drozdiak, Thomas and Mary Edsall, Edward Jay Epstein, Jim and Deb Fallows, Jeffrey Frank, Tom Geoghegan, Ben Gerson, Todd Gitlin, Danny Goldberg, Karen Greenberg, Rick Hertzberg, Stephen Holmes, Scott Horton, John Judis, Dan Morgan and Elaine Shannon, Mark Medish, James Mann, Jane Mayer, Richard Parker, Walter and Ann Pincus, Peter Pringle and Eleanor Randolph, Richard Rosen, Hillel Schwartz, Cody Shearer, Derek Shearer, Craig Unger, Nick Wapshott, Ralph Whitehead, and Jonathan Winer.

To Joseph C. Wilson IV, friend and patriot, who has dedicated his life to our country.

My sister Marcia has been an effervescent presence and staunch support for our whole family. Her husband, Stan Selinger, provides a touch of magic just when it's needed. My stepbrother, Anthony Miller, who is as concerned about the fate of the country as anyone I know, has been constantly encouraging.

To my invincible wife, Jackie, not least for being elected for the sixth time as Advisory Neighborhood Commissioner in the District of Columbia, my best reader, best everything. To our sons, Max and Paul, and Paul's wife, Alison, for their energy and engagement.

This volume is dedicated to our oldest friends in Washington, John Ritch and Christina Ritch, chieftains of what we call the tribe. John's storied career—West Point, Senate Foreign Relations Committee, U.S. ambassador to the International Atomic Energy Agency—made him a savant on foreign affairs, the environment, and art. Nobody who is acquainted with Christina's charm and style is surprised to learn that when she was nine years old living with her parents on a U.S. army base in Germany she drew the smile and greeting of "Little Darlin'" from then GI Elvis Presley. We have shared our lives together, weathered a literal hurricane as well as proverbial ones, snowbound and sunny birthdays, enjoyed the close relations of our children out of whose circle developed a marriage, mourned the loss of loved ones and mutual dear friends, and raised our glasses in the celebration of triumphs. From Washington to London, from Tuscany to Vienna, New York to Paris, and back again, the moveable feast goes on.

My thanks to the entire terrific team at Simon & Schuster who have made this book possible: its designer, Lewelin Polanco; production editor Lisa Healy and production manager Beth Maglione. I am also grateful for the efforts of Julia Prosser, deputy director of publicity, to bring my work to a broad audience of readers.

NOTES

CHAPTER ONE: THINGS FALL APART

3 *Most importantly, this new compromise:* William Earl Weeks, *John Quincy Adams and American Global Empire* (Lexington: University Press of Kentucky, 2002), 191; Sean Wilentz, *The Rise of American Democracy* (New York: W.W. Norton, 2005), 222–36.

4 *Jefferson's nightmare hung over the Senate:* Sidney Blumenthal, *Wrestling With His Angel, 1849–1856, The Political Life of Abraham Lincoln* (New York: Simon & Schuster, 2017), 56–66.

6 *Lincoln the "Proviso Man":* Roy Basler, ed., *The Collected Works of Abraham Lincoln* (New Brunswick, N.J.: Rutgers University Press) 1:439–40. Hereinafter *CW.*

6 *For Lincoln's criticism of the war:* Blumenthal, *Wrestling with His Angel,* 1.

7 *On March 1, 1853: CW,* 2:191.

7 *In a time of peace and prosperity:* Nathaniel Hawthorne, *Life of Franklin Pierce* (Boston: Ticknor, Reed, & Fields, 1852), 12.

7 *Pierce recited his inaugural address:* Franklin Pierce, "Inaugural Address," March 4, 1853, in Gerhard Peters and John T. Woolley, eds., *The American Presidency Project,* http://www.presidency.ucsb.edu/ws/?pid=25816; Paul F. Boller, *Presidential Anecdotes* (New York: Oxford University Press, 1996), 116.

8 *Southern senators welcomed Franklin Pierce:* Maunsell B. Field, *Memories of Many Men* (New York: Harper, 1874), 162.

8 *Jane Appleton Pierce:* Roy F. Nichols, *Franklin Pierce: Young Hickory of the Granite Hills* (Philadelphia: University of Pennsylvania Press, 1931), 86–87.

9 *Even before Pierce arrived in Washington:* Jonathan R.T. Davidson and Kathryn M. Connor, "The Impairment of Presidents Pierce and Coolidge After Traumatic Bereavement," *Comprehensive Psychiatry* 49 (2008): 413–15.

9 *Pierce's effortless ascent:* Field, *Memories of Many Men,* 162.

10 *From the beginning:* Larry Gara, *The Presidency of Franklin Pierce* (Lawrence: University Press of Kansas, 1991.

10 *Within a year of Pierce's:* John Robert Irelan, *History of the Life, Administration, and Times of Franklin Pierce, Fourteenth President of the United States* (Chicago: Fairbanks & Palmer), 246.

CHAPTER TWO: VAULTING AMBITION

14 *Even before Pierce's inauguration:* George Fort Milton, *The Eve of Conflict: Stephen A. Douglas and the Needless War* (New York: Octagon, 1963), 95.

16 *The first territorial governor:* William E. Connelley, *A Standard History of Kansas and Kansans* (Chicago: Lewis Publishing, 1918), 1:366–72.

16 *The first election in the territory:* House of Representatives, *Report of the Special Committee Appointed to Investigate the Troubles in Kansas* (Washington, D.C.: Cornelius Wendell, 1856), 3–68.

16 *Reeder's replacement as territorial governor:* William Phillips, *The Conquest of Kansas, by Missouri and Her Allies* (Boston: Phillips, Sampson, 1856), 117–18, 149.

16 *Abraham Lincoln feared: CW,* 2:321.

17 *Despite two invasions:* Phillips, *The Conquest of Kansas,* 122, 131; Leverett Wilson Spring, *Kansas, the Prelude to the War for the Union* (Boston: Houghton, Mifflin, 1885), 66, 84; John N. Holloway, *History of Kansas* (Lafayette, Ind.: James, Emmons, 1868), 188, 190.

17 *In late November 1855:* Spring, *Kansas,* 87–91; Holloway, *History of Kansas,* 215–27.

18 *The Ruffians descended on Lawrence:* James Ford Rhodes, *History of the United States from the Compromise of 1850* (New York: Macmillan, 1892–1927), 2:105; Henry Wilson, *History of the Rise and Fall of the Slave Power in America* (Boston: Houghton, Osgood, 1874), 2:474.

18 *In February, Lincoln attended a meeting:* William Henry Herndon, *Herndon's Lincoln: The True Story of a Great Life* (Springfield, Ill.: Herndon's Lincoln Publishing, 1888), 379.

18 *Under Douglas's exalted: Report of the Special Committee Appointed to Investigate the Troubles in Kansas,* 67.

CHAPTER THREE: THE SPIRIT OF VIOLENCE

21 *"Who names Douglas":* "The Prophet on the Nebraska Question," *New York Times,* May 23, 1854.

21 *"I could then travel":* *Political Debates Between Lincoln and Douglas* (Cleveland: Burrows Bros., 1897), 55.

22 *Still, Douglas believed the leadership:* Milton, *The Eve of Conflict,* 212–18.

22 *When the 34th Congress reconvened:* Ibid., 209, 219.

25 *"our little grog drinking":* William E. Dodd, *Jefferson Davis,* Philadelphia, G.W. Jacobs, 1907, 190.

27 *Douglas's description of Massachusetts:* Stephen A. Douglas, "Affairs of Kansas," Report No. 34, in *The Reports of the Committees of the Senate of the United States for the First Session of the Thirty-Fourth Congress* (Washington, D.C.: A.O.P. Nicholson, 1856), 1–10.

28 *Douglas seized upon the gambling metaphor: Congressional Globe,* 34th Congress, 1st Session, 639.

28 *The* New York Tribune *reported:* "Kansas in the Senate," *New York Tribune,* March 12, 1856, reprinted in *Chicago Tribune,* March 17, 1856; *Congressional Globe,* 34th Congress, 1st Session, 639 (hereinafter *CG*); Brie Anna Swenson Arnold, " 'Competition for the Virgin Soil of Kansas': Gendered and Sexualized Discourse About the Kansas Crisis in Northern Popular Print and Political Culture, 1854–1860" (diss., University of Minnesota, 2008, ProQuest), 186.

28 *Two days later:* Horace White, *The Life of Lyman Trumbull* (Boston: Houghton Mifflin, 1913), 48.

29 *The Whig candidate:* Robert W. Johannsen, *Stephen A. Douglas* (New York: Oxford University Press, 1973), 463; *CW,* 2:306.

30 *Reading further portions: CG,* 34st Congress, 1st Session, 200–206.

33 *"Why do you not reprove": CG,* 34th Congress, 1st Session, 654–58.

33 *The following week:* Johannsen, *Stephen A. Douglas,* 495.

34 *Douglas built to a crescendo: CG,* 34th Congress, 1st Session, 280–88.

34 *Calmly and deliberately:* Gideon Welles, *Lincoln and Seward* (New York: Sheldon, 1874), 23, 10.

35 *Seward wore the badges:* Frederick W. Seward, *Seward at Washington as Senator and Secretary of State, 1846–1861* (New York: Derby & Miller, 1891), 246.

36 *At Syracuse:* De Alva Stanwood Alexander, *A Political History of the State of New York* (New York: Henry Holt, 1906), 2:211–13; William H. Seward, "The Dangers of Extending Slavery," in *Republican Campaign Documents of 1856* (Washington, D.C.: Lewis Clephane, 1857), 173–82.

37 *Back in Washington:* Seward, *Seward at Washington as Senator and Secretary of State,* 269.

37 *On April 9: CG,* 34th Congress, 1st Session, 399–405.

38 *To Douglas's intense displeasure:* Albert Gallatin Riddle, *The Life of Benjamin F. Wade* (Cleveland: W.W. Williams, 1886), 136–45, 197.

39 *Then Senator Henry Wilson:* Elias Nason and Thomas Russell, *The Life and Public Services of Henry Wilson* (Boston: B.B. Russell, 1876), 66.

41 *But if Wilson was not: CG,* 34th Congress, 1st Session, 384–94.

42 *But Stowe also noticed:* Rhodes, *History of the United States,* 2:128–29; Johannsen, *Stephen A. Douglas,* 499.

CHAPTER FOUR: WAR TO THE KNIFE

45 *When the 34th Congress arrived:* William E. Gienapp, *The Origins of the Republican Party, 1852–1856* (New York: Oxford University Press, 1987), 240–48.

46 *The majority members:* Kristen Tegtmeier Oertel, *Bleeding Borders: Race, Gender, and Violence in Pre–Civil War Kansas* (Baton Rouge: Louisiana State University Press, 2009), 92.

46 *"The second month of spring":* Sara T.L. Robinson, *Kansas: Its Interior and Exterior Life* (Boston: Crosby, 1856), 196–98.

46 *Two days after the investigators:* Margaret L. Wood, *Memorial of S.N. Wood* (Kansas City: Hudson Kimberly, 1892), 56; Holloway, *History of Kansas,* 305.

47 *Jones arrested six:* Phillips, *The Conquest of Kansas,* 254; Holloway, *History of Kansas,* 317.

47 *Jones's deputies raided:* Holloway, *History of Kansas,* 308; Nicole Etcheson, *Bleeding Kansas: Contested Liberty in the Civil War Era* (Lawrence: University Press of Kansas, 2004), 102; John Sherman, *John Sherman's Recollection of Forty Years in the Senate and Cabinet* (Chicago: Werner, 1895), 1:129.

48 *On May 5:* Phillips, *The Conquest of Kansas,* 269; Franklin Benjamin Sanborn, *The Life and Letters of John Brown: Liberator of Kansas, and Martyr of Virginia* (Boston: Roberts Brothers, 1891), 232.

48 *Judge Lecompte:* Frank W. Blackmar, ed., *Kansas: A Cyclopedia of State History* (Chicago: Standard Publishing, 1912), 2:42.

48 *John Calhoun:* Richard Lawrence Miller, *Lincoln and His World* (Mechanicsburg, Penn.: Stackpole Books, 2006–2014), 1:215–20; John Carroll Power, *History of the Early Settlers of Sangamon County, Illinois* (Springfield, Ill.: Edwin A. Wilson, 1876), 168; Jack Henderson, "A Border Ruffian's Recollection of Kansas," Arkansas City, Kansas Traveler, March 5, 1879; *CW,* 2:229; Miller, *Lincoln and His World,* 1:115; Phillips, *The Conquest of Kansas,* 149–50.

49 *Former governor Reeder:* "Governor Reeder's Escape from Kansas," *Transactions of the Kansas State Historical Society,* Volume 3, *Diary of Gov. A.H. Reeder* (Topeka: Kansas Publishing, 1886), 205–6; *Report of the Special Committee Appointed to Investigate the Troubles in Kansas,* 66.

49 *On May 7:* "Governor Reeder's Escape from Kansas," 206; Charles Robinson, *The Kansas Conflict* (Lawrence: Journal Publishing Company, 1898), 262.

49 *Reeder fled disguised:* "Governor Reeder's Escape from Kansas," 222.

50 *Robinson escaped from Lawrence:* Sherman, *John Sherman's Recollection of Forty Years in the Senate and Cabinet,* 129; Hermann von Holst, *The Constitutional and Political History of the United States: 1854–1856* (Chicago: Callaghan, 1885), 297.

50 *When Reeder eluded arrest:* Holloway, *History of Kansas,* 320–22.

50 *The fog of impending violence:* Wilson, *History of the Rise and Fall of the Slave Power in America,* 2:478–79; Miller, *Lincoln and His World,* 4:139–40; "The Herbert Trial," *New York Times,* July 14, 1856.

51 *When Horace Greeley:* Don C. Seitz, *Horace Greeley,* Indianapolis: Bobbs Merrill, 1926, 170–1; "Latest Intelligence: Brutal Assaults of Rust upon Horace Greeley," *New York Times,* January 30, 1856.

51 *"The tyranny of the slave oligarchy":* Edward L. Pierce, *Memoir and Letters of Charles Sumner* (Boston: Roberts Brothers, 1898), 3:438–39; David Herbert Donald, *Charles Sumner and the Coming of the Civil War* (Chicago: University of Chicago Press, 1960), 279).

CHAPTER FIVE: THE PURITAN AS PROPHET

53 *Since Charles Sumner was elected:* Charles Francis Adams, *Charles Francis Adams, 1835–1915, An Autobiography* (Boston: Houghton Mifflin, 1916), 60–61.

54 *Neither Seward nor Lincoln:* John Greenleaf Whittier, "To C.S.," in *The Poetical Works of John Greenleaf Whittier* (Boston: Houghton Mifflin, 1892), 146; Hugh McCulloch, *Men and Measures of Half a Century: Sketches and Comments* (New York: Charles Scribner's Sons, 1889), 233–34; Frederic Bancroft, ed., *Speeches, Correspondence and Political Papers of Carl Schurz* (New York: G.P. Putnam's Sons, 1913), 39; Donald, *Charles Sumner and the Coming of the Civil War,* 271; Shelby M. Collum, *Fifty Years of Public Service* (Chicago: A.C. McClurg, 1911), 152.

54 *Sumner took painstaking care:* John Weiss, *Life and Correspondence of Theodore Parker* (New York: D. Appleton, 1864), 2:111.

55 *Sumner was absorbed:* Charles Sumner, *The Works of Charles Sumner* (Boston: Lee & Shepard, 1875), 3:275.

55 *Sumner's exalted oratory:* Bancroft, ed., *Speeches, Correspondence and Political Papers of Carl Schurz,* 3:30.

56 *In the Washington of the 1850s:* Eron Rowland, *Varina Howell: Wife of Jefferson Davis* (Gretna, La.: Pelican Publishing, 1927), 1:314; "Sumner's Unhappy Marriage," *New York Times,* October 19, 1884.

57 *Sumner's ostracism:* Charles Sumner, *The Works of Charles Sumner* (Boston: Lee & Shepard, 1870), 2:1, 4; Walter G. Shotwell, *Life of Charles Sumner* (New York: Thomas Y. Crowell, 1910), 205.

57 *In an age when oratory:* D.A. Harsha, *The Life of Charles Sumner: With Choice Specimens of His Eloquence* (New York: H. Dayton, 1858), 155–58.

57 *Despite his immersion:* Donald, *Charles Sumner and the Coming of the Civil War,* 281.

59 *Sumner was one:* C. Edwards Lester, *Life and Public Services of Charles Sumner* (New York: United States Publishing, 1874), 49.

59 *The Puritan as prophet:* Charles Sumner, *Orations and Speeches, 1845–1850* (Boston: Ticknor, Reed, & Fields, 1850), 2:256.

59 *Sumner's background:* Anne-Marie Taylor, *Young Charles Sumner and the American Enlightenment, 1811–1851* (Amherst: University of Massachusetts Press, 2001), 1–2.

60 *Sumner's roots:* Edward L. Pierce, *Memoir and Letters of Charles Sumner* (Boston: Roberts Brothers, 1893), 1:15; Taylor, *Young Charles Sumner and the American En-*

lightenment, 17–18; Elias Nason, *The Life and Times of Charles Sumner* (Boston: B.B. Russell, 1874), 11–13.

60 *The Federalist Party:* Pierce, *Memoir and Letters of Charles Sumner,* 1:2; Taylor, *Young Charles Sumner and the American Enlightenment,* 22–29, 74.

61 *Charles Sumner always considered:* Taylor, *Young Charles Sumner and the American Enlightenment,* 94, 17–18; Sumner, *Works,* 3:85.

61 *One of the beneficiaries:* Wendell Phillips Garrison and Francis Jackson Garrison, *William Lloyd Garrison, 1805–1879: The Story of His Life Told by His Children* (Boston: Houghton Mifflin, 1894), 1:224, 240, 495, 499–500.

62 *A month later, on September 17:* Ibid., 1:519, 2:29.

62 *Charles Sumner was one of the poorer:* Taylor, *Young Charles Sumner and the American Enlightenment,* 27; Shotwell, *Life of Charles Sumner,* 18–26; Moorfield Storey, *Charles Sumner* (Boston: Houghton Mifflin, 1900), 10, 14–15; Donald, *Charles Sumner and the Coming of the Civil War,* 82–83.

63 *Sumner fell under:* Taylor, *Young Charles Sumner and the American Enlightenment,* 139–43; Edward D. Jervey and C. Harold Huber, "The Creole Affair," *The Journal of Negro History* 65, no. 3 (Summer 1980): 196–211; William Ellery Channing, *The Duty of the Free States* (Boston: William Crosby, 1842), 8.

63 *Sumner steeped himself in antislavery literature:* Lydia Maria Child, *An Appeal in Favor of that Class of Americans Called Africans* (Boston: Allen & Ticknor, 1833), 228; Donald, *Charles Sumner and the Coming of the Civil War,* 131; Pierce, *Memoir and Letters of Charles Sumner,* 2:196, 203–4.

64 *In 1845:* Pierce, *Memoir and Letters of Charles Sumner,* 2:342, 348–53.

64 *At the traditional post-oration dinner:* Donald, *Charles Sumner and the Coming of the Civil War,* 110–11; Pierce, *Memoir and Letters of Charles Sumner,* 3:101–2.

65 *The censure of Sumner's:* Taylor, *Young Charles Sumner and the American Enlightenment,* 276–77.

65 *Sumner began meeting:* Ibid., 201; Donald, *Charles Sumner and the Coming of the Civil War,* 140; Sumner, *Works,* 1:149.

65 *Winthrop voted for the war:* Donald, *Charles Sumner and the Coming of the Civil War,* 141–46; Taylor, *Young Charles Sumner and the American Enlightenment,* 213–20.

66 *The Conscience Whigs:* Sumner, *Works,* 1:303–16, 331.

66 *Sumner's battle with Winthrop:* Donald, *Charles Sumner and the Coming of the Civil War,* 122–28, 112; Sumner, *Works,* 1:502; Pierce, *Memoir and Letters of Charles Sumner,* 3:79–97.

67 *As these controversies simmered:* Donald, *Charles Sumner and the Coming of the Civil War,* 129.

67 *The largest mansion:* George S. Hillard, *Life, Letters, and Journal of George Ticknor* (Boston: Houghton Mifflin, 1909), 1:390–2, viii–ix; Edwin Percy Whipple, *Recollections of Eminent Men* (Boston: Ticknor, 1886), 270; William Cullen Bryant

II and Thomas G. Voss, eds., *The Letters of William Cullen Bryant* (New York: Fordham University Press, 1992), 6:307.

68   *Ticknor had been Sumner's:* Katherine Wolff, *Culture Club: The Curious History of the Boston Athenaeum* (Boston: University of Massachusetts Press, 2009), 125; Pierce, *Memoir and Letters of Charles Sumner,* 3:7–8; Taylor, *Young Charles Sumner and the American Enlightenment,* 299; Charles Francis Adams, *Richard Henry Dana, Jr.* (Boston: Houghton Mifflin, 1891), 1:127–28; Carolyn L. Karcher, *The First Woman in the Republic: A Cultural Biography of Lydia Maria Child* (Durham, N.C.: Duke University Press, 1992), 39–40, 192; Hillard, *Life, Letters, and Journal of George Ticknor,* 1:ix.

68   *But the social insulation:* Taylor, *Young Charles Sumner and the American Enlightenment,* 246.

69   *Then Sumner led a contingent:* Ibid., 225; Pierce, *Memoir and Letters of Charles Sumner,* 3:144–46.

69   *In 1847:* Donald, *Charles Sumner and the Coming of the Civil War,* 161; Pierce, *Memoir and Letters of Charles Sumner,* 3:153; Taylor, *Young Charles Sumner and the American Enlightenment,* 248.

70   *"Be not Atticus:* James Spear Loring, *The Hundred Boston Orators* (Boston: John P. Jewett, 1852), 630.

70   *Sumner was already involved:* Samuel Longfellow, *Life of Henry Wadsworth Longfellow: With Extracts from His Journals and Correspondence* (Boston: Houghton Mifflin, 1891), 2:174; Donald, *Charles Sumner and the Coming of the Civil War,* 164–65; Pierce, *Memoir and Letters of Charles Sumner,* 3:161.

70   *When the Whigs nominated Zachary Taylor:* Sumner, *Works,* 2:80–81.

71   *In August, Sumner attended:* Edwin Percy Whipple, *The Great Speeches and Orations of Daniel Webster* (Boston: Little, Brown, 1889), 581; Sumner, *Works,* 2:144.

71   *The Boston Atlas:* Pierce, *Memoir and Letters of Charles Sumner,* 3:178; Donald, *Charles Sumner and the Coming of the Civil War,* 161.

71   *Sumner was drafted to run:* Longfellow, *Life of Henry Wadsworth Longfellow,* 129, 131, 134.

72   *Sumner's advocacy:* Donald, *Charles Sumner and the Coming of the Civil War,* 163.

72   *Samuel Lawrence, Abbot's brother:* Ibid., 170; Pierce, *Memoir and Letters of Charles Sumner,* 3:181–82.

72   *Nathan Appleton:* Nathan Appleton, *Introduction of the Power Loom, and Origin of Lowell* (Lowell: B.H. Penhallow, 1858), 29; Pierce, *Memoir and Letters of Charles Sumner,* 3:181; Donald, *Charles Sumner and the Coming of the Civil War,* 170.

73   *Sumner always believed:* Robert L. Hall, "Massachusetts Abolitionists Document the Slave Experience," in Donald M. Jacobs, ed., *Courage and Conscience: Black & White Abolitionists in Boston* (Bloomington: Indiana University Press, 1993), 85; Stephen Kendrick and Paul Kendrick, *Sarah's Long Walk: The Free Blacks of Boston and How Their Struggle for Equality Changed America* (Boston: Beacon Press,

2004), 13–20; Hillary J. Moss, *Schooling Citizens: The Struggle for African American Education in Antebellum America* (Chicago: University of Chicago Press, 2010), 181.

73   *On December 4, 1849:* Sumner, *Works,* 2:327–76.

74   *In 1850: Reports of Cases Argued and Determined in the Supreme Judicial Court of the Commonwealth of Massachusetts,* Volume 59 (Boston: Little, Brown, 1853), 209; Taylor, *Young Charles Sumner and the American Enlightenment,* 253.

74   *The demarcation line:* Daniel Webster, *Webster's Speeches* (Boston: Ginn & Company, 1897), 103–56; John Niven, *Salmon P. Chase: A Biography* (New York: Oxford University Press, 1995), 135.

75   *The Whig Party of Massachusetts:* Ralph Waldo Emerson, *The Complete Works* (Boston: Houghton, Mifflin, 1904), 11:202–4; Taylor, *Young Charles Sumner and the American Enlightenment,* 291, 298; Adams, *Richard Henry Dana, Jr.,* 127–28.

75   *On the eve of the election:* Sumner, *Works,* 2:398–424.

76   *Sumner's electrifying speech:* Donald, *Charles Sumner and the Coming of the Civil War,* 196.

76   *The balloting that began:* Henry David Thoreau, *The Writings of Henry David Thoreau* (Boston: Houghton Mifflin, 1893), 10:174; Henry Adams, *The Education of Henry Adams* (Boston: Houghton Mifflin, 1918), 51.

77   *In mourning Whigs wore black:* Adams, *The Education of Henry Adams,* 51; Benjamin Robbins Curtis, *A Memoir of Benjamin Robbins Curtis* (Boston: Little, Brown, 1879), 138–50.

77   *"He was sent to work":* Thomas Wentworth Higginson, *Contemporaries* (Boston: Riverside Press, 1900), 283.

77   *Sumner soon encountered the overriding reality:* Ibid., 282; Donald, *Charles Sumner and the Coming of the Civil War* 222; *CG,* 32nd Congress, 1st Session, 1952; Pierce, *Memoir and Letters of Charles Sumner,* 3:290; Seward, *Seward at Washington as Senator and Secretary of State,* 190.

78   *Sumner would envision the future:* Sumner, *Works,* 6:307.

78   *Sumner, meanwhile, wrote:* Ibid., 3:50; Daniel Drayton, *Personal Memoir of Daniel Drayton* (Boston: Bella Marsh, 1853), 116–17.

78   *Sumner argued that the slave was "a person":* Sumner, *Works,* 3:87–196; James Oakes, *Freedom National: The Destruction of Slavery in the United States, 1861–1865* (New York: W.W. Norton, 2013), 32–33.

79   *When Sumner took his seat: CG,* 32nd Congress, 1st Session, Appendix, 113–25.

79   *At the Massachusetts Free Soil Party convention:* Sumner, *Works,* 3:205.

CHAPTER SIX: CYCLOPS

81   *"This Congress is the worst":* Pierce, *Memoir and Letters of Charles Sumner,* 3:361.

81   *The outsiders at the fringe:* Ibid., 3:350; *CG,* 33rd Congress, 1st Session, 275–82.

82   *Sumner resumed his opposition: CG,* 33rd Congress, 1st Session, 108–9.

82 *After his disquisition: CG,* 33rd Congress, 1st Session, 116–17.

84 *But it was not strictly a play: CG,* 33rd Congress, 1st Session, 232–34.

84 *Butler may have been more familiar:* David S. Reynolds, *Mightier Than the Sword: Uncle Tom's Cabin and the Battle for America* (New York: W.W. Norton, 2011), 137–47.

84 *The exact Latin line:* Harriet Beecher Stowe, *Uncle Tom's Cabin: Or, Life Among the Lowly* (Boston: Houghton Mifflin, 1879), 374.

85 *Butler offered his own:* Frances Smith Foster, *Witnessing Slavery: The Development of Ante-bellum Slave Narratives* (Madison: University of Wisconsin Press, 1979), 130; J. Blaine Hudson, *Fugitive Slaves and the Underground Railroad in the Kentucky Borderland* (Jefferson, N.C.: McFarland, 2002), 37.

85 *The reality, however:* Howard Bodenhorn, *The Color Factor: The Economics of African-American Well-Being in the Nineteenth Century South*, New York: Oxford University Press, 71.

86 *Butler concluded his two-day marathon: CG,* 33rd Congress, 1st Session, 240.

86 *But the surprise obscure quotation:* "Queries Respecting the Slavery and Emancipation of Negroes in Massachusetts, Proposed by the Hon. Judge Tucker of Virginia, and Answered by the Rev. Dr. Belknap," *Collections of the Massachusetts Historical Society,* Series 1 (Boston: Massachusetts Historical Society, 1835; reprint of 1795 publication), 4:191–211, http://www.masshist.org/database/viewer.php?item_id=693&br=1; Justin Winsor, ed., *The Memorial History of Boston* (Boston: James R. Osgood, 1881), 2:485–86; Jeremy Belknap, *Life of Jeremy Belknap* (New York: Harper & Brothers, 1847), 160; C. Vanderford, "A Dissertation on Slavery: With a Proposal for the Gradual Abolition of It, in the State of Virginia" (1796), February 4, 2015, *Encyclopedia Virginia,* online, http://www.EncyclopediaVirginia.org/A_Dissertation_on_Slavery_With_a_Proposal_for_the_Gradual_Abolition_of_It_In_the_State_of_Virginia_1796; Winthrop D. Jordan, *White Over Black: American Attitudes Toward the Negro, 1550–1812* (Chapel Hill: University of North Carolina Press, 1968), 555–60.

87 *"Sir, the bill":* Sumner, *Works,* 3:340–44.

87 *Two nights later, on May 26:* Wilson, *History of the Rise and Fall of the Slave Power in America,* 2:435–41.

87 *The pro-Pierce newspapers:* Archibald Henry Grimké, *The Life of Charles Sumner: The Scholar in Politics* (New York: Funk & Wagnalls, 1892), 231–32.

88 *"Southern Men Threatening Personal Danger":* "Southern Men Threatening Personal Danger to Senator Sumner," *New York Times,* May 31, 1854.

88 *The article in the* Washington Union: "Abolition Mob and Murder in Boston," *Washington Union,* May 28, 1854.

88 *"If you really think there is any danger":* Grimké, *The Life of Charles Sumner,* 233.

89 *"Slavery," Sumner pledged:* Donald, *Charles Sumner and the Coming of the Civil War,* 262; Pierce, *Memoir and Letters of Charles Sumner,* 3:377.

89 *After Southern senators objected: CG,* 33rd Congress, 1st Session, 1517.

89 *Two days later, Sumner again spoke: CG,* 33rd Congress, 1st Session, 1011–15.

90 *But the effort to remove Sumner:* "Effort to Expel Senator Sumner," *New York Times,* June 30, 1854.

90 *In late 1854:* Mary Niall Mitchell, *Raising Freedom's Child: Black Children and Visions of the Future After Slavery* (New York: NYU Press, 2010), 72–74; "Letter from Hon. Charles Sumner—Another Ida May," *New York Times,* March 1, 1855; Henry Greenleaf Pearson, *The Life of John A. Andrew: Governor of Massachusetts, 1861–1865* (Boston: Houghton Mifflin, 1904), 1:57–58.

91 *Sumner had "created quite a sensation":* "A White Slave from Virginia," *New York Times,* March 9, 1855.

92 *Two months after Mary Mildred Botts:* Sumner, *Works,* 4:12.

CHAPTER SEVEN: A VOICE FROM THE GRAVE

94 *Even before his election:* Niven, *Salmon P. Chase,* 173.

94 *"Good! Good! Good!":* Richard H. Sewell, *Ballots for Freedom: Antislavery Politics in the United States, 1837–1860* (New York: Oxford University Press, 1976), 273; Niven, *Salmon P. Chase,* 174–79.

95 *Chase and his political agents:* Gienapp, *The Origins of the Republican Party,* 248–50; Niven, *Salmon P. Chase,* 177–78, 53, 78.

95 *Chase was not the sole person:* Lewis Clephane, *Birth of the Republican Party, With a Brief History of the Important Part Taken by the Republican Association of the National Capital* (Washington, D.C.: Gibson Bros., 1889), 8–9.

96 *Since the passage of the Nebraska Act:* Gienapp, *The Origins of the Republican Party,* 319–21.

96 *Blair arranged with the Republican Association:* Clephane, *Birth of the Republican Party,* 9.

97 *Blair placed Douglas:* Ibid., 19–23.

98 *"FRANCIS P. BLAIR TURNED BLACK REPUBLICAN":* "FRANCIS P. BLAIR TURNED BLACK REPUBLICAN," *Washington Union,* December 11, 1855; "The Administration Organ on Blair," *New York Times,* December 12, 1855.

98 *The dinner party:* Gienapp, *The Origins of the Republican Party,* 250–51; Niven, *Salmon P. Chase,* 178–79; Sewell, *Ballots for Freedom,* 277; Sumner, *Works,* 4:78; Pamela Herr and Mary Lee Spence, eds., *The Letters of Jessie Benton Frémont* (Urbana: University of Illinois Press, 1993), 66; Seward, *Seward at Washington as Senator and Secretary of State,* 264.

99 *The year 1856:* Pleasant A. Stovall, *Robert Toombs* (New York: Cassell Publishing Company, 1892), 128–39; Betty G. Farrell, *Elite Families: Class and Power in Nineteenth-Century Boston* (Albany: State University of New York Press, 1993), 60–63; Alexander H. Stephens, *A Constitutional View of the Late War Between the States* (Philadelphia: National Publishing, 1868), 1:625–47.

100 *After Blair's Christmas summit:* Walter C. Clephane, "Lewis Clephane: A Pioneer Washington Republican," *Records of the Columbia Historical Society, Washington, D.C.* (Washington, D.C.: The Society, 1918), 21:271; Sewell, *Ballots for Freedom,* 279; Francis P. Blair, *A Voice from the Grave of Jackson!* (Washington: Buell & Blanchard, 1856); Arthur M. Schlesinger, Jr., *The Age of Jackson* (Boston: Little, Brown, 1945), 478.

100 *When Jackson died:* Blair, *A Voice from the Grave of Jackson!*; Milton, *The Eve of Conflict,* 16; James W. Sheahan, *The Life of Stephen A. Douglas* (New York: Harper & Brothers 1860), 59–72.

101 *Pierce's vacuum:* Nichols, *Franklin Pierce,* 454; Alexander H. Stephens and Howell Cobb, eds., *The Correspondence of Robert Toombs* (Washington, D.C.: U.S. Government Printing Office, 1913), 368–72.

101 *The only way for Douglas: Quincy Daily Whig,* May 10, 1856; Milton, *The Eve of Conflict,* 224; Gienapp, *The Origins of the Republican Party,* 290–91.

102 *"Doing Him Honor,":* "Doing Him Honor," *Illinois State Journal,* May 3, 1856.

102 *"An Evil Genius":* "An Evil Genius," *New York Times,* May 3, 1856.

103 *By mid-May:* Johannsen, *Stephen A. Douglas,* 515; Milton, *The Eve of Conflict,* 225; Murat Halstead, *Trimmers, Trucklers & Temporizers: Notes of Murat Halstead from the Political Conventions of 1856,* eds., William B. Hesseltine and Rex G. Fisher (Madison: State Historical Society of Wisconsin, 1961), 19.

103 *In Washington, on May 18:* William C. Davis, *John C. Breckinridge: Statesman, Soldier, Symbol* (Lexington: University Press of Kentucky, 2015), 142.

104 *Newspapers across the country: Annals of Kansas,* Territorial Kansas Online, http://www.territorialkansasonline.org/cgiwrap/imlskto/index.php?SCREEN=view_image&file_name=annals_000082&document_id=102054&FROM_PAGE=; Albert J. Beveridge, *Abraham Lincoln, 1809–1858* (Boston: Houghton Mifflin, 1928), 2:334; Wilentz, *The Rise of American Democracy,* 688.

104 *On May 19: New York Tribune,* May 19, 1856.

104 *As Charles Sumner carefully prepared:* Nason, *The Life and Times of Charles Sumner,* 213.

CHAPTER EIGHT: THE HARLOT SLAVERY

105 *"In this dark midnight hour":* Anna Laurens Dawes, *Charles Sumner* (New York: Dodd, Mead, 1892), 88–89; Pierce, *Memoir and Letters of Charles Sumner,* 3:441.

105 *The authors of the Kansas debacle:* Donald, *Charles Sumner and the Coming of the Civil War,* 220, 263, 236; George Henry Haynes, *Charles Sumner* (Philadelphia: G.W. Jacobs, 1909), 165.

106 *Sumner scorned the Southern:* Pierce, *Memoir and Letters of Charles Sumner,* 3:433; "Reminiscences of Sumner," James Redpath to Elias Nason, April 10, 1874, http://www.wvculture.org/history/wvmemory/jbdetail.aspx?Type=Text&Id=1023.

106 *But any speculative search:* Sumner, *Works,* 3:131; Alan Heimert and Andrew

Delbanco, eds., *The Puritans in America* (Cambridge: Harvard University Press, 2009), 91.

106   *No less than George Washington:* John C. Fitzpatrick, ed., *The Writings of George Washington* (Washington, D.C.: U.S. Government Printing Office, 1931–1944), 25:484–85.

107   *"Notwithstanding the heat":* Pierce, *Memoir and Letters of Charles Sumner,* 3:441.

109   *The crime he described:* Dawes, *Charles Sumner,* 91–92.

109   *His particular targets:* Wilson, *History of the Rise and Fall of the Slave Power in America,* 2:480

112   *In pointing to slavery's:* Samuel May, *The Fugitive Slave Law and Its Victims* (New York: American Anti-Slavery Society, 1861), 50–60; Sally Gregory McMillen, *Lucy Stone: An Unapologetic Life* (New York: Oxford University Press, 2015), 133; Levi Coffin, *Reminiscences of Levi Coffin, Reputed President of the Underground Railroad* (Cincinnati: Robert Clarke, 1880), 563.

113   *The "pious matron":* Margaret Douglass, *Educational Laws of Virginia: The Personal Narrative of Mrs. Margaret Douglass* (Boston: John P. Jewett, 1854), 35, 62–64; Michael D. Pierson, "'All Southern Society Is Assailed by the Foulest Charges': Charles Sumner's 'The Crime Against Kansas' and the Escalation of Republican Anti-Slavery Rhetoric," *The New England Quarterly* 68, no. 4 (December 1995): 531–57.

114   *Sumner's picture of the domestic:* C. Vann Woodward, ed., *Mary Chesnut's Civil War* (New Haven: Yale University Press, 1981), 29.

115   *Butler had intervened:* Pierce, *Memoir and Letters of Charles Sumner,* 3:271.

118   *"the most un-American":* Jesse Macy, *The Anti-Slavery Crusade: A Chronicle of the Gathering Storm,* New Haven: Yale University Press, 1920, 176.

118   *"Is it his object":* Ibid., 176.

120   *Douglas took offense:* Charles Sumner, *Recent Speeches and Addresses, 1851–1855* (Boston: Higgins & Bradley, 1856), 542–43.

120   *Sumner now faced Mason:* Sumner, *Works,* 4:125–256.

120   *Thirteen years later:* Milton, *The Eve of Conflict,* 233.

120   *"You had better go down":* "Alleged Assault on Senator Sumner," House of Representatives, 34th Congress, 1st Session, Report No. 182 (Washington, D.C.: U.S. Government Printing Office, 1856), 25, 42, 45.

121   *The next day, on the floor of the House:* CG, 34th Congress, 1st Session, 1363, 1365.

CHAPTER NINE: THE ASSASSINATION OF CHARLES SUMNER

123   *David Rice Atchison:* David M. Potter, *The Impending Crisis: 1848–1861* (New York: Harper & Row, 1976), 239; P. Orman Ray, *The Repeal of the Missouri Compromise: Its Origin and Authorship* (Cleveland, Ohio: Arthur H. Clark, 1908), 225–26.

124   *Atchison sent a scouting party:* Spring, *Kansas, the Prelude to the War for the Union,* 122; Phillips, *The Conquest of Kansas, by Missouri and Her Allies,* 297.

124 *The Ruffians broke into the offices:* Phillips, *The Conquest of Kansas, by Missouri and Her Allies,* 297–99; Ray, *The Repeal of the Missouri Compromise,* 225–26.

124 *"LAWRENCE TAKEN!":* Daniel W. Wilder, *The Annals of Kansas* (Topeka: George W. Martin, 1875), 100.

124 *"Important From Kansas":* "Important from Kansas: A General Reign of Terror," *New York Times,* May 22, 1856; "General Jackson Vindicated Against Mr. Blair's Imputation of Black Republicanism," and "The Testimony of an Enemy on the Kansas Question," *Washington Union,* May 22, 1856; "To the Citizens of San- gamon County," *Illinois State Journal,* May 22, 1856.

125 *As Sumner's crime against Kansas speech:* "Alleged Assault on Senator Sumner," 43.

125 *The next evening, with news:* Arnold Burges Johnson, "Recollections of Charles Sumner," *Scribner's Monthly* 8 (New York: William H. Cadwell, 1874), 482.

126 *As the natural crucible:* Orville Vernon Burton, *In My Father's House Are Many Mansions: Family and Community in Edgefield, South Carolina* (Chapel Hill: Uni- versity of North Carolina Press, 2000), 65–73; Richard Maxwell Brown, *Strain of Violence: Historical Studies of American Violence and Vigilantism* (New York, Oxford University Press, 1975), 67–85.

126 *Preston Smith Brooks:* Ken Deitreich, " 'Ever Able, Manly, Just and Heroic': Pres- ton Smith Brooks and the Myth of Southern Manhood," *The Proceedings of the South Carolina Historical Association* (Columbia: South Carolina Historical As- sociation, 2011), 27–38; Thomas John Balcerski, "Intimate Contests: Manhood, Friendships, and the Coming of the Civil War," (PhD diss. Cornell University, 2014), 337, https://ecommons.cornell.edu/bitstream/1813/39014/1/tjb36.pdf; Ste- phen Berry and James Hill Welborn III, "The Cane of His Existence: Depression, Damage, and the Brooks–Sumner Affair," *Southern Cultures* 20, no. 4 (Winter 2014): 5–21; Stephen Puleo, *The Caning: The Assault That Drove America to Civil War* (Yardley, Penn.: Westholme, 2014), 93.

127 *Then an exceptional opportunity appeared:* George Frisbie Hoar, *Autobiography of Seventy Years* (New York: Charles Scribner's Sons, 1903), 1:24–26; Sumner, *Works,* 3:382.

128 *Hammond had ordered:* Drew Gilpin Faust, *James Henry Hammond and the Old South: A Design for Mastery* (Baton Rouge: Louisiana State University Press, 1982), 252; Carol K. Bleser, ed., *Secret and Sacred: The Diaries of James Henry Hammond, a Southern Slaveholder* (New York: Oxford University Press, 1989), 140.

128 *The declaration of war:* Deitreich, "Ever Able, Manly, Just and Heroic,' " 27–38; Berry and Welborn, "The Cane of His Existence," 5–21; Burton, *In My Father's House,* 96.

128 *Seeking the distinction:* Balcerski, "Intimate Contests," 348; Manisha Sinha, *The Counter-Revolution of Slavery: Politics and Ideology in Antebellum South Carolina* (Chapel Hill: University of North Carolina Press, 2000), 188–89; Lacy K. Ford, *Origins of Southern Radicalism: The South Carolina Upcountry, 1800–1860* (New York: Oxford University Press, 1991), 346; Ulrich B. Phillips, ed., *The Correspon-

dence of Robert Toombs, Alexander H. Stephens, and Howell Cobb (Washington, D.C.: U.S. Government Printing Office, 1911), 2:368.

129 *Within the House: CG,* 33rd Congress, 1st Session, 374, 77.

130 *As Brooks was being squeezed:* Paul Quigley, *Shifting Grounds: Nationalism and the American South, 1848–1865* (New York: Oxford University Press, 2014), 61; W.T. Thayer, "Assault Upon Senator Sumner," *New York Evening Post,* May 23, 1856.

130 *Laurence M. Keitt:* Berry and Welborn, "The Cane of His Existence"; *CG,* 33rd Congress, 1st Session, 1073–74.

131 *"Between the South and these men": CG,* 34th Congress, 1st Session, 442–43.

131 *A few days later, Brooks and Keitt joined:* Berry and Welborn, "The Cane of His Existence," 21.

132 *On May 8, 1856:* Balcerski, "Intimate Contests," 359.

132 *Brooks' intimate circle:* Blumenthal, *Wrestling with His Angel,* 315; Sara B. Bearss, "Henry Alonzo Edmundson," *Dictionary of Virginia Biography,* Library of Virginia, 2016, http://www.lva.virginia.gov/public/dvb/bio.asp?b=Edmundson_Henry_Alonzo; *CG,* 34th Congress, 1st Session, 253.

132 *Edmundson recalled:* "Alleged Assault on Senator Sumner," 59.

133 *While Edmundson and Brooks talked:* Elsie M. Lewis, "Robert Ward Johnson: Militant Spokesman of the Old-South-West," *The Arkansas Historical Quarterly* 13, no. 1 (Spring 1954): 16–30; James M. Wood, "Robert Ward Johnson," *The Encyclopedia of Arkansas History and Culture,* http://www.encyclopediaofarkansas.net/encyclopedia/entry-detail.aspx?entryID=1682.

133 *Early on the morning of the 22nd:* "Alleged Assault on Senator Sumner," 59–60; Burton, *In My Father's House,* 94.

134 *Edmundson noticed that Brooks was hovering:* "Alleged Assault on Senator Sumner," 60, 63.

135 *Sumner was bent over:* Ibid., 25.

135 *"At the concluding words":* Burton, *In My Father's House,* 94.

135 *But Sumner made no effort:* Sumner, *Works,* 4:268–70; "Alleged Assault on Senator Sumner," 37.

135 *While Brooks beat Sumner:* "Alleged Assault on Senator Sumner," 29, 34, 38–39, 47–49, 57.

136 *Congressman Edwin Morgan:* Ibid., 40, 24; "New York for Free Speech," *New York Tribune,* May 31, 1856.

136 *The three men:* Miller, *Lincoln and His World,* 4:147.

136 *Senator John Slidell: CG,* 34th Congress, 1st Session, 1304–5.

137 *Standing over Sumner:* "Alleged Assault on Senator Sumner," 49–50.

137 *Bassett the doorkeeper:* Isaac Bassett, "A Senate Memoir," unpublished manuscript. U.S. Senate Historical Office, https://www.senate.gov/artandhistory/art/special/Bassett/tdetail.cfm?id=17.

137 *The nearest physician:* Ibid., 51; William James Hoffer, *The Caning of Charles Sumner: Honor, Idealism, and the Origins of the Civil War* (Baltimore: Johns Hopkins University Press, 2010), 75; Haynes, *Charles Sumner,* 208.

138 *The doorkeeper of the House:* "Alleged Assault on Senator Sumner," 54–55.

138 *Even before Sumner delivered:* Ibid., 59; *CG,* 34th Congress, 1st Session, 1347.

139 *Butler described Brooks's "temperament":* CG, 34th Congress, 1st Session, 630–35.

140 *Brooks later told a friend:* Avery Craven, *The Coming of the Civil War* (Chicago: University of Chicago Press, 1942), 367.

140 *For all the reasons Brooks:* "Alleged Assault on Senator Sumner," 61.

141 *While there are no first-hand narratives:* "Slave Schedules, Edgefield County, S.C.," *1850 Federal Census,* Ancestry.com.

141 *Brooks was tapped to enforce:* CG, 34th Congress, 1st Session, 630–35; "The Ruffianly Assault of Senator Sumner," *New York Times,* May 24, 1856.

141 *Brooks had done his work:* Johnson, "Recollections of Charles Sumner," 482.

CHAPER TEN: ARGUMENTS OF THE CHIVALRY

143 *After leaving Sumner:* Wilson, *History of the Rise and Fall of the Slave Power in America,* 2:482–83.

144 *His appeal was greeted:* CG, 34th Congress, 1st Session, 1279–80.

144 *Five days later, on May 28:* CG, 34th Congress, 1st Session, 1317.

144 *On the same day that the Senate committee was formed:* Puleo, *The Caning,* 144–45.

144 *"The feeling is pretty much sectional":* Ford, *Origins of Southern Radicalism,* 348.

144 *"This is not an assault, sir":* "Attack on Sumner," *New York Tribune,* May 28, 1856.

145 *Brooks was acclaimed:* Sumner, *Works,* 4:277.

145 *"The whole South sustains Brooks":* "Washington," *Charleston Mercury,* May 28, 1856; Sumner, *Works,* 4:278–79.

146 *Southern newspapers boldly made the threats:* "Doings in Congress," *New York Tribune,* May 23, 1856.

146 *Douglas's purported threat:* "We Mean to Subdue You," *Illinois State Journal,* May 26, 1856.

146 *Across the North:* "The Sumner Outrage," *New York Tribune,* May 31, 1856; Sumner, *Works,* 4:305–6.

147 *On the Sunday after the attack:* Francis Power Cobbe, ed., *The Collected Works of Theodore Parker,* Volume 4 (London, Trübner, 1863), 288–91.

147 *"It is the best":* Ralph Waldo Emerson, *The Works of Ralph Waldo Emerson, Miscellanies* (Boston: Houghton Mifflin, 1883), 11:236.

147 *"You can have little idea":* Gienapp, *The Origins of the Republican Party,* 301–2.

148 *The timing fell:* Ibid., 300–302; William E. Gienapp, "The Crime Against Sumner: The Caning of Charles Sumner and the Rise of the Republican Party," *Civil War History* 25, no. 3 (September 1979): 218–45.

148 *"By great odds":* Alexander K. McClure, *Colonel Alexander K. McClure's Recollection of Half a Century* (Salem, Mass.: Salem Press, 1902), 393–94; Gienapp, *The Origins of the Republican Party,* 300.

149 *Edward Everett:* Tyler Anbinder, *Nativism and Slavery: The Northern Know Nothings and the Politics of the 1850's* (New York: Oxford University Press, 1992), 215–16.

149 *The Massachusetts legislature's resolution:* CG, 34th Congress, 1st Session, 1306; Wilson, *History of the Rise and Fall of the Slave Power in America,* 2:487–88.

149 *On June 2:* "Alleged Assault on Senator Sumner," 1–5.

150 *The minority report:* Ibid., 19.

150 *On June 12:* CG, 34th Congress, 1st Session, 625–26.

150 *The next day Henry Wilson:* CG, 34th Congress, 1st Session, 1399–1405.

150 *Senator Clement Clay:* CG, 34th Congress, 1st Session, 1405.

151 *Congressman Anson Burlingame:* CG, 34th Congress, 1st Session, 656.

151 *Brooks promptly sent word:* Wilson, *History of the Rise and Fall of the Slave Power in America,* 2:491–93; "Brooks and Burlingame Difficulty," *New York Tribune,* July 28, 1856.

151 *Brooks faced criminal charges:* "Brooks Defence of Himself," *New York Times,* July 10, 1856; Pierce, *Memoir and Letters of Charles Sumner,* 3:487.

152 *Two days later the House debate:* CG, 34th Congress, 1st Session, 734–39, 913–14.

152 *The House on July 14:* CG, 34th Congress, 1st Session, 831–33; "More About Bully Brooks and His Exit," *New York Tribune,* July 15, 1856.

153 *Since the assault:* "Another 'Painful Occurrence' in the City of Washington," *New York Times,* May 28, 1856; "Intelligence from Washington," *New York Times,* July 10, 1856.

153 *"Today I speak for South Carolina":* CG, 34th Congress, 1st Session, 833–38.

153 *Three weeks later, on August 1:* Puleo, *The Caning,* 174.

154 *On his thirty-seventh birthday:* J.F.H. Claiborne, *Life and Correspondence of John A. Quitman* (New York: Harper & Brothers, 1860), 2:318–20.

154 *Brooks went on a tour:* Hoffer, *The Caning of Charles Sumner,* 93; Michael W. Cluskey, ed., *The Political Text-book, Or Encyclopedia: Containing Everything Necessary for the Reference of the Politicians and Statesmen of the United States* (Philadelphia: J.B. Smith, 1859), 85–86.

154 *Brooks had overnight become an iconic figure:* Sumner, *Works,* 4:275.

154 *Throughout his life, Brooks:* Berry and Welborn, "The Cane of His Existence"; Wilson, *History of the Rise and Fall of the Slave Power in America,* 2:495.

155 *Brooks caught a cold:* Berry and Welborn, "The Cane of His Existence"; Virginia Clay-Clopton, *A Belle of the Fifties: Memoirs of Mrs. Clay of Alabama, Covering Social and Social and Political Life in Washington and the South* (London: Wm. Heinemann, 1905), 51.

155 *Privately, James Henry Hammond reflected:* "Hon. Preston S. Brooks," *Southern Quarterly Review* 30 (November 1856): 369; Berry and Welborn, "The Cane of His Existence."

155 *Later that year, just before Christmas:* Puleo, *The Caning,* 266.

155 *In Edgefield's Willowbrook Cemetery:* Ibid., 222–23.

CHAPTER ELEVEN: EXTERMINATING ANGEL

157 *Two days after the sack:* George Washington Brown, *The Truth at Last: History Corrected. Reminiscences of Old John Brown* (Rockford, Ill.: Abraham E. Smith, 1880), 69–70.

158 *Earlier that day, Brown:* Oswald Garrison Villard, *John Brown: 1800–1859: A Biography After Fifty Years* (Boston: Houghton Mifflin, 1910), 151–56.

158 *John Brown had followed:* James Redpath, *The Public Life of Capt. John Brown* (Boston: Thayer & Eldridge, 1860), 82.

158 *Brown heard the voice of God:* Ibid., 69.

159 *Brown viewed antislavery politics:* John Edwin Cook, *The Life, Trial, and Execution of Captain John Brown* (New York: Robert M. DeWitt, 1859), 15, 21.

159 *Just as Brown had no use:* Frederick Douglass, *Life and Times of Frederick Douglass* (Hartford: Park Publishing, 1882), 337–41.

160 *As much as Brown pored:* Zoe Trodd and John Stauffer, eds., *Meteor of War: The John Brown Story* (Maplecrest, N.Y.: Brandywine Press, 2004), 84; Ted A. Smith, *Weird John Brown: Divine Violence and the Limits of Ethics* (Stanford: Stanford University Press, 2014), 166.

160 *Brown's self-flagellation:* Cook, *The Life, Trial, and Execution of Captain John Brown,* 8.

160 *John Brown presented himself:* David Reynolds, *John Brown, Abolitionist: The Man Who Killed Slavery, Sparked the Civil War, and Seeded Civil Rights* (New York: Alfred A. Knopf, 2005), 19–25; Jonathan Edwards, *The Injustice and Impolicy of the Slave Trade and of the Slavery of the Africans* (Boston: Wells & Lilly, 1822), 3.

161 *John Brown, born in 1800:* Reynolds, *John Brown, Abolitionist,* 33, 43; Villard, *John Brown,* 4; James Oakes, *The Radical and the Republican: Frederick Douglass, Abraham Lincoln, and the Triumph of Antislavery Politics* (New York: W.W. Norton, 2007), 95.

161 *In 1839:* Richard J. Hinton, *John Brown and His Men* (New York: Funk & Wagnalls, 1894), 23.

162 *Brown had by now begun:* Reynolds, *John Brown, Abolitionist,* 66–94; Edward J. Renehan, Jr., *The Secret Six: The True Tale of the Men Who Conspired with John Brown* (Columbia: University of South Carolina Press, 1997), 23.

162 *The greater his adversity:* Reynolds, *John Brown, Abolitionist,* 56–57.

162 *He moved to Springfield:* Stephen B. Oates, *To Purge This Land with Blood* (Amherst: University of Massachusetts Press, 1984), 58; Hinton, *John Brown and His Men,* 27; Louis A. Decaro, Jr., *"Fire from the Midst of You": A Religious Life of John Brown* (New York: NYU Press, 2005), 149; Imani Kazini, "Black Springfield: A Historical Study," *Contributions in Black Studies* 1, no. 2; http://ourpluralhistory. stcc.edu/resistingslavery/thomas.html.

163 *Through his relationships:* Reynolds, *John Brown, Abolitionist,* 103; Henry High-

land Garnet, "An Address to the Slaves of the United States of America," 1843, digitalcommons.unl.edu/etas/8.

163   *On a speaking tour:* Douglass, *Life and Times,* 277–81.

164   *Douglass claimed from that moment:* Ibid., 282.

164   *Through Douglass, Brown met Willis Hodges:* Theodore Hamm, ed., *Frederick Douglass in Brooklyn* (New York: Akashic Books, 2017), 16–17; Trodd and Stauffer, eds., *Meteor of War,* 56–58.

165   *Nearly broke and scrambling:* Oates, *To Purge This Land with Blood,* 65–66; Franklin B. Sanborn, *The Life and Letters of John Brown* (Boston: Roberts Brothers, 1891), 59.

165   *Brown called the North Elba colony:* Nichole M. Christian, "North Elba Journal; Recalling Timbuctoo, A Slice of Black History," *New York Times,* February 19, 2002.

165   *Back in Springfield in 1851:* Sanborn, *Life and Letters,* 124–26; Oates, *To Purge This Land with Blood,* 74.

166   *When Senator Charles Sumner spoke:* Charles Henry Barrows, *The History of Springfield in Massachusetts for the Young* (Springfield, Mass.: Connecticut Valley Historical Society, 1909), 138.

166   *By May 7, 1855:* Reynolds, *John Brown, Abolitionist,* 133; Villard, *John Brown,* 84.

166   *As the nascent Republican Party was organizing:* G.W. Brown, *Reminiscences of Old John Brown: Thrilling Incidents of Border Life in Kansas* (Rockford, Ill.: Abraham E. Smith, 1880), 5; Frederic May Holland, *Frederick Douglass: The Colored Orator* (New York: Funk & Wagnalls, 1891), 247–48; John R. McKivigan and Madeleine Leveille, "The 'Black Dream' of Gerrit Smith, New York Abolitionist," *Syracuse University Library Associates Courier* 20, no. 2 (Fall 1985), New York History Net, http://www.nyhistory.com/gerritsmith/dream.htm.

167   *By the time Brown arrived at Osawatomie:* Etcheson, *Bleeding Kansas,* 108–9; Redpath, *The Public Life of Captain John Brown,* 86, 88, 92; G.W. Brown, *Reminiscences of Old John Brown,* 8.

167   *But after the free state leaders were charged:* Villard, *John Brown,* 151; Sanborn, *Life and Letters,* 337.

168   *At two in the morning: Report of the Special Committee Appointed to Investigate the Troubles in Kansas,* 105–7.

168   *Brown and his men washed:* Sanborn, *Life and Letters,* 273; Villard, *John Brown,* 165–66.

169   *After the Pottawatomie massacre:* Villard, *John Brown,* 114, 184; Sanborn, *Life and Letters,* 259.

169   *John Brown was an outlaw:* Ibid., 439.

169   *"War! War!":* Villard, *John Brown,* 189, 193–97; Etcheson, *Bleeding Kansas,* 114.

170   *John Brown went into hiding:* Villard, *John Brown,* 248.

170   *The romantic legend:* Redpath, *The Public Life of Capt. John Brown,* 112–14, 119.

170   *The proslavery forces: Squatter Sovereign,* August 26, 1856.

170   *The* New York Times *reported:* "Reported Battle at Osawatomie," *New York Times,* September 6, 1856.

171   *"God sees it":* Villard, *John Brown,* 248.

171   *On July 20:* Richard D. Webb, *Life and Letters of Captain John Brown* (London: Chapman & Hall, 1861), 426.

CHAPTER TWELVE: DEMOCRACY IN AMERICA

173   *Once Charles Sumner felt capable:* Seward, *Seward at Washington as Senator and Secretary of State,* 282.

173   *Sumner consulted four physicians:* Donald, *Charles Sumner and the Coming of the Civil War,* 315–17.

174   *Though he was an invalid:* New York *Tribune,* August 17, 1856; Gienapp, "The Crime Against Sumner," 245.

174   *On November 3, 1856:* Sumner, *Works,* 4:368–85.

175   *The Massachusetts General Assembly:* Frank P. Stearns, *Cambridge Sketches* (Philadelphia: J.B. Lippincott, 1905), 162–74; Pearson, *The Life of John A. Andrew,* 58–61.

176   *In early January 1857:* Franklin Benjamin Sanborn, *Memoirs of John Brown* (Concord, Mass.: J. Munsell, 1878), 45; Renehan, *The Secret Six,* 109.

176   *The enraptured Sanborn:* Wendell Phillips Garrison and Francis Jackson Garrison, *William Lloyd Garrison, 1805–1879: The Story of His Life Told by His Children* (Boston: Houghton Mifflin, 1894), 487; Renehan, *The Secret Six,* 111.

176   *George Luther Stearns:* Hinton, *John Brown and His Men,* 721.

176   *On January 8:* George L. Stearns to John Brown, January 8, 1857, Boyd B. Stutler Collection, West Virginia Archives and History, http://www.wvculture.org/history/jbexhibit/bbsms10-0022.html; Renehan, *The Secret Six,* 116; Sanborn, *Life and Letters,* 368.

177   *Brown returned to Boston:* Ibid., 372–74.

177   *Sanborn took Brown to Concord:* Franklin Sanborn, "John Brown in Massachusetts," *The Atlantic Monthly,* April 1872; Renehan, *The Secret Six,* 118; Henry David Thoreau, *Journals* (Boston: Houghton Mifflin, 1949), 12:437.

177   *After the legislature rejected his request:* James Redpath to Elias Nason, April 10, 1874, West Virginia Archives and History, http://www.wvculture.org/history/wvmemory/jbdetail.aspx?Type=Text&Id=1023.

178   *A week later, Sumner returned:* "Charles Sumner in Washington," *Chicago Tribune,* March 7, 1857; Donald, *Charles Sumner and the Coming of the Civil War,* 327.

178   *On March 7, 1857:* Alexis de Tocqueville, *Democracy in America* (New York: Alfred A. Knopf, 1941), 1:394–97.

179   *The ancient Château de Tocqueville:* Johnson, "Recollections of Charles Sumner," 299.

179   *"Mr. Sumner is a remarkable man":* Carl Schurz, *Eulogy on Charles Sumner* (Boston: Rockwell & Churchill, 1874), 32.

CHAPTER THIRTEEN: CREATION

183   *"For it is the solecism of power":* Henry C. Whitney, *Life on the Circuit with Lincoln* (Boston: Estes & Lauriat, 1892), 126.

183   *On May 26, 1856:* Ibid., 53.

184   *Before he rode the railroads:* Henry C. Whitney, *Lincoln the Citizen, Volume 1 of a Life of Lincoln* (New York: Baker & Taylor, 1909), 189, 233–34.

184   *A few months earlier:* Walter Stahr, *Stanton: Lincoln's War Secretary* (New York: Simon & Schuster, 2017), 78; Whitney, *Lincoln the Citizen,* 234.

185   *"His awkwardness of manner":* Whitney, *Lincoln the Citizen,* 212.

186   *After spending the night:* J.O. Cunningham, "The Bloomington Convention of 1856 and Those Who Participated in It," in *Transactions of the Illinois State Historical Society for the Year 1905* (Springfield: Illinois State Journal, 1906), 104; Louis A. Warren, *Lincoln's Youth: Indiana Years, 1816–1830* (Indianapolis: Indiana Historical Society, 1991), 208–9; Whitney, *Life on the Circuit with Lincoln,* 74.

186   *"Most men forget":* Henry B. Rankin, *Personal Recollections of Abraham Lincoln* (New York: G.P Putnam's Sons, 1916), 31–32.

186   *With daylight remaining:* Cunningham, "The Bloomington Convention of 1856," 104.

187   *"I am a Whig":* CW, 2:323.

189   *Before the Kansas-Nebraska Act:* Cunningham, "The Bloomington Convention of 1856," 101.

189   *After Lincoln delivered his speech:* CW, 2:288.

189   *"Finding himself drifting":* Herndon, *Herndon's Lincoln,* 311.

189   *But after his failed run:* CW, 2:316–17; Mitchell Snay, "Abraham Lincoln, Owen Lovejoy, and the Emergence of the Republican Party in Illinois," *Journal of the Abraham Lincoln Association* 22, no. 1(Winter 2001): 82–99; Edward Magdol, *Owen Lovejoy: Abolitionist in Congress* (New Brunswick, N.J.: Rutgers University Press, 1967), 143.

190   *Since 1854:* Blumenthal, *Wrestling with His Angel,* 386; David Herbert Donald, *Lincoln's Herndon* (New York: Alfred A. Knopf, 1948), 79.

191   *Herndon served as Lincoln's useful agent:* Donald, *Lincoln's Herndon,* 54–55, 88–89.

191   *Despite the apparent consensus:* Cunningham, "The Bloomington Convention of 1856," 103.

191   *While on the one hand Lincoln:* Orville Hickman Browning, *The Diary of Orville Hickman Browning, Volume 1, 1850–1864,* eds., Theodore Calvin Pease and James G. Randall (Springfield: Illinois State Historical Library, 1927), 237, xvi.

192   *Lincoln was acutely aware:* CW, 1:108–15.

192   *The Little Giant: CW,* 1:108–15; Allen C. Guelzo, *Lincoln and Douglas* (New York: Simon & Schuster, 2008), 30; *CW,* 3:382–83.

193   *Douglas had done the work: CW,* 4:67.

193   *Lincoln's stark naturalness:* Henry C. Whitney, "Abraham Lincoln: A Study from Life," *Arena,* no. 19 (January–June, 1898), 479.

193   *Traveling around central Illinois:* Whitney, *Life on the Circuit with Lincoln,* 126.

194   *Francis Bacon:* Francis Bacon, *Essay* (New York: E.P. Dutton, 1909), 159–61.

194   *A politician intent:* Ibid., 31–34; Whitney, "Abraham Lincoln: A Study from Life," 474–75. Also see Robert Bray, *Reading with Lincoln* (Carbondale: Southern Illinois University Press, 2010), 194–98.

195   *Lincoln applied the empirical:* Whitney, "Abraham Lincoln: A Study from Life," 468.

195   *In drawing up his cases:* Douglas L. Wilson, Rodney O. Davis, and Terry Wilson, eds., *Herndon's Informants: Letters, Interviews, and Statements About Abraham Lincoln* (Urbana: University of Illinois Press, 1998), 167.

196   *Boarding an early morning train:* Whitney, *Life on the Circuit with Lincoln,* 75.

196   *The town swarmed with delegates:* Cunningham, "The Bloomington Convention of 1856," 104–5; *CW,* 2:321; Jay Monaghan, *The Man Who Elected Lincoln* (Indianapolis: Bobbs-Merrill, 1956), 77.

197   *Upon his arrival Lincoln walked:* Whitney, *Life on the Circuit with Lincoln,* 75; Browning, *Diary,* 237; Joseph Medill, "Lincoln's Lost Speech: The Circumstances and Effect of Its Delivery," *McClure's Magazine,* no. 7 (June–October 1896), 321.

197   *As the alpha and omega of unity:* Medill, "Lincoln's Lost Speech," 321; "Official Record of Convention," in *Transactions of the McLean County Historical Society,* ed., Ezra Morton Prince (McLean County, Ill.: McLean County History Society, 1900), 3:161–63.

197   *That evening Lincoln wandered:* Whitney, *Life on the Circuit with Lincoln,* 75; Whitney, *Lincoln as Citizen,* 259.

198   *At Bloomington:* Whitney, *Life on the Circuit with Lincoln,* 177–78.

198   *"The Southerners are":* James L. Huston, *Stephen A. Douglas and the Dilemmas of Democratic Equality* (Lanham, MD: Rowman & Littlefield, 2007), 73; Frank M. Elliott, "Biographical Sketch of Governor Bissell," in Prince, *Transactions,* 134–3.

198   *At the editors' organizing meeting:* Ibid., 134–39.

199   *At first Bissell was receptive:* Michael Burlingame, *Abraham Lincoln: A Life* (Baltimore: Johns Hopkins University Press, 2008), 1:415–16.

199   *Early on the morning of the 29th:* Cunningham, "The Bloomington Convention of 1856," 105.

199   *The convention opened:* Whitney, *Life on the Circuit with Lincoln,* 76

199   *Before the chairman proceeded:* Cunningham, "The Bloomington Convention of 1856," 105–6; "Official Record of Convention," 158.

201   *Browning was summoned:* "Official Record of Convention," 172; Medill, "Lincoln's Lost Speech," 321.

201   *As Browning was the safest:* Medill, "Lincoln's Lost Speech," 321; Cunningham, "The Bloomington Convention of 1856," 106–7; "Official Record of Convention," 174.

201   *"As I stepped aside":* Cunningham, "The Bloomington Convention of 1856," 106–7.

201   *"At first":* Medill, "Lincoln's Lost Speech," 321–22.

201   *Several patchy descriptions:* Burlingame, *Abraham Lincoln,* 1:418–19.

202   *But Lincoln's speech:* "The Lost Speech," in Prince, *Transactions,* 3:180

202   *It seems likely though that two:* Cunningham, "The Bloomington Convention of 1856," 108.

202   *About his closing remark:* Ibid.

202   *Herndon's reaction:* William Henry Herndon, *Herndon's Life of Lincoln* (Cleveland: World, 1942), 312–13.

203   *A number of observers:* Medill, "Lincoln's Lost Speech," 322.

203   *Another delegate, Eugene F. Baldwin:* Burlingame, *Abraham Lincoln,* 1:420.

203   *The controversy flared:* Blumenthal, *Wrestling with His Angel,* 451; Wilson, *Herndon's Informants,* 163.

204   *"Your party is so mad":* Don E. Fehrenbacher, *Chicago Giant: A Biography of "Long John" Wentworth* (Madison, WI: American History Research Center, 1957), 140; Whitney, *Lincoln the Citizen,* 160-1; Whitney, *Life,* 78.

204   *But Dubois was finally won over:* Don E. Fehrenbacher, *Chicago Giant: A Biography of "Long John" Wentworth* (Madison, Wisc.: American History Research Center, 1957), 140; Whitney, *Lincoln the Citizen,* 160–61; Whitney, *Life on the Circuit with Lincoln,* 78.

CHAPTER FOURTEEN: MISS FANCY

205   *The Democratic Party convention:* Halstead, *Trimmers, Trucklers & Temporizers,* 16; Gienapp, *The Origins of the Republican Party,* 305; John W. Forney, *Anecdotes of Public Men* (New York: Harper & Brothers, 1873), 2:254.

206   *Alexander H. Stephens:* Phillips, *The Correspondence of Robert Toombs, Alexander H. Stephens, and Howell Cobb,* 367–68.

206   *Stephen A. Douglas's strategy:* Johannsen, *Stephen A. Douglas,* 507, 515, 510.

206   *Douglas fielded a formidable organization:* John Sergeant Wise, *The End of an Era* (Boston: Houghton Mifflin, 1901), 71; Milton, *The Eve of Conflict,* 222; Rhodes, *History of the United States from the Compromise of 1850,* 2:170.

207   *Douglas convinced himself:* Alice Elizabeth Malavasic, *The F Street Mess: How Southern Senators Rewrote the Kansas-Nebraska Act* (Chapel Hill: University of North Carolina Press, 2017), 88.

208   *Through a strange political alchemy:* Halstead, *Trimmers, Trucklers & Temporizers,* 17.

208 *"Mr. Buchanan":* August C. Buell, *History of Andrew Jackson* (New York: Charles Scribner's Sons, 1904), 2:404.

208 *Henry Clay intensely disliked him:* Forney, *Anecdotes of Public Men,* 1:67, 324, 182; Charles Francis Adams, ed., *Memoirs of John Quincy Adams: Comprising Portions of His Diary from 1795 to 1848* (Philadelphia: J.B. Lippincott, 1877), 12:25; Jean H. Baker, *James Buchanan* (New York: Macmillan, 2004), 58.

208 *Buchanan was briefly engaged:* Philip S. Klein, *President James Buchanan* (University Park: Pennsylvania State University Press, 1962), 30, 129–31; Elbert B. Smith, *The Presidency of James Buchanan* (Lawrence: University Press of Kansas, 1975),13; Charles Grier Sellers, *James K. Polk,* Volume 2, *Continentalist, 1843–1846* (Princeton: Princeton University Press, 2015), 34; Robert P. Watson, *Affairs of State* (Lanham, Md.: Rowman & Littlefield, 2012), 246.

209 *The highest accolade:* Henry S. Foote, *Casket of Reminiscences* (Washington, D.C.: Chronicle Publishing, 1874), 111–13.

210 *Buchanan had always been a boilerplate partisan:* Baker, *James Buchanan,* 53–57; Klein, *President James Buchanan,* 73.

210 *His head tilted:* Klein, *President James Buchanan,* 21.

210 *Buchanan was pedantic:* Roy F. Nichols, *The Disruption of American Democracy* (New York: Macmillan, 1948), 87–88.

211 *His tastes were epicurean:* Boller, *Presidential Anecdotes,* 117–19.

211 *He appeared hale:* Nichols, *The Disruption of American Democracy,* 89.

211 *Senator John Slidell:* Forney, *Anecdotes of Public Men,* 156; Charles Francis Adams, "The Trent Affair: An Historical Retrospective," *Proceedings, Massachusetts Historical Society,* Volume 45, 1911 (Boston: Liberty Reprints, 1912), 8.

212 *In 1853:* Albert Lewie Diket, "John Slidell and the Community He Represented in the Senate, 1853–1861," (PhD diss., Louisiana State University, 1958), 99–100, 107, 119–20.

212 *In October 1854:* Ibid., 157–59.

212 *At Slidell's direction:* Michael Todd Landis, *Northern Men with Southern Loyalties: The Democratic Party and the Sectional Crisis* (Ithaca, N.Y.: Cornell University Press, 2014), 144, 149.

213 *On the convention's eve:* Benjamin Brown French, *Witness to the Young Republic: A Yankee's Journal, 1828–1870,* eds., Donald B. Cole and John J. McDonough (Hanover, N.H.: University Press of New England, 1989), 269; Milton, *The Eve of Conflict,* 224.

213 *The Buchaneers:* Paul R. Cleveland, "The Millionaires of New York, Part II," *Cosmopolitan Magazine* (October 1888); "Obituary: Samuel L.M. Barlow," *New York Times,* July 11, 1889; Stephen W. Sears, *George B. McClellan: The Young Napoleon* (New York: Ticknor & Fields, 1988), 51.

213 *Breaking down Douglas began with Indiana:* Milton, *The Eve of Conflict,* 226, 106, 96, 223.

214 *Next came the demolition:* George Ticknor Curtis, *Life of James Buchanan: Fifteenth President of the United States* (New York: Harper & Brothers, 1883), 2:171–72.

214 *From the first ballot:* Halstead, *Trimmers, Trucklers & Temporizers,* 51–53 Milton, *The Eve of Conflict,* 227–29.

214 *In the battle for the vice presidency:* Halstead, *Trimmers, Trucklers & Temporizers,* 61–62.

214 *Douglas's withdrawal:* Benjamin F. Butler, *The Candidature for the Presidency in Eight Years of Stephen A. Douglas* (Lowell: Hildreth & Hunt, 1860), 8–9.

215 *Never leaving the bucolic surroundings:* Baker, *James Buchanan,* 71.

215 *Buchanan did not bother:* Johannsen, *Stephen A. Douglas,* 433.

215 *Outwardly, Douglas sustained his enthusiasm:* "Douglas Repudiating Buchanan," *Illinois State Journal,* October 15, 1856.

CHAPTER FIFTEEN: THE FORBIDDEN WORD

217 *Five days after:* Donald, *Lincoln's Herndon,* 90.

217 *Herndon's description:* Albert J. Beveridge, *Abraham Lincoln,* 2:384; Herndon, *Herndon's Life of Lincoln,* 315; *CW,* 2:344.

218 *"I don't sympathize":* Beveridge, *Abraham Lincoln,* 2:385, 172.

219 *Joseph Gillespie:* Arthur Charles Cole, *The Centennial History of Illinois, The Era of the Civil War, 1848–1870* (Springfield: Illinois Centennial Commission, 1919), 3:149; Beveridge, *Abraham Lincoln,* 2:282–83.

219 *James H. Matheny: CW,* 3:107–9.

220 *Matheny swore:* Beveridge, *Abraham Lincoln,* 2:401–2.

220 *John M. Palmer:* Burlingame, *Abraham Lincoln,* 1:425.

220 *Certain prominent Democrats:* Fehrenbacher, *Chicago Giant,* 140.

221 *Mary wrote her younger half sister:* Justin G. Turner and Linda Levitt Turner, *Mary Todd Lincoln: Her Life and Letters* (New York: Alfred A. Knopf, 1972), 46.

222 *Millard Fillmore:* Holst, *The Constitutional and Political History of the United States,* 5:438.

223 *At the beginning of June:* Benjamin W. Dreyfus, "A City Transformed: Railroads and Their Influence on the Growth of Chicago in the 1850s," 1995, https://www.hcs.harvard.edu/~dreyfus/history.html#footnote.

CHAPTER SIXTEEN: VICE PRESIDENT LINCOLN

225 *Lincoln was fixated: CW,* 2:342–43.

226 *Lincoln had been chosen:* Miller, *Lincoln and His World,* 4:165.

226 *John McLean:* Niven, *Salmon P. Chase,* 83; John Livingston, *Eminent Americans Now Living* (New York: Livingston's Monthly Law Magazine, 1854), 4:75; Thomas E. Carney, "The Political Judge: Justice John McLean's Pursuit of the Presidency," *Ohio History* 111 (Summer–Autumn 2002), 121–44.

227 *McLean was more than a jurist:* Adams, ed., *Memoirs of John Quincy Adams,* 8:537, 11:352.

228 *It was more than a little ironic:* Michael F. Holt, *The Rise and Fall of the American Whig Party: Jacksonian Politics and the Onset of the Civil War* (New York: Oxford University Press, 2003), 914.

228 *McLean's ambiguity: CW,* 1:474; Carney, "The Political Judge"; Wilson, Davis, and Wilson, eds., *Herndon's Informants,* 643–44; Miller, *Lincoln and His World,* 4, 165.

229 *"The fact is":* Halstead, *Trimmers, Trucklers & Temporizers,* 89.

229 *The natural candidate:* Thurlow Weed Barnes, *Memoir of Thurlow Weed* (Boston: Houghton Mifflin, 1884), 2:245; Gienapp, *The Origins of the Republican Party,* 316.

229 *The Republican convention:* Halstead, *Trimmers, Trucklers & Temporizers,* 95, 92.

230 *Frémont carried the aura:* James Fenimore Cooper, *The Pathfinder: or, The Inland Sea* (Boston: Houghton Mifflin, 1876), 14–15; Tom Chaffin, *Pathfinder: John Charles Frémont and the Course of American Empire* (Norman: University of Oklahoma Press, 2014), 7.

230 *Frémont fulfilled the dreams:* John Bigelow, *Memoir of the Life and Public Services of John Charles Frémont* (New York: Derby & Jackson, 1856), 327; Gienapp, *The Origins of the Republican Party,* 321–29; Halstead, *Trimmers, Trucklers & Temporizers,* 88.

231 *The platform was the first:* "Republican Party Platform of 1856," June 18, 1856, in *The American Presidency Project,* eds., Gerhard Peters and John T. Woolley, http://www.presidency.ucsb.edu/ws/?pid=29619; "Republican National Convention," *New York Herald,* June 19, 1856.

231 *Then suddenly there was dissension:* Horace Greeley, *Proceedings of the First Three Republican Conventions of 1856, 1860 and 1864* (Minneapolis: C.W. Johnson, 1893), 67.

232 *Their leader was a former Know Nothing:* Hans L. Trefousse, *Thaddeus Stevens: Nineteenth Century Egalitarian* (Mechanicsburg, Penn.: Stackpole, 2001), 94; Fergus Bordewich, "Digging Into a Historic Rivalry," *Smithsonian Magazine,* February 2004.

232 *Stevens rose at the convention:* "Republican National Convention," *New York Herald,* June 19, 1856; Holst, *The Constitutional and Political History of the United States,* 363–65.

233 *Stevens's editing of the resolution:* Halstead, *Trimmers, Trucklers & Temporizers,* 90–94.

233 *Before the final vote:* "Republican National Convention," *New York Herald,* June 19, 1856.

234 *The formal vote:* Halstead, *Trimmers, Trucklers & Temporizers,* 96.

234 *"On being defeated":* John P. Senning, "The Know-Nothing Movement in Illinois from 1854–1856," *Journal of the Illinois State Historical Society* 7 (April 1914): 24; Halstead, *Trimmers, Trucklers & Temporizers,* 98–99.

234 *The next day, June 19:* "The Peoples' Convention," *New York Tribune,* June 20, 1856.

234 *When the roll was called:* Halstead, *Trimmers, Trucklers & Temporizers,* 98; Jesse W. Weik, "Lincoln's Vote for Vice-President: In the Philadelphia Convention of 1856," *The Century Magazine* 76, May–October, 1908 (New York: Century Company, 1908), 189.

235 *But Lincoln brightened:* Whitney, *Life on the Circuit with Lincoln,* 78–81.

CHAPTER SEVENTEEN: THE BIRTHER CAMPAIGN

237 *"IMMENSE ENTHUSIASM":* "Republican National Convention," and "The Flag-Bearer of the Republicans," *New York Times,* June 19, 1856.

238 *"There is no mistake":* "The Effect of Fremont's Nomination," *New York Herald,* June 27, 1856.

238 *The Republican campaign:* Klein, *President James Buchanan,* 257.

238 *Fillmore said not a word:* Frank H. Severance, ed., *Millard Fillmore Papers* (Buffalo: Buffalo Historical Society, 1907), 2:2022.

239 *But the question of illegitimacy:* Gienapp, *The Origins of the Republican Party,* 369.

239 *The nativist pamphleteers:* "Fremont's Romanism Established" (No publisher, 1856), https://archive.org/details/fremontsromanism00sl.

239 *Frémont's illegitimacy:* Chaffin, *Pathfinder,* 446; Andrew F. Rolle, *John Charles Frémont: Character As Destiny* (Norman: University of Oklahoma Press, 1991), 168, 172.

240 *Frémont's wife:* Bigelow, *Memoir of the Life and Public Services of John Charles Frémont,* 11–22.

240 *Fremont, in fact, was illegitimate:* Rolle, *John Charles Frémont,* 2–5.

241 *By creating a personal counter-narrative:* Pamela Herr, *Jessie Benton Frémont* (New York: Franklin Watts, 1987), 263.

241 *Some years earlier, Benton:* Sally Denton, *Passion and Principle* (New York: Bloomsbury, 2007), 233, 59, xiii.

242 *Jessie was as much a trailblazer:* Ibid., 135.

242 *Jessie handed the president a letter:* Milo Milton Quaife, ed., *The Diary of James K. Polk During His Presidency, 1845–1849* (Chicago: A.C. McClurg, 1910), 52–53.

243 *Jessie ran the campaign:* Denton, *Passion and Principle,* 234–48; Herr and Spence, eds., *The Letters of Jessie Benton Frémont,* 98.

243 *Jessie called the campaign:* Rolle, *John Charles Frémont,* 173; Elizabeth Benton Frémont, *Recollections of Elizabeth Benton Frémont: Daughter of the Pathfinder* (New York: Frederick H. Hitchcock, 1912), 77; Gienapp, *The Origins of the Republican Party,* 376–77; Denton, *Passion and Principle,* 252–57.

243 *Republican leaders were confounded:* "Col. Fremont's Religion. The Calumnies Against Him Exposed by Indisputable Proofs" (No publisher, 1856), https://books.google.com/books?id=O7xcAAAAcAAJ&printsec=frontcover#v=onepage&q&f=false; Gienapp, *The Origins of the Republican Party,* 369.

244 *Neither facts nor clerical authority:* Seward, *Seward at Washington as Senator and Secretary of State,* 287; Gienapp, *The Origins of the Republican Party,* 370, 416.

245 *Wise called for a meeting:* Wilson, *History of the Rise and Fall of the Slave Power in America,* 2:520; Beveridge, *Abraham Lincoln,* 2:429; Eric H. Walther, *The Shattering of the Union: America in the 1850s* (Lanham, Md.: Rowman & Littlefield, 2004), 111; Potter, *The Impending Crisis,* 263; Barton H. Wise, *The Life of Henry A. Wise of Virginia, 1809–1876* (New York: Macmillan, 1899), 209; Horace Greeley and John F. Cleveland, eds., *A Political Text-Book for 1860* (New York: Tribune Association, 1860), 170–71.

245 *The* Richmond Enquirer*:* "Fremont and Disunion," *Richmond Enquirer,* August 29, 1856.

245 *John Minor Botts:* "Botts' Hegira," *Richmond Enquirer,* September 23, 1856.

246 *Several days after Botts:* James A. Hamilton, *Reminiscences of James A. Hamilton: Or, Men and Events, at Home and Abroad* (New York: Charles Scribner, 1869), 449; Chaffin, *Pathfinder,* 447.

246 *Throughout the North:* Denton, *Passion and Principle,* 247; Beveridge, *Abraham Lincoln,* 2:426–28; *New York Tribune,* November 1, 1856.

246 *Walt Whitman:* Walt Whitman, *Complete Poetry and Collected Prose,* ed., *Justin Kaplan* (New York: Library of America, 1982), 1307–25.

CHAPTER EIGHTEEN: THE GREAT AWAKENING

249 *Judge David Davis:* Browning, *Diary,* 245; Willard L. King, *Lincoln's Manager David Davis* (Chicago: University of Chicago Press, 1960), 72.

250 *Davis was used:* King, *Lincoln's Manager David Davis,* 72, 51.

250 *Davis believed:* Magdol, *Owen Lovejoy,* 154–55.

250 *"We learned yesterday":* King, *Lincoln's Manager David Davis,* 113.

251 *The split over Lovejoy:* CW, 2:346–47; Clark E. Carr, *My Day and My Generation* (Chicago: A.C. McClurg, 1908), 275–81.

251 *Upon his return after sharing the podium:* Bill Kemp, "Gridleys Obscured in Local Legend and Lore," *Daily Pantagraph,* September 28, 2014; Magdol, *Owen Lovejoy,* 156; Isabel Wallace, *Life and Letters of General W.H.L. Wallace* (Chicago: R.R. Donnelly, 1909), 73.

252 *Lincoln wasted little time:* King, *Lincoln's Manager David Davis,* 112–13; CW, 2:347; Whitney, *Life on the Circuit with Lincoln,* 62–63.

253 *Lincoln's attitude:* "Don't Like It," *Illinois State Journal,* July 7, 1856.

253 *Another friend of Lincoln:* King, *Lincoln's Manager David Davis,* 21.

253 *The bolters' convention:* Ezra M. Prince and John H. Burnham, eds., *Historical Encyclopedia of Illinois and History of McLean County* (Chicago: Munsell, 1908), 2:1029; William F. Moore and Jane Ann Moore, eds., *His Brother's Blood: Speeches and Writings, 1838–64: Owen Lovejoy* (Urbana: University of Illinois Press, 2004), 130–31; Frances Milton I. Morehouse, *The Life of Jesse W. Fell* (Urbana: University of Illinois Press, 1916), 55.

254   *Two days later a ratification meeting:* Magdol, *Owen Lovejoy,* 157–59.

254   *Dickey's candidacy cratered:* Ibid., 159–65; King, *Lincoln's Manager David Davis,* 113–14.

254   *Throughout the drama: CW,* 2:347–48; Stephen Hansen and Paul Nygard, "Stephen A. Douglas, the Know-Nothings, and the Democratic Party in Illinois, 1854–1858," *Illinois State Historical Journal* 87, no. 2 (Summer 1994): 118.

255   *Lincoln was aware of the rumors:* Emanuel Hertz, *The Hidden Lincoln: From the Letters and Papers of William H. Herndon* (New York: Blue Ribbon Books, 1940), 265.

255   *Lincoln, however, kept devising: CW,* 2:374; Beveridge, *Abraham Lincoln,* 2:437.

256   *The diehard Whigs:* Beveridge, *Abraham Lincoln,* 2:385.

256   *The Germans:* Frederic Bancroft and William A. Dunning, eds., *The Reminiscences of Carl Schurz* (New York: McClure, 1908), 2:91.

257   *After the Bloomington convention:* Gustave Koerner, *Memoirs of Gustave Koerner, 1809–1896* (Cedar Rapids, Iowa: Torch Press, 1909), 1:531; Sabine Freitag, *Friedrich Hecker: Two Lives for Liberty,* trans., Steven Rohan (St. Louis: University of Missouri Press, 2006), 181, 167–69, 173–77; *CW,* 2:376.

257   *Lincoln launched himself: CW,* 2:367–68; Rankin, *Personal Recollections of Abraham Lincoln,* 207–9.

259   *"Do you think we shall": CW,* 2:367–68; Rankin, *Personal Recollections of Abraham Lincoln,* 207–9.

260   *Then Lincoln grabbed: CW,* 2:361–66; Blumenthal, *Wrestling with His Angel,* 373–75.

260   *Douglas, too, was out:* Paul M. Angle, *"Here I Have Lived," A History of Lincoln's Springfield, 1821–1865* (Chicago: Abraham Lincoln Book Shop, 1971), 219; Octavius Brooks Frothingham, *Theodore Parker: A Biography* (New York: Putnam's, 1880), 447.

261   *The results of the Electoral College vote:* Beveridge, *Abraham Lincoln,* 2:441.

261   *Fillmore, who had railed:* William W. Freehling, *The Road to Disunion,* Volume 2, *Secessionists Triumphant, 1854–1861* (New York: Oxford University Press, 2007), 95.

262   *The fire-eating Charleston Mercury:* Holst, *The Constitutional and Political History of the United States,* 464–65.

262   *The 1856 results:* John Moses, *Illinois, Historical and Statistical* (Chicago: Fergus Printing, 1892), 2:602–3; Angle, *"Here I Have Lived,"* 223; Senning, "The Know-Nothing Movement in Illinois," 24.

262   *After the election:* "next Senator": Ian Hand, research director of the Abraham Lincoln Presidential Library, Springfield, Illinois.

264   *For the Republicans: CW,* 2:385–86.

265   *"Upon those men": CW,* 2:391.

CHAPTER NINETEEN: THE WHITE MAN

267 *Pennsylvania was the reason:* Curtis, *Life of James Buchanan,* 185.

268 *Buchanan had always been:* Klein, *President James Buchanan,* 141.

268 *John W. Forney:* Ibid., 265; John F. Coleman, *The Disruption of Pennsylvania Democracy, 1848–1860* (Harrisburg: Pennsylvania Historical and Museum Commission, 1975), 103.

269 *An enraged and alcohol fueled Forney:* Alexander K. McClure, *Old Time Notes of
Pennsylvania* (Philadelphia: John C. Winston, 1905), 1:254–62; Kenneth Stampp,
America in 1857 (New York: Oxford University Press, 1990), 52–55.

269 *Simon Cameron:* Allan Nevins, *The Emergence of Lincoln: Douglas, Buchanan, and
Party Chaos, 1857–1859* (New York: Scribner's Sons, 1950), 1: 79–81.

269 *Thaddeus Stevens:* Trefousse, *Thaddeus Stevens,* 89–90, 94–95; Klein, *President
James Buchanan,* 265.

270 *The Democratic caucus:* Coleman, *The Disruption of Pennsylvania Democracy,* 105;
Klein, *President James Buchanan,* 266; "Cabinet Struggles in Pennsylvania," *New
York Tribune,* February 11, 1857; McClure, *Old Time Notes of Pennsylvania,* 262.

270 *Buchanan cast around:* John W. Forney, *Anecdotes of Public Men,* Volume 2 (New
York: Harper & Brothers, 1881), 237, 421; Forney, *Anecdotes,* 1:146.

271 *Washington still seethed:* Nevins, *The Emergence of Lincoln,* 1:79; Nichols, *The Disruption of Pennsylvania Democracy,* 80.

271 *Virginia Clay:* Clay-Clopton, *A Belle of the Fifties,* 58–61.

272 *The Southerners' sense:* Lydia Maria Child, *Letters of Lydia Maria Child* (Boston:
Houghton Mifflin, 1882), 88.

272 *One man appeared:* James F. Simon, *Lincoln and Chief Justice Taney: Slavery, Secession, and the President's War Powers* (New York: Simon & Schuster, 2006), 91, 99.

272 *Taney was yet another breathing relic:* Paul Finkelman, "Hooted Down the Pages
of History: Reconsidering the Greatness of Chief Justice Taney," *Journal of Supreme Court History* 18 (1994): 83–102.

273 *Taney was the first Catholic:* Paul Finkelman, *Supreme Injustice: Slavery in the Nation's Highest Court* (Cambridge: Harvard University Press, 2018), 179; Samuel
Tyler, *Memoir of Roger Brooke Taney, LL.D.: Chief Justice of the Supreme Court of
the United States* (Baltimore: John Murphy, 1872), 359.

273 *Eighty years old:* Clay-Clopton, *A Belle of the Fifties,* 74.

273 *With the advent of 1857:* James Shepherd Pike, *First Blows of the Civil War* (New
York: American News, 1879), 355.

274 *The man in the vise:* Walter Ehrlich, *They Have No Rights: Dred Scott's Struggle
for Freedom* (Westport, Conn.: Greenwood, 1979), 7–35; Simon, *Lincoln and Chief
Justice Taney,* 100–101; Brooks Simpson, *Ulysses S. Grant: Triumph over Adversity, 1822–1865* (Boston: Houghton Mifflin, 2000), 71–72; Lea VanderVelde, *Mrs.
Dred Scott: A Life on Slavery's Frontier* (New York: Oxford University Press, 2010),
205–7.

275   *The Dred Scott case:* Wilentz, *The Rise of American Democracy,* 709; Ehrlich, *They Have No Rights,* 36–37; William Cathcart, *The Baptist Encyclopedia* (Philadelphia: Louis H. Everts, 1881), 33.

276   *By the time the Missouri Supreme Court ruled:* Melvin I. Urofsky, *Supreme Decisions: Great Constitutional Cases and Their Impact* (Boulder, CO: Westview Press, 2012), 81.

276   *Mrs. Emerson transferred control:* Ehrlich, *They Have No Rights,* 86–89.

277   *Montgomery Blair:* Urofsky, *Supreme Decisions,* 83–84.

277   *The justices descended into confused colloquy:* Ehrlich, *They Have No Rights,* 102–4.

277   *The court reconvened:* Ibid., 114–18.

278   *The next day Senator Geyer:* Ibid., 1180–20; Pike, *First Blows of the Civil War,* 353.

278   *The Southern justices:* Nevins, *The Emergence of Lincoln,* 1:107–9; Richard Malcolm Johnston and William Hand Browne, *Life of Alexander H. Stephens* (Philadelphia: J.B. Lippincott, 1884), 318.

279   *President-elect James Buchanan:* Nichols, *The Disruption of American Democracy,* 75–76; Smith, *The Presidency of James Buchanan,* 23.

279   *Catron was among the cadres:* Nevins, *The Emergence of Lincoln,* 103; Loren Schweninger, ed., *From Tennessee Slave to St. Louis Entrepreneur: The Autobiography of James Thomas* (Columbia: University of Missouri Press, 1984), 2, 7, 60.

279   *On February 3:* Nichols, *The Disruption of American Democracy,* 76–77; Nevins, *The Emergence of Lincoln,* 1:108–10; Simon, *Lincoln and Chief Justice Taney,* 117–18.

280   *Catron asked Buchanan: United States v. Hanway,* No. 15,299 Fed. Cas., 174.

280   *If Grier as a Northerner:* Nevins, *The Emergence of Lincoln,* 1:110–11; Nichols, *The Disruption of American Democracy,* 77–78.

281   *Buchanan was anxious:* Nevins, *The Emergence of Lincoln,* 1:111.

281   *Buchanan left his home:* Klein, *President James Buchanan,* 271.

281   *At noon on March 4:* Ibid., 272.

282   *After throat clearing*: James Buchanan, "Inaugural Address," March 4, 1857, *The American Presidency Project,* eds., Gerhard Peters and John T. Woolley, http://www.presidency.ucsb.edu/ws/?pid=25817.

282   *All sides understood Buchanan's message:* Pike, *First Blows of the Civil War,* 366.

282   *Two days later, on the morning of March 6:* "The Dred Scott, Case," *New York Times,* March 9, 1857.

284   *Taney presented his judgment:* Roger Taney, *The Dred Scott Decision: Opinion of Chief Justice Taney* (New York: Van Evrie, Horton, 1860).

284   *When Taney finished his reading:* "Justice Catron," *American History from Revolution to Reconstruction and Beyond,* http://www.let.rug.nl/usa/documents/1826-1850/ dred-scott-case/justice-catron.php; Schweninger, ed., *From Tennessee Slave to St. Louis Entrepreneur,* 80–81, 252; Leon Schweninger, "Thriving Within the Lowest Caste: The Financial Activities of James P. Thomas in the Nineteenth-Century South," *Journal of Negro History* 63 (Fall 1978): 353–64.

284 *Justice McLean read:* Ehrlich, *They Have No Rights,* 161–64.

285 *Justice Benjamin R. Curtis:* "Justice Catron."

285 *Curtis's masterful opinion:* Curtis, *A Memoir of Benjamin Robbins Curtis,* 214, 219, 222, 249–50; Simon, *Lincoln and Chief Justice Taney,* 131.

286 *"We believe it is settled":* Nevins, *The Emergence of Lincoln,* 1:118.

286 *The individuals involved:* Wilentz, *The Rise of American Democracy,* 714.

286 *The day after Taney read:* Ibid., 713; Pike, *First Blows of the Civil War,* 367; Nevins, *The Emergence of Lincoln,* 1:114; Thomas Hart Benton, *Historical and Legal Examination of That Part of the Decision of the Supreme Court of the United States in the Dred Scott Case* (New York: D. Appleton, 1858), 193, 185.

287 *Among Republicans the sense: CG,* 35th Congress, 1st Session, 941.

288 *Reverdy Johnson:* Tyler, *Memoir of Roger Brooke Taney,* 385–90.

288 *Southerners embraced Taney's ruling:* Jefferson Davis, *The Rise and Fall of the Confederate Government* (New York: D. Appleton, 1881), 1:84–85.

288 *Years later, after the Civil War:* Tyler, *Memoir of Roger Brooke Taney,* 391.

CHAPTER TWENTY: ALL THE POWERS OF EARTH

289 *James Buchanan was renowned:* Johannsen, *Stephen A. Douglas,* 538; Klein, *President James Buchanan,* 259.

290 *When Buchanan visited Washington:* Johannsen, *Stephen A. Douglas,* 551–52.

290 *From Buchanan, Douglas immediately:* Milton, *The Eve of Conflict,* 259.

290 *Slidell wrote Buchanan:* Johannsen, *Stephen A. Douglas,* 552; Smith, *The Presidency of James Buchanan,* 21; Milton, *The Eve of Conflict,* 259.

290 *"He is a stubborn old gentleman":* Klein, *President James Buchanan,* 285.

290 *The clash between Buchanan and Douglas:* "Harriet Lane," *National First Ladies Library,* http://www.firstladies.org/biographies/firstladies.aspx?biography=16; Smith, *The Presidency of James Buchanan,* 85; Clay-Clopton, *A Belle of the Fifties,* 114; Mrs. Roger A. Pryor, *Reminiscences of Peace and War* (New York: Grosset & Dunlap, 1904), 53.

291 *The early years of Adele Cutts:* Virginia Tatnall Peacock, *Famous American Belles of the Nineteenth Century* (Philadelphia: J.B. Lippincott, 1901), 177–81.

292 *Adele's lineage:* Pryor, *Reminiscences of Peace and War,* 68.

292 *In the three years since the death:* Johannsen, *Stephen A. Douglas,* 541–43; Pryor, *Reminiscence of Peace and War,* 68–69.

292 *Douglas commissioned the building:* John Ferrari, "Douglas Row," https://www.popville.com/2018/03/streets-of-washington-presents-douglas-row-the-lost-homes-of-politicians-generals-war-wounded-and-orphans/; Clay-Clopton, *A Belle of the Fifties,* 36.

292 *Douglas' marriage rankled:* "Senator Douglas on the Division of the Spoils," *New York Herald,* October 18, 1857; Klein, *President James Buchanan,* 284.

293 *When the Congress adjourned:* Beveridge, *Abraham Lincoln,* 2:500.

295 *Douglas played a deck:* Stephen A. Douglas, *Remarks of the Hon. Stephen A. Douglas on Kansas, Utah, and the Dred Scott Decision* (Chicago: Daily Times Book and Job Office, 1857).

296 *"The curtain of 1860":* "The Springfield Speech of Senator Douglas—His Card for 1860," *New York Herald,* June 24, 1857.

304 *The* Illinois State Register: Beveridge, *Abraham Lincoln,* 2:517–18.

304 *The case was a perversely refracted version:* Richard Campanella, *Lincoln in New Orleans: The 1828–1831 Flatboat Voyages and Their Place in History* (Lafayette: University of Louisiana at Lafayette Press, 2010), 187–90.

305 *Learning of the imminent danger:* J.G. Holland, *The Life of Abraham Lincoln* (Springfield, Mass.: Gurdon Bill, 1866), 128; Herndon, *Herndon's Life of Lincoln,* 308.

305 *But there was someone in New Orleans:* Jonathan D. Sarna and Benjamin Shapell, *Lincoln and the Jews: A History* (New York: St. Martin's, 2015), 14–27.

305 *Abraham Jonas's brother:* Charles M. Segal, "Lincoln, Benjamin Jonas and the Black Code," *Journal of the Illinois State Historical Society* 46 (Autumn 1853), 277–82; Wilson, Davis, and Wilson, eds., *Herndon's Informants,* 376.

CHAPTER TWENTY-ONE: THE WIZARD OF MISSISSIPPI

307 *Buchanan assumed that the troubles:* Curtis, *Life of James Buchanan,* 2:176.

307 *The parade of presidentially appointed territorial governors:* Robinson, *Kansas,* 291.

308 *The next governor, John W. Geary:* John H. Gihon, *Geary and Kansas: Governor Geary's Administration in Kansas* (Philadelphia: Chas. C. Rhodes, 1857), 104–5.

308 *Geary's peace:* Holst, *The Constitutional and Political History of the United States,* 60; Nevins, *The Emergence of Lincoln,* 2:135.

309 *On February 15, 1857:* Gihon, *Geary and Kansas,* 260.

309 *The legislature overrode his veto:* Wilentz, *The Rise of American Democracy,* 715; Holloway, *History of Kansas,* 410; Nevins, *The Emergence of Lincoln,* 1:137.

309 *Calhoun traveled to Washington:* Holloway, *History of Kansas,* 439.

309 *The free state convention meeting:* George Washington Brown, *Reminiscences of Gov. R.J. Walker* (Rockford, Ill.: Published by the author, 1902); 15–16; Nevins, *The Emergence of Lincoln,* 1:140.

310 *Geary traveled to Washington:* "Governor Geary's Last Interview with Mr. Buchanan," *New York Times,* April 26, 1857.

310 *The* New York Times *correspondent in Washington:* "Hon. R.J. Walker's Appointment as Governor of Kansas," *New York Times,* April 26, 1857.

311 *After conferring with Walker:* Seward, *Seward at Washington as Senator and Secretary of State,* 299.

311 *Walker's initial political mentor:* Dunbar Rowland, ed., *Encyclopedia of Mississippi History* (Madison, Wisc.: Selwyn A. Brant, 1907), 2:443–45, 583, 642; William

Edward Dodd, *Robert J. Walker, Imperialist* (Chicago: Chicago Literary Club, 1914), 7–17.

312 *Under Walker's guidance:* Dodd, *Robert J. Walker, Imperialist,* 20–22.

312 *Walker stridently demanded:* Edward P. Crapol, *John Tyler, The Accidental President* (Chapel Hill: University of North Carolina Press, 2012), 227; Frederick Merk, *Slavery and the Annexation of Texas* (New York: Alfred A. Knopf, 1972), 9–11.

312 *Walker played kingmaker:* Dodd, *Robert J. Walker, Imperialist,* 23–29.

313 *After the Polk administration:* Nichols, *The Disruption of American Democracy,* 58, 69–70; Johannsen, *Stephen A. Douglas,* 552; *Congressional Serial Set, Thirty-Sixth Congress, First Session, Elections, Etc., No. 1* (Washington, D.C.: Thomas H. Ford, 1860), 473.

313 *When Buchanan appeared:* "The Covode Investigation," *House of Representatives, 36th Congress, 1st Session, Volume V, No. 648* (Washington, D.C.: U.S. Government Printing Office, 1860), 105–6.

313 *Douglas desperately needed:* Douglas, *Remarks of the Hon. Stephen A. Douglas on Kansas, Utah, and the Dred Scott Decision,* 5–6.

314 *Walker was Douglas's:* Johannsen, *Stephen A. Douglas,* 315.

314 *Walker's condition:* "The Covode Investigation," 106–7; Rowland, *Encyclopedia of Mississippi History,* 2:893.

314 *"I should have preferred that":* "The Covode Investigation," 109.

315 *Walker said "the only plan":* Ibid., 107–8.

315 *In a letter to Buchanan:* George D. Harmon, "Buchanan's Betrayal of Governor Walker," *Pennsylvania Magazine of History* (1929), 52.

315 *Frederick P. Stanton:* Nevins, *The Emergence of Lincoln,* 148–49.

315 *On his way west:* J. Madison Cutts, *A Brief Treatise upon Constitutional and Party Questions* (New York: D. Appleton, 1866), 111; Holloway, *History of Kansas,* 450; Nevins, *The Emergence of Lincoln,* 152; Alice Nichols, *Bleeding Kansas* (New York: Oxford University Press, 1954), 146.

316 *That evening John Calhoun:* Nevins, *The Emergence of Lincoln,* 155.

316 *The Lecompton legislature:* Holst, *The Constitutional and Political History of the United States,* 64; John Bach McMaster, *A History of the People of the United States* (New York: D. Appleton, 1913), 8:304; Brown, *Reminiscences of Gov. R.J. Walker,* 44.

316 *Congressman Robert Toombs:* Phillips, ed., *The Correspondence of Robert Toombs, Alexander H. Stephens, and Howell Cobb,* 400–404.

317 *Senator Jefferson Davis:* Rhodes, *History of the United States from the Compromise of 1850,* 2:275; Nevins, *The Emergence of Lincoln,* 1:163–66; Harmon, "Buchanan's Betrayal of Governor Walker," 73; "'Kansas,' Editorial reprinted from the Richmond Enquirer," *Washington Union,* June 27, 1857.

317 *Despite the gale:* "The Covode Investigation," 112–13.

317 *Walker pledged:* Harmon, "Buchanan's Betrayal of Governor Walker," 63.

317 *Congressman Laurence M. Keitt:* "Letter from Hon. L.M. Keitt," *New York Times,* August 17, 1857.

318 *By the end of July:* Phillips, ed., *The Correspondence of Robert Toombs, Alexander H. Stephens, and Howell Cobb,* 407; Harmon, "Buchanan's Betrayal of Governor Walker," 66.

318 *Walker relied upon Buchanan:* Harmon, "Buchanan's Betrayal of Governor Walker," 68.

318 *Walker had failed:* Robinson, *Kansas,* 355; Holloway, *History of Kansas,* 305–6.

319 *On September 7:* Blackmar, *Kansas,* 856–57; Nevins, *The Emergence of Lincoln,* 1:173–74.

319 *Back in Washington:* Samuel Boykin, ed., *A Memorial Volume of the Hon. Howell Cobb, of Georgia* (Philadelphia: J.B. Lippincott, 1870), 29; Howell Cobb, *A Scriptural Examination of the Institution of Slavery in the United States* (Georgia: Printed for the Author, 1856), 2, 8, 12.

320 *The other frequent guests:* Nevins, *The Emergence of Lincoln,* 75–76; Nichols, *Bleeding Kansas,* 91; Mrs. N.G. Deupress, "Some Historic Homes of Mississippi," *Publications of the Mississippi Historical Society* 6, ed., Franklin L. Riley (Oxford: Mississippi Historical Society, 1902), 261; Jacob Thompson, *"Address, Delivered on Occasion of the Opening of the University of the State of Mississippi: In Behalf of the Board of Trustees, November 6, 1848"* (Memphis: Franklin Book and Job Office, 1848), 5; P.L. Rainwater, "Letters to and from Jacob Thompson," *The Journal of Southern History* 6, no. 1 (February 1940): 102–4; J.F.H. Claiborne, *Mississippi, as a Province, Territory, and State* (Jackson, Miss.: Power & Barksdale, 1880), 1:453.

321 *Throughout September and October:* Phillips, ed., *The Correspondence of Robert Toombs, Alexander H. Stephens, and Howell Cobb,* 424.

321 *Cobb summoned:* "The Covode Investigation," 103, 318, 158–68, 315, 160; Stampp, *America in 1857,* 269.

322 *For weeks before the Lecompton convention:* Holst, *The Constitutional and Political History of the United States,* 87–89.

322 *The difficult part was how to frame:* Rhodes, *History,* 2:279; Nevins, *The Emergence of Lincoln,* 235; "The Covode Investigation," 170, 168.

323 *Calhoun paid:* "The Covode Investigation," 110–11.

323 *Walker was anything but:* Harmon, "Buchanan's Betrayal of Governor Walker," 82; Rhodes, *History of the United States from the Compromise of 1850,* 280.

324 *Rolling down the Missouri River:* "Kansas and Her Constitution," *Washington Union,* November 18, 1857.

324 *Reading the editorial:* Nevins, *The Emergence of Lincoln,* 1:244.

324 *For months, Buchanan had been trying:* Ibid., 1:243–44; John G. Nicolay and John Hay, *Abraham Lincoln: A History* (New York: Century Company, 1890), 2:111–12; Horace Greeley, *Recollections of a Busy Life* (New York: J.B. Ford, 1868), 356.

324 *More than confusion:* Wilentz, *The Rise of American Democracy,* 719; Stampp, *America in 1857,* 221–23; James L. Huston, *The Panic of 1857 and the Coming of the Civil War* (Baton Rouge: University of Louisiana Press, 1999), 14; Karl Marx, "The British Revulsion," *New York Tribune,* November 30, 1857.

325 *Buchanan blamed the depression:* Huston, *The Panic of 1857 and the Coming of the Civil War,* 175; Klein, *President James Buchanan,* 314–15; "James Buchanan: First Annual Message to Congress on the State of the Union," December 8, 1857, *The American Presidency Project,* eds., Gerhard Peters and John T. Woolley, http://www.presidency.ucsb.edu/ws/?pid=29498; Stampp, *America in 1857,* 229–30.

326 *"The revulsion":* Rhodes, *History of the United States from the Compromise of 1850,* 281–82, 275; Foote, *Casket of Reminiscences,* 116.

326 *"The President was informed":* Nevins, *The Emergence of Lincoln,* 1:243.

326 *John Forney:* "The Covode Investigation," 296; Nevins, *The Emergence of Lincoln,* 1:246–47.

327 *Almost every Northern Democratic newspaper:* "The Democracy must Submit the Constitution or be Damned," *Chicago Times,* November 19, 1857.

327 *Walker met on November 26:* Holst, *The Constitutional and Political History of the United States,* 96.

327 *Walker formally resigned:* Nicolay and Hay, *Abraham Lincoln,* 2:116–18.

328 *"So disappears":* "Governor Walker and Secretary Stanton," *The National Era,* December 24, 1857.

CHAPTER TWENTY-TWO: THE UNMAKING OF THE PRESIDENT

329 *After meeting with the president:* Nevins, *The Emergence of Lincoln,* 1:250; "Douglas and the Administration," *Chicago Tribune,* December 4, 1857.

329 *Douglas was in an aggressive:* Anonymous, *The Diary of a Public Man: An Intimate View of the National Administration, December 28, 1860 to March 15, 1861* (Chicago: Abraham Lincoln Book Shop, 1945).

330 *Douglas's platform:* Milton, *The Eve of Conflict,* 273; Johannsen, *Stephen A. Douglas,* 584.

330 *Norman B. Judd:* Milton, *The Eve of Conflict,* 272–73.

331 *Lincoln first raised his concern:* CW, 2:428.

331 *Before he set off for Washington:* Nevins, *The Emergence of Lincoln,* 1:252; "From Washington," *Chicago Tribune,* December 2, 1857.

331 *On December 3:* Nevins, *The Emergence of Lincoln,* 1:253; Beveridge, *Abraham Lincoln,* 2:538.

332 *Douglas returned:* Greeley, *Recollections of a Busy Life,* 356.

332 *He quietly went:* Johnston and Browne, *Life of Alexander H. Stephens,* 327.

332 *On December 8:* "James Buchanan: First Annual Message to Congress on the State of the Union."

332 *The same day, Douglas rose:* CG, 35th Congress, 1st Session, 14–18.

333   *On the Senate floor:* "From Washington," *New York Tribune,* December 9, 1857; Johannsen, *Stephen A. Douglas,* 599.

333   *The nefarious plot:* "The Great Conspiracy to Rule or Ruin Mr. Buchanan's Administration," *New York Herald,* December 15, 1857.

334   *Just as the Buchanan administration:* Guelzo, *Lincoln and Douglas,* 47; Burlingame, *Abraham Lincoln,* 1:446; "Douglas on the Lecompton Fraud," *New York Tribune,* December 10, 1857; O.J. Hollister, *Life of Schuyler Colfax* (New York: Funk & Wagnalls, 1886), 119; Potter, *The Impending Crisis,* 321; Rhodes, *History of the United States from the Compromise of 1850,* 305–6; Johannsen, *Stephen A. Douglas,* 632.

335   *Douglas invited more Republicans:* Hollister, *Life of Schuyler Colfax,* 119–20, 124; Johannsen, *Stephen A. Douglas,* 603; White, *The Life of Lyman Trumbull,* 78–79; Beveridge, *Abraham Lincoln,* 2:545.

335   *As Douglas performed:* Holloway, *History of Kansas,* 476–77.

335   *At the dawn of the New Year:* Hollister, *Life of Schuyler Colfax,* 121; "The Administration vs. Douglas," *Chicago Tribune,* January 27, 1858.

336   *On February 2:* "James Buchanan, Message to Congress Transmitting the Constitution of Kansas, February 2, 1858," *The American Presidency Project,* eds., Gerhard Peters and John T. Woolley, http://www.presidency.ucsb.edu/ws/?pid=68298.

336   *Just before Buchanan sent:* Johnston and Browne, *Life of Alexander H. Stephens,* 329.

336   *Congressman Thomas Harris:* Miller, *Lincoln and His World,* 4:218.

336   *Rough times manifested themselves:* "Detailed Account of the Keitt and Grow Fight," *New York Times,* February 8, 1858.

337   *In early February:* Spring, *Kansas,* 230; Stampp, *America in 1857,* 324; Nevins, *The Emergence of Lincoln,* 1:289, 293–94.

338   *Douglas opened his offensive:* Johannsen, *Stephen A. Douglas,* 605.

338   *Jefferson Davis:* Varina Davis, *Jefferson Davis: Ex-president of the Confederate States of America* (New York: Belford, 1890), 1:530.

338   *In the winter of 1858:* Ibid., 574–75, 579.

339   *Still weak, Davis's speech:* Davis, *The Rise and Fall of the Confederate Government,* 541–45.

339   *On February 15:* Lyon Gardiner Tyler, *The Letters and Times of the Tylers* (Richmond: Whitter & Shepperson, 1885), 2:543.

339   *On March 3:* CG, 35th Congress, 1st Session, 939–45.

341   *If, as Seward threatened:* James Henry Hammond, *Selections from the Letters and Speeches of the Hon. James H. Hammond, of South Carolina* (New York: John F. Trow, 1866), 311–22.

341   *Hammond's rise as governor:* Faust, *James Henry Hammond and the Old South,* 314–17, 302; Rosellen Brown, "Monster of All He Surveyed," *New York Times,* January 29, 1989; Martin Duberman, "'Writhing Bedfellows' in Antebellum South Carolina," *The Journal of Homosexuality* (Fall–Winter, 1980–81).

342 *Following his early idol:* Faust, *James Henry Hammond and the Old South,* 300; Sinha, *The Counter-Revolution of Slavery,* 192.

342 *Douglas's speech on March 22:* Johannsen, *Stephen A. Douglas,* 609.

342 *The action turned:* Ibid., 610.

343 *Alexander Stephens:* C.M. Barnes, *James Buchanan* (Oswego, N.Y.: No publisher, ca. 1881), 44; Wilson, *History of the Rise and Fall of the Slave Power in America,* 561–62.

343 *Full-scale bribery:* "The Covode Investigation," 138–59, 184–97; Nichols, *The Disruption of American Democracy,* 179.

343 *Under the weight of corruption:* James A. Rawley, *Race and Politics: Bleeding Kansas and the Coming of the Civil War* (Lincoln: University of Nebraska Press, 1989), 249; Philip G. Auchampaugh, "The Buchanan-Douglas Feud," *Journal of the Illinois State Historical Society* 25, nos. 1–2 (April–July 1932), 5–48.

344 *Before he issued his statement:* Rawley, *Race and Politics,* 249.

344 *Speaking to the Senate:* Nevins, *The Emergence of Lincoln,* 1:301.

344 *"I expected that":* Johnston and Browne, *Life of Alexander H. Stephens,* 428.

344 *Buchanan moved:* Sheahan, *The Life of Stephen A. Douglas,* 420.

345 *Under Cook:* Nichols, *The Disruption of American Democracy,* 215–17; Johannsen, *Stephen A. Douglas,* 535, 602, 622–24; Milton, *The Eve of Conflict,* 295; Foote, *Casket of Reminiscences,* 135; Miller, *Lincoln and His World,* 4:221; "The Platforms of the Two Conventions," *Illinois State Journal,* April 23, 1858.

345 *Buchanan's interference:* "Democratic Conventions," *Washington Union,* May 27, 1858.

345 *Douglas girded himself:* White, *The Life of Lyman Trumbull,* 89; Guelzo, *Lincoln and Douglas,* 75.

CHAPTER TWENTY-THREE: A HOUSE DIVIDED

347 *Lincoln's law partner:* Beveridge, *Abraham Lincoln,* 2:544; Donald, *Lincoln's Herndon,* 110–11.

347 *Lincoln, however, was less certain:* Herndon, *Herndon's Life of Lincoln,* 321.

348 *Lincoln nervously wondered:* CW, 2:431.

348 *Through early 1858:* Herndon, *Herndon's Life of Lincoln,* 320.

349 *Lincoln wrote out the words:* CW, 2:452–53.

349 *Lincoln filed this fragment:* Donald, *Lincoln's Herndon,* 114; Herndon, *Herndon's Life of Lincoln,* 322.

350 *Herndon proceeded to see:* Herndon, *Herndon's Life of Lincoln,* 321–22.

350 *In New York:* Ibid., 322–23; Donald, *Lincoln's Herndon,* 115.

350 *In Boston:* Herndon, *Herndon's Life of Lincoln,* 395.

350 *On his Boston sojourn:* Ibid., 323.

351 *Back in Springfield:* Johannsen, *Stephen A. Douglas,* 633–34.

351 *"We want to be our own masters":* Miller, *Lincoln and His World,* 4:227; Joseph Fort Newton, *Lincoln and Herndon* (Cedar Rapids, Iowa: Torch Press, 1910), 164.

351   *There were some defections:* Beveridge, *Abraham Lincoln,* 2:547; Don E. Fehrenbacher, *Prelude to Greatness: Lincoln in the 1850's* (Stanford: Stanford University
Press, 1962), 62.

351   *Lincoln monitored the situation: CW,* 2:443–44, 456.

352   *Another of Lincoln's regular informants: CW,* 2:457.

353   *"My judgment": CW,* First Supplement, 29–30.

353   *Douglas staged a convention:* Fehrenbacher, *Prelude to Greatness,* 64; *CW,* 2:444.

353   *The factional divisions: CW,* 2:435–36.

354   *In May, Lyle Dickey's:* King, *Lincoln's Manager David Davis,* 117–19; *CW,* 2:458–59;
Wallace, *Life and Letters of General W.H.L. Wallace,* 84.

355   *"It is true":* Ida M. Tarbell, *The Life of Abraham Lincoln* (New York: Lincoln History Society, 1903), 2:82; Paul M. Angle, ed., "The Recollections of William Pitt
Kellogg," *Abraham Lincoln Quarterly* 3, no. 7 (September 1945); *CW,* 2:318.

356   *Now Lincoln told Herndon:* Herndon, *Herndon's Life of Lincoln,* 398.

357   *Just before the convention:* Ibid., 325–26; Fehrenbacher, *Prelude to Greatness,* 72,
180.

357   *The Republican convention gathered:* "Official Proceedings," *Illinois State Journal,*
June 17, 1858.

358   *The next night, before perspiring delegates:* Donald, *Lincoln's Herndon,* 206.

360   *"Our cause": CW,* 2:462–69.

361   *Immediately after concluding:* Beveridge, *Abraham Lincoln,* 2:584–85.

361   *But John L. Scripps:* "John L. Scripps to Abraham Lincoln, June 22, 1858," *House
Divided: The Civil War Research Engine at Dickinson College,* http://hd.housedi
vided.dickinson.edu/node/27455.

361   *A few weeks later, Norman Judd:* Wilson, Davis, and Wilson, eds., *Herndon's Informants,* 267.

362   *Swett recalled:* Ibid., 163.

CHAPTER TWENTY-FOUR: THE HIGHER OBJECT

363   *The Little Giant:* Rhodes, *History of the United States from the Compromise of 1850,*
296; Beveridge, *Abraham Lincoln,* 2:543.

364   *As soon as he left:* "The Douglas Demonstration," *Chicago Tribune,* July 10, 1858.

365   *In early July:* Donald, *Lincoln's Herndon,* 213.

366   *Douglas's paper:* Burlingame, *Abraham Lincoln,* 1:466–67.

369   *Lincoln looked to the crowd: CW,* 2:495–501; Guelzo, *Lincoln and Douglas,* 79–83.

370   *"Disgusting":* Burlingame, *Abraham Lincoln,* 1:471–72; Beveridge, *Abraham Lincoln,* 2:626.

370   *Douglas began a triumphant procession:* Whitney, *Life on the Circuit with Lincoln,*
305; Beveridge, *Abraham Lincoln,* 2:613.

370   *Lincoln took the same train:* Sheahan, *The Life of Stephen A. Douglas,* 417.

371   *The* Chicago Times *compared:* Beveridge, *Abraham Lincoln,* 2:619, 623.

371 *The Republican State Committee:* Guelzo, *Lincoln and Douglas,* 91, 73.

371 *The day of the State Committee meeting:* CW, 2:522; Beveridge, *Abraham Lincoln,* 2:629.

372 *Not once did Trumbull bother: Speech of Hon. Lyman Trumbull, of Illinois, at a Mass Meeting in Chicago, August 7, 1858* (Washington, D.C.: Buell & Blanchard Printers, 1858), 5, 12–13; Johannsen, *Stephen A. Douglas,* 675; Mark M. Krug, "Lyman Trumbull and the Real Issues in the Lincoln-Douglas Debates," *Journal of the Illinois State Historical Society* 57, no. 4 (Winter 1964).

373 *Lincoln invoked the names:* CW, 2:483.

374 *It is possible that Lincoln was familiar: The Parliamentary History of England, From the Earliest Period to the Year 1803,* Volume 29 (London: T.C. Hansard, 1817), 278.

374 *At about the same time that Lincoln wrote:* CW, 2:476–82.

CHAPTER TWENTY-FIVE: THE MORAL LIGHTS

375 *No one had more faith:* Newton, *Lincoln and Herndon,* 186.

376 *Douglas's agreement:* Edwin Erle Sparks, *The Lincoln-Douglas Debates of 1858, Lincoln Series* (Springfield: Illinois State Historical Library, 1908), 1:24.

376 *His attention to political detail:* Koerner, *Memoirs,* 2:68; CW, 2:416.

377 *Suffering the defection:* Beveridge, *Abraham Lincoln,* 2:402; Hertz, *The Hidden Lincoln,* 112.

377 *Stuart's law partner:* Koerner, *Memoirs,* 2:62; "Reception of Mr. Douglas by the Democracy of All the Central Countries," *Illinois State Journal,* July 19, 1858; Whitney, *Life on the Circuit with Lincoln,* 541.

378 *Rumor reached Lincoln:* CW, 2:483–84.

378 *Crittenden replied:* David Zarefsky, *Lincoln, Douglas and Slavery: In the Crucible of Public Debate* (Chicago: University of Chicago Press, 1993), 162.

379 *Two days after misleading Lincoln:* Mrs. Chapman Coleman, ed., *The Life of John J. Crittenden* (Philadelphia: J.B. Lippincott, 1873), 2:162–66.

379 *Lincoln's paper:* "A Letter from Judge Dickey," *Illinois State Journal,* August 10, 1858.

379 *Since Lincoln's Chicago speech:* Milton, *The Eve of Conflict,* 332.

379 *In Bloomington:* Burlingame, *Abraham Lincoln,* 1:473–77; "Douglas at Havana," *Chicago Tribune,* August 20, 1858; CW, 2:545.

380 *In fact Douglas never had:* Milton, *The Eve of Conflict,* 324.

381 *Before the debates:* "Letter from Illinois," *Richmond Enquirer,* August 10, 1858.

381 *From his placid summer:* Milton, *The Eve of Conflict,* 328.

381 *Douglas had choreographed:* Ibid., 336–39; Sparks, *The Lincoln-Douglas Debates of 1858,* 124–26, 133.

386 *Partisans on each side: New York Tribune,* August 26, 1858; Harold Holzer, *Lincoln and the Power of the Press* (New York, Simon & Schuster, 2014), 178–81.

387 *Lincoln in private:* Jesse W. Weik, *The Real Lincoln* (Boston: Houghton Mifflin, 1922), 231–32.

388 *Post-debate Republican newspapers:* Guelzo, *Lincoln and Douglas,* 143–44.

388 *The Douglas team:* Sheahan, *The Life of Stephen A. Douglas,* 432.

388 *On the night before the next debate:* Guelzo, *Lincoln and Douglas,* 144–45.

389 *Douglas quoted again:* John Stauffer, *Giants: The Parallel Lives of Frederick Douglass and Abraham Lincoln* (New York: Twelve Books, 2008), 158–59.

389 *Douglass was a foil:* Matthew Norman, "The Other Lincoln-Douglas Debate: The Race Issue in a Comparative Context," *Journal of the Abraham Lincoln Association* 31, no. 1 (Winter 2010): 1–21.

391 *The long-term effects:* "The Senator from Mississippi Attacks the Senator from Illinois," *Illinois State Journal,* November 29, 1858.

392 *"It is impossible":* Nicolay and Hay, *Abraham Lincoln,* 2:164.

392 *The "Freeport Doctrine":* "Judge Douglas Repudiates the Dred Scott Decision," *Washington Union,* September 4, 1858.

392 *Jonesboro:* Cole, *The Centennial History of Illinois,* 178.

394 *After the Jonesboro debate:* Miller, *Lincoln and His World,* 4:261.

394 *Under the headline:* "Negro Equality," *Chicago Tribune,* September 28, 1858.

394 *The fourth debate:* Charles H. Coleman, *Abraham Lincoln and Coles County* (New Brunswick, Ill.: Scarecrow Press, 1955), 165–66.

395 *Both candidates entered:* Ibid., 172–76.

395 *Just as the debate was about to begin:* Ibid., 180.

396 *Richard Mentor Johnson:* Richard Shenkman and Kurt Reiger, "The Vice-President Who Sold His Mistress At Auction," in *One-Night Stands with American History: Odd, Amusing, and Little-Known Incidents* (New York: HarperCollins, 2003), 71–72.

398 *"Republicans saw it":* Isaac N. Arnold, *The Life of Abraham Lincoln* (Chicago: Jansen, McClurg, 1885), 1:148–49.

398 *Lincoln's pandering:* Guelzo, *Lincoln and Douglas,* 204; Lew Wallace, *An Autobiography* (New York: Harper & Brothers, 1906), 1:253–56.

398 *It was three weeks:* "Poor Little Dug!," *Chicago Tribune,* September 28, 1858.

399 *The debates turned north:* Hermann R. Muelder, "Galesburg: Hot-Bed of Abolitionism," *Journal of the Illinois State Historical Society* 35, no. 3 (September 1942): 216–35; Guelzo, *Lincoln and Douglas,* 217–18.

399 *The candidates marched:* Sparks, *The Lincoln-Douglas Debates of 1858,* 375; Guelzo, *Lincoln and Douglas,* 219.

399 *Douglas was physically struggling:* Guelzo, *Lincoln and Douglas,* 221.

401 *Douglas's anger grew:* Sparks, *The Lincoln-Douglas Debates of 1858,* 385.

405 *In Schurz's telling:* Bancroft and Dunning, eds., *The Reminiscences of Carl Schurz,* 2:90–96.

412 *Douglas continued his mockery:* For the debates, see National Park Service, "The Lincoln-Douglas Debates of 1858," https://www.nps.gov/liho/learn/historycul ture/debates.htm; Sparks, *The Lincoln-Douglas Debates of 1858.*

413 *"I was really shocked":* Koerner, *Memoirs,* 2:65–68.

414 *Douglas signaled:* Guelzo, *Lincoln and Douglas,* 275.

414 *A week after the last debate:* Ibid., 271.

414 *Douglas traveled in luxury:* Ibid., 272.

414 *"The planting":* CW, 3:334.

414 *On November 1:* "Mississippi or Illinois—Which?," *Chicago Tribune,* November 1, 1858; Sheahan, *The Life of Stephen A. Douglas,* 438–42; Michael E. Woods, "Was There a Plot to Kill Stephen Douglas?," *The Journal of the Civil War Era,* January 30, 2018; *Claim of Rob't M. and Stephen A. Douglas of Rockingham County, North Carolina* (Washington: Powell & Ginck, 1872).

415 *Election Day was November 2:* Johannsen, *Stephen A. Douglas,* 677; Guelzo, *Lincoln and Douglas,* 284; Fehrenbacher, *Prelude to Greatness,* 119; Nevins, *The Emergence of Lincoln,* 1:398.

415 *Had the Republicans carried three:* Hansen and Nygard, "Stephen A. Douglas, the Know-Nothings, and the Democratic Party in Illinois," 129; Bruce Collins, "The Lincoln: Douglas Contest of 1858 and Illinois' Electorate," *Journal of American Studies* 20, no. 3 (December 1986): 391–420

416 *Late on election night:* Allen Guelzo, *Abraham Lincoln: Redeemer President* (Grand Rapids, Mich.: W.B. Eerdmans, 1999), 226.

416 *Lincoln's friends:* Abraham Lincoln Papers at the Library of Congress, transcribed and annotated by the Lincoln Studies Center, Knox College, Galesburg, Illinois. Letter from David Davis to Abraham Lincoln, November 7, 1858.

416 *He felt no regret:* CW, 3:339.

417 *Within a week, Lincoln was calculating:* CW, 3:336–37.

417 *"The fight must go on":* CW, 3:337.

417 *Lincoln tried to rouse Ray:* CW, 3:341–42.

417 *Within a month, Lincoln had collected transcripts:* Holzer, *Lincoln and the Power of the Press,* 183.

418 *On January 6:* Cole, *The Centennial History of Illinois,* 180.

418 *On the day of Douglas's election:* Whitney, *Life on the Circuit with Lincoln,* 467.

418 *But a clerk:* Charles S. Zane, "A Young Lawyer's Memories of Lincoln," *Journal of the Illinois State Historical Society* 14, nos. 1–2 (April–July, 1921): 79.

CHAPTER TWENTY-SIX: THE PHOENIX

419 *Four days before the election:* Villard, *Memoirs of Henry Villard: Journalist and Financier, 1835–19001* (Boston: Houghton Mifflin, 1904), 1:96.

420 *Mary Todd Lincoln:* Turner and Turner, *Mary Todd Lincoln,* 264.

420 *Trumbull, who was the beneficiary:* White, *The Life of Lyman Trumbull,* 427–31.

421 *To others who knew Lincoln:* Allen Thorndike Rice, *Reminiscences of Abraham Lincoln by Distinguished Men of His Time* (New York: North American Publishing, 1886), 443.

421 *A year later, in 1859:* Ibid., 446.

422   *Two years later, in 1860:* Sparks, *The Lincoln-Douglas Debates of 1858,* 205–6.

422   *Two days after the election:* William Baringer, *Lincoln's Rise to Power* (Boston: Little, Brown, 1937), 52–53; Jeriah Bonham, *Fifty Years' Recollections* (Peoria, Ill.: J.W. Franks & Sons, 1883), 178–79.

422   *On November 5:* "Horace White to Abraham Lincoln, November 5, 1858," *House Divided: The Civil War Research Engine at Dickinson College,* http://hd.housedi vided.dickinson.edu/node/27477.

424   *"Fell, I admit":* Osborn Hamiline Oldroyd, ed., *The Lincoln Memorial: Album-Immortelles* (New York: G.W. Carleton), 472–76.

424   *On November 24:* "Death of Maj. Thos. L. Harris," *Illinois State Journal,* November 25, 1858; Miller, *Lincoln and His World,* 4:273; *CW,* 3:344–45.

425   *On the evening of January 5:* Whitney, *Life on the Circuit with Lincoln,* 83; Chas. C. Chapman & Co., *History of Knox County, Illinois* (Chicago: Blakely, Brown & Marsh, 1878), 410; Emanuel Hertz, *Lincoln Talks: A Biography in Anecdote* (New York: Viking, 1939), 164–65.

425   *Shortly after the election:* Francis Fisher Browne, *The Every-Day Life of Abraham Lincoln* (Chicago: Browne & Howell, 1913), 209–10.

426   *A few months later, that spring:* Ibid., 228–29.

426   *At the onset of the Senate campaign:* Newton, *Lincoln and Herndon,* 222–23.

426   *Just days after Lincoln's loss:* Ibid., 234.

427   *Herndon's conflation:* "The Illinois Election—Triumph of Douglas," *New York Times,* November 5, 1858.

427   *Toward the end of the campaign:* William H. Seward, *The Irrepressible Conflict* (New York: The New York Tribune, 1860).

427   *In New York, the speech:* Nichols, *The Disruption of American Democracy,* 222; Seward, *Seward at Washington as Senator and Secretary of State,* 353.

428   *Seward's speech: CG,* 35th Congress, 2nd Session, 244.

428   *Senator Hammond:* Barnes, *James Buchanan,* 83.

428   *Herndon, while angry:* Donald, *Lincoln's Herndon,* 132; Walter Stahr, *Seward: Lincoln's Indispensable Man* (New York: Simon & Schuster, 2014), 176.

428   *The fury in Illinois:* "A Matter with Messrs. Greeley & Co.," *Chicago Press and Tribune,* February 2, 1859.

429   *Lincoln returned to his law practice: CW,* 3:397.

429   *Lincoln always maintained his focus: CW,* 3:344–45.

431   *Again and again, he hammered: CW,* 3:364–70.

432   *Lincoln ended: CW,* 3:375–76.

433   *Lincoln's stupendous ideological reinvention: CW,* 3:377.

433   *The Republican State Central Committee:* Koerner, *Memoirs,* 2:80.

433   *On April 20:* Baringer, *Lincoln's Rise to Power,* 80–82.

434   *Throughout the spring:* Carl Schurz, *Speeches of Carl Schurz* (Philadelphia: J.B. Lippincott, 1865), 51–75; "Massachusetts Citizenship—Speech of Wm. H. Herndon,"

Illinois State Journal, May 17, 1859; Alison Clark Efford, "Abraham Lincoln, German-Born Republicans, and American Citizenship," *Marquette Law Review* 93, no. 4 (Summer 2010): 93, http://scholarship.law.marquette.edu/mulr/vol93/iss4/37.

434 *Days after the Springfield protest:* "Mr. Lincoln on the Massachusetts Amendment," *Illinois State Journal,* May 19, 1859; *CW,* 3:380.

434 *Immediately after Lincoln's letter:* Holzer, *Lincoln and the Power of the Press,* 187–93; Baringer, *Lincoln's Rise to Power,* 84–85; William E. Barton, *The Life of Abraham Lincoln* (Indianapolis: Bobbs-Merrill, 1925), 420–3; Paul M. Angle, ed., *New Letters and Papers of Lincoln* (Boston: Houghton Mifflin, 1930), 204–7.

435 *Without personal familiarity: CW,* 3:284.

436 *Chase wrote back:* Salmon P. Chase to Abraham Lincoln, June 13, 1859, Letter, *Abraham Lincoln Papers,* Library of Congress, https://cdn.loc.gov/service/mss/mal/017/0174800/0174800.pdf.

436 *Lincoln replied on June 20: CW,* 3:386.

436 *In July 1857:* Miller, *Lincoln and His World,* 4:200–201.

437 *In September 1859:* R.J.M. Blackett, *The Captive's Quest for Freedom: Fugitive Slaves, the 1850 Fugitive Slave Law, and the Politics of Slavery* (New York: Oxford University Press, 2018), 173–76; Monaghan, *The Man Who Elected Lincoln,* 146–52; Browne, *The Every-Day Life of Abraham Lincoln,* 248.

437 *Out of the blue:* Josiah Lucas to Abraham Lincoln, June 13, 1859, Letter, Abraham Lincoln Papers, Library of Congress, https://cdn.loc.gov/service/mss/mal/017/0175300/0175300.pdf.

438 *Sargent was at the center:* Nevins, *The Emergence of Lincoln,* 1:59–63.

438 *Lincoln heard from Sargent:* Nathan Sargent to Abraham Lincoln, Letter, June 13, 1859, *Abraham Lincoln Papers,* Library of Congress, https://cdn.loc.gov/service/mss/mal/017/0175600/0175600.pdf.

438 *Lincoln's response: CW,* 3:387–88.

439 *On the Fourth of July: CW,* 3:390–91.

440 *Colfax wrote back:* Schuyler Colfax to Abraham Lincoln, Letter, July 14, 1859, *Abraham Lincoln Papers,* Library of Congress, https://cdn.loc.gov/service/mss/mal/017/0177300/0177300.pdf.

441 *Galloway observed:* Samuel Galloway to Abraham Lincoln, Letter, July 23, 1859, *Abraham Lincoln Papers,* Library of Congress, https://cdn.loc.gov/service/mss/mal/017/0178500/0178500.pdf.

441 *Lincoln replied on July 28: CW,* 3:394–95.

442 *Jesse Fell:* Morehouse, *The Life of Jesse W. Fell,* 58.

CHAPTER TWENTY-SEVEN: ICARUS

443 *James Buchanan had accepted:* Curtis, *Life of James Buchanan,* 241.

443 *"There is no such entity":* Holst, *The Constitutional and Political History of the United States,* 352; "The Democratic Party," *Washington Union,* February 25, 1859.

444 *Douglas believed his victory:* Johannsen, *Stephen A. Douglas,* 682.

445 *Douglas appealed:* Ibid., 680–85; Stephen A. Douglas, *Speeches of Senator S.A. Douglas* (Washington, D.C.: Lemuel Towers, 1859), 4–7, 14.

445 *Buchanan's blithe spirit:* Klein, *President James Buchanan,* 329.

445 *Buchanan's war:* Milton, *The Eve of Conflict,* 372–75.

446 *While Douglas was steaming:* Johannsen, *Stephen A. Douglas,* 684–87.

446 *The* Chicago Press and Tribune *reported:* "Our Washington Letter," *Chicago Press and Tribune,* December 22, 1858.

446 *Upon returning to Washington:* "Our Washington Correspondence," *New York Times,* January 13, 1859; Johannsen, *Stephen A. Douglas,* 690.

446 *Douglas was cut:* Woods, "Was There a Plot to Kill Stephen Douglas?," "The Duello," *Harper's Weekly,* January 9, 1859; Milton, *The Eve of Conflict,* 364.

447 *The Slidell affair: Washington Union,* January 25, 1859.

447 *On February 23:* Johannsen, *Stephen A. Douglas,* 695–97.

448 *Davis had risen:* William J. Cooper, Jr., *Jefferson Davis, American* (New York: Alfred A. Knopf, 2000), 288–96.

449 *Then Davis laid down the conditions:* Dunbar Rowland, ed., *Jefferson Davis, Constitutionalist* (Jackson: Mississippi Department of Archives and History, 1923), 348, 356.

449 *Douglas piped up: CG,* 35th Congress, 2nd Session, 1246–60.

449 *James M. Mason:* Johannsen, *Stephen A. Douglas,* 695–97.

451 *It had become a truism:* Milton, *The Eve of Conflict,* 379, 382.

451 *Visiting Chicago:* Ibid., 384.

452 *The Douglas bandwagon:* Nichols, *The Disruption of American Democracy,* 260–1; "Meeting of the New York Democratic State Committee," *New York Herald,* August 4, 1859.

452 *Buchanan's peevishness:* Klein, *President James Buchanan,* 333–35.

453 *Refreshed from his summer vacation:* Nevins, *The Emergence of Lincoln,* 2:47.

453 *Douglas decided to publish:* Sheahan, *The Life of Stephen A. Douglas,* 468–98.

454 *The most important lasting effect:* Johannsen, *Stephen A. Douglas,* 710; Jeremiah Black, *Observations on Senator Douglas's Views of Popular Sovereignty* (Washington, D.C.: Thomas McGill, 1859), 5, 20.

455 *Gwin was Broderick's antagonist:* Arthur Quinn, *The Rivals: William Gwin, David Broderick, and the Birth of California* (Lincoln: University of Nebraska Press, 1994), 12–16; Sheahan, *The Life of Stephen A. Douglas,* 500–501.

455 *The antislavery Broderick:* Jeremiah Lynch, *The Life of David C. Broderick: A Senator of the Fifties* (New York: Baker & Taylor, 1911), 161–229; Edward Dickinson Baker, *Oration of Colonel Edward D. Baker, Over the Dead Body of David C. Broderick, a Senator of the United States, 18th September, 1859* (New York: De Vinne Press, 1889); Milton, *The Eve of Conflict,* 391; Nevins, *The Emergence of Lincoln,* 2:121.

456   *When Broderick was struck down:* William T. Bascom to Abraham Lincoln, Letters, September 1, 1859, http://hdl.loc.gov/loc.mss/ms000001.mss30189a.0185300; September 9, 1859, http://hdl.loc.gov/loc.mss/ms000001.mss30189a.0187200, *Abraham Lincoln Papers,* Library of Congress.

457   *In his private jottings:* Gary Ecelbarger, *The Great Comeback: How Abraham Lincoln Beat the Odds to Win the 1860 Republican Nomination* (New York: St. Martin's, 2013), 53; *CW,* 3:198–99.

457   *Lincoln again stalked Douglas:* Rice, *Reminiscences of Abraham Lincoln by Distinguished Men of His Time,* 446.

458   *In Ohio:* "Mr. Lincoln in Ohio," *Chicago Press and Tribune,* September 19, 1859.

460   *Again, he reprised himself:* *CW,* 3:423–25.

460   *On his way to Cincinnati:* Bert S. Bartlow, William H. Todhunter, et al., *Centennial History of Butler County, Ohio* (Indianapolis: B.F. Bowen, 1905), 123–24.

461   *While Southerners and proslavery Northern Democrats:* *CW,* 3:438–62.

461   *Lincoln's Cincinnati speech:* Gary Ecelbarger, "Before Cooper Union: Abraham Lincoln's 1859 Cincinnati Speech and Its Impact on His Nomination," *Journal of the Abraham Lincoln Association* 30, no. 1 (Winter 2009): 13.

462   *On his way home:* *CW,* 3:462–63.

462   *Lincoln wrote Chase:* *CW,* 3:470–71.

462   *On October 13:* *CW,* 3:490; Burlingame, Abraham *Lincoln,* 1:570; Samuel Galloway to Abraham Lincoln, Letter, October 13, 1859, *Abraham Lincoln Papers,* Library of Congress, http://www.loc.gov/resource/mal.0196800; William T. Bascon to Abraham Lincoln, Letter, October 13, 1859, *Abraham Lincoln Papers,* Library of Congress, http://www.loc.gov/resource/mal.0196700.

463   *The day before:* James A. Briggs to Abraham Lincoln, Letter, October 12, 1859, *Abraham Lincoln Papers,* Library of Congress, http://www.loc.gov/resource/mal.0196600.

463   *Lincoln "came rushing":* Herndon, *Herndon's Life of Lincoln,* 367; Harold Holzer, *Lincoln at Cooper Union: The Speech That Made Abraham Lincoln President* (New York: Simon & Schuster, 2004), 13–14.

464   *At 7:05: Correspondence Relating to the Insurrection at Harper's Ferry, 17th October, 1859* (Annapolis: B.H. Richardson, 1860), 5; Klein, *President James Buchanan,* 334.

CHAPTER TWENTY-EIGHT: THIS GUILTY LAND

465   *In early May of 1858: Report [of] the Select Committee of the Senate Appointed to Inquire into the Late Invasion and Seizure of the Public Property at Harper's Ferry* (Washington, D.C.: U.S. Congress, 1860), 253.

465   *Hugh Forbes:* Renehan, *The Secret Six,* 122–28; Villard, *John Brown,* 285–87.

467   *Forbes proposed:* Villard, *John Brown,* 313–14; Renehan, *The Secret Six,* 128.

467   *Seward said Forbes:* "Senate Select Committee Report on the Harper's Ferry Invasion," 36th Congress, 1st Session, Senate. Rep. Com. No. 278, 253–54.

467   *Forbes went to the Senate chamber:* Ibid., 140–41.

468   *After Forbes defected:* Renehan, *The Secret Six,* 133–35.

468   *For a month, from January 28, 1858:* Douglass, *Life and Times,* 275–76; John Brown, *Provisional Constitution and Ordinances for the People of the United States* (St. Catherines, Ont.: William Howard Day, 1858).

468   *Brown wrote his Boston benefactors:* Villard, *John Brown,* 320; Franklin Sanborn, *Life and Letters of John Brown, Liberator of Kansas, and Martyr of Virginia* (Cambridge, Mass.: Sampson Low, 1885), 438–40.

469   *Sanborn raced to Boston:* Maud Howe Elliott, *Lord Byron's Helmet* (Boston: Houghton Mifflin, 1927), 24–25; J.C. Furnas, *The Road to Harpers Ferry* (New York: William Sloan Associates, 1959), 341; Franklin Sanborn, *Recollections of Seventy Years* (Boston: R.G. Badger, 1900), 182.

469   *And there was Parker himself:* Theodore Parker, *The Collected Works of Theodore Parker* ed., Frances Power Cobbe (London: Trubner, 1865), 12:164–77.

470   *Brown represented a stab:* Renehan, *The Secret Six,* 113, 147, 151; Villard, *John Brown,* 181–82.

470   *On May 8:* Reynolds, *John Brown, Abolitionist,* 261–65; Villard, *John Brown,* 330–36.

471   *Even while Brown recited:* Villard, *John Brown,* 339, 341.

471   *Sanborn was already frantically writing:* Renehan, *The Secret Six,* 151–53; Villard, *John Brown,* 338–40.

472   *Brown arrived in Boston:* Villard, *John Brown,* 340.

472   *Brown's expedition:* Helen Delay, "Richard Realf, Poet and Soldier," *The Home Monthly* 8, nos. 10–11 (May 1899); "Senate Select Committee Report on the Harper's Ferry Invasion," 144; Renehan, *The Secret Six,* 166–68.

473   *Brown resurfaced:* Redpath, *The Public Life of Capt. John Brown,* 199; Villard, *John Brown,* 355; Reynolds, *John Brown, Abolitionist,* 274–75; Joel Tyler Headley, *The Life of Oliver Cromwell* (New York: Charles Scribner's Sons, 1888), 234–61; Hinton, *John Brown and His Men,* 370–75.

473   *For months, Brown suffered:* Reynolds, *John Brown, Abolitionist,* 274; Villard, *John Brown,* 202–3.

474   *Hearing that a slave:* Reynolds, *John Brown, Abolitionist,* 278–79; Villard, *John Brown,* 367–73; Robinson, *Kansas,* 406–7.

475   *He launched into the history:* William A. Phillips, "Three Interviews with Old John Brown," *The Atlantic Monthly,* December 1879.

475   *Brown's fixation:* Sanborn, *Brown,* 444–45.

475   *Brown's raid:* Sanborn, *Recollections of Seventy Years,* 164.

476   *Brown came to Boston:* Renehan, *The Secret Six,* 179–87.

476   *Brown strangely appeared:* "Senate Select Committee Report on the Harper's Ferry Invasion," 144.

476   *That night Brown had dinner:* Renehan, *The Secret Six,* 188.

477 *On about July 12:* Reynolds, *John Brown, Abolitionist,* 304; Hinton, *John Brown and His Men,* 271; John Stauffer and Zoe Trodd, eds., *The Tribunal: Responses to John Brown and the Harpers Ferry Raid* (Cambridge, Mass.: Belknap Press, 2012), 38–43.

477 *On August 25:* B.F. Gue, "John Brown and His Iowa Friends," *The Midland Monthly,* February 1897 (Des Moines, Iowa: Johnson Brigham), 103–13.

477 *In early September:* Sanborn, *Recollections of Seventy Years,* 182–83.

478 *Brown summoned Frederick Douglass:* Douglass, *Life and Times,* 277–79.

478 *The sudden arrival of a windfall:* McClure, *Old Time Notes,* 24–25; Sandra Harbert Petrulionis, *To Set This World Right: The Antislavery Movement in Thoreau's Concord* (Ithaca, N.Y.: Cornell University Press, 2006), 142; Villard, *John Brown,* 421.

479 *Another trigger appeared:* Hinton, *John Brown and His Men,* 278.

479 *Some within the company:* Sanborn, *Recollections of Seventy Years,* 184; Osborne P. Anderson, *A Voice from Harper's Ferry: A Narrative of Events at Harper's Ferry* (Boston: Published by the Author, 1861), 27–28.

479 *Early on Sunday morning:* Anderson, *A Voice from Harper's Ferry,* 27–32.

480 *Upon entering Harpers Ferry:* "Senate Select Committee Report on the Harper's Ferry Invasion," 22, 29–37.

480 *The next man killed:* Alexander R. Boteler, "Recollections of the John Brown Raid," *The Century Monthly* 26, no. 4 (New York: The Century Co., 1883): 405–6; "Senate Select Committee Report on the Harper's Ferry Invasion," 39.

481 *Brown boasted:* Villard, *John Brown,* 432–37.

481 *Feeling secure:* Renehan, *The Secret Six,* 199–200; Villard, *John Brown,* 437–38; Anderson, *A Voice from Harper's Ferry,* 38.

481 *Brown sent:* Renehan, *The Secret Six,* 201–2; Boteler, "Recollections of the John Brown Raid," 407; Villard, *John Brown,* 439–44.

482 *Oliver Brown:* Villard, *John Brown,* 446–48.

482 *Before midnight:* Boteler, "Recollections of the John Brown Raid," 409; Villard, *John Brown,* 450–55; Renehan, *The Secret Six,* 204; "Senate Select Committee Report on the Harper's Ferry Invasion," 40.

483 *Through his self-control:* Headley, *The Life of Oliver Cromwell,* 245, 249, 250, 254.

486 *Brown had lost:* Sanborn, *Life and Letters,* 561–72.

487 *The nation's press:* "The Virginia Rebellion. The Trial of the Insurgents," *New York Times,* October 28, 1859; Villard, *John Brown,* 487–88, 496; Sanborn, *Life and Letters,* 588; Wise, *The End of an Era,* 130–31.

488 *Judge Parker:* Villard, *John Brown,* 498–99.

488 *Over the next month John Brown:* Sanborn, *Life and Letters,* 598–99.

489 *"Brown had his arms tied":* Mary Anna Jackson, *Life and Letters of General Thomas J. Jackson (Stonewall Jackson)* (New York: Harper & Brothers, 1892), 130–31.

489 *"So perish":* Nevins, *The Emergence of Lincoln,* 2:97.

489 *Standing about thirty feet:* Terry Alford, *Fortune's Fool: The Life of John Wilkes Booth* (New York: Oxford University Press, 2015), 81–82.

490 *As John Brown left:* Sanborn, *Life and Letters,* 620.

CHAPTER TWENTY-NINE: WITCH HUNT

491 *John Brown's initial legacy:* Villard, *John Brown,* 467; Redpath, *The Public Life of Capt. John Brown,* 270; "The Exposure of the Nigger-Worshipping Insurrectionists," *New York Herald,* October 28, 1859.

492 *Seward was on a Grand Tour:* "The 'Irrepressible Conflict,'" *New York Herald,* October 19, 1859; "Most Important Disclosures," *New York Herald,* October 27, 1859; "What is Treason?—Who are Traitors?," *New York Herald,* October 29, 1859.

492 *On November 18:* New York Democratic Vigilant Association, *Rise and Progress of the Bloody Outbreak at Harper's Ferry* (New York: John F. Trow, 1859), 10, 17.

493 *Seward was traveling:* Stahr, *Seward,* 180; Seward, *Seward at Washington as Senator and Secretary of State,* 440.

493 *Frederick Douglass:* Douglass, *Life and Times,* 391–97.

493 *Gerrit Smith:* "Gerrit Smith and the Harpers Ferry Outlook," *New York Herald,* October 31, 1859; Renehan, *The Secret Six,* 224; Reynolds, *John Brown, Abolitionist,* 341.

494 *Upon hearing that Brown's letters:* Sanborn, *Recollections of Seventy Years,* 187–92.

494 *The day Sanborn came back:* Renehan, *The Secret Six,* 227–29; Reynolds, *John Brown, Abolitionist,* 342–43.

494 *Higginson was infuriated:* Renehan, *The Secret Six,* 227–29; Reynolds, *John Brown, Abolitionist,* 343.

494 *Theodore Parker:* Parker, *Collected Works,* 165; Renehan, *The Secret Six,* 232–33.

494 *On the morning of Brown's hanging:* Frank Preston Stearns, *The Life and Public Services of George Luther Stearns* (Philadelphia: J.B. Lippincott, 1907), 198–201.

495 *At two in the afternoon:* Henry David Thoreau, *Political Writings,* ed., Nancy L. Rosenblum (Cambridge: Cambridge University Press, 1996), 133; Reynolds, *John Brown, Abolitionist,* 366; James Redpath, ed., *Echoes of Harper's Ferry* (Boston: Thayer & Eldridge, 1860), 437–54.

495 *Virginia governor Henry A. Wise's:* Forney, *Anecdotes of Public Men,* 1:144; Clement Eaton, "Henry A. Wise and the Virginia Fire Eaters of 1856," *The Mississippi Valley Historical Review* 21, no. 4 (March 1935): 495–512; Villard, *John Brown,* 504; Trodd and Stauffer, eds., *Meteor of War,* 267, 257; *Governor's Message* (Richmond, Va.: William F. Ritchie, 1859), 29.

496 *Edmund Ruffin:* Nevins, *The Emergence of Lincoln,* 2:102; Peter Wallenstein, "Incendiaries All: Southern Politics and the Harpers Ferry Raid," in *His Soul Goes Marching On: Responses to John Brown and the Harpers Ferry Raid,* Paul Finkelman, ed. (Charlottesville: University Press of Virginia, 1995), 166.

497 *Wise's handling:* Stauffer and Trodd, eds., *The Tribunal,* 308–10.

497 *The Southern reaction:* Virginia Mason, *The Public Life and Diplomatic Correspondence of James M. Mason* (New York: Neale Publishing, 1906), 148; Villard, *John Brown,* 566.

498 *Brown's sanctification:* Wise, *The End of an Era,* 133–34.

498 *The logic of disunion:* Henry D. Capers, *The Life and Times of C.G. Memminger* (Richmond: Everett Waddey, 1893), 239–74; Nevins, *The Emergence of Lincoln,* 2:111.

499 *A great fear:* Nevins, *The Emergence of Lincoln,* 2:106–12, 122; William Asbury Christian, *Richmond, Her Past and Present* (Richmond: L.H. Jenkins, 1912), 204.

499 *On December 5:* Holst, *The Constitutional and Political History of the United States,* 70; Potter, *The Impending Crisis,* 386.

500 *The day after Republicans unified: CG,* 36th Congress, 1st Session, 16; Potter, *The Impending Crisis,* 387.

500 *Listening to Clark: CG,* 36th Congress, 1st Session, 21.

501 *Congressman Laurence Keitt: CG,* 36th Congress, 1st Session, 24.

501 *This brought Thaddeus Stevens: CG,* 36th Congress, 1st Session, 24.

501 *Hinton Helper:* David Brown, "Attacking Slavery from Within: The Making of 'The Impending Crisis of the South,' *The Journal of Southern History* 70, no. 3 (August 2004): 541–76.

503 *Helper unapologetically called:* Hinton Rowan Helper, *The Impending Crisis: How to Meet It* (New York: Burdick Brothers, 1857), 111-23.

503 The Impending Crisis: "The Opening of Congress—The Vital Question of the Day," *New York Herald,* December 8, 1859.

504 *Roger Pryor: CG,* 36th Congress, 1st Session, 30; Sherman, *Recollections of Forty Years in the Senate and Cabinet,* 172, 83–84.

504 *The* New York Tribune: "Helper's Crisis," *New York Tribune,* December 27, 1859.

504 *Over a biblical forty days and nights:* Nevins, *The Emergence of Lincoln,* 2:120.

504 *The game of smearing:* Phillips, ed., *The Correspondence of Robert Toombs, Alexander H. Stephens, and Howell Cobb,* 461.

506 *"The meanest slave": CG,* 36th Congress, 1st Session, 202–7.

506 *After Lovejoy finished:* Rhodes, *History of the United States from the Compromise of 1850,* 2:439.

506 *On the day Lovejoy defended free speech:* Michael Kent Curtis, "The 1859 Crisis over Hinton Helper's Book, *The Impending Crisis:* Free Speech, Slavery, and Some Light on the Meaning of the First Section of the Fourteenth Amendment," *Chicago Kent Law Review* 68, no. 3 (June 1998): 1141–67.

506 *On the same day the House:* Trodd and Stauffer, eds., *Meteor of War,* 260.

507 *After Stearns testified:* Stearns, The *Life and Public Services of George Luther Stearns,* 209–10.

507 *As the House was embroiled:* "Great Speech of Senator Douglas," *New York Times,* January 24, 1860.

507 *In his first statement on Harpers Ferry: CG,* 36th Congress, 1st Session, 553.

508 *Harpers Ferry: CG,* 36th Congress, 1st Session, 554–59.

508 *Douglas's proposal:* Milton, *The Eve of Conflict,* 393, 404, 407; William Garrett, *Reminiscences of Public Men in Alabama: For Thirty Years* (Atlanta: Plantation Publishing, 1872), 693.

509 *The day after Pennington's election:* Holst, *The Constitutional and Political History of the United States,* 114–15; *CG,* 36th Congress, 1st Session, 658.

509 *Douglas had already announced:* Milton, *The Eve of Conflict,* 411; Phillips, ed., *The Correspondence of Robert Toombs, Alexander H. Stephens, and Howell Cobb,* 461.

509 *Again, on February 29:* Henry B. Stanton, *Random Recollections* (New York: Harper & Brothers, 1887), 213.

510 *Seward ended with a pastoral vision: CG,* 36th Congress, 1st Session, 910–14.

511 *"His speech":* "Mr. Seward's Speech," *New York Times,* March 1, 1860.

511 *"So calm in temper":* "The Speech of Mr. Seward," *New York Tribune,* March 1, 1860.

511 *Immediately upon Seward finishing: CG,* 36th Congress, 1st Session, 915.

511 *Then Jefferson Davis rose: CG,* 36th Congress, 1st Session, 916–17; "The Presidential Contest: 'Glittering and Sounding Generalities,'" *New York Times,* October 30, 1856.

512 *Seward was confident:* Stanton, *Random Recollections,* 213.

512 *Seward's tone:* F.I. Herriott, "The Conference in the Deutsches Haus Chicago, May 14–15, 1860, A Study of Some of the Preliminaries of the National Republican Convention of 1860," *Transactions, Illinois State Historical Society, 1928* (Springfield: Phillips Bros., 1928), 116.

CHAPTER THIRTY: RIGHT MAKES MIGHT

515 *They had last seen each other:* Henry Villard, "Recollections of Lincoln," *The Atlantic Monthly* 93 (Boston: Houghton Mifflin, 1904), 168.

516 *Lincoln's invitation:* Whitney, *Life on the Circuit with Lincoln,* 375.

516 *Just hours after he encountered Villard: CW,* 3:496–97.

517 *Lincoln refused to act: CW,* 3:503.

517 *The next day he observed the election:* "Abraham Lincoln in Kansas," Kansas Historical Society, https://www.kshs.org/kansapedia/abraham-lincoln-in-kansas/12132; "Hon. A. Lincoln," *Illinois State Journal,* December 10, 1859; Gilbert Tracy, ed., *Uncollected Letters of Abraham Lincoln* (Boston: Houghton Mifflin, 1917), 134–35.

517 *Once he was back home: CW,* 3:511.

518 *Jesse Fell:* Morehouse, *The Life of Jesse W. Fell,* 59–60.

519 *The conflict was a struggle:* King, *Lincoln's Manager David Davis,* 128; White, *The Life of Lyman Trumbull,* 149.

519 *On December 16:* Nathaniel Niles to Abraham Lincoln, Letter, December 16,

1859, *Abraham Lincoln Papers,* Library of Congress, www.loc.gov/resource/mal.0215400.

519   *Wentworth and Judd:* "The Sedgwick Street Humbug," *Chicago Press and Tribune,* April 2, 1859.

519   *Lincoln was already enmeshed: CW,* 2:428–29.

520   *Judd, close to Trumbull:* King, *Lincoln's Manager David Davis,* 128–29; *CW,* 3:390.

520   *In November 1859:* Norman Judd to Abraham Lincoln, Letter, December 1, 1859, *Abraham Lincoln Papers,* Library of Congress, www.loc.gov/resource/mal.0209800.

521   *That same day Judd wrote Trumbull:* Don E. Fehrenbacher, "The Judd-Wentworth Feud," *Journal of the Illinois State Historical Society* 45, no. 3 (Autumn 1952): 197–211; Thomas J. Pickett, "A Group of Country Editors Champion Mr. Lincoln," *Intimate Memories of Lincoln,* Rufus Rockwell Wilson, ed. (Elmira, Ill.: Primavera Press, 1945), 193–94.

521   *After he returned from his Kansas trip: CW,* 3:505, 507–8.

521   *Wentworth slyly asked Lincoln:* Norman B. Judd to Abraham Lincoln, Letter, February 21, 1860, *Abraham Lincoln Papers,* Library of Congress, www.loc.gov/resource/mal.0240800; David Davis to Abraham Lincoln, Letter, February 21, 1860, *Abraham Lincoln Papers,* Library of Congress, www.loc.gov/resource/mal.0239600; Fehrenbacher, *Prelude to Greatness,* 150–51.

522   *"I know":* Herndon, *Herndon's Life of Lincoln,* 370.

522   *The* Chicago Press and Tribune *reported:* "The Lincoln-Douglas Debates," *Chicago Press and Tribune,* January 10, 1860; "Mr. Lincoln and the Presidency," *Illinois State Journal,* January 14, 1860; Baringer, *Lincoln's Rise to Power,* 136, 141.

523   *On the last week of January:* Wilson, Davis, and Wilson, eds., *Herndon's Informants,* 247; Burlingame, *Abraham Lincoln,* 1:581; Baringer, *Lincoln's Rise to Power,* 142–43.

523   *Almost all of those in this caucus:* Hollister, *Life of Schuyler Colfax,* 143; Frederic Bancroft, *The Life of William H. Seward* (New York: Harper & Brothers, 1900). 1:528–30.

524   *About two weeks after the secret:* Browning, *Diary,* 394–95.

524   *Lincoln was alarmed: CW,* 3:517.

525   *A week later, on February 16:* "The Presidency—Abraham Lincoln," *Chicago Press and Tribune,* February 16, 1860; Burlingame, *Abraham Lincoln,* 1:581.

525   *On February 22: CW,* 3:509; Koerner, *Memoirs,* 2:80.

525   *Between law cases:* Holzer, *Lincoln at Cooper Union,* 204, 51–53.

526   *"The finished speech":* Rankin, *Personal Recollections of Abraham Lincoln,* 245; Herndon, *Herndon's Life of Lincoln,* 367.

527   *Bryant had closely followed: CW,* 2:346–47; John Drury, *Old Illinois Houses* (Chicago: Chicago Daily News, 1948), 152–54.

527   *According to George H. Putnam:* Parke Godwin, *Life and Works of William Cullen Bryant* (New York: D. Appleton, 1883), 2:124; Gilbert H. Muller, *Abraham Lincoln and William Cullen Bryant: Their Civil War* (New York: Palgrave, 2017), 257.

528   *Salmon P. Chase:* Holzer, *Lincoln at Cooper Union,* 83; Rice, *Recollections,* 298.

528   *Lincoln arrived in the city:* Villard, *John Brown,* 519; Thomas Wallace Knox, *The Life and Work of Henry Ward Beecher* (Hartford, Conn.: Park Publishing, 1887), 158.

528   *On the morning of February 27:* Wilson, *Intimate Memories,* 250–51.

529   *Lincoln's handler:* Louis DeCaro, Jr., *Freedom's Dawn: The Last Days of John Brown in Virginia* (Lanham, Md.: Rowman & Littlefield, 2015), 123.

529   *Lincoln was escorted:* Wilson, *Intimate Memories,* 251.

529   *Once Lincoln entered:* Mary Panzer, *Mathew Brady* (New York: Phaidon, 2001), 59.

530   *At eight in the evening:* Muller, *Abraham Lincoln and William Cullen Bryant,* 15.

530   *The audience applauded:* Wayne Whipple, *The Story-Life of Lincoln: A Biography Composed of Five Hundred True Stories* (Philadelphia: John C. Winston, 1908), 308; Gilbert H. Muller, *William Cullen Bryant: Poet of America* (Albany: State University Press of New York, 2008), 257.

530   *Lincoln's hair:* Holzer, *Lincoln at Cooper Union,* 108–14; Henry M. Field, *The Life of David Dudley Field* (New York: Charles Scribner's Sons, 1898), 123; Noah Brooks, *Abraham Lincoln and the Downfall of Slavery* (New York: G.P. Putnam's Sons, 1896), 186.

537   *Finally, unapologetically:* CW, 3:522–50.

537   *The crowd that had been taken aback:* Holzer, *Lincoln at Cooper Union,* 146.

537   *Noah Brooks:* Brooks, *Abraham Lincoln and the Downfall of Slavery,* 187.

537   *After a celebratory dinner:* Holzer, *Lincoln at Cooper Union,* 157.

538   *On his way to visit his son:* CW, 4:7.

538   *The* Chicago Press and Tribune *beat: Illinois State Journal,* March 8, 1860; Bancroft, *The Life of William H. Seward,* 1:531.

CHAPTER THIRTY-ONE: WALPURGISNACHT

539   *James Sheahan:* Johannsen, *Stephen A. Douglas,* 733–34; Sheahan, *The Life of Stephen A. Douglas,* 528.

540   *"There will be no serious":* Nevins, *The Emergence of Lincoln,* 2:206.

540   *The optimistic signs:* Nichols, *The Disruption of American Democracy,* 278–80; Milton, *The Eve of Conflict,* 411–13; "The Jeff. Davis Correspondence," *New York Times,* September 20, 1863; Johannsen, *Stephen A. Douglas,* 743–44; Douglas R. Egerton, *Year of Meteors: Stephen Douglas, Abraham Lincoln, and the Election That Brought on the Civil War* (New York: Bloomsbury, 2010), 58.

541   *Before the convention:* Milton, *The Eve of Conflict,* 421; Freehling, *The Road to Disunion,* 2:296.

542   *In his biography of Douglas:* Sheahan, *The Life of Stephen A. Douglas,* 1.

542   *But even as Sheahan's hagiography:* Milton, *The Eve of Conflict,* 423–24; Austin L. Venable, "The Conflict Between the Douglas and Yancey Forces in the Charleston Convention," *The Journal of Southern History* 8, no. 2 (May 1942): 237.

543 *Nothing Douglas could say:* William J. Cooper, ed., *Jefferson Davis: Essential Writings* (New York: Modern Library, 2004), 175–76.

543 *Douglas had ceaselessly attempted:* "Editorial," *New York Tribune,* April 14, 1860.

545 *Davis returned to the issue: CG,* 36th Congress, 1st Session, 424–26.

545 *But no one was letting it go:* Phillips, ed., *The Correspondence of Robert Toombs, Alexander H. Stephens, and Howell Cobb,* 450.

545 *Buchanan had issued a statement:* Klein, *Buchanan,* 341; Davis, *Essential Writings,* 175–76; Milton, *The Eve pf Conflict,* 416–19.

546 *The team that had secured:* Klein, *President James Buchanan,* 341; Milton, *The Eve of Conflict,* 419; Nevins, *The Emergence of Lincoln,* 2:206.

546 *At a Faneuil Hall rally:* John M. Belohlavek, *Broken Glass: Caleb Cushing and the Shattering of the Union* (Kent, Ohio: Kent State University Press, 2005), 302–3, 309; Richard Taylor, *Destruction and Reconstruction: Personal Experiences of the Late War* (New York: D. Appleton, 1879), 4.

546 *Charleston had been designated:* Johannsen, *Stephen A. Douglas,* 748; "The Democratic Party," Charleston Mercury, April 16, 1860.

547 *Douglas urged:* Nevins, *The Emergence of Lincoln,* 2:204; Rhodes, *History of the United States from the Compromise of 1850,* 2:441.

547 *Murat Halstead:* Murat Halstead, *Caucuses of 1860: A History of the National Political Conventions* (Columbus, Ohio: Follett, Foster, 1860), 6.

548 *"Imagine a crowded barroom":* New York Herald, April 26, 1860.

548 *A cloud of dread:* Klein, *President James Buchanan,* 337–38; Nevins, *The Emergence of Lincoln,* 2:197–99; "The Covode Investigation," 8.

548 *"The reception:* "Gossip from Charleston," *New York Times,* April 27, 1860; "Charleston Convention," *New York Herald,* April 23, 1860.

549 *Yet at the same time the disclosure:* "Our Special Washington Despatch," *New York Herald,* April 23, 1860; "Charleston Convention," *New York Times,* April 23, 1860; "From Charleston," *New York Tribune,* April 24, 1860.

549 *More than three thousand delegates:* Halstead, *Caucuses of 1860,* 5.

549 *On April 23:* Ibid., 23.

550 *The senatorial claque:* Milton, *The Eve of Conflict,* 432; Nichols, *The Disruption of American Democracy,* 296–97.

550 *" 'Bubble, bubble":* New York Herald, April 26, 1860.

550 *On April 27:* Nichols, *The Disruption of American Democracy,* 298.

551 *Jefferson Davis:* Rhodes, *History of the United States from the Compromise of 1850,* 2:445; "Charleston Convention," *New York Times,* April 27, 1860.

551 *The Charleston convention:* Halstead, *Caucuses of 1860,* 32.

551 *Both resolutions:* Ibid., 68.

552 *Faced with splitting the convention:* Venable, "The Conflict Between the Douglas and Yancey Forces in the Charleston Convention," 238–39; Halstead, *Caucuses of 1860,* 68–69.

552 *Henry B. Payne:* Johannsen, *Stephen A. Douglas,* 754.

552 *Yancey's motive:* Eric H. Walther, *William Lowndes Yancey and the Coming of the Civil War* (Chapel Hill: University of North Carolina Press, 2006), 14–17.

553 *In 1838:* John Witherspoon DuBose, *The Life and Times of William Lowndes Yancey* (Birmingham, Ala.: Roberts & Son, 1892), 73–74, 141–43.

553 *From 1848:* Chauncey Samuel Boucher, "South Carolina and the South on the Eve of Secession, 1852 to 1860," *Washington University Studies* 6, no. 2 (April 1919): 131.

554 *In anticipation of the election year:* DuBose, *the Life and Times of William Lowndes Yancey,* 440–42.

554 *Finally, he bid farewell: Proceedings of the Conventions at Charleston and Baltimore* (Washington: National Democratic Executive Committee, 1860), 66–78.

555 *Yancey spoke:* Halstead, *Caucuses of 1860,* 49.

555 *But the vanity: Proceedings of the Conventions at Charleston and Baltimore,* 79–81.

555 *On April 28:* Nichols, *The Disruption of American Democracy,* 301.

555 *On April 29:* Ibid., 302.

556 *On Monday, April 30:* Halstead, *Caucuses of 1860,* 70.

556 *While the Douglas majority passed:* Ibid., 73.

556 *That night was the Walpurgisnacht:* Ibid., 75.

556 *Late that night Richard Taylor:* Taylor, *Destruction and Reconstruction,* 4–5.

557 *In the sober light:* Halstead, *Caucuses of 1860,* 87, "Charleston Conventions," *New York Times,* May 3, 1860; "The Convention Breaking Up," *Charleston Mercury,* May 1, 1860.

557 *The certainty and poise:* Alexander, *A Political History of the State of New York,* 2:276–78.

558 *Richmond's faithlessness:* Halstead, *Caucuses of 1860,* 84–85.

558 *After fifty-six ballots:* Johannsen, *Stephen A. Douglas,* 757–58.

558 *While the regular Democratic convention:* "Proceedings of the Seceders," *New York Times,* May 2, 1860; Halstead, *Caucuses of 1860,* 97–100; Johannsen, *Stephen A. Douglas,* 758–59.

559 *One week after the suspension:* Halstead, *Caucuses of 1860,* 109.

559 *Declaring itself the party:* Rhodes, *History of the United States from the Compromise of 1850,* 2:454; Michael F. Holt, *The Election of 1860* (Lawrence: University Press of Kansas, 2017), 85.

559 *The Constitutional Unionists:* Holt, *The Election of 1860,* 85–86.

560 *The next day, May 4:* Edgar Eugene Robinson, ed., "The Day Journal of Milton S. Latham," *California Historical Society Quarterly* 11, no. 1 (March 1932): 17–18.

561 *On the day the Charleston convention:* "The Disruption of the Democratic Party," *New York Times,* May 4, 1860.

562 *Alexander Stephens:* Johnston and Browne, *Life of Alexander H. Stephens,* 355–57.

562 *The Douglas men:* Halstead, *Caucuses of 1860,* 87.

CHAPTER THIRTY-TWO: THE RAILSPLITTER

563   *On April 29: CW,* 4:45.

563   *The* Chicago Press and Tribune *had raised the banner:* "Chicago Convention—The Nominee," *Illinois State Journal,* March 13, 1860.

564   *"The Illinois State Journal":* "Seward and Lincoln," *Chicago Press and Tribune,* March 15, 1860.

564   *The* Tribune's *tentative tone:* Ecelbarger, *The Great Comeback,* 169–70, 174.

564   *Medill's candidate shopping:* Baringer, *Lincoln's Rise to Power,* 172.

565   *Wentworth and Davis:* John Wentworth to Abraham Lincoln, Letter, April 21, 1860, *Papers of Abraham Lincoln,* Library of Congress, https://cdn.loc.gov/service/mss/mal/026/0260300/0260300.pdf.

565   *Two days later, on April 23:* David Davis to Abraham Lincoln, Letter, April 23, 1860, *Papers of Abraham Lincoln,* Library of Congress, https://cdn.loc.gov/service/mss/mal/026/0260700/0260700.pdf.

566   *The day after Davis's letter:* Lyman Trumbull to Abraham Lincoln, Letter, April 24, 1860, *Papers of Abraham Lincoln,* Library of Congress, https://cdn.loc.gov/service/mss/mal/026/0261200/0261200.pdf.

566   *"A word now": CW,* 4:45–46.

566   *The election of delegates:* "The County Convention," *Chicago Press and Tribune,* May 1, 1860; Norman B. Judd to Abraham Lincoln, Letter, May 2, 1860, *Papers of Abraham Lincoln,* Library of Congress, https://cdn.loc.gov/service/mss/mal/026/0262500/0262500.pdf.

567   *Wentworth had in fact:* Ecelbarger, *The Great Comeback,* 173.

567   *Lincoln's men moved up:* Ibid., 172.

567   *The chief of convention planning:* J. McCan Davis, *How Abraham Lincoln Became President* (Springfield, Ill.: Henry O. Shepard, 1908), 55–58; Jane Martin Johns, "The Nomination of Abraham Lincoln to the Presidency, An Unsolved Psychological Problem," *Journal of the Illinois State Historical Society* 10, no. 4 (January 1918): 562–64.

567   *Thousands of delegates:* Wilson, Davis, and Wilson, eds., *Herndon's Informants,* 462–63.

568   *Oglesby calmed:* Davis, *How Abraham Lincoln Became President,* 59; Wilson, Davis, and Wilson, eds., *Herndon's Informants,* 463.

568   *Again, the crowd went wild:* Isaac N. Phillips, ed., *Abraham Lincoln, By Some Men Who Knew Him* (Bloomington, Ill.: Pantagraph Printing, 1910); Johns, "The Nomination of Abraham Lincoln to the Presidency," 564; 115.

568   *"How are you Abe?":* Davis, *How Abraham Lincoln Became President,* 59.

568   *"The whole scene":* Ward Hill Lamon, *The Life of Abraham Lincoln* (Boston: James R. Osgood, 1872), 446; Wilson, Davis, and Wilson, eds., *Herndon's Informants,* 463.

568   *The convention moved:* "Illinois Republican Convention," *Chicago Press and Tribune,* May 11, 1860.

569   *The next day, the Decatur convention:* Otto R. Kyle, *Lincoln in Decatur* (New York: Vantage Press, 1957), 113–14; Osborne H. Oldroyd, *Lincoln's Campaign: Or, the Revolution of 1860* (Chicago: Laird & Lee, 1896), 71; "Illinois Republican Convention," *Chicago Press and Tribune,* May 11, 1860.

569   *After the first day of the convention:* Arnold, *The Life of Abraham Lincoln,* 163; Burlingame, *Abraham Lincoln,* 2:599–600; "Illinois Republican Convention," *Chicago Press and Tribune,* May 11, 1860.

570   *As for John Hanks:* Davis, *How Abraham Lincoln Became President,* 59.

CHAPTER THIRTY-THREE: THE WIGWAM

571   *Thurlow Weed:* Robert H. Browne, *Lincoln and the Men of His Time* (Cincinnati: Jennings & Pye, 1901), 2:412.

573   *The former fur trading post:* Donald L. Miller, *City of the Century: The Epic of Chicago and the Making of America* (New York: Simon & Schuster, 1996), 89–121.

573   *In the counting rooms:* "The Council and the Slave Law," *Weekly Chicago Journal,* May 28, 1850.

573   *All sorts of Lincoln's friends:* Andrew Taylor Call, *Jacob Bunn: Legacy of an Illinois Industrial Pioneer* (Lawrenceville, Va.: Brunswick, 2005), 71.

574   *The rise of Chicago:* John M. Palmer, ed., *The Bench and Bar of Illinois: Historical and Reminiscent* (Chicago: Lewis Publishing, 1899), 2:643.

574   *In late March of 1860:* Stacy Pratt McDermott, "A Little Sandbar in Chicago," *History for the Present Blog,* January 5, 2017, https://stacyprattmcdermott.com/2017/01/05/a-little-sandbar-in-chicago/; Reinhold H. Luthin, *The Real Abraham Lincoln* (Englewood Cliffs, N.J.: Prentice-Hall), 170–71.

575   *The day after the trial ended:* Robert D. Sheppard and Harvey B. Hurd, *History of Northwestern University and Evanston* (Chicago: Munsell Publishing, 1906), 474–75.

575   *In January 1861:* Leonard Volk, "The Lincoln Life-Mask and How It Was Made," *The Century Illustrated Monthly* 23, no. 2 (December 1881): 225–28.

576   *After sitting for Volk:* Baringer, *Lincoln's Rise to Power,* 212; Halstead, *Caucuses of 1860,* 140.

576   *Delegation by delegation:* "The Opening of Convention Week," *Chicago Press and Tribune,* May 14, 1860.

576   *David Davis:* King, *Lincoln's Manager David Davis,* 135; A.T. Andreas, *History of Chicago: From 1857 Until the Fire of 1871* (Chicago: A.T. Andreas, 1885), 2:141; Leonard Swett, "The Life and Services of David Davis," *Proceedings of the Illinois State Bar Association* (Springfield: Illinois State Bar Association, 1887), 79.

577   *Davis created a political machine:* King, *Lincoln's Manager David Davis,* 135–36;

577   *Judd and Davis:* Davis, *How Abraham Lincoln Became President,* 65; Ecelbarger, *The Great Comeback,* 195–99.

577   *"No one ever thought":* Michael S. Green, *Lincoln and the Election of 1860* (Carbon-

dale: Southern Illinois University Press, 2011), 52; King, *Lincoln's Manager David Davis,* 136.

577 *"He seated himself":* Swett, "The Life and Services of David Davis," 79; Wilson, *Intimate Memories,* 296.

578 *"The gods help":* "The Choice of Illinois," *Chicago Press and Tribune,* May 14, 1860.

578 *"Availability":* "The Winning Man—Abraham Lincoln," *Chicago Press and Tribune,* May 15, 1860; "The Doubtful States," *Chicago Press and Tribune,* May 16, 1860.

579 *"Dined":* Howard K. Beale, ed., *The Diary of Edward Bates,* American Historical Association Annual Report, Volume 4, 1930 (Washington, D.C.: U.S. Government Printing Office, 1930), 11.

580 *The Illinois platform:* Herriott, "The Conference in the Deutsches Haus Chicago," 140–91.

580 *Bates's most visible promoter:* Baringer, *Lincoln's Rise to Power,* 205–6, 224; Wilson, *Intimate Memories,* 279–80; Barnes, *Life of Thurlow Weed,* 2:268; Oldroyd, *Lincoln's Campaign,* 71; James Parton, *The Life of Horace Greeley, Editor of "The New York Tribune": From His Birth to the Present Time* (Boston: Houghton Mifflin, 1889), 444–45.

581 *Another editor:* Abram J. Dittenhoefer, *How We Elected Lincoln; Personal Recollections of Lincoln and Men of His Time* (New York: Harper & Brothers, 1916), 20–21.

582 *Neither Indiana nor Pennsylvania:* A.K. McClure, *Abraham Lincoln and Men of War-Times* (Philadelphia: Times Publishing, 1892), 33–35.

582 *Indiana was the first target:* CW, 4:46–47; Oldroyd, *Lincoln's Campaign,* 71.

582 *"Things are working":* Mark Delahay to Abraham Lincoln, Letter, May 14, 1860, *Papers of Abraham Lincoln,* Library of Congress, https://cdn.loc.gov/service/mss/mal/026/0265300/0265300.pdf; William Butler to Abraham Lincoln, Letters, May 14, 1860, *Papers of Abraham Lincoln,* Library of Congress, https://cdn.loc.gov/service/mss/mal/026/0264900/0264900.pdf, https://cdn.loc.gov/service/mss/mal/026/0265100/0265100.pdf.

583 *Joseph Medill:* Tarbell, *The Life of Abraham Lincoln,* 1:347; Oldroyd, *Lincoln's Campaign,* 71; Monaghan, *The Man Who Elected Lincoln,* 162–63; Ecelbarger, *The Great Comeback,* 196–97.

583 *Overly enthusiastic and impatient:* Charles H. Ray to Abraham Lincoln, Letter, May 14, 1860, *Papers of Abraham Lincoln,* Library of Congress, https://cdn.loc.gov/service/mss/mal/026/0266000/0266000.pdf).

584 *The impulse to cut deals:* Bancroft and Dunning, eds., *The Reminiscences of Carl Schurz,* 176–77.

584 *Weed's operation:* Halstead, *Caucuses of 1860,* 121.

584 *The New York boosters:* Peter Gammie, "Pugilists and Politicians in Antebellum New York: The Life and Times of Tom Hyer," *New York History* 75, no. 3 (July 1994): 265–96.

584　*The New York crowd:* Francis Fessenden, *Life and Public Services of William Pitt Fessenden* (Boston: Houghton Mifflin, 1907), 1:112.

585　*The head of the Connecticut delegation:* Welles, *Lincoln and Seward*, 27–29.

585　*Weed invited Henry S. Lane:* McClure, *Abraham Lincoln and Men of War-Times*, 31.

585　*Then Weed sent Senator Prescott King:* Halstead, *Caucuses of 1860*, 142.

586　*Orville Browning:* Wilson, *Intimate Memories*, 194; Wilson, Davis, and Wilson, eds., *Herndon's Informants*, 348; Browning, *Diary*, 406–7.

586　*While Weed was promising:* John McAuley Palmer, *Personal Recollections of John Palmer: The Story of an Earnest Life* (Cincinnati: Robert Clarke, 1901), 81; Tarbell, *The Life of Abraham Lincoln*, 1:351.

587　*"We are quiet":* David Davis and Jesse K. Dubois to Abraham Lincoln, Telegram, May 15, 1860, *Papers of Abraham Lincoln*, Library of Congress, https://cdn.loc.gov/service/mss/mal/026/0266800/0266800.pdf; William Butler to Abraham Lincoln, Letter, May 15, 1860, *Papers of Abraham Lincoln*, Library of Congress, https://cdn.loc.gov/service/mss/mal/026/0266500/0266500.pdf).

587　*The proceedings began:* "The Great Wigwam," *Chicago Press and Tribune*, May 14, 1860; P. Orman Ray, *The Convention That Nominated Lincoln* (Chicago: University of Chicago Press, 1916), 6.

587　*Just past noon:* Halstead, *Caucuses of 1860*, 130; Michael Burlingame, ed., *An Oral History of Abraham Lincoln: John G. Nicolay's Interviews and Essays* (Carbondale: Southern Illinois University Press, 2006), 46–47.

588　*On Thursday morning, May 17:* Halstead, *Caucuses of 1860*, 132.

589　*The bell began to toll:* Ibid., 140.

589　*Throughout the day, the Seward forces:* Douglas H. Maynard, "Dudley of New Jersey and the Nomination of Lincoln," *The Pennsylvania Magazine of History and Biography* 82, no. 1 (January 1958): 103.

589　*"So confident":* Halstead, *Caucuses of 1860*, 140–41; Ray, *The Convention That Nominated Lincoln*, 26.

590　*Lincoln placed the newspaper:* Whitney, *Lincoln the Citizen*, 289; Herndon, *Herndon's Life of Lincoln*, 374.

590　*Lane of Indiana:* Halstead, *Caucuses of 1860*, 143; A.K. McClure, "Curtin Elected Governor—1860," in *Life and Times of Andrew Gregg Curtin*, William H. Egle, ed. (Philadelphia: Thompson Publishing, 1896), 103.

590　*"The Bates men":* Koerner, *Memoirs*, 2:87–89.

591　*At the same time, the Committee of Twelve:* Halstead, *Caucuses of 1860*, 142.

591　*But once Greeley left:* Maynard, "Dudley of New Jersey and the Nomination of Lincoln," 104.

591　*Even later that night:* Ecelbarger, *The Great Comeback*, 211–14; David Davis to Abraham Lincoln, Telegram, May 17, 1860, *Papers of Abraham Lincoln*, Library of Congress, https://cdn.loc.gov/service/mss/mal/026/0268600/0268600.pdf/

592　*Lane also came:* Halstead, *Caucuses of 1860*, 142.

592 *The morning edition:* "A Last Entreaty," *Chicago Press and Tribune,* May 18, 1860.

592 *Daylight broke:* Francis B. Carpenter, "How Lincoln Was Nominated," *The Century Illustrated Monthly* 24 (October 1882): 857.

592 *The Seward throng:* Morehouse, *The Life of Jesse W. Fell,* 71; Reinhard H. Luthin, *The First Lincoln Campaign* (Cambridge: Harvard University Press, 1944), 161; Swett, "The Life and Services of David Davis," 79.

593 *After the invocation:* Halstead, *Caucuses of 1860,* 145.

593 *On the first ballot:* Ibid., 146; Baringer, *Lincoln's Rise to Power,* 285.

593 *On the second ballot:* Halstead, *Caucuses of 1860,* 147.

594 *Without stop the roll:* Tarbell, *The Life of Abraham Lincoln,* 1:355.

594 *"The deed":* Baringer, *Lincoln's Rise to Power,* 287–88; Halstead, *Caucuses of 1860,* 149; Ecelbarger, *The Great Comeback,* 231; Franklin Johnson, "Nominating Lincoln," *The Youth's Companion,* February 8, 1917.

594 *Weed was "completely unnerved":* Halstead, *Caucuses of 1860,* 271; McClure, *Abraham Lincoln and Men of War-Times,* 40–41.

595 *Stanton believed:* Stanton, *Random Recollections,* 214–16; Bancroft and Dunning, eds., *The Reminiscences of Carl Schurz,* 2:221.

595 *While Chicago was delirious:* Barnes, *Life of Thurlow Weed,* 292–93, 296.

596 *Edward Bates:* Beale, ed., *The Diary of Edward Bates,* 129–30; Browning, *Diary,* 411, 416.

596 *On the day that the struggle:* Baringer, *Lincoln's Rise to Power,* 289–90; Ecelbarger, *The Great Comeback,* 233; Wilson, Davis, and Wilson, eds., *Herndon's Informants,* 492; Charles S. Zane, "Lincoln As I Knew Him," *Journal of the Illinois State Historical Society* 14, nos. 1–2 (April–July 1921): 74–84.

597 *Volk asked Lincoln:* Volk, "The Lincoln Life-Mask and How It Was Made," 228–29.

CHAPTER THIRTY-FOUR: A FALLEN STAR

599 *Three days after the Democratic convention:* CG, 36th Congress, 1st Session, 1942.

599 *It took the ill:* Johannsen, *Stephen A. Douglas,* 765; CG, 36th Congress, 1st Session, 313–14.

600 *Douglas, according to Davis:* CG, 36th Congress, 1st Session, 453.

602 *On the eve of the second Democratic convention:* Johannsen, *Stephen A. Douglas,* 766–67.

602 *After the debacle:* Ibid., 762.

602 *On June 18:* Halstead, *Caucuses of 1860,* 159, 176, 178.

603 *On the fifth agonizing day:* Ibid., 195, 229.

604 *The Southern bolters:* Ibid., 218.

604 *"Yancey! Yancey!":* Ibid., 226.

604 *Late in the evening of June 23:* Johannsen, *Stephen A. Douglas,* 772.

604 *The close of the two disastrous conventions:* Ibid., 775.

604 *Two days after the Baltimore convention:* Egerton, *Year of Meteors,* 170; Davis, *The Rise and Fall of the Confederate Government,* 1:52; Davis, *John C. Breckinridge,* 224–26; Nevins, *The Emergence of Lincoln,* 2:285.

605 *Davis's far-fetched notion:* John Cochrane, "The Charleston Convention," *The Magazine of American History* 14 (July–December 1885): 150–52.

605 *John Cabell Breckinridge:* Davis, *John C. Breckinridge,* 277; Davis, *Jefferson Davis,* 1:685; Nevins, *The Emergence of Lincoln,* 2:284.

606 *As Buchanan's vice president:* "The Baltimore Convention—The Democratic Candidates," *New York Times,* June 25, 1860.

607 *Douglas had expected:* Johannsen, *Stephen A. Douglas,* 776–77.

607 *But he started delivering:* Nichols, *The Disruption of American Democracy,* 341; "The Bomb from the Breckinridge Battery," *New York Times,* August 22, 1860.

607 *Douglas's campaign:* "Speech of John C. Breckinridge," *New York Times,* September 6, 1860.

608 *Cushing spoke:* "Gen. Cushing on the Canvas," *New York Times,* September 17, 1860.

608 *Dean Richmond:* "The Fusion Movement," *New York Times,* September 17, 1860; "Ruin of the Regency," *New York Times,* September 19, 1860.

608 *The Constitutional Unionist campaign:* Holt, *The Election of 1860,* 146; "Visit to the Home of John Bell," *New York Herald,* August 8, 1860.

608 *Douglas had a brief delusional episode:* Allen Johnson, *Stephen A. Douglas: A Study in American Politics* (New York: Macmillan, 1908), 745–45; Wilson, *History of the Rise and Fall of the Slave Power in America,* 2:699.

609 *On August 31:* Johannsen, *Stephen A. Douglas,* 790.

609 *Douglas conflated his fate:* Louis Howland, *Stephen A. Douglas* (New York: Scribner, 1920), 354; Johannsen, *Stephen A. Douglas,* 790–91.

610 *"The sky is dark":* Percy Scott Flippin, *Herschel V. Johnson of Georgia, State Rights Unionist* (Richmond: Dietz Printing, 1931), 126; Johannsen, *Stephen A. Douglas,* 784, 793.

610 *In late September:* Adams, *Autobiography,* 64–66; Milton, *The Eve of Conflict,* 495.

610 *"I'm no alarmist":* Milton, *The Eve of Conflict,* 496; Wilson, *History of the Rise and Fall of the Slave Power in America,* 700; "Movements of Senator Douglas," *New York Times,* October 17, 1860.

611 *The day after the catastrophic early elections:* Nichols, *The Disruption of American Democracy,* 345–46.

611 *Douglas went south:* DuBose, *The Life and Times of William Lowndes Yancey,* 529; Johnson, *Stephen A. Douglas,* 759; Lionel Crocker, "The Campaign of Stephen A. Douglas in the South, 1860," in *Antislavery and Disunion, 1858–1861,* J. Jeffery Auer, ed. (New York: Harper & Row, 1963), 262–78.

612 *Douglas defended:* David R. Barbee and Milledge L. Bonham, Jr., "The Montgomery Address of Stephen A. Douglas," *The Journal of Southern History* 5, no. 4 (November 1939): 527–52.

613   *Among those listening:* DuBose, *The Life and Times of William Lowndes Yancey,*
      534–35.

613   *Another face in the crowd:* Alford, *Fortune's Fool,* 95–96.

614   *On November 6:* Wilson, *History of the Rise and Fall of the Slave Power in America,*
      2:700; Johannsen, *Stephen A. Douglas,* 808–9.

614   *On his way back to Washington:* John W. Forney, *Eulogy upon the Hon. Stephen A.
      Douglas* (Philadelphia: Kingwalt & Brown, 1861), 12.

CHAPTER THIRTY-FIVE: WIDE-AWAKE

615   *Lincoln did not campaign:* William H. Herndon, *Herndon on Lincoln: Letters,*
      eds., Douglas L. Wilson and Rodney O. Davis (Champaign: University of Illinois
      Press), 13.

615   *The Wide-Awake Clubs:* Oldroyd, *Lincoln's Campaign,* 105–7; Joe Grinspan,
      "'Young Men for War': The Wide Awakes and Lincoln's 1860 Presidential Cam-
      paign," *Journal of American History* (September 2009): 357–78.

616   *"I have observed":* William Cullen Bryant to Abraham Lincoln, Letter, June 16,
      1860, *Papers of Abraham Lincoln,* Library of Congress, https://cdn.loc.gov/service/
      mss/mal/031/0310500/0310500.pdf.

617   *Lincoln's eyes: CW,* 4:90.

617   *The crisis had begun: CW,* 4:95.

618   *Lincoln did his best:* Burlingame, *Abraham Lincoln,* 1:672; Holzer, *Lincoln and the
      Power of the Press,* 249–51; "The Republican Mecca," *New York Herald,* October
      20, 1860.

619   *Lincoln quietly:* Joseph Medill to Abraham Lincoln, Letter, July 5, 1860, *Pa-
      pers of Abraham Lincoln,* Library of Congress, https://cdn.loc.gov/service/mss/
      mal/032/0326700/0326700.pdf.

619   *The unscrupulous Bennett:* Holzer, *Lincoln and the Power of the Press,* 248; "Tre-
      mendous Uprising of the People," *New York Herald,* October 24, 1860.

619   *The* Herald *also hyped:* "Notes of the Contest," *New York Times,* June 8, 1860;
      Garrison and Garrison, *William Lloyd Garrison,* 503.

620   *Phillips's speech:* James M. McPherson, *The Struggle for Equality: Abolitionists and
      the Negro in the Civil War and Reconstruction* (Princeton: Princeton University
      Press, 2014), 18–20; George W. Julian, *The Life of Joshua R. Giddings* (Chicago:
      A.C. McClurg, 1892), 376; Burlingame, *Abraham Lincoln,* 1:638; Richard J. Hin-
      ton, *The Life and Public Services of Hon. Abraham Lincoln, of Illinois* (Boston:
      Thayer & Eldridge, 1860), 9–10.

620   *Lincoln was known:* Henry Mayer, *All on Fire: William Lloyd Garrison and the
      Abolition of Slavery* (New York: St. Martin's, 1998), 486–87; Lucia A. Stevens,
      "Growth of Public Opinion in the East in Regard to Lincoln Prior to Novem-
      ber 1860," in *Transactions of the Illinois State Historical Society for the Year 1906*
      (Springfield: Illinois State Journal, 1906), 300.

621   *The Illinois abolitionists:* William F. Moore and Jane Ann Moore, *Collaborators for Emancipation: Abraham Lincoln and Owen Lovejoy* (Urbana: University of Illinois Press, 2014), 96; Owen Lovejoy to Abraham Lincoln, Letter, June 10, 1860, *Papers of Abraham Lincoln,* Library of Congress, https://cdn.loc.gov/service/mss/mal/030/0305200/0305200.pdf; Ichabod Codding, *A Republican Manual for the Campaign: Facts for the People, The Whole Argument in One Book* (Princeton, Ill.: "Republican" Book and Job Printing, 1860), 5; N. Dwight Harris, *The History of Negro Servitude in Illinois, and of the Slavery Agitation in That State, 1719–1864* (Chicago: A.C. McClurg, 1904), 223.

622   *Lincoln's nomination:* CW, 4:78; Bancroft, ed., *Speeches, Correspondence and Political Papers of Carl Schurz,* 1:120–21.

623   *Germans in every city:* Karl Obermann, *Joseph Weydemeyer: Pioneer of American Socialism* (New York: International Publishers, 1947), 109–11; Robin Blackburn, *Marx and Lincoln: An Unfinished Revolution* (London: Verso, 2011), 25.

623   *On September 1:* Adams, *Autobiography,* 64–65; *CW,* 4:126–27.

624   *On October 20:* David Hunter to Abraham Lincoln, Letter, October 20, 1860, *Papers of Abraham Lincoln,* Library of Congress, https://cdn.loc.gov/service/mss/mal/040/0407400/0407400.pdf; *CW,* 4:132; Edward A. Miller, *Lincoln's Abolitionist General: The Biography of David Hunter* (Columbia: University of South Carolina Press, 1997), 50.

624   *As his election appeared imminent: CW,* 4:134–35.

625   *On November 1:* David Hunter to Abraham Lincoln, Letter, November 1, 1860, *Papers of Abraham Lincoln,* Library of Congress, https://cdn.loc.gov/service/mss/mal/042/0423700/0423700.pdf).

625   *On November 4:* Donn Piatt, *Memories of the Men Who Saved the Union* (New York: Belford, Clarke, 1887), 30.

626   *Again, Lincoln explained:* Nicolay and Hay, *Abraham Lincoln,* 3:279–82.

627   *"The South":* "The South and the Revolutionary Consequences of Lincoln's Election," *New York Herald,* November 6, 1860; "The Secession Movement in the South," *New York Herald,* November 6, 1860.

627   *Dawn on Election Day:* Oldroyd, *Lincoln's Campaign,* 138–40; Nevins, *The Emergence of Lincoln,* 2:313–15.

628   *Lincoln walked:* Tarbell, *The Life of Abraham Lincoln,* 1:386; Harold Holzer, *Lincoln President-Elect: Abraham Lincoln and the Great Secession Winter, 1860–1861* (New York: Simon & Schuster, 2008), 44; Whipple, *The Story-Life of Lincoln,* 345.

628   *The day after the election:* Nevins, *The Emergence of Lincoln,* 2:318.

628   *On December 20:* Yates Snowden and H.G. Cutler, eds., *History of South Carolina* (New York: Lewis, 1920), 1:662–63; "Declaration of the Immediate Causes Which Induce and Justify the Secession of South Carolina from the Federal Union," http://avalon.law.yale.edu/19th_century/csa_scarsec.asp.

BIBLIOGRAPHY

BOOKS AND GOVERNMENT DOCUMENTS

Adams, Charles Francis. *Charles Francis Adams, 1835–1915, An Autobiography.* Boston: Houghton Mifflin Company, 1916.

———. *Richard Henry Dana, Jr.* Boston: Houghton Mifflin, 1891.

Adams, Charles Francis, ed. *Memoirs of John Quincy Adams: Comprising Portions of His Diary from 1795 to 1848.* Philadelphia: J.B. Lippincott, 1877.

Adams, Henry. *The Education of Henry Adams.* Boston: Houghton Mifflin, 1918.

Alexander, De Alva Stanwood. *A Political History of the State of New York.* New York: Henry Holt, 1906.

Alford, Terry. *Fortune's Fool: The Life of John Wilkes Booth.* New York: Oxford University Press, 2015.

Anbinder, Tyler. *Nativism and Slavery: The Northern Know Nothings and the Politics of the 1850's.* New York: Oxford University Press, 1992.

Anderson, Osborne P. *A Voice from Harper's Ferry: A Narrative of Events at Harper's Ferry.* Boston: Published by the Author, 1861.

Andreas, A.T. *History of Chicago: From 1857 Until the Fire of 1871.* Chicago: A.T. Andreas, 1885.

Angle, Paul M. *"Here I Have Lived," A History of Lincoln's Springfield, 1821–1865.* Chicago: Abraham Lincoln Book Shop, 1971.

Angle, Paul M., ed. *New Letters and Papers of Lincoln.* Boston: Houghton Mifflin, 1930.

Anonymous. *The Diary of a Public Man: An Intimate View of the National Administration, December 28, 1860 to March 15, 1861.* Chicago: Abraham Lincoln Book Shop, 1945.

Appleton, Nathan. *Introduction of the Power Loom, and Origin of Lowell.* Lowell: B.H. Penhallow, 1858.

Arnold, Isaac N. *The Life of Abraham Lincoln.* Chicago: Jansen, McClurg, 1885.

Bacon, Francis. *Essay.* New York: E.P. Dutton, 1909.

Baker, Edward Dickinson. *Oration of Colonel Edward D. Baker, Over the Dead Body of David C. Broderick, a Senator of the United States, 18th September, 1859*. New York: De Vinne Press, 1889.

Baker, Jean H. *James Buchanan*. New York: Macmillan, 2004.

Bancroft, Frederic. *The Life of William H. Seward*. New York: Harper & Brothers, 1900.

Bancroft, Frederic, ed. *Speeches, Correspondence and Political Papers of Carl Schurz*. New York: G.P. Putnam's Sons, 1913.

Bancroft, Frederic, and William A. Dunning, eds. *The Reminiscences of Carl Schurz*. New York: McClure, 1908.

Baringer, William. *Lincoln's Rise to Power*. Boston: Little, Brown, 1937.

Barnes, C.M. *James Buchanan*. Oswego, N.Y.: No publisher, ca. 1881.

Barnes, Thurlow Weed. *Memoir of Thurlow Weed*. Boston: Houghton Mifflin, 1884.

Barrows, Charles Henry. *The History of Springfield in Massachusetts for the Young*. Springfield, Mass.: Connecticut Valley Historical Society, 1909.

Bartlow, Bert S., William H. Todhunter, et al. *Centennial History of Butler County, Ohio*. Indianapolis: B.F. Bowen, 1905.

Barton, William E. *The Life of Abraham Lincoln*. Indianapolis: Bobbs-Merrill, 1925.

Basler, Roy, ed. *The Collected Works of Abraham Lincoln*. New Brunswick, N.J.: Rutgers University Press, 1953–1955.

Beale, Howard K., ed. *The Diary of Edward Bates*, American Historical Association Annual Report. Washington, D.C.: U.S. Government Printing Office, 1930.

Belknap, Jeremy. *Life of Jeremy Belknap*. New York: Harper & Brothers, 1847.

Belohlavek, John M. *Broken Glass: Caleb Cushing and the Shattering of the Union*. Kent, Ohio: Kent State University Press, 2005.

Benton, Thomas Hart. *Historical and Legal Examination of That Part of the Decision of the Supreme Court of the United States in the Dred Scott Case*. New York: D. Appleton, 1858.

Beveridge, Albert J. *Abraham Lincoln, 1809–1858*. Boston: Mifflin, 1928.

Bigelow, John. *Memoir of the Life and Public Services of John Charles Frémont*. New York: Derby & Jackson, 1856.

Black, Jeremiah. *Observations on Senator Douglas's Views of Popular Sovereignty*. Washington, D.C.: Thomas McGill, 1859.

Blackburn, Robin. *Marx and Lincoln: An Unfinished Revolution*. London: Verso, 2011.

Blackett, R.J.M. *The Captive's Quest for Freedom: Fugitive Slaves, the 1850 Fugitive Slave Law, and the Politics of Slavery*. New York: Oxford University Press, 2018.

Blackmar, Frank W., ed. *Kansas: A Cyclopedia of State History*. Chicago: Standard Publishing, 1912.

Blair, Francis P. *A Voice from the Grave of Jackson!* Washington: Buell & Blanchard, 1856.

Bleser, Carol K., ed. *Secret and Sacred: The Diaries of James Henry Hammond, a Southern Slaveholder*. New York: Oxford University Press, 1989.

Blumenthal, Sidney. *Wrestling With His Angel, 1849–1856, The Political Life of Abraham Lincoln*. New York: Simon & Schuster, 2017.

Boller, Paul F. *Presidential Anecdotes*. New York: Oxford University Press, 1996.

Bonham, Jeriah. *Fifty Years' Recollections*. Peoria, Ill.: J.W. Franks & Sons, 1883.

Boykin, Samue, ed. *A Memorial Volume of the Hon. Howell Cobb, of Georgia*. Philadelphia: J.B. Lippincott, 1870.

Bray, Robert. *Reading with Lincoln*. Carbondale: Southern Illinois University Press, 2010.

Brooks, Noah. *Abraham Lincoln and the Downfall of Slavery*. New York: G.P. Putnam's Sons, 1896.

Brown, George Washington. *Reminiscences of Gov. R.J. Walker*. Rockford, Ill.: Published by the Author, 1902.

———. *Reminiscences of Old John Brown: Thrilling Incidents of Border Life in Kansas*. Rockford, Ill.: Abraham E. Smith, 1880.

———. *The Truth at Last: History Corrected. Reminiscences of Old John Brown*. Rockford, Ill.: Abraham E. Smith, 1880.

Brown, John. *Provisional Constitution and Ordinances for the People of the United States*. St. Catherines, Ont.: William Howard Day, 1858.

Brown, Richard Maxwell. *Strain of Violence: Historical Studies of American Violence and Vigilantism*. New York: Oxford University Press, 1975.

Browne, Francis Fisher. *The Every-Day Life of Abraham Lincoln*. Chicago: Browne & Howell, 1913.

Browned, Robert H. *Lincoln and the Men of His Time*. Cincinnati: Jennings & Pye, 1901.

Browning, Orville Hickman. *The Diary of Orville Hickman Browning*, eds., Theodore Calvin Pease and James G. Randall. Springfield: Illinois State Historical Library, 1927.

Bryant, William Cullen II, and Thomas G. Voss, eds. *The Letters of William Cullen Bryant*. New York: Fordham University Press, 1992.

Buell, August C. *History of Andrew Jackson*. New York: Charles Scribner's Sons, 1904.

Burlingame, Michael. *Abraham Lincoln: A Life*. Baltimore: Johns Hopkins University Press, 2008.

Burlingame, Michael, ed. *An Oral History of Abraham Lincoln: John G. Nicolay's Interviews and Essays*. Carbondale: Southern Illinois University Press, 2006.

Burton, Orville Vernon. *In My Father's House Are Many Mansions: Family and Community in Edgefield, South Carolina*. Chapel Hill: University of North Carolina Press, 2000.

Butler, Benjamin F. *The Candidature for the Presidency in Eight Years of Stephen A. Douglas*. Lowell: Hildreth & Hunt, 1860.

Call, Andrew Taylor. *Jacob Bunn: Legacy of an Illinois Industrial Pioneer*. Lawrenceville, Va.: Brunswick, 2005.

Campanella, Richard. *Lincoln in New Orleans: The 1828–1831 Flatboat Voyages and Their Place in History.* Lafayette: University of Louisiana at Lafayette Press, 2010.

Capers, Henry D. *The Life and Times of C.G. Memminger.* Richmond, Va.: Everett Waddey, 1893.

Carr, Clark E. *My Day and My Generation.* Chicago: A.C. McClurg, 1908.

Cathcart, William. *The Baptist Encyclopedia.* Philadelphia: Louis H. Everts, 1881.

Chaffin, Tom. *Pathfinder: John Charles Frémont and the Course of American Empire.* Norman: University of Oklahoma Press, 2014.

Channing, William Ellery. *The Duty of the Free States.* Boston: William Crosby & Company, 1842.

Chas. C. Chapman & Co. *History of Knox County, Illinois.* Chicago: Blakely, Brown & Marsh, 1878.

Child, Lydia Maria. *An Appeal in Favor of That Class of Americans Called Africans.* Boston: Allen & Ticknor, 1833.

_____. *Letters of Lydia Maria Child.* Boston: Houghton Mifflin, 1882.

Christian, William Asbury. *Richmond, Her Past and Present.* Richmond: L.H. Jenkins, 1912.

Claiborne, J.F.H. *Life and Correspondence of John A. Quitman.* New York: Harper & Brothers, 1860.

_____. *Mississippi, as a Province, Territory, and State.* Jackson, Miss.: Power & Barksdale, 1880.

Claim of Rob't M. and Stephen A. Douglas of Rockingham County, North Carolina. Washington: Powell & Ginck, 1872.

Clay-Clopton, Virginia. *A Belle of the Fifties: Memoirs of Mrs. Clay of Alabama, Covering Social and Social and Political Life in Washington and the South.* London: Wm. Heinemann, 1905.

Clephane, Lewis. *Birth of the Republican Party, With a Brief History of the Important Part Taken by the Republican Association of the National Capital.* Washington, D.C.: Gibson Bros., 1889.

_____. "Lewis Clephane: A Pioneer Washington Republican." *Records of the Columbia Historical Society,* Volume 21.*Washington, D.C.* Washington, D.C.: The Society, 1918.

Cluskey, Michael W., ed. *The Political Text-book, Or Encyclopedia: Containing Everything Necessary for the Reference of the Politicians and Statesmen of the United States.* Philadelphia: J.B. Smith, 1859.

Cobb, Howell. *A Scriptural Examination of the Institution of Slavery in the United States.* Georgia: Printed for the Author, 1856.

Cobbe, Francis Power, ed. *The Collected Works of Theodore Parker.* London, Trübner, 1863.

Codding, Ichabod. *A Republican Manual for the Campaign: Facts for the People, The*

Whole Argument in One Book. Princeton, Ill.: "Republican" Book and Job Printing, 1860.

Coffin, Levi. *Reminiscences of Levi Coffin, Reputed President of the Underground Railroad.* Cincinnati: Robert Clarke, 1880.

Cole, Arthur Charles. *The Centennial History of Illinois, The Era of the Civil War, 1848–1870.* Springfield: Illinois Centennial Commission, 1919.

Coleman, Charles H. *Abraham Lincoln and Coles County.* New Brunswick, Ill.: Scarecrow Press, 1955.

Coleman, Mrs. Chapman, ed. *The Life of John J. Crittenden.* Philadelphia: J.B. Lippincott, 1873.

Coleman, John F. *The Disruption of Pennsylvania Democracy, 1848–1860.* Harrisburg: The Pennsylvania Historical and Museum Commission, 1975.

Collum, Shelby M. *Fifty Years of Public Service.* Chicago: A.C. McClurg, 1911.

Congressional Serial Set, Thirty-Sixth Congress, First Session, Elections, Etc., No. 1. Washington, D.C.: Thomas H. Ford, 1860.

Connelley, William E. *A Standard History of Kansas and Kansans.* Chicago: Lewis Publishing, 1918.

Cook, John Edwin. *The Life, Trial, and Execution of Captain John Brown.* New York: Robert M. DeWitt, 1859.

Cooper, James Fenimore. *The Pathfinder: or, The Inland Sea.* Boston: Houghton Mifflin, 1876.

Cooper, William J., Jr. *Jefferson Davis, American.* New York: Alfred A. Knopf, 2000.

Cooper, William J., ed. *Jefferson Davis: Essential Writings* (New York: Modern Library, 2004).

Correspondence Relating to the Insurrection at Harper's Ferry, 17th October, 1859. Annapolis: B.H. Richardson, 1860.

"The Covode Investigation." *House of Representatives, 36th Congress, 1st Session, Volume V, No. 648.* Washington, D.C.: U.S. Government Printing Office, 1860.

Crapol, Edward P. *John Tyler, The Accidental President.* Chapel Hill: University of North Carolina Press, 2012.

Craven, Avery. *The Coming of the Civil War.* Chicago: University of Chicago Press, 1942.

Crocker, Lionel. "The Campaign of Stephen A. Douglas in the South, 1860," in J. Jeffery Auer, ed., *Antislavery and Disunion, 1858–1861.* New York: Harper & Row, 1963.

Curtis, Benjamin Robbins. *A Memoir of Benjamin Robbins Curtis.* Boston: Little, Brown, 1879.

Curtis, George Ticknor. *Life of James Buchanan: Fifteenth President of the United States.* New York: Harper & Brothers, 1883.

Cutts, J. Madison. *A Brief Treatise upon Constitutional and Party Questions.* New York: D. Appleton, 1866.

Davis, J. McCan. *How Abraham Lincoln Became President.* Springfield, Ill.: Henry O. Shepard, 1908.

Davis, Jefferson. *The Rise and Fall of the Confederate Government.* New York: D. Appleton, 1881.

Davis, Varina. *Jefferson Davis: Ex-president of the Confederate States of America.* New York: Belford, 1890.

Davis, William C. *John C. Breckinridge: Statesman, Soldier, Symbol.* Lexington: University Press of Kentucky, 2015.

Dawes, Anna Laurens. *Charles Sumner.* New York: Dodd, Mead, 1892.

Decaro, Louis A., Jr. *"Fire from the Midst of You": A Religious Life of John Brown.* New York: NYU Press, 2005.

———. *Freedom's Dawn: The Last Days of John Brown in Virginia.* Lanham, Md.: Rowman & Littlefield, 2015.

Denton, Sally. *Passion and Principle.* New York: Bloomsbury, 2007.

Dittenhoefer, Abram J. *How We Elected Lincoln; Personal Recollections of Lincoln and Men of His Time.* New York: Harper & Brothers, 1916.

Dodd, William Edward. *Robert J. Walker, Imperialist.* Chicago: Chicago Literary Club, 1914.

Donald, David Herbert. *Charles Sumner and the Coming of the Civil War.* Chicago: University of Chicago Press, 1960.

———. *Lincoln's Herndon.* New York: Alfred A. Knopf, 1948.

Douglas, Stephen A. "Affairs of Kansas," Report No. 34, in *The Reports of the Committees of the Senate of the United States for the First Session of the Thirty-Fourth Congress* Washington, D.C.: A.O.P. Nicholson, 1856.

———. *Remarks of the Hon. Stephen A. Douglas on Kansas, Utah, and the Dred Scott Decision.* Chicago: Daily Times Book and Job Office, 1857.

———. *Speeches of Senator S.A. Douglas.* Washington, D.C.: Lemuel Towers, 1859.

Douglass, Frederick. *Life and Times of Frederick Douglass.* Hartford, Conn.: Park Publishing, 1882.

Douglass, Margaret. *Educational Laws of Virginia: The Personal Narrative of Mrs. Margaret Douglass.* Boston: John P. Jewett, 1854.

Drayton, Daniel. *Personal Memoir of Daniel Drayton.* Boston: Bella Marsh, 1853.

Drury, John. *Old Illinois Houses.* Chicago: Chicago Daily News, 1948.

DuBose, John Witherspoon. *The Life and Times of William Lowndes Yancey.* Birmingham, Ala.: Roberts & Son, 1892.

Ecelbarger, Gary. *The Great Comeback: How Abraham Lincoln Beat the Odds to Win the 1860 Republican Nomination.* New York: St. Martin's, 2013.

Edwards, Jonathan. *The Injustice and Impolicy of the Slave Trade and of the Slavery of the Africans.* Boston: Wells & Lilly, 1822.

Egerton, Douglas R. *Year of Meteors: Stephen Douglas, Abraham Lincoln, and the Election That Brought on the Civil War.* New York: Bloomsbury, 2010.

Ehrlich, Walter. *They Have No Rights: Dred Scott's Struggle for Freedom.* Westport, Conn.: Greenwood, 1979.

Elliott, Maud Howe. *Lord Byron's Helmet.* Boston: Houghton Mifflin, 1927.

Emerson, Ralph Waldo. *The Complete Works.* Boston: Houghton, Mifflin, 1904.

_____. *The Works of Ralph Waldo Emerson, Miscellanies.* Boston: Houghton Mifflin, 1883.

Etcheson, Nicole. *Bleeding Kansas: Contested Liberty in the Civil War Era.* Lawrence: University Press of Kansas, 2004.

Farrell, Betty G. *Elite Families: Class and Power in Nineteenth-Century Boston.* Albany: State University of New York Press, 1993.

Faust, Drew Gilpin. *James Henry Hammond and the Old South: A Design for Mastery.* Baton Rouge: Louisiana State University Press, 1982.

Fehrenbacher, Don E. *Chicago Giant: A Biography of "Long John" Wentworth.* Madison, Wisc.: American History Research Center, 1957.

_____. *Prelude to Greatness: Lincoln in the 1850's.* Stanford: Stanford University Press, 1962.

Fessenden, Francis. *Life and Public Services of William Pitt Fessenden.* Boston: Houghton Mifflin, 1907.

Field, Henry M. *The Life of David Dudley Field.* New York: Charles Scribner's Sons, 1898.

Field, Maunsell B. *Memories of Many Men.* New York: Harper, 1874.

Finkelman, Paul. *Supreme Injustice: Slavery in the Nation's Highest Court.* Cambridge: Harvard University Press, 2018.

Fitzpatrick, John C., ed. *The Writings of George Washington.* Washington D.C.: U.S. Government Printing Office, 1931–1944.

Flippin, Percy Scott. *Herschel V. Johnson of Georgia, State Rights Unionist.* Richmond: Dietz Printing, 1931.

Foote, Henry S. *Casket of Reminiscences.* Washington, D.C.: Chronicle Publishing, 1874.

Ford, Lacy K. *Origins of Southern Radicalism: The South Carolina Upcountry, 1800–1860.* New York: Oxford University Press, 1991.

Forney, John W. *Anecdotes of Public Men.* New York: Harper & Brothers, 1873.

_____. *Eulogy upon the Hon. Stephen A. Douglas.* Philadelphia: Kingwalt & Brown, 1861.

Foster, Frances Smith. *Witnessing Slavery: The Development of Ante-bellum Slave Narratives.* Madison: University of Wisconsin Press, 1979.

Freehling, William W. *The Road to Disunion,* Volume 2, *Secessionists Triumphant.* New York: Oxford University Press, 2007.

Freitag, Sabine. *Friedrich Hecker: Two Lives for Liberty,* trans., Steven Rohan. St. Louis: University of Missouri Press, 2006.

Frémont, Elizabeth Benton. *Recollections of Elizabeth Benton Frémont: Daughter of the Pathfinder.* New York: Frederick H. Hitchcock, 1912.

French, Benjamin Brown. *Witness to the Young Republic: A Yankee's Journal, 1828–1870*, eds., Donald B. Cole and John J. McDonough. Hanover, N.H.: University Press of New England, 1989.

Frothingham, Octavius Brooks. *Theodore Parker: A Biography*. New York: Putnam's, 1880.

Furnas, J.C. *The Road to Harpers Ferry*. New York: William Sloan Associates, 1959.

Gara, Larry. *The Presidency of Franklin Pierce*. Lawrence: University Press of Kansas, 1991.

Garrett, William. *Reminiscences of Public Men in Alabama: For Thirty Years*. Atlanta: Plantation Publishing, 1872.

Garrison, Wendell Phillips, and Francis Jackson Garrison. *William Lloyd Garrison, 1805–1879: The Story of His Life Told by His Children*. Boston: Houghton Mifflin, 1885–1894.

Garrison, Wendell Phillips, and Francis Jackson Garrison. *William Lloyd Garrison, 1805–1879*. Boston: Houghton Mifflin, 1894.

Gienapp, William E. *The Origins of the Republican Party, 1852–1856*. New York: Oxford University Press, 1987.

Gihon, John H. *Geary and Kansas: Governor Geary's Administration in Kansas*. Philadelphia: Chas. C. Rhodes, 1857.

Godwin, Parke. *Life and Works of William Cullen Bryant*. New York: D. Appleton, 1883.

"Governor Reeder's Escape from Kansas." *Transactions of the Kansas State Historical Society,* Volume 3, *Diary of Gov. A.H. Reeder.* Topeka: Kansas Publishing, 1886.

Governor's Message. Richmond, Va.: William F. Ritchie, 1859.

Greeley, Horace. *Proceedings of the First Three Republican Conventions of 1856, 1860 and 1864.* Minneapolis: C.W. Johnson, 1893.

———. *Recollections of a Busy Life.* New York: J.B. Ford, 1868.

Greeley, Horace, and John F. Cleveland, eds. *A Political Text-Book for 1860.* New York: Tribune Association, 1860.

Green, Michael S. *Lincoln and the Election of 1860* (Carbondale: Southern Illinois University Press, 2011).

Grimké, Archibald Henry. *The Life of Charles Sumner: The Scholar in Politics.*

Guelzo, Allen C. *Abraham Lincoln: Redeemer President.* Grand Rapids, Mich.: W.B. Eerdmans, 1999.

———. *Lincoln and Douglas.* New York: Simon & Schuster, 2008.

Hall, Robert L. "Massachusetts Abolitionists Document the Slave Experience," in *Courage and Conscience: Black & White Abolitionists in Boston,* Donald M. Jacobs, ed. Bloomington: Indiana University Press, 1993.

Halstead, Murat. *Caucuses of 1860: A History of the National Political Conventions.* Columbus, Ohio: Follett, Foster, 1860.

———. *Trimmers, Trucklers & Temporizers: Notes of MURAT HALSTEAD from the Political Conventions of 1856,* eds., William B. Hesseltine and Rex G. Fisher. Madison: State Historical Society of Wisconsin, 1961.

Hamilton, James A. *Reminiscences of James A. Hamilton: Or, Men and Events, at Home and Abroad.* New York: Charles Scribner, 1869.

Hamm, Theodore, ed. *Frederick Douglass in Brooklyn.* New York: Akashic Books, 2017.

Hammond, James Henry. *Selections from the Letters and Speeches of the Hon. James H. Hammond, of South Carolina.* New York: John F. Trow, 1866.

Harris, N. Dwight. *The History of Negro Servitude in Illinois, and of the Slavery Agitation in That State, 1719–1864.* Chicago: A.C. McClurg, 1904.

Harsha, D.A. *The Life of Charles Sumner: With Choice Specimens of His Eloquence.* New York: H. Dayton, 1858.

Hawthorne, Nathaniel. *Life of Franklin Pierce.* Boston: Ticknor, Reed, & Fields, 1852.

Haynes, George Henry. *Charles Sumner.* Philadelphia: G.W. Jacobs, 1909.

Headley, Joel Tyler. *The Life of Oliver Cromwell.* New York: Charles Scribner's Sons, 1888.

Heimert, Alan, and Andrew Delbanco, eds. *The Puritans in America.* Cambridge: Harvard University Press, 2009.

Helper, Hinton Rowan. *The Impending Crisis: How to Meet It.* New York: Burdick Brothers, 1857.

Herndon, William Henry. *Herndon on Lincoln: Letters,* eds., Douglas L. Wilson and Rodney O. Davis. Champaign: University of Illinois Press.

———. *Herndon's Life of Lincoln.* Cleveland: World, 1942.

———. *Herndon's Lincoln: The True Story of a Great Life.* Springfield, Ill.: Herndon's Lincoln Publishing, 1888.

Herr, Pamela. *Jessie Benton Frémont.* New York: Franklin Watts, 1987.

Herr, Pamela, and Mary Lee Spence, eds. *The Letters of Jessie Benton Frémont.* Urbana: University of Illinois Press, 1993.

Hertz, Emanuel. *The Hidden Lincoln: From the Letters and Papers of William H. Herndon.* New York: Blue Ribbon Books, 1940.

———. *Lincoln Talks: A Biography in Anecdote.* New York: Viking, 1939.

Higginson, Thomas Wentworth. *Contemporaries.* Boston: Riverside Press, 1900.

Hillard, George S. *Life, Letters, and Journal of George Ticknor.* Boston: Houghton Mifflin, 1909.

Hinton, Richard J. *John Brown and His Men.* New York: Funk & Wagnalls, 1894.

———. *The Life and Public Services of Hon. Abraham Lincoln, of Illinois.* Boston: Thayer & Eldridge, 1860.

Hoar, George Frisbie. *Autobiography of Seventy Years.* New York: Charles Scribner's Sons, 1903.

Hoffer, William James. *The Caning of Charles Sumner: Honor, Idealism, and the Origins of the Civil War.* Baltimore: Johns Hopkins University Press, 2010.

Holland, Frederic May. *Frederick Douglass: The Colored Orator.* New York: Funk & Wagnalls, 1891.

Holland, J.G. *The Life of Abraham Lincoln.* Springfield, Mass.: Gurdon Bill, 1866.

Hollister, O.J. *Life of Schuyler Colfax*. New York: Funk & Wagnalls, 1886.

Holloway, John N. *History of Kansas*. Lafayette, Ind.: James, Emmons, 1868.

Holst, Hermann von. *The Constitutional and Political History of the United States: 1854–1856*. Chicago: Callaghan, 1885.

Holt, Michael F. *The Election of 1860*. Lawrence: University Press of Kansas, 2017.

_____. *The Rise and Fall of the American Whig Party: Jacksonian Politics and the Onset of the Civil War*. New York: Oxford University Press, 2003.

Holzer, Harold. *Lincoln and the Power of the Press*. New York: Simon & Schuster, 2014.

_____. *Lincoln at Cooper Union: The Speech That Made Abraham Lincoln President*. New York: Simon & Schuster, 2004.

_____. *Lincoln President-Elect: Abraham Lincoln and the Great Secession Winter, 1860–1861*. New York: Simon & Schuster, 2008.

House of Representatives. *Report of the Special Committee Appointed to Investigate the Troubles in Kansas*. Washington, D.C.: Cornelius Wendell, 1856.

Howland, Louis. *Stephen A. Douglas*. New York: Scribner, 1920.

Hudson, J. Blaine. *Fugitive Slaves and the Underground Railroad in the Kentucky Borderland*. Jefferson, N.C.: McFarland, 2002.

Huston, James L. *The Panic of 1857 and the Coming of the Civil War*. Baton Rouge: University of Louisiana Press, 1999.

_____. James L. Huston, *Stephen A. Douglas and the Dilemmas of Democratic Equality*. Lanham, Md.: Rowman & Littlefield, 2007.

Irelan, John Robert. *History of the Life, Administration, and Times of Franklin Pierce, Fourteenth President of the United States*. Chicago: Fairbanks & Palmer.

Jackson, Mary Anna. *Life and Letters of General Thomas J. Jackson (Stonewall Jackson)*. New York: Harper & Brothers, 1892.

Johannsen, Robert W. *Stephen A. Douglas*. New York: Oxford University Press, 1973.

Johnson, Allen. *Stephen A. Douglas: A Study in American Politics*. New York: Macmillan, 1908.

Johnston, Richard Malcolm, and William Hand Browne. *Life of Alexander H. Stephens*. Philadelphia: J.B. Lippincott, 1884.

Jordan, Winthrop D. *White Over Black: American Attitudes Toward the Negro, 1550–1812*. Chapel Hill: University of North Carolina Press, 1968.

Julian, George W. *The Life of Joshua R. Giddings*. Chicago: A.C. McClurg, 1892.

Karcher, Carolyn L. *The First Woman in the Republic: A Cultural Biography of Lydia Maria Child*. Durham, N.C.: Duke University Press, 1992.

Kendrick, Stephen, and Paul Kendrick. *Sarah's Long Walk: The Free Blacks of Boston and How Their Struggle for Equality Changed America*. Boston: Beacon Press, 2004.

King, Willard L. *Lincoln's Manager David Davis*. Chicago: University of Chicago Press, 1960.

Klein, Philip S. *President James Buchanan*. University Park: Pennsylvania State University Press, 1962.

Knox, Thomas Wallace. *The Life and Work of Henry Ward Beecher.* Hartford, Conn.: Park Publishing, 1887.

Koerner, Gustave. *Memoirs of Gustave Koerner, 1809–1896.* Cedar Rapids, Iowa: Torch Press, 1909.

Kyle, Otto R. *Lincoln in Decatur.* New York: Vantage Press, 1957.

Lamon, Ward Hill. *The Life of Abraham Lincoln.* Boston: James R. Osgood, 1872.

Landis, Michael Todd. *Northern Men with Southern Loyalties: The Democratic Party and the Sectional Crisis.* Ithaca, N.Y.: Cornell University Press, 2014.

Lester, C. Edwards. *Life and Public Services of Charles Sumner.* New York: United States Publishing, 1874.

Lincoln, Abraham, and Stephen Douglas. *Political Debates Between Lincoln and Douglas.* Cleveland: Burrows Bros., 1897.

Livingston, John. *Eminent Americans Now Living.* New York: Livingston's Monthly Law Magazine, 1854.

Longfellow, Samuel. *Life of Henry Wadsworth Longfellow: With Extracts from His Journals and Correspondence.* Boston: Houghton Mifflin, 1891.

Loring, James Spear. *The Hundred Boston Orators.* Boston: John P. Jewett, 1852.

Luthin, Reinhard H. *The First Lincoln Campaign.* Cambridge: Harvard University Press, 1944.

_____. *The Real Abraham Lincoln.* Englewood Cliffs, N.J.: Prentice-Hall.

Lynch, Jeremiah. *The Life of David C. Broderick: A Senator of the Fifties.* New York: Baker & Taylor, 1911.

Magdol, Edward. *Owen Lovejoy: Abolitionist in Congress.* New Brunswick, N.J.: Rutgers University Press, 1967.

Malavasic, Alice Elizabeth. *The F Street Mess: How Southern Senators Rewrote the Kansas-Nebraska Act.* Chapel Hill: University of North Carolina Press, 2017.

Mason, Virginia. *The Public Life and Diplomatic Correspondence of James M. Mason.* New York: Neale Publishing, 1906.

May, Samuel. *The Fugitive Slave Law and Its Victims.* New York: American Anti-Slavery Society, 1861.

Mayer, Henry. *All on Fire: William Lloyd Garrison and the Abolition of Slavery.* New York: St. Martin's, 1998.

McClure, A.K. *Abraham Lincoln and Men of War-Times.* Philadelphia: Times Publishing, 1892.

_____. *Colonel Alexander K. McClure's Recollection of Half a Century.* Salem, Mass.: Salem Press, 1902.

_____. "Curtin Elected Governor—1860," in *Life and Times of Andrew Gregg Curtin,* William H. Egle, ed. Philadelphia: Thompson Publishing, 1896.

_____. *Old Time Notes of Pennsylvania.* Philadelphia: John C. Winston, 1905.

McCulloch, Hugh. *Men and Measures of Half a Century: Sketches and Comments.* New York: Charles Scribner's Sons, 1889.

McMaster, John Bach. *A History of the People of the United States*. New York: D. Appleton, 1913.

McMillen, Sally Gregory. *Lucy Stone: An Unapologetic Life*. New York: Oxford University Press, 2015.

McPherson, James M. *The Struggle for Equality: Abolitionists and the Negro in the Civil War and Reconstruction*. Princeton: Princeton University Press, 2014.

Merk, Frederick. *Slavery and the Annexation of Texas*. New York: Alfred A. Knopf, 1972.

Miller, Donald L. *City of the Century: The Epic of Chicago and the Making of America*. New York: Simon & Schuster, 1996.

Miller, Edward A. *Lincoln's Abolitionist General: The Biography of David Hunter*. Columbia: University of South Carolina Press, 1997.

Miller, Richard Lawrence. *Lincoln and His World*. Mechanicsburg, Penn.: Stackpole Books, 2006–2014.

Milton, George Fort. *The Eve of Conflict: Stephen A. Douglas and the Needless War*. New York: Octagon, 1963.

Mitchell, Mary Niall. *Raising Freedom's Child: Black Children and Visions of the Future After Slavery*. New York: NYU Press, 2010.

Monaghan, Jay. *The Man Who Elected Lincoln*. Indianapolis: Bobbs-Merrill, 1956.

Moore, William F., and Jane Ann Moore. *Collaborators for Emancipation: Abraham Lincoln and Owen Lovejoy*. Urbana: University of Illinois Press, 2014.

Moore, William F., and Jane Ann Moore, eds. *His Brother's Blood: Speeches and Writings, 1838–64: Owen Lovejoy*. Urbana: University of Illinois Press, 2004.

Morehouse, Frances Milton I. *The Life of Jesse W. Fell*. Urbana: University of Illinois Press, 1916.

Moses, John. *Illinois, Historical and Statistical*. Chicago: Fergus Printing, 1892.

Moss, Hillary J. *Schooling Citizens: The Struggle for African American Education in Antebellum America*. Chicago: University of Chicago Press, 2010.

Muller, Gilbert H. *Abraham Lincoln and William Cullen Bryant: Their Civil War*. New York: Palgrave, 2017.

————. *William Cullen Bryant: Poet of America*. Albany: State University Press of New York, 2008.

Nason, Elias. *The Life and Times of Charles Sumner*. Boston: B.B. Russell, 1874.

Nevins, Allan. *The Emergence of Lincoln: Douglas, Buchanan, and Party Chaos, 1857–1859*. New York: Scribner's Sons, 1950.

Newton, Joseph Fort. *Lincoln and Herndon*. Cedar Rapids, Iowa: Torch Press, 1910.

New York Democratic Vigilant Association. *Rise and Progress of the Bloody Outbreak at Harper's Ferry*. New York: John F. Trow, 1859.

Nichols, Alice. *Bleeding Kansas*. New York: Oxford University Press, 1954.

Nichols, Roy F. *The Disruption of American Democracy*. New York: Macmillan, 1948.

————. Roy F. Nichols, *Franklin Pierce: Young Hickory of the Granite Hills*. Philadelphia: University of Pennsylvania Press, 1931.

Nicolay, John G., and John Hay. *Abraham Lincoln: A History.* New York: Century Company, 1890.

Niven, John. *Salmon P. Chase: A Biography.* New York: Oxford University Press, 1995.

Oakes, James. *Freedom National: The Destruction of Slavery in the United States, 1861–1865.* New York: W.W. Norton, 2013.

———. *The Radical and the Republican: Frederick Douglass, Abraham Lincoln, and the Triumph of Antislavery Politics.* New York: W.W. Norton, 2007.

Oates, Stephen B. *To Purge This Land with Blood.* Amherst: University of Massachusetts Press, 1984.

Obermann, Karl. *Joseph Weydemeyer: Pioneer of American Socialism.* New York: International Publishers, 1947.

Oertel, Kristen Tegtmeier. *Bleeding Borders: Race, Gender, and Violence in Pre–Civil War Kansas.* Baton Rouge: LSU Press, 2009.

Oldroyd, Osborne H. *Lincoln's Campaign: Or, the Revolution of 1860.* Chicago: Laird & Lee, 1896.

Oldroyd, Osborn Hamiline, ed. *The Lincoln Memorial: Album-Immortelles.* New York: G.W. Carleton, 1882.

Palmer, John McAuley. *Personal Recollections of John Palmer: The Story of an Earnest Life.* Cincinnati: Robert Clarke, 1901.

Palmer, John M., ed. *The Bench and Bar of Illinois: Historical and Reminiscent.* Chicago: Lewis Publishing, 1899.

Panzer, Mary. *Mathew Brady.* New York: Phaidon, 2001.

Parker, Theodore. *The Collected Works of Theodore Parker,* ed., Frances Power Cobbe. London: Trübner, 1865.

The Parliamentary History of England, From the Earliest Period to the Year 1803. London: T.C. Hansard, 1817.

Parton, James. *The Life of Horace Greeley, Editor of "The New York Tribune": From His Birth to the Present Time.* Boston: Houghton Mifflin, 1889.

Peacock, Virginia Tatnall. *Famous American Belles of the Nineteenth Century.* Philadelphia: J.B. Lippincott, 1901.

Pearson, Henry Greenleaf. *The Life of John A. Andrew: Governor of Massachusetts, 1861–1865.* Boston: Houghton Mifflin, 1904.

Petrulionis, Sandra Harbert. *To Set This World Right: The Antislavery Movement in Thoreau's Concord.* Ithaca, N.Y.: Cornell University Press, 2006.

Phillips, Isaac N., ed. *Abraham Lincoln, By Some Men Who Knew Him.* Bloomington, Ill.: Pantagraph Printing, 1910.

Phillips, Ulrich B., ed. *The Correspondence of Robert Toombs, Alexander H. Stephens, and Howell Cobb.* Washington, D.C.: U.S. Government Printing Office, 1911.

Phillips, Ulrich B., ed. *The Correspondence of Robert Toombs, Alexander H. Stephens, and Howell Cobb.* Washington, D.C.: American Historical Association, 1913.

Phillips, William. *The Conquest of Kansas, by Missouri and Her Allies*. Boston: Phillips, Sampson, 1856.

Piatt, Donn. *Memories of the Men Who Saved the Union*. New York: Belford, Clarke, 1887.

Pierce, Edward L. *Memoir and Letters of Charles Sumner*. Boston: Roberts Brothers, 1893.

Pierce, Edward L. *Memoir and Letters of Charles Sumner*. Boston: Roberts Brothers, 1898.

Pike, James Shepherd. *First Blows of the Civil War*. New York: American News, 1879.

Potter, David M. *The Impending Crisis: 1848–1861*. New York: Harper & Row, 1976.

Power, John Carroll. *History of the Early Settlers of Sangamon County, Illinois*. Edwin A. Wilson & Company, 1876.

Prince, Ezra M., and John H. Burnham, eds. *Historical Encyclopedia of Illinois and History of McLean County*. Chicago: Munsell, 1908.

Proceedings of the Conventions at Charleston and Baltimore. Washington: National Democratic Executive Committee, 1860.

Pryor, Mrs. Roger A. *Reminiscences of Peace and War*. New York: Grosset & Dunlap, 1904.

Puleo, Stephen. *The Caning: The Assault That Drove America to Civil War*. Yardley, Penn.: Westholme, 2014.

Quaife, Milo Milton, ed. *The Diary of James K. Polk During His Presidency, 1845–1849*. Chicago: A.C. McClurg, 1910.

Quigley, Paul. *Shifting Grounds: Nationalism and the American South, 1848–1865*. New York: Oxford University Press, 2014.

Quinn, Arthur. *The Rivals: William Gwin, David Broderick, and the Birth of California*. Lincoln: University of Nebraska Press, 1994.

Rankin, Henry B. *Personal Recollections of Abraham Lincoln*. New York: G.P Putnam's Sons, 1916.

Rawley, James A. *Race and Politics: Bleeding Kansas and the Coming of the Civil War*. Lincoln: University of Nebraska Press, 1989.

Ray, P. Orman. *The Convention That Nominated Lincoln*. Chicago: University of Chicago Press, 1916.

———. *The Repeal of the Missouri Compromise: Its Origin and Authorship*. Cleveland: Arthur H. Clark, 1908.

Redpath, James. *The Public Life of Capt. John Brown*. Boston: Thayer & Eldridge, 1860.

Redpath, James, ed. *Echoes of Harper's Ferry*. Boston: Thayer & Eldridge, 1860.

Renehan, Edward J., Jr. *The Secret Six: The True Tale of the Men Who Conspired with John Brown*. Columbia: University of South Carolina Press, 1997.

Report [of] the Select Committee of the Senate Appointed to Inquire into the Late Invasion and Seizure of the Public Property at Harper's Ferry. Washington, D.C.: U.S. Congress, 1860.

Reynolds, David S. *John Brown, Abolitionist: The Man Who Killed Slavery, Sparked the Civil War, and Seeded Civil Rights*. New York: Alfred A. Knopf, 2009.

_____. *Mightier Than the Sword: Uncle Tom's Cabin and the Battle for America.* New York: W.W. Norton, 2011.

Rhodes, James Ford. *History of the United States from the Compromise of 1850.* New York: Macmillan, 1892–1927.

Rice, Allen Thorndike. *Reminiscences of Abraham Lincoln by Distinguished Men of His Time.* New York: North American Publishing, 1886.

Riddle, Albert Gallatin. *The Life of Benjamin F. Wade.* Cleveland: W.W. Williams, 1886.

Robinson, Charles. *The Kansas Conflict.* Lawrence: Journal Publishing Company, 1898.

Robinson, Sara T.L. *Kansas: Its Interior and Exterior Life.* Boston: Crosby, 1856.

Rolle, Andrew F. *John Charles Frémont: Character As Destiny.* Norman: University of Oklahoma Press, 1991.

Rowland, Dunbar, ed. *Encyclopedia of Mississippi History.* Madison, Wisc.: Selwyn A. Brant, 1907.

_____. *Jefferson Davis, Constitutionalist.* Jackson: Mississippi Department of Archives and History, 1923.

Rowland, Eron. *Varina Howell: Wife of Jefferson Davis.* Gretna, La.: Pelican Publishing, 1927.

Sanborn, Franklin Benjamin. *The Life and Letters of John Brown: Liberator of Kansas, and Martyr of Virginia.* Boston: Roberts Brothers, 1891.

_____. *Memoirs of John Brown.* Concord, Mass.: J. Munsell, 1878.

_____. *Recollections of Seventy Years.* Boston: R.G. Badger, 1900.

Sarna, Jonathan D., and Benjamin Shapell. *Lincoln and the Jews: A History.* New York: St. Martin's, 2015.

Schlesinger, Arthur M., Jr. *The Age of Jackson.* Boston: Little, Brown, 1945.

Schurz, Carl. *Eulogy on Charles Sumner.* Boston: Rockwell & Churchill, 1874.

_____. *Speeches of Carl Schurz.* Philadelphia: J.B. Lippincott, 1865.

Schweninger, Loren, ed. *From Tennessee Slave to St. Louis Entrepreneur: The Autobiography of James Thomas* (Columbia: University of Missouri Press, 1984).

Sears, Stephen W. *George B. McClellan: The Young Napoleon.* New York: Ticknor & Fields, 1988.

Sellers, Charles Grier. *James K. Polk,* Volume 2, *Continentalist, 1843–1846.* Princeton: Princeton University Press, 2015.

Severance, Frank H., ed. *Millard Fillmore Papers.* Buffalo: Buffalo Historical Society, 1907.

Seward, Frederick W. *Seward at Washington as Senator and Secretary of State, 1846–1861* (New York: Derby & Miller, 1891.

Seward, William H. "The Dangers of Extending Slavery," in *Republican Campaign Documents of 1856.* Washington, D.C.: Lewis Clephane, 1857.

_____. *The Irrepressible Conflict.* New York: The New York Tribune, 1860.

Sewell, Richard H. *Ballots for Freedom: Antislavery Politics in the United States, 1837–1860.* New York: Oxford University Press, 1976.

Sheahan, James W. *The Life of Stephen A. Douglas.* New York: Harper & Brothers, 1860.

Shenkman, Richard, and Kurt Reiger. "The Vice-President Who Sold His Mistress At Auction," in *One-Night Stands with American History: Odd, Amusing, and Little-Known Incidents.* New York: HarperCollins, 2003.

Sheppard, Robert D., and Harvey B. Hurd. *History of Northwestern University and Evanston.* Chicago: Munsell Publishing, 1906.

Sherman, John. *John Sherman's Recollections of Forty Years in the Senate and Cabinet.* Chicago: Werner, 1895.

Shotwell, Walter G. *Life of Charles Sumner.* New York: Thomas Y. Crowell, 1910.

Simon, James F. *Lincoln and Chief Justice Taney: Slavery, Secession, and the President's War Powers.* New York: Simon & Schuster, 2006.

Simpson, Brooks. *Ulysses S. Grant: Triumph over Adversity, 1822–1865.* Boston: Houghton Mifflin, 2000.

Sinha, Manisha. *The Counter-Revolution of Slavery: Politics and Ideology in Antebellum South Carolina.* Chapel Hill: University of North Carolina Press, 2000.

Smith, Elbert B. *The Presidency of James Buchanan.* Lawrence: University Press of Kansas, 1975.

Smith, Ted A. *Weird John Brown: Divine Violence and the Limits of Ethics.* Stanford: Stanford University Press, 2014.

Snowden, Yates, and H.G. Cutler, eds. *History of South Carolina.* New York: Lewis, 1920.

Sparks, Edwin Erle. *The Lincoln-Douglas Debates of 1858, Lincoln Series.* Springfield: Illinois State Historical Library, 1908.

Speech of Hon. Lyman Trumbull, of Illinois, at a Mass Meeting in Chicago, August 7, 1858. Washington, D.C.: Buell & Blanchard Printers, 1858.

Spring, Leverett Wilson. *Kansas, the Prelude to the War for the Union.* Boston: Houghton, Mifflin, 1885.

Stahr, Walter. *Seward: Lincoln's Indispensable Man.* New York: Simon & Schuster, 2014.

————. *Stanton: Lincoln's War Secretary.* New York: Simon & Schuster, 2017.

Stampp, Kenneth. *America in 1857.* New York: Oxford University Press, 1990.

Stanton, Henry B. *Random Recollections.* New York: Harper & Brothers, 1887.

Stauffer, John. *Giants: The Parallel Lives of Frederick Douglass and Abraham Lincoln.* New York: Twelve Books, 2008.

Stauffer, John, and Zoe Trodd, eds. *The Tribunal: Responses to John Brown and the Harpers Ferry Raid.* Cambridge, Mass.: Belknap Press, 2012.

Stearns, Frank P. *Cambridge Sketches.* Philadelphia: J.B. Lippincott, 1905.

————. *The Life and Public Services of George Luther Stearns.* Philadelphia: J.B. Lippincott, 1907.

Stephens, Alexander H. *A Constitutional View of the Late War Between the States.* Philadelphia, National Publishing, 1868.

Stephens, Alexander H., and Howell Cobb, eds. *The Correspondence of Robert Toombs.* Washington, D.C.: U.S. Government Printing Office, 1913.

Storey, Moorfield. *Charles Sumner.* Boston: Houghton Mifflin, 1900.

Stovall, Pleasant A. *Robert Toombs.* New York: Cassell Publishing Company, 1892.

Stowe, Harriet Beecher. *Uncle Tom's Cabin: Or, Life Among the Lowly.* Boston: Houghton Mifflin, 1879.

Sumner, Charles. *Orations and Speeches, 1845–1850.* Boston: Ticknor, Reed, & Fields, 1850.

_____. *Recent Speeches and Addresses, 1851–1855.* Boston: Higgins & Bradley, 1856.

_____. *The Works of Charles Sumner,* Volume 2. Shepard, 1870.

_____. *The Works of Charles Sumner,* Volume 3. Boston: Lee & Shepard, 1875.

Taney, Roger. *The Dred Scott Decision: Opinion of Chief Justice Taney.* New York: Van Evrie, Horton, 1860.

Tarbell, Ida M. *The Life of Abraham Lincoln.* New York: Lincoln History Society, 1903.

Taylor, Anne-Marie. *Young Charles Sumner and the American Enlightenment, 1811–1851.* Amherst: University of Massachusetts Press, 2001.

Taylor, Richard. *Destruction and Reconstruction: Personal Experiences of the Late War.* New York: D. Appleton, 1879.

Thompson, Jacob. *"Address, Delivered on Occasion of the Opening of the University of the State of Mississippi: In Behalf of the Board of Trustees, November 6, 1848."* Memphis: Franklin Book and Job Office, 1848.

Thoreau, Henry David. *Journals.* Boston: Houghton Mifflin, 1949.

_____. *Political Writings,* ed., Nancy L. Rosenblum. Cambridge: Cambridge University Press, 1996.

_____. *The Writings of Henry David Thoreau.* Boston: Houghton Mifflin, 1893.

Tocqueville, Alexis de. *Democracy in America.* New York: Alfred A. Knopf, 1941.

Tracy, Gilbert, ed. *Uncollected Letters of Abraham Lincoln.* Boston: Houghton Mifflin, 1917.

Trefousse, Hans L. *Thaddeus Stevens: Nineteenth Century Egalitarian.* Mechanicsburg, Penn.: Stackpole, 2001.

Trod, Zoe, and John Stauffer, eds. *Meteor of War: The John Brown Story.* Maplecrest, N.Y.: Brandywine Press, 2004.

Turner, Justin G., and Linda Levitt Turner. *Mary Todd Lincoln: Her Life and Letters.* New York: Alfred A. Knopf, 1972.

Tyler, Lyon Gardiner. *The Letters and Times of the Tylers.* Richmond: Whitter & Shepperson, 1885.

Tyler, Samuel *Memoir of Roger Brooke Taney, LL.D.: Chief Justice of the Supreme Court of the United States.* Baltimore: John Murphy, 1872.

Urofsky, Melvin I. *Supreme Decisions: Great Constitutional Cases and Their Impact.* Boulder, Colo.: Westview Press, 2012.

VanderVelde, Lea. *Mrs. Dred Scott: A Life on Slavery's Frontier.* New York: Oxford University Press, 2010.

Villard, Henry. *Memoirs of Henry Villard: Journalist and Financier, 1835–1900.* Boston: Houghton Mifflin, 1904.

Villard, Oswald Garrison. *John Brown: 1800–1859: A Biography After Fifty Years.* Boston: Houghton Mifflin, 1910.

Wallace, Isabel. *Life and Letters of General W.H.L. Wallace.* Chicago: R.R. Donnelly, 1909.

Wallace, Lew. *An Autobiography.* New York: Harper & Brothers, 1906.

Wallenstein, Peter. "Incendiaries All: Southern Politics and the Harpers Ferry Raid," in *His Soul Goes Marching On: Responses to John Brown and the Harpers Ferry Raid,* Paul Finkelman, ed. Charlottesville: University Press of Virginia, 1995.

Walther, Eric H. *The Shattering of the Union: America in the 1850s.* Lanham, Md.: Rowman & Littlefield, 2004.

———. *William Lowndes Yancey and the Coming of the Civil War.* Chapel Hill: University of North Carolina Press, 2006.

Warren, Louis A. *Lincoln's Youth: Indiana Years, 1816–1830.* Indianapolis: Indiana Historical Society, 1991.

Watson, Robert P. *Affairs of State.* Lanham, Md.: Rowman & Littlefield, 2012.

Webb, Richard D. *Life and Letters of Captain John Brown.* London: Chapman & Hall, 1861.

Webster, Daniel. *Webster's Speeches.* Boston: Ginn & Company, 1897.

Weeks, William Earl. *John Quincy Adams and American Global Empire.* Lexington: University Press of Kentucky, 2002.

Weik, Jesse W. *The Real Lincoln.* Boston: Houghton Mifflin, 1922.

Weiss, John. *Life and Correspondence of Theodore Parker.* New York: D. Appleton, 1864.

Welles, Gideon. *Lincoln and Seward.* New York: Sheldon, 1874.

Whipple, Edwin Percy. *The Great Speeches and Orations of Daniel Webster.* Boston: Little, Brown, 1889.

———. *Recollections of Eminent Men.* Boston: Ticknor, 1886.

Whipple, Wayne. *The Story-Life of Lincoln: A Biography Composed of Five Hundred True Stories.* Philadelphia: John C. Winston, 1908.

White, Horace. *The Life of Lyman Trumbull.* Boston: Houghton Mifflin, 1913.

Whitman, Walt. *Complete Poetry and Collected Prose,* ed., *Justin Kaplan.* New York: Library of America, 1982.

Whitney, Henry C. *Life on the Circuit with Lincoln.* Boston: Estes & Lauriat, 1892.

———. *Lincoln the Citizen.* New York: Baker & Taylor, 1908.

Whittier, John Greenleaf. "To C.S.," in *The Poetical Works of John Greenleaf Whittier.* Boston: Houghton Mifflin, 1892.

Wilder, Daniel W. *The Annals of Kansas.* Topeka: George W. Martin, 1875.

Wilentz, Sean. *The Rise of American Democracy.* New York: W.W. Norton, 2005.

Wilson, Douglas L., Rodney O. Davis, and Terry Wilson, eds. *Herndon's Informants: Letters, Interviews, and Statements About Abraham Lincoln.* Urbana: University of Illinois Press, 1998.

Wilson, Henry. *History of the Rise and Fall of the Slave Power in America*. Boston: Houghton, Osgood, 1874.

Wilson, Rufus Rockwell, ed. *Intimate Memories of Lincoln*. Elmira, Ill.: Primavera Press, 1945.

Winsor, Justin, ed. *The Memorial History of Boston*. Boston: James R. Osgood, 1881.

Wise, Barton H. *The Life of Henry A. Wise of Virginia, 1809–1876*. New York: Macmillan, 1899.

Wise, John Sergeant. *The End of an Era*. Boston: Houghton Mifflin, 1901.

Wolff, Katherine. *Culture Club: The Curious History of the Boston Athenaeum*. Boston: University of Massachusetts Press, 2009.

Wood, Margaret L. *Memorial of S.N. Wood*. Kansas City: Hudson Kimberly, 1892.

Woodward, C. Vann, ed. *Mary Chesnut's Civil War*. New Haven: Yale University Press, 1981.

Zarefsky, David. *Lincoln, Douglas and Slavery: In the Crucible of Public Debate*. Chicago: University of Chicago Press, 1993.

ARTICLES

Adams, Charles Francis. "The Trent Affair: An Historical Retrospective." *Proceedings, Massachusetts Historical Society* 45, 1911. Boston: Liberty Reprints, 1912.

Angle, Paul M., ed. "The Recollections of William Pitt Kellogg." *Abraham Lincoln Quarterly* 3, no. 7 (September 1945).

Auchampaugh, Philip G. "The Buchanan-Douglas Feud," *Journal of the Illinois State Historical Society* 25, nos. 1–2 (April–July 1932).

Barbee, David R., and Milledge L. Bonham, Jr. "The Montgomery Address of Stephen A. Douglas." *The Journal of Southern History* 5, no. 4 (November 1939).

Berry, Stephen, and James Hill Welborn III. "The Cane of His Existence: Depression, Damage, and the Brooks–Sumner Affair." *Southern Cultures* 20, no. 4 (Winter 2014).

Bordewich, Fergus. "Digging Into a Historic Rivalry." *Smithsonian Magazine,* February 2004.

Boteler, Alexander R. "Recollections of the John Brown Raid. *The Century Monthly* 26, no. 4. New York: The Century Co., 1883.

Boucher, Chauncey Samuel. "South Carolina and the South on the Eve of Secession, 1852 to 1860." *Washington University Studies* 6, no. 2 (April 1919).

Brown, David. "Attacking Slavery from Within: The Making of 'The Impending Crisis of the South.'" *The Journal of Southern History* 70, no. 3 (August 2004).

Carney, Thomas E. "The Political Judge: Justice John McLean's Pursuit of the Presidency." *Ohio History* 111 (Summer–Autumn 2002).

Carpenter, Francis B. "How Lincoln Was Nominated." *The Century Illustrated Monthly* 24 (October 1882).

Cochrane, John. "The Charleston Convention." *The Magazine of American History* 14 (July–December 1885).

Collins, Bruce. "The Lincoln: Douglas Contest of 1858 and Illinois' Electorate." *Journal of American Studies* 20, no. 3 (December 1986).

Cunningham, J.O. "The Bloomington Convention of 1856 and Those Who Participated In I," in *Transactions of the Illinois State Historical Society for the Year 1905*. Springfield: Illinois State Journal, 1906.

Curtis, Michael Kent. "The 1859 Crisis over Hinton Helper's Book, *The Impending Crisis*: Free Speech, Slavery, and Some Light on the Meaning of the First Section of the Fourteenth Amendment." *Chicago Kent Law Review* 68, no. 3 (June 1998).

Davidson, Jonathan R.T., and Kathryn M. Connor. "The Impairment of Presidents Pierce and Coolidge After Traumatic Bereavement." *Comprehensive Psychiatry* 49 (2008).

Deitreich, Ken. "'Ever Able, Manly, Just and Heroic': Preston Smith Brooks and the Myth of Southern Manhood." *The Proceedings of the South Carolina Historical Association*. Columbia: South Carolina Historical Association, 2011.

Deupress, Mrs. N.G. "Some Historic Homes of Mississippi." *Publications of the Mississippi Historical Society* 6, ed., Franklin L. Riley. Oxford: Mississippi Historical Society, 1902.

Duberman, Martin. "'Writhing Bedfellows' in Antebellum South Carolina." *The Journal of Homosexuality* (Fall–Winter, 1980–81).

Eaton, Clement. "Henry A. Wise and the Virginia Fire Eaters of 1856." *The Mississippi Valley Historical Review* 21, no. 4 (March 1935).

Ecelbarger, Gary. "Before Cooper Union: Abraham Lincoln's 1859 Cincinnati Speech and Its Impact on His Nomination." *Journal of the Abraham Lincoln Association* 30, no. 1 (Winter 2009).

Efford, Alison Clark. "Abraham Lincoln, German-Born Republicans, and American Citizenship." *Marquette Law Review* 93, no. 4 (Summer 2010), http://scholarship.law.marquette.edu/mulr/vol93/iss4/37.

Fehrenbacher, Don E. "The Judd-Wentworth Feud." *Journal of the Illinois State Historical Society* 45, no. 3 (Autumn 1952).

Finkelman, Paul. "Hooted Down the Pages of History: Reconsidering the Greatness of Chief Justice Taney." *Journal of Supreme Court History* 18 (1994).

Gammie, Peter. "Pugilists and Politicians in Antebellum New York: The Life and Times of Tom Hyer." *New York History* 75, no. 3 (July 1994).

Gienapp, William E. "The Crime Against Sumner: The Caning of Charles Sumner and the Rise of the Republican Party." *Civil War History* 25, no. 3 (September 1979).

Grinspan, Joe. "'Young Men for War': The Wide Awakes and Lincoln's 1860 Presidential Campaign." *Journal of American History* (September 2009).

Hansen, Stephen, and Paul Nygard. "Stephen A. Douglas, the Know-Nothings, and the Democratic Party in Illinois, 1854–1858." *Illinois State Historical Journal* 87, no. 2 (Summer 1994).

Harmon, George D. "Buchanan's Betrayal of Governor Walker." *Pennsylvania Magazine of History* (1929).

Herriott, F.I. "The Conference in the Deutsches Haus Chicago, May 14–15, 1860, A Study of Some of the Preliminaries of the National Republican Convention of 1860." *Transactions, Illinois State Historical Society,* 1928. Springfield: Phillips Bros., 1928.

"Hon. Preston S. Brooks." *Southern Quarterly Review* 30 (November 1856).

Jervey, Edward D., and C. Harold Huber. "The Creole Affair." *The Journal of Negro History* 65, no. 3 (Summer 1980).

Johns, Jane Martin. "The Nomination of Abraham Lincoln to the Presidency, An Unsolved Psychological Problem." *Journal of the Illinois State Historical Society* 10, no. 4 (January 1918).

Johnson, Arnold Burges. "Recollections of Charles Sumner." *Scribner's Monthly* 8. New York: William H. Cadwell, 1874.

Kazini, Imani. "Black Springfield: A Historical Study." *Contributions in Black Studies* 1, no. 2.

Krug, Mark M. "Lyman Trumbull and the Real Issues in the Lincoln-Douglas Debates." *Journal of the Illinois State Historical Society* 57, no. 4 (Winter 1964).

Lewis, Elsie M. "Robert Ward Johnson: Militant Spokesman of the Old-South-West." *The Arkansas Historical Quarterly* 13, no. 1 (Spring 1954).

Maynard, Douglas H. "Dudley of New Jersey and the Nomination of Lincoln." *The Pennsylvania Magazine of History and Biography* 82, no. 1 (January 1958).

McKivigan, John R., and Madeleine Leveille. "The 'Black Dream' of Gerrit Smith, New York Abolitionist." *Syracuse University Library Associates Courier* 20, no. 2 (Fall 1985), New York History Net, http://www.nyhistory.com/gerritsmith/dream.htm.

Medill, Joseph. "Lincoln's Lost Speech: The Circumstances and Effect of Its Delivery." *McClure's Magazine* 7 (June–October 1896).

Muelder, Hermann R. "Galesburg: Hot-Bed of Abolitionism." *Journal of the Illinois State Historical Society* 35, no. 3 (September 1942).

Norman, Matthew. "The Other Lincoln-Douglas Debate: The Race Issue in a Comparative Context." *Journal of the Abraham Lincoln Association* 31, no. 1 (Winter 2010).

Pierson, Michael D. "'All Southern Society Is Assailed by the Foulest Charges': Charles Sumner's 'The Crime against Kansas' and the Escalation of Republican Anti-Slavery Rhetoric." *The New England Quarterly* 68, no. 4 (December 1995).

Rainwater, P.L. "Letters to and from Jacob Thompson." *The Journal of Southern History* 6, no. 1 (February 1940).

Robinson, Edgar Eugene, ed. "The Day Journal of Milton S. Latham." *California Historical Society Quarterly* 11, no. 1 (March 1932).

Schweninger, Leon. "Thriving Within the Lowest Caste: The Financial Activities of

James P. Thomas in the Nineteenth-Century South." *Journal of Negro History* 63 (Fall 1978).

Segal, Charles M. "Lincoln, Benjamin Jonas and the Black Code." *Journal of the Illinois State Historical Society* 46 (Autumn 1853).

Senning, John P. "The Know-Nothing Movement in Illinois from 1854–1856." *Journal of the Illinois State Historical Society* 7 (April 1914).

Snay, Mitchell. "Abraham Lincoln, Owen Lovejoy, and the Emergence of the Republican Party in Illinois." *Journal of the Abraham Lincoln Association* 22, no. 1 (Winter 2001).

Stevens, Lucia A. "Growth of Public Opinion in the East in Regard to Lincoln Prior to November 1860," in *Transactions of the Illinois State Historical Society for the Year 1906.* Springfield: Illinois State Journal, 1906.

Swett, Leonard. "The Life and Services of David Davis." *Proceedings of the Illinois State Bar Association.* Springfield: Illinois State Bar Association, 1887.

Venable, Austin L. "The Conflict Between the Douglas and Yancey Forces in the Charleston Convention." *The Journal of Southern History* 8, no. 2 (May 1942).

Volk, Leonard. "The Lincoln Life-Mask and How It Was Made." *The Century Illustrated Monthly* 23, no. 2 (December 1881).

Weik, Jesse W. "Lincoln's Vote for Vice-President: In the Philadelphia Convention of 1856." *The Century Magazine* 76 (May–October 1908). New York: Century Company, 1908.

Whitney, Henry C. "Abraham Lincoln: A Study from Life." *Arena* 19 (January–June 1898).

Woods, Michael E. "Was There a Plot to Kill Stephen Douglas?" *The Journal of the Civil War Era*, January 30, 2018.

Zane, Charles S. "Lincoln As I Knew Him." *Journal of the Illinois State Historical Society* 14, nos. 1–2 (April–July 1921).

———. "A Young Lawyer's Memories of Lincoln." *Journal of the Illinois State Historical Society* 14, nos. 1–2 (April–July, 1921).

THESES

Arnold, Brie Anna Swenson. "'Competition for the Virgin Soil of Kansas': Gendered and Sexualized Discourse About the Kansas Crisis in Northern Popular Print and Political Culture, 1854–1860." Diss., University of Minnesota, 2008, ProQuest.

Balcerski, Thomas John. "Intimate Contests: Manhood, Friendships, and the Coming of the Civil War." PhD diss., Cornell University, 2014, https://ecommons.cornell.edu/bitstream/1813/39014/1/tjb36.pdf.

Diket, Albert Lewie. "John Slidell and the Community He Represented in the Senate, 1853–1861." PhD diss., Louisiana State University, 1958.

NEWSPAPERS AND PERIODICALS

Atlantic Magazine

The Atlantic Monthly

Charleston Mercury

Chicago Press and Tribune

Chicago Times

Chicago Tribune

Congressional Globe

Cosmopolitan Magazine

Daily Pantagraph

Harper's Weekly

The Home Monthly

Illinois State Journal

Kansas Traveler

The Midland Monthly

The National Era

New York Evening Post

New York Herald

New York Times

New York Tribune

Quincy Daily Whig

Richmond Enquirer

Scribner's Monthly

Smithsonian Magazine

Washington Union

Weekly Chicago Journal

The Youth's Companion

SELECT ONLINE RESOURCES

Dictionary of Virginia Biography, Library of Virginia, 2016, http://www.lva.virginia.gov.

The Encyclopedia of Arkansas History and Culture, http://www.encyclopediaofarkansas. net.

Encyclopedia Virginia, Online, http:// www.EncyclopdiaVirginia.org.

House Divided: The Civil War Research Engine at Dickinson College, http://hd.house divided.dickinson.edu.

Papers of Abraham Lincoln, Library of Congress, https://www.loc.gov/collections /abraham-lincoln-papers.

Peters, Gerhard, and John T. Woolley, eds. *The American Presidency Project*, http:// www.presidency.ucsb.edu.

Territorial Kansas Online, http://www.territorialkansasonline.org.

The Encyclopedia of Arkansas History and Culture, http://www.encyclopediaofarkansas. net.

ILLUSTRATION CREDITS

Page 267   Beinecke Rare Book & Manuscript Library; Yale University
Page 275   Wikipedia
Page 282   Library of Congress
Page 289   Historic New Orleans Collection
Page 293   National First Ladies Library
Page 306   Wells Family Collection
Page 307   Library of Congress
Page 320   Library of Congress
Page 329   Chicago History Museum
Page 342   Wikimedia Commons
Page 347   Wikimedia Commons
Page 363   Library of Congress
Page 374   Leeds Museums and Galleries
Page 375   National Portrait Gallery
Page 402   University of Illinois
Page 419   Library of Congress
Page 442   Library of Congress
Page 443   Library of Congress
Page 448   Library of Congress
Page 451   Tulsa's Gilcrease Museum
Page 463   Library of Congress
Page 465   Library of Congress
Page 489   http://wvutoday-archive.wvu.edu/resources/1/1255372862.jpg
Page 490   Chicago Historical Society
Page 491   Wikimedia Commons
Page 500   Library of Congress
Page 515   Library of Congress
Page 520   The Life of Abraham Lincoln by Ward H. Lamon
Page 539   Wikimedia Commons
Page 553   Wikimedia Commons
Page 562   Wikimedia Commons
Page 563   http://www.chicagonow.com/show-me-chicago/2018/04lincolns-undying
            -words-at-the-chicago-history-museum
Page 571   Library of Congress
Page 572   Harper's Weekly
Page 577   McLean County Museum of History
Page 588   Library of Congress
Page 597   Metropolitan Museum of Art
Page 599   Library of Congress
Page 606   National Archives
Page 615   Wikimedia Commons
Page 617   Library of Congress
Page 629   Library of Congress

INDEX

———◆———

Page numbers of photographs appear in italics.

ABOUT THE AUTHOR

———————

SIDNEY BLUMENTHAL is the acclaimed author of *A Self-Made Man*, and *Wrestling With His Angel*, volumes one and two of his five-volume biography, *The Political Life of Abraham Lincoln*. He is the former assistant and senior adviser to President Bill Clinton and senior adviser to Hillary Clinton. He has been a national staff reporter for *The Washington Post* and Washington editor and writer for *The New Yorker*. His books include the bestselling *The Clinton Wars, The Rise of the Counter-Establishment,* and *The Permanent Campaig*n. Born and raised in Illinois, he lives in Washington, D.C.